For Stuart Graham

with kind regards

Andrea Strunk.
6/2013

Stability of the Financial System

Stability of the Financial System

Illusion or Feasible Concept?

Edited by

Andreas Dombret

Deutsche Bundesbank

Otto Lucius

Austrian Society for Bank Research

Edward Elgar

Cheltenham, UK • Northampton, MA, USA

Published by
Edward Elgar Publishing Limited
The Lypiatts
15 Lansdown Road
Cheltenham
Glos GL50 2JA
UK

Edward Elgar Publishing, Inc.
William Pratt House
9 Dewey Court
Northampton
Massachusetts 01060
USA

A catalogue record for this book
is available from the British Library

Library of Congress Control Number: 2013931632

This book is available electronically in the ElgarOnline.com Economics Subject Collection, E-ISBN 978 1 78254 784 6

ISBN 978 1 78254 783 9

Printed by MPG PRINTGROUP, UK

Contents

List of Contributors   vii

Preface   xvii

Stability of the Financial System – An Introduction
   Mark Carney   1

PART I: ABOUT FINANCIAL STABILITY

1. Financial and Fiscal Stability beyond the Crisis Years: Two Paradigm
    Shifts and their Consequences
       Martin Blessing   7
2. Criteria for Financial Stability – The European View
       Andreas Dombret   27
3. Criteria for Financial Stability – A US View
       Nathan Sheets   46
4. Financial Stability in Brazil
       Luiz Awazu Pereira da Silva, Adriana Soares Sales and
       Wagner Piazza Gaglianone   65
5. From the Stability Pact to ESM – What Next?
       Claudia M. Buch   127
6. Economic Convergence – The Need for Economic Cooperation and
    Coordination
       Walter Rothensteiner and *Valentin Hofstätter*   159
7. Banking System and Financial Stability
       Andreas Ittner   180
8. Competition, the Pressure for Returns, and Stability
       Paul Tucker   200
9. Measuring Systemic Risk
       Jaime Caruana   215

PART II: THE CONSEQUENCES OF FINANCIAL INSTABILITY

10. Sovereign Risk
       Lorenzo Bini Smaghi   237

11. Default of Systemically Important Financial Intermediaries:
   Short-Term Stability vs. Incentive Compatibility
   Yves Mersch   258
12. Systemically Important Banks – Possible Options for Policy Makers
   Klaas H.W. Knot and *Hanne van Voorden*   288
13. A Paradigm Shift: Resolution of Banks
   Jean-Pierre Landau   310
14. Consequences of Financial Shocks for the Real Economy
   Hiroshi Nakaso   318

PART III: PREVENTION OF FINANCIAL INSTABILITY

15. The Economics of Financial Regulation
   Ewald Nowotny   337
16. A Strategic Approach to Post Crisis Regulation –
   The Need for Pillar 4
   David T. Llewellyn   358
17. Regulation of Banks and the "Level Playing Field" –
   The Case of Shadow Banking
   Otto Lucius   388
18. Enhancing Financial Stability – A Global Bank's Perspective
   Ulrich Körner   407
19. Stable Liquidity and Funding Flows
   José Manuel Campa Fernández   425
20. How to Avoid Contagion and Spillover Effects in the Euro Zone?
   Michael C. Burda   440
21. The New European Supervisory System – Harmonisation and
   Macroprudential Oversight
   Sabine Lautenschläger   457
22. Macroprudential, Microprudential and Monetary Policies: Conflicts,
   Complementarities and Trade-Offs
   Paolo Angelini, Sergio Nicoletti-Altimari and *Ignazio Visco*   474
23. Why Central Banks need a Macroeconomic Toolkit
   Philipp M. Hildebrand   502
24. Lender of Last Resort – Which Institution Could Best Fulfil this
   Function?
   Gertrude Tumpel-Gugerell   513

Stability of the Financial System: Illusion or Feasible Concept?
An Epilogue
   Christine Lagarde   527

Index   533

Contributors

Paolo Angelini joined the Bank of Italy in 1990. At present he heads the newly created Financial Stability Unit. His research has covered issues related to monetary policy, the interbank money market, credit rationing and firms' growth, and banks and interbank payment systems, and has been published in leading journals (American Economic Review, Journal of Monetary Economics, Journal of Money, Credit and Banking). He obtained a Ph.D. in Economics from Brown University in 1994. He is a member of the Advisory Technical Committee of the European Systemic Risk Board and the Financial Stability Committee of the European System of Central Banks.

Lorenzo Bini Smaghi is currently Visiting Scholar at Harvard's Weatherhead Center for International Affairs and Chairman of the Boards of SnamReteGas. From June 2005 to December 2011 he was a Member of the Executive Board of the European Central Bank. He started his career as an Economist at the Research Department of the Banca d'Italia (in 1983) and became Head of the Policy Division of the European Monetary Institute (in 1994) and then Director General for International Affairs in the Italian Treasury (in 1998). He holds a Bachelor's degree in Economics from the Université Catholique de Louvain (Belgium), a Master's degree from the University of Southern California and a Ph.D. from the University of Chicago.

He is author of several articles and books on international and European monetary and financial issues. He is currently member of the A-List of Commentators for the Financial Times.

Martin Blessing is Chairman of the Board of Managing Directors of Commerzbank of which he has already been a member since end of 2001. Prior to this position, he was Chairman of the Board of Advance Bank AG, Munich, Joint Manager at the Private Customers Section of Dresdner Bank AG, Frankfurt and Partner at McKinsey.

He studied Business Administration at the University of Frankfurt and the University of St.Gallen and holds an MBA of the University of Chicago.

Claudia M. Buch studied Economics at Bonn University. From 1992 to 2003, she was research associate at the Kiel Institute for the World Economy where she became head of the research area "Financial Markets" in 1998. She finished her doctorate in 1996 and her habilitation (postgraduate qualification) in 2002, both at the Christian-Albrechts-University, Kiel. In 2004, she became Professor in Economics, focusing on money and currency, at Tuebingen University. She has been the Scientific Director of the Institute for Applied Economic Research (IAW) in Tuebingen since 2005. In March 2012 she was appointed Member of German Council of Economic Experts (Sachverständigenrat).

Michael C. Burda is professor of economics at the Humboldt University Berlin, where he has held the chair in macroeconomics and labour since 1993. He received his Ph.D. from Harvard University and taught from 1987-1993 at INSEAD in Fontainebleau, France. His research interests lie in the role played by labour economics in macroeconomic dynamics as well as European integration. He is research fellow at the Centre for Economic Policy Research (CEPR London), CES-Ifo, and Institut zur Zukunft der Arbeit (IZA Bonn), and is a Fellow of the European Economic Association. Since September 2011, he is President of the Verein für Socialpolitik, the professional association of economists in Germany, Austria and Switzerland. He has consulted for a number of governments and international organisations.

José Manuel Campa Fernández, Ph.D., M.A. in Economics, Harvard University and B.A. Law and Economics, University of Oviedo, is Professor of Finance and Economics at IESE Business School. He was Secretary of State for Economic Affairs in the Government of Spain (May 2009 – December 2011). He has been a professor at New York University and Columbia University. He was the Spanish member of Liikanen High Level Expert Group, serves on the board of Bruegel and has been Research Associate at the National Bureau of Economic Research and Research Fellow at the Center for Economic Policy Research. He has been a consultant to multiple international institutions and has also served as an expert witness for arbitration disputes on financial issues and corporate valuation.

Mark Carney was appointed Governor of the Bank of Canada effective 1 February 2008, for a term of seven years. As Governor, he is also Chairman of the Board of Directors of the Bank. In addition he serves as Chairman of the Financial Stability Board (FSB) and as a member of the Board of Directors of the Bank for International Settlements (BIS). He is also a member of the Group of Thirty, and of the Foundation Board of the World Economic Forum.

Mr. Carney received a Bachelor's degree in economics from Harvard University in 1988. He received a Master's degree in economics in 1993 and a doctorate in economics in 1995, both from Oxford University. Prior to joining the public service, Mr. Carney had a thirteen-year career with Goldman Sachs in its London, Tokyo, New York and Toronto offices. In November 2004, he left the Bank to become Senior Associate Deputy Minister of Finance – a position he held until his appointment as Governor of the Bank. Mr. Carney was nominated for Governor of the Bank of England from mid-2013 on.

Jaime Caruana became General Manager of the Bank for International Settlements on 1 April 2009. Previously, Mr. Caruana was Financial Counsellor to the Managing Director and Director of the Monetary and Capital Markets Department of the International Monetary Fund.

From 2000 to 2006, Mr. Caruana was the Governor of the Bank of Spain, Spain's central bank, and in that capacity, served on the Governing Council of the European Central Bank. He was also the Chairman of the Basel Committee on Banking Supervision from 2003 to 2006 and has been a member of the Financial Stability Forum since 2003. From 2004 to 2006, he chaired the Coordination Group, a senior group of supervisory standard setters from the Basel Committee, the International Organization of Securities Commissions (IOSCO), the International Association of Insurance Supervisors (IAIS), and the Joint Forum. Prior to joining the Bank of Spain, Mr Caruana served as Director General of the Spanish Treasury and headed an investment services company and a fund management company for nearly 10 years.

Andreas Dombret has been a member of the Executive Board of the Deutsche Bundesbank since May 2010. Previously, he worked in the private banking sector at Deutsche Bank, JP Morgan, Rothschild and Bank of America. He holds a Ph.D. in banking from the University of Nürnberg and was awarded an honorary professorship from the European Business School in Wiesbaden in 2009 and sits, among others, on the Board of Trustees of the Center for Financial Studies in Frankfurt and the Austrian Society for Bank Research in Vienna. In addition, he is a member of the Board of Directors of the Bank for International Settlements, of the Board of the International Center of Monetary and Banking studies in Geneva as well as the treasurer of the Verein für Sozialpolitik and Atlantik-Brücke. He is also a co-editor of the Zeitschrift für das gesamte Kreditwesen. His main responsibility at the Bundesbank is in the area of Financial Stability.

Wagner Piazza Gaglianone has been working at the Central Bank of Brazil since 2000, first as Inspector of the Department of Banking Supervision and then as Advisor and Analyst of the Research Department. Former Assistant Professor of Economics at Fucape Business School (Brazil), he holds a Ph.D. and a Master's degree in Economics from the Getulio Vargas Foundation (Brazil) and was a Visiting Research Student at the London School of Economics and Political Science (UK). Prior to joining the Central Bank of Brazil, he worked as Structural Engineer at Engevix Engineering (Brazil) after graduating in Civil Engineering from the Federal University of Rio de Janeiro (Brazil).

Philipp M. Hildebrand is Vice-Chairman of BlackRock. Most recently, he was a Senior Visiting Fellow at Oxford University's Blavatnik School of Government. Until January 2012, he served as Chairman of the Governing Board of the Swiss National Bank. Philipp Hildebrand graduated from the University of Toronto in 1988. In 1990, he received a Master's degree from the Graduate Institute of International Studies in Geneva. In 1994, he completed his doctoral studies at the University of Oxford with a D.Phil in International Relations. Philipp Hildebrand is a member of the Group of Thirty and an Honorary Fellow of Lincoln College, Oxford.

Valentin Hofstätter finished his Ph.D. programme in economics at Vienna University of Economics and Business Administration (Thesis: Quantitative Early Warning System for Emerging Market Currency Crises), and then joined Raiffeisen Bank International (at that time still RZB) as economist and financial markets analyst in January 2000. The CFA programme was successfully concluded in 2003. Since 2005 he is heading the department for Economics, Fixed Income & Currency Research within RBI.

Andreas Ittner has been a member of the Governing Board of the Oesterreichische Nationalbank (OeNB) since 2008 and is in charge of the OeNB's financial stability, banking supervision and statistics functions. Recently he was appointed Vice Governor of OeNB. Previous positions at the OeNB include that of Director of the Financial Stability and Bank Inspections Department. In addition, Mr. Ittner holds numerous national and international functions related to banking supervision, e.g., with the European Systemic Risk Board, the European Banking Authority and the Austrian Financial Market Authority.

Klaas H.W. Knot has been President of De Nederlandsche Bank since 1 July 2011. In this capacity he is a member of the Governing Council and the General Council of the ECB, as well as being Governor of the IMF.

Mr. Knot is also a member of the Board of Directors of the BIS and Economics of Central Banking Professor at the University of Groningen. He was Deputy Treasurer-General and Director of Financial Markets at the Dutch Ministry of Finance (2009–11). From 1995 to 2009 he held several positions at DNB. During this period, Knot was seconded with the IMF (1998-99) and the then Pensions and Insurance Supervisory Authority (2003-04).

Ulrich Körner is CEO UBS Group EMEA, Group Chief Operating Officer and CEO Corporate Center of UBS AG. Mr. Körner has been with UBS since 2009, following a 10-year career at Credit Suisse Group where he last held the position of CEO for Switzerland. Prior to his banking career, he worked for both Price Waterhouse and McKinsey & Company.

Mr. Körner holds a Master's degree and a Ph.D. in Business Administration from the University of St. Gallen in Switzerland.

Christine Lagarde graduated from law school at University Paris X, and obtained a Master's degree from the Political Science Institute in Aix en Provence. After being admitted to the Paris Bar, Christine Lagarde joined the international law firm of Baker & McKenzie, becoming Chairman of the Global Executive Committee of Baker & McKenzie in 1999, and of the Global Strategic Committee in 2004. Christine Lagarde joined the French government in June 2005 as Minister for Foreign Trade. After a brief stint as Minister for Agriculture and Fisheries, in June 2007 she became the first woman to hold the post of Finance and Economy Minister of a G-7 country. In July 2011, Christine Lagarde became the eleventh Managing Director of the IMF.

Jean-Pierre Landau is currently visiting at Princeton University. He has worked in the French Treasury and Central Bank for most of his career, including as Executive Director of the International Monetary Fund (IMF) and the World Bank and Deputy Governor of the French Central Bank. He also served as Associate Professor at Sciences Po (Paris) and Visiting Professor at SAIS (Johns Hopkins – Washington DC). His main fields of interest include monetary policy, financial regulation and international macroeconomics.

Sabine Lautenschläger is Deputy President of the Deutsche Bundesbank and the President's Alternate in the Governing Council of the ECB. She is responsible for the Banking and Financial Supervision and the Audit Department. Ms Lautenschläger is a member of the Basel Committee on Banking Supervision (BCBS) and co-chairs the Core Principles Group (CPG) of the BCBS. Prior to joining the Bundesbank in June 2011, she was Chief Executive Director of Banking Supervision and a member of the Executive Board of the Federal Financial Supervisory Authority (BaFin).

David T. Llewellyn is Professor of Money and Banking at Loughborough University in the UK, Visiting Professor at the Vienna University of Economics and Business, External Member, Kellogg College Oxford, and a Senior Visiting Research Fellow at the Centre for European Policy Studies (CEPS) in Brussels. He is Vice Chair of the Banking Stakeholder Group of the European Banking Authority and a member of the Academic Board of the International Centre for Financial Regulation in London. He also serves as consultant Economist to ICAP plc. He is a Council Member (and former President) of SUERF: the European Money & Finance Forum.

Otto Lucius is CEO of the Austrian Society for Bank Research and editor of BankArchiv (Journal of Banking and Financial Research), the leading reviewed monthly journal in German. He is lecturing at the University of Graz and FH JOANNEUM in Graz, in Behavioural Finance, Investment Counselling and Financial Planning.

Mr. Lucius was educated at the University of Vienna in Law, holding a Master's degree in law, and at the Economic University of Vienna in Business Administration. He was appointed manager of BankAkademie Wien, an independent educational and training institution in 1983. In 1995 he joined the educational staff at University of Applied Sciences in Wiener Neustadt as Head of Department Investment Counselling and Corporate Finance. Editor of several books and author of numerous articles.

Yves Mersch has been President of the Luxembourg Central Bank since 1998. In this capacity he contributed the chapter in this volume. Currently he is Member of the Executive Board of the European Central Bank (ECB). Since 2011 he has been elected Co-Chair of the Financial Stability Forum's Regional Consultative Group for Europe.

He holds post-graduate degrees in both international public law and political science from the University of Paris 1 Panthéon-Sorbonne. He started his career at the Ministry of Finance in the budget department before leaving for two years for Washington at the IMF. He was reinstated in the Ministry of Finance dealing with fiscal affairs and structural policies.

In 1980, Mr. Mersch was seconded to the Ministry of Foreign Affairs where he became a member of Luxembourg's permanent representation at the United Nations in New York. The following years, he covered the fields of monetary affairs and international financial relations as Adviser in the Ministry of Finance. In 1985 he became Government Commissioner to the Luxembourg Stock Exchange, then Director of the Treasury in 1989, a post which he held for nearly ten years.

Hiroshi Nakaso joined the Bank of Japan in 1978 after finishing his course in Economics at the University of Tokyo. His main areas of responsibility at the Bank have been crisis management during Japan's financial crisis in the 1990s and subsequently market operation, which involved international dimensions in dealing with the global financial crisis. He was promoted Executive Director in 2008 and now serves as Assistant Governor for international affairs. In his current capacity he chairs the Markets Committee, a standing committee at the BIS. In 2011, he also chaired the G20 Study Group on Commodities under the French Presidency.

Sergio Nicoletti-Altimari is Deputy Head of the Central Bank Operations Department at the Bank of Italy. In 2006-2008, he was Economic Adviser to the Minister of the Economy and Finance of Italy. Previously, he worked at the European Central Bank as Deputy Head of the Monetary Policy Strategy Division. He is alternate member of the Economic and Financial Committee (European Union). His main research interests are macroeconomics, monetary policy and macroprudential regulation. He obtained a Ph.D. in Economics from the University of Pennsylvania.

Ewald Nowotny is the Governor of the Oesterreichische Nationalbank (OeNB) and a Member of the Governing Council of the European Central Bank (ECB).

Before taking on his current position in September 2008, he was CEO of the Austrian BAWAG P.S.K. banking group, served as Vice-President and Member of the Management Committee of the European Investment Bank (EIB), and in the seventies was first a Member and then President of the Governing Board of Österreichische Postsparkasse (P.S.K.). Mr. Nowotny was an elected Member of the Austrian Parliament from 1978 to 1999 and served as chairman of the parliamentary Finance Committee from 1985 to 1999.

He studied law and political science at the University of Vienna and economics at the Institute for Advanced Studies (IHS) in Vienna. In 1967, he received his doctorate in law from the University of Vienna. After working as assistant to Professor Kurt W. Rothschild at the University of Linz, from 1968 to 1973, he received his postdoctoral qualification (tenure-track professorship – "Habilitation") in General Economics and Public Economics in 1973, and subsequently held research tenures and professorships at Harvard University, TH Darmstadt, Germany, and the Johannes Kepler University Linz, Austria. From 1981 to 2008, Mr. Nowotny served as Full Professor at the Vienna University of Economics and Business Administration, where he also held the position of Vice Rector from 2003 to 2004. He has published numerous articles in refereed journals. He has also authored or coauthored nine books.

Luiz Awazu Pereira da Silva is currently Deputy-Governor, in charge of International Affairs and of Financial Regulation, at the Central Bank of Brazil. Before that he was Deputy-Finance Minister, in charge of International Affairs, Ministry of Finance – Brazil, Chief Economist, Ministry of Budget and Planning – Brazil, Regional Country Director and Advisor to the Chief Economist of the World Bank. He also worked as Visiting Scholar, Institute of Fiscal and Monetary Policy (IFMP) of the Ministry of Finance, Tokyo (Japan) and Director, Country Risk and Economic Analysis Department (CREAD) at the Export-Import Bank of Japan, Tokyo (Japan).

He holds a Ph.D. in Economics and a Master of Philosophy from the Université De Paris-I Sorbonne, Paris (France). He graduated from the Ecole des Hautes Etudes Commerciales (HEC) – Paris (France) and from the Institut d'Etudes Politiques (Science-Po) Paris (France).

Walter Rothensteiner has been CEO of Raiffeisen Zentralbank Österreich AG since June 1995 and Chairman of the Austrian Raiffeisen Association since June 2012. Among others, he chairs the Supervisory Boards of Raiffeisen Bank International AG and Uniqa Versicherungen AG. Furthermore he is Chairman of the Federal Division for Bank and Insurance in the Austrian Federal Economic Chamber, Member of the General Council of Oesterreichische Nationalbank, Member of the Federal Council of the Federation of Austrian Industries.

He studied at Vienna University of Economics and Business Administration, obtaining a Phd. Beyond his business functions he plays an active role at Austrian Red Cross (Vice President), Vienna State Opera (Supervisory Board), Friends of Grafenegg Music Festival (President).

Adriana Soares Sales is currently head of research, mainly in charge of making inflation projections to the Monetary Policy Committee at the Central Bank of Brazil (BCB). Prior to that, she was senior advisor to the Deputy Governor for Monetary Policy. She had also been deputy head of the Department of Banking Operations and Payment System at the BCB when she took part in the launch of the Brazilian Real-Time Gross Settlement System. She holds a Ph.D. in Economics from University of Brasília (Brazil) and a M. A. from Yale University (US).

Nathan Sheets joined Citigroup as Global Head of International Economics in September 2011. Previously, he served as Director of the Federal Reserve Board's Division of International Finance. In that position, he advised the Board and the FOMC on macroeconomic and financial developments in other countries, as well as on the outlook for US trade, the dollar, and global commodity prices. He also was a member of the Committee on the Global Financial System sponsored by the BIS. Mr. Sheets received his Ph.D. from the Massachusetts Institute of Technology and has published research on a wide range of international and macroeconomic issues.

Paul Tucker was appointed as Deputy Governor of Bank of England, Financial Stability in March 2009. He is a member of the Bank of England's Monetary Policy Committee, Financial Policy Committee and Court of Directors. In April 2012 he was appointed chair of the Committee for Payment and Settlement Systems. He is a member of the G20 Financial Stability Board Steering Committee, and chairs the Financial Stability Board's group on resolving large and complex banks. From June 2002 until his current appointment, he was Executive Director for Markets.

Gertrude Tumpel-Gugerell was a Member of the Executive Board of the European Central Bank from June 2003 to June 2011, responsible for market operations (until 2006), human resources, budget and organisation and for payment systems. In the past, she held a number of positions at the Oesterreichische Nationalbank and was nominated Vice Governor, responsible for the Economics and Financial Markets Department. She is currently a Member of the University Council of the University of Vienna and non-executive Member of the Board of several companies. Dr. Tumpel-Gugerell graduated in economics and social sciences from the University of Vienna.

Hanne van Voorden has been working for De Nederlandsche Bank since early 2010. She is an economist at the Financial Stability Division. In this capability, she is responsible for, inter alia, macro prudential analysis and implementation of the policy framework for systemically important financial institutions in the national and international context. In 2009, Hanne van Voorden graduated with honours in Economics at the University of Amsterdam.

Ignazio Visco was appointed Governor of the Bank of Italy in November 2011, after a long career with the Bank that began in 1972. He is also a member of the Governing Council and General Council of the European Central Bank and the Board of Directors of the Bank for International Settlements. From 1997 to 2002 he was Chief Economist and Head of the Economics Department of the OECD. Mr Visco graduated from the University of Rome and obtained a Ph.D. in Economics from the University of Pennsylvania. An author of numerous articles and books on economics and finance, he also taught Econometrics and Economic Policy at "La Sapienza" University of Rome.

Preface

Treasuries, politicians, bankers, central bankers as well as supervisors all share an inherent interest in a stable financial system, both at home and globally. They are all aware of how important it is that the financial system is able to perform key macroeconomic functions smoothly at all times. This holds true especially for periods of stress.

More than five years after the outbreak of the global financial crisis, one thing has become very clear: financial stability encompasses more than the sum of individual risks that exist in a financial system. We have learned the hard way that the threat to the financial system posed by macro risks is considerably greater than that of the individual micro risks. This is why the Financial Stability Board, or FSB for short, has gained so much importance over the past few years in proposing to the G20 a new and comprehensive framework for the reform of financial market regulation. And while this new financial market regulation is being implemented, more and more countries are establishing new legislation for macroprudential oversight.

It is against this background that the editors of this book – an Austrian academic and a German central banker – have decided to publish an anthology on financial stability, bringing together the views of leading experts on the topic. With this book as a platform, we intend to stir a global public debate about the issues which will be occupying us for the near future. Therefore, it was crucial to form a truly international group of well respected academics, bankers, supervisors and central bank officials in order to discuss financial stability from a wide variety of perspectives. Needless to say, we are extremely grateful to all 30 authors for the truly outstanding 24 contributions they have made to this anthology. All of them have invested their valuable time in this undertaking and have supported us throughout the project. It is less the intentions behind this publication than the long list of insightful and thought-provoking ideas produced by the expert authors which make this book so significant. Also, we wish to thank both the Chairman of the FSB and the Managing Director of the IMF for lending their weight and authority to this publication by writing an introduction and an epilogue respectively.

In this two-year project, we have received assistance from many sources. We would like to take this opportunity to thank our publisher, Edward Elgar, who has worked with us diligently on this publication and who has taken great care in preparing the end product. Distribution will be global, which was our main intention in choosing this publisher. We highly appreciate the valuable input from David Llewellyn and the fruitful debates we had during the initial phase of this project. Thilo Liebig of the Bundesbank's Financial Stability Department has performed a useful service in acting as our expert adviser. Our deeply felt gratitude also goes to Elisabeth Zivota of Österreichische Bankwissenschaftliche Gesellschaft who was responsible for all the typesetting and incorporated all the authors' changes and amendments before the proofs were finished. We would also like to thank Renate Schultz and Janina Brandt of the Bundesbank for their valuable assistance.

We really do hope that this volume will find a favourable response among its readers and thus serve as a modest contribution to the debate on the extremely important issue of financial stability.

Andreas Dombret   *Otto Lucius*

Stability of the Financial System – An Introduction

Mark Carney

Although the concept of financial stability may, at first glance, seem illusive and difficult to define, the global financial crisis of 2007-8 provided a stark and very concrete example of its antonym – financial instability. The crisis also demonstrated the importance of financial stability for economic stability as the economic fallout was horrendous: no country was left unscathed, 50 million jobs were lost and many countries have still not yet recovered to pre-crisis levels of output and employment. One positive consequence of the crisis is that the G20 assumed the leadership role as the premier global economic policy-making forum. The G20 has given the FSB an enhanced mandate to coordinate efforts to develop and consistently implement a comprehensive set of new global standards and regulations. The objective of these reforms is not to eliminate all financial crises but to lessen their likelihood and reduce their severity by increasing the resilience of the global financial system.

The breadth and scope of the chapters in this volume reflect the challenge of developing and consistently implementing a coherent set of financial re-forms to promote financial stability. They make an important contribution to deepening our understanding of the many facets of financial stability. They will promote the development of financial reforms that are effective in striking the optimal balance between realising the enormous benefits that the financial sector brings in to efficient financial intermediation, capital allocation and risk management, on the one hand, and controlling systemic risks and maintaining financial stability, on the other.

Substantial progress has been made on developing and implementing the programme of financial reforms mandated by the G20. To date, the most im-portant accomplishments are:

- Defining a new capital regime (Basel III) for banks;
- Agreeing to the core elements of a framework to end "Too-Big-To-Fail";
- Strengthening the plumbing of core financial markets;
- Placing more attention to the consistent national implementation of these reforms; and

- Putting the FSB on a firmer institutional footing.

While much has been accomplished in recent years, what is still to come is just as important, especially in four priority areas:

- Building resilient financial institutions;
- Ending Too-Big-To-Fail;
- Creating Continuously Open Core Markets; and
- Moving from Shadow Banking to Market-Based Financing.

BUILDING RESILIENT FINANCIAL INSTITUTIONS

Achieving a stronger, more resilient banking system is an overriding priority. The full implementation of Basel 2.5/III capital and liquidity standards will significantly increase the quantity and quality of bank capital and produce more robust funding structures. Although risks to financial stability are elevated and the macro-economic environment is challenging, large parts of the system are sounder than they were before the crisis. For example, the largest banks have the capacity to meet readily the new capital adequacy targets through earnings retention over the six-year transition period from 2013 to 2019.

In addition, a simple, but effective, leverage standard has been imported from Canada to protect the system from risks that banks think are low, but, in fact, are high. Sensible liquidity measures, including the Liquidity Coverage Ratio (LCR) and the Net Stable Funding Ratio (NSFR), have also been put in place. The LCR promotes short-term resilience by ensuring a bank holds sufficient liquid assets to survive intense stress lasting for one month, while the NSFR encourages a compatible maturity structure of assets and liabilities and thus prevents significant maturity mismatches over longer-term horizons. Both measures are currently under observation with the goal of fully implementing the LCR in January 2015 and the NSFR in January 2018.

Finally, supervisory intensity is being stepped up to strengthen risk management practices and disclosure. Across FSB member jurisdictions, supervisory expectations for risk governance at financial institutions have increased.

ENDING TOO-BIG-TO-FAIL

It is essential that large financial institutions can be resolved in the event of future failure without resorting to taxpayer support, while at the same time avoiding significant disruption to the wider financial system. Ending the problem of "too-big-to-fail" requires the full implementation of a number of agreed measures, including a marked step-up in resolution planning and cross-border cooperation. In particular, the FSB's new *Key Attributes for Effective Resolu-*

tion Regimes need to be fully implemented to establish effective resolution regimes in FSB member jurisdictions.

The FSB has identified a list of globally systemically important banks (G-SIBs). Cross-border crisis management groups have been established for the majority of these G-SIBs and resolution strategies and plans and cross-border co-operation agreements are being put in place to ensure their resolvability. This framework for regulating and supervising systemic global banks is being extended to domestic banks, global insurers, and key shadow banks.

CREATING CONTINUOUSLY OPEN MARKETS

To help end the problem of "too-big-to-fail", core financial markets should be able to withstand the failure of systemic firms. Achieving such resilience requires sounder market infrastructures and practices, increased transparency, and better data for firms and supervisors to monitor exposures and emerging risks.

Over-the-counter derivatives (OTCD) markets are immense and critical to the stable and efficient functioning of the financial system. To date, much of the policy development work has been completed on OTCD market infrastructures and practices to promote increased standardisation, and greater use of central clearing, trade repositories, and trading platforms, and to specify the rules for margining and capital. An important example is a new set of safeguards (fair and open access, cross border liquidity, cooperative regulatory oversight) for a resilient and efficient global framework for clearing OTC derivatives.

Many of these OTCD market infrastructures are operational and in use for different asset classes. Their usage will increase in the future as more jurisdictions enact the necessary legislation and regulation to support the implementation of these reforms. Progress to date has been the greatest in the jurisdictions with the largest OTC derivatives markets, namely the United States, European Union and Japan.

The reform agenda for OTCD markets is a good example of the FSB's role of coordinating the work of international standard-setting bodies in areas of overlapping responsibility. The margining requirements of CCPs are set by CPSS-IOSCO and those of bilateral trades by IOSCO, and the capital standards for centrally and bilaterally cleared trades are set by the BCBS.

MOVING FROM SHADOW BANKING TO MARKET-BASED FINANCE

Given the central role shadow banking activities played in the financial crisis, the FSB is working to strengthen the oversight and regulation of shadow banking so that it is a source of competition and diversity to the regulated sector.

The shadow banking sector needs to be converted from a source of vulnerabilities to a force for competition, efficiency and systemic resilience.

These reforms will require changes to the management of money-market funds, the terms of securitisation and, most importantly, the involvement and exposure of the regulated banking sector to shadow banking activities. These measures will aim to mitigate the spillovers between the regular banking system and the shadow banking system; reduce the susceptibility of money market funds and other shadow banking entities to runs; better align the incentives associated with securitisation; and dampen risks and pro-cyclical incentives associated with securities lending and repo activities.

CONCLUDING REMARK: THE IMPORTANCE OF TIMELY AND CONSISTENT IMPLEMENTATION

Although the development of global standards for financial stability is important, full and consistent implementation is absolutely essential to preserving the advantages of an open and globally integrated financial system. Market participants and authorities need to have confidence in the strength of financial institutions and markets in other countries. Moreover, to realise fully the benefits of openness and competition, there must be a level playing field. Recent post-crisis experience demonstrates that when mutual confidence is lost, the retreat from an open and integrated system can occur rapidly. A return to a nationally segmented global financial system would reduce both financial capacity and systemic resilience, with major consequences for output and employment growth.

The FSB is placing more emphasis on the timely, full and consistent implementation of major reforms, with reviews of progress in implementing Basel III, compensation standards and OTC derivatives reforms. This implementation monitoring is being conducted within a coordination framework that leverages the expertise and resources of the standard setting bodies.

G20 Leaders have endorsed significant proposals to strengthen the capacity, resources and governance of the FSB. In particular, the Leaders supported proposals to put the FSB on an enduring organisational footing, with legal personality and greater financial autonomy, and increased accountability. These changes will enhance the FSB's ability to coordinate among standard setters to effectively monitor and promote timely, full and consistent implementation across FSB members.

It is important to stress that financial stability is not an end to itself. To achieve the ultimate G20 goal of strong, sustainable and balanced global growth will require coherent monetary, fiscal, and financial policy frameworks within and across G20 countries.

PART I:

About Financial Stability

1. Financial and Fiscal Stability beyond the Crisis Years: Two Paradigm Shifts and their Consequences

Martin Blessing

1. INTRODUCTION

Debt crises in most industrial countries have held the world in thrall for several years now. The US subprime crisis morphed into the global financial crisis, which in turn was followed by the current sovereign debt crisis in Europe, still far from being resolved in mid-2012.

The crisis years have shown – in dimensions never seen before in earlier debt crises – that the stability of the financial sector and the stability of government finances are closely linked, and actually depend on each other. Instabilities in one system quickly spill over to the other. Financial and government systems both serve the real economy, and thus, ultimately, the well-being of everyone. This is why deleveraging is crucial to restore the stability of the financial and fiscal systems on a sustainable basis. And this will also be key for industrial countries to face the challenges ahead – the rise and catching up of the emerging markets (in part accelerated by the crisis years in the industrial countries), as well as massive demographic changes that necessitate a lot of saving, investment and financial intermediation over the coming decades.

It is not yet discernible just when and how the crisis years will end, but major insights have already been gained, and some conclusions can already be drawn. Two such major insights – paradigm shifts to be more precise – are presented and discussed here.

First, before the crisis years – and probably even now – the *systemic risk* which debt and other financial instruments pose *was underestimated*, be it for a subprime mortgage derivative or for a Euro area government bond. There was a widespread expectation that, individually, debt contracts would not endanger the financial system as a whole. This turned out to be a grave error, and led to excessively low risk premia and interest rates, i.e. the price of debt. In other words: interest rates were too low, making debt too cheap and thus the amount

7

of debt incurred globally was too high, and threatened systemic stability. As such, efforts to prevent debt crises in future have to focus on finding the correct price of debt, which fully reflects the risk it poses to systemic stability.

Second, it seems there is *no longer* any such thing as *a "risk-free" asset*. Apart from the obvious errors in the AAA-rating of some subprime securities, investor trust in this notion relied primarily on post-war industrial country experience. Up to 2008, the general wisdom prevailed that the governments of these countries would never really come under pressure to default on their debt. The sovereign debt crisis of several European countries has put an end to this notion. For instance, the possibility of a euro exit has triggered a re-emergence of country risk in Europe. On their way to regaining pre-crisis levels of trust, governments will appear to have several "easy" political options, while in fact, if they really try to shore up financial *and* fiscal stability, they only have one option – and a tough one, at that.

Before discussing these options, as well as how to ensure that debt is more adequately priced, it is necessary to understand the true nature of the two paradigm shifts. This will be done by describing the reasons as to why debt levels rose before and during the crisis years, as well as the economic and regulatory environment in which mountains of debt were allowed to grow.

2. THE EFFECTS OF MISPRICED DEBT IN A FRAGILE GLOBAL FINANCIAL WEB

Public and private debt has been rising in the industrial countries since the 1970s, all the way in the run up to, and during the crisis years. This happened in all non-financial sectors of the economy: households, corporates, as well as governments. In each of these sectors, debt levels rose in terms of their weight in the respective economies (measured by gross domestic product, or GDP, see figure 1.1).

Even if the crisis had not struck, debt levels would in many cases have come near to or exceeded a threshold of 80-90 percent in each of the non-financial sectors, a point at which empirical analysis shows that the level of debt could become a burden on the economy and hamper growth (Cecchetti et al. 2011). The reasons for the rise in debt are different for each of the sectors mentioned – and have already been well documented elsewhere (for instance, Reinhart and Rogoff 2009; and Sinn 2011). Therefore, a brief summary suffices here, but with a focus on how systemic risk was wrongly perceived in the respective debt pile-ups:

- *For all non-financial sectors*, a key factor was US monetary policy before 2007, for instance, when in 2003, the Fed lowered its funds rate to 1 percent for an extraordinarily long period of time. As US monetary policy has a signalling function for the rest of the world, the central banks of

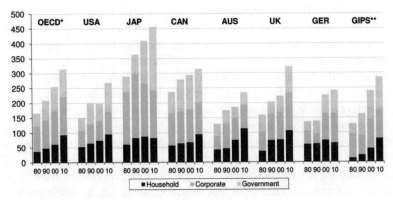

*Figure 1.1: Rising debt in the non-financial sectors 1980-2010
Gross debt levels, in % of GDP*

*Non-weighted average of 18 OECD countries
**Non-weighted avgerage of Greece, Italy, Portugal and Spain

Source: Cecchetti, Mohanty and Zampolli (2011).

other countries – including the Euro area – to a large extent mirrored this expansionary stance (otherwise they would have risked their currencies appreciating too strongly for their economies). Since inflation did not rise, but in some cases actually came down further from the already improved price stability conditions of the 1990s, there was a general consensus that global monetary stability had improved. By now, it became clear that the risks of asset price bubbles had been severely underestimated, including the negative impact on systemic stability. Thus, monetary policy distorted the price of debt in general, since the cost of increased systemic risk had not been included in the key central bank interest rates.

In the Euro area, trust in monetary policy received an additional boost due to the single currency. For the euro countries, this became a double-edged boon, since systemic risk was mispriced even further. The reason is that some of the additional trust was probably based on a tacit expectation that the no-bail-out rule of the European Monetary Union would be waived in the event of a crisis. As such, the interest paid on rising debt in Southern European countries, for instance, was too low, and did not price in this potential support by the whole Euro area or the European Central Bank (ECB). The crisis then put an end to this euro-driven interest rate anomaly.

- *Household debt* became the breeding ground for the subprime crisis in 2007 in the US, and in many countries, household debt was likewise driven by a boom in the housing market. Apart from the role of monetary policy, public subsidies likely contributed to the severity of the housing price bubbles, particularly in the US, but also in the euro sovereign debt crisis countries: Portugal, Ireland, Spain, Greece and Italy. However, the influence of the single currency may have taken a backseat here. Since there were also housing booms (or even bubbles) in non-euro industrial countries, such as the UK, Canada, Sweden and Australia (as discernible in OECD 2011, annex table 59), domestic factors – monetary policy or subsidies and regulatory incentives – were apparently the dominant feature of rising household debt in the decade before the crisis.

- *Corporate debt* rose, as increased debt financing often offered a better return on equity, a benchmark for many investment decisions in listed companies. Tax regimes favouring debt financing may also have influenced corporate finance decisions, lowering the after-tax cost of debt financing below levels appropriate for the systemic risk they could cause. Meanwhile in Europe, the euro made corporate bond issuance more attractive. Currency risk between monetary union members was removed, thus creating a deeper, more liquid capital market. However, lower interest rates resulting from this improvement in liquidity risk and economies of scale probably did not increase systemic risk, but merely reflected improved market conditions. A notable development was observed in the past decade in Germany, where the proportion of those small and medium enterprises ("*Mittelstand*") that had strong own capital ratios of 30% or more (measured by balance sheet volume) increased from 17% in 2002 to 29% in 2011 (Creditreform 2012, p. 23).

  As figure 1.1 illustrates, the rise in corporate debt from 1980 to 2010 by about 50% in industrial countries was the least pronounced of all sectors – but the corporate sector still has on average the largest debt burden of the non-financial sectors.

- Finally, *states and their governments*, in a political compromise common for industrial country parliamentary democracies, have since the 1970s increasingly relied on debt instead of just taxes to finance public spending. This development comprises all levels of government: central government, regional and local governments, as well as social security institutions (summarised as general government debt in the above and following statistics). The largest chunk of current sovereign debt was accumulated in industrial countries before 2007. As such, long before the crisis, there were a lot of question marks over fiscal stability and sustainability. A main theme in this regard since the 1990s has been the growing concern over unfunded public pension liabilities, estimated to equal several multiples of GDP alone (see, for instance, Moog et al. 2010).

  Industrial country gross government debt rose by only some 20% of GDP during the global financial crisis years of 2007-2009 and the recession year 2009 – mostly due to adjustments owing to lower government tax revenues and higher spending, but also economic stimulus packages and aid for the financial sector.

Still, in combination with a general reassessment of risk and risk appetite in the wake of the subprime crisis, the higher debt levels were obviously vulnerable enough to trigger a sovereign debt crisis in the Euro area.

The role of the euro in the accumulation and outbreak of the sovereign debt crisis is unclear: on the one hand, there were European countries with sovereign debt problems outside the Euro area (Iceland and Hungary). On the other hand, the severe crisis phase started in Greece in October 2009. Even countries where euro membership had led to massively lower government debt – Ireland and Spain – were struck by a sovereign debt crisis, as the private sector had used cheap credit to buy assets – mostly real estate – whose values proved to be unsustainable, causing a recession and raising the burden on government finances.

Apart from the non-financial sector, though, the financial sector – and banks in particular – were key in channelling the increased debt to the real economy, and thus contributed to the rise in systemic risk before the crisis.

- The activity of *banks and other financial institutions* even appeared to be detached from the debt levels in the non-financial sectors in the years before and during the crisis. Total bank assets in Europe alone as a % of GDP rose continuously and exceeded the levels of debt by households, corporates and governments. Meanwhile, the practice of asset sales and securitisation (in particular in the US), for instance, meant that a substantial share of credit originating in the bank sector was moved off-balance, largely not included in the official statistics. The massive rise in credit derivatives is also a symptom of financial sector debt growth, with worldwide credit default swap notional amounts outstanding rising from 15% of GDP at the end of 2004 to over 100% at the end of 2007 (as per BIS OTC Derivatives markets activity statistics).

It is impossible to say how much of the increased debt due to intra-financial sector connections was (non-financial) client-driven financial intermediation for hedging purposes – which would not add additional systemic risk. Other activities of the financial sector, however, could have well increased systemic risks, such as increased interbank connections that were not transparent enough for financial market participants (leading to more contagion risk).

A key aspect in understanding the role of the financial sector in contributing to systemic risk is that excessively low interest rates made *gross* debt rise. *Net* debt levels, for example, as discernible by net government debt and net financial household wealth, moved less dramatically (see the data provided by OECD 2011, Tables 33 and 58). However, it is *gross debt* which is the *main issue for systemic risk*, for every single debt counterparty that fails to fulfil its obligations can shake confidence in other borrowers' willingness

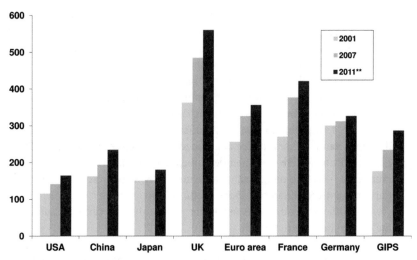

Figure 1.2: Financial intermediation by banks in the years 2001–2010
Bank assets, % of GDP*

* GIPS: non-weighted average of Greece, Italy, Portugal and Spain; data are as reported by central banks, or IMF (China), aggregation of Fed data on various banking groups (USA), Japanese Bankers Association (Japan – fiscal years).

**2010 latest available data for USA and China.

Sources: National central banks, ECB, IMF, EU Commission, Japanese Bankers Association, own calculations.

and ability to pay back their debt (e.g., the collapse of Lehman Brothers whose gross debt had been hedged with numerous methods but to no avail).

In principle, gross debt may have increased inside the financial sector, as it spread debt originating in the real economy to those in the financial sector (and, in many cases, eventually private investors) most willing to shoulder it. Unfortunately, the global financial crisis illustrated that, ultimately, those willing to shoulder debt and its associated credit risk were not necessarily those able to stomach losses without problems for systemic stability.

An important example is the securitisation of subprime mortgage debt and its transformation into collateralised debt obligations (CDO), plus their subsequent variants (CDO^2, CDO^3), as well as other credit derivatives and synthetic structured products. This financial innovation had carried the promise of removing credit risk from bank balance sheets, diversifying it to more investors able to individually bear such a risk. As it turned out, though, a lot of the credit risk had remained in the banking system (e.g., when held in the trading book with less capital requirements), or implicitly remained (e.g., by connections to special purpose vehicles). And the credit risk which was outside the banking system still proved to be a risk to overall financial stability (e.g., the credit derivatives sold by non-banks). The deteriorating credit risk of the underlying assets outweighed the stabilisation effect that diversification through securitisation had had on systemic risk.

One systemic weak spot with respect to stability is that the banking sector in its financial intermediation bears the highest systemic risk in the financial sector – incurred when performing credit-risk and maturity transformation, as well as when transforming the size of credit between savers and investors (convenience denomination for the real economy). However, such systemic risk would not vanish even if banks were abolished. As long as there is demand for it in the economy, credit intermediation would still occur, but simply elsewhere in the financial sector.

The common theme of the individual sector increases in debt has been that, barring central bank actions, they were fuelled by too low interest rates. These interest rates did not include the full price for the risk that each debt factor would contribute to the instability of the system as a whole. In other words, the systemic risk was long underestimated. Individually, the increase in each debt instrument did not raise any suspicions. The overall rise in debt levels was widely believed to be manageable in the industrial countries, where consumer price stability was continually improving. And, in fact, low interest rates and high debt were considered to be positive signs of greater trust in the system and mature capital markets. Only in retrospect – despite some warnings by a very few analysts – did the true extent of the problems regarding systemic stability become apparent.

These problems surfaced brutally during the crisis years, necessitating central bank and fiscal interventions to stabilise the system ("bailouts"), even across borders. Such bailouts are necessary at a time of crisis, since a crisis ultimately affects everyone – not just those first in the line of impact, such as mortgage debtors and banks. But those same bailouts eventually hurt taxpayers if they are able to restore confidence only by bearing true losses, and not just by providing temporary credit and guarantees. Moreover, they can create a moral hazard when market participants take on more debt than they would without the expectation of a bailout in a crisis – a threat to systemic stability. Thus, as far as possible, bailouts must be prevented from happening – by finding the correct price for debt that reflects the risk it poses to overall systemic stability.

On the one hand, there is a danger to systemic stability that can be portrayed like a web of growing debt connections with a growing risk that at some point, a counterparty will no longer pay back a debt, and thus possibly set into motion a meltdown of the whole system.

On the other hand, that same global financial web would benefit everyone with sustainably competitive states and financial systems endowed with a healthy amount of trust, domestically and across borders. Both financial and fiscal stability need to be assured for the web to work.

How fragile is this web when things go wrong? Six cases are shown in figure 1.3:

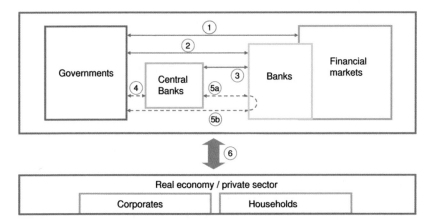

Figure 1.3: Financial linkages of financial markets, banks, governments, central banks and the real economy

- Governments which accumulate excessive debts or even go into default lose the trust of *financial markets* as a whole. Markets, in turn, may suffer from severe distortions and contagion effects (e.g., "investor strikes", increased cost of capital and interest rate hikes, which also affect other debtors). Conversely, governments have to sometimes support the financial sector with bailouts for debtors and even whole states (e.g., guarantees for debt securities), when they are the only ones left to restore general trust in the system (case 1).
- Similarly, governments – and ultimately society as a whole – also rely on stable *banks* that provide sufficient credit and channel reliable investment opportunities. The mutual interdependence at times of crisis mirrors the case of financial markets: if the banking system becomes distorted – for instance, due to the subprime crisis – governments with the same reasoning will support banks to prevent bank runs and preserve systemic stability. Conversely, banks can come under pressure due to credit exposure to governments with unstable finances – e.g., Greece or earlier crises in Emerging Markets (case 2).
- Both financial market and banking crises can trigger *central bank* measures to massively ease bank refinancing and monetary policy conditions (e.g., quality requirements for repo collateral). For instance, in a bid to re-instil

trust into the system, central banks during the crisis years ballooned their balance sheets by issuing liquidity. This way, they were able to take up ailing debt securities from the rest of the economy, either by outright purchases or by accepting the securities as collateral for repo operations. Such measures endanger, at least in the long run, the primary goal of price stability (case 3).

- In this respect, the sovereign debt crisis in Europe has jeopardised the iron principle that central banks should not finance *governments*. Granted, the European Central Bank (ECB) so far has not bought up government debt on the primary market, but, through its security market programme, it has intervened heavily on the secondary market (case 4). Additionally, ECB interventions on the market for government bonds were also done indirectly, e.g., through extreme long-term refinancing operations (LTRO), since the additional liquidity was used by many banks to buy domestic government bonds (cases 5a and 5b).
- In the end, all of the cases of different distortions and ensuing crises eventually find their way into the main parts of the *real economy – the household and corporate sectors* (case 6). The ways the real economy suffers from frictions in the linkages between the state and financial sector are manifold. Just to name a few examples: disruptions of payment flows; write-downs on securities and savings; credit shortages and even credit crunches through a sudden risk aversion of investors, depositors and banks; central banks stepping on monetary policy brakes; interest rate and tax hikes; austerity policies.

The crisis years have stressed the fragility of the web of financial interconnections and interdependencies, possibly more than ever before. The latest – and potentially most severe – phase of the crisis, the Euro area sovereign debt crisis, deserves particular focus.

The link between banks and governments is extremely narrow and vulnerable, since an erosion and a build-up of necessary trust for the links to function properly is near-binary in nature. Once trust is lost through the decision of politicians not to pay back government debt, or even to force default only on private creditors (as was the case with Greece in early 2012), critical stress on the whole financial system is the immediate result.

Even before the crisis years, the share of euro government debt as a percentage of overall Euro area bank balance sheets declined (from 14% in 1998 to 7% in 2008, as per ESCB statistics). Meanwhile, the proportion of Euro area monetary financial institutions (MFIs) holding government debt in the euro area countries started to recede since the mid-2000s, while domestic MFIs holding domestic government debt even receded in % of GDP before the crisis years (see figure 1.4). Providing government debt became more of a focus for specialised banks.

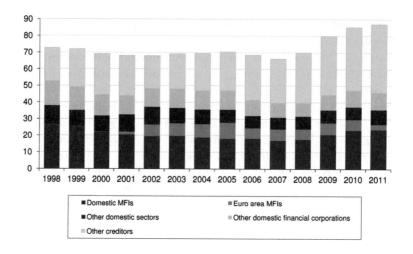

Figure 1.4: Importance of banks as a provider of credit to governments in the Euro area
Holders* of government debt, % of GDP Euro area

*Domestic holders denote holders resident in the country whose government has issued the debt.

Sources: ECB, Deutsche Bundesbank, own calculations.

As such, in the time since the introduction of the euro there are signs of fewer links between governments and banks in the Euro area (also in line with the trend over the past decades that banks in many countries are increasingly in private ownership). The diversification of debt among holders is something that might have even been able to limit the severity of any sovereign debt crisis. Nevertheless, the exposure to (crisis country) sovereign debt on European bank balances was too high still to prevent the crisis. Following the losses from the subprime crisis, the European banking sector simply did not have enough reserves to convince financial markets it could withstand substantial defaults in Europe unscathed.

Still, the path to fewer interconnections between banks and governments points to more stability. In this regard, the recent longer-term refinancing operations (LTROs) by the ECB had the side effect that some banks in crisis countries again increased their links to – and thus dependence on – domestic government debt (continuing the renewed rise of government debt on domestic MFI balance sheets in the crisis years, figure 1.4). This may run counter to the ECB's intention to prop up both the fiscal and bank stability of the crisis countries. Reducing the interdependence between banks and governments, is a healthy and understandable reaction of financial market participants, and can make the financial web more robust.

A similarly healthy reaction of the financial web is to review the notion of "risk-free" assets once investors doubt even those considered the safest debtors – industrial country governments. The amount of securities still receiving the highest rating (AAA), including that of governments, has indeed receded as a result of the crisis.

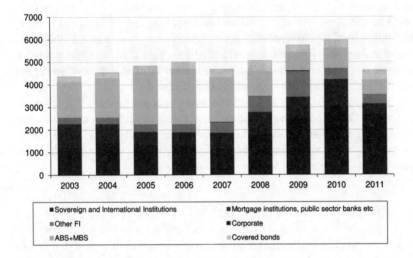

Figure 1.5: AAA issues in recent years (in USD bn)

Source: BIS.

However, this market reaction is not without problems. When only a few "safe havens" for debt investments remain during a time of crisis, even these "safe havens" can develop into an asset bubble. As an example, the extremely low interest rates the German government had to pay in early 2012 on its new debt issues are not only a mirror of excellent return on investment for the risk associated with Bunds. It also mirrors the fact that investors are trying to insure themselves against a break-up of the Euro area. In all conceivable scenarios, interest rates on German government debt close to zero percent do not appear to be sustainable.

So what does this boil down to? Can the global financial web repair itself from the damage of the crisis? And repair itself in such a way as to not lay the ground for future crises?

The answer is – probably not. We have to do more to return the whole system to sustainable stability.

The first paradigm shift showed that debt was mispriced, not adequately taking into account systemic risk. More importantly, it probably is still mispriced, despite regulatory lessons learnt from the crisis regarding the need for more financial resilience, as well as measures taken thus far to ensure greater European fiscal stability. Before the crisis, there was a widespread belief that globalisation – including major financial innovations, such as the securitisation of subprime loans and the introduction of the euro – would mean a greater tolerance for higher debt levels. The reasoning: the bigger and deeper financial markets are, the less market distortions loom, and more resilience to shocks would be the hoped-for result. Innovations, such as the euro or collateralised debt obligations, would remove risk from the system, or at least distribute it in a more stable way. This was an intellectually elegant view, and was not without some theoretic justification, but proved insufficient nonetheless: contagion potential and systemic risk were still underestimated.

Subsequently, the crisis revealed the second paradigm shift: that there are less "risk-free" assets than previously expected. This shift can massively impair the way the financial web develops beyond the crisis years. In particular, it may prevent governments from reacting the way they should to the new financial web environment left behind by the crisis.

3. HOW TO DEAL WITH THE TWO PARADIGM SHIFTS

As debt levels prior to the crisis were deemed to be too high, a period of deleveraging had to start. A certain degree of progress was made in some countries in 2011 (see Roxburgh et al. 2012). This is all the more remarkable, as any such deleveraging faces obstacles:

- Credit crunches may result if there is excess demand for credit while banks attempt to reduce their risk-weighted assets (which they do in a bid to please their investors pushing for lower risk, and also due to the new Basel accord regulations and stress testing).
- When debt is reduced, it can hamper growth. Lower growth usually leads to political conflict. This is particularly true in Europe, where the role the euro has played in the crisis, and rescue packages for crisis countries, have already entailed a lot of controversy.
- In the process of deleveraging, there can be a reversal of cross-border flows, as market participants may perceive international claims as more risky than domestic assets, and thus reduce their cross-border credit exposure first (as suggested by international banking data in BIS, 2007-2012, table 9A). This could mean a less optimal global asset allocation, and may support political views favouring protectionism.

Rising public debt supports the deleveraging process in the private sector, but is largely a zero-sum game for the whole economy when no further consolidation steps are taken and the road to growth and economic recovery remains elusive.

The deleveraging path can likewise be eased by a central bank policy that achieves a very delicate balance between doing too little and prolonging the crisis and doing too much and risking inflation. The major central banks of the industrial countries have so far executed a very impressive crisis management, replacing dried up interbank money markets and making up for lost investor trust. But the big challenge they face is to find the correct exit strategy out of the crisis measures all the way to quantitative easing, with part of the deleveraging challenge and the aforementioned obstacles basically now becoming a monetary policy challenge.

Even so, additional liquidity supply by central banks can only buy time; time which is needed to implement the necessary changes to the global financial web so that it no longer misprices debt and can handle the reduction of risk-free assets. Furthermore, all of those sectors connected by debt linkages have to use the time to adjust – the household and corporate sectors, banks and financial markets, as well as governments.

The *two major players involved* in the current sovereign debt crisis are *banks* and *governments*.

Banks have already done quite a lot with the changes they have made to their business models, both in reaction to the global financial crisis since 2007 directly, as well as to regulatory changes (see reports by IIF 2011; FSB 2011; BCBS 2012). Higher and stricter capital requirements for banks, for instance, represent a major correction of mispriced debt. The extent of the changes demanded from the banking sector can also serve to illustrate what still lies ahead for other sectors.

A crucial consequence of the sovereign debt crisis in this respect, though, is that the pre-crisis trend of relatively less and less bank financing for governments will likely continue.

How are governments going to react to such a reduction in the number of potential investors in sovereign debt, while at the same time, their demand for debt financing remains high as long as the crisis continues?

The situation of a *government debtor* is, to a certain extent, the same as that of a private debtor. In order to get debt under control, there is always the possibility to raise income and reduce spending. Raising income necessitates a boost to productivity and competitiveness (both usually by way of structural reform), but is difficult to achieve, and takes time before results are seen. Spending cuts are faster and more reliable, but reduce overall GDP in the short term, and are likely to encounter more political resistance. Even the government-only option to raise taxes encounters similar problems as spending cuts, and is even somewhat less reliable in its effect due to potential reactions and adjustments by the private sector. Consequently, the option to reduce spending and increase income like a private debtor appears to be a tough one for governments.

There are also four additional, easier options for governments. The *easier options* are:

1. Governments force central banks to allow *higher inflation* (boosting their tax take and reducing the real value of debt outstanding). This is an option available only to governments with national central banks that lack independence from political interference, and thus with access to the money printing press.
2. Governments resort to severe market interventions to obtain financing from the private sector beyond tax hikes (e.g., legally forcing investment in government bonds). This has been termed *"financial repression"* and has been used – alongside inflation – quite often in past sovereign debt crises of the 20th century (Reinhart and Sbrancia 2011).
3. Closely related to financial repression is the potential for governments to get credit from those parts of the financial sector that are less regulated than banks, and can provide credit: the *shadow banking sector*. The substantial increase in regulation in the banking sector following the global financial crisis makes this potential option even more attractive.
4. Finally, as the numerous *international fiscal bailout* programmes by the IMF and European governments have shown, a country can also try to continuously secure debt financing from other, more stable countries, once it loses the trust of the markets.

All of these four easy options share one major problem: they would not enhance the stability of the global financial web, but rather weaken it: investor confidence would take a blow, rather than be restored. The true price of debt cannot be found this way; in fact, it would become even more obscured.

Governments would face the following *drawbacks* of the easy options:

1. Inflation, apart from the obvious detrimental effects on financial market stability in the long term, runs the risk of not working at all in terms of improving a government's fiscal position – if everyone in the financial web from institutional investor to individual workers and investors anticipate higher inflation and demand a higher interest rate to compensate for it. Reducing debt with everything but hyperinflation would take years – a time during which everyone would be able to adjust to inflation surprises. Thus, on the whole, trust would not be strengthened but rather ultimately shaken.

   It should be borne in mind, however, that a temporary increase in inflation during crisis years is not a sign of alarm, but merely the way economies react to more volatile financial market conditions. It is only when inflation is there to *stay* – used for government debt purposes – that the trouble starts. Furthermore, within a monetary union, regional differences in inflation should be allowed – at least temporarily.
2. Using sovereign power to exert financial repression could work better than inflation, in that a government could obtain financing without private sector anticipation able to prevent it. However, the damage to the real economy may also be counterproductive over the long run. The financial web is built on trust. If rules are changed suddenly, and property rights are ignored when

convenient, trust is lost. In this regard, a finely balanced introduction, transition period and calibration of the new international liquidity standards is of key importance for banks and insurances.

3. Getting more debt finance from the shadow banking sector would also not be of much help. A government, which, with its regulation and behaviour, forces banks to provide less credit for its finances, and then simply turns to different parts of the financial sector, would be suffering from self-delusion. Worse, it would also lower financial stability, not support it.

4. This leaves the easy option to hope for indefinite bailouts from more stable governments in the global financial web. This, of course, is the exact opposite of a contribution to financial stability, an attempt to perpetuate a moral hazard situation that can only provide the wrong incentives.

As such, with the easy options clearly not helpful in restoring financial stability and lowering systemic risk, only the *tough option* for governments remains – *budget consolidation* from high levels of debt, with reforms and spending reductions. This is not without historical precedence (for instance, the impressive reduction of the government debt of Belgium from the 1990s to the eve of the crisis years in 2007). But such measures typically encounter political resistance, since ultimately, any sovereign debt reduction affects the distribution of income and wealth within an economy, and is decided by a democratic political process. Thus, while the easy options of debt reduction are ultimately detrimental to fiscal and financial stability, they may still be taken in an effort to achieve a political compromise.

Table 2.1: Redistribution effects of different measures to reduce government debt

Measure for reducing debt	Economic area/part of society burdened
Default	All creditors of the respective debt
Devaluation of currency	All foreign creditors, importers
Inflation	All creditors, all with rel. less pricing power
Taxes on	
Labour income/wages	All domestic employed
Value added	All consumers (to a linear degree)
Financial assets and capital gains	All savers/holders of financial assets
Real estate/property	Landowners and houseowners
Reduction of spending	
Subsidies	Respective industries
Social spending	Low income/unemployed/families

In this respect, *international support* for crisis countries, e.g., by the IMF and the new European Stability Mechanism (ESM), can play a key role. Although, as mentioned earlier, such help can threaten to create moral hazard, and delay adjustments for too long, it can create a compromise between crisis country domestic efforts to adjust to lower levels of debt, and economic and political upheaval in the process. Moreover, it is through such international agreements and negotiations that more binding fiscal rules and a commitment to a fiscally sustainable path may be found, as aid would only be provided after securing clear commitments from the crisis countries, and once these have taken specific actions to underpin their commitment to reform.

However, long-term international solidarity should not go so far as to attempt to mutualise national debt (example: "euro bonds" and, more recently, "project bonds"). This is too similar to the easy options out of debt mentioned earlier: continuous transfers and bailouts for those who are not able to handle debt financing properly in the long run. Such transfers would only be feasible within a national state prepared to continuously finance poorer regions for political reasons, and with the intention to jointly issue debt for better liquidity and technical efficiency (e.g., "Deutschlandbonds" within a fiscal federal state like Germany can make sense, where in any case, the centre ultimately takes full responsibility for all public liabilities of the regions. Also, within national borders, a central government is usually entitled – and practically able to – discipline regional authorities as part of its sovereign power). Therefore, a mutualisation of national debt via instruments like euro bonds can only be a solution after much more political integration in Europe is achieved.

However, avoiding pitfalls along the adjustment paths that governments must take is by far not the only means to restore stability to the global financial web. *Systemic risk and debt need to be correctly priced again*, with various improvements to regulation beyond that already underway.

- Generally, there is the task to *reduce leverage, interconnectedness and complexity* in the global financial web.

  As illustrated, when the financial sector piles up debt in excess of the credit it intermediates for the real economy, there may be problems, since the *interconnectedness* in the global financial web creates interdependencies and potential for contagion.

  Additionally, the kind of *leverage* that is not client-driven and merely speculative needs to be tackled. Massive losses from speculation – be it by rogue traders or whole financial institutions strategies going wrong – can pose a serious systemic risk, while not creating any corresponding economic value. Such investment bank activity amounts to a zero-sum game within the financial sector that should be stopped by regulation.

  As for *complexity*, the subprime crisis has shown how quickly complicated structured products with opaque risk exposures can cause a loss of trust in larger sections of financial activity. It would be an understandable general strategy for regulation and supervision to rather err on the safe side before allowing such products in such large amounts. After all, complexity in financial markets makes regulating them all the more difficult. Another lesson learnt would be to provide incentives for the originators of such products to never be able to shed all of the risks associated with them. This way, their motivation for monitoring the original credit remains intact. Complexity is also an issue for technical developments, such as high frequency trading, which is vulnerable to breakdowns and distortions.

- The *Euro* needs a political and fiscal union with binding rules for debt ceilings on government debt, also taking into account private sector debt (which, as seen during the crisis, can turn into implicit or explicit government debt due to bailouts). The failure of the Stability and Growth Pact serves as a reminder as to how binding these rules have to be to work. After abandoning their own currencies, monetary union member countries should either be willing to *relinquish even more sovereignty in other political areas* to a European supranational level as necessary, or not participate in a single currency at all. The tricky part is to determine precisely which areas are necessary? And what is the proper level of political and fiscal union in Europe?
  - First of all, maximum government debt levels need to be ascertained in such a way that *national parliaments no longer have the right to exceed* such *debt limits*. As such, this kind of fiscal union would limit debt, but not interfere with how taxes and public spending are handled (i.e. no "transfer or social union"). It is also useful to compare this core subsidiarity principle of the European integration process with similar checks and balances within national states: only rarely does political union mean a centralisation of all aspects of fiscal and economic policy (for instance, in Germany, it is the municipalities that implement various aspects of social policy, not all is done by the central government in Berlin).
  - Second, some Euro area governments had to step in with debt-making and fiscal bailouts for their banking systems, since their respective *national supervisory authorities* had failed to recognise systemic risk in their country of jurisdiction, which was big enough to spill over to other countries (prominent example: Ireland). This is best solved by advancing a pan-European financial supervisory structure. Note that this does not mean that the road to this new structure will always be a smooth one (as the European Banking Authority has shown with its stress tests).
  - Finally, rising private sector debt may also trigger a fiscal bailout that spills over to peripheral Euro area countries, even if the government had very low government debt before the bailout (example: Spain). Once again, in such a case, more scrutiny by a centralised financial supervision can be crucial – only that this time it would concentrate on macro

and systemic risks (as the *macroprudential supervision* so far attached to the ECB in the form of the European Systemic Risk Board).

However, all these steps towards further European integration need to be supported by the democratic, political will of the individual countries – and in particular their citizens – or they are bound to fail. If Europe fails to obtain the necessary emotional backing, no single currency or improved institutions to reinforce systemic stability can help. This also pertains to concerns that may come up in the event that a Euro area member leaves the monetary union. Any such exits should not be allowed to call into question the idea of monetary union and European integration per se, as long as the political will and convictions are behind it.

- *Shadow banks* have to be regulated in a way that addresses the same systemic risk concerns as has been the case for banks so far – as soon as they provide and receive credit like banks. The core principle here is that whatever causes systemic risks – inside and outside the banking sector – has to be regulated in the same way. An alternative is to create firm firewalls between the regulated banking sector and the shadow banking sector, obstructing any financial links, in particular those established by credit. This way, financial turmoil in shadow banking would not spill over to the banking sector. Without such a safeguard, the latter would be more prone to systemic risk.
- *Government debt* as an asset has long received special treatment in terms of *regulation*. In the crisis countries, such preferential treatment was apparently misplaced – and this might potentially prove to be the case in other countries as well. Regulation favouring government debt needs to be put on the regulatory agenda, including: zero risk weights for capital requirements in the Basel and CRD accords; exceptions from large credit exposures; lack of predictable and orderly resolution mechanisms for defaulting.

4. CONCLUSION AND OUTLOOK

Two paradigm shifts have emerged as a result of the crisis: systemic risk from individual debt contracts is higher than expected before the crisis, and the notion of risk-free assets has come under serious doubt. The consequences are also two-fold.

First, measures need to be taken to ensure that interest rates for individual debt-making – be it in the financial or non-financial sector, including banks and governments – henceforth factor in the systemic risk potential such debt-making has, in order to prevent excessive debt accumulation in future.

Second, many governments need to restore investor trust in their fiscal stability. On the path to stability, it is essential that they avoid easy options for debt reduction as much as politically possible. This is because the easy options would endanger the very fiscal and financial stability that debt consolidation aims to restore. Instead, governments need to focus on structural reforms and spending reductions, possibly helped by the international community to avoid too much domestic political resistance, but only as long as that international assistance is temporary, and with a firm agenda to support domestic reforms.

Even with all these measures, risk and volatility will remain in the system. *After all, the successful management of such risk is the very reason why financial markets and intermediation exist in the first place!*

Likewise, systemic risk itself will never vanish completely. This is because all debt obligations are based on expectations for the future, which by its very nature is uncertain. Such uncertainty can only be overcome with trust – and trust is indeed systemic in nature: Once trust is lost in an individual debtor or debt security, it can trigger crises of confidence in anything deemed similar to that product, or indeed in the act of lending itself.

The art is to achieve financial and fiscal stability that allows a sustainable degree of risk amplitude and crisis frequency in the system, while avoiding wholesale crises that may cause its breakdown.

BIBLIOGRAPHY

Bank for International Settlements (BIS) 2007-2012, *Quarterly Reviews*, Basel. Internet link: http://www.bis.org/publ/qtrpdf/r_qt1203.htm.

Basel Committee on Banking Supervision (BCBS) 2012, *Progress Report on Basel III Implementation*, April, Basel. Internet link: http://www.bis.org/publ/bcbs215.pdf (*accessed 24 May 2012*).

Cecchetti, S. G., M. S. Mohanty and F. Zampolli 2011, "The real effects of debt", *BIS Working Papers* No. 352, Basel: Bank for International Settlements. Internet link: http://www.bis.org/publ/work352.pdf (*accessed 24 May 2012*).

Creditreform Wirtschaftsforschung 2012, *Wirtschaftslage und Finanzierung im Mittelstand*, Frühjahr, Neuss. Internet link: http://www.creditreform.de/Deutsch/Creditreform/Presse/Archiv/Wirtschaftslage_Mittelstand_DE/2012-04/2012-04-16_Wirtschaftslage_Mittelstand_DE.pdf (*accessed 24 May 2012*).

Financial Stability Board (FSB) 2011, *Overview of Progress in the Implementation of the G20 Recommendations for Strengthening Financial Stability*, 4 November 2011, Basel. Internet link: http://www.financialstabilityboard.org/publications/r_111104.pdf (*accessed 24 May 2012*).

Institute of International Finance (IIF) 2011, *The Cumulative Impact of the Global Economy of Changes in the Financial Regulatory Framework*, Washington, D.C.: IIF.

Moog, S., C. Müller and B. Raffelhüschen 2010, "Ehrbare Staaten? Die deutsche Generationenbilanz im internationalen Vergleich: Wie gut ist Deutschland auf die demografische Herausforderung vorbreitet?", Diskussionsbeiträge des Forschungszentrums Generationenverträge, Albert-Ludwigs-Universität Freiburg, 44, also published in: *Argumente zu Marktwirtschaft und Politik, Stiftung Marktwirtschaft*, 110. Internet link: http://www.fiwi1.uni-freiburg.de/publikationen/258.pdf (*accessed 24 May 2012*).

Organisation for Economic Co-operation and Development (OECD) 2011, OECD Economic Outlook, December 2011, Paris: OECD.

Reinhart, C. and K. Rogoff 2009, *This Time is Different – Eight Centuries of Financial Folly*, Princeton: Princeton University Press.

Reinhart, C. and B. Sbrancia 2011, "The liquidation of government debt", *NBER Working Paper* No. 16893. Internet link: http://www.imf.org/external/np/seminars/eng/2011/res2/pdf/crbs.pdf (*accessed 24 May 2012*).

Roxburgh, C., S. Lund, T. Daruvala, J. Manyika, R. Dobbs, R. Forn and K. Croxson 2012, *Debt and Deleveraging: Uneven Progress on the Path to Growth*, McKinsey Global Institute. Internet link: http://www.mckinsey.com/Insights/MGI/Research/Financial_Markets/Uneven_progress_on_the_path_to_growth (*accessed 24 May 2012*).

Sinn, H-W. 2011, *Kasino-Kapitalismus – Wie es zur Krise kam, und was jetzt zu tun ist*, Berlin: Ullstein Buchverlage, 2nd edition.

2. Criteria for Financial Stability – The European View

Andreas Dombret

---

1. FINANCIAL STABILITY IN EUROPE

When Andrew Crockett gave a speech in 2000 about "Marrying the micro-prudential and macroprudential dimension of financial stability" it was almost impossible to guess more than a decade ago how prophetic his seminal contribution would turn out to be. At that time, South Asian countries were only just recovering from a severe currency crisis and the Argentine crisis was about to unfold. Some years before, the world had already witnessed the bursting of property bubbles in Japan and in some Scandinavian countries. And two years before Crockett published his marriage speech the world had gasped as the Long Term Capital Management hedge fund had to be bailed out. At this time, financial stability started to become a priority in international policy forums, and central banks as well as supervisory authorities started to publish financial stability reports.

As financial stability was a new concept, the general discussion was initially ambivalent. There was the general feeling that globalisation had changed the world economy and its financial system in a profound way. Most commentators, however, were hailing the benefits of globalisation, while financial crises were largely seen as a problem of emerging economies or a local phenomenon. At all events, many observers held the view that banking crises were best addressed through adequate minimum capital requirements.

The worldwide financial crisis that ensued after the Lehman Brothers default and the ongoing European debt crisis have changed that view completely. The former shows how an originally regional problem in a segment of the US housing market can have global impact. Likewise, in the European debt crisis a local phenomenon became systemic (Dombret 2012a).

There are some specific European characteristics which afford a European view on financial stability. Firstly, the financial market in Europe is highly integrated, with financial intermediaries heavily engaged in cross-border and cross-sector activities. For this reason, a problem in one sector of the financial sector can easily be transmitted across borders and across sectors and lead to widespread contagion. Secondly, despite years of ongoing financial integration in Europe, financial supervision was fragmented with different national authorities remaining in charge of their respective institutions and markets. It became evident that a lack of cooperation between national supervisors can cause severe problems. Thirdly, notwithstanding the fact that markets became more integrated, important differences in the financial culture and the financial structure between the EU member states remain. This is a fact that outsiders often tend to ignore, particularly with regard to the European debt crisis. Fourthly, the single currency has brought huge benefits but – due to the lack of a political union – has also created problems of its own.

Against this backdrop, Europe's establishment of a new supervisory framework, the *European System of Financial Supervision* (ESFS) in January 2011, taking up the warnings of Andrew Crockett and implementing the recommendations of the *De Larosière Report* (2009), marked a milestone. The ESFS has a microprudential and a macroprudential pillar, with the European Supervisory Authorities (ESAs) in charge of microprudential supervision and the European Systemic Risk Board (ESRB) having responsibility for macroprudential oversight.

Marrying the microprudential and macroprudential dimensions of financial stability requires a clear concept of these two dimensions. Whereas microprudential regulation has traditionally concentrated mainly on the regulation of individual institutions, the macroprudential dimension emphasises systemic risks arising from the collective behaviour of market participants. The EU and the ESRB define systemic risk as "*the risk of disruption in the financial system with the potential to have serious negative consequences for the internal market and real economy*". Effective macroprudential oversight of the financial system affords specific analytical tools as well as a range of macroprudential instruments to address systemic risks.

2. BANKING REGULATION AND FINANCIAL INTEGRATION IN EUROPE

The EU is based on the idea that member countries establish a common market for goods, services, capital and people out of formerly closed national markets. In order to foster financial integration, the EU has started several initiatives to reduce differences in national banking regulations and supervisory regimes that constitute obstacles to integration.

The first important initiative was the implementation of the *First Banking Directive* in 1977, which introduced the principle of "home country control" in banking supervision. According to this principle the member state licensing a bank is also responsible for supervising its activities throughout the EU. Another important step was the introduction of a single passport for European banks by the *Second Banking Directive* in 1989. The European passport grants all banks in the EU the right to offer services, either through the cross-border provision of services or through the establishment of branches, in any other member state without seeking authorisation from the host countries. To prevent regulatory arbitrage and to ensure a level playing field, the EU set common standards for the regulation of financial institutions, such as minimum standards for capital regulation, large exposures or deposit insurance (Barth et al., 2006). Further initiatives were outlined in the *Financial Services Action Plan* of 1999 and the *White Paper* of 2005. Finally, the introduction of the Euro in 1999 was a huge step in the process of creating an integrated financial market in Europe as it eliminated currency risk among euro-area countries and made it easier for borrowers and investors to take advantage of borrowing and investment opportunities.[1]

Large differences in the degree of integration across markets remain, however. While wholesale markets already show a higher degree of integration, retail markets are still highly fragmented (see, e.g., ECB 2011). In Germany, for example, cross-border lending to the real sector represented only slightly more than 20% of total non-bank lending before the crisis. By contrast, cross-border lending to banks accounted for 53% of total interbank lending. On the other hand, cross-border assets in wholesale markets levelled off during the crisis, while retail banking markets have been much less affected. It remains to be seen whether this development, which hints at some re-nationalisation of bank activities, is only temporary.

All in all, the integration of wholesale markets is driven by large cross-border banks that have operations in several EU countries and hold a large proportion of total assets abroad. Internal capital markets allow these banks to isolate their lending from fluctuations in funding and to continue lending in economic upswings if growth in deposits does not keep pace with lending growth (Navaretti et al. 2010).[2]

For some time, the increasing cross-border nature of banking in the EU was not adequately reflected in an appropriate regulatory and supervisory framework. The increased interconnectedness of banks in the EU has led to a rise in the risk of contagion across countries (Degryse et al. 2010). The speed at which a shock spreads through the system has risen in line with financial integration. This became apparent in the crisis when cross-border banking activities appeared to be among the most vulnerable and were subject to a cross-border deleveraging process.[3]

---

[1] Kalemli-Ozcan et al. (2010) find that the primary driver of the euro's impact on financial integration in Europe is the elimination of currency risk. Legislative and regulatory reforms undertaken in parallel with the introduction of the euro also contributed to financial integration. Trade in goods, by contrast, did not explain the positive effect of the euro on financial integration.
[2] See Goldberg (2009) for a survey on internal capital markets.
[3] This corresponds to the literature that shows that the effect of the financial crisis on the real economy varied in line with the degree of financial integration (Kalemli-Ozcan et al., forthcoming).

According to the *De Larosière Report* (2009), national authorities did not sufficiently cooperate and coordinate their actions with regard to cross-border institutions. The old supervisory framework was evidently ill equipped to deal with these problems. Not only was cooperation often difficult to achieve during the crisis, it sometimes failed completely at the resolution stage when national authorities tried to minimise the impact on their respective country and to ring-fence assets. These problems point to the "trilemma" of maintaining national responsibility, financial integration and financial stability at the same time (Schoenmaker 2011).

It also became evident – and not only in Europe – that the regulatory and supervisory framework was too focused on the stability of individual institutions rather than on the stability of the system as a whole. Broadly speaking, the microprudential concept treats risk largely as an exogenous parameter (Borio 2011). Risks to financial stability, however, often arise endogenously. For instance, if one bank decides to shed risky assets – for example in response to regulatory pressure – this can result in financial instability if done collectively by all banks.[4]

There can be no doubt that systemic risk has increased significantly over the past two decades. A greater move is therefore needed towards a macroprudential oversight which is clearly oriented towards the stability of the financial system including all parts of the financial system, taking cross-sectional interdependencies into account. The shadow banking sector is an important example in this context. While this sector largely evaded regulatory attention before the crisis it proved to be a main contributor to the propagation of financial instability (Dombret 2012b). The challenge in the European context will be to strike the right balance between strengthening the macroprudential pillar of supervision and keeping a level playing field. It is crucial to correctly identify and accurately measure systemic risks, since the outcome will be a prerequisite and basis for the development of suitable instruments.

3. SYSTEMIC RISKS IN THE EUROPEAN FINANCIAL SECTOR

Potential threats to the stability of the financial system have different origins, and risks are transmitted via various channels. Each of the different "dimensions" of systemic risk has specific characteristics which have to be taken into account by future macroprudential oversight schemes.

---

[4] See Hördahl and King (2008) and Gorton and Metrick (forthcoming) for a more detailed analysis of repo runs during the crisis.

3.1. Cyclical Imbalances

One potential source of financial instability stems from the build-up of aggregate financial imbalances over time. The hypothesis of mutually reinforcing cycles of "booms" and "busts" in the real economy and the financial sector has existed for a long time (see, e.g., Minsky 1982). Until the outbreak of the 2007-2009 global financial crisis, however, many held the view that central banks should not aim to "lean" against growing imbalances, but instead just "mop up" the aftermath of a financial collapse.[5] This prevailing view has been challenged as the crisis revealed the huge potential costs of a systemic disruption in modern financial markets. For example, it has been estimated that the cumulative negative impact of the crisis on the real economy exceeded 10 percent of GDP in advanced economies (Drehmann et al. 2011). Other estimates (Haldane 2010) even calculate the present value of global output losses at between USD 60 trillion and USD 200 trillion, i.e. between one and more than three times the global annual GDP.

The central problem is how to measure the gradual build-up of imbalances and vulnerabilities and which macroprudential instruments can be implemented to mitigate the associated risks to system-wide stability. The problem is aggravated by the "*paradox of financial instability*" which says that the system appears strongest precisely when it is most vulnerable (Borio and Drehmann 2009). For instance, risk premiums and volatilities tend to be below their long-term averages just before the onset of a crisis. Consequently, measures of risk based on raw market prices such as probabilities of default or unconditional value-at-risk figures give an incomplete picture of the current level and structure of systemic risk (Borio 2011).

Financial leverage appears to be a better measure of imminent systemic risks (Schoenmaker and Wierts 2011). As a case in point, the burst of the dot-com bubble in 2000, which was predominantly equity financed, had a limited impact on the financial system, while things were significantly different in the aftermath of the mainly debt financed US housing market bubble of 2007. The credit-to-GDP gap, i.e. the difference between the ratio of the indebtedness of the household and corporate sectors to GDP and its long-term trend, is often considered a measure of whether growth is excessively financed by debt.

Based on this idea, the new Basel III framework (BCBS 2011a) has introduced a countercyclical capital buffer which rises during periods of credit expansion and declines at times of incipient financial stress with the aim of limiting the amplitude of financial cycles (Borio 2011). These buffers enhance the resilience of the financial sector to systemic events and can, in the event of a crisis, interrupt the domino effect of the sequential default of institutions and mitigate contagion. Capital buffers reduce

---

[5] For a critical review of the pre-crisis literature see, e.g., White (2009).

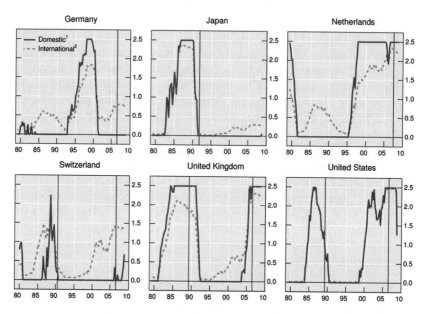

Figure 2.1: Countercyclical capital buffers

The vertical lines denote the beginning of a crisis.

[1] Buffer based on credit-to-GDP gap of the specific country (it would reflect the total charge for banks located there if they did not have any international exposures). [2] Buffer of a hypothetical bank whose portfolio of domestic and cross-border credit corresponds to that of the banking system in the given jurisdiction.

Source: Drehmann, Borio and Tsatsaronis (2011).

procyclicality in the system because financial institutions are less inclined to offload risky assets and curb their lending during an economic downturn. Regarding the future implementation at EU level, the European Commission (2011) has recently proposed a new Capital Requirements Directive (CRD IV) which is currently being discussed by European policy-makers. In this context, a crucial point particularly in the European environment will be the question of how to adequately apply such buffers for institutions with major cross-border activities. The ESRB has recognised the importance of sufficient flexibility, stating that macroprudential authorities *"need discretion to require additional disclosures and to tighten temporarily a diverse range of calibration"* (ESRB 2012). From a European perspective the challenge is to find enough flexibility when implementing instruments without jeopardising the level playing field in the single market (Dombret 2012a). Figure 2.1 presents the calculated capital buffers for six countries based on both domestic and global exposures and reveals a large amount of heterogeneity among the examined jurisdictions.

Another potential macroprudential instrument to mitigate the procyclicality related to lending is the introduction of time-varying restrictions on loan-to-value and debt-to-income ratios. By cyclically tightening/easing the eligibility criteria for real estate loans, the aim is to reduce the likelihood and/or magnitude of an unhealthy housing price boom and to improve the system's resilience to the negative impacts of a real estate bust (Crowe et al. 2011). Similarly, it has been proposed that excessive credit expansion could be restricted by adopting a rules-based dynamic (time-varying) loan loss provisioning framework requiring banks to build up buffers during an upswing which can be drawn down in a recession (IMF 2011a). In order to address cyclicality, particularly in intra-financial system activity, variations in margining requirements have also been suggested (Bank of England 2011).

Maturity transformation has been identified as another potentially harmful source of cyclical systemic risks. As banks tend to lend long-term and borrow short-term, they increase the likelihood of bank runs, liquidity hoarding and asset fire sales (Bank of England 2011). While the new Basel III framework (BCBS 2011a) contains two static liquidity measures, i.e. the liquidity coverage ratio and the net stable funding ratio, some observers propose introducing potentially time-varying liquidity risk charges, e.g., a levy on non-core short-term funding (Perotti and Suarez 2011) or a prudential risk surcharge on the gap between a bank's current liquidity position and the new Basel III norms (Goodhart and Perotti 2012). Finally, reserve requirements have been discussed, and have in fact been used in the past by emerging market economies as a macroprudential tool to guard against time-varying liquidity risks and excessive credit growth (Gray 2011; Lim et al. 2011). Moreover, since unhedged loans in foreign currency might entail potential risks if the common exposure is large, restrictions on foreign lending may be used to limit vulnerability to sudden exchange rate shifts (Lim et al. 2011).

In summary, a set of potential macroprudential instruments is currently being discussed in international forums with the aim of mitigating the cyclical component of system-wide risks to financial stability. While they primarily focus on the banking system, it is equally important to adequately address all other potential sources of instability, e.g., the "shadow banking" sector (credit intermediation provided by entities hitherto outside the regulated system).

3.2. Structural Externalities

A potential threat to financial stability might arise from common exposures and interlinkages within the financial system. For any given level of time-varying risk as discussed in the last section, the systemic consequences of a shock depend strongly on the structural features of the financial sector (Bank of England 2011). Consequently, macroprudential tools addressing the cross-sectional dimension should be calibrated according to the contribution of each institution to systemic risk with the aim of internalising the externality it imposes on the system (Borio 2011).

In the real world, the various contagion channels are difficult to isolate. This is also reflected in the variety of approaches to measuring endogenous systemic risk, which each emphasise different aspects.[6] These approaches should be understood as a set of analytical instruments which investigate different aspects of systemic risk. These measures are often less relevant as policy tools, as important micro data for measuring contagion risk is lacking. The situation has improved since the creation of the ESFS but important challenges concerning data confidentiality remain.

To address the systemic and moral hazard risks associated with systemically important financial institutions, SIFIs in short, the G20 leaders have agreed to introduce capital surcharges for international banks subject to their degree of global systemic importance (FSB 2011c; BCBS 2011b; Dombret 2012c). The methodology currently proposed for assessing the level of systemic importance is based on a set of five broad indicators – cross-jurisdictional activity, size, interconnectedness, substitutability/financial institution infrastructure and complexity. The precise definition of the requirements may be refined in the future in light of new research. In the European context, national SIFIs need to be included in the respective regulatory framework.

Systemic risks might also arise from the opacity and complexity of markets and infrastructures (Bank of England 2011). The design of market mechanisms can, for instance, amplify or dampen the transmission of shocks, while it is crucial to have robust infrastructures, e.g. payment and settlement systems, including central counterparties, in order to mitigate cross-sectional systemic risks. Examples of current macroprudential regulatory issues in this field include new rules for the trading of over-the-counter derivatives (FSB 2011a; Heller and Vause 2012) or the question of how to adequately monitor and supervise the "shadow banking" sector, i.e. the system of credit intermediation that involves entities and activities outside the regulated banking system (FSB-IMF-BIS 2011; FSB 2011b).

---

[6] A prominent proposal has recently been made by Adrian and Brunnermeier (2011) who advocate the so-called "conditional value-at-risk" measure which can be calculated and compared under different conditions. Another approach is presented by Acharya et al. (2012) who propose the so-called "systemic expected shortfall" measure which is based on the concept of marginal expected shortfall. Brownlees and Engle (2011) use a similar method to estimate the percentage of capital shortfall that can be expected in a future crisis. Drehmann and Tarashev (2011) present a "contribution approach", rooted in the Shapley value methodology, to target banks' risk contributions. Finally, Huang, Zhou and Zhu (2011) propose a so-called "distress insurance premium" and provide a comparison with the CoVaR and MES measures. Several further methodologies are presented and critically discussed in Deutsche Bundesbank (2011).

3.3. Integrated Monitoring and Governance

The last two sections discussed the two main sources of systemic risks. A coherent, comprehensive monitoring system is needed in order to fully benefit from the measures of systemic risk (FSB-IMF-BIS 2011).

The literature discusses several definitions of an integrated framework for the measurement and treatment of systemic risks. Various stress indexes have been developed for various regions.[7] Calculating common indicators for Europe or the Euro area requires harmonised data from member countries. Statistical experts thus have to agree on common definitions and frequencies, which is a field where we can expect to benefit from European cooperation.

Macro stress testing is often used to examine the stability of the financial system under specific adverse conditions. By defining different hypothetical scenarios, this technique models how various shocks are propagated through the system in order to discover potential vulnerabilities and imbalances.

An integrated approach is currently being developed by the ESRB.[8] The envisaged "*risk dashboard*" will cover market, credit and liquidity risks as well as exposures and interlinkages and aims to provide an up-to-date picture of the current level and composition of systemic risk with regard to both its cyclical and structural dimension. The results will be presented, notably, in the form of "heat maps" depicting the evolution of systemic risks over time and providing the basis for cross-country comparisons. From the European perspective, a challenge for all of the mentioned approaches is to find a balance between both capturing heterogeneous developments in the different jurisdictions and providing a meaningful overview of systemic risks in Europe as a whole.

3.4. Risk and Uncertainty

These tools are important and helpful in preventing and managing systemic risks. Nevertheless, the question remains whether they actually are sufficient. This seems questionable given the high level of complexity that has arisen in globally integrated financial markets. This complexity leads to non-linear dynamics in the system which are difficult to handle, both for the risk management of financial institutions and for supervisors. It is also characterised by "Knightian uncertainty" (Knight 2002; Caballero 2010; Dombret 2012a), named after Chicago economist Frank Knight. Knight argued: "*There are known knowns;*

---

[7] Illing and Liu (2006) develop a stress index for the Canadian financial system, Hakkio and Keeton (2009) present the "Kansas City Financial Stress Index" (KCFSI) and Cardarelli, Elekdag and Lall (2009) construct an index of financial stress for seventeen advanced countries. More recent contributions include Slingenberg and de Haan (2011), who analyse thirteen OECD countries, and Oet et al. (2011), who present the "Cleveland Financial Stress Index" (CFSI), which provides a continuous signal and broad coverage of financial stress.

[8] More information on the ongoing development can be found on the ESRB's homepage (http://www.esrb.europa.eu/about/tasks/html/index.en.html).

there are things we know we know. We also know there are known unknowns; that is to say we know there are some things we do not know. But there are also unknown unknowns – the ones we don't know we don't know."

For example, prior to the financial crisis a shadow banking system emerged which found itself at the centre of the crisis. This shadow banking system also has some elements of "unknown unknowns". As a consequence, risks stemming from this system were broadly ignored or underestimated. Even if systemic risks are calculated successfully, we cannot ultimately be sure that we have identified all relevant risks, because "unknown unknowns" may well also exist in another area of the financial system which we are not observing.

To give another example, there are a large number of regulatory target variables which involve the use of complex risk-adjusting methods. For instance, the core capital ratio is the ratio of core capital to risk-weighted assets. Yet the models used for adjusting the risk did not perform perfectly and underestimated the true risks stemming from CDOs. As a result, financial institutions were undercapitalised when Lehman Brothers became insolvent.

This argumentation has consequences for instruments. If there had been a robust target such as a leverage ratio which is not risk-adjusted, financial institutions would have been better prepared on the eve of the Lehman Brothers bankruptcy. Such robust targets and measures are independent of risk assessment errors and provide additional buffers to absorb risks stemming from the "unknown unknowns" (Dombret 2012a).

3.5. Successful Mitigation

In order to successfully implement the discussed macroprudential tools to measure and mitigate systemic risks, several aspects have to be taken into account (Lim et al. 2011). The first point relates to the question of whether a specific risk should be tackled using a single instrument or a combination of multiple tools. The latter approach could be more effective if there are several sources of risk, but it may be harder to calibrate and more expensive to implement. The next step is to decide whether a specifically targeted or a more broad-based approach is preferable. A broad-based approach might have a wider impact and smaller scope for circumvention, but may also imply larger distortions. For the instruments to address cyclical risks there is a choice between fixed and time-varying tools; the latter will be better able to "lean" against the wind, but only if the cycle is "timed" correctly. One issue affecting all instruments is the level of discretion. While in specific cases discretionary measures might provide a higher degree of flexibility, a rule-based approach is generally more transparent and tends to ensure better predictability and commitment. Other areas of fiscal and economic policy benefit from rules-based instruments since discretionary intervention itself is fraught with a number of problems, and the same applies to macroprudential policy: its decision makers are not omniscient when it comes to systemic interrelationships. Not least in light of the novelty of systemic issues, it makes sense in this policy area, where possible, to institute rule-based procedures and instruments which act primarily as automatic stabilisers. This is precisely why countercyclical capital buffers are a suitable instrument for mitigating macroprudential risk.

Finally, all elements of macroprudential regulation should also take account of policy measures from other bodies, notably microprudential supervision, monetary policy and fiscal policy, in order to enhance general policy effectiveness by adequately addressing potential interactions and feedback effects. To ensure that macroprudential policy is credible, means need to be clearly assigned to targets. This includes awareness that monetary policy instruments are not macroprudential instruments. It is a generally recognised principle of economic policy theory that an instrument should be assigned to only one target. Applied to the relationship between monetary policy and macroprudential policy, monetary policy remains committed to price stability, which means that macroprudential policy requires its own instruments and institutional rules. Over the longer term, the aims of price stability and financial stability do not stand in conflict with one another – quite the opposite: price stability is a key precondition for financial stability as monetary policy needs a functioning transmission process and a healthy financial system in order to succeed. By using their own specific instruments to pursue their own targets, each of these two policy areas indirectly promotes the other area's objective; the targets are complementary in that respect. If used appropriately, macroprudential instruments will help to increase policy credibility by influencing expectations (as monetary policy did after the 1970s). Once market participants know that macroprudential tools will step in to stabilise imbalances, these imbalances may decline or not actually arise in the first place (Schoenmaker and Wierts 2011).

4. A NEW ARCHITECTURE FOR FINANCIAL SUPERVISION IN EUROPE

One crucial lesson learned from the financial crisis is the knowledge that the only way to ensure financial stability is to regard and to treat the financial system as an interdependent system as well as viewing it in the context of its interaction with the real economy. This enhances financial supervision by adding the perspective of macroprudential oversight, which aims to identify and mitigate systemic risk. The creation of the European Systemic Risk Board at the beginning of 2011 represented a key cornerstone at European level in the efforts to construct a credible framework for identifying and mitigating systemic risk. Through the ESRB, macroprudential policy has acquired its own institutional rules. The EU regulation establishing the ESRB states that "[t]he ESRB's task should be to monitor and assess systemic risk in normal times for the purpose of mitigating the exposure of the system to the risk of failure of systemic components and enhancing the financial system's resilience to shocks."

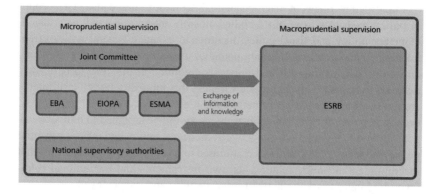

Figure 2.2: The European System of Financial Supervision
Source: Deutsche Bundesbank (2012).

Figure 2.2 provides an overview of the new framework for financial supervision in the EU. The first pillar of the *European System of Financial Supervision* comprises a network of three newly established European supervisory authorities (ESAs): the *European Banking Authority* (EBA), the *European Insurance and Occupational Pensions Authority* (EIOPA) and the *European Securities and Markets Authority* (ESMA). The ESMA is responsible for the supervision of securities markets and consumer protection, while the EIOPA is in charge of supervising insurance companies. Both institutions work closely with the EBA, which is responsible for supervising EU banks. The EBA, EIOPA and ESMA replace the former Committee of European Banking Supervisors, the Committee of European Insurance and Occupational Pensions Committee and the Committee of European Securities Regulators, respectively. The ESAs are to enhance microprudential supervision at the EU level and work in tandem with the national supervisors.

4.1. Strengthening Macroprudential Oversight: The European Systemic Risk Board

The second pillar of the ESFS is the *European Systemic Risk Board*. The ESRB is responsible for the oversight of the financial system in the EU. Its main tasks are to monitor and assess systemic risk in the EU financial system and to issue warnings and recommendations where systemic risks are deemed to be significant. Macroprudential and microprudential surveillance require co-operation and coordination and thus close synchronisation – not only at the European level, but also at the national level. It is essential that authorities exchange material information and findings in an orderly and timely manner. Macroprudential supervisors should therefore alert microprudential supervisors to recognised threats in due time and provide the latter with the appropriate background information and analyses. Conversely, microprudential supervisors should forward systemically important information and findings to macroprudential supervisors. This is the only way to ensure mutually beneficial cooperation.

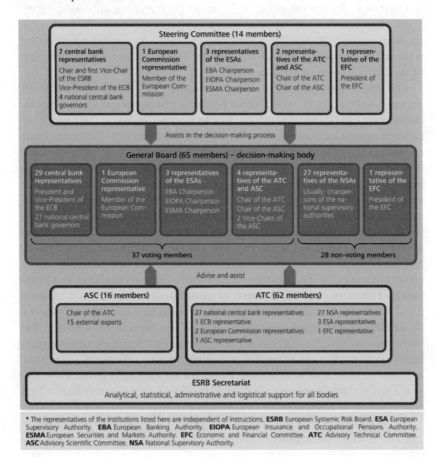

Figure 2.3: The organisational structure of the ESRB
Source: Deutsche Bundesbank (2012).

Given their experience with financial markets and their responsibility for macroprudential issues, central banks play a dominant role in the ESRB's decision-making body, the *General Board*. The board is chaired by the President of the European Central Bank. He works in close cooperation with the governors of the EU national central banks, who are the other voting members of the Board. Furthermore, non-voting members of the Board are mainly representatives of the national supervisory authorities.

To efficiently prepare the General Board's discussions and decision-making process, a smaller *Steering Committee* assists the Board by preparing its meetings and by monitoring ongoing work. The ESRB also has an *Advisory Technical Committee* and an *Advisory Scientific Committee*. The ATC provides advice and assistance relevant to the work of the ESRB. The members of the ATC are typically from the level of the head of the financial stability or supervisory department, while the ASC consists of academic experts in the field of financial stability. It provides advice and assistance on issues relevant to the work of the European Systemic Risk Board. Figure 2.3 provides an overview of the ESRB's organisational structure.

The ESRB issues warnings and recommendations based on these committees' analyses. Both can be either public or private. Warnings and recommendations can be addressed to the EU, to member states, to the ESAs or to national supervisory authorities. Warnings should make the addressees aware of systemic risks to the financial system within the EU, while recommendations include proposals on how the addressees should deal with the identified risks. Although the ESRB's recommendations are not legally binding, the mechanism of "comply or explain" puts pressure on the addressees to implement certain measures as proposed in the recommendation. This mechanism forces the addressees to state their reasons if they do not implement measures as recommended by the ESRB. Together with the "moral suasion" of a public recommendation this should provide strong incentives for the addressees to comply. However, if the ESRB draws the conclusion that the addressee has not followed the recommendation or that the justification for inaction is inadequate it will inform the Council and, where applicable, the ESA concerned. To ensure the ESRB's credibility, it is important that its members accept warnings and recommendations. To achieve this, its assessments and recommendations must be of a high quality and presented in a timely manner. Warnings and recommendations must also be efficiently communicated either in public or in private. Only if these conditions are met can the ESRB gain the credibility which is essential for macroprudential oversight in Europe.

4.2. The ESRB's First Year

The European Systemic Risk Board has published a set of recommendations on foreign currency lending reflecting financial stability concerns arising from foreign currency lending to the non-financial private sector. The ESRB states that this phenomenon is currently present to different degrees in the EU countries and has led in some cases to a build-up of substantial mismatches between the currencies in which the non-financial private sector receives its income and those in which it pays back loans, thus making it more vulnerable to unfavourable movements in the exchange rate. The ESRB regards these risks as systemically important.

The recommendations are intended to limit such risks and to mitigate the consequences. Borrowers should be given the appropriate information to make well-informed decisions. Moreover, credit institutions should properly incorporate foreign currency lending risks into their internal risk management systems. National supervisors are to issue guidelines so that financial institutions can better weave the risks from foreign currency lending into their internal risk management systems.[9] The deadline for implementing the recommendations is 31 December 2012. Some of these recommendations are subject to special deadlines.

Another recommendation refers to US dollar funding risks. The US dollar is an important funding source for European banks, but exposes them to currency and funding risk. This became apparent when US money market funds withdrew from European banks during the sovereign debt crisis. In addition, the maturities of US dollar-denominated liabilities shortened. The ESRB has come to the conclusion that the vulnerability of European credit institutions' US dollar funding harbours significant liquidity risk for banks and, in the medium term, for the real economy. It therefore recommends that national supervisory authorities monitor maturity mismatches and counterparty risks and expand their oversight of US dollar swaps and intra-group exposures. Suitable measures should be taken whenever banks' exposures become excessive. Moreover, credit institutions' contingency funding plans should be able to handle US dollar funding shocks in such a manner that systemic risk is avoided.[10]

The third recommendation refers to the design of national macroprudential mandates. Although the recommendations lay important cornerstones, they leave enough scope for adjustment to the structures of the financial sector and the national supervisory regime. Member states should assign responsibility for macroprudential oversight to a designated authority. Cooperation within the macroprudential authority and with other institutions would need to be regulated and coordinated. It is recommended that central banks have a significant role in macroprudential oversight, especially in independent macroprudential analysis. The competent authority should act on its own initiative and should also follow up, for instance, on warnings and recommendations issued by the

---

[9] See ESRB recommendation 2011/1 for more information on the measures recommended by the ESRB for lending in foreign currencies.
[10] See ESRB recommendation 2011/2 for more information on the measures recommended by the ESRB for lending in foreign currencies. The recommendation was made in December 2011. The publication followed in January 2012.

ESRB. The authority, in cooperation with microprudential supervisors, should name systemically important institutions and structures. It should receive access to all necessary data and recommend the use of the required instruments. According to the ESRB, independence is intended to shield the macroprudential authority from external pressure. This is essential in order to preserve its credibility. Moreover, the authority should have a mandate that permits it to act in a forward-looking manner and prevent systemic risk from building up before it is too late. The ESRB has called on the EU member states to take the necessary action before July 2013 and to communicate their intentions with respect to implementation and report on developments by June 2012.

5. CONCLUSIONS

By establishing the European System of Financial Supervision and the European Systemic Risk Board, Europe seems to have succeeded in marrying the microprudential and macroprudential dimensions of financial stability as Andrew Crockett (2000) demanded in his seminal contribution, solving the trilemma between national authority, financial integration and financial stability at least partly.

As in real life, of course, marriage does not necessarily mean "happily ever after". It has to prove its worth day by day. This remains challenging in a European Union with a high level of financial integration and differences in financial structures and cultures. Macro- and microprudential surveillance require cooperation. It is essential that authorities exchange material information and findings in a timely manner. Macroprudential supervisors should alert microprudential supervisors to recognised threats. Equally, microprudential supervisors should forward systemically important information and findings to macroprudential supervisors. This is the only and best way to ensure that cooperation will be mutually beneficial. The credibility of the ESRB hinges on the quality of its risk analyses and the relevance of its warnings and recommendations. It remains to be seen whether it can prove its credibility.

Regarding potential instruments for identifying and mitigating systemic risks in the European financial sector, a set of macroprudential tools is currently being discussed. One of the primary means of addressing the cyclical dimension of system-wide risks will be the adoption of countercyclical capital buffers in order to prevent, or at least diminish, the build-up of aggregate financial imbalances due to excessive credit growth. The structural cross-sectional risk dimension will be tackled, notably, by introducing additional loss absorbency requirements for systemically important financial institutions.

Establishing macroprudential policy instruments is a complex act. A balance needs to be struck between a sophisticated system fine-tuned to marginal changes in systemic risk on the one hand and an approach based on easy-to-implement rules on the other. The discussion is far from complete and future experiences with practical implementations will help to improve the envisaged European regulatory instruments to successfully mitigate system-wide risks in the financial sector.

Even though future systemic crises cannot be ruled out *a priori*, the new architecture will be better able to monitor and address system risk than the old one. Overall, therefore, the ESFS will contribute to a more stable financial system in Europe.

BIBLIOGRAPHY

Acharya, V., L. H. Pedersen, T. Philippon and M. Richardson 2012, "Measuring Systemic Risk", *CEPR Discussion Paper* No. 8824, February 2012.

Adrian, T. and M. K. Brunnermeier 2011, "CoVaR", *Working paper*, Princeton University, September 2011.

Bank of England 2011, "Instruments of Macroprudential Policy", *Discussion Paper*, ISSN 1754-4262, December 2011.

Barth, J. R., G. Caprio and R. Levine 2006, *Rethinking Bank Regulations – Till Angels Govern*, Cambridge University Press, Cambridge.

Basel Committee on Banking Supervision 2010, *Guidance for National Authorities Operating the Countercyclical Capital Buffer*, December 2010.

Basel Committee on Banking Supervision 2011a, *Basel III: A Global Regulatory Framework for More Resilient Banks and Banking Systems*, June 2011.

Basel Committee on Banking Supervision 2011b, *Global Systemically Important Banks: Assessment Methodology and the Additional Loss Absorbency Requirement*, November 2011.

Beck, T., R. Todorov and W. Wagner 2011, "Bank Supervision Going Global? A Cost-Benefit Analysis", *European Banking Center Discussion Paper*, No 2011-033.

Borio, C. 2011, "Rediscovering the Macroeconomic Roots of Financial Stability Policy: Journey, Challenges and a Way Forward", *Annual Review of Financial Economics*, Vol. 3, pp. 87-117 (also published as BIS Working paper No. 354, September 2011).

Borio, C. and M. Drehmann 2009, "Towards an Operational Framework for Financial Stability: 'Fuzzy' Measurement and its Consequences", *BIS Working Paper* No. 284, June 2009.

Brownlees, C. T. and R. Engle 2011, "Volatility, Correlation and Tails for Systemic Risk Measurement", *Working Paper*, New York University, June 2011.

Caballero, R. 2010, "Crisis and Reform: Managing the systemic risk", Prepared for the Angelo Costa Lecture delivered in Rome, March, 2010.

Cardarelli, R., S. Elekdag and S. Lall 2009, "Financial Stress, Downturns, and Recoveries", *IMF Working Paper* WP/09/100, May 2009.

Crockett, A. 2000, "Marrying the micro- and macro-prudential dimensions of financial stability", Eleventh International Conference of Banking Supervisors, Basel, September 2000.

Crowe, C., G. Dell' Ariccia, D. Igan, and P. Rabanal 2011, "How to Deal with Real Estate Booms: Lessons from Country Experiences", *IMF Working Paper* WP/11/91, April 2011.

Degryse, H., M. A. Elahi and M. F. Penas 2010, "Cross-Border Exposures and Financial Contagion", *International Review of Finance*, Vol. 10(2), pp. 209-240.

De Larosière Group 2009, *Report of the High-Level Group of Financial Supervision in the EU.*

Deutsche Bundesbank 2011, *Monthly Report*, March 2011.

Deutsche Bundesbank 2012, "The European System Risk Board", *Monthly Report*, April 2012.

Dombret, A. 2012a, "How to manage financial crisis from a systemic viewpoint", speech at 40th OeNB Economics Conference, European Monetary Union: Lessons from the Debt Crisis, May 2012.

Dombret, Andreas 2012b, "Systemic risk analysis and crisis prevention", speech at the High-level Eurosystem seminar with central banks and monetary agencies of the Gulf Cooperation Council, January 2012.

Dombret, Andreas 2012c, "Europe's solution to the Too-Big-To-Fail", speech at the Institute of Law and Finance, Goethe-University, May 2012.

Drehmann, M., C. Borio and K. Tsatsaronis 2011, "Anchoring Countercyclical Capital Buffers: The Role of Credit Aggregates", *International Journal of Central Banking* 7(4), 189-240 (also published as BIS Working Paper No. 355, November 2011).

Drehmann, M. and N. Tarashev 2011, "Measuring the Systemic Importance of Inter-connected Banks", *BIS Working Paper* No. 342, March 2011.

ECB 2011, *Financial Integration in Europe*, May 2011.

ESRB 2012, *Principles for the development of a macro-prudential framework in the EU in the context of the capital requirements legislation*, ESRB/2012/0050, April 2012.

European Commission 2011, "Proposal for a Directive on Capital Requirements", COM(2011) 453 final, July 2011.

Financial Stability Board 2011a, *OTC Derivatives Market Reforms*, October 2011.

Financial Stability Board 2011b, *Shadow Banking: Strengthening Oversight and Regulation*, October 2011.

Financial Stability Board 2011c, *Policy Measures to Address Systemically Important Financial Institutions*, November 2011.

FSB, IMF and BIS 2011, *Macroprudential Policy Tools and Frameworks*, October 2011.

Goldberg, L. 2009, "Understanding Banking Sector Globalization", *IMF Staff Papers*, Vol. 56(1), pp. 171-197.

Goodhart, C.A.E. and E. Perotti 2012, "Preventive Macroprudential Policy", *Working Paper*, February 2012.

Gorton, G. and A. Metrick (forthcoming), "Securitized Banking and the Run on Repo", *Journal of Financial Economics*.

Gray, S. 2011, "Central Bank Balances and Reserve Requirements", *IMF Working Paper* WP/11/36, February 2011.

Hakkio, C. S. and W. R. Keeton 2009, "Financial Stress: What Is It, How Can It Be Measured, and Why Does It Matter?", Federal Reserve Bank of Kansas City, July 2009.

Haldane, A. G. 2010, "The $100 Billion Question", *BIS Review* 40/2010, March 2010.

Heller, D. and N. Vause 2012, "Collateral Requirements for Mandatory Central Clearing of Over-the-Counter Derivatives", *BIS Working Paper* No. 373, March 2012.

Hördahl, P. and M. R. King 2008, "Developments in Repo Markets During the Financial Crisis", *BIS Quarterly Review*, December 2008.

Huang, X., H. Zhou and H. Zhu 2011, "Systemic Risk Contributions", *Working Paper*, Federal Reserve Board, January 2011.

Illing, M. and Y. Liu 2006, "Measuring Financial Stress in a Developed Country: An Application to Canada", *Journal of Financial Stability* 2, 243–265.

IMF 2011a, *Macroprudential Policy: An Organizing Framework*, March 2011.

IMF 2011b, *The European Systemic Risk Board: Effectiveness of Macroprudential Oversight in Europe*, in Euro Area Policies – Selected Issues, July 2011.

Kalemli-Ozcan, S., E. Papaioannou and F. Perri (forthcoming), "Global Banks and Crisis Transmission", *Journal of International Economics*.

Kalemli-Ozcan, S., E. Papaioannou and J.-L. Peydro 2010, "What Lies Beneth the Euro's Effect on Financial Integration: Currency Risk, Legal Harmonization, or Trade?", *Journal of International Economics*, Vol. 81(1), pp. 75-88.

Knight, F. H. 2002, *Risk, Uncertainty and Profit*, Beard Books, Washington D.C.

Lim, C., F. Columba, A. Costa, P. Kongsamut, A. Otani, M. Saiyid, T. Wezel, and X. Wu (2011), "Macroprudential Policy: What Instruments and How to Use Them?", *IMF Working Paper* WP/11/238, October 2011.

Minsky, H. P. (1982), *Can "It" Happen Again? – Essays on Instability and Finance*, M. E. Sharpe, Inc.

Navaretti, G. B., G. Calzolari, A. F. Pozzolo and M. Levi 2010, "Multinational Banking in Europe – Financial Stability and Regulatory Implications: Lessons from the Financial Crisis", *Centre for European Policy Research Discussion Paper*, No. 7823.

Oet, M. V., R. Eiben, T. Bianco, D. Gramlich, and S. J. Ong 2011, *The Financial Stress Index: Identification of Systemic Risk Conditions*, Federal Reserve Bank of Cleveland, November 2011.

Perotti, E. and J. Suarez 2011, "A Pigovian Approach to Liquidity Regulation", *International Journal of Central Banking* 7(4), 3-41.

Schoenmaker, D. (2011), "The Financial Trilemma", *Economic Letters*, Vol. 111, pp. 57-59.

Schoenmaker, D. and P. Wierts 2011, "Macroprudential Policy: The Need for a Coherent Policy Framework", *DSF Policy Paper* No. 13, July 2011.

Slingenberg, J. W. and J. de Haan 2011, "Forecasting Financial Stress", *DNB Working Paper* No. 292, April 2011.

White, W. R. 2009, "Should Monetary Policy 'Lean or Clean'?", *Working Paper* No. 34, Federal Reserve Bank of Dallas, August 2009.

3. Criteria for Financial Stability – A US View

Nathan Sheets

1. INTRODUCTION

Perspectives as to how financial stability is best achieved have shifted significantly since the years before the global financial crisis. Stated bluntly, previously there was a strong faith in the invisible hand and its capacity to guide financial markets. The prevailing view among US regulators and other policy-makers was that financial markets and institutions, if left to function on their own and with a minimum of intervention, would tend to generate outcomes that were generally stable and efficient. The upshot was a commitment to "light touch" regulation and supervision. The authorities were prepared to address cases of outright fraud and abuse but were often hesitant to question the decisions and practices of institutions and investors.

In addition, most regulation was explicitly microprudential in nature, focusing on the safety and soundness of individual firms, and concerned only to a lesser extent with the integrity of the system as a whole. Well-developed mechanisms were not in place to assess the inter-linkages between the financial sector and the macroeconomy or how those inter-linkages should be reflected in the stance of monetary, fiscal, or supervisory policies.

The eruption of the financial crisis and the sustained stresses that followed has dramatically shifted perspectives on these issues. There is still general agreement among policy-makers that financial markets should be free and open. But there is now a deeper conviction that excesses and distortions may arise in the financial sector and that, accordingly, regulators must be prepared to occasionally step in to preserve the stability of the system. The presumption is not that the authorities necessarily know best. But there is a sense that regulators can provide a complementary and dispassionate perspective and are well positioned to think broadly about the integrity of the entire financial system.

The discussion in this chapter will examine the shifting perspectives of policy-makers as to how financial stability can be best achieved. We will focus in particular on the US experience, but the journey has been broadly similar in many other countries. As much as anything, the shift that has occurred has been one of ideology and philosophical orientation. But in addition, policy-makers have put in place important legal and regulatory reforms, including the Dodd-Frank legislation and the new Basel III rules, in an effort to make the financial system more robust to crises in the future. This chapter also considers what financial stability means, what kinds of metrics should be used in gauging the presence or absence of financial stability, and the potential challenges for monetary policy and fiscal policy that may arise in the pursuit of financial stability.

2. PERSPECTIVES BEFORE THE FINANCIAL CRISIS

The thinking of US regulators and policy-makers before the crisis erupted tended to emphasise the natural stability of financial markets and the self-corrective features of these markets. It was argued that financial markets reflect the collective judgments of thousands of investors who are putting actual resources at risk. As such, investors should have strong incentives to assess the underlying fundamentals of the securities that they purchase and to carefully calibrate the risks embedded in their portfolios. Similarly, it was emphasised that financial institutions should have incentives to pursue stable profit-maximising strategies over time. A failure to do so would jeopardise franchise value and put shareholders, managers, and employees at risk. This perspective tended to emphasise the efficiency properties of freely functioning financial markets and to down-weight the extent of market frictions, failures, and inefficiencies. Janet Yellen (2010) summarised the thinking before the crisis this way: "Financial markets were not held to be perfect, of course. But they were viewed as self-correcting systems that tended to return to a stable equilibrium before they could inflict widespread damage on the economy."

This perception was reinforced by the very strong performance of the financial system from the early 1990s through the eruption of the global financial crisis. In November 2002, Alan Greenspan – the most influential advocate of this perspective – observed,

"Despite the draining impact of a loss of $8 trillion of stock market wealth, a sharp contraction in capital investment and, of course, the tragic events of September 11, 2001, our economy is still growing. Importantly, despite significant losses, no major US financial institution has been driven to default. ... These episodes suggest a marked increase over the past two or three decades in the ability of modern economies to absorb unanticipated shocks." (Greenspan 2002)

It was further argued that ongoing market innovations and the evolution of technology were making the financial system more efficient, liquid, and robust. This was facilitated by a whole range of sophisticated financial products that facilitated the transfer of risk. In the same November 2002 speech, Greenspan noted, "The development of our paradigms for containing risk has emphasised dispersion of risk to those willing, and presumably, able to bear it."

These "paradigms for containing risk" to which Greenspan referred largely involved a shift in intermediation from simple deposit-taking and loan-making activities within the banking system to a much more complex and varied set of instruments that were bought and sold on financial markets. The increasing prominence of market-based finance was seen as a triumph for more flexible approaches to intermediation and risk management. Dan Tarullo has argued that this rise of market-based finance brought with it strong pressures to deregulate the banking sector, in order to maintain the franchise value of the banks (see, e.g., Tarullo 2012a). In any event, the two decades before the global financial crisis saw *significant deregulation of the financial system*, including the repeal of Glass-Steagall, and the emergence of larger financial institutions in the United States.

Given their underlying confidence in the efficiency and functioning of the financial system, coupled with the perception of its strong track record, the authorities were generally reluctant to intervene in the financial system. First, who were regulators to question the judgments and perspectives of thousands of investors who were actually putting their money at risk? This perspective was reinforced by intellectual arguments supporting market efficiency. If markets were mispriced or misaligned, certainly investors had incentives to arbitrage away the mispricings.

Second, even if there were notable problems with financial market performance, it was not at all clear that regulatory interventions would actually make the situation better. Instead, regulatory interventions could further disrupt the functioning of these markets, distort incentives, and reduce – rather than enhance – the efficiency and resilience of the markets. On the subject of credit-risk transfer, Greenspan noted in May 2005,

"Market participants usually have strong incentives to monitor and control the risks they assume in choosing to deal with particular counterparties. In essence, prudential regulation is supplied by the market through counterparty evaluation and monitoring rather than by authorities. Such private prudential regulation can be impaired – indeed, even displaced – if some counterparties assume that government regulations obviate private prudence." (Greenspan 2005)

Dan Tarullo (2010) has argued, in addition, that during this period

"the attention of banking regulators around the world had been heavily oriented toward elaborating capital requirements to reflect more precisely the particular risks faced by a financial institution. Capital requirements had, to a considerable extent, become the dominant prudential regulatory tool. The financial crisis showed that the concentrated, almost all-consuming regulatory focus on refining bank capital requirements in Basel II had come at the expense of attention to other risks in the financial system."

The authorities' reluctance to intervene in the financial sector was seen by some observers as appropriate humility and as recognition of the limits of what supervisors could legitimately do. We note that these views were advanced with particular forcefulness in the United States, but the US experience was hardly unique. Quite the contrary, similar views were held by policy-makers and bank regulators throughout the world.

All this said, the US economy in the years before the financial crisis was beset by one very notable government intervention in the financial system – namely, the central role of the government-sponsored enterprises (GSEs) in facilitating housing finance. The GSEs operated with an implicit government guarantee that made their debt relatively attractive to investors, allowing them to fund at rates lower than would have otherwise been the case. While it is difficult to fully parse out the counterfactual, it seems safe to conclude that the *GSEs contributed meaningfully to the scale of the housing bubble* and, hence, to the eventual intensity of the financial crisis.

3. THE EMERGENCE OF THE FINANCIAL CRISIS

As the financial crisis took hold, it rapidly became clear that the supervisory community had an *inadequate understanding* of *where the risks* in the financial system *were actually lodged.* As such, the regulators' most notable failure in the years before the crisis was perhaps a failure of curiosity. If risks were indeed being transferred to those who, in Greenspan's words were "willing, and presumably, able" to bear them – who was now holding the underlying exposures? How did this new plumbing for dispersing risks actually work?

Speaking in May 2007, at the onset of the financial crisis, Don Kohn – then Vice Chairman of the Federal Reserve Board – noted these challenges: "Market-intermediated finance also requires us to live with less control and less knowledge than we had when banks were dominant. Greater uncertainty about where risks are lodged is the flip side of better dispersion of those risks, especially to less regulated sectors." (Kohn 2007). But he concluded, hopefully, "We need to have faith in the invisible hand." Even so, Kohn was not sanguine. By this time, he was seeing a range of concerns that were later to manifest themselves even more intensively, including vulnerabilities associated with embedded leverage, compressed risk premiums, and heightened exposure to shifts in market liquidity.

While we do not have scope in this essay to provide a detailed accounting of the underlying drivers of the financial crisis, we will make a few brief observations on this score, drawing on a watershed report published by the Financial Stability Forum (FSF) in the spring of 2008 (FSF 2008). As underlying weaknesses in the financial system that contributed to the global crisis, this report identified poor underwriting standards, weaknesses in firms' risk management processes, inadequate due diligence by investors, and the poor performance of the credit rating agencies. In addition, the FSF emphasised the role of distorted incentives, including problems with the originate-to-distribute model and compensation schemes, and inadequate disclosure practices. Finally, the report noted that *"weaknesses in regulatory frameworks"* also played a role and admitted that the authorities "may have overestimated the strength and resilience of the financial system."

As the financial crisis progressed, it became increasingly clear that the consensus that prevailed before the crisis had placed too much emphasis on the equilibrium features of markets and not enough on market imperfections, including principal-agent problems, information asymmetries, and perverse incentives arising from the structure of compensation, the process of securitisation, and distortions in the credit-rating process.

The claim had been that various sophisticated financial products were transferring risks to investors that were most capable of absorbing them. As the crisis proliferated, evidence emerged that *underwriters had actually sold a sizable chunk of this risk to off-balance-sheet vehicles that they themselves were responsible for backstopping.* The upshot was that much of this risk came back onto their balance sheets as the crisis deepened. In addition, issuers had sometimes held on to so-called "super-senior" exposures, as they had found it difficult to sell these tranches at the desired spreads. Underwriters had taken steps to hedge some of the risk that remained on their balance sheets through insurance contracts with monoline insurers, but once the crisis emerged the financial position of the monolines quickly deteriorated, undercutting the effectiveness of these hedges (see, e.g., Kohn 2008). This was hardly the process of risk dispersion that had been contemplated in the years before the financial crisis.

In short, as Greenspan famously observed in October 2008, it became increasingly clear that there had been a flaw in the collective thinking of the financial regulatory community. Accordingly, since the onset of the crisis, a fundamental shift in perspective regarding approaches to financial oversight has occurred. Before, it was believed that financial stability would grow naturally out of freely functioning financial markets and a market economy. The key was mainly to keep out of the way and to not interfere. Financial innovation, evolving technology, and ongoing deregulation were all broadly stabilising factors. But in recent years, a much different perspective has taken hold. The experience of the crisis underscores that *financial stability objectives* must be pursued as an *explicit policy goal*. The intention is not to blunt the power of the invisible hand. Rather, the objective is to foster an environment that garners the efficiency gains of freely functioning markets but also one that identifies and disciplines excesses, with an eye toward ensuring the stability of the economy and the financial system over the medium term.

4. DEFINING FINANCIAL STABILITY

In formulating structural reforms to address the causes of the financial crisis and, more generally to build a more durable and stable financial system, a first step is to adequately define what is meant by the term "financial stability". A minimum definition is to ensure that the structure of the financial system, as well as its ongoing functioning, serve to minimise the frequency and intensity of crises. We note, as a philosophical matter, that the more ambitious objective of eliminating crises entirely is almost certainly not realistic. The boom-bust-cycles that are observed in market economies are reflective of the mood swings that seem to inevitably characterise human nature.

Moreover, even as a purely economic matter, significant shocks, regime shifts, and the arrival of new information may trigger upward or downward surges in asset prices, and this may bring with it implications for the rest of the financial system and the economy more generally. Similarly, although pursuing financial stability requires efforts to make financial institutions as robust to failure as possible, even with the most reliable policies in place, some institutions will inevitably fail and others will experience losses on their investments. *Market discipline should remain intact.*

For this reason, the objective of financial stability is not to stabilise or even necessarily to reduce the volatility of asset prices. In the limit, such outcomes could easily be achieved by repressing the financial system through heavy government regulations. But this kind of heavy-handed financial repression is the antithesis of the kinds of financial stability objectives that policy should be geared to achieve. *Instead, the goal of financial stability should be seen as fostering financial conditions that minimise financial imbalances and that support the sustainable medium-term growth of the economy.*

The irony is that financial stability may at times be best achieved through sharp re-alignments of asset prices. Specifically, to the extent that shocks are absorbed by movements in exchange rates, bond yields, and equity prices, rather than in employment, production, and pricing decisions by firms on the real side of the economy, such an outcome will likely be welfare enhancing for the vast majority of the population. As discussed below, the daunting practical challenge in pursuing financial stability is differentiating between moves in assets prices that are responding to developments in the underlying real economy – the so-called fundamentals – and movements that are driven by mispricing and the like. Our view is that defined in these terms, the pursuit of financial stability will generally be consistent with other macroeconomic objectives.

Accordingly, the ultimate criteria by which financial stability should be judged relate on the one hand to *minimising the frequency and intensity of financial crises and on the other hand to the achievement of sustainable economic growth and rising employment.*

4.1. The Macroprudential Perspective

A clear lesson from the crisis is that achieving financial stability will require a philosophical reorientation of financial supervision and regulation. This is true for traditional microprudential supervision, which focuses on ensuring that individual financial institutions are operating in a way that is safe and sound, that they are effectively managing current and prospective risks, and that they are holding sufficient capital and liquidity to absorb a range of shocks. As noted below, the Basel III regulations are broadly geared to address these issues.

Effective microprudential supervision – understanding the risks facing the financial system on an institution-by-institution basis – is a necessary foundation for financial stability more broadly. Assuming that such efforts are in place, *macroprudential regulation, in turn, is primarily focused on the linkages across financial institutions and on the inter-linkages between the financial system and the economy.* For example, even if individual institutions seem to be well capitalised and hence strong from a microprudential standpoint, it may be undesirable for these institutions to all be gearing their lending to a single sector, such as real estate. Such behaviour would undesirably expose financial institutions to common vulnerabilities in the event of a shock to the real estate market, and the resulting flood of credit to the sector might boost real estate prices in an unsustainable way. Similarly, macroprudential supervision should carefully consider the potential channels of feedback from the real economy and asset prices back into the financial sector. As we discuss in more detail below, this will require macroprudential regulators to carefully *monitor a range of financial and economic indicators*, sometimes even taking a stand as to whether a given level of asset prices is likely to prove sustainable.

In this context, we would argue that the recent financial crisis emerged for two reasons. First, microprudential regulation was inadequate, both in tracking the behaviour of individual institutions and in ensuring that institutions maintained sufficient capital buffers. As we have discussed, this at least in part reflected an ideological predisposition toward "light touch" regulation and a presumption that financial institutions had incentives to behave efficiently. But a second factor causing the crisis was that there was no systematic effort in the United States, or really in most other countries, to pursue macroprudential regulation. The prevailing thinking was that markets would tend toward equilibrium, which raised the bar for regulatory intervention. In addition, large swaths of the financial system – and many sizable financial institutions – were not receiving much (or any) supervisory scrutiny.

As microprudential supervision is reformed and strengthened and as macroprudential initiatives are further fleshed out and put in place, it is *imperative that these efforts do not become heavy handed or interventionist*, effectively repressing decision making in the financial sector, appropriate risk taking, or innovation. While the macroprudential approach requires exquisitely difficult judgments, attitudes toward regulation tend to have features of a swinging pendulum. In reforming financial supervision, it is important that we do not compensate for past mistakes by allowing the pendulum to swing too far in the opposite direction. The crisis highlights that governance by the invisible hand has limits, but by the same token the invisible hand is still a powerful paradigm. The challenge is to balance these considerations in a pragmatic and sophisticated way.

Ultimately, the prospects for financial stability cannot depend principally on interventions by the official sector. *Efforts to restructure the financial sector to make it more stable will be helpful.* In addition, initiatives by regulators to formulate rules of the road that will support a safer financial sector and more effective policing of those rules once they are in place will also play an important role. But stronger market discipline is also indispensable. Even over and above regulatory considerations, financial institutions will need to manage risk more prudently. Boards of directors will need to more thoroughly examine the views of management, asking deeper and more probing questions. And participants in financial markets should be more aggressive in combing through financial statements and punishing firms that are not fully forthcoming about their finances and their business strategies. The losses sustained by investors over the past five years provide strong incentives for more thorough scrutiny going forward.

4.2. Structural Reforms to Strengthen the US Financial System

We now turn to two broad classes of financial stability reforms that the US authorities have recently put in place. The first of these includes structural measures designed to make the financial system more resilient to crisis. The leading examples are the *Dodd-Frank Act* and efforts to implement the internationally agreed *Basel III standards*, which seek to bolster bank capital and liquidity. The second class of reforms focuses on bringing a macroprudential perspective to financial supervision. With this preface, the remainder of this section highlights some key features of the Dodd-Frank Act, while the following section focuses on efforts by the US authorities to implement macroprudential supervision. (We do not offer a summary of the Basel III reforms, since they are covered in detail in other chapters in this volume.)

For the sake of brevity, we will focus on just those elements of the expansive Dodd-Frank Act that pertain most directly to our theme of financial stability. The first of these is the establishment of the *Financial Stability Oversight Council (FSOC)*, which is composed of ten voting members, including the Secretary of the Treasury, the Chairman of the Federal Reserve, and the heads of other regulatory agencies. The FSOC is tasked with monitoring the financial system to identify systemic risks and gaps in supervision. Consistent with this responsibility, the FSOC is mandated to prepare an annual report assessing developments in the financial sector. The FSOC also is required to identify non-bank financial institutions that it views as systemically important, a process which is ongoing.

As a second and related reform, Dodd-Frank requires that the *non-bank financial institutions that the FSOC designates as systemically important* – as well as bank holding companies with assets of USD 50 billion or more – must be *subject to intensified supervision* by the Federal Reserve Board, including higher capital standards than are applied to other institutions. This feature of Dodd-Frank is designed to strike a blow at not only the "too big to fail" problem, because large institutions are now subject to tougher requirements than other institutions, but also at vulnerabilities arising from the "shadow banking system", as intensified regulation will be applied to all systemically important financial firms, including those outside the banking system. In addition, the Federal Reserve Board is required to perform an *annual stress test* on these institutions, with the results released to the public, and these firms are required to stress test their own balance sheets at least twice a year.[1]

A third key element of Dodd-Frank, which is also intended to mitigate the "too big to fail" problem, is the establishment of a *resolution mechanism for non-bank financial institutions*. The basic idea is to give the FDIC powers to resolve these institutions that are broadly similar to those that it already holds for commercial banks (see Fitzpatrick and Thomson 2011). Triggering this regime requires a two-thirds vote of both the Federal Reserve Board and the FDIC Board of Directors and a determination from the Secretary of the Treasury (in consultation with the President) that the institution is in danger of default and that resolution under this regime (rather than under the bankruptcy code) would limit financial stability risks. Once this authority is triggered, the FDIC is appointed the receiver for the failed entity and has a range of powers, including the possibility of creating a bridge bank, selling the assets or the operations of the firm, and imposing haircuts on unsecured creditors. Such powers would have been very useful during the financial crisis. This authority might have provided scope for Lehman to be resolved in a more orderly way. And the presence of such powers might have allowed AIG to be taken into bankruptcy and smoothly restructured, rather than being bailed out.

Two other aspects of the Dodd-Frank Act should be mentioned as well. Both of these are designed to constrain the activities and risk taking of commercial banks (which have access to the public safety net, including deposit insurance). One of the more controversial provisions of Dodd-Frank is the so-

---

[1] A debate has recently arisen as to whether designating a financial firm as systemically important will simply codify the perception that the firm is, in fact, too-big-to-fail. An alternative view is that the size of such firms is already well known and that these large institutions will now be subject to more intense scrutiny by the supervisors, which offers the opportunity to mitigate any perverse incentives that may arise. This clearly is an issue that deserves careful monitoring going forward.

called "*Volcker rule*" that prohibits banks from engaging in proprietary trading. The underlying rationale for this provision is to limit the risks that banks take onto their balance sheets. In practice, however, defining proprietary trading has proven notoriously difficult. And some have voiced concerns that the Volcker rule may prompt banks to curtail their market-making activities, possibly leading to less liquid financial markets. Second, Dodd-Frank also included *provisions* designed *to make the OTC derivatives market more robust and stable*, including enhanced regulation, and tighter mandates for central clearing, exchange trading, and reporting. The Act also expanded capital and margin requirements in many instances, and banks are now required to "push out" broad classes of their derivatives activities into separately capitalised affiliates.

In summary, we see much of the Dodd-Frank Act as broadly geared to addressing the problems associated with "too big to fail" and vulnerabilities arising in the shadow banking system. The Act also notably seeks to discipline the proprietary trading and derivatives exposures of commercial banks. In each case, the intended objectives and the suggested solutions are reasonable and defensible. But only time and experience will allow us to judge whether these measures actually deliver enhanced financial stability or, alternatively, whether these moves will generate unpalatable unintended consequences. One specific concern is that by constraining the activities of the commercial banks, market-making activity may migrate into the shadow banking system. This could have the effect of making the shadow banking system more central, rather than less central, to the overall functioning of the financial system.

5. ASPECTS OF MACROPRUDENTIAL MONITORING AND SUPERVISION

We now turn to the issue of macroprudential monitoring and supervision. As we have noted, there is broad agreement that macroprudential approaches to supervision must be increasingly prominent in the years ahead. However, what is still lacking from this consensus is a detailed plan as to how macroprudential supervision should actually be done in practice. In particular, what tools are available? With this in mind, this section briefly sketches out some thoughts as to how macroprudential supervision might be implemented, but also offers some views regarding the range of potential challenges.

The first – and probably the most powerful – pillar of the macroprudential approach is intensified real-time monitoring of financial developments, in search of variables that are behaving in some way differently than they have in the past. This effort requires huge quantities of information to better assess the ongoing behaviour of markets and asset prices. This will include data such as the following:

- *Market Prices.* Potentially including residential and commercial real estate prices, mortgage rates, equity prices, the sovereign yield curve (both TIPS and nominal Treasuries), spreads on risky debt, bank lending rates, money market rates, exchange rates, commodity prices, and CDS spreads.
- *Market Quantities.* Volumes of transactions in a range of markets (both primary and secondary) including equities, sovereign debt, corporate bonds, money markets (including repo), foreign exchange, and derivatives. This also should include disaggregated data on bank lending volumes.
- *Balance Sheets of Financial Institutions.* This would include both aggregated and disaggregated data on balance sheet size, leverage, liquidity, features of maturity transformation, concentrations of exposures, value at risk, funding strategies, and the quality and composition of capital.
- *Market functioning.* Information on market liquidity, bid-ask spreads, haircut and collateral policies, credit standards, and robustness of architecture.

As part of this monitoring process, substantial quantities of data will be examined at various frequencies in terms of both levels (e.g., is the level of asset prices out of line with fundamentals?) and growth rate (e.g., does the growth of issuance look unsustainable?)

What makes this process particularly difficult is the lack of clarity as to what mounting financial vulnerabilities and imbalances may actually look like in practice. Even as the recent global financial crisis erupted, many top-notch analysts explained away various movements in the data and did not successfully connect the dots. While the lessons of the financial crisis have emphasised the need to be more vigilant in monitoring for signs of imbalances, every indication suggests that effective monitoring will be a very challenging undertaking.

At any rate, this monitoring will require searching the data for signs of a notable shift in the behaviour of some series or set of series. The goal is to identify financial developments that have deviated from their past behaviour in striking and sizable ways. In some cases, this might involve a run-up in the price of an asset that leaves it outside its historical range. Alternatively, a clue may come from an outsized shift in bank lending volumes or more generous credit standards. While none of these developments necessarily suggests financial stability risks or the presence of asset bubbles, the trends of such variables and the way that they may – or may not – move together, should at times be useful in signalling a change in financial conditions.

This monitoring process will be speculative by its very nature. There are many factors shaping financial market conditions, and it may be difficult for supervisors to understand all of the underlying dynamics at any point in time. As such, the intention of this monitoring exercise is not to second guess the markets or to categorically identify unsustainable financial developments. Rather, this effort must be approached with humility but also with a willingness to probe. This will require asking deeper questions as to what is driving financial market variables and market dynamics than was the case in the years before the financial crisis.

In the long-standing policy debate regarding rules versus discretion, this approach falls somewhere in between. To support macroprudential supervision, a series of "rules of thumb", i.e., expected ranges for financial variables, would need to be developed. But when a variable breaches these rules of thumb, it should only be taken as a signal that deeper scrutiny is necessary. And it may very well be that the underlying fundamentals have shifted in a way that justifies the variable's move outside the anticipated range.

In our view, there is a compelling case for regularly sharing with the public the analysis and conclusions generated by this macroprudential monitoring process. The annual report produced by the FSOC would seem to be one natural venue for reporting such work.

The next issue is how supervisors should proceed once they identify financial developments that appear significantly out of line with perceived fundamentals. *What are the actual, hands-on tools to be used in macroprudential supervision?* This issue remains very much work in progress for the official sector. To date, however, US supervisors have found the "horizontal review" and the "stress test" to be powerful instruments. The basic idea is to employ supervisory powers to systematically scrutinise the balance sheets of a cross-section of large banks and to assess the vulnerabilities of these balance sheets to a range of severe shocks. On this score, Chairman Bernanke (2012) remarked, "We have supplemented the traditional firm-by-firm approach to supervision with a routine use of horizontal, or cross-firm, reviews to monitor industry practices, common trading and funding strategies, balance sheet developments, interconnectedness, and other factors with implications for systemic risk. ... [We have] also made increasing use of improved quantitative methods for evaluating the condition of supervised firms as well as the risks that they may pose for the broader financial system."

Governor Dan Tarullo, who has played a key role in recent efforts to strengthen the Federal Reserve's supervisory efforts, observed that "the stress testing that the Federal Reserve has instituted during the past few years has become an important part of our horizontal, interdisciplinary approach to supervising the largest bank holding companies." (Tarullo 2012b). He further argued that the public release of the parameters of these stress tests – including their assumptions and methods – offers useful insights into the nature and effectiveness of supervision. In addition, the features of the stress test, as well as the eventual results, provide information for markets and investors about vulnerabilities in the financial sector, and the very process of completing the stress test prompts stronger risk management inside financial institutions.

In some cases, emergent financial stability concerns may relate specifically to exposures or behaviours of the banking system (e.g., bank vulnerabilities to stresses in Europe or capital distribution policies). In other cases, the concerns may be more broadly a market phenomenon (e.g., the behaviour of agricultural land prices). But in either event, the balance sheets of these large institutions provide a useful window into conditions in the financial system. And, if financial imbalances are to create macroeconomic stresses, they will typically be transmitted through the banking system, making the degree of bank vulnerability a pivotal consideration.

To the extent that large financial institutions are driving the imbalances in question, horizontal reviews and stress tests may provide supervisors with information that will allow them to devise appropriate interventions. Such efforts may also highlight regulatory and legal changes that are necessary to ensure greater stability in the banking system. Indeed, in the speech cited above, Chairman Bernanke noted that "macroprudential considerations are being incorporated into the development of new regulations as well as into supervision." In short, the intensified macroprudential monitoring that we have outlined, coupled with the strategic use of horizontal reviews and stress tests, strikes us as providing a practical backbone for a pragmatic and judgment-based approach to macroprudential supervision.

Two further thoughts on these issues seem appropriate. First, as an alternative (and more rules-based) approach to macroprudential supervision, regulators might work to develop capital and liquidity requirements that they could actively calibrate to ease or tighten overall financial conditions through the business cycle. Although this idea deserves further consideration, there seem to be limits to its practical usefulness. During periods of economic weakness or financial stress, market participants typically show heightened concerns regarding the capital levels of banks. As such, regulators may find it difficult to convince banks to release capital during such times – and markets are likely to demand more capital, not less capital.

Second, the following section examines in some detail the scope for using monetary policy as a macroprudential tool. The key conclusion is that in some situations financial stability considerations may be fully compatible with a central bank's traditional macroeconomic objectives; in such instances, monetary policy has the capacity to support the pursuit of financial stability. However, in other instances, this may not be the case. As such, other tools – such as those outlined earlier in this section – are likely to be necessary to achieve financial stability on a sustained basis.

Going forward, regulators should carefully bear in mind the painful lessons that were learned through the years of the global financial crisis. The financial system does occasionally veer off track. Even so, the macroprudential approaches that we have described are not a panacea and will no doubt require ongoing refinements. The objective is not to second guess the markets but to independently monitor and assess potential systemic risks. And, admittedly, macroprudential supervision may at times be mistaken or misdirected in its prescriptions. However, the financial crisis highlights that the only thing worse than forming such difficult judgments, is not addressing these issues at all.

6. TRADE-OFFS BETWEEN FINANCIAL STABILITY AND OTHER POLICY OBJECTIVES

This section considers some potential trade-offs between financial stability and other policy objectives. We focus in particular on the implications for the Federal Reserve but also briefly consider what this discussion might suggest for US fiscal policy.

The Federal Reserve has a statutorily prescribed dual mandate, which requires it to pursue price stability and maximum sustainable employment. That said, the Fed's aggressive response to the global financial crisis highlights that implicitly at least there is a third pillar in the mandate – a responsibility for financial stability. This view is also consistent with the increased responsibilities for financial stability that were assigned to the Federal Reserve by the Dodd-Frank Act.

From a historical perspective, the Fed's responsibilities for financial stability are hardly new. Indeed, the Federal Reserve was created a century ago particularly to pursue objectives related to financial stability. The Fed was commissioned to provide "an elastic currency", i.e., to ensure that credit could flexibly expand and contract in line with shifting economic and seasonal conditions. Financial stability is also at the heart of Bagehot's famous dictum that central banks should be prepared to lend freely against good collateral during times of stress. More generally, a central bank's role in ensuring financial stability seems to grow almost unavoidably from its responsibility to act as a lender of last resort.

The key question then is how do these objectives interact? As a general matter, the Fed's dual mandate and its responsibilities for financial stability should be broadly consistent and reinforcing. In particular, efforts to reduce inflation should contribute over time to stronger economic growth and enhanced financial stability. Similarly, financial stability should generally tend to support economic growth and help foster an environment conducive to stable credit and prices.

Even so, trade-offs between the pursuit of financial stability and other objectives may very well arise. How worrisome are such conflicts? And how can they best be managed? As a background point, we note that such tensions also arise within the context of the dual mandate. Specifically, in the face of supply shocks, the Fed must balance concerns for stabilising inflation against efforts to preserve levels of employment.

This noted, the following scenarios highlight some possible tensions that may arise between financial stability objectives and the Fed's traditional dual mandate. A key conclusion is that successfully achieving these various objectives will likely require the use of macroprudential tools such as those that were discussed in the previous section.

Scenario 1. In response to weak growth and deflationary pressures, the central bank is pursuing an extraordinarily stimulative monetary policy. Given the weakness of the economy, investors become increasingly convinced that these policies will remain in place indefinitely. Investors borrow aggressively at low prevailing short-term rates and invest at longer-term horizons and in risky assets. Term and risk premiums become highly compressed, creating concerns about an abrupt and potentially destabilising re-pricing of asset values when the need to tighten monetary policy eventually arrives.

In this scenario, the central bank's policy stance is consistent with its mandates for inflation and employment, but it arguably is not meeting its financial stability goals. Given the weak performance of the economy, the decision to reduce the extraordinary stimulus that is in place would be – at the very least – a complicated one. In this instance, the central bank would need to rely on its macroprudential tools to address the emerging financial imbalances.

Scenario 2: Growth has been strong and inflation low for many years, causing expectations of macroeconomic volatility to decline sharply. In pricing assets, investors incorporate expectations that these benign macroeconomic conditions will continue indefinitely.

The central bank is meeting its mandates for inflation and economic activity, indeed doing so in a very sustained and convincing way. The economy, however, is becoming a victim of its own success and is vulnerable to a sharp realignment of asset prices. Again, the regulators should use macroprudential tools to encourage appropriate risk assessments and financial stability.

Scenario 3: A central bank concerned about financial stability introduces a new tougher set of capital and liquidity requirements. But these new requirements are criticised on the grounds that they will reduce the flow of credit from financial institutions to the real economy and, accordingly, lower the level of economic activity and employment going forward.

Occasional choices between the various legs of the mandate may be unavoidable. How much growth is the central bank willing to sacrifice in the pursuit of financial stability? In some sense, these trade-offs are not new. As we noted above, the Fed already has to accept the fact that there may be trade-offs between the growth and inflation legs of its mandate, particularly in the aftermath of supply shocks; the key question in such instances is what trajectory of policy will provide the best path for the economy over the medium to long run, in terms of both the level and volatility of output and inflation? Similarly, the central bank should pursue its macro-prudential policies with an eye toward best achieving financial stability and its other mandates over the medium term. This may at times entail sacrificing some growth today in exchange for greater financial stability in the future.

Scenario 4: A central bank with a financial stability mandate is hesitant to tighten monetary policy as inflationary pressures emerge and the labour market reaches full employment. Commercial banks are in the process of strengthening their balance sheets in the aftermath of a financial crisis, and the central bank worries that a tightening of monetary policy will bring a marked flattening of the yield curve. The upshot will be reduced earnings and renewed stresses for many of the banks.

As we noted, it is important for the central bank to cast its mandate in a medium-term perspective. The tightening of monetary policy may pose stresses for the banks in the near-term, but an upswing in inflationary pressures and a more aggressive policy tightening down the road could create even greater financial tensions. The central bank could ease macroprudential requirements if the banking system does in fact come under stress.

A related concern is that as the central bank is handed multiple mandates, at least without a clear ordering among those mandates, it may *become vulnerable to persuasion – or domination – by politicians.* For example, after World War II, the Federal Reserve's mandate was much less clearly defined than is the case today. The Fed worried about stability in the bond markets and the government's debt-servicing costs, as well as about inflation, growth, employment, and its regulatory responsibilities. Ambiguity as to which of these objectives was senior left the Fed vulnerable to pressure from the Treasury, since any number of policies could be justified given the broad set of objectives. This highlights that a clear anchoring mandate is a necessary condition for central bank independence.

We see two broad kinds of solutions to these potential conflicts. The first, as we have discussed, is to reserve monetary policy for the achievement of macroeconomic objectives. Macroprudential tools could then be utilised as necessary, given the setting of macro policies, to achieve financial stability. Second, there may be a case for the Federal Reserve's mandate to be more hierarchical, indicating which of these objectives should take precedence if there is a conflict. The Fed can legitimately argue that it sees the two parts of its dual mandate as being of equal importance. But the increasing emphasis on a third pillar may make such a framework more difficult to manage.

We conclude this section with a couple of additional thoughts. First, the pursuit of financial stability may ultimately require more interaction and coordination between the central bank and the government than is the case with conventional monetary policy. For example, as was the case during the financial crisis, efforts to stabilise the financial system may at times require a fiscal backstop for troubled institutions. Is it possible for the central bank to closely cooperate with the government in one dimension of its policies but fully preserve its independence in other dimensions? To date, the answer to this question appears to be a qualified yes. Even so, this is ground that central banks should traverse with the greatest of caution, establishing careful protocols and firewalls detailing the acceptable parameters for this interaction.

As a final issue, we briefly consider some channels through which fiscal policy may help foster financial stability. As a general matter, fiscal policy will best contribute to stable financial conditions by ensuring that spending and taxes – and, hence, the level of the debt – are on disciplined and predictable paths. Strong and sustainable fiscal performance, which avoids sharp lurches in the trajectory of policy, will support confidence in the private sector and the functioning of the economy. In addition, as noted above, fiscal resources may be necessary during times of stress to recapitalise institutions and otherwise backstop the financial system. The government should be prepared to provide these resources in extreme circumstances, with appropriate regard for blunting moral hazard and ensuring the safety of taxpayer resources.

7. SOME CONCLUDING THOUGHTS

There is clear commitment among US policy-makers to continue to develop key aspects of macroprudential regulation and supervision, with an eye toward avoiding financial crises and encouraging the financial system to develop in a direction that best supports economic growth and low and stable inflation. Driven by the jarring experience of the financial crisis and codified in the Dodd-Frank Act, many concrete reforms are in the pipeline. And the Federal Reserve and other regulators are moving to implement an approach that is firmly macroprudential in its orientation.

These are all encouraging developments, and it is important that this work continue and, indeed, move as quickly as possible toward implementation. But there is no shortage of challenges. *One key concern is that macroprudential efforts should not become heavy-handed, thus short-circuiting the functioning of markets.* Striking an appropriate balance will require a deference to market outcomes on the one hand, but also a willingness to occasionally intervene when financial markets have moved distinctly out of line with perceived fundamentals.

An even more vexing concern is that the collective memory of the financial crisis will eventually fade. This raises the question of whether it is possible to embed the macroprudential approach so deeply in the financial architecture that it will continue to be operative into the indefinite future. Although we are doubtful that financial crises can be eliminated entirely, there are good reasons to believe that the reforms currently being put in place are likely to increase the robustness and resilience of the financial system. Continuing with a broad range of implementation efforts represents an important challenge for policy-makers in the years ahead.

BIBLIOGRAPHY

Bernanke, B. 2012, "Fostering Financial Stability", speech at the 2012 Federal Reserve Bank of Atlanta Financial Markets Conference, Stone Mountain, Georgia, April 9, 2012.

Financial Stability Forum 2008, *Report of the Financial Stability Forum on Enhancing Market and Institutional Resilience*, April 7, 2008.

Fitzpatrick, T. and J. Thomson 2011, "An End to Too Big to Let Fail? The Dodd–Frank Act's Orderly Liquidation Authority", *Federal Reserve Bank of Cleveland, Economic Commentary*, January 5, 2011.

Greenspan, A. 2002, "International Financial Risk Management", remarks before the Council on Foreign Relations, Washington, D.C., November 19, 2002.

Greenspan, A. 2005, "Risk Transfer and Financial Stability", remarks to the Federal Reserve Bank of Chicago's Forty-first Annual Conference on Bank Structure, Chicago, May 5, 2005.

Kohn, D. 2007, "Financial Stability and Policy Issues", speech at the Federal Reserve Bank of Atlanta's 2007 Financial Markets Conference, Sea Island, Georgia, May 16, 2007.

Kohn, D. 2008, "The Changing Business of Banking: Implications for Financial Stability and Lessons from the Recent Market Turmoil", speech at the Federal Reserve Bank of Richmond's Credit Market Symposium, Charlotte, North Carolina, April 17, 2008.

Tarullo, D. 2010, "Next Steps in Financial Regulatory Reform", speech at the George Washington University Center for Law, Economics, and Finance Conference on the Dodd-Frank Act, Washington, D.C., November 12, 2010.

Tarullo, D. 2012a, "Regulatory Reform since the Financial Crisis", speech delivered at the Council on Foreign Relations C. Peter McColough Series on International Economics, New York, May 2, 2012.

Tarullo, D. 2012b, "Dodd-Frank Act Implementation", testimony before the Committee on Banking, Housing, and Urban Affairs, US Senate, Washington, D.C., June 6, 2012.

Yellen, J. 2010, "Macroprudential Supervision and Monetary Policy in the Post-crisis World", speech at the Annual Meeting of the National Association for Business Economics, Denver, Colorado, October 11, 2010.

4. Financial Stability in Brazil

Luiz Awazu Pereira da Silva, Adriana Soares Sales and Wagner Piazza Gaglianone

INTRODUCTION

The global financial crisis identified, among many, at least four specific issues for supervisors and regulators of financial systems worldwide. First, micro-prudential tools[1] are insufficient to ensure financial stability. Before the crisis, the common view was that the existing financial regulation and supervision could maintain the stability of all individual institutions. The crisis showed that ensuring compliance at the individual institution level does not guarantee that the financial system as a whole is stable. Therefore and second, an overarching policy framework was absent before the crisis, which would be responsible for systemic financial stability; this systemic approach is now labelled macro-prudential policy. But then, the third issue is what exactly do we mean by "financial stability"? In most cases, what implicitly comes to one's mind are features of financial "instability" such as bubbles in asset prices, excessive leverage by banks, etc. This lack of precision calls for a clear definition of financial stability in order to define an objective for macroprudential policy. The last and fourth issue is whether macroprudential policy needs to complement other policies (for example monetary policy) to ensure financial (and simultaneously) price stability.

Indeed, regarding financial stability, there is so far no agreed upon definition despite numerous instruments to conduct direct intervention in markets and many indicators of financial instability. Instruments range from liquidity or credit control measures, up to requirements for margin and capital adjustments, among many others. Moreover, the transmission mechanisms of such instruments are not well understood (Agénor and Pereira da Silva 2011) and

The views expressed herein are those of the authors and do not necessarily reflect those of the Central Bank of Brazil. The authors are grateful to the IBRE/FGV for kindly providing the commercial property price IGMI-C index. Any remaining errors are ours.

[1] We define hereby microprudential instruments as any regulatory provision that sets binding constraints to the balance sheet of individual financial institutions and affects its behaviour (e.g., minimum regulatory capital, maximum leverage ratio, maximum loan-to-value ratio, debt-to-income of potential borrowers, etc.)

the Financial Stability Reports (FSR) exhibit worldwide different views regarding areas of financial system fragility and the likelihood of crises in specific markets (for a detailed discussion see Goodhart 2011).

In Brazil, the global financial crisis has spurred renewed efforts in the task of monitoring financial stability. In order to address the issue, the Central Bank of Brazil (BCB) established in 2011 a Financial Stability Committee[2] to coordinate and strengthen the supervision of the financial industry and reduce systemic risk. In addition, BCB has been publishing a semi-annual FSR that describes the dynamics of the National Financial System (SFN) and, analyses its resilience to eventual shocks, as well as its projected evolution.

In this chapter we provide our specific definition of financial stability (section 1), using existing definitions, including the associated notion of systemic risk, in the current literature and reports. Then we proceed in section 2, to define the time and cross-section dimensions of systemic risk. In section 3, the areas of vulnerabilities and of financial (in)stability are discussed. In section 4 a comparison of systemic risk indicators is provided for Brazil, the US and the Euro area offering a perspective of vulnerabilities and systemic risks based on selected credit market indicators. In section 5, we examine financial conditions in Brazil in light of the current macroeconomic setup, and we detail a frequent indicator of financial (in)stability, focusing in the credit market. In section 6, a broad synthetic indicator of financial stability is constructed in relation to systemic risk with an estimated probability of disruption of financial services. That probability, in turn, could be used to define policy guidelines and objectives.

1. A "WORKING" DEFINITION FOR "FINANCIAL STABILITY"

"Financial stability" has become, especially in the light of the global financial crisis, an explicit objective of central banks and other public authorities (see Allen and Wood 2005). For instance, the Bank of England used the term in 1994 to denote those of its objectives which were distinct from price stability or from the efficient functioning of the financial system. Many central banks and/or regulatory agencies have within their mandate the obligation to ensure "financial stability".

---

[2] The duties of the new committee are to guide the central bank's committee on regulation and supervision of financial markets, capital, insurance, private pension plans and other similar national and international forums, maintain financial stability by defining strategies and guidelines for the conduct of the central bank, allocate responsibilities between the internal units involved, to ensure integrated and coordinated action, and to order ongoing studies, research and work on financial stability and preventing systemic risk. See http://www.bcb.gov.br/?FINANCSTAB for further details.

Mishkin (1991), *apud* Allen and Wood (2005), defines financial stability as *"the prevalence of a financial system, which is able to ensure in a lasting way, and without major disruptions, an efficient allocation of savings to investment opportunities."* More recently, Houben et al. (2012) argue that financial stability refers to the ability of the financial system to help the economic system allocate resources, manage risks and absorb shocks. But now almost twenty years after these proposed definitions, there is still no widely-accepted definition of "financial stability" and therefore, equally, no consensus across central banks and regulatory agencies on what policies should be pursued in the interest of financial stability.

Indeed, according to BIS-CGFS (2010), there is no commonly shared definition of financial stability, towards which macroprudential policies would be geared. Alternative definitions would include robustness of the financial system to external shocks or to shocks originating within the financial system, and the vulnerability to financial distress in response to normal-sized shocks (or even larger ones).[3] We therefore propose the following definition.

Definition 1 of financial stability:[4] A financial system is "stable" when it continues performing its functions (e.g., maturity transformation, allocation of savings, etc.) across a time dimension (e.g., growing in a sustainable way across the financial cycle) without building-up systemic risk measured across its cross-section dimension. "Stability" requires also that when the system is submitted to a normal-sized shock (or even larger shocks up to a certain defined threshold) it would be resilient and return – within some timeframe – to its previous functioning pattern.

This definition requires, in turn, specifying "what is systemic risk"? One definition from the post-crisis work by the IMF, FSB and BIS for the G20 defines it as "a *risk of disruption to financial services*[5] *that is caused by an impairment of all or parts of the financial system and has the potential to have serious negative consequences for the real economy"*. Indeed, the notion of financial stability is often discussed in terms of the concept of systemic risk and its sources, for which again there is no consensus definition. The above-mentioned definition of systemic risk translates into the mapping of vulnerabilities by components (the "parts") of the financial sector that can cause potentially

---

[3] Alternative definitions for financial stability could also be proposed within an analytical equilibrium setup including, for example, welfare and social costs issues, externality mechanisms and related policy instruments, efficiency issues (e.g., financial deepening and/or more complete markets increasing welfare), among many other relevant and related topics (see Borio and Drehmann, 2009, for further details).

[4] In physics and in asynchronous distributed decision-making (ADDM) systems, a complex system is defined as a stable system if it returns to a steady state in finite time, following a shock or perturbation, provided that it is initiated in a steady state. Equilibrium or steady state have to be defined by measurement as well as "perturbation".

[5] See BIS-CGFS (2010), for these purposes, "financial services" include credit intermediation, risk management and payment services.

the "impairment" of the system mentioned above. We therefore propose our own definition of "systemic risk".

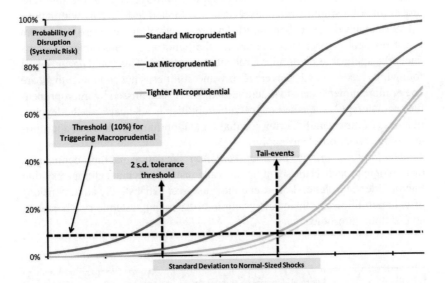

Figure 4.1: Stylized probability of disruption in a financial system due to systemic risk

Definition 2 of systemic risk: Systemic risk is measured by the probability of disruption of financial services, when the system is submitted to shocks, related to vulnerabilities such as inadequate leverage and levels of liquidity, and highly correlated co-movements of asset quality in the balance sheet of financial institutions, exacerbated by their interconnectedness and occurring despite the set of microprudential regulatory constraints that individual institutions have to comply with.

Therefore, systemic risk should be captured by a "probability of disruption" given a set of risk dimensions (e.g., time and cross-sectional), measured within an institutional and regulatory microprudential setup[6] and estimated according to the magnitude of shocks. Suppose that we define a tolerance level of 2 standard deviations (s.d.) from normal-sized shocks (observing the past history of a financial system) as a reference to test a system's stability. Suppose also that we have – through stress-tests – a mapping of the probability of disruption of the system and we define a tolerance threshold of say 10%. In a normal financial cycle, a financial system by itself and under its own set of standard microprudential regulations, should have its level of endogenously

---

[6] Stress tests are supposed to capture this probability (depending on how they are conducted).

Stability of the Financial System

generated systemic risk below the agreed upon threshold. This corresponds, respectively, in figures 4.1 and 4.2, to the blue line and situations of type I. There could be, however, situations of type II portrayed by the red line. The probability of disruption might exceed a reasonable threshold (say within the 2 s.d. normal-sized shocks boundary). That may arise either because the system is not resilient or because potential for the build-up of vulnerabilities exists under the applicable set of microprudential regulation. This could occur for the following reasons: (1) the coverage of vulnerabilities is not complete: there are one or more dimensions of vulnerability that has been missed by microprudential regulators; (2) the coverage of vulnerabilities is adequate but the level or tightness of the overall microprudential regulation framework is not appropriate; and (3) both problems apply.

Definition 3 of macroprudential regulation: We define macroprudential regulation or approach as the set of policies and instruments that calibrate existing microprudential rules and/or extend them to cover exhaustively all dimensions of vulnerabilities in a financial system in order to put systemic risk below an agreed upon threshold.

		Normal Financial Cycle	Normal-sized Shock < 2 s.d.	Larger Shock > 2 s.d. & < 4 s.d.	Tail Event > 4 s.d.
Situation of Type I	Microprudential regulation	System Stable, Probability of disruption small	System Stable, Probability of disruption higher	System Stable (?), Probability of disruption (?)	System Unstable, Probability of disruption > threshold
	Macroprudential regulation	No need	No need	Some need	Imperative Requirement
Situation of Type II	Microprudential regulation	System Stable (?), Probability of disruption (?)	System Stable (?), Probability of disruption (?)	System Unstable, Probability of disruption > threshold	System Unstable, Probability of disruption > threshold
	Macroprudential regulation	Some need	Some need	Imperative Requirement	Imperative Requirement

Figure 4.2: Diagram of macroprudential regulations

For example, in our figure 4.1, a tightening of regulations, i.e. the utilisation of a macroprudential approach is portrayed by the green line. It should reduce the probability of disruption significantly, perhaps even in areas beyond the occurrence of "tail events". Therefore, there is a relationship between financial stability and systemic risk in the sense that we recognise that any financial system builds inherently some degree of systemic risk across the cycle but there is a level of systemic risk beyond which the probability of "disruption" becomes too high. For policy-makers defining the threshold beyond which this probability is indeed too high and the specific vulnerabilities associated with it is paramount in order to trigger macroprudential policy action.

Regardless of the definition adopted,[7] financial stability is difficult to measure, and is clearly affected by other policy areas such as monetary policy and fiscal policy. As a result, macroprudential policy can contribute to financial stability, but it cannot guarantee the delivery of this objective on its own. The focus of macroprudential policy is on systemic risks, which is investigated in the following section along distinct dimensions.

2. TIME AND CROSS-SECTION DIMENSIONS OF SYSTEMIC RISK

Systemic risk is usually divided for analytical purposes into a time dimension and a cross-section dimension.

According to Houben et al. (2012) the time dimension deals with the evolution of aggregate risk in the financial system over time. Looking at figure 4.2, it means understanding the dynamics of the "blue curve" (representing systemic risk under standard microprudential regulations): would the curve shift towards the "red line" over the financial cycle, i.e. building more vulnerabilities endogenously? This property refers to "pro-cyclicality", a tendency of financial agents to assume excessive risk in the upswing and then to become overly risk averse in the downswing. Accordingly, this characteristic is illustrated by the cyclical patterns in the leverage and maturity mismatch positions in the financial system — a credit and liquidity cycle. The cross-section dimension, on the other hand, is related to the distribution of risk across the financial system at a given point in time, and has to be understood looking at the interconnectedness and resilience of the market structure.

Smets (2011) in turn argues that although the time dimension of systemic risk consists in investigating the build-up of financial imbalances in booms and its unravelling features in busts, while the cross-section dimension analyses contagion in interconnected financial systems, the real challenge is how to properly link these two perspectives.

Borio (2011) brings to the discussion the so-called *"paradox of financial instability"*: the system appears robust precisely when it is in fact the most vulnera-

---

[7] See Allen and Wood (2005) for a detailed discussion on desirable features of a definition of financial stability.

ble. According to the author, credit growth and asset prices are unusually strong, leverage measured at market prices artificially low, and risk premia and volatilities unusually low precisely when risk is at its highest. What looks like a low level of systemic risk is, in fact, a sign of aggressive risk-taking by agents. The experience of the recent global financial crisis provides a good example. This perspective is somehow discouraging because it means that assessing the probability of disruption using existing market price signals would be misleading.

In this context, the best leading indicators of financial distress in its time dimension try to turn the Borio paradox to the policy-makers' advantage. Borio (2011) stresses that indicators such as credit-to-GDP gaps and asset prices calculated using as benchmarks their historical norms provide reasonably reliable signals of systemic financial distress over horizons that vary between two-to-four years. Unfortunately, using similar approaches, macro-stress tests have so far failed to effectively identify these risks, probably due to their inability to capture the highly non-linear behaviour of prices and quantities during crises owing to the shortcomings of existing macro models.

Nonetheless, while the "paradox of financial instability" advises us to not use raw market prices in the time dimension, it does not prevent policy-makers using them to assess the cross-sectional dimension of systemic risk. In fact, there is a vast empirical literature suggesting that market prices have the ability to measure relative risk, which can be a powerful tool for policy-makers to help calibrating prudential tools with respect to the systemic significance of individual financial institutions (see Borio, 2011). In practice, several cross-section measures of systemic risk (such as correlations or other measures of interdependence) are indeed based on market prices, and are usually complemented with inputs from supervisors, such as probabilities of default.

3. AREAS OF VULNERABILITIES AND OF FINANCIAL (IN)STABILITY

Houben et al. (2012) state that making macroprudential policy operational is a major policy challenge. It means *inter alia* specifying – according to our definition of financial stability and systemic risk – what are the policy-makers' acceptable thresholds for the probability of disruption of its financial system (e.g., 10%? 20%? etc.) associated with an acceptable level of stress (e.g., 2 s.d., 3 s.d. for shocks) and under the existing set of microprudential regulations. Our definition 3 states that a macroprudential approach simply tightens the existing microprudential rules and/or extends their reach to cover all the areas of vulnerabilities in a given financial system.

One of the steps involved is to specify a policy strategy, which links the objectives of macroprudential policy to intermediate objectives and presumptive indicators for risk identification and instrument selection. *Operational macroprudential policy requires concrete intermediate objectives*, effective and efficient policy instruments for achieving these indicators that prompt policy implementation and accountability mechanisms. Those, in turn, validate the much needed operational independence of regulators and central banks.

According to the authors, in essence, there are three groups of intermediate policy objectives, the first comprising leverage and credit, the second liquidity and funding and the third the resilience of the market structure. The third can be further divided into common exposures, "too-big-to-fail" bail-out expectations and interconnectedness through the financial infrastructure.

In this regard, the Basels Committee on the Global Financial System (CGFS) segregates the *vulnerabilities* of financial stability into three main categories: *leverage, liquidity* (or market risk) *and interconnectedness*. Addressing the mentioned time series and cross-sectional dimensions of systemic risk requires different types of instruments. Ideally, a relatively small set of indicators would provide reliable early warning signals of financial fragilities. In practice, however, given the elevated uncertainty regarding the build-up of risk according to several indicators, enhancing the toolkit available to policymakers might be a good approach.

According to BIS-CGFS (2010), a key element of developing macroprudential instruments is to adapt existing microprudential tools, such as strong prudential standards and limits on activities that increase systemic vulnerabilities and risks. These standards and limits might be occasionally altered, or adjusted in a countercyclical manner, especially with a view to "leaning against the financial cycle". When that is the objective, the instruments would be properly adjusted (dynamically) in response to changing assessments of financial risks. Adjustments would need to occur both on the upswing, when vulnerabilities are growing, and on the downswing, when risks of a destabilising credit contraction or crunch are rising.

The referred to CGFS document also argues that existing microprudential instruments could be used for promoting financial system resilience. They can be recalibrated to limit the financial system's exposure to shocks. In this category, instruments include capital and liquidity requirements, leverage limits, constraints on currency mismatches, and measures that strengthen financial infrastructure. Table 4.1 presents some examples of macroprudential instruments, classified by the main risk factors they influence (or constrain) and by the financial system component they apply to.

In order to guide the adequate utilisation of macroprudential instruments, systemic risk indicators are necessary to properly map the potential areas (or sectors) of increasing risk across the financial system. The key question is whether (in practice) the available indicators are sufficiently reliable. Both Goodhart (2011) and Borio (2011), *apud* Houben et al. (2012), point to readily available data related to leverage, credit growth, housing and property prices, and perhaps also funding and liquidity. Indeed, these data are regularly used in Financial Stability Reports (FSRs) to indicate emerging risks. However, these available indicators might not be adequate to deal with extreme (tail) events, in which the relationship between macroeconomic and financial variables might change dramatically. In this case, tail risk measures would be indicated.[8] Apart from the difficulty of adequately identifying when a risk becomes excessive (and how much policy intervention is needed), empirical research is necessary in order to deepen our understanding of leading indicators and transmission channels.

Table 4.1: Macroprudential instruments by vulnerability and financial system component

		Financial system component				
		Individual bank or deposit-taker		Non-bank investor	Securities market	Financial infrastructure
		Balance sheet*	Lending contract			
Vulnerability	Leverage	capital ratio risk weights provisioning profit distribution restrictions credit growth cap	LTV cap debt service / income cap maturity cap margin			
	Liquidity or market risk	Liquidity / reserve FX lending restriction currency mismatch limit open FX position limit	Valuation rules (eg. MMMFs)	local currency or FX reserve requirements	central bank balance sheet operations	exchange trading
	Interconnect-edness	concentration limits systematic capital surcharge subsidiarisation				Central counterparties (CCP)

*Capital and other balance sheet requirements also apply to insurers and pension funds, but we restrict our attention here to the types of institutions most relevant for credit intermediation.
Source: BIS-CGFS (2010).

---

[8] There is a fast growing literature on systemic risk, especially on tail risk related indicators. Just to mention some recent papers: Schechtman and Gaglianone (2012) shift the focus of financial stability monitoring from the usual conditional mean of a specific credit indicator to the conditional tail of this indicator based on quantile regressions. Adrian and Brunnermeier (2011) propose a measure for systemic risk so-called CoVaR, which is the value-at-risk (VaR) of the financial system conditional on institutions being under distress. More recently, Lopez-Espinosa et al. (2012) extended the CoVaR measure to capture the asymmetric response of the banking system to positive and negative shocks, capturing non-linear tail co-movement between system-wide and individual bank returns.

4. COMPARISON BETWEEN FINANCIAL SYSTEMIC VULNERABILITIES IN BRAZIL AND THE US AND THE EURO ZONE

In this section, we present a selected set of systemic risk indicators according to BIS-CGFS (2010) for Brazil, United States and Euro area.[9] We use as proxy for leverage the credit-to-GDP gap, and for liquidity the loan-to-deposit (LTD) ratio. Interconnectedness is also analysed based on individual network data from interbank transfers. A broad view of asset prices (stocks and property prices) along the three considered regions is also provided with the objective of investigating a possible temporal (lagged) relation between credit-to-GDP gap and asset prices, as often suggested in the literature (e.g., Borio 2011). Finally, non-performing loan (NPL) series together with selected indicators (e.g., capital adequacy) are presented for comparison purposes.

4.1. Leverage

Financial development is commonly measured by the credit-to-GDP ratio. A useful leverage indicator[10] extracted from this series is the *credit-to-GDP gap*, which is defined by the difference between the observable credit-to-GDP ratio and its estimated trend. According to Smets (2011), the credit-to-GDP gap can also be used as an early warning indicator and be helpful to calibrate macroprudential policy responses (e.g., countercyclical capital buffers).

Several methods can be used to obtain the credit-to-GDP trend, such as linear trend techniques, quadratic or cubic trends, cubic splines and time series filters (e.g., Hodrick-Prescott (HP) and band-pass filters). In this chapter, we adopt the HP filter for practical purposes despite its well known drawbacks (e.g., end-point unreliable estimation).[11] In addition, this is the trend extraction method often used in the MVTF's Consultative Documents.[12]

A broad picture of the credit-to-GDP ratio of the three considered regions (based on annual data from World Bank) is shown in figure 4.3. We can note the relatively low level of Brazilian credit in comparison to that of the US and

---

[9] The Euro area (Euro zone) refers to a monetary union among the European Union member states that have adopted the euro as their sole official currency. It currently consists of 17 countries: Austria, Belgium, Cyprus, Estonia, Finland, France, Germany, Greece, Ireland, Italy, Luxembourg, Malta, Netherlands, Portugal, Slovakia, Slovenia, Spain.

[10] A drawback of this indicator is that credit-to-GDP gap possibly accounts for risk-taking on both the asset and liability sides of the financial institutions' balance sheet.

[11] A deeper empirical investigation should consider, for instance: (i) a robustness analysis of the credit gap estimation based on competing trend extraction techniques; (ii) recalibration of the adopted filters according to relevant credit cycle frequencies (which are often different from the business cycle ones); (iii) a forecast device to deal with the end-point issue by using (for example) an out-of-sample projection instead of the (in-sample) last HP-filtered trend point.

[12] Basel Committee's Macro Variables Task Force (MVTF).

the Euro area. Indeed, the domestic credit to the private sector (in % of GDP) in Brazil was reported by World Bank at 57% in 2010, in sharp contrast to figures for the US (201%) and the Euro area (134%). Domestic credit to the private sector refers to all financial resources provided to the private sector, through loans, purchases of nonequity securities, and trade credits and other accounts receivable that establish a claim for repayment.

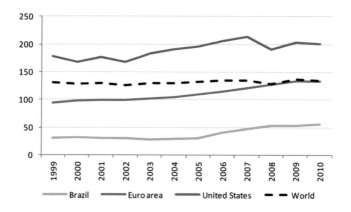

Figure 4.3: Domestic credit to private sector (% of GDP)

Source: World Bank (annual data).

Credit-to-GDP increased in Brazil, US and Euro area in comparison to its 2000 levels, but the underlying picture is very different across these regions. Lending conditions tightened noticeably in the Euro area recently, and credit growth slumped in late 2011. Developments were more positive in the United States. In Brazil, it exhibited a significant increase in past years but still remains on a sustainable path.

These developments are better understood when *real GDP growth rates* are analysed. According to the IMF-WEO (2012), European GDP real growth has slowed sharply, and many economies in the region are now in or close to recession. The United States has seen a spate of encouraging economic news, with GDP growth increasing and unemployment falling. Latin America (and Brazil in particular) has shown resilience to the swings in risk aversion following the developments of the European crisis over recent months.

In order to construct credit-to-GDP gap measures, we use quarterly frequency series. The credit-to-GDP ratio for Brazil is calculated by using financial system credit operations (% of GDP). For the US, we followed Edge and Meisenzahl (2011), in which the credit-to-GDP ratio is based on nominal credit (in the numerator) as the volume of credit market debt outstanding of the non-financial corporate business sector and household and non-profit organisation sector.[13] For the Euro area, we adopt the definition of Smets (2011) based on total loans to Euro area residents over nominal GDP. Although these series might not be perfectly comparable, in the sense of using not exactly the same definitions for "credit", and distinct databases, we believe they are able to generate proper gap dynamics, provided that our objective here is to identify periods in which the observed credit-to-GDP series deviated from the estimated trends.

Table 4.2: Real GDP growth rate (annual percent change)

									IMF Projections		
	2004	2005	2006	2007	2008	2009	2010	2011	2012	2013	2017
Brazil	5.7	3.2	4.0	6.1	5.2	−0.3	7.5	2.7	3.0	4.1	4.1
Euro area	2.2	1.7	3.3	3.0	0.4	−4.3	1.9	1.4	−0.3	0.9	1.7
United States	3.5	3.1	2.7	1.9	−0.3	−3.5	3.0	1.7	2.1	2.4	3.3

Source: IMF–WEO, April 2012.

Table 4.3: Correlations between Credit-to-GDP gaps

	Brazil	Euro area	USA
Brazil	1,00	-	-
Euro area	0,83	1,00	-
USA	0,64	0,84	1,00

Note: Sample period 2001Q1-2011Q4.

Some interesting features arise from the normalised credit-to-GDP gap comparison. First, one should note the high correlation of Euro area and US gaps, suggesting synchronic credit cycles between the two regions. Moreover, both gap series exhibit end-points with significant negative values, suggesting that their credit-to-GDP ratios could be below their respective trends.[14] The Brazil-

---

[13] Nonetheless, the authors argue that *ex-post* revisions to the US credit-to-GDP ratio gap are sizeable and as large as the gap itself, and that the main source of these revisions stems from the unreliability of end-of-sample estimates of the series' trend rather than from revised estimates of the underlying data. In this sense, the authors point out for potential costs of gap mismeasurement.
[14] According to IMF-WEO (2012), bank deleveraging is affecting primarily Europe. While such deleveraging does not necessarily imply lower credit to the private sector, the evidence suggests that it is contributing to a tighter credit supply. IMF estimates are that it may subtract another 1 percentage point from Euro area growth this year.

ian credit cycle seems to be more connected to that of the Euro area. Its credit-to-GDP gap appears to be close to zero, indicating that Brazil's recent credit growth path might be close to its potential.

Panel A – Brazil

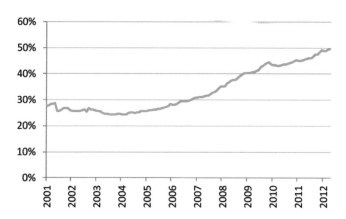

Panel B – Euro area and United States

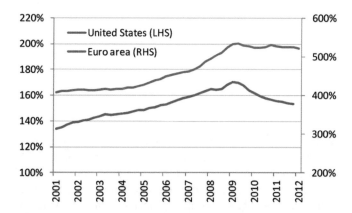

Figure 4.4: Credit (% of GDP)

Source: Brazil: Central Bank of Brazil – Financial system credit operations (% of GDP). Earmarked and non-earmarked resources are included. Euro area: MFI Consolidated Balance Sheets (ECB Monetary Statistics) and Quarterly National Accounts (Eurostat). Data refer to the changing composition of the Euro area. USA: Nominal credit (in the numerator) from Federal Reserve Board (FRB) in the Flow of Funds Accounts (FOFAs) and nominal GDP (in the denominator) from the Bureau of Economic Analysis (BEA) in the National Income and Product Accounts (NIPAs).

According to Borio (2011), the financial cycle can be longer than the business cycle and empirical evidence could shed some light on how different monetary and financial regimes affect the relationship between financial and business cycles. This comparison between financial and business cycles can also be a guide to the more theoretical analysis. In this sense, we provide in figure 4.6 and table 4.4 a short comparison involving credit-to-GDP, output and industrial production gaps for Brazil, US and Euro zone, using the HP filter.

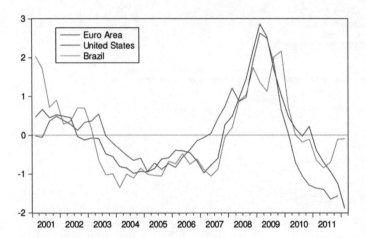

Figure 4.5: Credit-to-GDP gaps (normalised)

Source: Authors' calculations. Credit-to-GDP gaps are based on the previously presented quarterly credit-to-GDP series and HP-filter to extract the trends. Gap series are normalized (zero mean and unit variance) for comparison purposes.

Table 4.4: Correlations between "gap" measures

	Brazil	Euro area	USA
Credit-to-GDP gap and Output gap	-0.06	-0.20	-0.44
Credit-to-GDP gap and Industrial produ-ction gap	-0.20	-0.44	-0.46
Output gap and Industrial production gap	0.94	0.95	0.95

Source: Authors' calculations. Sample period 2001Q1-2011Q4.

The negative signs obtained from correlations between the credit-to-GDP gaps and output (or industrial production) gaps indicate that *financial and business cycles are indeed not synchronised.* One possible explanation would be

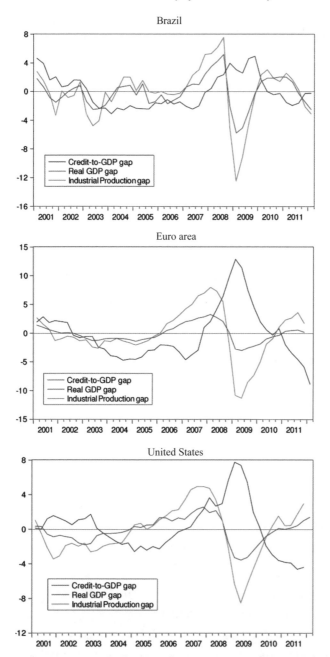

Figure 4.6: Gap comparison: Credit, GDP and industrial production

Source: Authors' calculations. Credit-to-GDP gap for Euro area is divided by two for comparison purposes. For Brazil it is multiplied by two.

the (possible) longer duration of financial cycles. In addition, note that the 2008/2009 crisis imposed, firstly, a negative shock in the business cycles (closing the output gaps by the end of 2008), whereas the credit gaps continued to increase in the same period. Secondly, a few quarters later, only when the business cycles reached its (local) lowest levels, then the credit gaps suffered the negative crisis impact, leading the credit-to-GDP trajectory towards its historical trend.

On the other hand, it is worth mentioning that the referred negative signs are higher (in absolute terms) when considering correlation between credit gaps and industrial production gaps than the respective correlations between credit gaps and output gaps. One possible explanation is that output gap includes other sectors besides industrial production (e.g., services) with distinct interactions in respect to credit market dynamics. Finally, it is also worth highlighting that correlations for Brazil are closer to zero, in comparison the US and Euro zone, which is probably due to its relatively lower level of credit-to-GDP and the relevant differences in financial depth across these regions.

4.2. Liquidity

We adopt the *loan-to-deposit (LTD) ratio as our indicator for liquidity risk*. Aggeler and Feldman (1998) argue that the liquidity of a bank is usually evaluated by using a host of tools and techniques, but the traditional loan-to-deposit (LTD) ratio is a measure that often receives the most attention by analysts and regulators. According to the authors, it captures the bank's ability to repay depositors and other creditors without incurring excessive costs[15] and while continuing to fund its expansion. An increase in the LTD ratio may indicate that a bank exhibits less of the needed cushion to fund its business growth and to protect itself against a sudden recall of its funding, especially a financial institution that relies on deposits to fund growth.

Although we present LTD series based on different definitions[16] we believe their growth rates can perfectly depict the broad liquidity characteristics of the financial sectors in the three regions.

It should be remembered that European banks historically present high loan-to-deposit ratios, meaning that they are more leveraged than, for instance, the US banks. One element to highlight is the sharp increase of LTD in Brazil in the past few years, mainly due to the nature of bank financing.[17] In addition,

---

[15] Based on a survey of US banks and regression analysis the authors found that the LTD ratio was statistically highly significant and robust in explaining the likelihood that a bank would refuse a loan: The higher the LTD the more likely a bank would refuse a loan (probably due to liquidity constraints).

[16] Given the scarcity of database covering the three regions altogether.

[17] The main issue with Brazil's credit boom over recent years has been the nature of bank financing, with loans backed more by debt issuance than deposits. This has led to a rapid increase in commercial banks' loan-to-deposit ratio (one of the highest in the world) and has created a system where many lenders (particularly smaller-sized banks) to a great extent are reliant on government-backed loans.

the significant decrease in the US LTD series since 2009 is noticeable, confirming the fact that most US banks are currently highly liquid.

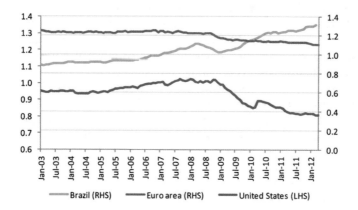

Figure 4.7: Loan-to-deposit ratio (LTD)

Sources: ECB Monetary Statistics (MFI Consolidated Balance Sheets): Total Loans (and Deposits) to (from) Euro area residents. Board of Governors of the Federal Reserve System (Assets and Liabilities of Commercial Banks in the United States – H.8): All commercial banks' LTD is defined as the ratio between loans (and leases) in bank credit and deposits. Central Bank of Brazil: LTD is defined as the ratio between loans and deposits of the financial system.

Table 4.5: Loan-to-deposit ratio (annual percent change)

	2004	2005	2006	2007	2008	2009	2010	2011
Brazil	1.6%	1.2%	3.7%	7.8%	4.0%	-0.9%	12.6%	4.5%
Euro area	-0.4%	-0.1%	0.8%	-0.6%	-1.6%	-4.9%	-1.4%	-0.8%
United States	-0.7%	1.9%	2.8%	2.1%	0.5%	-8.1%	-6.3%	-5.3%

The most recent IMF's Global Financial Stability Report (IMF-GFSR, 2012) states that advanced economy banks have been under pressure to reduce leverage since the outbreak of the subprime crisis, as many institutions had entered the crisis with thin capital cushions and a heavy reliance on wholesale funding. According to the Report, progress has varied in this adjustment process. While institutions in the United States have reduced their leverage and reliance on wholesale funding, Euro area banks still rely more on wholesale funding and, though leverage has been reduced, levels remain elevated. *This has left the European banking system more exposed to structural and cyclical deleveraging pressures.*

4.3. Interconnectedness

Banking lending networks are one of the most important aspects of financial systems and are the main channel of transmission of systemic risk. In fact, small shocks limited only to a few banks can spread by contagion and affect the entire system (Allen and Gale 2000, *apud* Tabak et al. 2011). In this sense, Georg (2010) argues that one of the lessons from the recent crisis is that the network structure of the banking system has to be taken into account to assess systemic risk.

The fast growing literature on *financial networks* (see De Nicolò et al. 2012) suggests that high interconnectedness mitigates the impact of small shocks by spreading them but, on the other hand, amplifies large shocks since they can reach more counterparties. According to the referred authors, banks operate in an interconnected system and, consequently, distress or failure of a single bank can affect other institutions. In this sense, spillover effects arise because of asset price movements, bilateral interbank market exposures or feedback from the real economy.[18]

The interconnectedness of a financial institution inside a network can be measured by the number of other institutions with which it is connected (see Georg (2010, p.6) for a technical discussion). In this section, we present the *interconnectedness of the Brazilian, US and Euro area banking system* to assess interbank overall exposure.

The *Brazilian analysis* is based on two interbank fund transfer systems (STR and SITRAF) and considers interbank transfers of financial institutions and conglomerates (transfers between institutions of the same conglomerate are not included). We use data on daily transfers made between financial institutions within the Brazilian financial system for all financial institutions (and conglomerates) that have exposures in the interbank market.

The 25 more connected institutions provided over 90% of total transfers (and eight institutions were responsible for 76% of total transfers in 2011Q4). This evidence indicates a large heterogeneity[19] across banks and supports the hypothesis that Brazilian banking system interconnectedness has a fat tail distribution, in which there are few institutions that are highly connected and, thus, are key in the interbank exposure network.

---

[18] Moreover, externalities provoked by interconnectedness are particularly significant for systemically important financial institutions, since they are often "backbones" of the whole financial infrastructure. It is worth mentioning that, although "systemic importance" has been generally associated with the size of financial institutions, recent events suggest a more complex picture: The interconnectedness would be also determined by its interbank market linkages, and its effects amplified by high leverage (see Drehmann and Tarashev 2011). In addition, interconnectedness may also be present in nonbanking financial systems or institutions that support market infrastructure, such as central clearing counterparties.

[19] Tabak et al. (2011) present results which suggest that banks pursue different strategies within the interbank network, which may be due to diversity in obtaining funds domestically and internationally.

Stability of the Financial System

100 institutions (BRL 3.084 trillion)

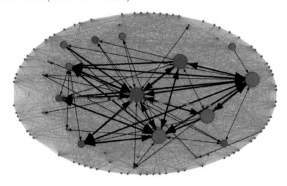

25 institutions (BRL 2.802 trillion)

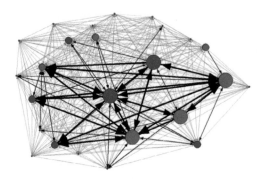

Figure 4.8: Interconnectedness diagrams of the Brazilian Banking System (2011Q4)

Banking system (B1 and B2) with individual exposure values above BRL 1 million. Blue (red) circle refers to positive (negative) net position in 2011Q4. Size of the circle indicates size of assets (big circle: above 5% of total assets, medium circle: between 0.5% and 5%, small circle: below 0.5%). Light-grey arrows refer to values up to quantile 50%, dark-grey arrows indicate values between quantiles 50% and 75% and black arrows refer to values above quantile 75%.

Source: Central Bank of Brazil.

Next we present some summary statistics of a broader Brazilian interbank network. The nodes (vertices) of the network are the commercial banks, and the edges are interbank loans between two banks. The value *in-degree* is a measure for the liabilities of a node while the value *out-degree* is a measure for its assets.

There is an increase in the number of edges (in comparison to the number of vertices) which might be a signal of financial deepening (and thus a signal of an augmented degree of complexity of the banking system as a whole).

Nonetheless, the ratio between exposures and funding has slightly decreased in the same period.

Table 4.6: Brazilian interbank network

Network statistics	2008Q4	2009Q4	2010Q4	2011Q4
Vertice	128	135	136	136
Edge	1.106	1.132	1.144	1.403
Max Out-degree	79	100	104	103
Max In-degree	48	43	48	64
Average Diameter	2.08	2.05	2.06	1.98
Exposure values (BRL billion)	114.4	95.2	115.4	137.9
Exposures/Fundings	5.7%	4.5%	4.2%	4.2%

Banking system (B1, B2 and B4).

Source: Central Bank of Brazil.

Tabak et al. (2011) provide more results on Brazilian interbank networks and investigate the concept of directed clustering coefficients as a measure of systemic risk in complex networks. The authors explore data from the Brazilian interbank network and show that the way through which banks make clusters of lending relationships has a different impact in terms of systemic risk, although systemic risk within this market seems to be very limited.

Drehmann and Tarashev (2011) develop a measure[20] of systemic importance for international banking systems that accounts for the extent to which a bank propagates shocks across the system and is vulnerable to propagated shocks. An empirical exercise based on 20 large internationally active banks suggests that systemic importance greatly depends on the bank's role in the interbank network, both as a borrower and as a lender. On the other hand, regarding the international banking systems' deleveraging process observed in latest years, a recent paper by Singh (2012) argues that it would be grounded on a decline in the interconnectedness in the pledged collateral market as well as on the overall shrinking of balance sheets.[21]

Regarding the *Euro area*, the ECB's 2012 Financial Stability Report (ECB-FSR 2012) presents a financial network (static) analysis based on existing data

---

[20] Based on Shapley values, this measure gauges the contribution of interconnected banks to systemic risk, in contrast to other measures proposed in the literature.

[21] Singh (2012) suggests a decomposition of deleveraging into two components: (i) the shrinking of balance sheets (due to increased haircuts/shedding of assets) and (ii) the reduction in the interconnectedness of the financial system, which has been contributing towards the higher credit cost to the real economy. In this sense, the author investigates the second aspect of deleveraging and shows that (post-Lehman) there has been a significant decline in the interconnectedness in the pledged collateral market between banks and nonbanks.

for the Euro area, showing a banking structure which is well integrated across countries, with some banks playing an important role at the Euro area level while others have a more domestic focus. On the other hand, the Report also shows a *dynamic network modelling approach*, which can illustrate important aspects and fragilities of interbank activity[22] in a simulated network (in the absence of real micro data) used for stress testing purposes.[23] It is worth mentioning that this is a *unique application of conceptual and analytical techniques* that have only recently been introduced in financial analysis.

Table 4.7: Euro area interbank network

Metrics at the network level

Average number of links	69.640
Density	0.005
Average path length	2.510
Cluster coefficient	0.126
Weighed cluster coefficient	0.291
Assortativity	-0.410
Diameter	7.000

Refers to March 2012.

Source: ECB-FSR (2012, p.128).

Overall, measures at the network[24] and node levels confirm that the security network has a centralised structure, with some important banks connected with many other peripheral ones. Moreover, the analysis of the securities network

---

[22] The ECB's 2011 Financial Stability Report (ECB-FSR 2011) argues that evidence from the collateral held at the ECB supports the image of a highly interconnected banking system with respect to cross-holdings of bank securities. In this sense, one finds evidence of the key importance of a few core institutions for drawing funding from "satellite" banks across the Euro area, as only disproportionately few banks' bonds continue to be widely used as collateral. This reveals the significant potential impact that the default of one such core issuer would have on the system.

[23] The idea is to exploit information on the microstructure of banking activities to characterise the robustness of the banking sector to operating shocks.

[24] The present analysis relies on observations which are available on a weekly basis starting in October 2008 (174 periods). The number of holding relationships (or links) of each bank with another bank is 17 on a simple average and 69 when using a value-weighted average (the value of securities representing the link). Thus, this network is characterised by a low density (very sparse network). Indeed the diameter (i.e., the greatest distance between any pair of nodes) comprises only seven nodes and the average path length is 2.51, indicating that typically banks are not "too distant" from each other in this type of relationship. This is a consequence of well-connected nodes being linked to less well-connected ones. While the concentration of banks in the network is also low (i.e., low clustering coefficient), the larger weighted coefficient implies strong relationships between the nodes.

shows that the structure is well integrated across countries, with some banks
playing an important role at the European level and others at the domestic
level. Single measures alone may not be sufficient to analyse the securities
network, as multiple levels of analysis are required to assess banks' network
fragility in a complex banking system.

Regarding the *United States* (the only major industrialised country that does
not publish a Financial Stability Report[25]), to our knowledge, there is *no publicly available official report about the US interbank network* following the
approach previously presented for Brazil and the Euro area. Nonetheless, some
few studies such as Markose et al. (2010) can help bridge this gap. The authors
present an *empirical exercise for the US-Credit Default Swap (CDS) market*,
based on 2008Q4 data and on 26 US banks.

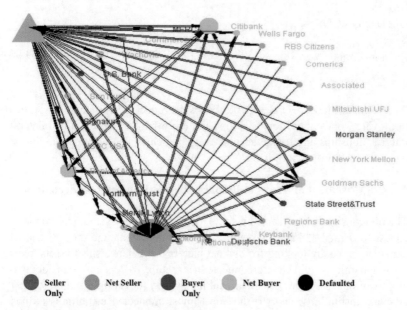

Figure 4.9: US CDS market network

The pure blue circles are banks that are sole buyers (these include Morgan Stanley, Merrill Lynch,
Northern Trust, State Street and Trust, Deutsche Bank, US Bank and Signature), while the light
blue nodes are net buyers and the larger of these represent Bank of America and Citigroup. An
entity that is exclusively a CDS protection seller is marked in red (there are no such entities)
while net sellers are marked in light pink. The pink triangular node represents the "outside entity"
constituted by (among others) non US banks involved in the CDS market and is a net seller as is
required. On the buy side, the outside entity accounts for about USD 3 trillion of CDS sold to it by
the US banks and on the sell side it accounts for about USD 3.2 trillion.

Source: Markose et al. (2010).

[25] Although the Federal Reserve and other regulatory authorities have regular surveillance and
monitoring programmes.

Within this sample, the top 5 US banks account for 92% of the US bank activity in the USD 34 trillion gross notional value of CDS for 2008Q4. Top 3 banks ranked in terms of their dominance in this market (JP Morgan, Citibank and Bank of America) account for 83% of the total CDS purchases. We present in figure 4.9 a diagram of their modelled US network, in which the largest pink node represents JP Morgan as dominant net seller in the system.

Table 4.8: Network statistics for degree distribution for US CDS network

Initial Network Statistics	Mean	Standard deviation	Skewness	Kurtosis	Connectivity	Clustering coefficient
In Degrees CDS Buyers	3.04	4.44	3.13	9.12	0.12	0.92
Out Degrees CDS Sellers	3.04	5.34	3.60	14.12	0.12	0.92
Random Graph	3.48	1.50	0.70	0.04	0.12	0.09

Source: Markose et al. (2010).

According to Markose et al. (2010), the results reflect the very high concentration of network connections[26] among the top 6 banks[27] in terms of bilateral interrelationships and triangular clustering, which is also underscored by the large cluster coefficient of 0.92.

4.4. Co-Movement of Assets in Balance Sheets given Interconnectedness

The previous section presented a comparison of banking system interconnectedness for Brazil, US and Euro zone. Now, we investigate the specific case of Brazilian banks by looking for distinct patterns of balance sheet assets' temporal dynamics within an interconnectedness setup. To do so, we consider two groups of banks: (i) the Brazilian banking system (covering a sample of 137 financial institutions) and (ii) the Top 8 most connected institutions (which represented, in 2011Q4, roughly 76% of total transfers – BRL 2.3 trillion), and a sample period from January 2000 until April 2012. Figure 4.10 shows the total amount of balance sheet assets as well as its main components for both the banking system and the Top 8 most interconnected banks.

---

[26] The highly asymmetric nature of the empirical CDS network is manifested in the large kurtosis or fat tails in degree distribution which is characterised by a few (two banks in this case) which have a relatively large number of in degrees (up to 14) while many have only a few. Note the asymmetries are greater in the out degree distribution in terms of bank activity as CDS protection sellers.

[27] According to Markose et al. (2010), the Top 6 ranking order in terms of dominance in the US CDS market is: JP Morgan, Citibank, Bank of America, Goldman Sachs, HSBC-USA and Wachovia. However, the authors recall that in terms of assets, Goldman Sachs is ranked in 11th place and Wells Fargo, which is the 4th largest in terms of assets (provided that Wachovia has been taken over), ranks only in 13th place in terms of CDS activity.

Banking System (BRL trillion, in constant prices of Jan2000)

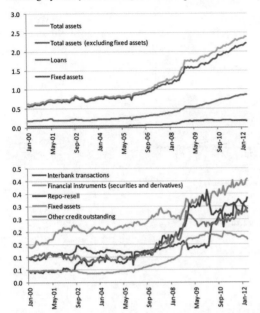

Top 8 most interconnected Banks (BRL trillion, in constant prices of Jan2000)

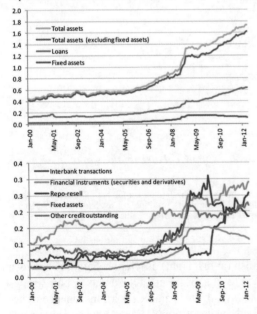

Sample period: 2000m1-2012m4. Banking system covers 137 financial institutions. The IPCA inflation index (Jan2000 = 100) is used as a deflator to convert nominal series into real series.

Source: Central Bank of Brazil.

Figure 4.10: Balance sheet assets (Brazil)

Banking System

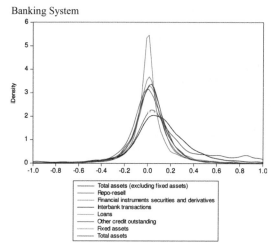

Top 8 most interconnected banks

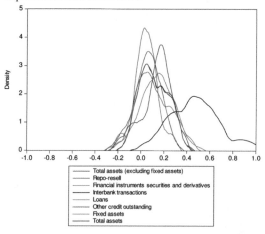

Figure 4.11: Co-movement of assets: Empirical distributions of pair wise correlations

Probability density functions (PDF) estimated via Epanechnikov kernel. Sample period: 2000m1-2012m4. Banking system covers 137 financial institutions, resulting in a total amount of 9,316 distinct pair wise sample correlations, whereas the Top8 banks group results in 28 pair wise correlations. *Source*: Authors' calculations.

Overall it is difficult to distinguish (at first sight) different behaviours between the Top8 and the banking system asset series. First, total assets in both groups significantly increased along the investigated sample (as a consequence of decreasing interest rates and, more broadly, a more stable macroeconomic environment), which is perfectly in line with the (previously discussed) augment of credit-to-GDP ratio in Brazil. Second, all asset series have been significantly impacted by the 2008/2009 crisis (e.g., temporary reduction of interbank transactions by the end of 2008, partially offset by an increase of repo-resell operations and financial instruments).

A more detailed investigation of assets co-movement is provided by using disaggregated data. In other words, we take the real value and compute all bank individual assets' (pair wise) correlations of monthly real growth rates for the referred assets' time series across the banking system. For instance, the first group of banks is composed of 137 financial institutions, which results in a total amount of 9,316 pair wise sample correlations for each considered asset series. For the second group, the Top 8 institutions generate an amount of 28 pair wise correlations. The empirical distribution of those correlations is presented in figure 4.11.

Table 4.9: Descriptive statistics of pair wise correlations (balance sheet assets)

	Banking System					Top 8				
	Mean	Median	Std. Dev.	Skewness	Kurtosis	Mean	Median	Std. Dev.	Skewness	Kurtosis
Total assets (excluding fixed assets)	0.02	0.03	0.17	-0.25	6.53	0.11	0.09	0.12	0.19	1.92
Repo-resell	0.00	0.00	0.18	-0.15	7.32	0.06	0.06	0.11	-0.32	2.84
Financial instruments securities and derivatives	0.02	0.01	0.19	-0.02	8.06	0.04	0.05	0.10	-0.01	3.54
Interbank transactions	0.10	0.10	0.28	-0.39	5.62	0.47	0.51	0.20	0.29	2.70
Loans	0.03	0.03	0.21	-0.22	7.46	0.14	0.13	0.14	-0.23	2.74
Other credit outstanding	0.17	0.10	0.30	0.85	3.75	0.13	0.16	0.13	-0.67	2.95
Fixed assets	0.01	0.01	0.18	0.33	10.35	0.11	0.07	0.14	0.42	2.44
Total assets	**0.03**	**0.03**	**0.17**	**0.05**	**6.94**	**0.11**	**0.09**	**0.12**	**0.23**	**2.02**

Sample period: 2000m1-2012m4. Banking system covers 137 financial institutions, resulting in a total amount of 9,316 distinct pair wise sample correlations, whereas the Top8 group results in 28 pair wise correlations.

Source: Authors' calculations.

The pair wise correlations analysis reveals clear differences of assets co-movements. First, note that mean correlation for total assets of the banking system is slightly below the respective figure for the Top 8 banks, indicating that more *connected banks tend to alter their total assets in a more synchronised way than the entire banking system* (in fact, this finding holds for all considered asset components, excepting other credit outstanding). Second (and most importantly) *interbank transactions for the Top 8 banks exhibit an average correlation of 0.47, in sharp contrast to the 0.10 value for the whole banking system.* Moreover, the distributions of correlations show a higher kurtosis (and an overall lower skewness) for the banking system, when compared to the Top 8 banks. These findings obtained from disaggregated data corroborate the hypothesis that interconnectedness indeed matters for understanding co-movement of assets. It also confirms that the more a system is concentrated and interconnected, the more it will be sensitive to changes in asset valuation, especially under tail event conditions.

4.5. Asset Prices

The statistical observation of the previous section explains why intuitively stock market and property prices are often used as proxies for analyses of the behaviour of asset prices and banks' balance sheet vulnerabilities. First we present *selected stock indexes* for Brazil, the US, Germany and France. Second, we also show some property price indexes for comparison purposes.

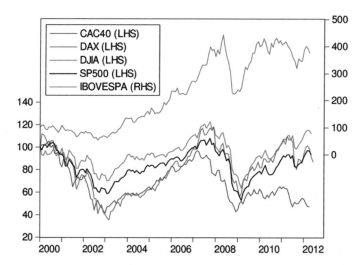

Figure 4.12: Stock indexes comparison (Jan 2000 = 100)
Source: Bloomberg.

As we know, the global correction in residential real estate markets has generated large declines in house prices and construction activity across a broad range of economies.[28] According to IMF-WEO (2012), there were about 2.4 million properties in foreclosure in the United States at the end of 2011, a nearly fivefold increase over the pre-crisis level. The "shadow inventory" of distressed mortgages suggests that this number could rise further. In Brazil, property prices have risen but there is no comprehensive and reliable indicator for property prices. In some specific areas of large cities (e.g., São Paulo, Rio de Janeiro, etc.) the rise in real estate prices (i.e. in listed offered prices) might suggest some localised pressure in the domestic housing market, which can be directly linked to the credit expansion path of recent years but it is difficult to assess the situation in the absence of rigorous indexes.

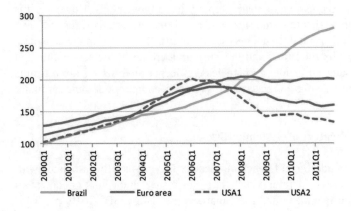

Figure 4.13: Property price indexes

Euro area index (XM:0:1:0:0:0:0): all types of dwellings (new and existing houses and flats, index 2007=100). USA1 index (US:0:1:1:2:0:1): all types of existing dwellings, single-family homes (attached and detached) and condominiums and cooperatives (index Jan2000=100). USA2 index (US:0:2:1:3:0:0): existing single-family houses (index 1980Q1=100). Brazilian real state IGMI-C index (capital return sub-index of commercial properties, index 2000Q1=100) provided by IBRE/FGV. USA2 index is divided by two (and Euro area index is multiplied by two) for graphical comparison purposes.

Source: BIS Property Price Statistics (Euro area and USA) and IBRE/FGV (Brazil).

One important and extensive discussion in the literature has been the *relationship between credit booms and bubbles*. Therefore we turn now briefly

---

[28] In this sense, the IMF-WEO (2009) report argues that at a conceptual level, the impacts of housing corrections on the real economy depend on the extent of house price misalignment, as estimated above; the impact of a given house price correction on macroeconomic variables – which could vary across economies due to differences in the characteristics of mortgage markets or because of differences in policy responses to housing shocks; and transmission and amplification mechanisms, such as the impact of defaults on bank balance sheets or the indirect effects on commercial real estate, which may not be fully captured in a standard macroeconomic model of the impacts of housing price shocks.

to the discussion about using credit gaps as early warning indicators for asset booms.[29] We analyse here solely statistical relationships based on Granger causality tests. Admittedly, in addition to existing literature (e.g., Borio and Lowe 2002; Alessi and Detken 2009), there is a need for a better understanding of the transmission mechanisms between these variables.[30]

Overall, in this simplified stylized overview, the results (not reported) seem to suggest that stock price rises precede credit surges, and that credit booms anticipate property price increases, partially corroborating the hypothesis that credit-to-GDP gaps might be able to anticipate asset booms. For instance, the results for the US suggest that movements in both S&P500 and Dow Jones Industrial Average (DJIA) stock market indexes precede the credit gap dynamics, which, in turn, seems to anticipate property price movements. However, it is worth mentioning that this empirical evidence is merely a statistical result (i.e., Granger causality) and does not necessarily imply "causality" in the economic sense. The results for Brazil and the Euro area are less conclusive, although point in the same direction. Nonetheless, a deeper analysis on these results focused on the transmission mechanisms remains an important topic for future research.

4.6. Other Indicators of Systemic Risk

There are many additional financial indicators that are usually associated with systemic risk in the literature, such as balance sheet indicators or indicators based on credit quantities and asset markets (see BIS-CGFS 2010, p. 18 for further details). Among them, and to continue our comparison of systemic risk indicators for Brazil, the US and the Euro area, we show below the respective *non-performing loans (NPL) ratios*.

Non-performing loans (or loan loss provisions) are essentially backward-looking (or at most contemporaneous) indicators of financial distress (see Bongini et al. 2002, *apud* BIS-CGFS 2010). Nonetheless, they might provide an *important picture about the overall credit quality* in the banking system, and can signal for possible excessive credit growth and/or fragile lending standards. The high NPL figures for the US and the Euro area observed in 2011 reflect the mentioned lower lending standards, as a direct consequence of

---

[29] According to Alessi and Detken (2009), the global private credit gap and the global M1 gap seem to be the best early warning indicators for asset price boom/bust cycles. In this sense, global variables would be adequate indicators since asset price cycles are largely international phenomena.

[30] According to IMF-WEO (2009), since 1985, house price busts have been typically preceded by large deviations in credit relative to GDP, the current account balance, and investment. Output and inflation, on the other hand, would not display such large deviations. These conventional components of monetary policy rules have little ability to predict house price busts. For stock price busts, output and inflation perform slightly better as leading indicators, but credit, the current account balance, and residential investment have much more predictive ability, as they do for house price busts.

the global economic and financial crisis. In Brazil, on the other hand, despite experiencing a temporarily hike in 2009, the NPL series decreased towards a moderate 3% level, suggesting that the (ongoing) global crisis did not impose a relevant change in domestic credit quality.[31] Finally, to conclude our comparisons, we show in table 4.10 below some additional indicators of financial conditions selected from the IMF – Financial Soundness Indicators, which can be interpreted as indicators of financial distress based on balance sheet data.

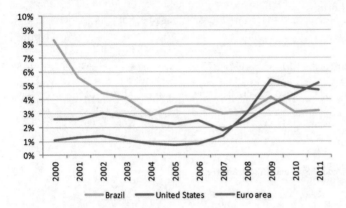

Figure 4.14: Bank non-performing loans to total gross loans (%)
Source: World Bank (annual data).

Firstly, note that Brazilian regulatory capital level is quite high in comparison to that of other (advanced) economies, and the NPL ratio is the lowest among the selected countries. In this sense, Brazilian banks have strong capital cushions and capital adequacy is well above the minimum required, enabling Brazilian banks to absorb large loan losses. Liquidity indicators for Brazil are slightly better than the average figures presented by the US and some European countries, whereas household debt, despite substantially increasing over the last few years, still accounts for less than 20% of GDP, in sharp contrast to the US (94% of GDP) and the Euro area (around 60% of GDP for France, Germany and Italy). Residential loans in Brazil are also quite low in comparison to other countries.

---

[31] The country's banking sector has strong capital buffers and should easily withstand the upswing in bad loans typically associated with fast credit growth.

Table 4.10: Other comparative indicators

Selected indicators	Period	Brazil	France	Germany	Italy	Portugal	Spain	USA
Regulatory Capital to Risk-Weighted Assets	2011 Q2	18%	13%	17%	13%	10%	12%	15%
Regulatory Tier 1 Capital to Risk-Weighted Assets	2011 Q2	14%	11%	13%	9%	8%	10%	13%
Non-performing Loans to Total Gross Loans	2011 Q2	3%	4%	-	11%	6%	5%	4%
Liquid Assets to Total Assets (Liquid Asset Ratio)	2011 Q2	32%	42%	43%	-	16%	-	13%
Liquid Assets to Short Term Liabilities	2011 Q2	108%	75%	138%	-	86%	-	61%
Household Debt to GDP	2010 Q4	16%	54%	60%	60%	104%	-	94%
Residential Real Estate Loans to Total Loans	2011 Q2	8%	-	17%	19%	33%	27%	36%

Source: IMF – Financial Soundness Indicators (FSI).

5. A FREQUENT INDICATOR OF FINANCIAL (IN)STABILITY: CREDIT

In this section, we analyse the patterns of the Brazilian credit market based on disaggregated credit growth gaps, in order to understand better the dynamics of the Brazilian credit market.

We present first a (short) macroeconomic overview of the Brazilian economy, which is important to argue that credit growth observed in past recent years is sustainable given its structural components and additional cyclical factors.

5.1. Macroeconomic Fundamentals

Long before the crisis – since the mid-1990s – Brazil adopted standard macroeconomic policies to control inflation and anchor expectations, including an inflation targeting framework. Fiscal policies were strengthened to ensure that markets perceived debt dynamics as sustainable. Together with many (though not all) emerging markets, Brazil opted for a flexible exchange rate regime as a first buffer against capital market mood swings and volatility. Last but not least, Brazil did not embark on the fashionable financial deregulation move-

Unemployment rate (%) and real income

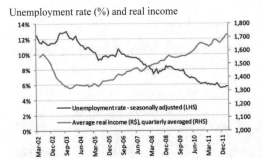

Net public debt (% GDP) – Consolidated public sector

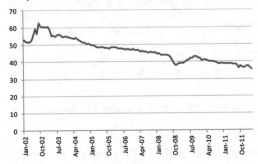

Inflation rate and inflation target (% p.a.)

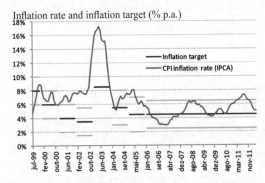

Interest rate and exchange rate

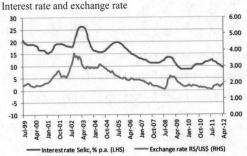

Figure 4.15: Selected Brazilian macro variables

Source: Central Bank of Brazil.

ment of the 1990s, keeping a conservative prudential regulatory framework for
its financial sectors, which remained tightly supervised and well-capitalised.

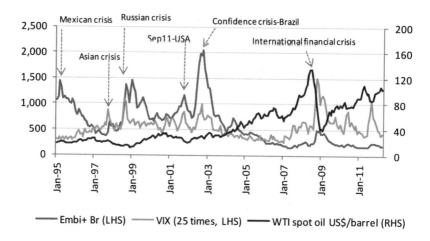

Figure 4.16: Emergent Markets Bonds Index (Brazil), VIX and Oil price.
VIX refers to Chicago Board Options Exchange Market Volatility Index.
Source: Bloomberg.

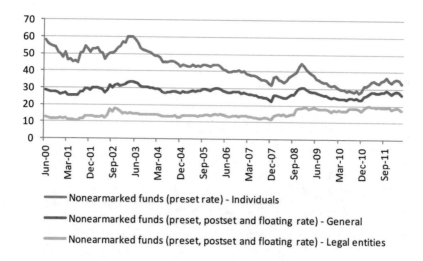

Figure 4.17: Credit operations average spread (p.p.)
Source: Central Bank of Brazil.

Therefore, several factors contributed to a sustainable credit expansion in the last ten years: the above mentioned macroeconomic stability led to an increase in formal employment and real income. Together with institutional reforms, social and financial inclusion policies, among other factors, led to a steady decline of the average domestic credit spread (and of the sovereign debt risk premium, measured by the Embi+Br index). The absence of significant external shocks in the 2003-2007 period must also be taken into account to understand the growth of credit in recent years.

With respect to financial deepening, according to IMF-GFSR (2012, Table 3.4) Brazil contributed in 2009 with only 1.63% to global financial depth[32] (and emerging markets as a whole with 17.97%), in sharp contrast to USA: 29.28%, UK: 7.73%, China: 7.13%, Germany: 6.04% and France: 5.40%; suggesting that Brazilian financial system is yet quite distant from financially-deep countries. These figures reveal the inability of emerging countries (in particular, Brazil) to contribute to the global supply of safe assets. According to the referred IMF Report, many emerging markets are still in the process of developing well-functioning financial systems, which are characterised by sound legal institutions and adequate property rights. Such limitations restrain the assets supply in local capital markets and limit the development of liquid financial markets.

Accordingly, although shrinking in recent years, the *disparity* in the degree of financial depth between emerging markets and advanced economies is *still considerable* (at the end of 2009, emerging markets accounted for roughly 40% of global GDP, although their contribution to financial depth was less than 20% that of advanced economies).

The 2008 crisis significantly affected the credit market in Brazil. As an immediate consequence, supply conditions were severely compromised, due to adverse external financial conditions, low levels of liquidity in domestic inter-bank market and higher risk aversion hampering the concession of new loans. At the same time, credit demand was naturally dampened by unfavourable evolution of the expectations of unemployment, income and production, with direct effects on consumption and investment.[33]

---

[32] Summing all assets and liabilities (held against residents and nonresidents) as a share of GDP gives a measure of the weight of total financial claims and counterclaims of an economy – both at home and abroad. Financial depth as a share of global depth is given by each country's contribution weighted by its GDP.

[33] The effects of the crisis were indeed severe. After the Lehman Brothers episode, in the last quarter of 2008, trade flows contracted 6.9% Year-Over-Year (YOY); industrial production fell by 27.0% Quarter-Over-Quarter (QOQ); capital outflows rose by 36.0% QOQ causing an exchange rate depreciation spike of 32% YOY; and credit growth fell by 35% YOY. In one month (October 2008), trade financing fell by 30% and the debt rollover ratio went down from 167% to 22%. From July to October, liquidity ratios in Brazilian banks also fell from 1.73 to 1.43.

Panel A – According to the source of funding

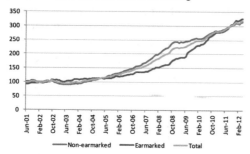

Panel B – Credit operations – Corporations

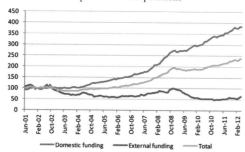

Panel C – According to destination

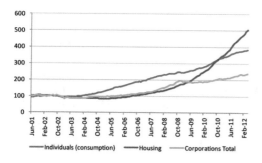

Figure 4.18: Financial system credit operations (real indexes)

Source: Central Bank of Brazil and authors' calculations.

The Brazilian authorities took immediate action in face of the shock (Mesquita and Torós 2010). First, they addressed liquidity problems both in domestic and foreign currencies: bank reserve requirements were lowered, injecting about BRL 116 billion worth of liquidity (or 4% of GDP) into the economy; lines of credit in foreign exchange were provided to the private sector; the Central

Bank of Brazil offered USD 14.5 billion (7% of total international reserves at the end of 2008) in spot market auctions. Foreign exchange swap contracts to the tune of USD 33 billion were also offered by the Central Bank, helping an orderly wind down of large foreign exchange derivatives exposures by domestic corporations (amounting to an estimated USD 37 billion at the end of September 2008).

Table 4.11: Real growth of credit operations (annual percent)

	2002	2003	2004	2005	2006	2007	2008	2009	2010	2011
Financial system credit operations	-2%	-5%	8%	13%	16%	19%	25%	15%	13%	12%
Earmarked	-5%	3%	6%	3%	10%	12%	18%	23%	25%	17%
Non-earmarked	0%	-9%	10%	19%	20%	23%	28%	12%	8%	10%
Corporations – Total	2%	-13%	6%	7%	11%	17%	32%	9%	5%	11%
Corporations – Domestic Funding	6%	-1%	11%	19%	15%	19%	35%	15%	13%	12%
Corporations – External Funding	-2%	-26%	-4%	-14%	2%	14%	24%	-13%	-31%	2%
Individuals – Consumption	10%	-4%	16%	28%	24%	18%	14%	8%	18%	17%
Housing	-39%	-11%	-4%	1%	16%	20%	25%	35%	43%	39%

Growth rates are based on annual averaged indexes.

Source: Central Bank of Brazil and authors' calculations.

The second line of action was to calibrate policy instruments to provide stimulus to economic activity: the monetary policy base rate was lowered by a total of 500 basis points, from 13.75% p.a. to 8.75% p.a.; a number of tax breaks were put in place and the fiscal surplus target was reduced from 3.8% in 2008 to 2.5% of GDP in 2009; credit extension by public financial institutions rose by BRL 105 billion (3.3% of GDP).

The response of the Brazilian economy was swift, and produced the expected V-shaped recovery pattern. In the credit market, the Central Bank of Brazil implemented several measures in order to re-establish credit market liquidity, especially for small and medium-size banks.[34] Moreover, state-owned banks

[34] Overall, throughout the global financial crisis, the Central Bank of Brazil has actively used a mix of monetary policy and macroprudential measures, for an account see Pereira da Silva and Harris (2012).

played an important role as anti-cyclic agents by providing extra supply of resources in domestic credit market. These actions combined with fiscal stimulus
contributed to boost sales of higher aggregate value and, therefore, domestic
consumption. But despite the strong policy-driven rebound throughout 2009,
GDP growth was still zero for that calendar year, but in 2010 GDP grew 7.5%
YOY, domestic demand by 10.3%, with private consumption expanding 7.2%
YOY and investment by 11.1% YOY

But in any event, credit for individuals and firms exhibited different dynamic patterns. In particular, firms' external funding sharply decreased after
2008, whereas consumption loans maintained a steady growth (mainly driven
by fiscal stimulus, increasing real income and low unemployment) and housing credit faced a significant augment,[35] mainly due to lower interest rates and
additional credit for this segment provided by state-owned banks.

5.2. Real Growth Credit Gaps

In order to illustrate the recent evolution of the Brazilian credit market, we construct real growth credit gap series, with the main objective of investigating potential imbalances between demand and supply in the credit market. Differently
from credit-to-GDP gaps, which are used as comparative indicators for leverage
in section 4, real growth credit gaps are used to investigate the Brazilian credit
market in a more precise way, without including possible output gap effects into
the credit gap measure. Eight real growth credit indexes (monthly data, seasonally adjusted) are constructed[36] to capture the Brazilian credit market across its
various components. An excess demand for credit is represented by a positive
gap, indicating that observed credit growth is above its potential growth (analo-
gous to the definition of output gap). The results are displayed in figure 4.19.

In the credit gap series by source of funding, it is worth noting that non-
earmarked and total financial system credit gaps exhibit similar patterns along
the investigated sample period, whereas the earmarked credit gap presents a
more volatile dynamic. Nonetheless, it is worth mentioning that all three gap
series end up close to the zero gap line. In the credit gap series for corporations,
for total and for domestic sources of funding, the gaps are very close to each
other. However, for external sources of funding the gap presents quite dramatic
changes since 2008. Finally, in the credit gap series by end-users, the credit
gaps are close to zero at their end-point, which might be a signal of a credit
market working close to its potential equilibrium.

---

[35] Real estate credit market has been the most dynamic sector of the Brazilian credit market in
recent years. Although exhibiting a fast growing path it still represents a small amount of total
credit in the financial system.

[36] Firstly, each monthly nominal credit series (in BRL currency) is converted into real series (at constant prices of July 2002). Then, a real credit index is constructed such that the average 2002 index =
100 (as a common base-value for all eight considered real credit indexes). Subsequently, each index
is seasonally adjusted (Census X12) and then HP filtered to generate both the trend and the gap series.

According to the source of funding

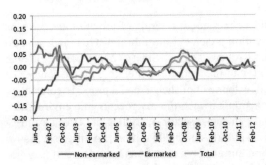

Corporations

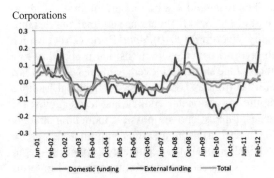

According to destination

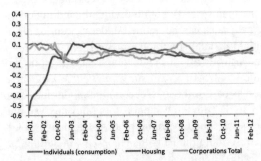

Figure 4.19: Financial system credit gaps

Source: Central Bank of Brazil and authors' calculations.

Nonetheless, it seems that the major risk to financial stability in Brazil, from the credit market perspective, still comes from exogenous foreign shocks rather than excessively rapid domestic credit growth. We examine this risk below.

5.3. Credit-to-GDP and Credit Growth Gaps based on GE Models

Ideally, the credit gap should be measured in terms of growth rates of loans from its steady-state values within a General Equilibrium (GE) model, based on fundamental and structural relationships.[37] Smets (2011) points out that credit gaps need a connection with the theoretical literature on the sources of systemic risk. However, the development of such a model properly connecting the real economy (e.g., interaction between the macroeconomic environment and the monetary policy) to the financial sector (including the effects of macroprudential tools) is a work-in-progress in the literature.[38] In this sense, Borio (2011) asks in which direction current Dynamic Stochastic General Equilibrium (DSGE) models should be modified? According to the author, the key would be to allow scope for the cross-sectional and inter-temporal coordination failures that lie at the heart of business fluctuations and financial instability. A possible route is given by Woodford (2010), *apud* Borio (2011), which discuss a DSGE model with credit that makes the transition probability to a bad state (e.g., crisis) a function of the amount of leverage in the system. It is a good example of how to modify current DSGE models with financial frictions so as to formalise the desirability of a monetary policy that leans against the build-up of financial imbalances. Finally, another possible modelling strategy is taken by Agénor et al. (2011a, 2012a) using a DSGE with imperfect credit markets and an explicitly modelled Basel III-type countercyclical capital regulatory rule in its financial sector. Macroeconomic stability is defined in terms of a weighted average of inflation and output gap volatility, whereas financial stability is defined in terms of three alternative indicators (real house prices, the credit-to-GDP ratio, and the loan spread), both individually and in combination. Steady state credit growth rates can be defined under any set of macroeconomic and macroprudential financial conditions.

With respect to Brazil, De Castro et al. (2011) develop a DSGE model for the Brazilian economy (so-called *SAMBA – Stochastic Analytical Model with a Bayesian Approach*) to be used as part of the macroeconomic modelling setup of the Central Bank of Brazil (BCB), providing support for policy analysis and forecasting. This model combines the main building blocks of standard DSGE models with specific features describing the Brazilian economy, including ex-

---

[37] For instance, by considering that financial cycles can have a much longer duration than business cycles.

[38] A good review is given by BIS-CGFS (2010, p.21), which identifies four strands in the literature focused on how macroprudential tools interact with monetary policy: (i) monetary policy in DSGE models augmented with financial intermediaries; (ii) dynamic equilibrium models in which the financial sector does not internalise all the costs associated with excessive risk taking; (iii) models considering the role of bank capital in the monetary transmission mechanism (e.g., risk taking channel); (iv) a very recent theoretical research that specifically examines the interaction between monetary policy and macroprudential policy (e.g., interaction between optimal monetary policy and endogenous bank risk).

ternal finance for imports and financially constrained households. However, the banking sector is not explicitly modelled and there is no credit gap variable, since SAMBA was not originally designed to address financial stability issues. Nonetheless, the development of a DSGE model properly considering the financial system is an ongoing project of the BCB, which might generate structurally-oriented credit growth gaps in the near future, as potential candidates for financial stability proxies. In the meantime, in this chapter (see below in section 6.3), we conduct an analysis using HP-filtered credit gaps to investigate empirical evidences of credit growth at equilibrium based on historical statistical relationships.

5.4. Credit Market External Vulnerabilities[39]

Brazil is an open economy and a sizeable player in global capital and commodity markets. As such, it remains vulnerable to sudden floods and sudden stops of capital flows, especially under the current conditions of volatility abroad. Due to its strong fundamentals, Brazil has been attracting large volumes of capital inflows, reflecting both economic factors at home (deep capital markets, the large interest rate differential between Brazil and advanced economies, and strong economic performance) and global trends (spillovers from advanced economies). Therefore, managing the effects of large capital flows has been one of the main policy challenges for Brazil since the global crisis. Brazil managed those massive inflows primarily in standard textbook fashion, with aggregate demand contraction through fiscal and monetary policies, allowing significant currency appreciation while smoothing movements through sterilised reserve accumulation – which reduced the volatility of the exchange rate, without, however, aiming at distorting its structural trend. But Brazil's credit market was affected by capital inflows and a set of macroprudential measures was consequently adopted to smooth the financial cycle. There was evidence that there were multiple sources of foreign funding that transmitted into credit markets, in addition to the confidence factors that are associated with periods of abundant liquidity. External funding at low cost, despite tight domestic prudential rules, creates incentives to increase risk taking and usually ends by distorting asset prices, including the exchange rate. In Brazil, excessive capital inflows contributed to the brisk pace of domestic credit growth, which fuelled inflationary pressures associated with domestic demand-supply mismatches and created fertile ground for the domestic transmission of pressures stemming from global commodity prices.

Capital inflows into Brazil intensified in particular after the beginning of the financial crisis around mid-2007, and portfolio flows hovered around 10

---

[39] This section uses information contained in the forthcoming Financial System Stability Assessment (FSSA) for Brazil (IMF-FSSA 2012).

Stability of the Financial System

percent of GDP at the end of 2009. As it is extensively reported in the literature
(figure 4.20), these short-term flows are volatile and can behave with episodes
of surges and reversals (sudden-floods and sudden stops). This in turn affects
the funding of banks and produces exchange rate volatility. Similarly, the equity and derivatives markets are also vulnerable to market sentiment, especially
if foreign investors are responsible for large shares of trading (see figure 4.21).

Capital Flows (in percent of GDP)

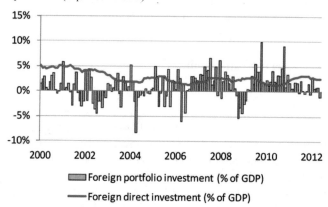

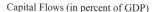

Volatility of Capital Flows (FPI): Conditional Variance of Garch (1,1)

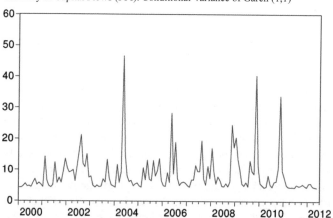

Figure 4.20: Capital flows and volatility

Source: Central Bank of Brazil and authors' calculations.

Brazil had to address these issues with pragmatism, since it was painfully
aware of the destabilising effects of excessive levels of global liquidity, in par-

ticular when it transmits to domestic credit growth. Excessive capital inflows present several risks to recipient countries. They are potentially disruptive for emerging markets' price and financial stability. In the absence of any policy response, the economy may lose competitiveness and experience unsustainable trade account deficits. There is also a risk of financial instability. Banks tend to increase their foreign currency exposure and become more lenient in their credit standards when faced with higher foreign liquidity. Surges in capital inflows can lead to higher inflation and to credit and asset price bubbles.

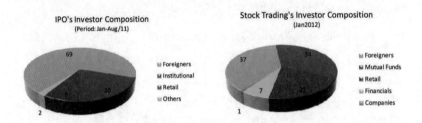

Figure 4.21: Investor composition in IPO and stock trading

Source: BM&F Bovespa.

Given the importance of commodities in Brazil's trade, fluctuations in commodity prices[40] can bring an additional source of vulnerability that affect both equity and credit markets. The share of commodity exports in exports has been growing in the 2000s and is important. The terms of trade and GDP growth in Brazil during the 2000s have been related to commodity prices, including oil (figure 4.22). Under the current scenario of a prolonged period of low global growth, due to the Euro zone crisis and its fallout in other major economies (e.g., the US and China), it is possible that commodity prices will experience a stabilisation and/or downturn. That could have a sizeable impact on Brazilian exporters and affect its financial sector.

Another traditional source of financial instability has been cross-border financial interconnectedness. That aspect has attracted considerable attention in the wake of the Euro zone debt crisis. In the case of Brazil, this risk is limited (figure 4.23). The Brazilian financial system is characterised by a relatively small share of foreign banks presence, small reliance on external sources of funding and limited foreign exposures. The financial system is rather geared toward the domestic market and its process of internationalisation is recent and affects only a very small number of large conglomerates.

Therefore, foreign lending and borrowing exposures hovered around 5 and 20 percent of GDP respectively, and Brazilian banks' exposure to Euro zone

---

[40] Commodity exports accounted for about 39-40% in Brazil's total exports in 2011.

crisis-affected countries is about 4% of its total loans by September 2011 (figure 4.24). Brazilian banks' funding is mostly domestic through deposits and repos, and Brazilian conglomerates dispose of a large and diversified domestic funding base. The exposure to foreign currency liabilities is small (9%). The major exposure to international markets comes from the large public sector banks that are backed by the government. Currency mismatches in balance sheets are limited by regulation and constantly monitored by the BCB. The banks' net open position in foreign exchange has been monitored and subject to further regulatory tightening in 2010-2012, averaging only about 7 percent of banks' capital by end-June 2011.

Share of commodity exports in total exports (in percent)

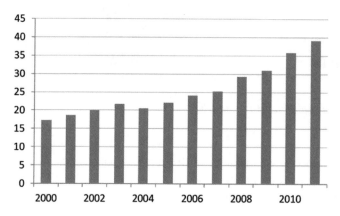

Commodity prices and terms of trade (in percent, YOY)

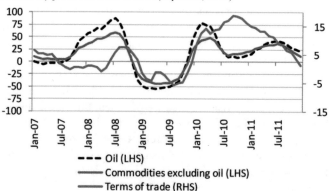

Figure 4.22: Commodity exports and terms of trade

Source: CEIC database and authors' calculations.

Selected 24 countries

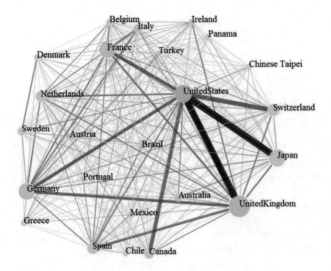

Brazil

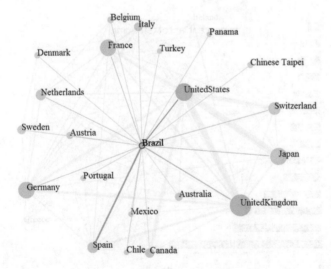

Figure 4.23: Cross-border interconnectedness[1/2/]

[1/] The size of a circle shows the amount of foreign bank's lending to each country and its colour gets greener as the amount of inflows to the country gets larger. Two-way flows, an outflow and inflow from country A to B, overlap each other with two different grey colours. [2/] We would like to acknowledge Financial Network Analytics for its web-based program of network analysis.

Source: BIS Consolidated Banking Sector Statistics (as of December 2011).

Lending and borrowing: Cross-border exposures (% of GDP)

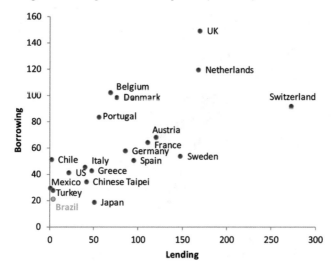

Banks' exposures to Euro-peripheral countries[1]

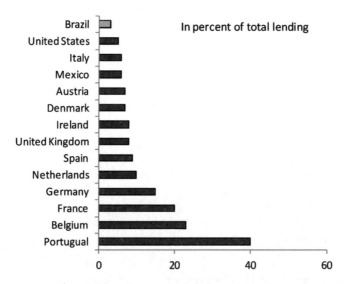

Figure 4.24: Cross-border banking exposures

[1] Includes Greece, Ireland, Portugal, Italy and Spain. This figure shows banks' exposure to Euro zone crisis-affected countries.

Source: BIS and authors' calculations (as of September 2011).

6. BROAD INDICATORS OF FINANCIAL (IN)STABILITY

6.1. Financial Stability Map

In Brazil, *systemic risk has declined* since the peak of the global financial crisis. There are many ways to capture an overall perception of systemic risk and one route is that of mapping factors related to systemic risk into a single chart. For illustrative purpose, we construct a financial stability map based on the following six systemic factors: leverage, liquidity, interconnectedness, external vulnerability, bank soundness and economic conjecture. Table 4.12 shows the proxies used for each dimension of the map as well as the respective figures by the end of past years. The signs presented in the second column of table 4.12 refer to the positive (or negative) correlation of the selected proxies in respect to the increase of risk (i.e., towards financial instability).[41]

Table 4.12: Dataset for financial stability map

Dimension	Proxy	2007Q4	2008Q4	2009Q4	2010Q4	2011Q4
Leverage	(+) Credit-to-GDP gap (normalised)	-0.06	2.00	2.48	-0.12	-0.13
Liquidity	(+) Loan-to-Deposit ratio	1.07	1.03	1.14	1.23	1.28
Interconnectedness	(+) δ index	3,448	3,444	3,450	3,449	3,443
External Vulnerability	(-) International reserves to short-term external debt ratio	4.6	5.3	7.7	5.0	8.8
Bank Soundness	(+) Non-performing loans to total gross loans	3.0%	3.1%	4.2%	3.1%	3.5%
Economic Conjecture	(-) Real GDP growth rate (YOY)	6.1%	5.2%	-0.3%	7.6%	2.7%

Sources: Authors' calculations based on data from Central Bank of Brazil, World Bank-Quarterly External Debt Statistics (QEDS/SDDS), IMF-Financial Soundness Indicators (FSI) and IBGE-SIDRA.

---

[41] In order to adequately compare the systemic risk factors within a single picture, they are first transformed to a common scale (i.e. demeaned and re-scaled to unit variance, excepting the loan-to-deposit ratio which is demeaned around the unit value, that represents a balanced amount between loans and deposits) and, then, logit-transformed to map the individual risks from the real line into the [0;1] interval. The logit function is given by $yt = 1/(1+\exp(-xt))$. Finally, the sign for each factor presented in table 4.12 is considered in order to build the map dimensions according to the proper direction (i.e., away from centre signifies higher risks).

Stability of the Financial System

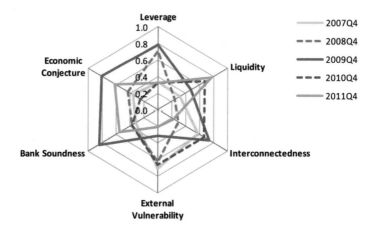

Figure 4.25: Financial stability map

Away from centre signifies higher risks.

Sources: Authors' calculations based on data from Central Bank of Brazil, World Bank-Quarterly External Debt Statistics (QEDS/SDDS), IMF-Financial Soundness Indicators (FSI) and IBGE-SIDRA.

A preliminary evaluation of Brazilian systemic risk factors in figure 4.25 shows that the relative importance of individual risks has changed in the recent years. For instance, the *leverage risk factor* had been relatively high in comparison to other factors along the 2008/2009 period. However, as the global financial crisis and its spillover effects impacted the Brazilian financial system, the *liquidity risk factor gained importance*, replacing the leverage risk factor during the 2010/2011 period, whereas the *interconnectedness risk factor*, which significantly rose by the end of 2009, returned to relatively low levels by the last quarter of 2011.

Looking at the *external vulnerability dimension*,[42] the indicator suggests a lower risk by the end of 2011, basically reflecting the sharp increase of international reserves during the last years, which more than compensate the rise in short-term obligations. The *bank soundness*[43] *proxy* (non-performing loans to total gross loans) exhibits a hike in the last quarter of 2009 and relatively

---

[42] Other alternative proxies for the external vulnerability are: (i) the Credit Default Swap (CDS) representing sovereign risk; (ii) the ratio of total external debt-to exports (goods and services); (iii) the ratio of Brazilian banks' investment in foreign sovereign debt securities to total assets; (iv) the ratio of external funding (loans, bonds and securities issued abroad) to total assets of the Brazilian banking sector.
[43] Other possible proxies for bank soundness are: regulatory capital to risk-weighted assets, liquid assets to total assets (liquid asset ratio), return on assets, and FX net open position to capital.

lower figures in other quarters, whereas the *economic conjecture*[44] depicts the domestic economic slowdown in recent years due to the impact of the global crisis in the Brazilian economy.

This framework can be used as a summary for assessing current systemic risk, and the preliminary impression conveyed by figure 4.25 is corroborated by a more in-depth analysis of selected risk factors.

6.2. Synthetic Indicators of Financial (In)Stability

Financial stability is measured by different components of the financial system. Indexes of overall financial conditions are often constructed as weighted (or simple) averages of a number of individual indicators, each representing one distinct aspect of systemic risk. Aggregate indexes of this sort have the advantage of capturing both the time series and cross-section dimensions of systemic risk mentioned throughout this chapter. The main idea is to summarise in a single index the overall conditions of the financial system in order to help policy-makers to monitor systemic risk, anticipate booms/crunches and develop adequate policy strategies.

Although there is no consensus in the literature (e.g., Borio and Lowe 2002; BIS-CGFS 2010; and De Nicolò et al. 2012)[45] about a unique indicator of financial stability, several of them can be constructed. Therefore, we generate three broad financial stability (synthetic) indicators, with the objective of summarising the systemic risk aspects of the Brazilian financial system. First, in order to deal with comparable components of the broad indicator, we transform the individual indicators (credit-to-GDP gap, loan-to-deposit ratio and interconnectedness α index,[46] which are our proxies for leverage, liquidity and

---

[44] Regarding economic conjecture, we assume for simplicity that an increase in overall economic conjecture (i.e., higher real GDP growth rate) improves contemporaneous financial stability, although there might be exceptions to this positive relationship (e.g., an overheated economy might be associated with price bubbles and, thus, could lead to a deterioration of financial stability). Other possible proxies for this dimension are: growth rate of industrial production, private consumption growth rate, average real income growth rate, unemployment rate, consumer price inflation and current account to GDP ratio.

[45] According to De Nicolò et al. (2012), systemic risk is a multi-faceted phenomenon and there are a variety of metrics that help either signal the gradual buildup of imbalances or flag the concentration of risk within the system. In respect to prudential frameworks, Borio and Lowe (2002) argue that: *"Despite very encouraging steps in recent years, we are still a long way from achieving a greater consensus on the nature of the problem and hence on the possible solutions."* In the same line, the BIS-CGFS (2010) report states that: *"In contrast to the monetary policy literature, research on macroprudential policy is still in its infancy and appears far from being able to provide a sound analytical underpinning for policy frameworks. This may be due to two main reasons. First, the macroprudential approach has come to play a visible role in policy discussions only very recently. Second, it reflects the lack of established models of the interaction between the financial system and the macroeconomy."*

[46] The degree of interconnectedness of the whole system can be summarised by an index (α) which is proportional to the size of the left tail of the distribution of interconnectedness across financial institutions. As long as α increases there are more highly connected institutions, indicating that the net is more concentrated (and the systemic risk has increased).

interconnectedness, respectively) to zero mean and unit variance series (ex-cepting the loan-to-deposit ratio, which is demeaned around the unit value, which represents a balanced amount between loans and deposits). A growing positive value for the transformed indicator represents an increase in financial instability. Second, we must decide how to aggregate these individual indica-tors into a single one.

The first synthetic indicator is a simple average of our normalised proxies for leverage, liquidity and interconnectedness, which are assumed to repre-sent both time series and cross-sectional dimensions. The second proposed synthetic indicator aims to capture common risk factors among the individual systemic risk indicators. The main idea is to use the Principal Component Analysis (PCA), in which an orthogonal transformation of the set of individual indicators is employed to generate the so-called principal components.[47] A third synthetic indicator, based on a weighted average of the first and second principal components is also suggested as an alternative indicator to summa-rise the common patterns from the investigated financial stability individual indicators (see Sales et al. 2012, for other indicators).

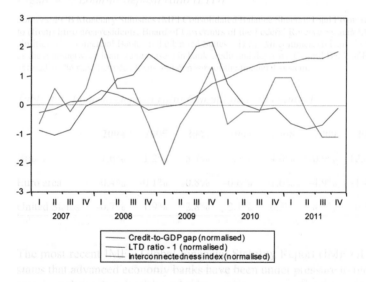

Figure 4.26: Individual components of a Brazilian synthetic indicator

Source: Authors' calculations.

---

[47] The first principal component accounts for most of the variation observed in the data and repre-sents common patterns (e.g., co-movements) of the set of systemic risk indicators.

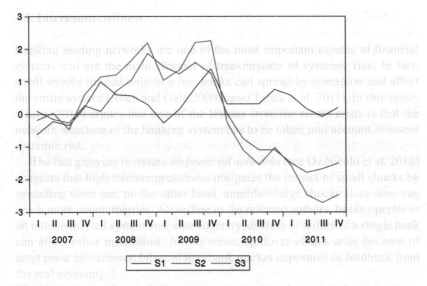

Figure 4.27: Synthetic indicators

S1 is a simple average of the three individual components, S2 is the first principal component (accounts for 44% of total variation) and S3 is a weighted average (based on eigenvalues) of the first and second principal components (cumulatively accounts for 78% of total variation).

Source: Authors' calculations.

We first note that the simple average indicator seems to differ significantly from the two others: one explanation is that two of its components (e.g., credit-to-GDP and LTD) appear to offset each other in the averaging process. Second, both the two PC-based indicators (S2 and S3) indicate – quite rightly – a significant increase in financial instability in the run-up to the 2009 global financial crisis until the Lehman Brothers event (fourth quarter of 2009). After the intensification of the 2008/2009 subprime financial crises triggered by the collapse of Lehman Brothers, the S2 and S3 synthetic indicators seem to suggest that financial instability in Brazil has decreased or that financial stability has improved. That seems to be related to the decline in the credit-to-GDP gap component, despite the worsening of global economic growth and international financial conditions (mainly in the US and in the Euro area). These features seemed to have induced a slowdown of domestic credit growth (e.g., via negative shocks in output), resulting in an overall balanced credit market, pictured here by a credit gap that falls into negative territory at the end of 2010-early 2011 and then rebounds to be close to zero by the end of 2011.

It is also noteworthy that by the end of 2011 the simple two S2-S3 principal component-based indicators are on the negative side, suggesting that financial stability is stronger despite a tightening of credit-to-GDP gap. In addition, the

Stability of the Financial System

two S2-S3 indicators show very similar dynamics since the last quarter of 2009, and they consistently change direction from 2011Q3 to 2011Q4 (as occurred in 2010Q4) which is in line with the recent bout of risk aversion in 2012Q2 and the tightening of credit conditions observed in the global economy.

How would the synthetic indicators relate to other business and financial cycle variables? In table 4.13 we present the sample correlations of the synthetic indicators S2 and S3 with our proxies for business and credit cycles.[48] First, note that output and industrial production gaps are negatively correlated with our synthetic indicators, which is an expected result given that credit and business cycles have not been synchronised in recent years (as discussed in section 4) and that our synthetic indicators (to a great extent) follow a credit gap dynamics. Second, it is noteworthy to see that the correlation for credit-to-GDP gap and for credit growth gaps (based on the whole financial system), is significant and positive in both cases. In fact, *the correlation of both S2 and S3 with the credit-to-GDP gap is high (around 0.8) which suggests that for Brazil the credit-to-GDP gap by itself appears to be a good proxy of "financial (in) stability".*

Table 4.13: Correlations for synthetic indicators

	S2	S3
Output gap	-0.36	-0.17
Industrial production gap	-0.39	-0.21
Credit-to-GDP gap	0.82	0.79
Credit growth gap (financial system)	0.45	0.39
Credit growth gap (earmarked)	-0.37	-0.34
Credit growth gap (non-earmarked)	0.54	0.49
Credit growth gap (housing)	-0.60	-0.59
Credit growth gap (individuals-consumption)	-0.48	-0.36
Credit growth gap (corporations-total)	0.51	0.43
Credit growth gap (corporations-external funding)	0.51	0.41
Credit growth gap (corporations-domestic funding)	0.38	0.32

Source: Authors' calculations. Sample: 2007Q1-2011Q4.

[48] The results are very similar for S2 and S3 as expected, since sample correlation between these two series is equal to 0.96.

It is also worth noting that the correlation is negative for credit gaps regarding earmarked, individuals (consumption) and housing loans, which suggest that rapid growth of these credit segments is not contemporaneous in respect to financial stability risks.[49] On the other hand, credit gaps for non-earmarked and corporations loans are positively correlated to S2 and S3, indicating that an increase of these credit lines above their potential growth might directly lead to a riskier environment and financial instability. Finally, excessive credit growth for corporations with external funding seems to be more damaging to financial stability in comparison to domestic funding. One reason would be that larger firms are more likely to access external funding, which in case of default impact the financial system in a riskier way than smaller/medium firms whose funding is based on domestic sources.

These empirical evidences should be properly viewed within the lens of theoretical models designed to understand the respective transmission channels and related threats to financial stability. As discussed in section 5.3., credit gaps measured in terms of deviations of the growth rate of loans from its steady-state value (i.e. structurally-based) generated from General Equilibrium (GE) models, instead of statistical HP-filtered credit gaps, are likely better proxies for financial stability. Nonetheless, this topic remains an open route for future research.

Finally, it should be stressed that these results are merely illustrative and do not represent (or summarise) the overall financial conditions of the Brazilian financial system. They should therefore be interpreted with caution.

6.3. Measure of Equilibrium Rate for the Credit Growth

In the absence of deriving credit gaps from a GE model, we propose in this section a simple measure for the equilibrium rate of the Brazilian credit growth. In table 4.14, we calculate the "potential" growth of the Brazilian financial system's total credit (based on the HP-filtered observed real growth): it indicates an 11.6% (annual) growth by the end of 2011, after reaching 20.6% before the 2008/2009 crisis.

When this potential credit growth rate is compared to the synthetic indicator S2, a positive sample correlation of 0.54 is obtained. A more in-depth analysis of the equilibrium rate is given by figure 4.28, which shows the estimated unconditional distributions for the synthetic indicator S2 and the above mentioned potential credit growth. Note that the distribution of S2 is centred on zero (by construction) whereas the potential credit growth fluctuates around the 10-23% (annual growth rate) interval.

---

[49] A possible explanation would be an indirect (lagged) channel for individuals impacting financial stability. For instance, an excess of credit for individuals (combined with lower lending standards) might lead a lagged increase of non-performing loans, affecting both firms and financial institutions some periods later and, thus, financial stability as a whole in a non-synchronous way.

Synthetic indicator (S2)

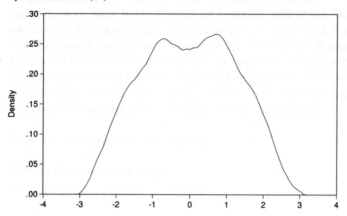

Potential credit growth (% annual)

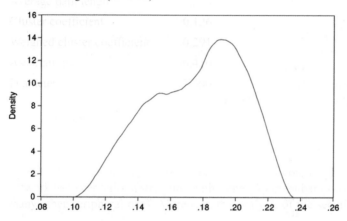

Figure 4.28: Probability density functions

Densities estimated via Epanechnikov kernel. Sample 2007Q1-2011Q4.

Source: Authors' calculations.

Now, we define our equilibrium measure of credit growth as the potential credit growth which is compatible with a null synthetic indicator.[50] To do so, we employ a simple conditional model in order to estimate (via OLS – Ordinary Least Squares) the respective equilibrium rate. The idea is to investigate the statistical relationship between the synthetic indicator S2 and the potential

---

[50] In other words, the "equilibrium" is here defined as the credit growth rate which is compatible with a zero credit-to-GDP gap, a loan-to-deposit ratio equal to one, and an interconnectedness α index equal to its unconditional mean.

credit growth.[51] *According to this definition, the estimated equilibrium rate for credit (real) growth is equal to a 16% annual growth rate.* Note that this rate is below the observed real growth rates for the pre-crisis period (see table 4.14); revealing a temporary higher credit growth trajectory until the aftermath of the global financial crisis of 2008/2009.

Table 4.14: Total financial system credit's growth rate (annual percent change)

	Real growth rate (% p.a.)	**HP-filtered trend's growth rate (% p.a.)**
2005	12.7%	14.8%
2006	16.3%	19.0%
2007	19.2%	20.6%
2008	24.7%	18.7%
2009	14.8%	15.3%
2010	13.1%	13.1%
2011	12.3%	11.6%

Growth rates are based on annual averaged indexes.

Source: Authors' calculations.

6.4. Synthetic Indicators of Financial (In)Stability

The synthetic indicators previously discussed can provide an important piece of information for a policy-maker, i.e. the probability of a financial stability disruption at a given time period.[52] Based on the synthetic indicator S2, we construct a conditional model using the individual risk factors (leverage, liquidity and interconnectedness) as covariates, and estimate it by using the quantile regression (QR) technique[53], which enables us to generate conditional density functions and, therefore, calculate the probability of a disruption. In addition, the following control variables (x_t) are considered in the model: real GDP growth rate, non-performing loans to total gross loans, and international reserves to short-term external debt ratio.[54]

---

[51] The estimated equation (sample: 2007Q1-2011Q4) is the following: *potential_credit_growth = 0.160029 + 0.015953*S2.*
[52] Borio and Lowe (2002) argue that sustained rapid credit growth combined with large increases in asset prices appears to increase the probability of an episode of financial instability.
[53] We follow the density estimation scheme of Schechtman and Gaglianone (2012), which uses quantile regression to compute tail risks for Brazilian household non-performing loans.
[54] These series stand for the following financial stability dimensions discussed in section 6 (respectively): economic conjecture, bank soundness and external vulnerability.

In this sense, the first step is to estimate the following QR model:

S2$_t$ = $\alpha_0(\tau) + \alpha_1(\tau)$ *leverage$_t$ + $\alpha_2(\tau)$*liquidity$_t$ + $\alpha_3(\tau)$*interconnected-ness$_t$ + $\beta(\tau)$*x$_t$ for a grid of selected quantiles $\tau \in [0;1]$.[55] Then, the estimated conditional quantiles are mapped into the zero-one interval (i.e., logit-trans-formed) and the respective probability density functions (PDF) are estimated for selected quarters via Epanechnikov kernel (see figures 4.29 and 4.30).

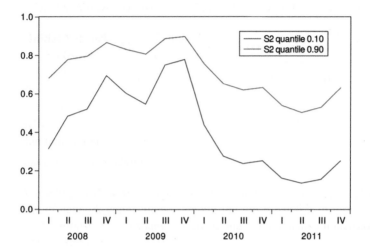

Figure 4.29: Estimated conditional quantiles for the (logit-transformed) syn-thetic indicator S2

Source: Authors' calculations.

Finally, the probability of disruption is computed (for each period) by identify-ing the respective quantile which corresponds to a selected threshold value. In this chapter, for illustrative purpose, we define the probability of a finan-cial stability "disruption" as the probability of the (logit-transformed) syn-thetic indicator S2 surpassing (in each period) the threshold level δ = 0.80 (or, alternatively, δ = 0.85, provided that S2 $\in [0;1]$).[56] The results are shown in figure 4.31. Note that some financial stress periods are revealed during the 2008/2009 global financial crisis period, indicating that *the probability of a financial stability disruption (considering δ = 0.80) reached 69% in 2008Q4; 60% in 2009Q4 and 9% in 2010Q4.* Considering a higher threshold δ = 0.85,

---

[55] Due to the model limited degrees-of-freedom (i.e., quarterly series) and taking into account only significant coefficients, the following covariates are used in the final specification: leverage and first principal component of the set of control variables xt.
[56] In other words, the probability of disruption (p) at period t is given by p=Prob(S2$_t\geq\delta$|F$_t$), which is equivalent to Q$_{\tau=p}$(S2t|F$_t$)= δ, in which F$_t$ represents the set of model covariates and Q$_{\tau=p}$(.) is the estimated conditional quantile of S2 at period t and quantile level τ=p.

these probabilities are 37%, 36% and 3%, respectively. It is worth noting that despite the recent rebound of some risk factors by the end of 2011, the synthetic indicator (and the respective probability of disruption) remained in quite low levels in recent quarters.

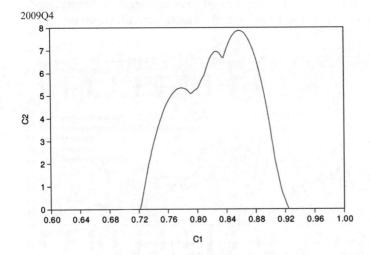

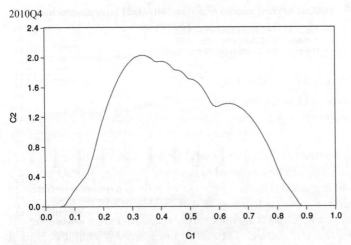

Figure 4.30: Probability density functions (PDF) of S2 at selected quarters

Densities estimated via Epanechnikov kernel.

Source: Authors' calculations.

As discussed in section 1, there is yet no consensus in the literature regarding the definition of financial stability (BIS-CGFS 2010) and (much less) about

Stability of the Financial System

how to compute the probability of "financial stability disruption".[57] In this sense, we propose a simple statistical definition for "disruption" which is not structurally derived within a general equilibrium model, but generated from selected risk factor variables. In other words, we compute the (*ex-post* and in-sample) probability of disruption based on an econometric (density) model, conditional on related risk factors and observable (control) variables.

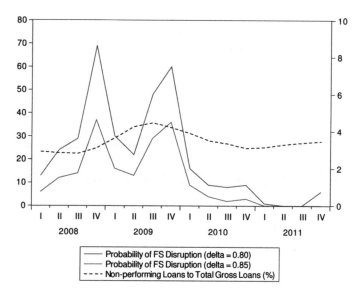

Figure 4.31: Probability of disruption (%)

Probabilities on left-hand scale and NPL ratio on right-hand scale.
Source: Authors' calculations.

Nonetheless, despite not being an observable variable, the computed probability of disruption can be compared to observed variables in order to reveal past periods of increased risk that might not be fully materialised in observed data. For instance, note on figure 4.31 that the lower NPL levels observed until the third quarter of 2008 are not entirely accompanied by lower financial stability disruption probabilities. In fact, the probability has significantly risen along 2008, due to the impacts of the global crisis in the Brazilian economy (expressed here through our synthetic indicator S2 dynamics), whereas the observed NPL series reacted only a few quarters later, due to possible lagged transmission mechanisms of real shocks to financial risk indicators.

---

[57] See Borio and Drehmann (2009) for a good discussion on financial instability measurement. See also N'Diaye (2009), which argues that binding countercyclical prudential regulations (e.g., capital adequacy rules) can help reduce output fluctuations and diminish the risk of financial instability.

This type of exercise might be useful as a monitoring tool for central banks or regulatory agencies, and possible extensions include: (i) to condition the model on macroeconomic policy variables, such as monetary policy interest rates or macroprudential variables. These proxies could be further included into the xt vector in order to analyse such policies in light of the probability of disruption, as discussed in section 1; and (ii) to adapt the estimated model to investigate stress scenarios by conditioning the model on distressed variables.

6.5. Financial (In)Stability and Monetary Policy

The previous section assumes that we succeed in identifying a "good" indicator for financial stability and systemic risk: either the synthetic indicator S2 (or as we saw the credit-to-GDP gap). We can therefore monitor the (logit-transformed) synthetic indicator and we can determine continuously when it surpasses an agreed upon (0.80 or 0.85) threshold which would then correspond to a probability of disruption of the financial system above the policy-maker's tolerance level (say 30% or 50%, etc).

The early identification of that specific point in time would be an indication for the Financial Stability Committee of a potential threat to financial stability above the policy-maker's tolerance level, thus suggesting the need for policy action including through the mobilisation of macroprudential (new) rules and the strengthening of regulations. Therefore, the proposed methodology contributes to identify quantitatively – in addition to other warning signals and the policy-maker's own perception – the precise moment where special attention to financial stability is necessary.

The final and (still unresolved) issue that we mentioned earlier is whether monetary policy itself needs to be expressly concerned with financial stability objectives. And then, if the answer is affirmative, (a) whether it should also begin acting in the specific moment identified above;[58] (b) what financial indicators – say the S2 or the credit-to-GDP gap – monetary policy should respond to, and (c) what would be the new set of instruments to be used as an additional component of the policy framework aimed at preventing financial crises. In short, to what extent should regulatory rules and monetary policy be combined to ensure both macroeconomic and financial stability?

That discussion is evolving alongside the emergence of analytical research, testing and studying how these policies interact.[59] This new analysis explores

---

[58] Or even earlier provided that the probability of disruption can be projected using the same methodology and given the time lags for monetary policy transmission.

[59] For a summary of the literature see Agénor and Pereira da Silva (2012a). For an analytical solution see Agénor et al. (2011, 2012). The stabilising effect of a central bank reaction function with a credit rule is stronger than that of alternative rules following a classical Taylor-rule specification even when augmented by a set of macroprudential regulations. These results hold for an open-economy with a flexible exchange rate, incorporating the interaction between capital inflows (sudden floods), credit creation and the macroeconomy.

the roles of macroprudential regulation and monetary policy in mitigating pro-cyclicality and promoting macroeconomic and financial stability. One avenue is to bring the qualitative insights into a typical dynamic stochastic general equilibrium framework with explicitly modelled credit markets featuring some counter-cyclical (Basel-type) rules. There are some promising results suggesting that when both macroeconomic stability and financial stability are properly defined by quantitative benchmarks (e.g., the volatility of stock or housing prices for the latter) monetary policy could go beyond its conventional mandate under inflation targeting frameworks and address the time-dimension of systemic risk – if only during a transitory period, while more is learnt about the implementation and performance of the new macroprudential rules that are currently being discussed. Hence, there are promising arguments in favour of monetary policy reacting in a state-contingent manner to a credit growth gap measure, because of financial stability considerations. Nevertheless, monetary policy is not a replacement for macroprudential regulation either – because monetary policy cannot, in any event, address the cross-section dimension of systemic risk.

The broad direction of the new strand of literature that emerged after the crisis can be summarised in the following way: "leaning against the financial cycle", (i.e. excessively rapid growth in credit) can be done through a combination of monetary and macroprudential policies to avoid financial fragility and some prevention is not only recommended but achievable in an effective way. A combination of policies is effective involving monetary and macroprudential policies to act in a complementary fashion to ensure both macroeconomic and financial stability.

7. CONCLUSION

According to Borio (2011), better policy calls for better analytics. The crisis has not just challenged policy-makers, but has also been a major wake-up call for the economic profession in general. This chapter presents quantitative indicators of financial stability in Brazil in comparison to the US and Euro zone. These indicators help in measuring systemic risk and explain the dynamics of financial distress.

We have proposed a working definition for "financial stability" together with that of systemic risk as "the probability of disruption of financial services, measured against an agreed upon threshold of shocks", exploring the respective time and cross-sectional dimensions of systemic risk and highlighting key areas of financial (in)stability (e.g., liquidity, interconnectedness and leverage). This definition allowed us to link systemic risk with synthetic indicators (e.g., S2 and/or a credit-to-GDP gap) of financial conditions and to calculate the probability of disruption of the financial system across its time dimension. At any point in time, we are therefore able to relate the cross-sectional dimension with the time dimension of systemic risk.

Therefore, this approach can link the probability of disruption with a tolerance level for "financial stability" set by the prudential regulator and thus enhances its capability of determining the precise moment when it should strengthen its set of analytical tools and calibrate operational instruments, such as countercyclical capital buffers, time-varying leverage ratios, changes in sectoral risk weights, limits to loan-to-value and loan-to-income ratios, capital surcharge, among many others (see Houben et al. 2012). The chapter also discusses whether this should be done in complement with monetary policy action.

Taking individually each dimension of financial vulnerability for Brazil, several factors guarantee the robustness and solidity of the Brazilian financial system: capital adequacy buffers above international standards, rigorous rules for credit provisioning, elevated liquidity levels (e.g., net assets/short-term liabilities), credit expansion with decreasing interest rates and bank spreads. Moreover, domestic non-performing loans (NPL) are expected to diminish in the upcoming quarters.[60]

To sum it up, Brazil is facing the new round of global financial crisis in a proper and adequate way. Resilience of the Brazilian economy comes from its macroeconomic and financial solid fundaments, and from an autonomous and prompt economic policy. The results clearly contrast with the ones observed in past decades, when external shocks of much less intensity used to produce more harmful effects in our economy.

BIBLIOGRAPHY

Adrian, T. and M. Brunnermeier 2011, "CoVaR", *NBER Working Papers* 17454, National Bureau of Economic Research; available at: http://www.nber.org/papers/w17454.pdf.

Agénor, P.-R., K. Alper, and L. A. Pereira da Silva 2009, "Capital Requirements and Business Cycles with Credit Market Imperfections", *Policy Research Working Paper* No. 5151, World Bank (December 2009). Forthcoming, Journal of Macroeconomics.

Agénor, P.-R., K. Alper, and L. A. Pereira da Silva 2011, "Capital Regulation, Monetary Policy and Financial Stability", *Centre for Growth and Business Cycles Research, Working Paper* No. 154, March. Forthcoming, *International Journal of Central Banking.*

---

[60] Mainly due to the following reasons: (i) new loans since 2011Q3 exhibit lower NPL levels (e.g., for automobile acquisitions); (ii) the current state of monetary (easing) cycle; (iii) lowering trajectories for interest rates and banking spreads; (iv) the perspective of a higher real GDP growth in the second semester of 2012; (v) the significant creation of new jobs; (vi) historically lower unemployment rates and rising real average income; (vii) declining inflation rate towards the target, preserving real wages; (viii) the relatively short-term maturities of domestic loans; among others.

Agénor, P.-R., K. Alper, and L. A. Pereira da Silva 2012, "Sudden Floods, Macroprudential Regulation and Stability in an Open Economy", *Working Paper* No. 267, Central Bank of Brazil, February.

Agénor, P.-R. and L. A. Pereira da Silva 2010, "Reforming International Standards for
Bank Capital Requirements: A Perspective from the Developing World", in *Interna-
tional Banking in the New Era: Post-Crisis Challenges and Opportunities*, ed. by S.
Kim and M. D. McKenzie, IFR Vol. No 11, Emerald, Bingley.

Agénor, P. R. and L. A. Pereira da Silva 2011, "Macroprudential Regulation and the
Monetary Transmission Mechanism", *Central Bank of Brazil Working Paper* No. 254,
November.

Agénor, P.-R., and L. A. Pereira da Silva, 2012a "Macroeconomic Stability, Financial
Stability, and Monetary Policy Rules", unpublished, forthcoming *Journal of International Finance*.

Agénor, P.-R. and L. A. Pereira da Silva 2012b, "Cyclical Effects of Bank Capital Requirements with Imperfect Credit Markets", *Journal of Financial Stability*, 8 (January
2012), pp. 43-56.

Aggeler, H.T. and R.J. Feldman 1998, "Is the loan-to-deposit ratio still relevant? A preliminary test says yes for many Ninth District banks", *Fed Gazette*, July 1998, available at: http://www.minneapolisfed.org/publications_papers/pub_display.cfm?id=2530.

Alessi, L. and C. Detken 2009, "Real time early warning indicators for costly asset
price boom/bust cycles: A role for global liquidity", *ECB Working Paper* 1039.

Allen, F. and D. Gale 2000, "Financial contagion", *The Journal of Political Economy*
108(1), pp. 1-33.

Allen, W.A. and G. Wood 2005, "Defining and achieving financial stability", *LSE Financial Markets Group Special Paper Series* 160, available at: http://www2.lse.ac.uk/
fmg/documents/specialPapers/2005/sp160.pdf.

BIS – Committee on the Global Financial System – CGFS 2010, "Macroprudential
instruments and frameworks: a stocktaking of issues and experiences", *CGFS Papers*
38, available at: http://www.bis.org/publ/cgfs38.pdf.

Bongini, P., L. Laeven and G. Majnoni 2002, "How good is the market at assessing
bank fragility? A horse race between different indicators", *Journal of Banking and
Finance* 26(5), pp. 1011–28.

Borio, C. 2011, "Rediscovering the macroeconomic roots of financial stability policy:
journey, challenges and a way forward", *BIS Working Papers* 354, September, available at: http://www.bis.org/publ/work354.pdf.

Borio, C. and M. Drehmann 2009, "Towards an operational framework for financial
stability: 'fuzzy' measurement and its consequences", *BIS Working Papers* 284, June,
available at: http://www.bis.org/publ/work284.pdf.

Borio, C. and P. Lowe 2002, "Asset prices, financial and monetary stability: Exploring
the nexus", *BIS Working Papers* 114, July.

De Castro, M.R., S.N. Gouvea, A. Minella, R.C. Santos and N.F. Souza-Sobrinho 2011,
"SAMBA: Stochastic Analytical Model with a Bayesian Approach", *Banco Central
do Brasil, Working Paper Series* 239.

De Nicolò, G., G. Favara and L. Ratnovski 2012, "Externalities and Macroprudential
Policy", *IMF Discussion Note*, SDN/12/05, June 7, 2012.

Drehmann, M. and N. Tarashev 2011, "Measuring the systemic importance of interconnected banks", *BIS Working Papers* 342, available at: http://www.bis.org/publ/
work342.pdf.

ECB-FSR 2011, *Financial Stability Review*, December 2011, available at: http://www.
ecb.int/pub/pdf/other/financialstabilityreview201112en.pdf?19b0b78aacfbb75dfb5f7
599c181a94b.

ECB-FSR 2012, *Financial Stability Review*, June 2012, available at: http://www.ecb. int/pub/pdf/other/financialstabilityreview201206en.pdf?82c8d663b48dbb6a9e8303f 70ae8bb27.

Edge, R.M. and R.R. Meisenzahl 2011, "The unreliability of credit-to-GDP ratio gaps in real-time: Implications for countercyclical capital buffers", Federal Reserve Board, *Staff Working Papers in the Finance and Economics Discussion Series*, 2011-37.

Georg, C.P. 2010, "The Effect of the Interbank Network Structure on Contagion and Financial Stability", *Working Papers on Global Financial Markets*, 12 September 2010, available at: http://pubdb.wiwi.uni-jena.de/pdf/wp_hlj12-2010.pdf.

Goodhart, C.A.E. 2011, "The macro-prudential authority: powers, scope and accountability", *OECD Journal: Financial Market Trends*, 2011 (2), available at: http://www. oecd.org/dataoecd/0/0/48979021.pdf.

Houben, A., R. van der Molen and P. Wierts 2012, "Making macroprudential policy operational", *Revue de Stabilité Financière*, Banque Centrale du Luxembourg, available at: http://www.bcl.lu/fr/publications/bulletins_bcl/RSF_2012/RSF_2012_Chapitre_1.pdf.

IMF-FSSA 2012, "Brazil: Financial System Stability Assessment". *IMF Country Report* No. 12/206, July 2012, available at: http://www.imf.org/external/pubs/ft/scr/2012/cr12206.pdf.

IMF-GFSR 2012, *The Quest for Lasting Stability*, April 2012, available at: http://www. imf.org/external/pubs/ft/gfsr/2012/01/pdf/text.pdf.

IMF-WEO 2009, *World Economic Outlook – Sustaining the Recovery*, October 2009, available at: http://www.imf.org/external/pubs/ft/weo/2009/02/pdf/text.pdf.

IMF-WEO 2012, *World Economic Outlook – Growth Resuming, Dangers Remain*, April 2012 available at: http://www.imf.org/external/pubs/ft/weo/2012/01/pdf/text. pdf.

IMF and World Bank 2012, "Brazil: Detailed Assessment of Observance of Basel Core Principles for Effective Banking Supervision", *IMF Country Report* No. 12/207, available at: http://www.imf.org/external/pubs/ft/scr/2012/cr12207.pdf.

Lopez-Espinosa, G., A. Moreno, A. Rubia and L. Valderrama 2012, "Systemic Risk and Asymmetric Responses in the Financial Industry", *IMF Working Paper* WP/12/152, June 2012, available at: http://www.imf.org/external/pubs/ft/wp/2012/wp12152.pdf.

Markose, S., S. Giansante, M. Gatkowski and A.R. Shaghaghi 2010, "Too Interconnected To Fail: Financial Contagion and Systemic Risk in Network Model of CDS and Other Credit Enhancement Obligations of US Banks", *University of Essex Discussion Paper Series* 683, available at: http://www.essex.ac.uk/economics/discussion-papers/ papers-text/dp683.pdf.

Mesquita, M. and M. Torós (2010) "Considerações sobre a Atuação do Banco Central na Crise de 2008", *Working Papers Series* WP 202, Central Bank of Brazil (March 2010).

Mishkin, F.S. 1991, "Anatomy of Financial Crisis", *NBER Working Paper* 3934, available at: http://www.nber.org/papers/w3934.pdf.

N'Diaye, P. 2009, "Countercyclical macro prudential policies in a supporting role to monetary policy", *IMF Working Paper* WP/09/257, November 2009, available at: http://www.imf.org/external/pubs/ft/wp/2009/wp09257.pdf.

Pereira da Silva L. A. and R. Harris 2012, "Sailing through the Global Financial Storm: Brazil's recent experience with monetary and macroprudential policies to lean against the financial cycle and deal with systemic risks", *Central Bank of Brazil, Working Papers Series* (forthcoming).

Sales, A., W. Aerosa and M. B. Aerosa 2012, "Some Financial Indicators for Brazil", *Working Paper Series* 287, available at: http://www.bcb.gov.br/pec/wps/ingl/wps249.pdf.

Schechtman, R. and W.P. Gaglianone 2012, "Macro Stress Testing of Credit Risk Focused on the Tails", *Journal of Financial Stability* 8(3), pp. 174-192.

Singh, M. 2012, "The (Other) Deleveraging", *IMF Working Paper* WP/12/179, July 2012, available at: http://www.imf.org/external/pubs/ft/wp/2012/wp12179.pdf.

Smets, F. 2011, "The credit-to-GDP gap and systemic risk", conference on Incorporating Financial Stability into Inflation Targeting, 25-26 November 2011, Istanbul. The Central Bank of the Republic of Turkey, available at: http://www.tcmb.gov.tr/yeni/konferans/financial_stability/Conference_files/Frank_SMETS.pdf.

Tabak, B.M., M. Takami, J.M.C. Rocha and D.O. Cajueiro 2011, "Directed Clustering Coefficient as a Measure of Systemic Risk in Complex Banking Networks", *Banco Central do Brasil, Working Paper Series* 249, available at: http://www.bcb.gov.br/pec/wps/ingl/wps249.pdf.

Woodford, M. 2010, "Inflation targeting and financial stability", presentation at the conference The future of monetary policy, Einaudi Institute for Economics and Finance, Rome, September.

5. From the Stability Pact to ESM – What Next?

Claudia M. Buch

1. HOW IT ALL BEGAN

The introduction of the euro marked a decisive moment in the process of European integration. Before the adoption of the euro, focus had been on deepening the Union through increased integration and the creation of a Common Market and on widening the Union by accepting new member countries in Central and Eastern Europe. In 1999, a core group of eleven member countries (Austria, Belgium, Finland, France, Germany, Ireland, Italy, Luxembourg, the Netherlands, Portugal, and Spain) formed the European Monetary Area and adopted a common currency. Greece (2000), Slovenia (2006), Cyprus and Malta (2007), the Slovak Republic (2008), and Estonia (2010) joined later on.

It was well understood that the sequence proposed by many, i.e. to form a monetary union only after a political union had been achieved, had not been followed. Yet, there was the hope that the requirements of the new currency would induce governments to pursue policies consistent with the common monetary regime. The facts that only countries fulfilling the Maastricht Criteria could join the euro and that member states had to adhere to the Stability and Growth Pact was considered to be a sufficient precondition for stability-oriented fiscal policies.

Parts of the analysis are based on reports written by the Economic Advisory Council to the German Federal Ministry of Economics on the European sovereign debt crisis and on the real economic conditions in the Euro area (Academic Advisory Council BWMi 2010a, 2010b). I am indebted to my colleagues in the advisory council as well as Manuel Buchholz, Jörn Kleinert, Wilhelm Kohler, Achim Wambach, and Benjamin Weigert for extremely fruitful discussions about European policy issues and for shaping my thinking about current developments in Europe. Lu Liu, Christof Weinmann, and Johannes Fleck have provided most efficient research assistance. But, of course, I am solely responsible for the text in this volume, and I bear full responsibility for any errors and inconsistencies.

Insufficient consideration was given to the potentially devastating feedback loops between misaligned incentives in the financial sector, overborrowing of the private and the public sector, and the evolution of persistent current account deficits. Yet, past experiences with currency and financial crises could have told a lesson: turbulence in the European Exchange Rate Mechanism and the speculation against the British Pound had happened less than a decade ago, and severe banking and exchange rate crises had just shaken the Asian countries as well as other emerging markets in the late 1990s. In fact, the Delors-Reports is quite explicit about the constraints financial markets can impose on economic policy.[1]

Now, more than a decade later, the European sovereign debt and banking crisis has revealed three main fault lines of the European institutional architecture.

First, incentives for structural reforms have been insufficient and, as one consequence, price and wage convergence has been limited. While nominal interest rates had converged across countries, relative prices and real interest rates have differed persistently. The resulting diverging trends in competitiveness and low risk premia have led to persistent current account imbalances in the Euro area and have created incentives to overborrow.

Second, links between sovereign risk and banking stability have not been addressed adequately. The Stability and Growth Pact was intended to create incentives for governments not to overborrow and to keep the official budget deficit in line with the Maastricht criteria. Yet, between 1999 and 2008, there have been 60 violations of the debt criterion and 33 violations of the deficit criterion.[2] Microprudential regulation of banks was used to keep checks and balances on private sector borrowing, but without adequately addressing feedback channels between private and public sector risk. Yet, recent experience particularly in Ireland and Spain has shown that financial sector stress can spill over into the fiscal sphere. Many banks in the crises countries have a significant and highly concentrated exposure to sovereign risk. Hence, the rescue measures that have been launched since May 2010 were motivated by the risk of contagion of sovereign risk into the banking sector – not only in the crises countries but also beyond.

---

[1] The Report states that "*However, experience suggests that market perceptions do not necessarily provide strong and compelling signals and that access to a large capital market may for some time even facilitate the financing of economic imbalances. Rather than leading to a gradual adaptation of borrowing costs, market views about the creditworthiness of official borrowers tend to change abruptly and result in the closure of access to market financing. The constraints imposed by market forces might either be too slow and weak or too sudden and disruptive. Hence countries would have to accept that sharing a common market and a single currency area imposed policy constraints.*" Committee for the Study of Economic and Monetary Union, Jacques Delors, Chairman, Report on Monetary and Economic Union in the European Community, April 1989, p. 10.

[2] These figures have been calculated on the basis of Eurostat data.

Third, the no-bail-out clause has lacked credibility. Article 125 of the Treaty on the European Union "The Lisbon Treaty" (2007) specifies a no-bail-out clause.[3] Article 100 of the EC Treaty stipulates that financial assistance might be granted, but only under exceptional circumstances.[4] Notwithstanding this modification, the strict adherence to the no-bail-out principle is one cornerstone of the institutional framework in the Euro area. Yet, recent experience shows that diverging trends in competitiveness and weaknesses in the financial systems can lead to speculation against the weaker countries in the Euro area which may ultimately render the no-bail-out principle to be time inconsistent. Since May 2010, several rescue measures have thus been launched, including bilateral loans to Greece, the successive support packages of the newly established European Financial Stability Facility (EFSF) for Greece and Portugal and the liquidity support provided by the European Central Bank (ECB). New rescue schemes have been established as well. Up to now, total support measures amount to approximately 800 billion EUR, consisting of 53 billion EUR of bilateral loans, 49 billion EUR (European Financial Stabilisation Mechanism or EFSM), 440 billion EUR (EFSF), and 500 billion EUR (European Stability Mechanism (ESM)) with the latter two being limited to a combined lending of not more than 700 billion EUR.

Correcting the imbalances that have built up in the Euro area requires deep structural reforms, involving labour market and product market reforms, lower national and international barriers to the entry of (new) firms, and measures to enhance the productivity of firms. In addition to policies improving the competitiveness of firms, reforms are needed that create a more credible framework for financial markets. These reforms should reduce incentives for private and public sector overborrowing while, at the same time, providing a mechanism to deal with financial stress in countries that have sound fundamentals but that come under pressure from financial markets.

In short, Europe stands at the doorstep of encompassing institutional reforms, and the ESM is one part of this reform package. In the following, I briefly summarise the scope of the ongoing institutional reforms, the struc-

---

[3] "*The Union shall not be liable for or assume the commitments of central governments, regional, local or other public authorities, other bodies governed by public law, or public undertakings of any Member State, without prejudice to mutual financial guarantees for the joint execution of a specific project. A Member State shall not be liable for or assume the commitments of central governments, regional, local or other public authorities, other bodies governed by public law, or public undertakings of another Member State, without prejudice to mutual financial guarantees for the joint execution of a specific project.*" Source: Consolidated version of the Treaty on the Functioning of the European Union, Article 125 (ex Article 103 TEC).

[4] "*Where a Member State is in difficulties or is seriously threatened with severe difficulties caused by natural disasters or exceptional occurrences beyond its control, the Council, acting by a qualified majority on a proposal from the Commission, may grant, under certain conditions, Community financial assistance to the Member State concerned.*" Source: Treaty establishing the European Community (Nice consolidated version) Article 100, second paragraph/ Article 103a – EC Treaty (Maastricht consolidated version), second paragraph.

ture of the ESM, and the conditions under which countries can draw on these funds (section 2). I then discuss the process of economic convergence in the Euro area and the mechanisms that have led to external imbalances (section 3). Section 4 discusses the implications for the ESM. I focus on four aspects: the extent to which the ESM can and should address the debt overhang problem, the extent to which the option of bank recapitalisation should be used, the need to focus the ESM on a mechanism that provides liquidity only under very narrowly defined circumstances, and the complementary reforms that are needed in order to strengthen the credibility of the ESM. Section 5 concludes.

2. THE EUROPEAN STABILITY MECHANISM (ESM)

The European Stability Mechanism (ESM) is a *permanent mechanism to ensure financial stability*. When designing the conditions under which countries can draw on funds provided by the ESM, two main questions need to be answered: First, how can the available funds be used most effectively, and which instruments should be at the disposal of the ESM? Second, how can financial assistance be provided without reducing the effectiveness of market signals for structural reforms?

These questions cannot be answered without taking into consideration that the ESM is part of an encompassing reform programme the EU has initiated in response to the (sovereign) debt crisis. This programme aims at reforming the Stability and Growth Pact, enhancing competitiveness and growth, and stabilising financial markets.

As regards fiscal policy, the so-called *Six Pack*, which went into force in December 2011, consists of five regulations and one directive addressing improved fiscal surveillance as well as a new programme of macroeconomic surveillance and coordination. The fiscal part of a new "Treaty on Stability, Coordination and Governance (TSCG)" is called the *Fiscal Compact*, signed by 25 EU member countries. It will enter into force after ratification by at least 12 countries of the Euro area. These amendments to the Stability and Growth Pact include the obligation for all contracting parties to introduce balanced budget rules at the national level, preferably in the national constitution, stricter surveillance and enforcement mechanisms with regard to the 3% deficit criterion of the Maastricht treaty for Euro area countries, mandatory debt reduction plans (i.e. a reduction of the differences between the 60% debt ceiling and the actual debt level), and sanctions in case of non-compliance (BMWi 2012, p. 18). As preventive measures, EU member countries must submit annual programs defining medium-term budgetary plans; the corrective arm consists of measures aimed at limiting excessive deficits. Sanctions can be imposed by the Ecofin-Council through simple majority votes (in the preventive arm) or through reverse majority voting (in the corrective arm). In the future, it will be necessary to have a majority *against* recommendations of the European Commission concerning the decision of whether an excessive deficit exists or whether, in case of non-compliance, further actions are needed. Furthermore, a new macroeconomic surveillance and coordination mechanism as well as the Euro-Plus-Pact include measures aimed at promoting growth and enhancing competitiveness. And, finally, comprehensive financial sector reforms are under way.[5]

All these policy measures aim at the prevention of crisis in the future. In parallel to that, the EFSF provides a temporary rescue scheme, which will be succeeded by the ESM as a permanent rescue scheme from mid-2012 onwards. The purpose of these rescue schemes is to provide financial assistance in times of crisis and under strict conditions of conditionality. For this purpose, the following paragraph is added to Article 136 of the Treaty on the Functioning of the European Union *"The Member States whose currency is the euro may establish a stability mechanism to be activated if indispensable to safeguard the stability of the Euro area as a whole. The granting of any required financial assistance under the mechanism will be made subject to strict conditionality."*[6]

Current policy discussions on the ESM have focused primarily on the volume of funds that are available to support Euro area countries. The effective lending capacity of the ESM is 500 billion EUR, while this amount initially also represented the original combined lending capacity of the EFSF and the EFSM. On March 30, 2012, it was decided to keep the EFSF operational until July 2013 and raising the combined lending capacity to a total of 700 billion EUR, of which approximately 200 billion EUR consists of the already agreed adjustment programmes in Greece, Portugal and Ireland, thereby raising the maximum additional lending capacity available as of now from 300 billion EUR to 500 billion EUR.[7] Generally, only countries that have ratified the Fiscal Compact qualify for funding under the ESM, and financial support can be granted only upon approval of a qualified majority of 86% of the votes.

The total subscribed capital of the ESM will be 700 billion EUR, which consists of 80 billion EUR be paid in capital and 620 billion EUR callable capital. Due to its overcollateralisation, the ESM shall obtain a top rating.

The ESM is activated upon application of one of its member countries for financial assistance. With this application, the specific financing instrument is specified as well. Details on the use of each instrument are defined by the directorate of the ESM in a set of guidelines. Generally, five instruments are available:

---

[5] A comprehensive review of these initiatives would be beyond the scope of the present chapter. See the website of the European Commission for an overview of the state of the legislative process (http://ec.europa.eu/internal_market/bank/index_en.htm).

[6] See ESM Treaty, p. 3, http://www.efsf.europa.eu/attachments/esm_treaty_en.pdf.

[7] See European Financial Stability Facility (EFSF), Frequently asked questions, http://www.efsf.europa.eu/attachments/faq_en.pdf, accessed on May 1, 2012.

1. *Precautionary Conditioned Credit Line (PCCL):* According to Article 14 of the ESM treaty, countries can draw on a PCCL (a) if they fulfil certain preconditions including measures to correct structural weaknesses, and (b) if they adhere to sound macroeconomic and fiscal policies. Countries which meet only criterion (b) get access to an *Enhanced* Conditions Credit Line (ECCL). Conditions that countries have to fulfil are specified in a memorandum of understanding (MoU).[8]

2. *Financial assistance for the recapitalisation of financial institutions of an ESM Member:* According to Article 15, the ESM can provide loans to the respective government that can be used to recapitalise financial institutions. Countries that qualify for such support must sign a memorandum of understanding which emphasises financial sector restructuring. Financial assistance for recapitalisation may also be granted to non-programme countries, i.e. it is not necessarily conditional upon a full macroeconomic adjustment programme.[9]

3. *ESM loans:* According to Article 16 of the ESM treaty, the fund may provide loans to support a macroeconomic adjustment programme. Details of this adjustment programme must be specified in a memorandum of understanding. ESM loans have preferred creditor status, similar to IMF funds. This is in contrast to EFSF loans, which have the same seniority as other holders of sovereign debt.

4. *Primary market support facility:* According to Article 17, the ESM may purchase securities on the primary market in order to ensure market access for one of its member countries or to ease a country's return to the capital market.

5. *Secondary market support facility:* According to Article 18, the ESM may buy securities on the secondary market in order to prevent financial contagion to other member countries and in case of the *"existence of exceptional financial market circumstances and risks to financial stability"*, as defined by the ECB. A memorandum of understanding again specifies the conditionality for the country affected.

Private sector involvement, an issue which has been highly contentious in the negotiations of the treaty, is mentioned only in the preamble of the ESM Treaty. Departing from the original drafts of the treaty, which had been agreed upon in July 2011, private sector involvement is not the rule, but *"In accordance with IMF practice, in exceptional cases an adequate and proportionate form of private sector involvement shall be considered in cases where stability*

---

[8] The PCCL and ECCL share similarities with new credit lines that the International Monetary Fund (IMF) has established after the Asian crisis. Use of these so-called Flexible Credit Line and the High Access Precautionary Credit Line has been limited because of the requirements of strict ex ante conditionality and the fear of a stigmatization effect for countries under these arrangements. See John and Knedlik (2011) for a discussion of the experience.

[9] See "EFSF Guidelines on Recapitalisation of Financial Institutions (FIs) via loans to non-programme countries", http://www.efsf.europa.eu/about/legal-documents/index.htm (accessed May 1, 2012).

support is provided accompanied by conditionality in the form of a macro-economic adjustment programme." (ESM Treaty, version as of 23.2.2012, p. 8). Financial support from the ESM is thus not conditional upon the initiation of debt restructuring negotiations. It is also not conditional upon a write down of debt, which would require bridge financing in order to maintain access to finance in times when access to private financial markets is temporarily shut off. Moreover, according to Article 12 of the ESM Treaty, collective action clauses shall be included in all new Euro area government securities with maturity of more than one year, beginning in January 2013.

3. REAL ECONOMIC DEVELOPMENTS IN THE EURO AREA[10]

The ESM is intended to stabilise financial markets resulting from sovereign risk and banking sector instability. But understanding the potential of the ESM to contain financial instabilities also requires a thorough understanding of the underlying state of the real economy and of the mechanisms that may lead to a build-up of unsustainable debt positions. In this section, I take a step back and discuss the economic developments that are behind the current crisis in the Euro area. I review trends in income and productivity in Europe (section 3.1.), the evolution of interest rates and prices (section 3.2.), the current account and capital flows (section 3.3.), and the role of fiscal transfers in existing currency unions (section 3.4.).

3.1. Income and Productivity

Many view the convergence of per capita incomes as a precondition for a functioning monetary union. Yet, economic convergence is a rather gradual process, and differences in per capita incomes are very persistent even within existing monetary unions.[11] In the case of Europe, an important issue has been whether the increased integration of markets through the Single Market Programme has speeded up or slowed down convergence. If technological progress is largely exogenous and if there are no significant barriers to the movement of capital and labour across borders, then market integration could increase the speed of economic convergence. If, in contrast, agglomeration advantages such as proximity to suppliers and customers are important and if this leads to endogenous technological progress, enhanced integration may rather lead to economic divergence.

---

[10] The following argument is a shortened and updated version of a report of the Academic Advisory Council BMWi (2011).
[11] Historical evidence shows that, on average, incomes per capita converge by about 2 percentage points annually (Barro and Sala-i-Martin 1991; Sala-i-Martin 1996).

Empirical evidence from the European Union (EU) as a whole shows that differences in per capita incomes have decreased gradually up until the 1970s (Boldrin and Canova 2001; Giannone et al. 2009). Convergence has slowed down in recent decades, while differences at the regional level have increased (Sapir et al. 2003). Since the 1980s, differences in per capita incomes of the core countries of the Euro area have remained relatively stable with a coefficient of variation of about 0.28.[12] These differences are slightly below comparable numbers for the US states (0.38).

Differences in unemployment rates are much more pronounced in Europe than across the individual states in the US. Prior to the financial crisis (in the year 2007), the average unemployment rate in Europe stood at 6.5% and thus above the US rate (4.6%); in the year 2011, average unemployment rates were 10.2% in the Euro area and 8.9% in the US.[13] Yet, dispersion of unemployment rates is much higher in Europe. While the coefficient of variation of regional unemployment rates was 0.25 in the US, the corresponding number was about twice as high in 2010 in Europe (0.47). Or, in absolute terms: while the highest unemployment rate in the US was registered in Nevada (13.5%),[14] the highest rate in Europe was recorded in Spain (more than 20%). There are many explanations for these differences, but insufficient regional mobility of labour, together with large inter-country variation in structural weaknesses on European labour markets, are certainly important factors.

In addition, productivity and innovation activity differ across European countries. According to *Eurostat*, labour productivity has diverged considerably across the Euro area with numbers for Greece (18 EUR), Spain (24 EUR) and Portugal (14 EUR) lying below the values for the Euro area as a whole (33 EUR) (data are for the year 2010). In terms of expenditure for research and development, European countries fall into three main groups. The highest expenditure relative to GDP are recorded in Germany and in the Scandinavian countries (about 3% of GDP), followed by Austria, the Benelux countries, Estonia, France, Ireland, Slovenia, and the UK (about 2% of GDP), and the southern and Eastern European countries with less than 1% (OECD 2011). Using the number of patents or employment in R&D gives a very similar picture. Interestingly, in countries with a low share of R&D investment, a relatively high share of these investments comes from the public sector.

---

[12] The coefficient of variation of real GDP per capita is the standard deviation relative to the mean of real GDP per capita for each individual year in US dollar. The Euro area comprises Austria, Belgium, France, Germany, Greece, France, Italy, Ireland, Netherlands, Portugal, and Spain. The numbers given in the text are based on (for Europe) International Monetary Fund, World Economic Outlook Database, April 2011, and (for the US) Bureau of Economic Analysis, Regional Economic Accounts.

[13] These numbers are based on Eurostat and refer to the annual average unemployment rates.

[14] This number refers to September 2011 and has been calculated by the Bureau of Labor Statistics.

3.2. Interest Rates and Relative Prices

While there has been no distinct trend towards real convergence in the Euro area in recent decades, nominal interest rates have quickly converged following the introduction of the euro (figure 5.1b). This nominal interest rate convergence has not only affected wholesale markets but also retail interest rates. Figure 5.2 shows that the standard deviation of interest rates on time deposits has been below 0.1 until the outbreak of the financial crisis in 2007; standard deviations of loan rates have been a bit higher. The graph also shows that the convergence of nominal interest rates has come to an abrupt end leading to a widening of spreads due to the sovereign debt and banking crises.

Nominal interest rate convergence reflected the elimination of exchange rate risk and a convergence of inflationary expectations (Ehrmann et al. 2011).[15] Interestingly, default risk has been priced in only after support measures had been granted, perhaps because these measures have been deemed insufficient. The widening interest rate spreads since the start of the financial crisis in the year 2007 certainly reflect increased risk premia. Over time, bail-out expectations have changed, but quantifying these effects empirically is hardly possible. There is evidence that the factors driving the pricing of government debt have differed before and after the crisis: before the crisis, sovereign risk in the Euro area was systematically under-priced; during the crisis, it was systematically overpriced (De Grauwe and Ji 2012).

a) Inflation (%)

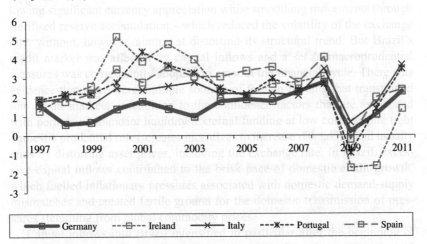

---

[15] This study does not capture the effects of the sovereign debt crisis. Schuknecht et al. (2009) also analyse interest rates and risk premia in the Euro area. Buiter and Sibert (2005) argue that the refinancing policies of the ECB have affected risk premia in the Euro area.

(b) Nominal interest rates (%)

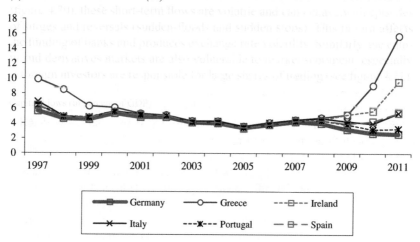

Figure 5.1: Inflation and nominal interest rates

Nominal interest rates are the annual average rates of return on fixed rate government bonds with a residual maturity of at least 3 years. The inflation rate refers to the harmonised consumer price index.

Sources: Sachverständigenrat, ECB Statistical Data Warehouse, own calculations.

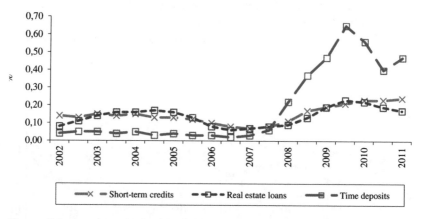

Figure 5.2: Divergence of nominal retail interest rates in the Euro area

The graph shows the coefficient of variation, i.e. the standard deviation relative to the mean interest rates, across Euro area countries. Short-term credits are those with a residual maturity of less than one year. Data for the year 2011 are as of September.

Sources: ECB Statistical Data Warehouse, own calculations.

Nominal interest rate convergence can be problematic if real economic developments diverge. Together with diverging price and wage developments, nominal interest rate convergence leads to differences in real interest rates. In countries where prices increase faster than in the rest of the currency area, real interest rates are low, and firms, households, or governments have incentives to borrow. Table 5.1 shows the evolution of private and public sector debt in % of GDP. In the Euro area as a whole, public debt has increased from about 73 to 81% from the second half of the 1990s until the crises years (2008-2011). Developments across countries differ. While the steepest increase occurred in Greece (from 96 to 138%), public debt in Ireland or Spain has been below the 60% threshold before the crisis but increased during the crisis because of the instabilities in the financial sector. Private sector debt increased by almost 20 percentage points as well for the Euro area as a whole (from 47 to 66%), with above-average values in Ireland, the Netherlands, Portugal, and Spain.

Table 5.1: Private and public debt in the Euro area (in % of GDP)

	Public debt			
	1995-1999	2000-2003	2004-2007	2008-2011
France	58.2	59.0	64.8	78.9
Germany	59.1	61.1	67.1	76.3
Greece	96.3	101.6	103.0	138.2
Ireland	63.7	33.8	26.5	77.5
Italy	117.1	106.4	104.5	115.1
Netherlands	69.0	51.8	49.2	61.9
Portugal	54.4	52.4	63.2	89.0
Spain	64.7	54.1	41.3	56.0
Euro area (total)	72.7	68.6	68.6	80.6

	Private debt			
	1995-1998	1999-2002	2003-2006	2007-2010
France	41.1	44.2	50.8	60.7
Germany	66.5	73.3	70.8	63.1
Greece	13.2	21.8	38.6	58.3
Ireland	n.a.	53.7	81.6	118.6
Italy	22.0	29.5	38.4	48.4
Netherlands	67.2	89.3	111.6	126.3
Portugal	48.0	73.7	88.6	102.5
Spain	43.2	55.4	75.0	90.0
Euro area (total)	46.5	53.0	59.5	65.8

This table shows average sovereign debt to GDP ratios (in per cent). Data for the Euro area start in 1995. Private debt to GDP ratios (in per cent) are measured as household liabilities to GDP. Data for Ireland start in 2001.

Sources: Eurostat; own calculations.

The central bank, in turn, has limited means to counteract such diverging developments because it sets its policy interest rates for the currency union as a whole. Hence, it cannot counteract diverging regional price and wage developments. Just as the ECB lacks instruments to affect regional prices and wage developments, it also lacks tools to directly supervise the banks that take recourse to its refinancing operations. Since the beginning of the European debt crisis in May 2010, the ECB has successively changed the conditions under which banks can obtain access to central bank refinancing by changing the collateral framework and the margin requirements. Several banks, the so-called "persistent bidders", rely on ECB funding almost exclusively.

The discussion about the role, the interpretation, and the possible policy implications of the Target II (im)balances is one facet of this debate. These balances are related to the underlying weaknesses of the real economies, i.e. current account imbalances within the Euro area which are not financed entirely by private capital flows. They also reflect weaknesses in the financial sector that leads to capital flight. Several commercial banks in the crisis countries cannot fund their operations on private capital markets and thus resort to liquidity support from the ECB.[16]

Diverging price developments not only lead to differences in real interest rates but also to changes in relative prices. Even within a currency union, in which nominal exchange rates are irrevocably fixed, relative prices (the "real exchange rate") can diverge. If prices, say, in Greece increase faster than in the rest of the Euro area, exports of Greek firms become relatively more expensive while imports from the Euro area into Greece become relatively cheaper. The Greek real exchange rate has thus appreciated in real terms, which corresponds to a loss in competitiveness of Greek firms on international markets.[17]

Differences in unit labour costs have been one main driver of these developments. In the run-up to the crisis, unit labour costs increased by 2.9% annually between 2001 and 2009. This number has been below average in Germany (1.8%) but above average in Greece (3.9%), Spain (4.5%), Italy (3.3%) or Portugal (3.1%), reflecting structural differences on product and labour markets (based on Eurostat; see Lebrun and Pérez 2011).

Figure 5.1a shows the evolution of consumer prices in selected Euro area countries. On average, consumer prices in Germany have increased by 0.5 percentage points less than in the rest of the Euro area; in the crises countries, consumer prices have increased by 1.28 percentage points more in Greece or 0.81 percentage points in Spain. Hence, these countries have appreciated in real terms vis-à-vis the other countries in the Euro area. Note that real exchange rate appreciation does not necessarily imply that the real exchange rate

---

[16] See Sinn and Wollmershaeuser (2011) and the references in ifo (2011).
[17] Neary (2006) discusses the link between the real exchange rate and the "competitiveness" of a country.

becomes overvalued. If price increases reflect an increase in (relative) productivity, there would be no misalignment of prices (the so-called Balassa-Samuelson effect).[18] But increasing and highly persistent bilateral current account imbalances in the Euro area are strong signals of an overvaluation of the real exchange rate.

There are two main adjustment mechanisms to realign real exchange rates. In the short run, prices and wages have to adjust (internal devaluation) or the nominal exchange rate can adjust (external devaluation). In the medium- to long-term, productivity needs to increase.

Countries that are members of the Euro area cannot use the nominal exchange rate to achieve the needed realignment of the real exchange rate. Hence, adjustment has to fall on prices and wages. The ability to achieve the required revaluation of wages and thus of real incomes depends on the political support for such measures and the institutional framework. In fact, many factors which obstruct internal devaluation could also prevent sustained effects of an external devaluation. (Kohler 2012, for instance, makes this point.)

Previous empirical work on the degree of wage flexibility in Europe hints at potential institutional shortcomings. Dickens et al. (2007) analyse the degree of wage flexibility in 16 OECD countries. According to their study, Greece, Italy, and Portugal have a low while Ireland has a comparatively high degree of wage flexibility. This may be one reason for the fact that, so far, Ireland has adjusted relatively successfully to the crisis. The study by Dickens et al. also provides information on the causes of wage (in)flexibility. Wages are relatively rigid in countries with strong employment protection legislation and with high minimum wages relative to the mean wage level. Wage flexibility is relatively high, in contrast, in countries where union density and the degree of centralised wage bargaining are high. These results indicate that deep structural reforms are required in the Euro area in order to realign prices and wages with economic fundamentals.

3.3. Current Accounts and Capital Flows

Although public discussions describe the current situation in Europe as a (sovereign) debt crisis, it can in fact also be seen as a full-fledged *intra-European balance of payments crisis*. Diverging patterns of real interest rates and of real exchange rates have been associated with widening current account imbalances in the Euro area. Generally, current account imbalances and the corresponding capital flows are one adjustment mechanism to shocks and to differences in real incomes. During a longer-term catching up process, poorer

---

[18] The link between real exchange rates and per capita incomes as a measure for productivity has been analysed in detail by Berka and Devereux (2010). They show that, in Europe, this link has become stronger with the introduction of the euro and that it is stronger for tradables than for non-tradables.

countries or regions should be expected to import foreign capital (and thus to run current account deficits) and to repay their foreign debts through current account surpluses in the future. Access to international capital markets can also provide countries with a short-run insurance mechanism, allowing them to buffer short-run fluctuations in incomes. Hence, in integrated financial markets, income shocks have a weaker impact on consumption patterns than in a closed economy.

Yet, reaping the benefits of international financial integration in the form of faster economic convergence and of insurance against income fluctuations is possible only if financial frictions and incentives to overborrow are limited. In addition to informational frictions that are prevalent on domestic capital markets as well, sovereign risk adds an additional friction on international capital markets: here, the borrower remains sovereign, and the collection of collateral in the case of default is often not possible. Hence, in an international context, it is not only the ability of borrowers to pay but also their willingness to pay that matters (Eaton et al. 1986). The threat not to repay and to default increases the borrower's bargaining power (Bulow and Rogoff 1989). The implicit price borrowers have to pay for this sovereignty is the risk of a *sudden stop* of capital flows in case creditors expect a sovereign default. The quite significant reversal of capital flows to some European countries suggests that these mechanisms have been at play in the Euro area.[19]

It is a key challenge for empirical research to disentangle the extent to which current account imbalances in the Euro area reflect a normal adjustment process and are thus a signal of increased market integration and to what extent they reflect excessive borrowing and lending on international capital markets. Table 5.2 shows that current account deficits in the Euro area have tended to widen since the introduction of the euro. Partly, these deficits reflect increased financial integration, but partly they also reflect excessive borrowing. While the current account of the euro area towards the rest of the world has largely been balanced since 1999, there are two distinct groups of countries. The capital exporters comprise the northern European countries, Germany, the Netherlands, and Austria. The capital importers (with current account deficits) comprise the southern European countries Greece, Italy, Portugal, and Spain. In the case of Spain and Ireland, capital imports have been accompanied by increased investment rates; in the case of Greece and Portugal, they were driven by an increase in consumption (Deutsche Bundesbank 2010). In the course of the crisis, the current account deficits in the Euro area have to some extent narrowed down. This adjustment has been driven primarily by a reduction in domestic demand rather than an adjustment of relative prices.

---

[19] See Kohler (2012) for a more detailed discussion of the situation in Europe as balance of payments crises. Merler and Pisani-Ferry (2012) show that sudden stops of capital flows have occurred in the Euro area.

Table 5.2: Current accounts in the Euro area (in % of GDP)

	1990-1995	1996-2000	2001-2005	2006-2010
France	0.12	2.26	0.86	-1.43
Germany	-0.51	-0.95	2.74	6.20
Greece	-1.74	-4.57	-6.72	-12.23
Ireland	1.46	1.43	-1.15	-3.33
Italy	-0.43	1.56	-0.94	-2.92
Netherlands	3.74	4.10	5.04	6.61
Portugal	-0.57	-7.01	-8.23	-10.12
Spain	-2.19	-1.68	-4.66	-7.78
Euro area (total)	n.a.	0.48	0.53	-0.02

This table shows average current account deficits relative to GDP. Data for the Euro area start in 1997.
Sources: IMF World Economic Outlook; own calculations.

The international indebtedness of the crisis countries has thus increased in recent years. Some countries carry a net foreign debt burden of a magnitude similar to their GDP (figure 5.3). Italy with a high debt burden of the government vis-à-vis domestic residents is an exception. The bulk of foreign liabilities is in the form of fixed income assets (bank debt plus bonds). The share of foreign direct investment and of other equity investments is relatively small, and it has declined over time.

Recent studies conclude that the introduction of the euro has promoted capital market integration in Europe (see, e.g., Baldwin et al. 2008; Demyanyk et al. 2008; Kalemli-Ozcan et al. 2007; or Okawa and van Wincoop 2010). However, most of these studies do not cover the crisis period. Empirical studies show that the tendency of lower-income countries to import and of higher-income countries to export capital has become stronger after the introduction of the euro (Schmitz and von Hagen 2011). In line with expectations, capital flows have contributed to a higher degree of economic convergence. There is also evidence that capital flows have helped countries to cushion negative shocks and to smoothen consumption over time (Artis and Hoffmann 2008; Gerlach and Hoffmann 2010). But, not only have capital flows increased, international borrowing patterns have also become more persistent (Berger and

(a) Net foreign liabilities (stocks) relative to GDP (%)

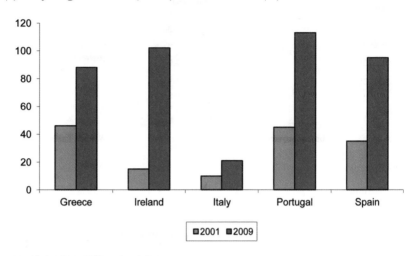

(b) Share of fixed income securities in total foreign liabilities (%)

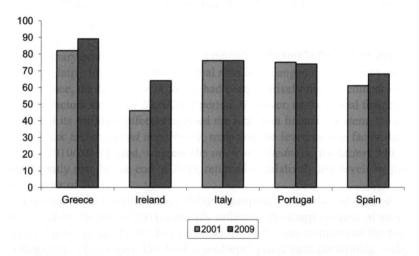

Figure 5.3: Foreign liabilities of selected Euro area countries

Net foreign liabilities are the difference between total foreign liabilities and assets as the sum of foreign direct investment, portfolio investment, and bank credits. Fixed income securities are bonds and bank credits.

Sources: IMF, International Financial Statistics; own calculations.

Nitsch 2010), indicating capital flows in excess of sustainable long-run positions. Consistent with this interpretation, Berger and Nitsch find that lack of structural reforms drives external imbalances. Countries with inflexible labour and product markets, with strong job protection legislation, with high fiscal deficits, and with volatile business cycles have had high external deficits.

3.4. Fiscal Transfers

In discussions about the future of the Euro area, it is often argued that successful currency unions have strong fiscal transfer systems which help cushioning shocks to short-term income. If a member country (or region) of a currency union is hit by an adverse shock, the nominal exchange rate cannot adjust to realign prices. Hence, fiscal transfers may be needed in order to provide a short-term insurance mechanism and to ensure a certain degree of burden sharing. Such fiscal insurance systems must be distinguished conceptually from long-run redistributive mechanisms which help reducing differences in per capita incomes. Such redistributive transfers are not necessarily motivated by the special conditions of a monetary union. But, of course, any transfer system will also have some redistributive elements, and it is thus a political question how much redistribution and risk sharing is desired.

Existing systems of interregional fiscal burden sharing differ. In the US, ad hoc transfers are relatively important. Here, transfers between the federal level and the level of the individual state account for about 3% of GDP or 15% of federal spending.[20] These shares have increased slightly during the crisis. In Germany, rule-based transfers dominate, but the federal transfer system (*Länderfinanzausgleich*) reached magnitudes similar to those in the US (2.4% of GDP in 1990, see Büttner 2002). This mechanism is used to redistribute the proceeds of value added taxes (*Umsatzsteueraufkommen*), but there are also horizontal and additional federal transfers (Büttner 2002, 2009).

Empirical studies analyse whether fiscal transfers serve the main purpose of insuring against short-term shocks or if they are contributing to smaller income differentials in the longer-run. These studies start by distinguishing short-run from long-run fluctuations of income and then ask to what extent households can shield consumption from such fluctuations of income, i.e. "insure" against them. In the US, only about 16% of short-term income fluctuations across states affect consumption while the corresponding number of long-run fluctuations is higher (49%) (Becker and Hoffmann 2006). But only a relatively small share of this consumption risk sharing is achieved via fiscal transfers; the bulk of insurance comes through the integration of capital and labour markets (Artis and Hoffmann 2011; or Becker and Hoffmann 2006). Cross-state-border ownership of firms and thus a relatively high degree of integration of equity markets, for instance, plays an important role. In addition, it is important to note

---

[20] See US Census Bureau, Statistical Abstract of the United States 2011, table 429, p. 268 "Federal Grants-in-Aid to State and Local Governments".

that the no-bail-out principle has been adhered to quite strictly in the United States. Most US states have constitutional balanced budget rules, and the states are treated as sovereign entities.

In Germany, the importance of different adjustment channels has changed over time. In the years 1970-1994, fiscal transfers have accounted for a share of 50% of consumption risk sharing across state borders Factor and credit markets accounted for insurance against about 36% of income shocks. In the post-unification period, about 63% (53%) of shocks have been smoothened via markets in West Germany (East Germany) and only 15% (19%) through fiscal insurance mechanisms. These numbers are roughly comparable to those observed for the US (Astrubali et al. 1995).

3.5. Summing Up

This section has shown that countries can share the same currency even though there are differences in per capita incomes. Real economic convergence is not a necessary precondition for a monetary union while, of course, a higher degree of convergence eases the adjustment to adverse shocks. Tensions can arise for the following reasons: First, diverging price and wage developments within a currency union can lead to persistent divergence in competitiveness. Second, because nominal exchange rates cannot be used as a buffer against adverse business cycle fluctuations, alternative mechanisms such as sufficiently integrated and flexible factor markets or fiscal transfer system are required. Third, if market participants expect bail-outs by other members of the currency area, interest rates may not fully reflect the underlying risk premia, which may create incentives for overborrowing.

These considerations have several implications for the environment in which the ESM will operate. The ESM per se will not affect the real economic conditions in the Euro area, but its institutional design may affect the incentives to engage in the structural reforms that are necessary to realign real developments. Moreover, the impact of ESM funding on financial market stability will depend on the credibility of establishing a new institutional regime for the Euro area addressing existing structural weaknesses.

4. THE ROLE OF THE ESM

Financial markets can contribute to greater economic convergence and to a smoothening of shocks across countries, thus bringing capital flows in line with underlying patterns of the real economy and stabilising a common currency area. However, financial markets may also overreact with regard to fundamentals and thus have destabilising effects. What are the options that are available for economic policy to strengthen the stabilising and to weaken the destabilising forces? While encompassing financial sector reform programmes and the necessary fiscal and structural reforms have been proposed elsewhere (e.g., Academic Advisory Council BMWi 2010a, 2010b; Sachverständigenrat 2011; or Academic Advisory Council BMF 2010), this section focuses on the potential contribution of the ESM.

I will argue that, in the current situation, financial stabilising requires taking account of the stock problem of non-performing assets (section 4.1.), that bank recapitalisation and restructuring can play an important role (section 4.2.), that the role of the ESM should be confined to the provision of liquidity under well-defined criteria for countries restructuring their debt (section 4.3.), and that complementary reforms of the financial system are needed (section 4.4.).[21]

4.1. Dealing with Debt Overhang

The scope of the ESM is defined fairly broadly. Article 18 states that "*Decisions on interventions on the secondary market to address contagion shall be taken on the basis of an analysis of the ECB recognising the existence of exceptional financial market circumstances and risks to financial stability.*" At the same time, the ESM shall provide financial support under well-defined criteria only: "*The granting of any required financial assistance under the mechanism will be made subject to strict conditionality.*" (Treaty Establishing the European Stability Mechanism, p.3.

One potential use of ESM funds is to deal with debt overhang. While the exact amount of debt overhang in Europe is not known, the mechanisms that have been described so far have caused excessive borrowing of the private and of the public sector. Some of this excess debt has been written off, but an excess debt burden is also likely to be carried forward on banks' and other investors' balance sheets. Quantifying potentially non-performing assets is difficult: information on loan forbearance is scarce, the quality of banks' assets crucially depends on the state of the economy and on interlinkages in the financial system, and there may be multiple equilibria. Hence, there might be a situation where economic fundamentals do not differ but, depending on the beliefs of market participants, a crisis may or may not occur. Not least, incentives of debtors and borrowers matter.

Hence, the ESM will become effective at a time when a large part of the bad debts are still outstanding. Inevitably, the ESM will deal not only with the flow but also with a stock problem of bad debts. However, if the ESM aims at preventing a fundamental revaluation of assets in the Euro area, it is hardly conceivable how this goal could be achieved. Recent experience rather sug-

---

[21] For a discussion of policies aimed at stabilising the real economy and promoting growth, see, e.g., Academic Advisory Council BMWi (2011).

gests that there will be continued pressure on the ECB to support malfunctioning financial markets and banks through the provision of liquidity support. It has in fact been argued that the ECB is the only institution in Europe which can prevent a meltdown of asset prices in case the financial crisis worsens by, for instance, announcing that it will buy up all government bonds up to a certain percentage of a country's GDP.[22] The ESM may not only lack the funding to buy up a sufficient volume of assets and thus to stabilise asset prices, decision making will also be too slow in times of acute financial stress. This limits the potential for the ESM to act as a lender of last resort. (Kohler 2012 makes a similar point.)

The decisions of the ECB to purchase government bonds directly or to relax collateral standards indicate its willingness and ability to act as a lender of last resort. According to the so-called Bagehot principle, however, a lender of last resort should lend at a sufficiently high penalty rate to solvent but illiquid banks that have adequate collateral. In the current crisis, both of these conditions have been violated: the ECB currently lends at a low rate, and the quality standards for collateral in ECB refinancing operations have been weakened over time.

There is thus a growing concern that risks have been shifted from the financial and from the public sector onto the ECB's balance sheets. Recent announcements of the ECB to tighten lending standards and to induce governments to restructure banks essentially acknowledge these risks. At the same time, the ECB has practically no instruments at its disposal to enforce strict fiscal rules or to impose prudential regulations on banks. Hence, the task of stabilising the banks should gradually be moved from the ECB to the fiscal authorities.

With the ESM having limited funds to address the stock problem of outstanding debt and the adoption of additional risks through the ECB being problematic, *alternative solutions* need to be found. One proposal of how to deal with the public debt overhang has been made by the German Council of Economic Experts.[23] Its *redemption fund* has two core elements. First, eligible countries would transfer their outstanding public debt in excess of the 60% debt ceiling of the Maastricht treaty to a common redemption fund. Second, a clear repayment schedule would have to be defined, and countries need to credibly transfer tax proceeds or other financial sources to the Fund as collateral in order to repay their debts. Hence, the proposal includes a limited transfer of sovereign rights to the Fund. As regards the potential debt overhang problem in the private sector, additional measures would be required though.

---

[22] According to these proposals, support from the ECB should be granted only under the conditionality that the country in question adheres to strict fiscal discipline in the future. See, e.g., Charles Wyplosz http://voxeu.org/index.php?q=node/7031 or Paul DeGrauwe http://www.voxeu.org/index.php?q=node/6884.
[23] See, e.g., the proposal by the German Council of Economic Experts to establish a debt redemption fund (Doluca et al. 2012; Sachverständigenrat 2011).

4.2. Bank Recapitalisation and Restructuring

There is a long-standing tradition of discussing whether conditions in the real economy affect conditions in the financial sector, or vice versa. In the current situation in Europe, this discussion is largely an academic one. Clearly, problems on European debt markets cannot be addressed without, in the long run, improving the underlying real economic conditions while, in the short run, ensuring a sufficient capitalisation of European banks is crucial in order to prevent negative feedback effects for the real economy. Evidence from other world regions, in particular from Japan during the past two decades, shows that delaying a solution might be costly in terms of misaligned incentives in the financial system that can lead to a misallocation of real resources (see, e.g., Caballero et al. 2008; or Peek and Rosengren 2005). Recent policy decisions to improve the capitalisation of banks are thus a step into the right direction, although care should be taken that regulations are not tightened during the crisis and that banks have a sufficient adjustment period.

Private funds either in the form of retained earnings or through new issuances of equity should certainly have priority in strengthening the capital buffer of banks. In line with this, funds for recapitalisation are available under the EFSF and the ESM only if other, private and public, sources of funds are not available. Yet, these private funds may turn out to be insufficient, and a deterioration of the economic environment may require a higher volume of recapitalisation. In such a situation, the case can be made that governments should stand ready to support ailing financial institutions in order to prevent contagion effects (Academic Advisory Council BMWi 2008). This would also reduce pressure on the ECB to support distressed banks. Bank recapitalisation in the crisis countries may also be desirable from the point of view of overall financial stability. Hence, solutions for the Euro area as a whole must be sought.

Bank recapitalisation through the national government may not be forthcoming at a sufficient scale for several reasons though. Most importantly, countries in which banks are in need of capital support are also the countries in which governments have the least room to manoeuvre, given their own dire financial state. Therefore, governments in the crisis countries may be unable to support their banks on a stand-alone basis. While funding for bank recapitalisation is in principle available through the ESM, the incentives of governments to apply for bank recapitalisation funds under Article 15 are thus limited. Taking up such support could be taken as a negative signal to financial markets concerning the financial state of the sovereign, thus negatively affecting market access for banks and sovereigns.[24] Moreover, funding for bank recapitalisation is conditional upon the specification of a plan on how to restructure the coun-

---

[24] Empirical evidence shows that the risk profiles of the sovereign and of the banks converge if the sovereign assumes guarantees or supports banks through other means (BIS 2009).

try's banking system. In order to be effective, such a bank restructuring plan may require the consolidation of a country's financial system thus raising opposition by affected stakeholders. Finally, bank recapitalisation in one country might induce competitive distortions. Banks in the non-crisis countries might thus lobby against support for crisis banks if they fear that such support measures might distort the competitive environment on European banking markets.

Hence, there is the risk that, although bank recapitalisation may be desirable for overall financial stability, such considerations might prevent a concerted solution. These arguments speak in favour of taking concerted action at the EU level and of closely involving European competition authorities in order to prevent a distortion of market structures.

No matter whether bank restructuring and supervision is a national or an international task, the rules under which public capital support is granted must be clearly defined, and it must be clear that public ownership in the banks is a crisis management tool. The goals of any bank recapitalisation programme should be (i) to restore the functioning of financial markets as quickly and as broadly as possible, (ii) to generate the least possible distortions facing private market participants, and (iii) to keep costs to the tax payer as small as possible (see Academic Advisory Council BMWi 2008 for details).

In addition, the following aspects need to be considered:

First, bank restructuring and recapitalisation should take place in the context of a well-defined cross-border resolution regime for banks. In the medium to longer run, this also requires the establishment of a European deposit insurance and resolution fund.

Second, using the financial resources available under the ESM to recapitalise banks might solve the problem that a European solution requires sufficient funding in the short run. By affecting the liabilities' side of banks' balance sheets rather than trying to support asset values through purchases on the primary or secondary market, a given volume of funds could be used more efficiently. Banks would obtain leeway to restructure their balance sheets and to write off non-performing assets, which may be loans to the private sector as well as government bonds.

Third, under the present legal framework, application for a specific financial instrument is done by the countries themselves. For reasons outlined above, the individual country may not have an incentive to apply for recapitalisation funds. Markets could take such an application as a signal that the government has insufficient funds to support its country's banks. Instead, pressure to apply for bank recapitalisation funds could come through the ECB or the EBA, which already call for national governments to provide backstop facilities for their banking systems. As regards application for recapitalisation funds, it could be considered to assign a more active role to the European Banking Authority (EBA).

Fourth, bank recapitalisation is no panacea. Instead, it needs to go hand in hand with a thorough review of the quality of banks' assets, with a restructuring of banks, and, if needed, adjustment of market structures. Evidence from Japan is particularly instructive in this context.[25] Hoshi and Kashyap (2010) review the experience from bank restructuring in Japan and derive the following lessons: banks often refrain from accepting capital support measures because they fear negative signalling effects and thus lack of access to private capital markets; rescue packages need to have a sufficient scale; asset purchase programmes are of limited effectiveness; a thorough audit of banks' assets and a restructuring of non-performing assets are required; a powerful and adequate resolution authority must be in place; capital support measures through the government run the risk of promoting politically motivated lending; and, finally, macroeconomic growth is crucial for a recovery of banks.

Fifth, the conditions under which public support is given to banks should be clearly specified. Under a high degree of uncertainty about the conditions of public involvement, private investors are unlikely to provide sufficient additional funds. Moreover, if banks do not meet regulatory capital requirements, payments of dividends and other payments to shareholders should be restricted in order to prevent the depletion of funds.

Finally, institutions receiving financial support from their government should be supervised by politically independent institutions. Many governments in Europe face a conflict of interest: on the one hand, the domestic banks are important buyers of domestic sovereign debt. There is in fact evidence of a substantial degree of home preference in banks' (sovereign debt) portfolios, which has even tended to increase during the crisis (Giannetti and Laeven 2011; Hildebrand et al. 2012; Rose and Wieladek 2011). On the other hand, institutions linked to the government are assigned the task to supervise the banks and to disclose potential problems. These considerations strengthen the case for an independent European supervisor.

4.3. Limiting the Role of the ESM to a Crisis Mechanism

It has been argued above that the ESM lacks resources and sufficient speed in decision making to serve as a general lender of last resort. Hence, the question remains as to what the actual role of the ESM should be. The ESM is part of a new institutional framework which builds on strengthened fiscal surveillance, enforced fiscal policy rules, and strengthened banking regulations. But even if all these policies succeeded, there would still be the risk that situations of (fiscal) distress occur because of unforeseen shocks or changes in market

---

[25] Misallocation of credit continued in some Japanese banks after recapitalisation (Giannetti and Simonov 2009), and weak corporate governance and regulatory forbearance lengthened the recovery of the real economy (Kanaya and Woo 2000). See also Caballero et al. (2008) or Peek and Rosengren (2005).

sentiment. In order to avoid being taken by surprise, the credibility of the new framework can be enhanced by establishing clear guidelines of how to deal with countries in distress. This is, in essence, the purpose of an insolvency regime for countries. Such a regime needs to establish clear mechanisms for debt restructuring and a mechanism to provide bridge-financing for countries undergoing such restructuring. While outlining the details of an insolvency regime is beyond the scope of this contribution, most proposals that have been made involve some type of credit mechanism providing such sources of finance. (see, e.g., Academic Advisory Council BMWi 2010a; Sachverständigenrat 2011; or Bruegel 2010).

Such a credit mechanism as part of an insolvency regime must be distinguished from funds that are used to generally stabilise prices of government bonds of selected Euro area member countries. Buying bonds on the secondary market in order to ensure the proper functioning of financial markets is likely to prove insufficient in situations of financial market distress. It is likely to generate speculation on further interventions, and eventually render the funds available to the ESM as being insufficient. The ongoing discussions about leveraging the ESM, to increase the firewalls, and to provide the ESM with direct access to central bank refinancing by giving it a banking licence show that this mechanism is already at work. Unless the causes of the debt problems, i.e. the weaknesses of the real economies and the resulting banking sector problems are addressed, there will be continued pressure on the ECB to assume the role of a "lender of last resort". Not least, overburdening the ESM might eventually also have negative effects for the borrowing capacities of the stronger Euro area members.

Instead, lending through the ESM should take place only under strict conditionality and only in the context of a well-defined debt restructuring procedure. Lending through the ESM will always involve an element of moral hazard because it allows sharing the burden of excessive borrowing in the past. It is thus all the more important to ensure that creditors have the right incentives in the future.

The claim that ESM funding should provide short-term liquidity assistance only to countries undergoing debt restructuring is often considered unrealistic, given the difficulties with private sector involvement in the case of Greece. Yet, this argument overlooks that the Greek debt restructuring took place in a situation in which most outstanding government bonds did not include collective action clauses. Hence, such clauses had to be imposed ex post and in the context of a high degree of pre-existing uncertainty on financial markets. In future debt restructuring cases, collective action clauses would be the norm, thus reducing uncertainty on the part of creditors and ensuring a more orderly debt restructuring. Also, debt restructuring in the case of Greece was announced in parallel to other policy measures at the European level, such as the decision of the EBA in autumn of 2011 to increase capital requirements for banks. Hence it is difficult to isolate the impact of debt restructuring on bond markets and prices.

Limiting the role of the ESM to well-defined cases of liquidity support implies that the ESM would not play a major role as a redistributive or shock absorbing mechanism. It will not substitute for a system of fiscal transfers. There are several reasons why a higher volume of fiscal transfers – be it through the ESM, through a system comparable to the German inter-state fiscal transfer system (*Länderfinanzausgleich*), or be it through some form of Eurobonds is neither desirable nor necessary at the European level. It has already been argued above that fiscal transfers in existing currency unions play a limited role when it comes to the smoothing of short-run business cycle fluctuations (section 3.4.). In addition, there are four arguments which need to be considered when discussing the role of fiscal transfers in Europe.

First, there are good reasons to believe that the full potential for countries to insure against income fluctuations via capital and labour markets remains unexploited in Europe. Enhanced labour market integration and the opening up of protected sectors such as in services can provide additional flexibility. Enhanced integration of equity markets can provide an insurance mechanism through cross-border profit sharing. Obviously, market-based insurance mechanisms are not available to or not used by all households. For households not benefiting from direct participation in international capital markets, social security systems can provide the necessary within-country insurance mechanisms. Within-country insurance mechanisms can provide insurance against, for instance, unemployment to the extent that shocks hitting firms and workers are sector-specific or region-specific but not country-specific.

Second, enforcement of stricter fiscal rules through the Fiscal Compact and the strengthened Stability and Growth Pact will certainly limit the ability of governments to use anti-cyclical fiscal policies quantitatively. But these new rules do not prevent governments from running fiscal surpluses in goods times, which can be used to buffer adverse income shocks in bad times, and from allowing automatic stabilisers to work.

Third, fiscal transfers bear the risk of reducing incentives to reform and thus to become persistent. Empirical evidence shows that fiscal transfers have tended to delay labour market adjustment (Boldrin and Canova 2001; Obstfeld and Peri 1998), that social transfers in Europe have contributed to a convergence of incomes only in some countries (Bouvet 2010), and that income levels in poorer regions tend to converge to those in richer regions while differences in productivity or in employment growth tend to persist (Becker et al. 2010a; Checherita et al. 2009).

Last but not least, adopting existing fiscal transfer systems in Europe to levels comparable to, for instance, the German situation would be very costly, and this is likely to lack political support. Across German states, about 90% of differences in per capita tax receipts are redistributed (Konrad and Zschäpitz 2011). Implementing a similar system of tax equalisation in Europe would imply a massive increase of the EU budget. This is likely to be opposed politically not only among the existing members of the Euro area. It may also raise the issue of whether increased fiscal transfers should be confined to the core Euro area countries or whether other EU members – notably in Eastern Europe – should be included as well

4.4. Improved Banking Regulation as a Complementary Reform

For the ESM to become part of an efficient and credible crisis resolution mechanism in the longer run, it needs to be backed by a stronger and more resilient financial and banking system. In this regard, three reforms are crucial.

First, strengthening the capital base of banks not only reduces the probability of individual bank failures; it also strengthens the stability of the financial sector as such and reduces the probability of a systemic crisis (see also Hellwig 2010; Academic Advisory Council BMF 2010). Poorly capitalised banks, if hit by a negative shock, need to divest a large share of their assets in order to restore solvency and to prevent regulatory intervention in the short run. If all banks are hit by similar shocks and adjust in a similar fashion, this will trigger downward spirals of prices and markets.[26] Hence, higher bank capital can reduce the large multipliers seen in the recent crisis that translate seemingly small initial shocks into system-wide distress of financial institutions.

Second, the current framework of calculating the capital requirements of banks on the basis of risk-weighted assets should be reformed. Risk weights are based on banks' internal risk models which, by definition, cannot take system-wide developments and counterparty risk sufficiently into account. Risk weights are backward-looking by their very nature because they are calculated based on past data. This suggests that a capital requirement, which is not based on risk weights, the so-called leverage ratio, should be implemented. In the context of the ESM, the current plans to maintain zero risk weights on government bonds issued by Euro area governments when translating the new Basel III regime into European law (CRD IV) are particularly problematic. For a given set of assets with similar default probabilities, banks will have an incentive to invest into government bonds. Additional incentives to invest into government bonds result from liquidity regulations and from the ability to use these assets as collateral for central bank refinancing. Yet, the current situation shows that sovereign exposures are risky, and this should be reflected in risk weights. Moreover, applying zero risk weights to sovereign debt could prove inconsistent with future private sector involvement in debt restructuring.

---

[26] For a more detailed discussion of this multiplier effect and the role of bank capital, see Academic Advisory Council BMWi (2010a).

Third, higher capital requirements alone will not make the banking and financial system more stable. Instead, complementary reforms are needed that include a special resolution regime for banks which eases the unwinding of balance sheet positions and imposes penalties on equity owners. Intervention and resolution mechanisms need to be coordinated internationally. Also, the Second Pillar of the Basel framework should be enhanced in order to strengthen discretionary power to detect and prevent regulatory arbitrage. This is particularly important in order to mitigate the incentives for regulatory arbitrage and for an evasion to the shadow banking system, which are inherent in any proposal for stricter regulations.

It is often argued that higher capital requirements are costly for the real economy because they increase banks' costs of funding, lower credit for the real economy, or increase the costs of borrowing for firms. Yet, higher capital requirements, being phased in gradually and backed by complementary reforms of the governance of the financial sector, need not be costly (see, e.g., Admati et al. 2010; or Kashyap et al. 2010). Banks can adjust to higher capital requirements not only by shrinking their balance sheets. They can also raise new equity to support unchanged or even higher total assets. When comparing the costs of debt and equity finance, it should also be taken into consideration that many tax systems favour debt finance compared to equity finance. If capital requirements are increased, the cost of equity finance might even fall: If, as a result of the regulatory change, banks invest into less risky assets, the risk premium on equity finance falls. Empirical studies show that the costs of higher capital requirements for the real economy in terms of higher lending rates are modest in the mid- to longer-term (see Kashyap et al. 2010, for a summary of the evidence). Moreover, these costs must be weighed against the benefits in terms of increased financial stability: for a given risk structure of assets, banking risks would be buffered by higher capital stocks. It is interesting to note in this context that, historically, capital levels of banks have been significantly above the levels currently observed (Alessandri and Haldane 2009) without impeding economic growth or innovation.

5. SUMMARY: WHAT NEXT?

The Euro area is in the transition to a new institutional regime. Policy-makers are currently setting the course for a future institutional framework combining more stringent crisis prevention tools with an explicit crisis resolution mechanism. In July 2013, the European Stability Mechanism (ESM) shall become operational with a maximum lending capacity of 500 billion EUR and a set of five financing tools. In this chapter, I have argued that a successful operation of the ESM has four key requirements:

First, in the medium to long run, the ESM should be restricted to being an institution that provides liquidity assistance to countries restructuring their (public) debt and thus losing temporary access to financial markets. In order to prevent the ESM from bailing out private investors, private sector involvement will be crucial. If financial support was not conditioned upon private sector involvement, the principle of liability in debt contracts would be violated. Under conditions of very tight ex ante conditionality, the case for access to precautionary credit lines has been made as well. Experience of the IMF with such credit lines as well as the difficulties of imposing ex ante conditionality suggests though that such credit lines are unlikely to be of much importance. In any case, measures to limit moral hazard associated with any credit mechanism must be taken. It is thus important to condition access to ESM funds on the implementation of the Fiscal Compact and of the European surveillance framework. Also, countries' access to ESM funds should be conditional upon the enforcement of a strict regime of banking regulation and supervision. If, in contrast, the aim is to use the ESM as a general mechanism to stabilise financial markets and to buy securities on primary or secondary markets, this would eventually overburden even its stronger members.

Second, in order to make the transition to a new institutional environment succeed, clear mechanisms need to be specified that prevent the ESM from being burdened with legacies from the past in the form of debt overhang. In the short run, policy-makers need to find loss-sharing mechanisms in order to deal with the debt overhang problem. This will involve difficult political decisions, but delaying a solution is unlikely to diminish the problem. Letting the ECB take over the losses might seem an easy solution – but the potential loss of central bank credibility will have detrimental effects. Pressure on the ECB to provide liquidity is unlikely to subside unless the problem of private and public sector debt overhang is addressed.

Third, using Euro area wide funds for the recapitalisation of banks is one possibility to deal with non-performing assets of banks and the debt overhang problem. It would also allow the banks to write off such assets. Yet, governments are unlikely to invoke the recapitalisation option within the current framework of the ESM because they risk sending out negative signals regarding their own financial situation. Therefore, mechanisms should be sought that move the decision of which banks to recapitalise at least partially away from the national level. At the same time, bank recapitalisation can succeed only if banks' portfolios are carefully audited, if corporate governance structures of banks are reviewed, and, if eventually market structures adjust. All this involves close cooperation between supervisory institutions at the national and at the EU level. In order to effectively recapitalise and restructure Euro area banks, the cross-border resolution regime needs to be improved.

Fourth, in order to address the underlying weaknesses and imbalances in the real economy, significant structural reforms are needed. This involves the removal of national and international barriers to entry, labour market reforms, and product market reforms. Enhanced fiscal rules need better enforcement than similar rules in the past. Complementary reforms in the financial sector are needed. In this context, zero risk weights in government bonds as currently envisaged in EU banking regulations are inconsistent with private sector involvement in future debt restructuring cases. Most importantly, better capitalised banks will contribute to enhanced financial stability, thus reducing the probability that ESM funds will have to be used in order to restore financial stability.

BIBLIOGRAPHY

Academic Advisory Council BMWi (German Federal Ministry of Economics) 2008, letter to Minister Michael Glos "Zur Finanzkrise", 10.10.2008, Berlin.

Academic Advisory Council BMWi (German Federal Ministry of Economics) 2009, letter to Minister Michael Glos "Zur Bankenregulierung in der Finanzkrise", 23.1.2009, Berlin.

Academic Advisory Council BMWi (German Federal Ministry of Economics) 2010a, *Reform von Bankenregulierung und Bankenaufsicht nach der Finanzkrise*, April, Berlin.

Academic Advisory Council BMWi (German Federal Ministry of Economics) 2010b, *Überschuldung und Staatsinsolvenz in der Europäischen Union*, Berlin.

Academic Advisory Council BMWi (German Federal Ministry of Economics) 2011, *Realwirtschaftliche Weichenstellungen für einen stabilen Euro*, Berlin.

Academic Advisory Council BMF (German Federal Ministry of Finance) 2010, letter to Minister Dr. Wolfgang Schäuble "Ohne Finanzmarktreformen keine Lösung der europäischen Staatsschuldenkrise", 20.9.2010, Berlin.

Admati, A.R., P.M. DeMarzo, M.F. Hellwig and P. Pfleiderer 2010, "Fallacies, Irrelevant Facts, and Myths in the Discussion of Capital Regulation: Why Bank Equity is Not Expensive", *Preprints of the Max Planck Institute for Research on Collective Goods*, Bonn 2010/42, Bonn.

Alessandri, P. and A. Haldane 2009, "Banking on the State", presentation delivered at the Federal Reserve Bank of Chicago twelfth annual International Banking Conference on "The International Financial Crisis: Have the Rules of Finance Changed?", Chicago, 25 September 2009. http://www.bis.org/review/r091111e.pdf.

Artis, M.J. and M. Hoffmann 2008, "Declining home bias and the increase in international risk sharing" in *Building the Financial Foundations of the Euro: Experiences and Challenges*, edited by Lars Jonung, Christoph Walker and Max Watson, Routledge, pp. 236-252.

Artis, M.J. and M. Hoffmann 2011, "The Home Bias, Capital Income Flows and improved Long-Term Consumption Risk Sharing between Industrialized Countries", *International Finance* 14(3), pp. 481-505.

Astrubali, P., B. Sorensen and O. Yosha 1995, "Channels of Interstate Risk-Sharing: United States. 1963-1990", *Quarterly Journal of Economics* 111, pp. 1081-1110.

Baldwin, R., V. DiNino, L. Fontagné, R.A. De Santis and D. Taglioni 2008, "Study on the Impact of the Euro on Trade and Foreign Direct Investment", *European Economic and Monetary Union Working Paper* 321.

Bank for International Settlements (BIS) 2009, "An Assessment of Financial Sector Rescue Programmes", *BIS Papers* 48, July, Basel.

Barro, R. J. and X. Sala-i-Martin 1991, "Convergence across States and Regions", *Brookings Papers on Economic Activity* 22(1), pp. 107-182.

Becker, S.O., P.H. Egger and M. von Ehrlich 2010a, "Going NUTS: The Effect of EU Structural Funds on Regional Performance", *Journal of Public Economics* 94, pp. 578-590.

Becker, S.O. and M. Hoffmann 2006, "Intra- and International Risk-sharing in the Short Run and the Long Run", *European Economic Review* 50, pp. 777-806.

Berger, H. and V. Nitsch 2010, "The Euro's Effect on Trade Imbalances", *IMF Working Paper* 10/226. Washington DC.

Berka, M. and M.B. Devereux 2010, "What Determines European Real Exchange Rates?", *NBER Working Paper* 15753. Cambridge MA.

Boldrin, M. and F. Canova 2001, "Inequality and Convergence in Europe's Regions: Reconsidering European Regional Policies", *Economic Policy* 16(32), pp. 205-253.

Bouvet, F. 2010, "EMU and the Dynamics of Regional Per Capita Income Inequality in Europe", *Journal of Economic Inequality* 8(3), pp. 323-344.

Bruegel 2010 (ed.), *A European mechanism for sovereign debt crisis resolution: a proposal*. Jürgen von Hagen, Jean Pisani-Ferry, André Sapir, Francois Gianviti, Anne O. Krueger, Brussels.

Bulow, J. and K. Rogoff 1989, "A Constant Recontracting Model of Sovereign Debt, *Journal of Political Economy* 97, pp. 155-178.

Büttner, T. 2002, "Fiscal Federalism and Interstate Risk Sharing: Empirical Evidence from Germany", *Economics Letters* 74, pp. 195-202.

Büttner, T. 2009, "The Contribution of Equalization Transfers to Fiscal Adjustment: Empirical Results for German Municipalities and a US-German Comparison", *Journal of Comparative Economics* 37, pp. 417-431.

Buiter, W. H. and A.C. Sibert 2005, *How the Eurosystem's Treatment of Collateral in its Open Market Operations Weakens Fiscal Discipline in the Eurozone (and what to do about it),* mimeo.

Bundesministerium für Wirtschaft und Technologie (BMWi) 2012, Jahreswirtschaftsbericht *"Vertrauen stärken – Chancen eröffnen – mit Europa stetig wachsen"*, Berlin.

Caballero, R.J., T. Hoshi and A. Kashyap 2008, "Zombie Lending and Depressed Restructuring in Japan", *American Economic Review* 98(5), pp. 1943-1977.

Checherita C., C. Nickel and P. Rother 2009, "The role of fiscal transfers for regional economic convergence in Europe", *ECB Working Paper* 1029, Frankfurt a.M.

De Grauwe, P. and Y. Ji 2012, "Mispricing of Sovereign Risk and Multiple Equilibria in the Eurozone", *CEPS Working Documents*.

Demyanyk, Y., C. Ostergaard and B.E. Sorensen 2008, "Risk sharing and portfolio allocation in EMU", *European Economy – Economic Papers* 334. Directorate General Economic and Monetary Affairs. European Commission. Brussels.

Deutsche Bundesbank 2010, "Zur Problematik makroökonomischer Ungleichgewichte im Euro-Raum", Monatsbericht, July, Frankfurt a.M.

Dickens, W.T., L. Goette, E.L. Groshen, S. Holden, J. Messina, M.E. Schweitzer, J. Turunen and M. Ward 2007, *The Interaction of Labor Markets and Inflation: Micro Evidence from the International Wage Flexibility Project*, Frankfurt a.M.

Doluca, H., M. Hübner, D. Rumpf and B. Weigert 2012, "The European Redemption Pact: An Illustrative Guide", *German Council of Economic Experts, Discussion Paper*, Wiesbaden.

Eaton, J., M. Gersovitz and J. Stiglitz 1986, "The Pure Theory of Country Risk", *European Economic Review* 30, pp. 481-513.

Ehrmann, M., M. Fratzscher, R.S. Gürkaynak and E.T. Swanson 2011, "Convergence and Anchoring of Yield Curves in the Euro Area", *Review of Economics and Statistics* 93(1), pp. 350-364.

Gerlach, S. and M. Hoffmann 2010, "The Impact of the Euro on International Stability and Volatility", in *The Euro: the first decade*, eds. M. Buti, S. Deroose, V. Gaspar and J.N. Martins, Cambridge University Press, pp. 648-670.

Giannetti, M. and A. Simonov 2009, "On the Real Effects of Bank Bailouts: Micro-Evidence from Japan", *FEEM Working Paper* 103.

Giannetti, M. and L. Laeven 2011, "The Flight Home Effect: Evidence from the Syndicated Loan Market During Financial Crises", *Journal of Financial Economics* 104(1), pp. 23-43.

Giannone, D., M. Lenza and L. Reichlin 2009, "Business Cycles in the Euro Area", *ECB Working Paper Series* 1010/February 2009, Frankfurt a.M.

Hellwig, M.F. 2010, "Capital Regulation after the Crisis: Business as Usual?", *Max Planck Institute Collective Goods Preprint*, No. 2010/31, Bonn.

Hildebrand, T., J. Rocholl and A. Schulz 2012, *Flight to Where? Evidence from Bank Investments During the Financial Crisis*, Warwick, mimeo.

Hoshi, T. and A.K. Kashyap 2010, "Will the US Bank Recapitalization Succeed? Eight Lessons from Japan", *Journal of Financial Economics* 97, pp. 398-417.

ifo 2011, "Die europäische Zahlungsbilanzkrise", *ifo Schnelldienst* 64 (16), pp. 1-94.

John, J. and T. Knedlik 2011, "New IMF Lending Facilities and Financial Stability in Emerging Markets", *Economic Analysis and Policy* 41(2), pp. 225-238.

Kalemli-Ozcan, S., B. Sorensen and B. Turan 2007, "Where does Capital Flow? A Comparison of US States and EU Countries 1950-2000", *European Economy, Economic Papers* No. 295.

Kanaya, A. and D. Woo 2000, "The Japanese Banming Crisis of the 1990s: Sources and Lessons", *IMF Working Paper* 00/7, Washington DC.

Kashyap, A.K., J.C. Stein and S. Hanson 2010, *An Analysis of "Substantially Heightened" Capital Requirements on Large Financial Institutions*, University of Chicago and Harvard University, mimeo.

Kohler, W. 2012, *Resolving Sovereign Debt Crises: Opening or Closing the Tap?* University of Tübingen, mimeo.

Konrad, K.A. and H. Zschäpitz 2011, "Die Zukunft der Eurozone", *Ökonomenstimme* 11. July 2011.

Lebrun, I. and E. Pérez 2011, "Real Unit Labor Costs Differentials in EMU: How Big, How Benign and How Reversible?", *IMF Working Paper* 11/109, Washington DC.

Merler, S. and J. Pisani-Ferry 2012, "Sudden stops in the euro area", *Bruegel Policy Contribution* 2012/06, Brussels.

Neary, P. 2006, "Measuring Competitiveness", *The Economic and Social Review*, 37(2), pp. 197-213.

Obstfeld, M. and G. Peri 1998, "Asymmetric shocks: Regional non-adjustment and fiscal policy", *Economic Policy*, pp. 207-247.

OECD 2011, *Main Science and Technology Indicators*, 2011(1), Paris.

Okawa, Y. and E. van Wincoop 2010, "Gravity in International Finance", *Hong Kong Institute for Monetary Research Working Paper* 07/2010, Hong Kong.

Peek, J. and E.S. Rosengren 2005, "Unnatural Selection: Perverse Incentives and the Misallocation of Credit in Japan", *American Economic Review* 95(4), pp. 1144-1166.

Rose, A.K. and T. Wieladek 2011, "Financial Protectionism: the First Test. National Bureau of Economic Research", *NBER Working Paper* 17073, Cambridge, MA.

Sachverständigenrat zur Begutachtung der gesamtwirtschaftlichen Entwicklung 2011, Jahresgutachten 2011: *Chancen für einen stabilen Aufschwung*, Wiesbaden.

Sala-i-Martin, X. 1996, "The Classical Approach to Convergence Analysis", *Economic Journal* 106(437), pp. 1019-1036.

Sapir, A., P. Aghion, G. Bertola, M. Hellwig, J. Pisani-Ferry, D. Rosati, J. Viñals and H. Wallace 2003, "An Agenda for a Growing Europe: Making the EU Economic System Deliver", *Report of an Independent High-Level Study Group established on the initiative of the President of the European Commission*, Brussels.

Schmitz, B. and J. von Hagen 2011, "Current Account Imbalances and Financial Integration in the Euro Area", *Journal of International Money and Finance* 30(8), pp. 1676-1695.

Schuknecht, L, J. von Hagen and G. Wolswijk 2009, "Government Risk Premiums in the Bond Market: EMU and Canada", *European Journal of Political Economy* 25(3), pp. 371-384.

Sinn, H.-W. 2010, "Rescuing Europe", *CESifo Forum 11. Special Issue*. August. Munich.

Sinn, H.-W. and T. Wollmershaeuser 2011, "Target Loans, Current Account Balances and Capital Flows: The ECB's Rescue Facility", *NBER Working Papers* 17626, Cambridge MA.

6. Economic Convergence – The Need for Economic Cooperation and Coordination

Walter Rothensteiner and Valentin Hofstätter

The currency union is one of the central pillars of European integration. For many citizens, the common currency, the euro, is one of the most visible symbols of European identity. Even back when the euro was introduced, it was clear that there had to be common convergence criteria in order to prevent imbalances in public finances. Now, however, the crisis that has erupted in recent years has shown that there is still a great need for reforms in this currency union in particular. Both in economic and political terms, clearer answers are needed to be able to continue pressing forward with European integration.

In this chapter, we would like to discuss possible alternatives with a view to public finances, financial markets and banking sector regulation. In order to draw lessons from the difficult situation that has developed in the last couple of years we will also discuss the handling of existing problems. In section 1 we discuss convergence as a necessity in a fixed currency regime. Section 2 deals with the question whether convergence is also the result of a common currency area, whereas section 3 tackles practical issues like convergence and coordination in Europe. Section 4 examines if flawed convergence is due to a failure of political coordination. In section 5 we show some lessons learned, and section 6 concludes.

1. CONVERGENCE AS A NECESSITY IN A FIXED CURRENCY REGIME

In the midst of the debt crisis in the Euro area, which is often described as a consequence of inadequate economic "convergence" or as the result of too much divergence, a good starting point is to first clarify the provocative question as to why economic convergence is a goal in its own right. After all, generally speaking, a lack of convergence between economic regions and countries is the normal situation (cf. China/USA/Japan), and convergence is not an explicit goal of the economic policies of these countries. In these countries, the explicit economic policy goals are more traditional, easily understood "primary" goals such as stronger economic growth, full employment and/or the individual country's definition of price stability.

Consequently, these countries neither move in synch with each other in terms of economic cycles nor does inflation develop at the same levels or "converge" without there being considerable complaints about this internally or externally or attempts to change it.

Naturally, in such cases, these differences in economic cycles, and thus also in the interest rate cycles and inflation rates (as well as differences in competitiveness over the long term) have consequences: this is reflected in the development of the exchange rates between these countries, which is often characterised by significant swings (e.g., USD versus JPY) or chronic, long-lasting appreciation trends (e.g., CNY versus USD).

As long as these movements in exchange rates are not considered to be a problem, there is no need for "convergence" of any kind.

Unfortunately, however, *developments in exchange rates* can certainly *lead to costs and problems*:

First, the ongoing volatility itself – which can be mitigated with hedging transactions – results in hedging costs and renders trade and investment decisions more expensive. In extreme cases, exchange rate volatility can become so severe, that it creates a barrier to economic transactions and hinders economic potential.

Second, the recent history of the financial markets is full of cases, in which free-float exchange rates between countries have proven to be completely inadequate for offsetting varying real economic developments (i.e. the concept of "fair" exchange rates) and in which chronic, significant under- or overvaluations have built up for long periods of time, initially hampering a country's real economy[1] and finally culminating in a crisis-like situation.

Third, there were and continue to be cases in which a country attempts to manipulate the exchange rate to its (at least ostensible) advantage; in practice, this generally involves keeping the exchange rate artificially low. In extreme cases, this can end up in a race to devalue inflicting significant economic damage, especially if it leads to countermeasures in the form of trade barriers, which subsequently inhibit trade completely. In part, this kind of scenario is seen as being partly responsible for the protracted and very severe nature of the Great Depression in the 1930s.

If this problem is to be avoided, one obvious solution is to implement exchange rate coordination or even fixing.

---

[1] Just consider a country with an overvalued currency, whose economy suffers due to this competitive disadvantage; at the same time, however, countries with undervalued currencies can also run into serious economic problems due to the boom triggered by undervaluation (potentially exacerbated by inflows of "hot money").

Viewed in this light, it is not surprising that a system of fixed exchange rates (Bretton-Woods) was created as a part of the world economic order following World War II, in order to address these problems. Within this system, the exchange rate of every national currency was fixed vis-à-vis the US dollar (with the dollar itself fixed to the gold price), and accordingly the exchange rates between two non-USD currencies were also set.

While this *removed exchange rate fluctuations*, it created the *need for "convergence"*. This system had some offsetting mechanisms (e.g., the exchange rate could be changed if it moved far away from fundamentals), and the widespread use of restrictions on flows of capital made it easier to defend the fixed exchange rate using intervention on the FX markets. Nonetheless, this system finally collapsed in the early 1970s, in part because the economic and monetary policy developments in the various countries (first and foremost in the USA, in contrast to the other industrialised countries) diverged so much that it was no longer possible to maintain a fixed exchange rate.

Whereas most of the rest of the world subsequently settled for the currently prevailing system of freely fluctuating exchange rates, European policy-makers quickly worked towards the establishment of a "European Exchange Rate Mechanism" (ERM) to be joined by all EC countries. This system was introduced on 1 January 1979 and remained in place until 31 December 1998 (when it was replaced by the euro and by the ERM II regime for the non-euro countries).

The decision in favour of a new system of interrelated exchange rates in *Europe* is understandable, because in light of the desired *close economic integration* and cooperation (especially in the common market) some of the *disadvantages of freely fluctuating exchange rates are particularly acute*. However, if one decides in favour of the advantages of such a system of fixed exchange rates, the coordination of economic policy essentially automatically arises as a necessary "secondary goal", in order for such a mechanism to be able to function.

This quickly became clear in the crisis that unfolded within the ERM system: the fixed exchange rates were unable to withstand the pressure exerted on the system, for example due to increasing differences in inflation and the reunification of Germany. Suddenly, Germany's public deficit was significantly larger and as a result of this interest rates rose dramatically, which in turn exerted intense pressure on interest rates throughout Europe. This was irreconcilable with the parities in ERM, in particular because the other ERM members were not able or did not wish to accept this. Market speculation against these fundamentally untenable exchange rate relationships increased the pressure, and in September 1992 the UK was no longer able to withstand and abandoned the exchange rate peg. Following another speculation crisis in July 1993, the exchange rate bands in the ERM system were eventually widened to 15%, thereby broadly removing the function of the mechanism ensuring exchange rate stability.

With regard to *introduction of the euro*, which involves an "irrevocable" pegging of exchange rates for the participating countries, these events taught policy-makers the importance of economic policy coordination, leading to the establishment of "convergence rules" which countries had to comply with before they were allowed to introduce the common currency.

2. IS CONVERGENCE ALSO THE RESULT OF A COMMON CURRENCY AREA?

It is important to note, however, that *the euro is more than just the result of irrevocably fixed exchange rates*. The single currency is part of the process of economic integration in Europe. First, this is politically desirable, as complete economic integration is supposed to essentially render military conflicts on the continent impossible. Second, the euro has a geo-political dimension, as it helps Europe negotiate its interests on par with the other major economic areas. Third, the euro must also be viewed as a response to an increasingly interconnected world. Even without the single currency, the coordination of international politics is a challenge that stems from globalisation. Fourth, an economic area with a common currency is a logical way of ensuring more growth and prosperity via economies of scale and stimulation of competition.

On the one hand, a certain minimum amount of economic commonality and political coordination is a prerequisite for a functioning currency union. On the other hand, however, *a currency union reinforces the process of economic convergence*. For less developed countries, it opens up the chance of a catching-up process, insofar as tested technologies, organisational structures and production procedures are transferred from more developed economies to less developed economies, in order to produce at a lower cost there and to access new markets. In other words, less developed countries import capital and know-how, which often leads to a deficit on the current account, which is financed by direct investment and long-term capital inflows. Over time, there should be convergence in the levels of key macroeconomic indicators such as per capita GDP, wages and productivity, as well as in price levels.

Thus, in fundamental terms, *economic convergence is not only a prerequisite* for a currency union, *it is also the result* of such a union in an ideal case.

3. PRACTICAL ISSUES: CONVERGENCE AND COORDINATION IN EUROPE

Fulfilment of the convergence criteria is the ticket to membership of the currency union. Following this, the necessary economic policy coordination and economic convergence has to be ensured by a relatively lean institutional setting in the currency union, which is based on the following *assumptions* (Pichelmann 2012):

Macroeconomic stability occurs automatically, if firstly public finances (budget deficit, debt) are sustainable and secondly the rate of inflation settles in at a low level. The Stability and Growth Pact was intended to ensure the former, and the European Central Bank was responsible for the latter. Furthermore, the Four Freedoms – free movement of goods, services, people and capital – are intended to ensure the most efficient market conditions. Taking this view, different developments in wages, prices or credit in individual regions or countries are seen as the efficient result of free, private markets in their decisions on the allocation of resources. Within this framework, economic fluctuations are to be mitigated by the usual monetary and fiscal policies. Finally, structural reforms are intended to drive long-term economic growth.

In fact, economic convergence is a prominent phenomenon in Europe. The region of "Wider Europe" (including Western Europe as well as Central and Eastern Europe, CEE) is one of the few major regions where something like economic convergence (in real and nominal terms) takes place. That means that there is a tendency that less wealthy countries are catching up over time. Therefore, it is not surprising that this issue has found the attention of international forecasters and institutions such as the International Monetary Fund or the World Bank. The latter even named Europe a "Convergence Machine".[2]

At the same time, the developments in Ireland and Greece provide a good example of how the achievement of the convergence within Europe over the long term can be a double-bladed sword. Both of these countries were natural candidates for a convergence process. From 1999 (introduction of the euro) until 2007, both posted average GDP growth rates which were in general far higher than the average growth rates registered in the Euro area. While per capita GDP in Germany only increased by 12.4% in the period 1999-2007, Ireland and Greece were able to catch up significantly, posting growth rates of 59.6% and 39.3%, respectively. Indeed, "Emerald Isle" in the north-western corner of the currency union was actually able to surpass Germany in absolute terms of GDP per capita.

On the other hand, there were also clear-cut signs of divergence from the currency union in these two countries, originating from higher inflation rates and excessive wage increases over the years. First, real interest rates were very low, which led to an unhealthy economic boom financed to an excessive degree by lending. Second, the elevated wage and inflation trends represented a real appreciation. In conjunction with excessive wage increases, competitiveness declined and this resulted in rising deficits on the current account. Par-

---

[2] World Bank, Press Release No 2012/240/ECA, http://web.worldbank.org/WBSITE/EXTERNAL/NEWS/0,,contentMDK:23094165~pagePK:64257043~piPK:437376~theSitePK:4607,00.html.

tially related to this aspect, the development of private sector debt (in Ireland) and public sector debt (in Greece) was completely unsustainable.

4. FAILED CONVERGENCE AS A FAILURE OF POLITICAL COORDINATION?

Many of the economic convergence trends in Europe are closely linked with European economic integration, i.e. the European Union (EU) and European Economic and Monetary Union (EMU). However, recent economic setbacks in Europe have also shown that economic convergence is neither given, nor a one way street. Prior to the crisis, a sort of convergence optimism was en vogue in South Western Europe and in CEE. An anticipation of a steady and "natural" catch-up of income levels to the income levels in "core" EMU countries prevailed. However, much of the recent convergence in Europe was based on excessively cheap financing and unsustainable intra-European capital flows. There is a valid question, however, as to *whether the assumptions were incorrect* in a number of ways and *whether the institutional setting was inadequate*:

Public finances: Monitoring of public deficits was guided more by power relationships than by clear-cut rules. The Stability and Growth Pact was undermined in the implementation of sanctions on Germany and France. Furthermore, there was no consolidation of public budgets with high levels of debt (Greece and Italy), and the focus was shifted too strongly to the budget balances.

Mitigation of cyclical divergencies: Differing GDP growth rates are the logical consequence of the path to convergence. Accordingly, by default, the uniform *monetary policy* is too expansive for the group of catching-up countries and often too restrictive for the group of countries which already enjoy high standards of living. In fact, in some countries this led to strongly expansive monetary policy stimulus, which was not countered by suitable fiscal measures.

The *four freedoms* are a prerequisite for efficient markets, but cannot prevent the *development of significant imbalances*. Indeed, these freedoms are found to be a catalyst for expectation bubbles, which lead to exaggerated developments in the real economy and the financial market. One important reason why these imbalances in the real economy are difficult to alleviate may be the overly low level of labour market mobility between countries in the Euro area; although this mobility is possible *de jure*, in *de facto* terms it is much lower than in the USA, for example (where there are no language barriers).

Against the backdrop of the relatively expansive economic policy management, the growth boom in some countries was misinterpreted as a long-term, sustainable growth trend within the framework of the convergence process. In other words, *potential growth was overestimated*, which had numerous *grave consequences*:

- First, strong wage growth expectations led to a lending boom. In relation to this, bubbles often developed in the real estate sector and there was a boom in private consumption demand.
- Second, wage developments outstripped the gains in productivity, which resulted in a deterioration of the relative competitiveness within the currency union. As a result, massive current account deficits were racked up, which were characterised more by consumer goods and less by capital goods.
- Third, the improvement in budget balances was not sustainable. The rising tax revenues were seen as being permanent (e.g., real estate tax in Ireland), and the development of spending did not move in harmony with the long-term possibilities. Accordingly, the fiscal policies in some countries did (too) little to counter the expansive monetary policy.

Far too often, efforts to move forward with *structural reforms* turned out to consist of empty promises in complex strategy papers at the EU level (Lisbon Agenda). Lacking real pressure or sanctions, the implementation of growth-stimulating reform measures by national policies remained limited. Furthermore, the needs in many countries were underestimated.

In this regard, it is impossible to adequately stress the importance of structural, supply-side reforms designed to increase the possible long-term growth path of an economy (e.g., more flexible labour market regulations, improvement of a country's attractiveness as a location for doing business, in terms of taxes as well, thus promoting inflows of FDI, which boost productivity and thus a country's potential economic growth via the related transfer of productive capital and know-how). Many examples in Eastern Europe in the last decade highlight how sustainable convergence and a process of economic catching-up can be successfully pursued with such reforms; unfortunately, there are also plenty of negative examples in Europe, featuring countries in which the failure to address such structural reforms has led to major economic problems over the long run and only allowed for a kind of temporary "false" convergence, based on a massive increase in debt.

Some *Western European* economies abused the cheap funding that came with their Euro zone entry to boost private and public spending beyond the economy's production capacity. Temporarily high growth rates pushed the need to counter country-specific economic weaknesses (e.g., a weak international competitiveness position or poor labour market conditions) to the background.

Consequently, growth was partially based on the accumulation of private debt and an overly expansive economic policy. The ensuing *self-enforcing boom cycle* was facilitated by the abundant inflow of (financial) capital. The robust economic growth also resulted in a distorted view of the fundamentals in relation to financing decisions by non-residents. Thus, the easy availability of external funding functioned like a massive bellows, inflating external imbalances (e.g., current account deficits) and unhealthy developments in the domestic economy (e.g., oversized construction sector). The boom finally came to an end when the real estate market bubble burst at the global level, and now these credit-fuelled excesses must be worked off.

Some *Eastern European* economies *also abused the cheap funding* that came with the integration of their banking systems into the global financial markets and the cheap funding of the last global leverage cycle. Consequently, there is some deleveraging need in some (mostly South-)Eastern European countries as well.

The developments on the capital markets in the course of the European economic and financial crisis can also be seen as another aspect of the *lack of economic policy governance and coordination mechanisms* at the overall European level. Confidence in the previous boom regions in Europe eroded, partly due to the persistent economic turmoil and partly due to the excessive budget deficits and mounting public debt levels. This occurred hand in hand with a *freeze in external financing*, and some countries are also facing the phenomenon of capital flight. Private creditors from Northern and Western Europe have been scaling back their transfers of capital, which had helped to finance private and public indebtedness, and the budget and current account deficits in the GIIPS countries in the past. This has resulted in high interest rates on new loans, the risk of a credit crunch and ultimately the risk of a depression, which undermines the efforts to consolidate private and public finances.

Since 2010, these flows of private capital have been replaced with public funds (safety nets with IMF support) and central bank liquidity, stemming from ad-hoc programmes which stretch the limits of legal legitimacy based on the EU contracts. By contrast, in the USA and the UK, which are actually in overall worse shape than the Euro area as a whole, there are no signs of a financing freeze in certain areas of the country or at the broader level of the national economy either. And it may turn out to be one of history's ironic footnotes that an important, successful step against the panicked withdrawal of private capital occurred not for the Euro zone countries, but rather for the European countries which were not members of the currency union: thanks to the "Vienna Initiative" it was possible to *avert the destructive phenomenon of capital flight in Central and Eastern Europe* with a coordinated approach by Western banks and public financing organisations.

Recent crisis events in Western Europe and CEE have shown that there are many *risks* during a longer-term *convergence process*, including *self-enforcing boom bust cycles in the private and financial sector* and a lack of fiscal discipline in the public sector. However, it is important to stress that there is not something like a "New Divide" in Europe. Some Western and Eastern European countries are just paying the price for past excesses or too much of an "intertemporal" income and consumption smoothing that was based on a shaky foundation in some cases. Therefore, it is clear that there is a *need for more economic cooperation and coordination* in Europe, given the idea that Europe wants to keep its status as a "Convergence Machine".

5. LESSONS LEARNED: MAKING ECONOMIC CONVERGENCE IN EUROPE SAFER

Economic convergence is a good thing. However, we should not be too over-ambitious. Pre-crisis, there was too much convergence optimism in Europe. This holds true for Western Europe and CEE. Convergence towards the wealth and income levels of the most developed Western European economies was seen as a rather easy, not very bumpy, journey. However, the optimism fostered by the pre-crisis convergence in Europe was smashed by some severe setbacks in CEE (in the years 2009-2011) and the EMU sovereign debt crisis (2010-2012). Some CEE countries had to seek international financial assistence to avoid worst-case scenarios in 2009 and 2010 (e.g., Hungary, Romania and Latvia). There had to be behind-the-scenes private and public sector co-ordination (the European Bank Coordination Initiative, or "Vienna Initiative") to stabilise the CEE region. Later on Greece, Portugal and Ireland had to seek support from the International Monetary Fund (IMF) and EU. With Greece, an EMU country essentially defaulted, which represents the first sovereign default in Europe in the last 60 years. The sovereign default of Greece was the largest in modern economic history in absolute USD-terms, outstripping even Argentina. Furthermore, sizeable financial bail-out mechanisms such as the European Financial Stability Facility (EFSF) and its permanent successor, the European Stability Mechanism (ESM), have been put in place. Such instruments and events would have been unthinkable before the crisis. They violate the "non-bail-out" clause inside the EMU. Moreover, risk sharing mechanisms such as the EFSF and ESM install sizeable (conditional) fiscal transfers inside the EMU. Furthermore, the European Central Bank (ECB) started to buy government bonds via its Securities Market Programme (SMP).

Going forward, we must acknowledge that nominal and real *economic convergence must be backed by economic fundamentals and reasonable economic policies, i.e. a sustainable degree of structural convergence*. For example, the current economic integration and institutional framework of the Euro zone is undoubtedly more than usual for a set of individual countries with a fixed exchange rate regime, but is apparently less than what is needed for a fully integrated monetary union. The deep crisis demands a decision either going half way back and abandoning the common currency or going all way through. More generally, at the EU level most experts perceive a lack of

- Economic policy governance (convergence criteria are not comprehensive and sustainable enough
- Fiscal discipline
- Integration of the financial/banking sector

In order to avoid setbacks as seen in CEE in 2009 and 2010 or in Western Europe and to make economic convergence in Europe safer, *several major reforms should be considered*:

A) Better Macroeconomic Surveillance and Governance

Firstly, all EU countries and especially EMU members should be part of transparent and rule-based *macroeconomic surveillance and governance* with adequate incentives (e.g., collective support mechanisms inside the EU and limited joint government refinancing inside the EMU) and sanctions (e.g., partial loss of sovereignty in certain areas). Tighter economic governance inside the EU/EMU will also require an upgrading of independent economic monitoring capabilities at EU level.

B) A Rule-based European Financial Stability Framework

Such a framework inside the EU (for EMU members and non-members) needs to be formalised to better cope with the current and potential future acute financing crises.

C) No Overambitious EMU Entry Timeframes

Moreover, EMU's expansion must be based on a broad-based economic surveillance which should apply to all EU members.

D) Reintroduction of Limited Liability Inside the EU and EMU

This would help to keep their attractiveness and to make tight economic governance work. The motivation to subscribe to tighter governance and limited liability could be enhanced via several incentives (e.g., limited common government (re-)financing in the EMU and eligibility for the proposed European Financial Stability framework).

In the following sections, we consider in broader detail the suggestions given above.

Ad A) Better Macroeconomic Surveillance and Governance

Going forward, economic trends in all EU countries need to be monitored following the same broad-based set of indicators. In the past, all EMU candidates and especially the CEE countries were closely monitored in terms of their readi-

ness to join EMU (published in the ECB "Convergence Reports"). This monitoring was based on the Maastricht criteria. However, other indicators to detect
possible external imbalances (reflected in the current account position or an
overvalued effective exchange rate) or internal disequilibria (e.g., credit or asset
price booms, unsustainable wage policies, deteriorating productivity) were also
watched. The performance of existing EU and EMU members in particular was
not monitored in such a coherent way. Implicitly, this procedure benefited EMU
members. This holds especially true since the "Convergence Reports" became
more comprehensive in comparison to the years 1998 or 2000.

The tight "Convergence Report" monitoring reflects the pre-crisis intellectual Western European position. Most European economists and EU officials
considered the eastward enlargement of EMU as its major challenge (i.e. as a
danger for the functioning of the single monetary policy). Boom-bust cycles in
new EMU member states were expected in case of a rapid EMU enlargement.
Therefore, it is an irony of fate that such problems were unfolding inside the
EMU, while most CEE countries were still outside the bloc. In fact, there is
certain evidence that the complex interplay between the current EMU and EU
design could facilitate an unbalanced economic integration with boom-bust
cycles or so called "rotating economic bubbles" inside the EMU (e.g., via the
single interest rate and unrestricted capital mobility). This holds especially true
for fast growing catching-up economies. Therefore, tighter economic governance inside the EMU/EU may also help to mitigate the macroeconomic volatility inside the EMU. This aspect is of importance as its unbalanced economic
integration seems to be one of the main reasons why EMU's long-term growth
performance had been rather poor.

Forceful economic governance inside the EU and EMU in particular must
apply the same standards to all EU countries. There are several proposals as to
which indicators might be included in such in-depth monitoring. Areas to be
covered would include: a public debt sustainability analysis, aspects related to
the overall competitiveness and productivity of an economy, the structure and
strength of domestic demand as well as private and public (external) indebtedness. Indicators to monitor may include: current account data, unit labour
cost and real effective exchange rate trends, external trade performance indicators such intra EU or world market shares as well as the net international
investment position. The indicators that are part of the newly introduced EIP
(Excessive Imbalance Procedure) framework (some of which featured in the
"Convergence Reports") point in this direction.

The appeal of including *current account data or other indicators of external
aspects* is that cheating at the national level would be much more difficult in
comparison to fiscal data. Moreover, problematic economic imbalances and
boom-bust cycles could be identified in a timely manner. The top performing
EMU/EU countries in terms of growth or low unemployment during the crisis

or post-crisis just avoided excessive economic imbalances. Although the focus of tighter governance within EMU/EU would be on macroeconomic aspects, it may also support some degree of minimum microeconomic harmonisation inside the EMU and EU.

Ad B) A Rule-based European Financial Stability Framework for Better Crisis Management in Europe (for EMU Members and Non-Member Countries)

Upgrading economic governance inside the EU should make the EMU and the whole EU less crisis prone. However, the EU must still be prepared for adverse scenarios. The EMU sovereign crisis has shown that the EU/EMU lacks centralised crisis management capacity that follows some principles which are known ex-ante. The latter was one of the reasons behind the delay of bankruptcy in the case of Greece. There had to be several ad-hoc stabilisation packages and measures in order to make the Greek (selective) sovereign default manageable and one of the most expected sovereign events in modern history.

Going forward, a *rule-based European financial stability framework* inside the EU, eligible for EMU members and non-members, should be established. The current EFSF is already a step in the direction of a broader European financial stability network. However, a more transparent safety net, focused on short-term and medium-term liquidity assistance (i.e. covering a time horizon of one year to three years) is needed, as the "no assistance at all" approach is not credible anyway. Moreover, an EU-wide financial stability network would also make rushing into the EMU because of instability considerations less attractive. It is obvious that outside the EMU and without the Emergency Liquidity Assistance (ELA) of the ECB framework, Ireland could have experienced a similar meltdown of its financial sector like Iceland. However, the current EFSF/ESM framework is clearly focused on the EMU (although the EFSF rules include a vague statement that the EFSF "could support all European Union Member States"). The same holds true regarding all the direct and indirect government financing and banking sector assistance via the ECB and the European Central Bank System. The creation of a formalised European financial stability framework (with the ECB, its European Systemic Risk Board and a newly created Euroean Monetary Fund (EMF) as important pillars) would also allow for the execution of medium-term, IMF-style stabilisation and reform programmes at country level inside the EU and EMU without the involvement of the IMF. This might be appropriate going forward as Europe must accept a decreasing influence in the IMF and the "European economic model" might be more and more questioned in such institutions such as the IMF or World Bank. However, the current EMU/EU crisis mechanisms are more or less based on participation of the IMF, or at least involvement of the IMF is more or less actively sought.

A rule-based European financial stability framework inside the EU would have to tackle issues such as: How much financial support can a national central bank or government obtain within the European financial stability framework? What would be eligible collateral for short-term liquidity support and possibly foreign exchange swap lines? In order to make the proposed EU-wide European financial stability framework setting effective, relevant institutions should not rely on external sovereign ratings in formulating collateral standards for EMU/EU government bonds that might be used for liquidity support and crisis lending. The ECB and proposed EMF should formulate their own internal standards through cycle creditworthiness assessments. In this regard, they should focus on stand-alone ratings for all EMU and EU countries. Moreover, not only government bonds from EMU members should be accepted within the European financial stability framework as collateral. For instance, it appears odd that the ECB accepts lower rated Greek, Portuguese or Irish government paper or lower rated private sector issuance (in EUR) as collateral, while higher rated (local currency) EU sovereign paper of EMU outsiders is not accepted. European financial stability framework collateral rules could well reflect (possible) currency risks of non-EMU local currency government bonds of European countries. *Such a move would also acknowledge that the European banking sector is well integrated beyond the EMU.* Western European banks from EMU countries dominate in CEE. Moreover, central banks and governments of EMU outsiders could also use their local currency bonds as collateral for swap lines to obtain foreign currency (EUR) within the European financial stability framework in order to secure financial stability. In some CEE countries outside the EMU the euro is in widespread use.

The newly created European financial stability framework should also introduce uncollateralised pre-emptive liquidity facilities for all EU countries. Such facilities should be designed along the lines of IMF's Flexible and Precautionary Credit Line (FCL, PCL) with tight eligibility criteria attached and no or only limited conditionality. It seems embarrassing why a solid EU country like Poland in 2009 (with its FCL application) or Cyprus in 2011 had to turn to the IMF and Russia respectively to secure their short-term foreign currency position or overall financing position. In order to avoid lengthy discussion with the EU/EMU, Cyprus turned to Russia to secure rather cheap and unbureaucratic financial support in 2011. The newly introduced credit lines within the EFSF framework – i.e. the Precautionary Conditioned Credit Line (PCCL), the Enhanced Conditions Credit Line (ECCL) and the Enhanced Conditions Credit Line with sovereign partial risk protection (ECCL+) – are pointing in the right direction. The PCCL and ECCL with a possible lending amount of 2% to 10% of GDP (for 1 year, renewable for 6 months twice) are designed along the lines of IMF's FCL and PCL (i.e. borrowing more or less the access criteria from the IMF rules). However, they are unfortunately limited to EMU members so far.

Ad C) No Overambitious EMU Entry Timeframes

The EMU crisis has shown that overly ambitious timeframes for EMU entry (in Western Europe) have turned out to be costly for the respective countries, for the whole EMU and some bona fide market participants who took disproportionally high risks. Accordingly, EMU entry should not be considered as a panacea for all economic risks and structural weaknesses at country level. Accordingly, there should be no overambitious EMU entry strategies. Recent adverse developments inside the European Monetary Union (EMU) have shown the *imperative need for a sufficient degree of real economic convergence*, in order to secure the sustainability of nominal convergence in EMU member countries. Otherwise the centralised monetary policy of the European Central Bank (ECB) may turn out to be inappropriate. The absence of monetary and nominal exchange rate flexibility as tools to stabilise the domestic economy in the case of economic shocks can cause a challenging situation in EMU members without a sufficient degree of nominal and real convergence. These lessons are of importance for all remaining EMU candidates, most of them being current or future EU members in Central and Eastern Europe (CEE). Even if an EMU candidate is able to fulfil the nominal Maastricht entry criteria at one point in time, entering EMU is not always an optimal strategy at every point in time. There is sufficient evidence that a sustainable degree of nominal and real convergence vis-à-vis the so-called "core" European countries is indispensable before joining EMU. We do not hint purely at criteria such as fiscal headline deficits, but also at external imbalances, other indicators of the international competitiveness position or the overall wealth level of a given economy. Otherwise, ECB's monetary policy stance – for the most part determined by the "core" EMU members – may turn out to be inappropriate. In the absence of basic tools (i.e. monetary policy or exchange rate flexibility) to smooth their domestic economic cycles, premature EMU members are at risk of excessive output volatility (i.e. boom-bust cycles and balance of payment crises).

However, Europe needs *better crisis management mechanisms open to non-EMU EU members* as well (as was dsicussed in the section about a proposed European financial stability framework) to avoid making a rush into the EMU a preferred strategy. Moreover, it must be stressed that some potential long-term benefits of EMU membership (e.g., efficiency gains and increasing competition) cannot be separated easily from the effects of European economic integration, i.e. the European Common Market. EMU is not a stand-alone project and is accompanied by a variety of economic integration efforts inside the EU. More important, EMU membership does not offer a "free lunch". Recent experience in the context of the EMU (sovereign debt) crisis made a paradigm change necessary. This holds especially true with regards to some of the frequently cited advantages of EMU membership (e.g., EMU as a sort of "safe haven" with low country risk premia). Nevertheless, weighing all the pros and cons, entering EMU remains an attractive option for well-prepared candidates.

More Sophisticated EMU Entry Test

Pricing on European government bond markets changed completely during the EMU sovereign debt crisis. The "convergence-trade" pricing changed to a pricing based on economic fundamentals and political risks at the country level. Country risk premia for some EMU members are back to pre-EMU (stand-alone) levels. Therefore, risk-wise some EMU outsiders from CEE are currently trading well below some EMU countries on international sovereign debt markets. This reasonable pricing reflects low public debt sustainability problems in EMU outsiders from CEE as well as more favourable international competitiveness positions. By contrast, some EMU member countries have lost their biggest benefit of entering EMU: financing costs close to the "risk-free" European benchmark (i.e. German Bunds). Hence, incentives to join EMU to profit from low interest rates have also decreased. Moreover, the introduction of tighter economic governance inside EMU – the enforcement power in EMU is higher than inside the EU – could also make EMU entry less attractive for some outsiders. In order to calm voters in "core" EMU countries, economic policy initiatives may spread to issues such as taxation, wages, harsh financial markets regulation, etc. However, some comparative advantages outside the EMU and in CEE are based on competitive taxation and wages or special financial sector regulation, as in the UK. Moreover, some catching-up CEE economies outside EMU have also managed the global crisis in good shape, due to their nominal exchange rate flexibility. Current EMU outsiders with an opt-out as well as the *de facto* opt-out of Sweden or countries like Czech Republic or Poland clearly demonstrated that being outside the EMU could be a feasible strategy. However, due to the formal duty to introduce the euro (the only formal exceptions are granted to UK and Denmark), remaining outside EMU was largely considered as bad in pre-crisis times. Going forward, membership should not be forced on countries not yet fit for handling the economic pressure inside EMU. Even if the nominal euro adoption criteria are fulfilled, the example of several peripheral countries shows that the hurdle for remaining fit once having joined EMU are higher than previously thought. Furthermore, from a moral point of view, Sweden and the CEE countries, which are still obliged to enter EMU, should have a fair choice. EMU and EU have changed since their EU entry. Moreover, some policy-makers in CEE were shocked by the formal and narrow interpretation of the ECB's mandate in the context of the EMU sovereign debt crisis. Furthermore, EMU membership is not rating positive *per se*. The rating agency Standard and Poor's rightly punished some peripheral EMU members in a recent upgrade of its sovereign rating methodology. Countries such as the EMU peripherals (i.e. which differ substantially from the core of the EMU) receive a lower score for monetary flexibility.

In case European integration (becoming a member of the European Union) is considered possible without EMU membership, issues related to the EU enlargement could be separated from issues related to EMU. This aspect may gain in importance going forward. It is unlikely that new EU members (e.g., from the Western Balkans, possibly Turkey) will be ready or willing to join EMU quickly. Separating EU and EMU membership may also help to stimulate more enlightened debates about the pros and cons of joining EMU. Candidates would be encouraged to ask themselves relevant questions beyond the (current) formal EMU entry criteria. For instance, the "British Euro test" was based on five aspects:

● *Economic harmonisation*: Is the economy sufficiently harmonised with EMU on a sustained basis (e.g., in terms of needed interest rates)?
● *Economic flexibility*: Is there enough flexibility to cope with a domestic recession (monetary and fiscal flexibility are limited inside EMU)?
● *Impact on investments*: Would joining EMU really create better conditions for (foreign) firms making long-term investment decisions?
● *Impact on domestic comparative and competitive advantages*: Would joining EMU fit the current economic (growth) model?
● *Impact on growth and labour market*: Would joining EMU lead to higher growth, macroeconomic stability and a lasting job increase?

As long as there is no straightforward "Yes" answer to *all* the aforementioned questions no candidate should subscribe to an "as soon as possible" EMU entry strategy. Entering EMU makes sense only for candidate countries which are structurally and mentally well-prepared. Therefore, EMU needs a proper assessment regarding the ability of candidates to join. Hence, the *EMU entry criteria must be harmonised in line with the proposed economic governance* inside the EU/EMU. The *sustainability of nominal and real economic convergence*, based on a broad-based monitoring, should become the *key entry test*. Such an upgraded qualification test would make sure that window-dressing aiming at fulfilling some criteria at one point in time would not help. Candidates would be motivated to pursue credible EMU entry strategies when their economies are closer to a sustainable equilibrium.

In this context it is important to assure that there is no discrimination between EMU members and non-members. For instance, EU member countries not part of the EMU felt not well informed about issues related to the EMU sovereign debt crisis. However, when Poland (holding the EU presidency in 2011) wanted to join Eurogroup meetings it received express rejection. Moreover, there is a certain disappointment with the EU/EMU crisis management policies in CEE. During the early phase of the global financial crisis (when CEE countries were in the focus of financial markets) EU institutions as well as the ECB were tough on respecting the institutional roadmap for entering EMU and the institutional limits for support among EU countries. The ECB remained rather tough on providing emergency liquidity to CEE countries. However, in the wake of the EMU sovereign debt crisis European institutions have started to interpret the governance principles of the EU/EMU in a much more flexible way.

Ad D) Limited Liability, EMU Exit and Debt Restructuring Mechanism

It is useful to distinguish between reforms induced by the desire to become a member of EU or EMU and the reform appetite once membership is secured. The Vice Governor of the Czech National Bank summed it up nicely in saying that EMU did not stimulate reforms in some countries. By contrast, EMU membership made it possible to "borrow like a thrifty German and spend like a profligate Greek".[3] However, *systemic bail-outs* of EMU members (as in the case of Greece) *must be avoided*. They are a worst case scenario for a monetary union. Hence, a reinforcement of the limited financial and fiscal liability principle among the EMU/EU members in case of an "unsustainability of debts" would serve as a logical step to foster the national ownership. Moreover, the proposed tighter economic governance would lack enforcement. At this juncture, it is also important to stress: historical experience shows that most currency unions did suffer from a gradual loosening of its founding principles.

Enforcement of a limited liability principle inside the EMU and EU would require the introduction of a European Sovereign Debt Restructuring Mechanism (ESDRM) for highly indebted governments. The costly ad-hoc Greek government debt restructuring is not a viable benchmark. It can be hardly applied to other or bigger EU/EMU countries. The planned introduction of collective action clauses (CACs), well established in emerging markets where there had been frequent public debt restructurings, into EMU sovereign bond contracts points in the right direction. CACs facilitate effective debt restructuring. In a worst case scenario, the ESDRM may lead to a general restructuring of all non-commonly financed national public debt. Creditors would be punished for imprudent investments based on moral hazard or utopian convergence assumptions. Moreover, Western European policy-makers and EU officials should also closely study past sovereign debt restructurings in Emerging Markets. Experience there shows that a well tackled sovereign debt restructuring must not lead *per se* to long-term capital flight and the inability to tap international financial markets.

There are some well developed proposals as to how an ESDRM scheme (e.g., in a so-called "Frankfurt Club" and with the inclusion of a proposed

---

[3] "Eastern Europe pushes back euro adoption", Financial Times, 12 June 2011.

EMF) might look like.[4] A well-designed sovereign debt resolution framework would also put the EMU/EU in a leading position in terms of economic governance. The introduction of such an insolvency regime for countries is a long-standing economic policy discussion. No progress has been achieved in this direction so far at the global level. However, a sovereign debt restructuring inside the EMU/EU should not come at too low economic and reputational costs. Otherwise it may create the wrong incentives. Moreover, the (re-)introduction of a limited liability must be clearly separated from short-term and medium-term liquidity assistance under the proposed European financial stability framework with a *strong and independent EMF* as an institution to distinguish between a liquidity and solvency problem.

Introducing the ESDRM would – to a certain extent – also help to avoid the discussion whether one or some members should leave EMU. Public debt stock problems could be solved within the ESDRM. Private sector debt restructurings are not a technical problem and the proposed economic governance should help to avoid serious structural economic weaknesses in EU/EMU countries anyway. *Nevertheless, exit clauses and exit procedures for leaving EMU should be made explicit.* They would make the exit costs relative to short-term political costs of harsh economic adjustments more transparent. An explicit EMU exit clause would also help to reap the advantages of a fixed exchange rate regime as a powerful incentive for fiscal discipline. If a country runs excessively lax fiscal policies under a unilateral fixed exchange rate regime imports are set to rise. In the end, this may become a threat for foreign exchange reserves and eventually the exchange rate itself. Risks to the exchange rate itself were precisely one reason for the successful consolidation and economic rebalancing in CEE countries such as Bulgaria or in the Baltic countries. Moreover, a serious exit clause will also require that the legal and practical consequences of an EMU exit are handled in level-headed way. Issues such as bank account freezes, bank holidays, capital controls or an orderly redenomination of EUR-denominated debt and claims of the ECB on a national bank of a country leaving the EMU would have to be addressed. Moreover, economically stronger EMU countries will not remain hostage of financially distressed member states, while the possibility of a limited EMU split-up (i.e. orderly exit of one or more EMU countries) may calm fears about a disorderly full-blown EMU break-up, due to a badly managed crisis in one or some economically weaker and not-committed member countries. Furthermore, ESDRM introduction would make an EMU exit a possible scenario.

Reinforcing the limited liability principle inside the EU and especially EMU would also ensure that the intra-EU or intra-EMU solidarity will not be overstretched. The solidarity of economically stronger EMU countries should not and cannot be overstretched. A lot of payer countries for the recent EMU rescue

---

[4] For the currently most famous and feasible proposal see Gros and Mayer (2010).

packages are also burdened with high public debts and long-term sustainability issues. Moreover, the *bail-out capacity of the EMU should not be overrated.* On average, EMU does not have a Triple "AAA" rating.[5] Currently, four to six "AAA" rated EMU members (out of 17 EMU members, depending on the criterion of having a Triple "AAA" rating by all three important agencies or not) shoulder the bulk of the EMU rescue costs. In terms of GDP, Germany represents 45% of this six-country alliance. Moreover, intra-European solidarity is not as strong as the solidarity within a sovereign nation. The EMU rescue packages caused a strong deterioration in pro-European attitudes in societies characterised by a certain degree of "political correctness" (e.g., Germany, Finland). Not to forget that all current EMU rescue packages were designed during an economic upturn cycle in payer countries. The willingness to provide support might not be the same in a downturn. Thus, reinforcing limited liability would also be a hedge against political risks, i.e. payer countries could refrain from supporting other EU/EMU countries due to domestic political pressure.

An effective cap on intra-EU transfers while tackling sovereign debt problems inside EMU with the help of an ESDRM would also make EMU membership more attractive. This holds especially true for many of the CEE countries. Most of them inherited low public debt stocks from the communist times. Moreover, the CEE region showed an impressive economic reform drive during the last 20 years. As most prominent and recent examples, the Baltic countries and Bulgaria embarked on a painful "internal devaluation", i.e. bringing down wages and prices relative to competitors via deflationary policies (including massive wage cuts in the public and private sector). These policies helped to rebalance the economies and to keep the fixed exchange rates versus the euro. These countries have well understood the constraints of a fixed exchange rate (as in EMU). Such adjustments would be also needed in hard hit and uncompetitive EMU economies. However, currently only the consolidation in Ireland seems to be along the lines of the efforts seen in CEE. Therefore, it is difficult to sell large-scale support schemes for Western European reform laggards in CEE. Interestingly, this holds partially also true in some Western European countries, such as Germany or Sweden, which carried out painful reforms in the last two decades.

---

[5] Currently the EMU would have a GDP-weighted average "AA-" rating (by Standard and Poor's), mostly driven by larger "AAA" countries. However, 13 out of the 17 members do not have an "AAA" rating (Standard and Poor's, January 2012). Hence the unweighted average rating of the EMU is even at a lower "A" level.

6. CONCLUSIONS

The governance reforms discussed in this chapter are in the best interest of the EU and especially EMU. They would help to secure sustainability and may help to boost internal credibility. They would also help to fully reap the economic benefits of EU and EMU. Going forward, both of these constellations will be increasingly measured in terms of their economic benefits rather than their historic "peace-keeping role". EU and EMU must prove their ability to function as a positive sum game. However, upgrading governance inside the EU/EMU will not be easy. There remains the political risk that such a move will be interpreted as capture of Europe and EMU by German economic policy ideas. By the way, the old EFSF (with its lean structure) was largely based on the support of the German Debt Management Office, i.e. the "Bundesfinanzierungsagentur".

Moreover, the enhanced macroeconomic governance should not result in a large-scale harmonisation and micro-management; otherwise another round of convergence optimism could re-emerge. However, the proposed European Sovereign Debt Restructuring Mechanism (ESDRM) should help to avoid another round of excessive "convergence speculation" on financial markets that is not backed by economic fundamentals on a country level.

Putting EMU/EU economic governance on a stronger footing could also help to re-establish its external credibility. A lot of cash-rich international investors prefer buying US government bonds instead of EMU government bonds (with the exception of German Bunds), although many indicators of the US economy look worse than for the EMU on aggregate. From a long-term perspective, Europe needs these investors. Going forward, major European capital exporters (e.g., Germany, the Netherlands) will have less capacity to export capital to other Euro countries due to their challenging demographic outlooks.

There are also several attempts to push forward regional economic and monetary integration outside of Europe. All these attempts (e.g., in the Middle East, CIS or Africa) are inspired by the EU and EMU. Recent crisis experience in Europe should be studied closely there. The EMU sovereign debt crisis has shown that a monetary union requires an extremely high degree of economic convergence, including a convergence of formal and informal institutions. Moreover, the EMU (sovereign debt) crisis has shown the risks of a low degree of institutional capacity at a later stage of an economic integration. If a regional economic integration were to accept monetary integration as an overriding goal more integrated economic, financial sector oversight and political structures than in the EU/EMU would be needed. If a regional grouping were to accept monetary integration as an overriding goal it would be also appropriate to allow for a multi-speed economic and monetary integration. Not all members of a regional grouping must join the respective monetary integration. The experience of EMU shows that the issue of being a member of a so-called "core" of a regional integration, such as EMU, must be depoliticised.

BIBLIOGRAPHY

Gros, D. and T. Mayer (2010), "How to deal with sovereign default in Europe: Create the European Monetary Fund now!", *CEPS Policy Briefs*, No. 202, 17. May 2010.

Merler, S. and J. Pisani-Ferry (2012), "Sudden stops in the Euro area", *Breugel policy contribution*, issue 2012/06, March 2012.

Oesterreichische Nationalbank (2011), "The future of European integration: some economic perspectives", in *Proceedings of the 39th Economics Conference 2011*.

Pichelmann, K. (2012), "Old dogs learning new tricks? Macroeconomic surveillance in EMU re-designed", Presentation WIFO, Vienna, 6 March 2012.

Raiffeisen RESEARCH (2010), *Divergenz in der Eurozone – Bedingungen für das Funktionieren einer Währungsunion*, Juni 2010.

7. Banking System and Financial Stability

Andreas Ittner

1. LESSONS FROM THE CRISIS

The causes behind the financial crisis, the aftermaths of which are still unfolding, are diverse and multifaceted. They range from macroeconomic conditions to flaws in firms' risk management and corporate governance, as well as to issues regarding regulation and supervision (De Larosière et al. 2009; Turner 2009). In addition, there is the central issue of pervasive incentive problems within the financial system, which comprises agency problems on the one hand between banks' investors and banks' management, and on the other hand between banks' stakeholders and the general public (Calomiris 2009).

From a supervisor's point of view, some of the underlying factors, arguably not the least important ones, are exogenous to their domain, and are likely to persist in the future. Financial supervisors cannot do much about issues such as global imbalances and an environment of low interest rates, ample liquidity and a general low risk perception coupled with a high risk appetite among participants in financial markets.

2. FINANCIAL HISTORY AND "THIS TIME IS DIFFERENT"

When credit spreads have been stable, volatility low, liquidity plentiful, and markets booming for quite a while, no one wants supervisors to get in the way. There is pervasive talk about regulatory pause, proficiency of risk management systems and efficiency of capital markets. Prudential backstops to the financial system are not deemed necessary. Supervisors are supposed to stand on the sidewalk and not to disturb the party going on in the markets. Typically, in such benign conditions systemic risks are overlooked or grossly underestimated. No one can, or wants to imagine that things could go severely wrong. A "This time is different mood" prevails and is easily coupled with a good story that sounds sufficiently plausible for the time being (Reinhardt and Rogoff 2009).

The author would like to thank Ulrich Gunter and Alexander Trachta, both with the Financial Markets Analysis and Surveillance Division of Oesterreichische Nationalbank, for their kind research assistance.

It is possible under such circumstances that supervisors too get lulled into a false sense of security and join the happy crowd, instead of resolutely leaning against the wind.

Historical evidence clearly indicates that unsustainable development in financial markets and the building up of severe systemic risk, which ultimately leads to financial crises, emanate in prolonged periods of economic and rapid credit growth. As has been prominently stated, banks "keep dancing while the music plays". Otherwise they would risk losing market shares. As a result, risk costs tend to be projected at the low end to enable "competitive" interest rates. Once the dynamics in financial markets decelerate, it turns out that pricing of credit was too low to cover the real risks. Then, banks need to urgently deleverage and increase credit margins sharply to cover not only the true risk costs of new loans, but also to recover some of the risk costs that were not priced into the existing loan portfolio. The pre-crisis credit boom breaks and suddenly turns into a post-crisis credit bust. These are repeated lessons from financial history, which supervisors must heed well.

Concerning the financial crisis, there were also shortcomings in the regulation and supervision of the banking sector. The amount and quality of capital in the banking system are generally within the remit of supervision. However, many big banks stumbled into the financial crisis with historically very low levels of capital. And the risk bearing capacity of much of the available capital base was found wanting under conditions of real stress. Deficiencies in banks' risk management and corporate governance have become further issues of concern to supervisors, as today it seems clear that often boards of directors did not comprehend either the nature or scale of the risks their institutions were facing, and risk management processes were flawed. And that corporate governance arrangements did not effectively correct agency problems between banks' top management and shareholders, let alone the public interest.

3. THE PROPER ROLE OF BANKING

Before trying to outline the most important areas for regulatory improvement from a supervisor's perspective, some considerations on the proper role of financial intermediation through the banking system are due.

Progress and growth of an economy are inextricably linked with uncertainty about the future. For instance, firms' investment projects such as research for new or improved products and services, on which progress and growth ultimately rely, are associated with risk. Since a single firm typically is not endowed with enough own funds to fully finance all its promising ideas on its own, it needs access to a source of external funding, which is not only able to provide the necessary financing today for the benefit of expected positive returns in the future, but which is also able to take over part of the risk associated with a possible failure of a particular investment project.

Hence, for the progress and growth of an economy, its single sectors such as households, firms, the government, or the financial system need to be involved in a risk-sharing process according to their capability and responsibility. In particular, the banking sector plays a crucial role as risk bearer, risk manager, and risk distributor by fulfilling its core functions of risk transformation, maturity transformation, and lot-size transformation via collecting deposits from households and granting loans to firms with a view to financing promising investment projects. Given that, conducting banking activities with zero risk is not possible.

High credit growth, however, that is based on lending spreads not covering the true risk costs is both detrimental to financial stability and economically inefficient. Ultimately, the purpose of banking intermediation is transforming short-term deposits into a stable and sustainable supply of long-term credit to the real economy. This is the policy goal that regulation must attempt to bolster and that supervisors must not lose sight of even under benign market conditions.

At the moment, traditional loan financing by banks is no longer perceived by corporates as the most reliable and stable form of financing as risk premia measured by credit default swap (CDS) spreads on European banks have been higher than those of European non-financial corporates for quite a while: as of mid-September 2012, the spread between the iTraxx Senior Financials 5Y and the iTraxx Corporates 5Y was still around 83 basis points. On the one hand, this development may suggest a certain regime shift towards a more market-based financing by creating the incentive for corporates to explore new funding sources by issuing bonds, thus increasing the importance of the corporate bond market. On the other hand, the question arises, why undiversified risks of single corporates should be better priced than the diversified risks incorporated in bank bonds. Most likely, this phenomenon constitutes a temporary anomaly, which is based on the current lack of confidence in banks rather than on long-term fundamentals.

4. WELL-DIVERSIFIED UNIVERSAL BANKS ARE MORE RESILIENT

Given the traditionally bank-based European financial system, we still need to draw a possible solution for making existing European banks' business models more sustainable and resilient in the future.

As noted in the ECB report on "EU Banking Structures" (ECB 2010) European universal banks characterised by a diversified business model (meaning banks that combine in their business portfolio commercial bank activities such as retail and corporate banking with private banking and investment bank activities) proved more resilient than specialised banks (e.g., pure investment banks whose business models rely exclusively on market-based services) through the height of the financial crisis as measured by net income for the years 2007 to 2009. These well-diversified banks could take advantage of the synergies obtained by combining the different bank activities.

The main reason for this greater resilience was more sustainable business models, which could be described by the following characteristics: strong customer relationships and more stable funding sources – such as customer deposits – making diversified banks less reliant on wholesale funding and on average more resilient to liquidity shocks, balanced sources of revenue resulting from the cross-selling of products, which helps to maintain profitability, as well as economies of scale resulting from cost-sharing across geographical areas and businesses.

Moreover, even though the average long-term profitability of specialised banks was higher than that of diversified commercial banks (14.8% vs. 13.1%) between 1997 and 2006, the profits of diversified commercial banks were less volatile and less affected by financial distress due to the aforementioned synergy effects.

5. SYSTEM STRUCTURE VERSUS SYSTEM GOVERNANCE

An interesting question is what the main drivers are of success or failure of financial systems in the financial crisis. Is it the structure of a financial system, or are issues of governance more important?

In light of the development of market-based indicators such as stock market capitalisation per GDP, the world share in derivative trading, or the issuance of asset-backed securities between 1980 and 2000 and even more so after the year 2000 until the onset of the global financial crisis in 2007, it seems that the traditionally bank- or relationship-based (continental) European financial system has gradually become more market-based over the last almost 30 years (Rajan and Zingales 2003). This evolution was fostered primarily by increases in international trade and capital movements (worldwide financial integration), the progress in information technology (availability of and easy access to market data), as well as the intensified monetary and political integration within the European Union, all of which are potentially able to make the bank-based European system more competitive.

Empirical findings based on BankScope data from 1997 to 2005 for the EU of 25 also back this view as too much concentration (in terms of the market share of the five largest domestic banks per banking sector) in national European banking sectors undermines their financial soundness as measured by their Z-score since fewer diversification opportunities are used (Uhde and Heimeshoff 2009).[1]

On the contrary, apart from traditional market-based financing via equity and bonds, not every market-based financial innovation such as residential and commercial mortgage-based securities whose large-scale default triggered the first wave of the ongoing crisis in the United States back in 2007 eventually proved a sustainable market-based alternative to bank-based financing (mostly due to a lack of transparency on the part of the investor and asymmetric information about the asset quality of the underlying mortgages).

Bank-based financing – or, in other words, financing through a financial intermediary – may generally have the advantage of a reduction of ex-post information asymmetry in terms of less costly state verification of the profitability of debtors' investment projects over a direct market-based relationship between creditor and debtor. The reason for this phenomenon as argued by Diamond (1984) is that financial intermediaries can realise economies of scale by jointly surveilling a large number of debtors and thus reduce the cost of state verification relative to the case when each debtor would have to be surveilled by its creditor in a purely market-based environment. However, the mere availability of (well-designed) market-based financing as an alternative to bank-based financing should, in principle, promote diversification and reduction of risk on the part of investors and borrowers and simultaneously reduce both banks' total assets and the systemic risk in the banking sector.

Both, purely bank-based and purely market-based financial systems as textbook models are characterised by specific deficiencies. A closer look at real-world financial systems is needed.

The financial sectors of many OECD countries experienced severe turbulences during the crisis, including countries such as the United States or the United Kingdom with a more market-based financial sector as well as countries such as Ireland or Spain with a more bank-based system. Hence, the structure of the market per se does not seem to be crucial to its resilience, fuelling the idea of a well-governed European bank-based financial system being fit for the future.

On the other hand, there are some countries that have weathered the crisis astonishingly well. Canada and the Czech Republic are such examples.

5.1. The Case of Canada

Like in many European countries the Canadian financial system is large compared to the economy, with total assets exceeding 300% of GDP considerably. The financial system is generally bank-based and the banking sector is dominated by six big banks. However, in their domestic market banks need to focus

---

[1] Z-score = (Return on average assets before taxes + Capital in per cent of total assets)/Standard deviation of the return on average assets before taxes.

on consumer and mortgage lending, where competition from regional banks and credit unions is intense. For larger corporate clients alternative sources of funding are available. They borrow mainly either directly from capital markets or from syndicates led by foreign banks.

It is generally acknowledged that the Canadian banking system has continued to perform well during the financial crisis compared to most other OECD countries. Indeed, the Financial Stability Board in its Peer Review Report of Canada (FSB 2012) noted that

"The strength of the economy and of the financial system at the onset of the crisis meant that no Canadian financial institution failed or required government support in the form of a capital injection or debt guarantees. This resilience, which was achieved in spite of Canada's relatively complex regulatory structure, highlights a number of key lessons for other jurisdictions – namely, the importance of having: pro-active and targeted macroeconomic policies, supported by adequate fiscal space and a flexible exchange rate to help absorb external shocks; prudent bank risk management, particularly a stable and well-diversified funding profile as well as conservative loan underwriting standards; and a comprehensive regulatory and supervisory framework that effectively addresses domestic prudential concerns, including (when necessary) by adopting regulatory policies that go beyond international minimum standards."

Likewise, since 2008 the Global Competitiveness Report of the World Economic Forum (WEF 2011) has constantly rated Canada as having the soundest financial system in the world.

This strong performance of the Canadian financial sector is attributed on the one hand to good macroeconomic fundamentals including monetary policy and fiscal management, but on the other hand to a conservative approach to banking, and a strong regulatory and supervisory regime (Northcott et al. 2009). The banking supervisor seems to enjoy substantial discretion in setting policy objectives.

Both the level and quality of capital in banks' balance sheets required by supervisory targets exceeded the internationally agreed minima. Additional operating cushions complemented the regulatory minima (Ratnovski and Huang 2009). And exposures to unregulated financial institutions required more capital for banks. Leverage in the financial system was seen as a supervisory issue and addressed by regulatory policies. According to the Canadian authorities (Northcott et al. 2009), these measures forced the banks to manage their leverage and helped to contain excessive leverage in the system. Furthermore, excesses in the residential mortgage market were contained by requiring insurance coverage for loans to borrowers with a loan-to-value ratio over 80%. Thus, for markets the non-prime mortgages remained limited.

An interesting feature of the Canadian supervisory culture is the principles-based approach to supervision. The supervisor states its regulatory objectives, leaving it to the institutions to achieve them. Risk-based supervision assesses the success. The Canadian authorities state that principles-based supervision can better deal with the problem of regulatory arbitrage, as banks do not merely need to comply with strict rules but must achieve certain results, whereby both the choice of means and the burden of proof is on the industry. This makes it harder to work around rules. Finally, corporate governance ranks high on the supervisory agenda with a dedicated corporate governance department within the authority.

5.2. The Case of the Czech Republic

The IMF noted in its staff report for the 2012 Article IV Consultation on the financial sector of the Czech Republic:

"The Czech financial system has proved resilient to the effects of the global crisis, but spillover risks remain elevated. Despite slow GDP growth at home and financial strains abroad, the performance of banks is very good, with strong capitalization, solid profits, and ample liquidity. This resilience, which has been confirmed by the FSAP stress tests, reflects to a large extent a relatively conservative structure of bank balance sheets (particularly low loan-to-deposit ratios) and relatively low indebtedness of the corporate and household sectors." (IMF 2012b).

Concerning the development of the regulatory framework in the Czech Republic, the IMF further highlights the assertive stance of the Czech National Bank (CNB) in terms of various measures already taken or envisaged for enhancing financial stability. Among these are efforts to improve bank reporting requirements, including on transactions between parents and subsidiaries, envisaged legal amendments aimed at broadening the mandate of the CNB and regulating the activities of credit unions, as well as the strengthening of the macroprudential policy framework and of stress testing.

The latest CNB stress testing results of February 2012 provided additional evidence for the resilience of the Czech banking sector. Using data available until the end of 2011, a "debt crisis" stress scenario assuming escalation of the Euro area debt crisis did not result in a decline of the aggregate capitalisation of the banking sector below the regulatory minimum of 8% for the forecasting period of 2012 to 2014 (CNB 2012). Only an even more severe, yet very unlikely stress scenario was able to push the aggregate capitalisation of the banking sector slightly below the regulatory minimum.

During the crisis, Czech banks, which are predominantly foreign-owned and typically have low loan-to-deposit ratios, were net creditors to their parent banks. According to Moody's the tightening of regulatory limits on group transfers proved credit positive for Czech banks (Moody's 2012).

Similarly to Canada, the Czech regulator has a relatively high level of discretion at its disposal and a relatively conservative stance on the sustainable way of banking.

5.3. Governance is the Key

These two examples underline the assumption that it is not primarily the structure of the financial system that matters for financial stability, but much more the way the specific system is supervised. A sound regulatory framework and a strong, proactive supervisory culture is a key to the stability of the banking system. This insight is also backed by recent research findings that a high capital regulatory index, measuring the overall capital stringency of supervisors, significantly and positively influences financial soundness of single banks and the banking sector as a whole (Uhde and Heimeshoff 2009).

6. REGULATORY REPAIR AND GOVERNANCE IMPROVEMENT

Drawing on the insight of the importance of system governance, we shall now turn to the issues of regulatory and supervisory improvement.

In the European Union the various regulatory efforts, which have been underway since 2009, are directed towards the goals of crisis prevention, crisis management and adapting the supervisory architecture to the realities of an EU single market for financial services.

Substantial progress has been achieved in the area of crisis prevention: the Basel III framework, which will be transposed in Europe into a single rule book of banking regulation, will require banks to hold much more and much better risk-absorbing capital. Whereas under Basel II banks could operate with as little as two per cent of common equity capital, they will have to hold at least seven per cent of equity capital in the future.

A theme from the history of banking supervision has been taken up again by the reintroduction of liquidity standards, requiring banks to provide for coverage of their short-term liquidity needs under a one month stress scenario and a stable funding base over a one year time horizon. As a backstop to possible flaws in the capture and measurement of risk in the Basel risk-based capital regime, a leverage ratio has been introduced that compares the amount of capital with the accounting value of exposures on banks' balance sheets, including off-balance sheet items. In addition, supervisors will have new powers to monitor banks more closely and take prudential measures where necessary.

With the establishment of three microprudential European Supervisory Authorities on Banking (EBA), on Securities and Markets (ESMA) and on Insurances and Occupational Pension Schemes (EIOPA) a common European perspective has been added to financial supervision, which is a great step to improving supervision under conditions of a single European market for financial services (for more details see Lautenschläger, chapter 21 in this volume).

7. OPEN ISSUES: MORAL HAZARD AND MACROPRUDENTIAL POLICY

Speaking particularly from the viewpoint of a banking supervisor, there are two main areas, in which further progress needs to be accomplished. These areas relate on the one hand to the incentive structure and on the other hand to the macroeconomic environment, under which financial institutions, and their stakeholders, conduct business.

7.1. Moral Hazard Issues

The most pressing open issue is addressing moral hazard connected with large cross-border banks (SIB), which are too systemically important to fail (Stern and Feldman 2004). The repercussions of the insolvency of Lehman Brothers in September 2008 to financial stability worldwide unfortunately demonstrated that currently there is no viable other option than the rescue of SIBs with tax-payers' money. Accordingly, the public support implicit to the status as a SIB was made explicit, at least as a temporary crisis measure, by political leaders, e.g., by the G20 summit in November 2008. This must change.

7.2. Stricter Rules for and Supervision of SIB

The existence of implicit or explicit public support to SIBs leads to bad incentives in the banking sector and finally to costly government bail-outs for a number of reasons. Competition is distorted and the functioning of the order of the market economy is undermined. SIBs generally enjoyed advantages in their credit ratings and funding conditions before the crisis (Haldane 2010; Kenichi and Weder di Mauro 2012). A market economy cannot function when the threat of failure and insolvency is removed from economic agents. When risk taking is incentivised and there is a bias towards underpricing of risk, massive systemic risks ensue. But such systemic risk often builds up only gradually and may remain hidden for some time. And it has been found by economic research that SIBs tend to "invest" their cost savings realised through, at least partially artificial, competitive advantages in greater risk-taking (Kenichi and Weder di Mauro 2012). It is not surprising, therefore, that in the past years the biggest banks have suffered relatively greater write-downs of assets than smaller ones. For a more theoretical discussion on the nature and systemic risk of systemically important financial institutions (SIFIs), see Nowotny, chapter 15 in this volume.

Overall, the "game" is conceived by the public as privatisation of gains and socialisation of losses and lowers public trust in the fairness of the system. This is incompatible with the rules of justice and the incentive structure necessary to maintain the order of market economies. There is, quite correctly, the notion among the public as well as among politicians that never again should taxpayers' money be used to bail out the financial giants. In some countries this proposition has even been embedded in legislation, see, e.g., section 214 of the Dodd-Frank Act in the US.

However, this good intention must be transferred into practice. What regulators and supervisors need to achieve is to limit both the probability of default and the impact given default of institutions, whose failure would likely lead to severe stress in financial markets. This, of course, applies to big banks (SIBs) as well as to other systemically important financial institutions (SIFIs). The focus here, however, is on banks.

To achieve the first aim of substantially lowering the probability of distress of a SIB, such institutes must be subjected to additional regulatory requirements that come on top of the new Basel III standards. To counter the so-called cross-sectional dimension of systemic risk surcharges of high quality capital would increase the loss bearing capacity and at the same time mitigate to some extent the artificial advantage in funding costs that SIBs typically enjoy. The Financial Stability Board (FSB) issued recommendations to that effect, which were endorsed at the G20 meeting in November 2011. Sensibly, the FSB also proposed that in addition to capital surcharges supervisors may require extra contingent capital instruments. The FSB recommendations must faithfully be adapted to the realities of the European banking sector and its SIBs.

Nonetheless, higher capital requirements are insufficient if they are not accompanied by more effective supervision. This includes enhanced supervisory mandates as well as resources and making good use of the new enhanced Pillar 2 of the EU capital requirements framework, in which the dimension of systemic risk is now explicitly included. All this needs to be embedded in a shift in supervisory culture towards stricter expectations and tougher challenges regarding banks' risk management practices, and their corporate governance and internal control environment.

7.3. SIB Resolution must be Viable

Generally, for economies based on free enterprise and competition, the exit of firms from markets is an indispensable element. It would be naïve to assume that in spite of all regulatory repair and lessons learned by supervisors there will never again occur another financial crisis, let alone a failure of a SIB. Entrepreneurial activity is never a zero-risk game. It is the incentives of economic agents that matter. Risk and reward must go together. However, in the event of a firm's failure, the potential fallout to society is to be minimised.

This calls for flanking the additional SIB requirements by enhanced crisis management and crisis resolution remedies. An orderly resolution of a SIB in severe distress must be a viable option in the future. This is the most important piece of financial regulation yet missing from the point of view of "Ordnungspolitik".

One first important step in this direction has been made with the FSB's requirements for resolvability assessments for global SIBs (G-SIBs) (FSB 2011). Many countries in which G-SIBs are domiciled have started projects on recovery and resolution planning, also called "living wills", for their biggest banks. Also supervisors in other countries should follow suit for their SIBs, even if their relevance is more of a domestic or regional nature as is the case in many EU Member States. Complementary institution-specific cross-border cooperation agreements are to be concluded, in order for home and host supervisors of cross-border SIBs to be able to cooperate effectively and quickly in a crisis situation.

7.4. Challenges of SIB Resolution

A SIB default triggers direct counterparty effects, when obligations vis-à-vis counterparties cannot be honoured. Downward spirals may arise from fire-sales in asset markets, when ailing SIBs experience liquidity problems. Widespread contagion effects may ensue when panic among market participants spreads to other SIBs. Government bail-outs in this crisis, however, have contributed to the deterioration of public finances in many countries. This resulted in the negative feedback effect that banks with large exposures to such sovereign debt now experience solvency problems. And government-assisted M&A deals have resulted in further concentrations in the banking sector, particularly in the US but also in Europe. The biggest European and US banks have become even bigger. The issue of SIBs being "too-big-to-fail" is worse than before. It is a vicious circle.

To be able to break it, a robust and effective resolution regime is needed. It ought to combine a number of resolution instruments. But it should be designed to preserve the going-concern of an institution, if anyhow possible, while at the same time making first and foremost equityholders take the losses, followed by certain creditors. Depending on the situation, also the responsible managers should be replaced.

A SIB restructuring process must balance delicate challenges. It must operate quickly and swiftly in order to reduce contagion risk as much as possible. Its aim must be to preserve the going-concern, i.e. the systemic business functions and asset values, of an institution. And finally, it should work as a private sector solution avoiding the use of public funds, or at least reducing it to an option of ultimate resort.

7.5. Bail-In as Resolution Instrument

One promising instrument to achieve these aims is "bail-in" (Gleeson 2012; IMF 2012a). Bail-in in this sense gives a supervisory, or a separate resolution authority statutory powers to restructure the liabilities of a distressed financial institution by writing down its unsecured debt and converting it to equity. The statutory bail-in power is intended to achieve a prompt recapitalisation of the distressed institution, ideally to a level sufficiently above regulatory requirements, so that it remains viable.

By wiping out or substantially diluting existing shareholders and including creditor claims in the write-down it would, from the perspective of "Ordnungspolitik", ameliorate the incentive structure of equity holders and investors in financial institutions. When the threats on the one hand of equity write down and debt conversion to shareholders and creditors and on the other hand of replacement to management are sufficiently credible, this should lead to behavioural changes more conducive to financial stability. Firms might generally raise the level of own funds they hold for unexpected risk in order to stay well above likely bail-in triggers. And in a situation of difficulties they might try harder themselves to raise capital or restructure debt voluntarily, before the supervisor activates its resolution powers.

7.6. Going-Concern Resolution is Preferable

There are a number of good arguments in favour of going-concern resolution (Gleeson 2012; IMF 2012a). Firstly, there is the immediate concern of spreading contagion and panic. Outright insolvency may result e.g., in a disorderly unwinding of derivative contracts or runs on repos and other forms of secured funding, causing severe knock-on effects among market participants. Secondly, it is an insight from insolvency practitioners that shutting down a productive enterprise destroys more value than when restructuring regimes permit business continuity, and asset values can be preserved that would otherwise be lost in a liquidation. Thirdly, successful bail-in does not involve finding purchasers and conducting intensive due diligence for a distressed SIB, which is very difficult in times of acute stress. Finally, and very importantly in the long run, in a going-concern resolution, if its business model is deemed sustainable, the institution would remain in the market as a competitor, with new equity and a new management. This would be a favourable outcome from the viewpoint of competition policy, preventing further market concentration as compared e.g., with M&A solutions often used. Only if a (full) going-concern restructuring were not an option would the authority initiate a (partial) gone-concern liquidation.

7.7. Details need further Consideration

In defining the trigger for activation of the supervisory bail-in powers it is important to avoid uncertainty and arbitrariness as much as possible both, for reasons of rule of law and to enable the market to price bail-in-able debt (Gleeson

2012). For these reasons, contingent capital instruments, where trigger events are ex ante defined in the respective contracts, may provide a higher level of certainty and should be a main building block of any resolution regime. Generally, as regards the height of the trigger it seems prudent to set it not too distant from the point in which the institute is technically insolvent. The trigger could be based on quantitative and qualitative conditions, which should be pre-specified by law, unless contractual arrangements are used. To make the use of the bail-in tool as predictable as possible, the powers of the competent authorities should only apply when the legal criteria are met. There should be the possibility for ex post judicial review, which, however, should not render the resolution decision invalid. Where necessary for reasons of equity, compensation for damages should be awarded.

As regards the scope of bail-in, subordinated and senior unsecured forms of debt should generally be subject to bail-in, while insured deposits, secured debt and repo agreements should be excluded. Discussions are ongoing if some forms of senior unsecured debt such as e.g., inter-bank deposits, payments, clearing and securities settlement system obligations and certain trade-finance obligations should be exempted (IMF 2012a). Here, a very difficult trade-off needs to be found between keeping the essential parts of a bank going and avoiding unintended consequences, e.g., by providing opportunities for circumvention or wrong incentives.

However, bail-in is not a panacea and should be considered to be but one element of a comprehensive, robust resolution framework. Depending on the facts of each case it might need to be supplemented by other resolution tools, such as good bank / bad bank solutions or arranged acquisitions.

The planned common crisis management framework for the European Union (European Commission 2010a) addresses these issues and will provide a last line of defence in supervision. However, as long as there is no European resolution authority in combination with a common European financing arrangement, cross-border issues such as effective coordination of home and host authorities as well as burden sharing remain on the agenda. Regulators and supervisors must faithfully strive to implement, improve and deploy the crisis management framework, if necessary, to end moral hazard in the financial sector. In any event, they must be able to manage the distress of all kinds of SIFIs better in the next crisis than in the past.

8. AND FINALLY: MACROPRUDENTIAL SUPERVISION

The other main issue that needs to be advanced is the area of so-called macroprudential supervision and policy. In short, macroprudential policy means adapting the pivotal parameters of prudential regulation in accordance with

changes in the macroeconomic environment (Calomiris 2009). The idea behind this approach is to complement the traditional microprudential perspective of supervisors with their main focus on the compliance with regulatory
norms by single institutions with a much stronger supervisory emphasis on
the detection and mitigation in due time of systemic risks to the financial system as a whole (Brunnermeier et al. 2009). A little uncouth, this approach has
also been named "big picture supervision". Macroprudential authorities will
conduct supervisory monitoring from a system-wide point of view and recommend or execute macroprudential policies that address the main propagation
channels of systemic risk, ideally at an early point in time. The predominant
concerns here arise from the time-varying dimension of systemic risk, which
manifests itself mainly in the development of leverage and maturity transformation in the financial system (Bank of England 2009).

8.1. What can be achieved by Macroprudential Supervision?

While it would, clearly, be overambitious to "manage" the financial cycle via
macroprudential supervisory policies, what can and should be achieved at least
is to make the banking system more resilient well before the turning point of
the cycle, and thus to reduce the height of fall and the collateral damage of a
systemic crisis as much as possible. To this purpose it is paramount that banking systems enter times of financial distress with a sound level of capital. A
decrease in the level of capital in the system should only occur, if at all, after a
severe crisis event has hit – not before. After all it is a major takeaway of this
crisis that it is in good times, when all risk indicators look fine, that the real
risks to financial stability accrue.

It is not yet clear how big the room for manoeuvre for macroprudential policies will finally be. However, in any case under Basel III there will be more
potential for counteracting exuberant developments in the financial sector as
under the previous regime (Caruana 2010). First, there is the capital conservation buffer. It can be seen as a rule-based microprudential tool with macroprudential implications, which improves system resilience in a downturn. Second,
there is the innovative instrument of an additional countercyclical buffer. The
sustainability of refinancing the real economy, and eventually also the sustainable profitability of financial intermediation, is improved by avoiding the
credit crunches that inevitably follow unsustainable credit booms. During periods of rapid credit growth banks would need to accumulate this buffer in order
to mitigate the build-up of systemic risk. This addresses an important aspect of
the time dimension of systemic risk, and might also help in avoiding the bias
towards underestimation of credit risk during credit booms. In times of strains,
supervisors would release the buffer that can then be used to absorb losses.

While the capital buffer regime of Basel III is a very important first step, additional instruments are needed in other areas of macroprudential policy. This

includes other tools that are aimed at leaning against exuberances in financial markets and help support sectoral policies (Bank of England 2011). The details of the "macroprudential tool box" will only be known once the legislative process regarding the Capital Requirements Directive and Regulation are finalised at the European level.

However, it is already clear that there will be additional flexibility to deploy macroprudential policy instruments in a meaningful way. These include the possibility to set higher risk-weights or minimum values of exposure-weighted average loss given default rates regarding mortgage credit on the basis of financial stability considerations and a reorganised Pillar II process, where systemic risk is taken into account. And in certain areas prudential requirements may be tightened either at Member State level or by the European Commission via delegated acts for a limited period of time, when justified by the build-up of risks to financial stability. A review clause will provide opportunity for further improvements of the European macroprudential framework. It is expected from the European Systemic Risk Board (ESRB) to be the driving force in Europe behind further developing our understanding of macroprudential policy and the refinement of its instruments.

8.2. Coordination in the Internal Market

Besides powers, governance of the framework is of great importance. A sound governance regime requires on the one hand clearly defined roles and responsibilities and on the other hand operational independence of the institutions involved (CGFS 2010; FSB, IMF and BIS 2011; Schoenmaker and Wierts 2011).

And information sharing and cooperation between authorities across borders is paramount to the success of this new strand of supervisory policy. Much speaks in favour of a key role of central banks. They have lots of expertise in macroeconomic analysis and they are well acquainted with financial markets through their role as lenders of last resort and as overseers of payment and settlement systems. And in the conduct of monetary policy similar issues of independence and accountability to the public ensue.

At EU level, a big step was made with the establishment of the ESRB as the body responsible for macroprudential oversight of the financial system within the Union. The ESRB is designed to complement the tasks of the three new European microprudential supervisory authorities (ESA) with a systemic risk perspective, and forms part of the European System of Financial Supervision (ESFS). While representatives of central banks have the majority of votes in its General Board, the ESRB nevertheless brings together all the institutions that have responsibilities for financial stability, both at Member State and Union level. And it is enriched by the outsight views of academics and other experts. The ESRB also provides a forum for cooperation of macroprudential policies across EU countries, which is so important from the perspective of an integrated common market for financial services in the EU.

In December 2011, the ESRB issued a recommendation providing guiding principles on core elements of macroprudential mandates for authorities in Member States. As the recommendation acknowledges, the responsibility for the initiation of macroprudential policy measures lies first and foremost within national authorities. It is, therefore, crucial that the national frameworks provide them with the necessary degree of independence from all kinds of lobbying pressures as well as with clear enough objectives that reduce the bias towards inaction in boom times.

But in spite of all institutional arrangements in the years to come it will be the task of supervisors, both micro- and macroprudential, to develop a strong supervisory culture that has a real impact on the way the supervised market actors conduct their businesses that is conducive to the fair and sustainable provision of financial services to customers and to overall financial stability in Europe. For this common goal supervisors in the EU will have to cooperate and join forces in the spirit of trust.

9. CONCLUDING REMARKS

For a sustainable development in the future Europe needs a resilient "financial system 2.0". In the continental European tradition this will have to be based primarily on well-diversified universal banks and require sustainable bank business models and a strong risk management culture. In the EU single market context there is the perspective that market-based forms of financing complement more and more the predominant role of bank lending. This would be desirable also from the point of view of banking supervision, because it would foster competition and diversification of risks and should, therefore, support the stability of the banking system.

A central issue for all Member States of the European Union is the availability of adequate forms of funding for European small and medium sized enterprises (SME). SME are the backbone of innovation and sustainable economic growth in the EU. They need sufficient external financing to introduce new or improved products and services. But they also need the chance of expanding their businesses and eventually grow to the size of global players in the longer run. To the extent that SME in Europe remain dependent on bank lending as primary source of external financing, they will be among the beneficiaries of a sounder and more sustainable banking system in the EU.

The overall experience in OECD countries during the financial crisis indicates that it is less important what kind of financial system, i.e. market- or bank-based, a country has. A more crucial factor is how the financial system is governed. Here, financial supervisors need to draw the right conclusions from

the crisis, and more generally from financial history. And they should not ab-
stain from looking elsewhere. Arguably, there is something to be learned from
jurisdictions that have fared comparatively better during the crisis than many
other peers.

In the field of banking regulation much progress has been achieved with
the conclusion of the Basel III agreement. The likelihood of bank failures is
reduced by comprehensive prudential requirements, particularly on own funds
and liquidity. But the successful implementation lies yet in front of us. Sin-
cere efforts to implement the new rules need to be supported by strong and
enhanced supervision of individual banks. Persevering supervision is needed
to ensure that banks operate with capital levels, liquidity buffers and risk management practices that are commensurate with the risks taken. New prudential
powers and instruments are granted to supervisors. They must use them well.

In the European Union the new supervisory architecture, the European System of Financial Supervision (ESFS), in both its micro- (ESA) and macroprudential (ESRB) dimension, must be filled with life and the common spirit of
all institutions involved of protecting the integrity and stability of the common
EU market for financial services.

There also needs to be a shift in supervisory culture towards stricter expectations and tougher challenges regarding firms' risk management practices, and
their corporate governance and internal control environment. Supervision must
become more proactive and more insistent. Recent quantitative results indicate
that a high capital regulatory index that measures the overall capital stringency
of supervisors significantly positively influences financial soundness of single
banks and the banking sector as a whole (Uhde and Heimeshoff 2009).

But regulatory repair is by no means simply about more or more intrusive
regulation and supervision. A targeted approach, first and foremost, deals with
internalising negative externalities that result from incentive structures, which
are not conducive to the common good. In this regard, more needs to be done
with respect to wrong incentives in the financial system. Moral hazard must
come to an end. Additional capital and possibly other prudential requirements
are needed to increase the loss bearing capacity of systemic banks (SIBs) and
other financial institutions (SIFIs) and to mitigate artificial competitive advantages they enjoy.

Moreover, recent research finds that a high degree of government ownership in the banking sector has negative effects on the financial soundness of
banks, which may be attributable to the probability of a public bail-out in distress being more explicit (Uhde and Heimeshoff 2009). As the issue of SIBs
being even larger and banking markets more concentrated, this is another corollary of the crisis we will have to deal with in the midterm.

But higher loss absorption and stricter supervision are not enough by themselves. Since economic activity means taking on risk and dealing with uncer-

tainty, failures of market actors frequently occur. But under conditions of a free market economy, market exit must always be a credible option. Without viable market exit options for financial firms incentive problems immediately occur. Therefore, resolution of systemically relevant financial institutions is the most crucial pillar of reforms outstanding from the perspective of "Ordnungspolitik".

A SIFI resolution process must balance delicate challenges. It must operate quickly and swiftly in order to reduce contagion risk as much as possible. Ideally it should preserve the going-concern, i.e. the systemic business functions and asset values, of an institution, while including shareholders, creditors and management in the resolution. Contingent capital instruments and bail-in powers are main building blocks of such a framework. And finally, the use of public funds should be avoided, or at least reduced to an option of ultimate resort. Supervisors must be able to manage SIFI failures better in the future than in the recent past.

Microprudential supervision with its focus on individual institutions needs to be complemented by a macroprudential perspective on the system as a whole. Macroprudential supervision will particularly have to address the main propagation channels of systemic risk, namely excessive leverage and maturity transformation. Macroprudential policy measures employed in due time would help to curb the building up of system wide risk, both in its time- and its cross-sectional dimension. The aim is, at least, to reduce the magnitude of financial crises and to limit the social losses associated with them. The "*Guideline to Strengthen the Sustainability of the Business Models of Large Internationally Active Austrian Banks*" issued by the Austrian authorities, Finanzmarktaufsichtsbehörde (FMA) and Oesterreichische Nationalbank (OeNB), in March 2012 is one recent attempt in this direction (OeNB 2012).

In any case, policies of these kinds must be resolutely employed in the future to lean against the wind, before it is too late. Supervisors should not be too afraid to use this new instrument. Since error is inevitable in human action, supervisors henceforth better err on the safe side.

Financial stability must be protected. Supervisory governance for sure is instrumental.

BIBLIOGRAPHY

Bank of England 2009, "The role of macroprudential policy", *Bank of England Discussion Paper*, November.

Bank of England 2011, "Instruments of macroprudential policy", *Bank of England Discussion Paper*, December.

Brunnermeier, M., A. Crocket, C. Goodhart, A. D. Persaud and H. Shin 2009, "The fundamental principles of financial regulation", *Geneva Reports on the World Economy*.

Calomiris, C. W. 2009, "Financial innovation, regulation, and reform", *Cato Journal*, Vol. 29, No. 1, Winter, pp. 65-91.

Caruana, J. 2010, "Macroprudential policy: working towards a new consensus", Remarks at the high-level meeting on "The Emerging Framework for Financial Regulation and Monetary Policy" jointly organised by the BIS's Financial Stability Institute and the IMF Institute, Washington DC, 23 April.

Committee on the Global Financial System 2010, "Macroprudential instruments and frameworks", *CGFS Paper* No 38, May.

Czech National Bank 2012, *Czech Banking Sector Stress Tests*, February 2012, Prague, http://www.cnb.cz/miranda2/export/sites/www.cnb.cz/en/financial_stability/stress_testing/2011/stress_test_results_2011_4q.pdf.

De Larosière, J. et al. 2009, *Report of the High-Level Group on Financial Supervision in the EU*, 25 February.

Diamond, D. W. 1984, "Financial intermediation and delegated monitoring", *Review of Economic Studies*, Vol. 51, pp. 393-414.

European Central Bank 2010, *EU Banking Structures*, September 2010, Frankfurt am Main, http://www.ecb.int/pub/pdf/other/eubankingstructures201009en.pdf.

European Commission 2010a, *An EU framework for crisis management in the financial sector*, Com(2010) 579 final, Brussels.

European Commission 2010b, *Green paper on corporate governance in financial institutions and remuneration policies*, Com(2010) 284 final, Brussels.

Financial Stability Board 2011, *Key attributes of effective resolution regimes for financial institutions*, October.

Financial Stability Board 2012, *Peer Review of Canada*, 30.1.2012: http://www.financialstabilityboard.org/publications/r_120130.pdf.

FSB, IMF and BIS 2011, "Macroprudential policy tools and frameworks", *Progress report to G20*, October.

Galati G. and R. Moessner 2011, "Macroprudential policy – a literature review", *BIS Working Paper* No 337, February.

Gleeson, S. 2012, "Legal aspects of bank bail-ins", *LSE Financial Markets Group Paper Series, Special Paper* 205, January.

Haldane, A. 2010, "The $100 Billion Question", speech to Institute of Regulation and Risk, Hong Kong, March.

IMF 2012a, "From bail-out to bail-in: mandatory debt restructuring of systemic financial institutions", *Staff Discussion Note*, April.

IMF 2012b, "Czech Republic 2012: Article IV Consultation – Staff Report", *IMF Country Report* No. 12/115, May 2012, Washington, D.C.

Kenichi, U. and B. Weder di Mauro 2012, "Quantifying Structural Subsidy Values for Systemically Important Financial Institutions", *IMF Working Paper* No. 12/128.

Moody's 2012, "Czech Banks: Tightening Regulatory Limits on Group Transfers is Credit Positive", *Sector Comment*, February 2012, London.

Northcott, C., G. Paulin and M. White 2009, "Lessons for banking reform: a Canadian perspective", *Central Banking*, Vol. 19, No. 4, pp. 43-53.

OeNB 2012, "Guideline to strengthen the sustainability of the business models of large internationally active Austrian banks", March 2012, Vienna, http://oenb.at/en/presse_pub/aussendungen/2012/2012q1/pa_aufsicht__nachhaltigkeitspaket_fuer_oesterreichs_banken__246091_page.jsp#tcm:16-246091.

Rajan, R. and L. Zingales 2003, "Banks and markets: the changing character of European finance", *NBER Working Paper* No. 9595, Cambridge, MA.

Ratnovski, L. and R. Huang 2009, "Why Are Canadian Banks More Resilient", *IMF Working Paper* No. 09/152.

Reinhardt, C. and K. Rogoff 2009, *This Time is Different: Eight Centuries of Financial Folly*, Princeton University Press.

Schoenmaker, D. and P. Wierts 2011, "Macroprudential policy: the need for a coherent policy framework", *DSF Policy Paper* No. 13, July.

Stern, G. and R. Feldman 2004, *Too Big To Fail: The Hazards of Bank Bailouts*, Washington: Brookings Institution Press.

Turner, A. 2009, *The Turner Review. A regulatory response to the global banking crisis*, Financial Services Authority (FSA), March.

Uhde, A. and U. Heimeshoff 2009, "Consolidation in banking and financial stability in Europe: Empirical evidence", *Journal of Banking and Finance*, Vol. 33, pp. 1299-1311.

World Economic Forum 2011, "The Global Competitiveness Report 2011-2012", September 2011: http://www.weforum.org/issues/global-competitiveness.

8. Competition, the Pressure for Returns, and Stability

Paul Tucker

Propelled by a deep and continuing crisis in the financial system, the international authorities are overhauling the 'rules of the game' for global finance.

The changes are profound.[1] But the goal is not to abolish risk or risk-taking. We need to find broadly the right balance between, on the one hand, safety and, on the other hand, the contribution that sound and honest finance can make to economic prosperity. In striking that balance, international policy-makers have maintained three beliefs:

- risk is an intrinsic and unavoidable part of the (monetary) services that banks provide to the economy, just as risk is intrinsic to the businesses that borrow from banks;
- competition in finance is in principle good, although the authorities need to be mindful that the drive for headline returns can contribute to excess;
- open financial borders and so a global financial system, including cross-border international banking, should be maintained, but the authorities need to contain the way that problems can be transmitted from one part of the globe to another.

History reveals repeated episodes of herd-like chasing of high headline returns during exuberant phases of the credit cycle. Eventually that will recur. Nor can we completely eliminate the interlinkages within the system that can propagate distress. But the emerging new rules of the game *can* lean against stability-threatening exuberance and *will* make the international financial system much more resilient.

In this chapter, I shall review why the international authorities think banking can be useful (section 1), before in section 2 turning to what drives its excesses, and how, internationally, we plan to arrest and contain them (section 3).

With thanks for conversations with Anil Kashyap, David Scharfstein and Jeremy Stein; and to Sarah Ashley and James Benford at the Bank of England.

[1] For an account of the international reform programme, see Tucker (2012a).

1. IS BANKING USEFUL?

The banking system is, in effect, a mechanism for monetising illiquid claims on the economy's capital stock. Banks make loans, and those loans are inherently risky. They are funded by issuing claims that circulate as a medium of exchange and as a source of liquidity for savers – 'inside money'. This works so long as there is confidence in the soundness – the solvency – of the banks. As the financial system deepens and more inside money issued by *sound* banks circulates, the door can be opened to more long-term investment, an enriched capital stock and higher levels of output.[2]

Most prosaically, the banking system allows households and firms to tie up less of their resources in liquid assets than otherwise. Bad things happen in the world – to individual households and firms, to sectors and regions, and even to the economy as a whole – and those adversely affected often need some liquidity to get them through the bad times. Banks provide households and businesses with liquidity insurance – through deposits that can be withdrawn on demand, and through committed lines of credit, or overdraft facilities, that can be drawn down on demand. By providing this insurance to lots of households and firms, and by providing it on both sides of their balance sheets, banks gain diversification benefits and so can economise on the liquid resources they themselves need to underpin (or reinsure against) the insurance they provide (Kashyap et al. 2002). That benefits everyone. It means that more of the economy's resources can be allocated to productive but, by their nature, risky enterprises.

All this turns on the ability of banks to create (broad) money when they make a loan. Something no mutual fund could do, for example. We, the international policy community, still believe in fractional reserve banking, which links the production of credit to the production of money, as an important part of the financial system.

We also believe in the importance of domestic and international capital markets. One of the key lessons of the late-90s' Asian crises was that economies could be safer if they had *domestic* capital markets that intermediated *local* savings and *local* investment projects. Vulnerabilities are greater if what should be local financial intermediation entails currency transformation because borrowers and savers have no choice but to meet via the international markets.

But we do also believe in *international* capital markets, because they can facilitate efficient and effective allocation of capital around the world. Global savings can in principle be channelled to the most productive set of investments available, facilitating specialisation and cross-border trade in goods and services: i.e. comparative advantage. And they can open the door to greater risk sharing. A country with investments that are not tied entirely to the future

---

[2] Kiyotaki and Moore's (2005) model of financial deepening, with roots in Holmstrom and Tirole (1997), seeks to capture this.

state of its domestic economy should have more resources to draw upon when bad times hit (Obstfeld and Rogoff 1996, ch. 5).

All that should be obvious.

Let me make another obvious statement. Policy-makers still believe in the social value of insurance – in the value of the ability of households and firms to transfer risk to others via well-specified contracts; and in insurance firms pooling risk in order to build up, though diversification, a portfolio with more stable returns.

Why am I saying such obvious things? Because the lion's share of innovations in finance over the past decade or so involved risk transfer and risk pooling via the international capital markets – derivatives, securitisation, and so on. In one sense, it should not be surprising that most innovations are in this area. While the technologies for payments and credit are not static, innovations mostly affect their mode and cost of delivery rather than *what* they deliver. Whereas for risk transfer, there are all sorts of still unexplored ways of transferring and bundling the risks that households, firms and governments bear. The economic world is far from comprising a complete set of markets and contracts (see, for example, Shiller 1993).

Financial innovations were at the heart of the crisis that broke in summer 2007. They added complexity to instruments and to chains of intermediation. This diluted incentives to monitor risk, and masked the likely spillovers from borrower distress (Bank of England 2007, p.22).

So an important question is how much we know about the benefits of financial innovation. It has to be said that there is not much robust research about the benefits of new modes of risk transfer. Anecdotally, it is striking that large companies are concerned about rising costs of hedging following various current and prospective regulatory reforms, which suggests the ability to insure against risks via capital markets is valued. But there is little research exploring whether meaningful benefits for society or the economy as a whole – through higher productivity, lower volatility of output or a more efficient distribution of available resources – can be pinned down empirically.

So what *do* we know from research?

The link between financial deepening and economic growth *is* well documented, notably by Ross Levine (2005). Much of that literature is, however, about economies with financial systems at an early stage of development. There is less evidence available on the value of additional financial deepening for already advanced economies. Lerner and Tufano (2011) attempt a counterfactual history around four types of financial innovation, largely drawn from the US. They reach the following conclusions:

(i)   the development of venture capital has helped firm start-ups;

(ii) the development of private equity increased management focus on returns to shareholders and so supported, it is suggested, the productivity of existing firms;

(iii) the development of the mutual fund industry enabled diversification of small investors' investment portfolios, possibly lowering the cost of capital for firms;

(iv) the early[3] development of securitisation – the conversion of packages of illiquid debt claims into tradable securities – was associated with improved access to mortgage credit and a rise in homeownership.

A deepening of lending markets is part of the story for at least three of those developments. But Lerner and Tufano remain largely silent on the benefits/costs of maturity transformation, as well as on any effects of risk transfer via derivatives. And their focus is the USA.

The expansion of the US financial services industry over the past 30 years is further examined in a forthcoming paper by Greenwood and Scharfstein (2012). They find that financial services outpaced the rest of the economy – accounted for by a rising share of national expenditure going to fees for asset management and to the servicing of secured household debt. On asset management, they favour the development of a low-cost mutual fund industry.

Perhaps especially in the US, the recent deepening in household debt markets was fuelled by an expansion of maturity transformation by non-banks – shadow banking. Greenwood and Scharfstein point out that it is hard to measure benefits associated with the production of these money-like claims. Many shadow banks turned out to be unsafe. They might have been meeting a wider demand for liquidity services, but no one was internalising the resultant increase in the fragility of the system.

As it happens, the increase in the capital-output ratio (capital deepening) in Europe over the postWar period was accompanied by a steady rise in the ratio of broad monetary liabilities to output – which is to say, an expansion of commercial banking. But it is hard to know the counterfactual: could we have had capital deepening unaccompanied by growth in deposits and bank credit?

And it is certainly clear that excessive maturity transformation and expansion by banks is perilous – for the economy and society as well as for banks themselves.

I rehearse all this because it is important that the official community should be open with the public that, in redrawing the rules of the game for finance, it is having to make tradeoffs without the extensive research base that would ideally be available. Policymaking is a real-world activity. Banking has been so much a part of the past two centuries of economic development that policymakers want to make it safe, not close it down. We want to make the financial system more resilient against tail risks *without* killing the lubricant of our economy.

This makes competitive and risk-taking excesses a very important problem.

---

[3] They are agnostic about the benefits/costs of the rapid growth of securitisation in the run-up to the crisis that began in 2007.

2. THE TENDENCY TO EXCESSIVE RISK IN THE SYSTEM

That excesses occurred in the run-up to the current crisis is not remotely in doubt. For many banks, return on equity rose above 20%. Meanwhile, return on assets fell, signalling clearly that the enhanced headline returns were generated largely by leverage, and hence that banks were becoming riskier. But their cost of debt did not rise to reflect the increased risks.

If anything, the story is worse than that. As leverage increased, asset prices tended to rise. That depressed the return earned on assets. And it gave intermediaries the confidence to lend secured on wider classes of securities, enhancing the day-to-day liquidity of markets, at least temporarily. That in turn depressed what banks could charge for providing liquidity services. Faced with earning lower returns from holding assets and from providing what should be their core services, even more leverage, with ever greater maturity transformation, was needed to sustain headline returns. And so on. In other words, leverage was not just a passive way of generating higher static headline returns. *Increasing* leverage was dynamic: feeding upon itself by necessitating ever greater risk-taking to sustain those headline returns.

The composition of bankers' asset portfolios changed. Big picture, as more types of loan became securitisable, commercial banks could be left with relatively concentrated portfolios of riskier loans. Some rating agencies pointed out nearly a decade ago that US regional banks were liable to become overly exposed to their local real-estate markets partly for that reason. Towards the other end of the spectrum, wholesale and investment banks ended up holding on to vast portfolios of *undistributed* tranches of securitisations.

What I have summarised poses deep and pressing questions about the efficiency and effectiveness of capital markets in monitoring and pricing risk. Why did investors in bank equity expect such high returns? Why didn't the capital markets reprice bank paper (downwards) as leverage and other sources of risk increased? Why didn't they distinguish more between banks?

It is easy to answer that debt holders relied on Too-Big-To-Fail – a public safety net. They did. It was terrible – the biggest problem we have to crack. But that won't do as a complete answer, because equity holders were surely exposed to risk, as many discovered. We need richer explanations of what drove the multitude of excesses.

They lie partly in layer upon layer of principal-agent problems; in myopia; and their interaction.

2.1. Agency Problems

Business is infected by a string of principal-agent problems: shareholders having the upside of returns but limited downside, and not being able to monitor management perfectly; households delegating their investment decisions, and voting rights, to asset managers. Even without the existence of a state-sponsored safety net, these problems are likely to be particularly pronounced in banking because it is, intrinsically, levered and complex.

Under limited liability, shareholders enjoy the upside, but the downside is capped. Shareholders have a *de facto* call option on the firm. That is true for all joint-stock companies, but the option is in principle worth more when, as in banking, returns are volatile.

That elides the distinction between controlling owners and management. By giving management equity and equity options, shareholders put management in a similar position to themselves. Given management's immediate and complete access to information, that can backfire on the owners. The problem is by no means unique to banking, though banks may be especially opaque. Given bankers have private information on the quality of their portfolios and their earnings streams, they are unable to commit to a safe investment strategy. This opens up an incentive to opt for risky investments, knowing they get the profits if the risks pay off, but that their losses are capped and shared with debt holders if downside risks crystallise (Jensen and Meckling 1976).

When we add in the fragmentation of shareholdings and relatively liquid markets in equity shares, few shareholders seem to have the incentive or wherewithal to monitor banks effectively. This can all too easily lead to what some call managerialism.[4]

And within the management structure of banks, there are pressing questions about how well different layers are able to monitor others, with all to a greater or lesser degree incentivised by contracts, and possibly accounting regimes, that reward short-term performance.

These problems are compounded by agency issues in the asset-management industry, which manages the investment portfolios that contain bank stocks and shares. First, nearly all investment portfolios are now managed by third-party asset managers. Second, there has been an increase in stock-index matching and tracking amongst managers of unlevered investment portfolios, which may impair shareholder stewardship. Why didn't investors act to constrain the management at various banks? Possibly because their individual stakes were too small. Possibly because they believed there were impediments in securities regulation to their acting as a group. Possibly because they held back from selling their holdings because they were reluctant to go underweight a large component of an index (or benchmark) they tracked (or were measured against). I am not sure that we can feel confident about shareholder stewardship without some active management – i.e. selling as well as buying (for a broader view see Kay 2012).

---

[4] Mount (2012) contains a lay description of Adolf Berles and Gardiner Means' 1932s description of managerialism.

Active management does, of course, thrive in the hedge-fund community, and it seems that some funds spotted incipient problems amongst the banks ahead of the 2007/08 phase of the crisis. But relying for market discipline entirely on investors who themselves are levered seems a slightly shaky foundation for a resilient financial system.

Each of these agency problems is individually well enough understood.[5] But there are so many layers that it is hard to frame a comprehensive account from which policy remedies drop out in a straightforward way.

2.2. Myopia

In any case, I doubt that agency problems and incentives are the whole of the problem of exuberance. Like Charles Goodhart (2010), I doubt that, in managing their banks' financial risks, many bankers deliberately or even consciously drove the system over the cliff. Rather, like others, they were mainly myopic about the risks in the system. Technology innovations, the opening up of the world economy, better macroeconomic policy frameworks, new markets for transferring risk – all of this encouraged a sense that the world had become a safer place.

Gennaioli et al. (2010) have described a world in which the myopia of agents – investors, bankers, intermediaries – leads them, and the economy more widely, towards trouble, sometimes disaster (see also Tucker 2011). Because they are effectively blind to certain lowish probability risks, they generate and invest too heavily in securities that carry precisely those risks, which in consequence become big risks. Investors are attracted to the extra return in good states of the world and do not see the small chance of a catastrophic loss.

During the good times, everyone feels that they are achieving a nice balance of risk and return. They are getting, they think, safety, liquidity and return! Worse, they have few incentives to wake up, for the reasons explained above. The effects of myopia and incentives are not independent.

But eventually something happens to cause them to wake up, to see the risks they have neglected. Investors are then liable to react in a dramatic way. They stop buying, sell; prices collapse, liquidity dries up, defaults occur, etc etc.

A large exogenous shock is not needed to generate that unravelling. If the overpriced securities have led to credit conditions being too loose, then somebody – households, firms, sovereigns, or all sectors of the economy – will have accumulated too much debt, and so eventually fundamentals assert themselves: defaults rise, and realisation sets in.

This highlights a special quality of exuberance in credit markets. When insurers underprice, say, hurricane risk and, in consequence, write too much

---

[5] See, for example, Part One of Shiller (2012) for a description of the various roles of the myriad players in today's financial system.

business, the *impact* on the industry of an unexpectedly bad hurricane season is greater. But the *probability* of a bad hurricane season is not affected. It is exogenous. By contrast, when lending markets became overly exuberant, not only do the lenders become overly exposed to default, the *probability* of default also becomes elevated because the *borrowers* become over indebted. And, as I discussed earlier, high levels of debt twist borrowers' incentives towards actions that put more risk onto their creditors. The problem here is more than just an increased vulnerability to bad events.

This makes excess in banking especially damaging. (And similarly, for shadow banking (see Tucker 2010, 2012b; Turner 2012.))

As risk-transfer instruments, derivatives are economically similar to insurance contacts. But trading in derivatives on financial products (whether interest rates, equities, currencies etc) can influence the value of the underlying financial instruments themselves. That might in some circumstances drive prices beyond fundamental values, increasing the *probability* of a correction and thus the riskiness of the derivative position. Writing derivatives (or insurance) on financial instruments is not the same as writing hurricane insurance.

What I am describing matters a lot to debates about risk measurement and management in finance and, therefore, to policies designed to preserve stability. It is not simply that Value-At-Risk makes assumptions, such as normally distributed returns, that are manifestly false, as highlighted by my colleagues Haldane and Nelson (2012). It is not just a matter of finding a better model of some underlying stochastic process. The challenge is that the observed (ex-post) stochastic process is *en*dogenous not exogenous. It is determined by the behaviour of the participants in the financial system. The problem of excess is not simply one of lots of Black Swans; it is that the system can itself generate the tail events that sow its own destruction – it can breed swans.

Central bankers have known this historically. It is what Federal Reserve Board Chairman McChesney Martin was talking about more than half a century ago when he explained our role as being to take away the punchbowl – the issue on which I shall conclude.

3. WHAT CAN AND SHOULD THE AUTHORITIES DO?

Confronted by the systemic risks that finance can generate but also by the benefits it can bring to economic life, society developed over the past century or more a complex Social Contract for banking comprising: (i) permissions to conduct banking; (ii) a safety net, in the form of deposit insurance and lender-of-last-resort lending by central banks; and (iii) regulation and supervision to contain the consequent moral hazard.

Each of the elements of that Social Contract are being overhauled.[6] And a crucial fourth element is being added: (iv) resolution regimes that leave the risks from bank failure with a bank's creditors rather than the taxpayer and which require banks to be structured to make resolution feasible.

On top of which, a completely new Social Contract is emerging for the risk-transfer (derivative) capital markets: (i) clearing via central counterparties; (ii) mutualisation of clearing house risk exposures amongst the firms who are their members, through mandated loss-sharing agreements and resolution regimes; and (iii) transparency so that market participants, customers and authorities can see what is going on.

I want to pick out just a few features of the new rules of the game.[7]

3.1. Expose Debt Holders to Losses: Resolution Regimes

First and foremost, we need holders of bank debt to be exposed to losses. This is not some macho thing. Leverage is especially hazardous to the economy and society if the debt holders are not exposed to loss from risk. If banks' cost of debt finance does not vary properly with the risks they are taking, an important check on the tendency to excess is badly diluted.

For the financial system to be safe, both commercial banking and investment banking operations need to be resolvable without taxpayer solvency support. Capital markets need sound intermediaries that can expire safely or be resurrected, just as the economy's payments system needs sound deposit-takers that can be resolved in an orderly way.

That is why around the world countries are introducing resolution regimes that enable them to put losses on to bondholders without all the problems of liquidation. Bail-in – a power for the Resolution Authority to write down and convert debt into equity – is one way of doing this (Tucker 2012c; Gruenberg 2012). It is included in the EU Commission's draft directive on recovery and resolution. It is not a silver bullet that can, on its own, cure every manifestation of Too-Big-To-Fail. For example, it will not work when a banking group's financial condition is rotten through and through. In those circumstances, the authorities have to focus on preserving continuity in its *most* critical (elemental) services – payments and deposit taking. The UK government's plans for ring-fencing retail banking are, therefore, a central element of building an effective resolution regime for large and complex banks. But bail-in without a break-up of the group will sometimes work, and that prospect gives debt holders a strong incentive to monitor banks' risk taking.

---

[6] On the second, for example, see Tucker (2009).
[7] For a further account, see the piece referenced in footnote 2.

3.2. Disclosure

No one can expect market discipline to work without adequate transparency. This is especially hard in banking given the inherent opacity of loan portfolios. But more could be done. Globally, the Financial Stability Board (2011) is considering this. Domestically in the UK, the Bank of England's Financial Policy Committee is embarking on doing so too (Bank of England 2012, p. 57). The authorities have a particular role in helping to avoid collective action problems, where one bank will disclose only if others do so; or in encouraging disclosures where there are wider benefits not valued sufficiently by banks. Examples include the requirements introduced by the Bank of England and the European Central Bank for transparency in the documentation of securities that are eligible as collateral in our respective monetary operations.

3.3. Expose Management to Tail Risk: Payment in Subordinated Debt

Once exposing debt holders to loss is embedded in the new rules of the game, the authorities need to consider whether management should be paid to a significant extent in subordinated debt. Giving managers a stake in an instrument whose value depends on the *survival* of their firm would helpfully heighten their incentive to maintain a safe and sound bank with robust risk management.

What I air here would probably entail revisiting the Financial Stability Board, European Union and, in the United Kingdom, Financial Services Authority codes on remuneration.

3.4. Industry Structure and Culture

Incentives may also be influenced helpfully by measures that constrain the *structure* of banking.

I have already noted that the UK's plans to ring-fence the more basic retail banking business will help to protect the core payments system in the event of a crisis that outstrips the application of group-wide resolution strategies. But it will do more than that. It effectively separates the domestic-intermediation part of banks' activities from the *entrepôt*, wholesale business centred in the City of London. The ring-fenced bank will make its own disclosures and have its own independent board of directors. As well as making it somewhat easier to see what is going on – where profits are coming from; how much capital is allocated to domestic intermediation etc. – this will help, at the margin, to maintain different cultures in domestic commercial banking and international wholesale banking.

But more will be needed to secure cultural change across all the dimensions needed.

The advent in London of a dedicated securities regulator, the Financial Conduct Authority, in 2013 will surely help – building on the work of the FSA on conduct and enforcement issues. Reviewing the structure of remuneration for desk-level bankers could also be useful – tying pay to the medium-term success of the firm so that, putting it bluntly, it is less easy to get rich quick irrespective of the quality of business transacted.

But there are even wider issues.

For example, in the area of core services to the domestic economy, we need somehow to unwind some of what I think of as the 'industrialisation of retail and business banking' that occurred during the years of plenty. During a prolonged economic upswing, branch and regional banking came too close to being seen as an exercise in sales and marketing. The role of local branch managers in granting loan applications has been diluted over recent decades. Banks' comparative advantage in making loans rests on the special information they gain from *knowing* their customers (Diamond 1984; Petersen and Rajan 1994). Recent experience reminds everybody that banking is about making credit *judgments*.

Competition policy may matter here too. Some countries – perhaps notably Australia and Canada – are sometimes characterised as shielding their main domestic commercial banks from competition, in order to dampen the temptation to launch out into risky international wholesale banking (Kent and Debelle 1999). Other countries – perhaps most obviously the US – have banned acquisitions of banks that would result in the acquirer controlling more than 10% of the country's insured deposits.

As we prepare for the transfer of prudential supervision to the Bank of England, we want to reduce barriers to entry somewhat, so that the banking system can, over time, become less concentrated. With more competitors around, the wider effects of the failure of an individual bank should be smaller.[8] That point may have received insufficient attention in stability policy.

But if supervisors are to ease the way to new banks, there needs to be confidence in the authorities' ability to resolve those banks that get into distress without dramatic spillovers. For smaller banks, that should be possible in the United Kingdom using the existing Special Resolution Regime. For larger banks, it should be delivered through the reforms agreed upon at the G20 Financial Stability Board and being implemented in the EU via a resolution directive.

We need to ensure that lowering the barriers to safe exit can also lower the barriers to entry.

---

[8] See Tucker (2012d): "The businesses making up Lloyds Banking Group and the Royal Bank of Scotland accounted for 40% of the stock of lending to UK firms in 2007.... The competition authorities care about [such concentrations] because of the quality of services provided during peacetime. But the stability authorities also need to be more alert to this source of vulnerability because it affects the economic costs of distress at individual banks".

3.5. A Cap on Leverage and Higher Risk-Based Capital Requirements

What I have described may not work. As I set out earlier, I do not subscribe to the view that distorted incentives alone caused this crisis. Myopia was part of the problem too. We cannot rule out that, after a long period of stability sometime in the future, bank managers, shareholders and debt holders will again take their eye off the big risks. Prudential supervision centred on making judgments about the big risks to safety and soundness can help – that is what the future Prudential Regulatory Authority will do in the UK.

But we also need a set of *regulatory* constraints to act as a check on risk-taking and balance sheet expansion. That is where the planned Basel leverage limit for bank balance sheet comes in. It will be a backstop to higher risk-based capital requirements.

As well as providing a bigger buffer against losses, higher capital requirements should help to change the incentives of equity investors to recapitalise a bank whose capital base is eroding. If, as when the crisis broke in 2007, the equity layer is thin, a fall in the value of banks' assets will quickly leave banks' debt trading well below par. In those circumstances recapitalisation effectively entails a substantial transfer of resources from the equity investors to debt holders. When in the future the equity layer is fatter, recapitalisation of a stressed but not chronically failing bank should be more in the interests of the equity holders themselves.

Higher capital requirements are likely to affect remuneration. As a matter of simple arithmetic, the first round effect of higher capital requirements will probably be to depress return on equity. I have thought for a while (Tucker 2011) that as the returns to shareholders decline, they will demand a larger share of the cake. Basically, I believe, but cannot prove, that so long as return on equity was persistently in the region of 20% and above, many institutional shareholders proceeded as if they did not care how much management were paid. Higher capital requirements might help to change that, and with it the incentives of bankers.

But for the frontline risk-based capital requirement to perform as intended, policy-makers need to be confident that risk-weights are determined robustly. Leaving banks completely free to choose risk-weights, using internal models, does not seem safe, given the incentives of management. Allowing banks effectively to determine their own regulatory capital requirements hardly fits with society's objectives for regulating banks. Floors on risk-weights *need*, therefore, to be debated in Basel.

3.6. Taking Away the Punchbowl: Macroprudential Policy

Much as I should like to, I do not think we can rely entirely on enhanced incentives and a *static* set of regulatory constraints. If, as I have argued, myopia plays a meaningful role in booms and busts, then markets can drive the system to the edge simply because they have misread the signals. Even when they become aware of the potential risks, a collective action problem can prevent key players from taking their foot off the accelerator.

A telling experience in the run-up to the crisis was of CROs in Wall Street talking openly about a dilemma between what they called financial risk and business risk. On the one hand, the Street was taking too much financial risk, which could end in tears. On the other hand, they were *not* certain that it *would* end in tears and they were worried that if they left the field too early, their customers would cross the street to their competition, destroying their franchise. This was highlighted by the Bank of England in 2006.[9]

The art of taking away the punchbowl – *one* crucial dimension of macroprudential policy – is to solve that collective action problem. *No* set of static rules, regulations and structures will keep the system safe. As time passes, the market will take the system to the edges of the box the authorities have tried to put it in. The authorities have to be able to respond flexibly, and we need the upfront support of society in designing a regime for doing so (Dombret and Tucker 2012). That is why the current debates in the UK Parliament about the Bank of England's new Financial Policy Committee, and in the European Union about national authorities having discretion to vary bank capital requirements for macroprudential reasons, are so important: in a word, legitimacy.

Accountability is crucial too. If the new macroprudential bodies are regularly asked by legislatures what they are doing to meet their objective of maintaining financial stability, the lessons of the current crisis are more likely to be remembered. Markets will, in time, forget about the risks, but the system should be safer if we can build official institutions that do not forget.

4. CONCLUDING REMARKS

When the financial tide goes out, it lays bare the problems that had been brewing during the 'good' times. Work to make the system safe and sound has made real progress in recent years, but it is not complete and absolutely must continue with energy.

We may not be able to abolish occasional waves of optimism that grip humanity and the tendency to excess they set off. But we can and must dampen

---

[9] See Bank of England 2006, p. 8: "Many may have believed that the price of certain assets had become too high and the premium for taking risk too low. But there are business risks associated with acting on that view when others are not; it may not only reduce profitability in the short run, but may also risk losing market share or failing to establish a foothold in a rapidly expanding market. These concerns often seem to have outweighed the risks to balance sheets associated with potentially overpriced assets. As a result, in the early part of this year, there appears to have been an extension of risk-taking activities by financial institutions, including some UK banks".

their effects on the financial system and economy. This must include changing the incentives that bankers face. It will include a simplification of the capital markets; and constraints on the effects of exuberance through policies on leverage, capital and liquidity – applied beyond banking where warranted. And it must include flexible, adaptive macroprudential regimes, which will make it easier for the authorities to step in to take away the punchbowl when the party threatens to get out of control. That will make for a safer and sounder financial system that can meet the abiding needs of the economy as a whole.

BIBLIOGRAPHY

Bank of England 2006, *Financial Stability Report*, June.
Bank of England 2007, *Financial Stability Report*, April.
Bank of England 2012, *Financial Stability Report*, June.
Berle, A. and G. Means 1932, *The Modern Corporation and Private Property*, Transaction Publishers.
Diamond, P. 1984, "Financial intermediation and delegated monitoring", *The Review of Economic Studies*, vol 51(3), pp 393-414.
Dombret, A. and P.M.W. Tucker 2012, "A Blueprint for resolving regulation", *The Financial Times*, 20 May 2012.
Financial Stability Board 2011, *Thematic Peer Review of Risk on Risk Disclosure Practices*.
Gennaioli, N., A. Shleifer and R. Vishny 2010, "Neglected risks, financial innovation, and financial fragility", *NBER Working Paper* no. 16068.
Goodhart, C.A.E. 2010, "Is a less pro-cyclical financial system an achievable goal?", *National Institute Economic Review*, 211 (1), pp. 81-90.
Greenwood, R. M. and D. S. Scharfstein 2012, "The Growth of Modern Finance", available at SSRN website: http://ssrn.com/abstract=2162179.
Gruenberg, M.J. 2012, Remarks given to the Federal Reserve Bank of Chicago Bank Structure Conference, Chicago.
Haldane, A.G. and B. Nelson 2012, *Tails of the unexpected*, given at "The Credit Crisis Five Years On: Unpacking the Crisis", conference held at the University of Edinburgh Business School.
Holmstrom, B. and J. Tirole 1997, "Financial intermediation, loanable funds, and the real sector", *The Quarterly Journal of Economics*, MIT Press, vol. 112(3), pp. 663-91.
Jensen, M.C. and W.H. Meckling 1976, "Theory of the firm: managerial behaviour, agency costs and ownership structure", *Journal of Financial Economics*, Elsevier, vol. 3(4), pp. 305-360.
Kashyap, A., R. Rajan and J. Stein 2002, "Banks as liquidity providers: an explanation for the coexistence of lending and deposit-taking", *Journal of Finance*, vol. 57(1), pp. 33-73.
Kay, J. 2012, *The Kay Review of UK Equity Markets and Long-Term Decision Making: Final Report*, London: Department for Business Innovation and Skills.
Kent, C. and G. Debelle 1999, "Trends in the Australian Banking System: Implication for Financial Stability and Monetary Policy", *Reserve Bank of Australia Discussion Paper* 1999-05.
Kiyotaki, N. and J. Moore 2005, "Financial deepening", *Journal of the European Economic Association*, vol. 3(2-3), pp. 701-713.

Lerner, J. and P. Tufano 2011, "The Consequences of Financial Innovation: A Counterfactual Research Agenda", *NBER Working Papers* 16780, National Bureau of Economic Research, Inc.

Levine, R. 2005, "Finance and Growth: Theory and Evidence", in *Handbook of Economic Growth*, eds. P. Aghion and S. Durlauf, The Netherlands: Elsevier Science.

Mount, F. 2012, *The New Few: Or a Very British Oligarchy*, Simon and Schuster.

Obstfeld, O. and K.S. Rogoff 1996, *Foundations of International Macroeconomics*, MIT Press Books, The MIT Press, edition 1, volume 1

Petersen, M. and R. Rajan 1994, "The benefits of lending relationships: Evidence from small business data", *Journal of Finance* 49, pp. 3-37.

Shiller, R.J. 1993, *Macro Markets: Creating Institutions for Managing Society's Largest Economic Risks*, Oxford University Press.

Shiller, R.J. 2012, *Finance and the Good Society*, Princeton: Princeton University Press.

Tucker, P.M.W. 2009, *The repertoire of official sector interventions in the financial system: last resort lending, market-making, and capital*, speech given at Bank of Japan's International Conference in Tokyo.

Tucker, P.M.W. 2010, *Shadow banking, financing markets and financial stability*, speech given at BGC Partners Seminar.

Tucker, P.M.W. 2011, *Discussion of Lord Turner's lecture "Reforming finance: are we being radical enough?"*. Clare Distinguished Lecture in Economics, Cambridge.

Tucker, P.M.W. 2012a, "Banking in a market economy – the international agenda", in *Investing in Change: A book of essays on financial reform in Europe*, ed. Association for Financial Markets in Europe, 2012.

Tucker, P.M.W. 2012b, *Shadow banking: thoughts for a possible policy agenda*, speech given at the European Commission High Level Conference, Brussels.

Tucker, P.M.W. 2012c, *Resolution: a progress report*, speech given at the Institute for Law and Finance Conference in Frankfurt.

Tucker, P.M.W. 2012d, *Property booms, stability and policy*. Alastair Ross Goobey Memorial Lecture given at the Investment Property Forum in London,

Turner, A. 2012,. *Shadow banking and financial instability*, speech to the Cass Business School.

9. Measuring Systemic Risk

Jaime Caruana

To manage it, you need to measure it. The dictum applies to many fields of public policy, since effectiveness depends critically on measuring the goal and performance towards it. An objective that can be quantified guides the deployment of tools, as well as making policy-makers more accountable and policy frameworks more transparent. But when it comes to financial stability policy, measurement poses a serious challenge. There are no clear quantifiable expressions of the objective, nor is there a generally agreed conceptual paradigm to guide the calibration and use of policy instruments.

This challenge has become all the more urgent, given rising financial volatility and the episodes of systemic financial distress that have become more frequent in the wake of financial liberalisation since the 1970s. These trends have pushed financial stability up the list of public policy priorities. Even before 2007, many countries were starting to build more robust and explicit policy frameworks. These efforts have been everywhere intensified in the wake of the most recent crisis, which has sharpened priorities, highlighted data gaps and triggered the revamping of existing policy frameworks. It has also boosted the interest of academic economists in the field and, with it, the pace of innovation.

This chapter aims to take stock of the progress made in the field of systemic risk measurement from the practical perspective of policy-makers. More specifically, it seeks to provide an overview of the main strands in the burgeoning literature. It is not meant to be a detailed technical survey, and it is selective rather than exhaustive in its coverage.[1] It identifies broad approaches and places them in a policy context. In doing so, it distinguishes between two dimensions of systemic risk: the time dimension, which focuses on how risk evolves over time, and the cross-sectional dimension, which focuses on the distribution of risk across the system at any given point in time.

---

[1] For more detail, see Bisias et al. (2012), who provide an excellent technical review of many analytical approaches. Gadanecz and Kaushik (2009) review different measures reported in the regular financial stability publications of central banks. BCBS (2012a, 2012b) report on work on the modelling and quantification of the interactions between the real and financial sectors and derive policy implications. For more narrowly focused reviews of particular strands in the literature, see the relevant sections below.

The overall message is unsurprising: despite recent progress, there is much scope for improvement in our understanding of the mechanisms behind financial distress and in the measurement of systemic risk. In a way, our situation is the opposite to that of weather forecasters. Meteorologists can precisely measure atmospheric conditions, such as temperature, pressure, and wind direction. They have elaborate models that can predict with relative, if varying, precision the evolution of weather systems, helping them to identify approaching storms. But they are virtually powerless to change the weather. By contrast, financial stability policy-makers are well equipped to influence the behaviour of financial markets and institutions through the use of prudential tools and monetary policy. However, they lag far behind meteorologists in their ability to measure and predict. Compared with that of meteorologists, the toolset available to policy-makers is imprecise. No less rudimentary in comparison with models of the weather is their understanding of the dynamics of the interaction between financial markets and institutions, as well as between the financial and real sectors of the economy. Narrowing this gap will take enormous effort. A side-benefit of reviews such as this one is to highlight areas where that effort can be most beneficial.

The rest of this chapter is organised as follows. The next section sets the stage by presenting a general definition of systemic risk and explaining the difference between its time and cross-sectional dimensions. The following four sections provide overviews of different categories of measurement approaches in the literature. These relate in turn to contemporaneous measures of systemic stress (section 2); early warning indicators (section 3); measures of the cross-sectional distribution of risk, including network analysis (section 4); and macro stress tests (section 5). The final section concludes.

1. SYSTEMIC RISK IN ITS TIME AND CROSS-SECTIONAL DIMENSIONS

Despite the all-pervasive references to systemic risk in the policy and academic literature, the notion remains elusive. There is no single, widely accepted, definition, let alone one that lends itself directly to measurement. The ECB (2010) defines it as a risk of financial instability "... *so widespread that it impairs the functioning of a financial system to the point where economic growth and welfare suffer materially*". Others tend to emphasise particular aspects, such as contagion (e.g., de Bandt et al. 2009), information disruptions (Mishkin 1999), or the negative impact on confidence (Billio et al. 2010). Reports by the FSB-IMF-BIS (2011) and the Group of Ten (2001) include related definitions.

Two important threads run through these definitions. The first is an emphasis on disruptions in the financial system as opposed to any particular component thereof. What is at stake is the capacity of the system to perform its services as opposed to the ability of any individual institution or market to function properly. The interactions between the components of the financial system are a key aspect of such instability. The second is the connection to the real economy and the potential for financial instability to weaken macroeconomic performance. The risk is not described purely in terms of potential losses to institutions or portfolios of investors; rather, it also includes the loss associated with wider economic disruptions, measured in terms of variables such as forgone growth and higher unemployment. While these observations are useful in understanding why we care about systemic risk, they render quantification and measurement very difficult.

Systemic risk, therefore, is a complex and multi-faceted concept. It thus makes sense to consider different aspects of risk separately, so as to obtain more precise, if necessarily less comprehensive, perspectives. One such approach that has received considerable support distinguishes between the time and the cross-sectional dimensions of risk (see Borio 2003; Caruana 2010).

The *cross-sectional dimension* refers to the way risk is distributed in the system at a given point in time. It relates to weaknesses in the organisation of markets and their infrastructure and to the concentration of risks in specific institutions or segments of the financial sector, for instance through large bilateral counterparty exposures or large exposures to similar risks. As in a securities portfolio, bulges of risk in the system result from insufficient diversification across institutions and give rise to vulnerabilities. An exogenous shock can spread quickly through a system that exhibits such weaknesses.

The *time dimension* refers to the dynamic profile of systemic risk. It is often referred to as financial system procyclicality and is closely related to the idea that finance, like the real economy, is characterised by cycles that include periods of growth and exuberance interrupted by periods of generalised strain. Booms are characterised by buoyant asset prices and rapid credit growth, which lift investors' expectations and boost their confidence. They often follow on the heels of innovation and liberalisation. Invariably, they are periods when market-based measures of risk are low and the tendency of investors to take on risks, including through leverage, is high. Imbalances that build up gradually during booms are righted abruptly in a bust, with potentially disastrous consequences for the financial and real sectors. In this sense, systemic risk in the time dimension is best understood as arising largely endogenously: the seeds of crises are sown during the boom.

This split (time versus cross-sectional dimension) is a useful device for arranging the metrics in more homogeneous groups and for facilitating comparisons. It also reflects the absence of a unified paradigm encompassing all the aspects of systemic risk. This issue is not limited to this field. For quite some time now the economics profession has lived with a qualitatively similar split between microeconomics and macroeconomics (see Borio 2003; Caruana 2010).[2] Attempts at reconciling the two have been far from perfect and, at times, even counterproductive.

2. QUANTITATIVE CONTEMPORANEOUS INDICATORS OF FINANCIAL STRESS

Over the past several years, efforts to develop metrics for financial stability (or rather financial stress) have intensified. Many of these initiatives, discussed in this section, provide what can be characterised as *contemporaneous* indicators of levels of financial stress: they point to financial strains that have already materialised or are emerging. And even when they include hints of potential future problems, they have not been specifically designed and validated to produce those results. These efforts are largely data-driven, with only limited reference to theory or specific structural explanations of financial instability dynamics.

Examples include the so-called "chartpacks" and "dashboards" that are routinely put together in policy institutions as inputs to qualitative assessments of financial stability at the country and international levels. They are organised displays of variables that relate to the performance of financial institutions, credit growth, the availability of liquidity, and asset price movements. The main idea is to combine information and to reveal common patterns without imposing too much structure. The value of such approaches derives from the way the information is organised and combined, and their ability to showcase different aspects of financial instability. The criterion for success is subjective and time-varying. It relates to whether the collection of information appears to cover the main areas of interest at the time. An example of such a set of variables is the list of Financial Soundness Indicators put together by the IMF (2008), which is intended to serve as a minimum benchmark for national authorities (see also IMF and World Bank 2003). This information is publicly disclosed.

Moving beyond the identification of relevant variables, the academic and policy literature includes many examples of composite indicators, which numerically combine several variables into a single number. Various combination methods have been proposed.[3] A popular one is to take simple averages, or weighted averages using weights inversely proportional to the variability of the series. More elaborate statistical techniques have also been used, such as principal components analysis, that distil common factors from the constituent variables.

---

[2] This comparison does not imply that the micro/macro split maps onto the time/cross-section split. After all, system-wide risk is all about the big picture, and it is in that sense a "macro" concept.
[3] See Oet et al. (2011b) for a short discussion of alternative methods of combination.

Typically, the current value of the combined indicator is benchmarked against its own past or against subjective thresholds that indicate periods of low, moderate or high stress.[4] A common validation approach compares spikes in the value of the indicator to the timing of well-known episodes of financial sector stress (e.g., the sudden failure of large financial institutions, large drops in asset prices, the 2001 terrorist attacks in New York etc.).

Financial stress indicators have become more sophisticated over time. An early example of the indicator approach is Bordo et al. (2000), who construct an index from bank charge-off rates, business failure rates, real interest rates and the spread between the interest rates paid by low and high quality borrowers. Other examples include Illing and Liu (2006), who develop an index from interest rate spreads and variables linked to stock prices for Canada, and Hanschel and Monnin (2005), who combine banks' balance sheet data (loan provisions, capitalisation etc.) with supervisory information on bank health to create a stress index for the banking sector in Switzerland.[5] More recently, Holló et al. (2012) have developed a composite stress indicator for the Euro area financial system that is itself based on five sub-indicators. The aggregation method they use puts added emphasis on the co-movement between sub-indicators.

A distinct group of stress indicators takes a more structured approach to measuring risk by looking at the financial system portfolio of securities, and treats financial firms as risky individual exposures subject to risk. The systemic supervisor, like an oversized portfolio investor, experiences (fictitious) losses in line with fluctuations in the value of those exposures. Particular outcomes in the performance of the portfolio are defined *a priori* as systemic events – situations in which the financial system is said to be under extreme duress. Systemic risk is then the likelihood that such outcomes materialise and the metric of (in-)stability is the one that summarises the losses to the portfolio in those outcomes. In some cases, this imaginary portfolio is taken to include the aggregate debt liabilities issued by the firms in the system. In those cases, the supervisor's loss resembles the pay-outs of a hypothetical deposit insurance fund that covers all of the banks' liabilities. In other cases, the loss is, in effect, defined in terms of the aggregate equity in the system. For instance, a systemic event would be an outcome in which banks' losses wipe out more than a certain percentage of the aggregate capital in the system. The assessment of systemic stress is done using the analytical techniques of portfolio credit risk management. The inputs to the analysis are the firms' balance sheets (size of assets, debt and capital) and market price information (e.g., share price volatility, CDS spreads etc.), which help pin down the value and risk of the assets of individual firms and their correlation across firms.

---

[4] Before combining them, the individual variables need to be defined so that higher numerical scores are indicative of greater stress.
[5] Nelson and Perli (2007), and Hakkio and Keeton (2009) are further examples of this approach.

Huang et al. (2009) apply this approach to derive a systemic distress insurance premium. They define as systemic events those in which banks' losses amount to at least 15% of the system's aggregate capital.[6] Acharya et al. (2012) identify systemic risk with the average decline in the equity value of banks during periods of generalised stress in the stock market.[7] Segoviano and Goodhart (2009) define a banking stability index (their proposed metric of systemic distress) as the likelihood that several banks become distressed simultaneously, with their equity falling below a minimum threshold. In these examples, interconnections among the firms in the system listed above are embedded in the asset correlation assumptions. There is no distinction between co-movement in the balance sheets of the firms that is due to common exposures and that due to exposures to each other. Drehmann and Tarashev (2011) add a matrix of bilateral exposures to the framework to better distinguish between these two sources of common risk.

3. EARLY WARNING INDICATORS

Quantitative indicators of systemic stress are most useful to policy-makers when they signal trouble well ahead of time, giving them a chance to take remedial action. By this standard, the indicators of financial distress just discussed above fall short of the mark. By the time they flash red, serious strains have already emerged or are emerging.[8] This is no coincidence. It is extremely difficult, if not impossible to predict systemic crises with any precision and with a sufficient lead. Episodes of generalised stress seem to hit the financial system with an intensity that invariably takes market participants and policy-makers by surprise. That said, and despite a badly incomplete understanding of the dynamics of the interactions between economic agents that lead to crises, policy-makers and researchers have made some progress in identifying the conditions that signal trouble ahead.

One popular line of enquiry relies on relatively simple early warning indicators (EWI). Following a similar approach to that used to build coincident financial stress indices, the idea behind EWIs is to identify variables, or combinations thereof, that provide useful signals of future distress. Again, the analysis does not deal in any depth with the question of how financial instability comes about and abstracts from the dynamics of transmission of stress across the system. It is a statistical approach that makes only limited references to theory or

---

[6] They define the hypothetical system as comprising 13 international banks. A similar measure applied on a different set of firms is reported in BIS (2008).
[7] Brownlees and Engle (2011) refine the approach in Acharya et al. (2012) by using more elaborate ways of assessing expected loss.
[8] Indeed, sometimes those contemporaneous indicators have been used as the variables to be predicted by the leading indicators discussed in this section.

structural models. The regular Early Warning Exercises conducted by the FSB in collaboration with the IMF provide an example at the international level. They offer an opportunity to assess global systemic vulnerabilities through a combination of indicators, international analysis of vulnerabilities and regulatory challenges coordinated by the FSB, and analysis of macroeconomic and macrofinancial risks produced by the IMF.

The loose link to theory and structural models is both an advantage and a disadvantage. EWIs exploit recurring patterns in the data that conform to basic intuition. These patterns can then guide the development of more formal, structural explanations of the mechanisms that produce the build-up of vulnerabilities and lead to crises. Critics argue, however, that data patterns which are not based on a solid understanding of the underlying economic mechanisms can prove unreliable as guides to action: they are prone to collapsing at the very moment that policy-makers attempt to use them.[9] From a practical viewpoint this suggests a dialectic process between policy design and EWIs – a process that employs healthy doses of judgment and that monitors the indicators' performance over time.

Analysts have engaged in a systematic investigation of a wide range of financial sector data, both prices and quantities, for their properties as EWIs. These include bank balance sheet items, such as capitalisation and measures of loan-book performance, or household and corporate balance sheet items, such as debt, liquidity and net wealth levels. These variables can certainly contribute to a more complete and nuanced picture of financial distress. They are important components for any structural explanation of how interactions between economic agents can lead to crises and, as such, they should be part of any dynamic model of this process. However, from a purely statistical perspective, and unless properly adjusted, they behave more like contemporaneous than leading indicators.

"Raw" asset prices have been of particular interest to researchers given that they embed market participants' expectations about the future performance of the underlying securities. The results are mixed, though. Asset prices tend to co-move closely with the financial cycle: growing vigorously in good times and declining precipitously in bad times. They might peak prior to the bust, but they do so unreliably. Equity prices give very little warning, with peaks that may occur just before systemic stress.[10] Credit spreads behave in a similar way.

These results suggest that, in order to provide reliable early warning signals, variables such as debt and asset prices have to be adjusted in ways that can account for their cyclical properties. In particular, if financial booms tend to

---

[9] This is the well-known critique associated with Lucas (1976) and also articulated by Goodhart (1975).

[10] See Borio and Drehmann (2009b); and Drehmann et al. (2012) for a discussion of the behaviour of asset prices prior to banking crises. Borio and McGuire (2004) analyse the determinants of the time between peaks in equity prices and banking crises.

precede and cause busts, then the trick is to identify those characteristics of the booms that make them unsustainable.

Credit has proved to be a particularly useful variable from this perspective. Financial busts tend to be preceded by persistent credit growth in excess of GDP growth. More specifically, periods when the ratio of credit to GDP exceeds its long-term trend are typically harbingers of crises. This pattern is most pronounced when one considers a horizon of one to three years prior to the event.[11]

While unusually strong cumulative credit growth has been the single most reliable indicator of impending systemic distress, its signalling power is substantially improved when combined with signals from asset prices and, in particular, from property prices. Borio and Drehmann (2009a) show that, for many countries observed over the past 40-odd years, a systemic banking crisis almost invariably followed periods when growth in both credit-to-GDP and an asset price index significantly outpaced the growth implied by their respective historical trends. The association between signals and crises is especially strong when a property price index, rather than a broad asset price index, is used. Interestingly, the pattern is similar when episodes of stress are identified with abrupt and precipitous drops in asset prices (Alessi and Detken 2011). Again, unusually strong increases in the credit-to-GDP ratio, especially when combined with unusually strong increases in asset prices, provide the most reliable signals.[12]

These observations confirm a pattern whereby the seeds of distress are sown during periods of financial euphoria. They shine a sceptical light on theories based on the premise that forward-looking investors make decisions by rationally incorporating all available information. If this were true, crises would have been fully unpredictable. Instead, the results point to systematic patterns in the dynamics of credit and asset prices that need to be better understood by economists and policy-makers. Of course, this is as far as the EWI analysis is able to go. Theorists and modellers need to take this further, explaining the nexus of incentives and perspectives that drive economic agents and give rise to instability.

---

[11] The pattern was first noted in Borio and Lowe (2002) and further documented in Borio and Drehmann (2009a).

[12] Research that uses financial stress indicators (described in section 1) as the variable to be forecast by EWIs finds broadly similar patterns. See Hanschel and Monnin (2005); Lo Duca and Peltonen (2011); and Oet et al. (2011a).

4. MEASURING THE CROSS-SECTIONAL DIMENSION: INDICATORS, NETWORKS AND SYSTEMIC CONTRIBUTION

The cross-sectional dimension of systemic risk has received less attention than the time dimension in the literature. This is not very surprising, given the difficulties in quantifying the aggregate level of risk at a given point in time. It is, after all, quite difficult to slice a cake that you cannot touch. Dealing with individual firms magnifies the practical and conceptual complications. Data issues become a more serious limitation. Consistent data on individual size and risk profiles are difficult to obtain. Information that may be available in aggregate form is confidential when it pertains to individual firms (e.g., positions in derivative contracts). And other information may not even be collected at firm level in a way that permits comparisons with other firms (e.g., bilateral risk exposures by asset class, maturity and currency). Conceptually, the analysis of the cross-sectional distribution of risk needs to distinguish between concentrations of risk due to the size of exposures of individual firms, due to the similarity of exposures across firms, and due to linkages arising from counterparty connections between firms.

These difficulties notwithstanding, quantitative analyses of the cross-sectional dimension of systemic risk can be classified in three different approaches: analysis of the relative size of firms; analysis of networks of interconnected firms; and analysis of the contribution of individual institutions to systemic or system-wide risk.

The first approach is the conceptual counterpart to the compilation of financial soundness indicators described in section 2 above. It amounts to the collection of data on the size and activity of individual firms, expressed as a share of the overall market. The underlying idea is that a firm's share in a financial activity is a proxy for its importance to the functioning of the system. The failure of a larger player is more likely to lead to serious disruptions to intermediation, not least because it will be difficult for others to step in and fill the void. This type of information is regularly published in financial stability reports. The rest of this section focuses on the other two groups of measures, which are also technically more elaborate.

Descriptions of financial crises often invoke falling dominoes as a metaphor for how financial distress spreads across the system, with each piece knocking down the next. The collapse of an important financial firm can set off a chain of counterparty failures that ripple across the system. This is especially pertinent when the failure is disorderly, as the fire-sale liquidation of positions is particularly destructive of value. Each successive round of failures destroys more of the capital that underpins finance, thus reducing the system's capacity to intermediate. Network analysis, the second type of approach, takes a similar perspective.

Network models study the transmission of stress across a system of interconnected firms. The connections between network members can be payments system exposures or counterparty relationships, such as those in the interbank market or the derivatives markets. The analysis relies on counterfactual simulations of how the system would respond to different shocks. In the typical setup, a shock originating outside the system (exogenous) hits one or more members of the network, often in the form of large losses that lead to sudden failure. The initial failure creates losses for other network participants, propagating strains through the system. When bankruptcy results in additional costs (because, for example, of value destruction in a disorderly liquidation) the eventual aggregate loss can far exceed the initial shock. Losses are even larger when many institutions are weakened at the same time, for instance because of similarities in their risk exposures. In this case the losses due to bilateral links (the key feature of the network) will add to those associated with the original shock, further undermining an already weakened capital base and tipping institutions into distress. A number of assumptions are necessary in order to perform the simulations. They relate to the way bilateral claims are cleared in the event of a failure, the loss-given-default, the reactions of network members etc. Upper (2007) provides an excellent review of the technical aspects of the simulation methodology as well as of ways to overcome data limitations, especially those concerning missing information about bilateral exposures in the network.

Models of networks have been studied in different contexts, with more applications becoming possible as more data have become available. Degryse and Ngyuen (2007), van Lelyveld and Liedrop (2006), Upper and Worms (2004), and Furfine (2003) have analysed the interbank markets in Belgium, the Netherlands, Germany and the United States, respectively. Wetherilt et al. (2010) study the network of 13 large players in the UK large-value payment system. McGuire and Tarashev (2008) and IMF (2008) use very similar methodologies to assess the robustness of the international banking market using aggregate exposures between national banking systems from the BIS international banking statistics.

The literature has also produced more general results based on theoretical explorations of how different network structures vary in their ability to withstand shocks. Allen and Gale (2000) show that a complete network (i.e. one characterised by symmetrical links across the participants) is more likely to withstand shocks than an incomplete one (i.e. one where each institution is directly connected only to a few neighbouring institutions). Freixas et al. (2000) show that the stability of a network where most players are connected with each other indirectly, for instance through a few money-centre institutions, depends on the relative size of the nodes and connections. Craig and von Peter (2010) quantify the effect of tiering in the German interbank market. Von Peter (2007) describes the characteristics of international banking centres in terms of network-based descriptive metrics applied to the exposures between national banking systems.

The strength of network models is that they provide a quantitative framework to analyse the robustness of various market structures. They produce results on the basis of straightforward computer simulations that require little information beyond counterparty exposures. Often, short or long exposures by an individual institution vis-à-vis the overall market would suffice to run the relevant simulation algorithm. It is not unusual for these data to be collected as part of the daily operations of the payments system or the central bank (e.g., payment system flows or bank-to-bank transactions in central bank reserves). The data may be useful for quite different purposes, such as market surveillance, as in the case of information on banks' participation in interbank funding markets.

Simplicity, however, also has its drawbacks. The information on exposures is unrealistically static, freezing the picture at a specific point in time. Wholesale funding positions can change rapidly, especially in the first stages of generalised financial stress. Changes in the pattern of bilateral exposures can have major implications for financial stability. For example, exposures may become more concentrated in a few key players that are perceived to be safer. Simulations are mechanical exercises with minimal assumptions about how the incentives of participants may affect their behaviour. This limits the reliability of the results.[13] Network analysis based on granular and up-to-date information is a tool better suited to crisis management, when the authorities are weighing the potential repercussions of an institution failing, rather than to crisis prevention, when the objective is to uncover systemic vulnerabilities to specific risks over the medium term.

The third group of approaches assesses the systemic importance of individual firms in terms of their contribution to the overall risk in the system. The approach builds on the portfolio risk measurement techniques discussed in section 2. The systemic supervisor attributes risk to financial firms much as a risk manager in a firm attributes firm-wide risk to individual positions or trading desks. The clear strength in this approach is the seamless connection between the time and cross-sectional dimensions of systemic risk. The drawback is that the metrics are linked to specific parametric models that are used to measure the overall risk in the system.

Tarashev et al. (2010, 2011) take a method developed by Lloyd Shapley in the context of game theory and adapt it to the allocation of system-wide risk to individual firms. They use the expected loss on the aggregate portfolio of firms' liabilities as a metric of risk and find that individual contributions to system risk increase at least proportionately with the firm's size. Huang et

---

[13] Elsinger et al. (2006a) found that common exposures across all banks are a much more important driver of system-wide risk than the network of bilateral links between banks.

al. (2010, 2011) use a similar metric of overall risk and a simpler allocation procedure to assess the systemic importance of a number of Asian banks and a group of international lenders, respectively.[14] Adrian and Brunnermeier (2011) extend the popular value-at-risk (VaR) metric of portfolio risk in defining the CoVaR (conditional VaR) as the VaR of the aggregate asset portfolio conditional on the individual bank's current state. The contribution of the individual bank to system-wide risk is the difference between its CoVaR when the bank is under stress and the same metric conditional on it being in its normal state.

5. MACRO STRESS TESTS

Stress testing is an approach adapted from engineering. Engineers routinely subject constructions and materials to extreme conditions, in a controlled environment, in order to assess their resistance to stress. The idea is to assess their physical limits and to understand their weaknesses. Stress tests in the context of financial stability analysis simulate the impact of specific economic scenarios on the balance sheet and earnings of financial institutions. They may also trace the shock's impact through the interactions of institutions and the feedback with the macroeconomy.

The basic design of a stress test involves four elements.[15] The first is the choice of the type of portfolios that will be shocked. This includes the choice of participating institutions and the relevant portion of their balance sheet. The second element is the stress scenario, i.e. a quantitative description of the shocks assumed to hit the economy and financial institutions. The third element can be loosely termed the "model". It covers how the exercise translates the shocks into losses for the institutions, how it captures the reaction of institutions to those losses and their interaction and, potentially, how it incorporates feedbacks between the financial system and the macroeconomy. The final element is the outcome of the test – the metric of the impact of the scenario. For example, this can be the overall impact on banks' capital position, or the impact on the supply of credit or even on output and growth.

Stress testing is better seen as a toolbox than a single tool. Stress tests come in various shapes and sizes. The *micro* variety is performed routinely by bank risk managers, who are interested in analysing the response to scenarios of single portfolios, or an institution's entire balance sheet. These tests can focus narrowly on specific risk types (e.g., credit, market, liquidity) or analyse richer "what if" scenarios concerning the macroeconomy or financial markets (e.g.,

---

[14] Acharya et al. (2012) use the same attribution approach as Huang et al. (2010, 2011) but their measure of risk is the expected decline in the value of the equity of the firm in a generalised market slump. Brownlees and Engle (2011) refine Acharya et al. (2012).

[15] For a more detailed discussion of the various components of stress tests, see Drehmann (2009) and references therein.

a recession, sharp asset price declines, drying up of funding liquidity). *Macro* stress tests, by contrast, are coordinated exercises across a number of institutions with a view to getting a better idea of how the system as a whole can cope with specific stress scenarios. These exercises can combine the outcomes of tests conducted by the institutions themselves on the basis of a common scenario, the so-called *bottom-up* approach, or alternatively, involve analysis of system-wide data carried out at a centralised location, the so-called *top-down* approach. The two approaches can also be combined (see below). In addition, the tools involved in the simulations vary widely, from simple equations that summarise stylised relationships between micro and macro variables to more sophisticated behavioural models that incorporate the incentives and reactions of different economic agents.

Macro stress tests are widely used policy tools, and the available techniques are well covered in the literature. The earlier approaches included a set of basic equations that linked measures of banks' performance (e.g., profits and losses, or loan loss reserves) to broad macroeconomic aggregates (see Blaschke et al. 2001; Bunn et al. 2005). Segoviano and Padilla (2006) describe how these approaches can be made more robust through more complex modelling. Elsinger et al. (2006a, b) develop a model to assess risk in the Austrian banking sector that can capture market, credit and counterparty risk. The model combines a credit register with interbank data to trace the effects of shocks across the system. Drehmann et al. (2010a) present a granular model that accounts for risks on both sides of banks' balance sheets and can accommodate different assumptions about how banks' investment decisions respond to fluctuations in profits. Bank of England staff have built a risk assessment model (named RAMSI) that fairly comprehensively covers different types of risk to banks' balance sheets and performance and that allows for feedback both within the financial system and between the financial and real sectors.[16] Feedback paths to the macroeconomy are also explored in the Swedish model, as described in Jacobsen et al. (2005). Finally, Gray et al. (2006), and Gray and Jobs (2010) adopt a different approach, based on contingent claims and the work of Merton (1974), that traces the behaviour of mark to market positions of different sectors (government, corporate, households, financial firms) under normal and stressed conditions. The link to non-linear option pricing can more easily accommodate non-linearities in the behaviour of these sectors.

The ability of stress tests to combine different analytical components is a strength of the approach. Linking partial models of different sectors can provide a more general picture of the financial sector and its interaction with the macroeconomy. That said, their output should be treated with caution given the limited progress in developing analytical techniques that capture the complexity of behaviour. In fact, experience has shown time and again that stress tests

---

[16] See Aikman et al. (2009); and Kapadia et al. (2011) for descriptions of RAMSI.

are not very good at uncovering vulnerabilities that develop in good times. Borio et al. (2012) attribute this to two related factors. The first is that, in practice, modelling technology remains fundamentally linear, and hence incapable of capturing the dynamics unleashed in periods of financial distress. The other is that tests conducted in good times are unable to distinguish between market estimates of risk (interest rate spreads, price volatility etc.) that are very low because the true risks are low and those that are very low because they reflect aggressive risk-taking.[17] Taking these initial conditions as given, a linear framework will be unable to produce sizeable losses, even when these are imminent, unless subjected to unreasonably large shocks.[18] When tests are conducted during periods of stress (as part of the efforts in crisis management and resolution) they tend to provide more reliable outcomes, because they start from already weakened initial conditions for the financial system. Even then the tests need to be based on realistic valuations that fully recognise those weaker conditions.

Despite these important caveats, macro stress tests are useful instruments in the policy toolbox. If properly designed, they help build a common understanding among private-sector risk managers and supervisors of how to think about risks; they can thus better support crisis resolution efforts. Their performance in assessing vulnerabilities in good times could also be improved, by combining the technology of macro stress tests with the information from EWIs as discussed above.

6. CONCLUSIONS

Efforts to develop quantitative measures to support financial stability policy have borne fruit. Much progress has been made in harnessing existing data, both at the macro and micro level, as well as in producing financial system stress indicators, measures of system-wide risk and early warning signals for financial imbalances that might lead to trouble down the road. This chapter has reviewed the major developments from a policy perspective.

A testimonial to the progress made is that such quantitative tools are finding their way into actual policymaking. One example is the countercyclical capital buffer embedded in the newly agreed Basel III framework. The requirement encourages banks to build capital during financial booms to help them deal with the subsequent bust. The buffer's design builds on the work done to establish early warning indicators that identify deviations of the credit-to-GDP ratio

---

[17] This is what Borio and Drehmann (2009b) label the paradox of financial instability: the system looks strongest precisely when it is most fragile.

[18] In fact, stress tests have repeatedly given a clean bill of health to financial systems just prior to a crisis. Borio et al. (2012) cite a few examples.

from its long-term trend as a robust harbinger of episodes of systemic stress.[19] Another example is the quantitative approach to addressing the risk posed by global systemically important banks (G-SIBs), as decided by the Group of Governors and Heads of Supervision and endorsed by the Financial Stability Board (see BCBS 2011). The assessment of systemic relevance is made on the basis of a set of simple indicators that are combined to produce a measure of an institution's contribution to systemic risk in the global financial system. Similar frameworks are expected to be put in place in individual jurisdictions to deal with financial firms deemed systemically important in their domestic financial systems.

At the same time, however, these examples also highlight the shortcomings in measurement technology and the need for further work to upgrade the measurement toolbox. The credit-to-GDP gap is not a rigid benchmark but just a guide that authorities can use in setting the countercyclical buffer: substantial discretion is allowed to policy-makers in making a richer assessment of the build-up of financial imbalances. Similarly, the G-SIB framework is based on simple indicators because the more structural, model-based approaches are still insufficiently robust for policy purposes. Lack of data on cross-exposures among financial firms is a major issue.

The crisis has galvanised efforts to develop analytical tools for financial stability policy. On-going work in academia and in policy organisations focuses on models that capture the interactions between the real and financial sectors (see surveys in BCBS 2012a, 2012b). At the same time, statisticians are making major efforts to improve data collection to support the monitoring of systemic stability at the national and international levels.

Better measurement is the prerequisite for better policy. Although the science of financial stability may inevitably lack the precision of meteorology, it is often said that everyone talks about the weather but nobody does anything about it. By improving our ability to measure systemic risk, we will also improve policy effectiveness, not least by enhancing policy-maker accountability and by clarifying the allocation of responsibilities across different areas of public policy. Yet it is essential to remain prudent in our risk management and acknowledge that our understanding of the financial system remains far from perfect.

---

[19] See references in BCBS (2010) to Drehmann et al. (2010b).

BIBLIOGRAPHY

Acharya, V., L. Pedersen, T. Philippon and M. Richardson 2012, "Measuring systemic risk", *CEPR Discussion Paper,* no DP8824, February. Available at SSRN: http://ssrn. com/abstract=2013815.

Adrian, T. and M. Brunnermeier 2011, "CoVaR", *NBER Working Paper*, no 17454, National Bureau of Economic Research.

Aikman, D., P. Alessandri, B. Eklund, P. Gai, S. Kapadia, E. Martin, N. Mora, G. Stern and M. Willison 2009, "Funding liquidity risk in a quantitative model of systemic stability", *Bank of England Working Paper*, no 372.

Alessi, L. and C. Detken 2011, "Quasi real time early warning indicators for costly asset price boom/bust cycles: a role for global liquidity", *European Journal of Political Economy*, 27 (3), September, pp. 520–33.

Allen, F. and D. Gale 2000, "Financial contagion", *Journal of Political Economy*, 108(1), pp. 1–33.

Bank for International Settlements 2008, 78th Annual Report, Chapter VII, Basel, June.

Basel Committee on Banking Supervision 2010, *Guidance for national authorities operating the countercyclical capital buffer*, December 2010.

Basel Committee on Banking Supervision 2011, *Global systemically important banks: Assessment methodology and the additional loss absorbency requirement – Final document*, November.

Basel Committee on Banking Supervision 2012a, "The policy implications of transmission channels between the financial system and the real economy", *BCBS Working Paper*, no 20, May.

Basel Committee on Banking Supervision 2012b, "Models and tools for macroprudential analysis", *BCBS Working Paper*, no 21, May.

Billio, M., M. Getmansky, A. Lo and L. Pelizzon 2010, "Econometric measures of systemic risk in the finance and insurance sectors", *NBER Working Paper*, no 16223, July.

Bisias, D., M. Flood, A. Lo and S. Valavanis, 2012, "A survey of systemic risk analytics", US Department of Treasury, *Office of Financial Research Working Paper Series*, no 1. Available at SSRN: http://ssrn.com/abstract=1983602 or http://dx.doi. org/10.2139/ssrn.1983602.

Blaschke, W., M. Jones, G. Majnoni and S. Peria 2001, "Stress testing of financial systems: an overview of issues, methodologies, and FSAP experiences", *IMF Working Paper*, 01/88.

Bordo, M., M. Dueker and D. Wheelock 2000, "Aggregate price shocks and financial instability: an historical analysis", *NBER Working Paper*, no 7652.

Borio, C, 2003, "Towards a macroprudential framework for financial supervision and regulation?", *CESifo Economic Studies*, vol 49, no 2/2003, pp. 181–216. Also available as *BIS Working Paper*, no 128, February.

Borio, C. and M. Drehmann 2009a, "Assessing the risk of banking crises – revisited", *BIS Quarterly Review*, March 2009, pp. 29–46.

Borio, C. and M. Drehmann 2009b, "Towards an operational framework for financial stability: 'fuzzy' measurement and its consequences", 12th Annual Conference of the Central Bank of Chile on *Financial stability, monetary policy and central banking*. Also available as *BIS Working Paper*, no 284, June.

Borio, C., M. Drehmann and K. Tsatsaronis 2012, "Stress testing macro stress testing: does it live up to expectations?", *BIS Working Paper*, no 369, January.

Borio, C. and P. Lowe 2002, "Assessing the risk of banking crises", *BIS Quarterly Review*, December, pp. 43–54.

Borio, C. and P. McGuire 2004, "Twin peaks in equity and housing prices?", *BIS Quarterly Review*, March, pp. 79–93.

Brownlees, C. and R. Engle 2011, "Volatility, correlation and tails for systemic risk measurement", mimeo. Available at SSRN: http://ssrn.com/abstract=1611229.

Bunn, P., A. Cunningham and M. Drehmann 2005, "Stress testing as a tool for assessing systemic risk", *Bank of England Financial Stability Review*, June, pp. 116–26.

Caruana, J. 2010, "Systemic risk: how to deal with it?", speech, BIS publications. www.bis.org/publ/othp08.htm.

Craig, B. and G. von Peter 2010, "Interbank tiering and money centre banks", *BIS Working Paper*, no 322, October.

De Bandt, O., P. Hartmann and J. L. Peydro 2009, "Systemic risk: an update", in *Oxford Handbook of Banking*, eds. A Berger et al., Oxford University Press.

Degryse, H. and G. Nguyen 2007, "Interbank exposures: an empirical examination of systemic risk in the Belgian banking system", *International Journal of Central Banking*, no 3(2), pp. 123–71.

Drehmann, M. 2009, "Macroeconomic stress testing banks: A survey of methodologies" in M. Quagliariello (ed.) Stress testing the banking system: Methodologies and applications, Cambridge University Press.

Drehmann, M., C. Borio, L. Gambacorta, G. Jimenez, and C. Trucharte 2010b, "Countercyclical capital buffers: exploring options", *BIS Working Paper*, no 317, July.

Drehmann, M., C. Borio and K. Tsatsaronis 2012, "Characterising the financial cycle: don't lose sight of the medium term!", *BIS Working Paper*, no 380, June.

Drehmann, M., A. Patton and S. Sorensen 2007, "Non-linearities and stress testing", in *Risk measurement and systemic risk: Proceedings of the fourth joint central bank research conference*, ECB.

Drehmann, M., S. Sorensen and M. Stringa 2010a, "The integrated impact of credit and interest rate risk on banks: a dynamic framework and stress testing application", *Journal of Banking and Finance*, no 34, pp. 735–51.

Drehmann, M. and N. Tarashev 2011, "Systemic importance: some simple indicators", *BIS Quarterly Review*, March, pp. 25–37.

ECB 2010, "Analytical models and tools for the identification and assessment of systemic risks", *Financial Stability Review*, June, pp. 138–46.

Elsinger, H., A. Lehar and M. Summer 2006a, "Risk assessment for banking systems", *Management Science*, no 52, pp. 1301–14.

Elsinger, H., A. Lehar and M. Summer 2006b, "Using market information for banking system risk assessment", *International Journal of Central Banking*, 2(1), pp. 137–65.

Freixas, X., B. Parigi and J. C. Rochet 2000, "Systemic risk, interbank relations and liquidity provision by the central bank", *Journal of Money, Credit and Banking*, 32(3), Part 2, pp. 611–38.

FSB-IMF-BIS 2009, *Guidance to assess the systemic importance of financial institutions, markets and instruments: initial considerations*, October 2009.

FSB-IMF-BIS 2011, *Macroprudential policy tools and frameworks, progress report to G20*, October.

Furfine, C. 2003, "Interbank exposures: quantifying the risk of contagion", *Journal of Money, Credit and Banking*, 35(1), pp. 111–28.

Gadanecz, B. and J. Kaushik 2009, "Measures of financial stability – a review", in *Irving Fisher Committee Bulletin*, no 31: Proceedings of the IFC Conference on Measuring Financial Innovation and its Impact, pp. 361–80, July.

Goodhart, C. 1975, "Problems of monetary management: the UK experience", *Papers in Monetary Economics*, Reserve Bank of Australia. Also published in *Inflation, de-*

pression, and economic policy in the West, Anthony Courakis (ed), Rowman & Littlefield, pp. 111-46.

Gray, D. and A. Jobst 2010, "New directions in financial sector and sovereign risk management", *Journal of Investment Management*, vol 8, no 1.

Gray, D., R. Merton and Z. Bodie 2006, "A new framework for analyzing and managing macrofinancial risks of an economy", *NBER Working Paper*, 12637.

Group of Ten 2001, *Report on consolidation in the financial sector*, January.

Hakkio, C. and W. Keeton 2009, "Financial stress: what is it, how can it be measured, and why does it matter?", *Economic Review*, Federal Reserve Bank of Kansas City, second quarter, pp. 5–50.

Hanschel, E. and P. Monnin 2005, "Measuring and forecasting the stress in the banking sector: evidence from Switzerland", *BIS Papers*, no 22, April, pp. 431–49.

Holló, D., M. Kremer and M. Lo Duca 2012, "CISS – a composite indicator of systemic stress in the financial system", *ECB Working Paper*, no 1426, March.

Huang, X., H. Zhou and H. Zhu 2009, "A framework for assessing the systemic risk of major financial institutions", *Journal of Banking and Finance*, vol 33, pp. 2036–49.

Huang, X., H. Zhou and H. Zhu 2010, "Assessing the systemic risk of a heterogeneous portfolio of banks during the recent financial crisis", *BIS Working Paper*, no 296, January.

Huang, X., H. Zhou and H. Zhu 2011, "Systemic risk contributions", mimeo. Available at SSRN: http://ssrn.com/abstract=1650436.

Illing, M. and Y. Liu 2006, "Measuring financial stress in a developed country: an application to Canada", *Journal of Financial Stability*, 2 (4), pp. 243–65.

IMF 2008, *Financial Soundness Indicators*.

IMF 2009, *Global Financial Stability Report*, April.

IMF and World Bank 2003, *Analytical Tools of the Financial Sector Assessment Program*, 24 February.

Jacobsen, T., J.Linde and K.Roszbach 2005, "Exploring interactions between real activity and the financial stance", *Journal of Financial Stability*, 1 (3), pp. 308–41.

Kapadia, S., M. Drehmann, J. Elliot and G. Stern 2011, "Liquidity risk, cash flow constraints and systemic feedbacks", in *Quantifying systemic risk*, J. Haubrich and A. Lo (eds), NBER, (forthcoming).

Lo Duca, M. and T. Peltonen 2011, "Macro-financial vulnerabilities and future financial stress: assessing systemic risks and predicting systemic events", *ECB Working Paper*, no 1311, March.

Lucas, R. 1976, "Econometric policy evaluation: a critique", in *The Phillips curve and labor markets*, K. Brunner and A. Meltzer (eds), Carnegie-Rochester Conference Series on Public Policy, no 1, American Elsevier, pp. 19–46.

McGuire, P. and N.Tarashev 2008, "Global monitoring with the BIS international banking statistics", *BIS Working Paper*, no 244.

Merton, R. 1974, "On the pricing of corporate debt: the risk structure of interest rates", *Journal of Finance*, 29, pp. 449–70.

Mishkin, F. 1999, "Global financial instability: framework, events, issues", *The Journal of Economic Perspectives*, vol 13(4), pp. 3–20.

Nelson, W. and R. Perli 2007, "Selected indicators of financial stability", *Risk Measurement and Systemic Risk*, ECB, pp. 343–72.

Nier, E., J.Yang, T. Yorulmazer and A. Alentorn 2007, "Network models and financial stability", *Journal of Economic Dynamics and Control*, vol. 31, issue 6.

Oet, M., R. Eiben, T. Bianco, D. Gramlich, S. Ong and J. Wang 2011a, "SAFE: An early warning system for systemic banking risk", *Federal Reserve Bank of Cleveland Working Paper* 11-29, November.

Oet, M. R. Eiben, T. Bianco, D. Gramlich, and S. Ong 2011b, "The financial stress index: identification of systemic risk conditions", *Federal Reserve Bank of Cleveland Working Paper*, 11-30, November.

Quagliarello, M. 2009, *Stress testing the banking system: methodologies and applications*, Cambridge University Press.

Segoviano, M. and C. Goodhart 2009, "Banking stability measures", *IMF Working Paper,* no 09/04.

Segoviano, M. and P. Padilla 2006, "Portfolio credit risk and macroeconomic shocks: applications to stress testing under data-restricted environments", *IMF Working Paper*, no 06/283.

Tarashev, N., C. Borio, and K. Tsatsaronis 2009, "The systemic importance of financial institutions", *BIS Quarterly Review*, September, pp. 75–87.

Tarashev, N., C. Borio, and K. Tsatsaronis 2010, "Attributing systemic risk to individual institutions", *BIS Working Paper*, no 308, May.

Upper, C. 2007, "Using counterfactual simulations to assess the dangers of contagion in interbank markets", *BIS Working Paper*, no 234, August.

Upper, C. and A. Worms 2004, "Estimating bilateral exposures in the German interbank market: is there a danger of contagion?", *European Economic Review*, 48(4), pp. 827–49.

Van Lelyveld, I. and F. Liedrop 2006, "Interbank contagion in the Dutch banking sector: a sensitivity analysis", *International Journal of Central Banking*, 2(2), pp. 99–133.

Von Peter, G. 2007, "International banking centres: a network perspective", *BIS Quarterly Review*, December, pp. 33–45.

Wetherilt, A., P. Zimmerman and K. Soramäki 2010, "The sterling unsecured loan market during 2006–08: insights from network theory", *Bank of England Working Paper*, no 398, July.

PART II:

The Consequences of Financial Instability

10. Sovereign Risk

Lorenzo Bini Smaghi

1. WHAT IS SOVEREIGN RISK AND DEFAULT?

Sovereign risk refers to the risk of a government defaulting on its debt (sovereign debt) or other obligations.

Before assessing sovereign default in more detail, we should first properly define it. Unfortunately, no off-the-shelf definition exists. Clearly, the concept of sovereign default has a legal dimension: it is when a scheduled debt service is not paid beyond a grace period specified in the debt contract.

However, in the literature and in the financial world many other definitions exist. For credit rating agencies, a "technical" default is when the sovereign makes a restructuring offer on terms that are less favourable than the original debt (see Hatchondo et al. 2007). "Default" has also been defined more broadly. Manasse and Roubini (2005), for example, also include episodes of incipient defaults which they believe were averted through large-scale international bailouts, such as in Mexico in 1995, Turkey in 2000 and Brazil in 2001. And Sy (2004) defines a sovereign debt crisis as being when sovereign spreads over US Treasuries rise to 1,000 basis points (10%) or more (see Hatchondo et al. 2007).

In this chapter, we will focus on the broad definition of sovereign default and sovereign risk. We will first compare the difference between the concept of sovereign default and corporate bankruptcy (section 2). In section 3 we will then consider the historical experience, also assessing how sovereign debt crises have been resolved (i.e. how sovereign debt restructuring was carried out in the past).[1] Thereafter, we will compare the difference between sovereign distress for emerging and for advanced economies (section 4). Finally, in section 5 we will consider the specific features of sovereign default risk in a monetary union.

---

[1] It is important to note that a sovereign debt crisis in some instances has been resolved through a restructuring of the sovereign debt without resulting in a sovereign default in the legal sense (i.e. when a scheduled debt service is not paid after a grace period specified in the debt contract). Such restructurings are called *pre-emptive debt restructurings* in this chapter. They contrast with debt restructurings which happened *after* a sovereign default, i.e. a missed payment (and are called post-default sovereign debt restructurings in this chapter). In some cases, however, a pre-emptive sovereign debt restructuring has provided insufficient debt relief and led nevertheless to a sovereign default.

2. CORPORATE BANKRUPTCY AND SOVEREIGN DEFAULT

'Countries don't go out of business... The infrastructure doesn't go away, the produc-tivity of the people doesn't go away, the natural resources don't go away. And so their assets always exceed their liabilities, which is the technical reason for bankruptcy. And that's very different from a company.' (Walter Wriston, Citicorp Chairman 1970-1984)

Sovereign defaults and debt workouts have always attracted special atten-tion. Such attention is warranted since the resolution of sovereign defaults is complicated and costly. Corporate debt workouts are different. If a corporate can no longer honour its obligations, creditors can go to court and seize its as-sets. A corporate debt workout can admittedly be costly too, but the costs tend to be much higher for the sovereign due to the externalities they may generate. Indeed, the debt restructuring of a sovereign may have severe implications for the debtor's domestic economy. It can affect the domestic banking sector to such an extent that it may lead to bank runs and bank failures, as many restruc-turings in the past have shown.

Sovereign debt workouts also tend to be more complicated than corporate ones. When a corporate goes bankrupt, the resolution is "relatively straightfor-ward": the firm is liquidated. It will be required to sell off all its assets and pay off all its debts. For sovereigns, the situation is different for several reasons.

First of all, unlike a company, a sovereign cannot be liquidated. If a sover-eign becomes insolvent – due to poor macroeconomic performance and poli-cies – it cannot simply be dissolved at the end of an insolvency procedure. It will continue to exist. This also makes it impossible to use existing insolvency codes to handle the financial failure of a state.

Second, there is often very little income or collateral that a country can credibly pledge in repayment to creditors (see Bolton and Jeanne 2008), and creditors have little or no control over the actions of the sovereign due to the concept of sovereign immunity. This is the concept in international law that a sovereign nation cannot be sued by private parties (or other sovereign au-thorities) against its own will. The concept is derived from the meaning of sovereignty.[2] Creditors have sought to strengthen their rights in the event of a sovereign default by including waivers of sovereign immunity in most loan contracts and bond covenants. However, creditors attempting to use litigation to enforce claims against defaulting sovereigns have rarely been successful.

---

[2] The English term *sovereignty* is derived from the French word *souverain*: "a supreme ruler not accountable to anyone, except perhaps to God". See Fowler and Bunck, supra note 7, at 4 (citing Ivo Duchacek, Nations and Men: International Politics Today 46 (1966), discussing the etymology of the English word *sovereign*) in Nagan and Hammer on *The Changing Character of Sovereignty in International Law and International Relations.*

Finally, and most importantly, there is greater uncertainty when it comes to assessing the sustainability of the debt of a sovereign than of a corporate. Making judgements about the sustainability of a country's debt is both an analytical and a political issue, as the capacity to service debt in part concerns the willingness and the ability to implement policies that will generate the resources needed to service the debt. In some abstract sense, debt can almost always be serviced. But there exists a threshold beyond which policies to force such an outcome become unacceptable. This threshold is country-specific and in the first instance a decision for the respective government. However, the international community has to judge whether to accept where the government has drawn the line (see Boorman 2002). Indeed, the sovereign may be inclined to "gamble for redemption". If so, the country should not be allowed to restructure but should be forced to make the domestic adjustment and possibly sell assets before engaging in a restructuring.

3. THE EXPERIENCE OF SOVEREIGN DEFAULTS

3.1. The Historical Incidence of Sovereign Defaults

History is replete with instances of sovereign default. Indeed, sovereign default is as old as sovereign debt. In Europe, during the mid-sixteenth century, for instance, the kingdoms of France, Spain and Portugal defaulted. In the case of Spain, Philip II defaulted four times on his short-term loans during his rule (1556-1598), thus becoming the first serial defaulter in history (see Drelichman and Voth 2009). Other European states followed in the seventeenth century, including Prussia in 1683 (see table 10.1).

Although debt crises are as old as sovereign debt itself, it was only in the mid-nineteenth century that the number and geographical incidence of debt crises, defaults and debt workouts increased sharply. Between 1824 and 2004, S&P reports 218 sovereign defaults. This rapid increase was mainly a by-product of increasing cross-border debt flows, newly independent governments and the development of modern financial markets. Defaults have been most frequent in Latin America and Africa; no advanced economy has defaulted since the inter-war period.

As noted by Sturzenegger and Zettelmeyer (2005), default episodes tend to come in temporal and regional clusters. Defaults were most common during the Great Depression of the 1930s and during the economic crises that struck developing countries in the 1980s.[3]

---

[3] From 1945 to 1975 there were just five sovereign defaults. Interestingly, during this period expropriation of foreign assets peaked. In 1970 alone, there were at least 25 nationalisations and expropriations of foreign assets (see Tomz and Wright 2008).

Table 10.1: European sovereign debt default history

Austria	England	France	Germany	Greece	Holland	Portugal	Spain
1796	1340	1558	1683	1826	1814	1560	1557
1938	1472	1624	1807	1843		1828	1560
1940	1594	1648	1813	1860		1837	1575
1945		1661	1932	1893		1841	1596
		1701	1939	1932		1845	1607
		1715				1852	1627
		1770				1890	1647
		1788					1809
		1812					1820
							1831
							1834
							1851
							1867
							1872
							1882
							1936
							1937
							1938
							1939

Sources: Reinhart and Rogoff (2009), and Drelichman and Voth (2009).

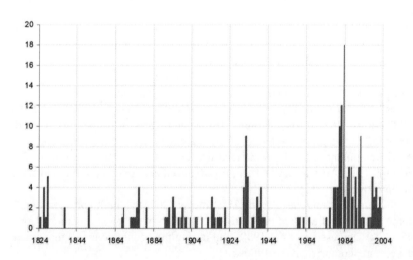

Figure 10.1: Sovereign defaults per year

Source: S&P data for foreign bank and bond defaults in Borensztein and Panizza (2008).

Whereas the number of countries defaulting reached a high in the early 1980s, the amount of sovereign debt in default instead peaked at more than USD 335 billion in 1990. This debt was issued by 55 countries (see Beers and Chambers, 2006). One of the largest defaults in history occurred in late December 2001, when Argentina defaulted on USD 82 billion.

3.2. Why does a Sovereign Default?

Broadly speaking, there are three main reasons why a sovereign decides to default, namely: i) a liquidity problem; ii) a sustainability problem, and iii) unwillingness to pay. Due to the mutually reinforcing interaction between the financial markets and sovereign debt sustainability, a liquidity problem can quickly turn into a sustainability problem. At the end of the day, however, the ultimate decision to default – though at some point unavoidable due to market forces – rests with the sovereign, i.e. no other party can decide on the default (see Baer et al. 2009). The three causes are discussed below in detail.

Liquidity problem. An economy faces a liquidity problem when its debt liabilities coming due in a given period exceed its liquid assets, including funds that it has borrowed from overseas. In other words, an economy faces a cash flow problem, although it might be solvent in the long run. Liquidity problems generally emerge when there is a sudden change in investor sentiment.

Sustainability problem. A solvency problem, by contrast, is when the sovereign (or in an even broader sense, the economy) may not be able to service its debt out of its own resources. For the sovereign, this could be assessed by verifying if the government is in compliance with the present value borrowing constraint (PVBC), also known as the intertemporal fiscal constraint. According to the PVBC, the current stock of government debt is less than or equal to the discounted sum of expected future government surpluses, which means that the government is not financing itself through a Ponzi scheme (see, for instance, Stoica and Leonte 2011). A solvency problem implies that government debt is unsustainable over the medium to long-term horizon. While a medium to longer-term solvency problem can result in a near-term liquidity problem, it is possible for a liquidity problem to arise independently of a solvency problem. Distinguishing the two is not straightforward.

Unwillingness to pay. In theory, a country may decide to repudiate its debt well before facing a sustainability problem. However, such a decision is highly controversial. In particular, while such a decision may be seen as welfare-improving in the short term, other effects from not servicing the debt (such as the implications for the bank sector, the macroeconomic consequences, the long-run financial costs) may well outweigh the prima facie short-term gains. The relatively small number of defaults observed to date implicitly also confirms the potentially high costs of defaulting.

3.3. Costs and Consequences of a Default

Sovereign lending is a risky business. Lenders put their fate in the hands of the sovereign. Given the lack of a third-party enforcement of the creditor's rights in the presence of sovereign immunity, we may even wonder why cross-border lending occurs at all. The sovereign debt literature has traditionally focused on two explanations: reputational costs/direct sanctions acting as a deterrent for the sovereign on the one hand and the broader costs to the domestic economy on the other hand. The reputational cost of default has a well-established theoretical and historical tradition (see, for instance, Eaton and Gersovitz 1981). However, the empirical evidence is inconclusive, although some studies do point to an adverse effect on the government's cost of future borrowing (see Özler 1993 and Reinhart et al. 2003). The broader losses for the economy – i.e. beyond those caused by a tightening of the terms and conditions imposed by foreign creditors – work via the impact on the domestic financial system and also on the corporate access to external finance. In both cases, the impacts can be significant and in this context the IMF (2006) found that on average, real GDP contracts by 7.5% in countries that underwent a sovereign default, whereas it only declined by 3.6% in countries that went through a crisis but restructured their debt prior to default. In addition, De Paoli et al. (2006) found that the longer a country is in arrears, the higher the output loss will be.

3.4. Sovereign Defaults versus Sovereign Pre-Emptive Debt Restructuring

When assessing sovereign debt crises, it is important to note that many did not result in an outright "default" (i.e. when a scheduled debt service is not paid beyond a grace period specified in the debt contract) but resulted from the decision of the sovereign to restructure the debt in a pre-emptive manner.

In principle, pre-emptive restructurings are considered to be aimed at liquidity problems, while outright defaults tend to be more associated with insolvency problems (see Díaz-Cassou et al. 2008). However, there exists no one-to-one link. Indeed, sovereign debt crises tend to be country-specific events and decisions on how to resolve them have an important country-specific element. Nevertheless, table 10.2 shows that preventive cases have indeed tended to be more associated with liquidity problems or ambiguous situations. Outright solvency crises in the sample considered by the authors have only been solved via post-default restructurings.

In terms of the outcome of pre-emptive versus post-default restructurings, the following features can be identified:
- Countries that restructured pre-emptively generally received less debt reduction than those that restructured post-default (see table 10.2). On average, pre-emptive cases receive net present value (NPV) reductions of no

more than 9.5%. The post-default cases received NPV reductions in the range of 9-75%, with an average of almost 54%.

- Debt restructuring negotiations tend to take longer in post-default than in pre-emptive cases. This is mainly related to the incentives of the debtor countries to finalise the negotiations swiftly. In a pre-emptive restructuring, debtor countries want to maintain their access to international capital markets. They decide to continue honouring their obligations. As a result, however, debt relief only occurs after the debt exchange has taken place. Moreover, debtor countries often choose to implement a pre-emptive restructuring as they wish to maintain good relations with their creditors. These factors explain why debtor countries aim to conclude restructuring negotiations quickly. By contrast, when a country starts negotiating after having defaulted, it has an incentive to hold out as long as possible and to obtain larger debt relief (see, inter alia, Díaz-Cassou et al. 2008 for a similar argumentation).

- Pre-emptive debt restructurings tended to result in a near-100% participation rate. Indeed, as table 10.2 shows, in the pre-emptive cases studied, the participation rate was above 97%. By contrast, in the post-default 2005 restructuring case of Argentina, participation rate was only 76%.

- While post-default cases have tended to receive more debt reductions, they also experienced on average deeper economic contractions than the pre-emptive cases. On average, real GDP in the pre-emptive restructuring cases contracted by 3.6% in the year of lowest growth during the sovereign debt crisis. This compares with an average contraction of 7.5% in post-default cases (see IMF 2006).

3.5. Sovereign Debt Crisis Resolution Mechanisms over Time

3.5.1. Debt restructurings pre-1990s

Sovereigns have borrowed and defaulted for more than 2,000 years. At the international level, extreme forms of debt contract enforcement have been seen in the past, often labelled as gunboat diplomacy or super-sanctions. In the late 1800s and early 1900s, it was considered reasonable for powerful countries to use military force to extract payments on delinquent debt. This was done, for example, by collecting taxes on trade.

However, the global political system embodied in the United Nations was designed to discourage the use of force to settle international disputes. As a result, the idea of international debt collection by force is widely disapproved of nowadays. Although this has arguably made sovereign debt workouts less costly and disruptive, the restructuring of sovereign debt remains a complex issue as there is no international bankruptcy regime equivalent to domestic bankruptcy regimes. One reason why such a regime is absent is that there is no world government. Likewise, the world has no parliament which can pass legislation relating to sovereign workouts. Moreover, there is no international judicial system which could enforce such legislation or adjudicate on claims.

Table 10.2: Key features of recent pre-emptive versus post-default debt restructuring cases

	Nature of problem		Debt restructured		Debt exchange				Access to intl. markets
	Debt/ GDP (%)	Liquidity vs Solvency	% of GDP	% of total debt	Duration (quarters)	NPV loss	Principal reduction	Participation (%)	1st intl. bond issuance
Pre-emptive									
Dom. Rep.	56	Liquidity	10	17.5	5	1-2	0.0	97	8
Pakistan	84	Ambiguous	31	61	12	8-27	-1	99	21
Ukraine	42	Liquidity	9	53	7	5	0.0	99	17
Uruguay	103	Ambiguous	43	42	1	8-20	1.0	99	3
Average	71.25		23.2	43.3	4	9.5	0	98	12.25
Post-default									
Argentina	130	Solvency	30	56	13	75	56	76	20
Ecuador	101	Solvency	45	44.5	4	9-25	37.3	97	24
Moldova						58	57.9		
Russia	52	Ambiguous	24	39	4	40-75	17.2	92	13
Serbia	64	Solvency	n.a.	n.a.		62	n.a.		Not yet
Average	86.75		33	47	7	53.9	42.1	88.3	19

Note: Access to international capital markets is measured in months.

Sources: Díaz-Cassou et al. (2008) and IMF (2006).

In the absence of such a judicial system (be it via law, statute, convention or treaty), creditors have formed ad hoc fora to facilitate the sovereign debt restructuring process. The first one was the Paris Club,[4] which was created in the 1950s and 1960s. Its aim was to restructure public and private debt owed to the public sector in advanced economies.

---

[4] Cosio-Pascal (2007) defines it as an informal forum, serviced by the French Treasury, in which the major creditors agree to take a common approach to restructuring the repayment schedules on each of the individual loans owed to each of the member countries' government agencies or offices, or sometimes they agree to reduce the amount of outstanding debt itself.

The 1970s saw a boom in the lending of advanced countries' commercial banks to developing countries. As a result, by the end of that decade, when these countries started facing debt servicing problems, there was a need for a forum like the Paris Club for commercial banks. It duly came into being – the Bank Advisory Committee – although the press informally called it the London Club.

Table 10.3 provides a summary of the various forums where debt restructuring negotiations can take place.

Table 10.3: Creditor and debtor categories and the restructuring forums

Debtors	*Creditors*					
	IMF	Multilateral development banks	Bilateral agencies	Commercial banks	Bond investors	Suppliers
Sovereigns	Preferential treatment		Paris Club	London Club	To be determined	Ad hoc
Public sector enterprises	No such debt exists	Special treatment				
Banks			No such debt exists	Special treatment		No such debt exists
Private companies	National corporate bankruptcy regime					

Source: Rieffel (2003).

3.5.2. Debt restructuring post 1990s

In the late 1990s and early 2000s, international institutions and forums paid considerable attention to strengthening the mechanisms of crisis prevention and resolution. This focus was triggered by various emerging market crises that had led to protracted debt restructuring processes in a number of cases. Indeed, with the transition from bank loans to expanded bond financing by emerging market sovereigns, the restructuring of sovereign debt had become more complicated. There are a number of factors that account for this. First, the rising mobility of bonds has made the identification of creditors increasingly difficult. Also, short-term financing has gained significantly in weight. Moreover, sovereign debtors have been faced with an increasingly fragmented investor base. This latter development has led to various potential collective action problems arising in the interactions between sovereign debtors and their private creditors. Concerns grew inter alia over actions by creditors such as litigation before and after the debt restructuring.

In the absence of a framework in the area of sovereign debt restructuring, the international policy debate has focused on two key approaches to ensuring that processes of sovereign debt restructuring are predictable and orderly. This reflects the broad agreement that full reliance on official support to fill countries' financing gaps is undesirable for a number of reasons, including simply the lack of resources as well as the risk of moral hazard behaviour on the part of private creditors and sovereign debtors alike.

The first approach, the so-called statutory approach, was based on an IMF proposal for a "Sovereign Debt Restructuring Mechanism" (SDRM), an early version of which was presented in late 2001. This mechanism, which was designed along the lines of Chapter 11 of the US bankruptcy code, was envisaged as a legal framework that would enable a qualified majority of creditors to make critical decisions, including the acceptance of final restructuring terms, which in turn would be binding on all private creditors holding external claims. While this approach initially received the backing of the international community, it quickly met with resistance from both the official and the private sectors. During the discussions on the SDRM, a non-statutory or market-based approach to sovereign debt restructuring emerged, consisting of two complementary legs: i) collective action clauses (CACs), included in international bond contracts and ii) the "Principles for stable capital flows and fair debt restructuring". Being a set of rules that can be applied to all key decisions in a debt restructuring process, CACs enable a decentralised response to collective action problems between bond creditors. As regards the Principles, they are voluntary and non-binding rules, jointly agreed by sovereign debtors and private creditors, and designed to provide guidance on cooperative actions between sovereign debtors and their private creditors.

Table 10.4: Duration of sovereign debt restructurings in months (1980-2006)

	Cases	Min.	Max.	Mean	Std. Dev.
Total duration (from start of debt distress to final deal)	90	3	189	29.2	32.6
Total duration (pre-Brady era: 1980 – Feb 1990)	53	3	79	17.7	15
Total duration (Brady era: Mar. 1990 to Feb. 1998)	26	9	189	59.4	43.8
Total duration (post-Brady era: since 1998)	11	3	41	13.6	12.4
Time until negotiations start: months from start of debt distress to start of negotiations/market sounding		1	150	9.5	18.4
Time of negotiations: months from start of negotiations to exchange offer		1	141	14.3	22.1
Time of implementation: months from exchange offer to final deal		1	32	7.7	5.7

Source: Trebesch (2008).

As table 10.4 shows, despite the more complex nature of the recent debt restructurings (inter alia due to the wider investor base), the resolution of sovereign debt crises has been much faster than in the past, taking an average of about 14 months.

A description of the evolving architecture of sovereign debt restructuring would of course not be complete without elaborating the role of the IMF in the resolution of sovereign debt crises. It should be noted that the IMF does not have specific instruments at its disposal to deal with sovereign debt restructurings. Rather, the Fund follows a case-by-case approach, usually involving a financial programme that is approved either before the sovereign's restructuring plan or as a result of it. A key element entails conducting a debt sustainability analysis and calculating the related financing needs of the country. While the decision to restructure sovereign debt lies with the country itself, the Fund does provide its expertise on a restructuring strategy to those countries that seek its advice.

4. COMPARING SOVEREIGN DEFAULTS IN ADVANCED ECONOMIES WITH THOSE IN EMERGING MARKET ECONOMIES

A sovereign cannot be forced to honour its debt obligations. However, the determination, since World War II, to fully honour the sovereign signature in advanced economies has implied that their government bonds have been considered as risk-free. Allowing for a sovereign default or debt restructuring in advanced economies would imply that government bonds lose their status as risk-free assets. As a result, those bonds will no longer be treated as purely interest rate products, thereby blurring the line between interest rate and credit product. Such changes can have a profound impact on investors' choices. Moreover, if government debt is deprived of its risk-free and hence safe haven, status, it will limit the ability of governments to use fiscal policy counter-cyclically as a macroeconomic stabilisation tool. Finally, it will result in a much closer interconnection between the health of the financial sector and the government.

Thus, in advanced economies, the risks related to a sovereign debt restructuring are much more acute than in emerging market economies. Indeed, given the high degree of economic and financial integration of advanced economies, global risks related to a sovereign default or debt workout are elevated. In this context, it is also important to note that there is a higher degree of foreign exposure to sovereign risk in advanced economies than in emerging market economies and that the closer integration of banking systems across advanced economies also increases financial stability risks.

5. DEFAULT IN A MONETARY UNION

The previous section has emphasised that sovereign default in advanced economies might have severe economic consequences in a globally integrated world. This section extends the analysis by considering a scenario in which the sovereign at risk of default is part of a monetary union such as EMU. To this end, it first considers some of the specificities of fiscal policy in EMU and then it turns to the consequences of sovereign default in a monetary union.

5.1. Specificities of EMU and the Sovereign Debt Crisis

EMU is a unique form of monetary union. It is characterised by a single monetary policy decided at supranational level, a common market, and decentralised fiscal policies. Fiscal policies remain within the competence of individual Member States, with no mutualisation of public liabilities across Member States.

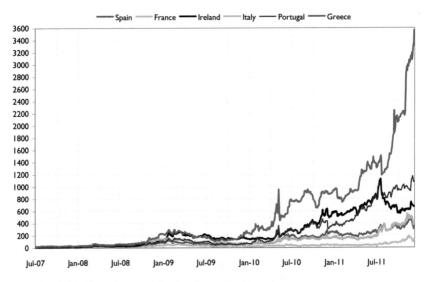

Figure 10.2: Sovereign yield spreads in the Euro area
(versus German 10-year government bond yields, daily data)
Last observation refers to 12 December 2011
Source: ECB.

The founding fathers of EMU well understood that the unique nature of EMU as a currency union with no political union required imposing policy constraints on each Member State in order to ensure the sustainability of individual members' public finances. The need for mutually consistent national policies was clearly expressed in the Delors Report:[5] *"An economic and monetary union could only operate on the basis of mutually consistent and sound behaviour by governments and other economic agents in all member countries. In particular, uncoordinated and divergent national budgetary policies would undermine monetary stability and generate imbalances in the real and financial sectors of the Community."*

This understanding led to the *no bail-out clause* (Article 125 of the Treaty on the Functioning of the European Union) and the *prohibition of monetary financing* (Article 123) being supplemented by the adoption of rules-based coordination procedures, as envisaged in the Stability and Growth Pact. In addition, peer pressure among Member States, competition between Member States for best practices, and market discipline were considered powerful mechanisms to ensure fiscal discipline, the competitiveness of each national economy and the stability of each national financial system.

In reality, the economic governance of EMU and especially its implementation turned out to fall short of expectations. On the fiscal side, the Stability and Growth Pact did not provide sufficient incentives to adopt prudent fiscal policies during times of favourable macroeconomic conditions and to substantially lower existing debt levels. The global financial crisis led to a further sharp deterioration in fiscal positions, owing to the effects on budgets of automatic stabilisers, the fiscal stimulus packages introduced to counter the economic downturn, and the support provided to the financial sector.

In addition, the mechanisms that the founding fathers of EMU expected to contribute to stability turned out to be ineffective. First, peer pressure was unable to address macroeconomic imbalances arising from divergent unit labour costs and other competitiveness measures. Second, markets failed to provide discipline and incentives. For instance, up to the start of the sovereign debt crisis yield differentials among Euro area countries were very small (see figure 10.2), notwithstanding large differences in the countries' fiscal strength.

As often happens in market dynamics, under-appreciation of risk suddenly turned into an over-reaction, spreading across an increasing number of countries. Although the markets' reaction might have been exacerbated by the decision of European political leaders to assign a role for private sector involvement in the resolution of the Greek debt crisis, it is clear that markets are inherently pro-cyclical and cannot be relied upon as a mechanism able to provide incentives in a timely manner.

---

[5] Committee for the Study of Economic and Monetary Union, Report on Economic and Monetary Union in the European Community, April 1989.

5.2. Macroeconomic Consequences of a Sovereign Default in a Monetary Union

While contemporary history offers several instances of sovereign defaults, it provides little insight into sovereign default by a member of a monetary union. Some historical instances do exist, but the different financial structures prevailing at the time limit the lessons that can be drawn. For instance, the American state debt crisis of the early 1840s is an episode in which nine state governments – after two decades of increasing public expenditures and debts – defaulted on their debts. While two of the defaulting states were able to resume debt payments by raising property taxes, four other states ultimately repudiated all or part of their debts and three went through substantial renegotiations.[6] The defaulting states appealed to the federal government for bailouts in an attempt to escape painful adjustment measures, but these calls were rejected.[7] Given the much greater depth of global financial integration now, this episode does not allow any inference of the potential for contagion across financial institutions, markets and countries that a similar episode could give rise to nowadays.

The rest of this section tries to assess the domestic impact on the country that defaults and then the possible consequences on the rest of the monetary union.

5.2.1. Domestic impact on the country that defaults

As documented in sections 1 and 2, sovereign default is generally associated with high costs for the domestic economy as a result of restricted access to external finance, higher costs of future government borrowing and broader output losses. One channel through which these losses are incurred is through the impact of the sovereign debt crisis on the domestic financial system.

Domestic banks, which are usually major creditors of a government, may be severely hit if that government defaults. The impact might be magnified by the increasing role played by banks in financing government debt in the run-up to a crisis when governments find it harder or more expensive to access external finance. The effect on the banking sector triggered by a default might lead to a fully-fledged banking crisis, with banks withdrawing from their normal intermediation role and a negative feedback loop emerging. Ultimately, bank runs might occur, as the government no longer has the credibility to assure the public that bank deposits are protected by a guarantee and will be honoured if banks fail. In addition, a government default might result in a fall in private sector wealth and have adverse effects on confidence, leading to a drag on private consumption and investment.

---

[6] Grinath et al. (1997) explain the differences between defaulting states as regards their response to fiscal pressures built around the revenue structures of those states.

[7] As stated by Bordo et al. (2011): "…the federal government sent a costly but clear signal regarding the limits to its commitment to fiscal support to the states".

It is possible that the severe turmoil in the domestic financial system will result in large capital outflows, especially within a monetary union where there are no capital controls. In turn, the associated imbalances would endanger the financial stability of the currency union as a whole.

While the costs to the country defaulting are likely to be high, the potential benefits appear to be limited in the case of a Euro area country. Defaults are usually partial and the defaulting country is likely to be excluded from borrowing, especially on international markets. As a result, a defaulting country still needs to run a primary surplus in order to finance the payments on the part of the debt not affected by restructuring.

Table 10.5: Primary balance and interest payments, Euro area and default episodes (% of GDP)

	Primary balance	Nominal interest payments	Government gross debt
Euro area and main advanced economies (average 2009-2010)			
Belgium	-1.4	3.5	96.0
Germany	-1.1	2.6	78.8
Estonia	-0.7	0.2	6.9
Ireland	-20.2	2.6	80.0
Greece	-7.8	5.4	137.1
Spain	-8.4	1.8	57.4
France	-4.9	2.4	80.7
Italy	-0.5	4.6	117.0
Cyprus	-3.3	2.4	60.0
Luxembourg	-0.6	0.4	16.9
Malta	-0.6	3.1	68.4
Netherlands	-3.2	2.1	61.8
Austria	-1.5	2.7	70.7
Portugal	-7.0	2.9	88.2
Slovenia	-4.5	1.5	37.0
Slovakia	-6.4	1.4	38.2
Finland	-1.4	1.1	45.8
Euro area	-3.5	2.8	82.7
United Kingdom	-8.5	2.4	74.8
European Union	-4.1	2.7	77.5
Japan	-5.1	2.6	195.8
USA	-8.5	2.6	90.5
Default episodes (median)	-0.4	4.3	46.9

Source: European Commission autumn 2011 forecast and Cottarelli et al. (2010); data reported for default episodes correspond to an average for the two years prior to default over the following sample of defaulting countries: Argentina (2002), Ecuador (1999), Indonesia (1999), Jamaica (2010), Mexico (1982), Moldova (2002), Pakistan (1999), Russia (1998), Ukraine (1998), Uruguay (2003).

Looking at a sample of countries that have defaulted in the last two decades, Cottarelli et al. (2010) find that the median primary surplus over the three years following default was about 2% of GDP.[8] When looking at the current fiscal position in Euro area countries, the striking feature is that the large primary deficit is greater than the interest payments (see table 10.5). For instance, in 2009-2010 the Euro area countries under an IMF/EC programme had primary deficits of around 11.2% of GDP on average, and nominal interest payments of around 3.6% of GDP on average. When comparing these figures with the ones in the sample of countries that defaulted, it shows that over the two years prior to default they were 0.4% and 4.3%, respectively. Hence, any default by a Euro area country would not, at the moment, significantly alter the sizeable adjustment in the primary balance needed to stabilise public debt.

5.2.2. Consequences on the rest of the union

In a monetary union a default may put at risk the financial stability of the currency area as a whole, given the higher propensity for cross-country spillovers. There are two main channels of contagion.

First, a default will not only affect the solvency of financial institutions in the defaulting country, but will also have adverse effects on the balance sheets of banks in other countries through cross-border financial exposure. The magnitude of this first, direct channel depends on the economic weight of the defaulting country and the degree of its exposure to the sovereign debt of other countries within the monetary union. More generally, the perception of the credit quality of financial institutions will deteriorate, leading to increasing refinancing costs and roll-over risks, which may become self-fulfilling.

Second, a decline in investors' tolerance of credit risk may spread to other countries' sovereign markets. Once the principle that a sovereign is bound to honour its debt has been infringed, expectations that other countries might do likewise to reduce their debt burden may be triggered. This change in perception is likely to increase – to different degrees – refinancing costs for other countries for a relatively long period of time. Increasing refinancing costs might cause rating agencies to downgrade the more vulnerable countries. The negative feedback loop between the sovereign and the banks' conditions may become entrenched. This would lead to a freezing-up of wholesale funding markets for banks deemed to be in a vulnerable position. Deposit runs might spread from one country to another.

Heightened financial tensions would be expected to move to the real economy through adverse confidence and wealth effects weighing on private spending, as well as restricted access to credit. Falling demand for imports in some

---

[8] Cottarelli et al. (2011) look at the following sample of countries that have defaulted: Argentina (2002), Ecuador (1999), Indonesia (1999), Jamaica (2010), Mexico (1982), Moldova (2002), Pakistan (1999), Russia (1998), Ukraine (1998), Uruguay (2003).

countries would affect the export performance of other countries, given the high degree of trade integration within the monetary union. Overall, these factors would most likely lead to a prolonged recession, with a negative feedback loop between the real and financial sector, dampening prospects for output growth and employment in the area as a whole.

The two channels of transmission just described interact along a negative feedback loop. The fiscal situation of the respective country may be adversely affected by the need to recapitalise the banking sector, which might lead to additional downgrades of the sovereign and in turn to further negative effects on the stability of the banking system.

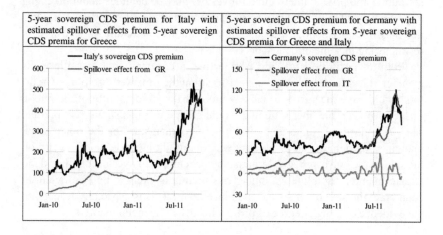

Figure 10.3: Euro area cross-country contagion effects

Source: Constâncio (2011).

In the Euro area, these contagion channels across countries' sovereign markets and from sovereign to financial institutions are potentially large, as the developments during the Euro area sovereign debt crisis have demonstrated. For instance, the downgrade of Portugal's sovereign rating by one particular rating agency in early July 2011 was attributed, among other factors, to adverse conditions in Greece. That downgrade and the lingering fears of a default in Greece were followed by a massive sell-off of Spanish and Italian government bonds, although there was no significant adverse news concerning these economies. Similarly, the Euro area sovereign crisis has affected funding availability and funding costs for banks in the Euro area.

One way of assessing contagion is to test whether country-specific shocks to the CDS premium help to predict CDS premia in other countries (see Constâncio 2011). For this purpose, the CDS premium is decomposed into shocks affecting the short term as opposed to the medium and long term. If the medium to long-term shocks of one country improve the forecasting of the CDS premia of other countries over and above their own idiosyncratic shocks, this may be taken as evidence of contagion. The empirical results show that the contagion emanating from Greece accounts for a large part of the Italian CDS premium. In turn, the joint medium to long-run shocks from Greece and Italy explain much of the German CDS premium, which increased after July 2011 (see figure 10.3).

The Euro area may have to bear additional costs from one of its members' default, affecting in particular reputation and currency volatility. In particular, public and private international investors may be cautious about investing large portions of their wealth in assets denominated in a currency of sovereigns that may not fully honour their obligations and may be willing to rely on debt restructuring in some circumstances.

From an institutional-design perspective, a currency area that allows its member states to default may appear to strengthen market discipline. Creditors would have incentives to closely monitor the sustainability of the public finances of each member state and would charge commensurate risk premia. This is, indeed, an important disciplinary mechanism. On the other hand, knowing that default can be an easy way out might increase moral hazard on the side of the borrower. A sovereign may be tempted to over-accumulate debt. Greater market discipline via higher risk premia is likely to be insufficient to counteract the sovereign's weakened incentives. This is especially true given the evidence of a high degree of pro-cyclicality in financial markets.

6. CONCLUSION

Sovereign defaults have been remembered for a long time afterwards, mainly because they have been costly and complex to resolve. This explains why default and debt restructurings have always been regarded as the last resort, i.e. when it is clear that the debtor country cannot repay its debt. Incidentally, this is the way the international community has functioned and cooperated since the Bretton Woods agreement, which led to the founding of the IMF. Indeed, the global political system embodied in the United Nations (to which the IMF belongs) was designed to discourage the use of force to settle international disputes. Although this has arguably made sovereign debt workouts less costly and disruptive, the restructuring of sovereign debt remains a complex and costly issue.

In recent history, sovereign debt crises have mainly been experienced by emerging market economies. They have shown that while some restructurings have indeed been successful and can arguably be said to have been conducted in an orderly fashion, they were often on a small scale and executed under special circumstances. The most striking and often-quoted case is Uruguay. However, more often than not, restructurings have been disorderly, harmful and fraught with difficulties. The average length of the negotiations is 2½ years and it can vary greatly. Empirical evidence also shows that private investors are likely to penalise a country which has a history of restructuring and to demand higher risk premia.

While these are some of the important lessons to be learned from the emerging market experience, several factors make a comparison with a potential debt workout in advanced economies different.

In advanced economies, the risks related to a sovereign debt restructuring are much more acute, given the high degree of economic and financial integration. The issue is even more complicated in the context of the monetary union.

This is why defaults and debt restructuring should not be considered as easy ways out from a situation of excessive debt. They should be only a last resort, when fiscal consolidation to regain control of the budget is considered impossible from an economic point of view. In any case, such extreme measures do not do away with the need to implement tight budgetary controls and structural reforms to improve growth potential. They do not do away with the need to provide external financial assistance to smooth out the adjustment and ensure debt sustainability.

As the adjustment to high levels of debt is long and painful, what a monetary union ultimately requires is first and foremost an effective framework aimed at avoiding and preventing the emergence of unsustainable debt.

BIBLIOGRAPHY

Arellano, C. 2005, "Default Risk and Income Fluctuations in Emerging Economies",Working paper, University of Minnesota.

Baer, W., D. Margot and G. Montes-Rojas 2009, "Argentina's Default and the Lack of Dire Consequences", *City University Department of Economics Discussion Paper Series* No 10/09.

Beers, D. and J. Chambers 2006, "Sovereign Defaults at 26-Year Low, To Show Little Change in 2007", Standard & Poor's Commentary, September 18.

Bolton, P. and O. Jeanne 2008, "Structuring and Restructuring Sovereign Debt: The Role of Seniority", *Review of Economic Studies*, Vol. 76(3), pp. 879-902.

Boorman, J. 2002, "Alternative Approaches to Sovereign Debt Restructuring", *CATO Journal*.

Bordo, M.D., L. Jonung and A. Markiewicz 2011, "A Fiscal Union for the Euro: Some Lessons from History", *NBER Working Paper* No. 17380, September 2011.

Borensztein, E. and U. Panizza 2008, "The Costs of Sovereign Default", *IMF Working Papers* 08/238.

Bulow, J. and K.S. Rogoff 1989, "Sovereign Debt: Is to Forgive to Forget?" *American Economic Review*, 79, pp. 43-50.

Chuhan, P. and F. Sturzenegger 2005, "Default Episodes in the 1980s and 1990s: What Have We Learned?" in *Managing Economic Volatility and Crises*, edited by Joshua Aizenman and Brian Pinto, Cambridge University Press.

Constâncio, V. 2011, "Contagion and the European Debt Crisis", keynote lecture at the Bocconi University, Intesa Sanpaolo conference on "Bank Competitiveness in the Post-crisis World", Milan, 10 October 2011.

Cosio-Pascal, E. 2007, Paris Club: "Intergovernmental Relations in Debt Restructuring", Initiative for Policy Dialogue, Working Paper under the Task Force for Sovereign Debt Restructuring and Sovereign Bankruptcy.

Cottarelli, C., L. Forni, J. Gottschalk and P. Mauro 2010, "Default in Today's Advanced Economies: Unnecessary, Undesirable, and Unlikely", *IMF Staff Position Note* Number 12, September 2010.

De Paoli, B., G. Hoggarth and V. Saporta 2006, "Costs of Sovereign Default", Bank of England Financial Stability Paper 1.

Díaz-Cassou, J., A. Erce-Domínguez and J. J. Vázquez-Zamora 2008, "The role of the IMF in recent sovereign debt restructurings: Implications for the policy of lending into arrears", *Banco de España Occasional Papers* 0805, Banco de España.

Drelichman, M. and H.-J. Voth 2009, "Lending to the Borrower from Hell: Debt and Default in the Age of Philip II, 1556-1598", *CEPR Discussion Papers* 7276.

Eaton, J. and M. Gersovitz 1981, "Debt with Potential Repudiation: Theoretical and Empirical Analysis", *Review of Economic Studies*, 48, pp. 89-309.

Eaton, J. and R. Fernandez 1995, "Sovereign Debt", *NBER Working Paper* 5131.

ECB 2011, "The European Stability Mechanism", *ECB Monthly Bulletin*, July 2011.

Eichengreen, B. and R. Portes 1989, "Dealing with Debt: The 1930s and the 1980s." in *Dealing with the Debt Crisis*, editors Ishrat Husain and Ishac Diwan, A World Bank Symposium.

Fowler, M. R. and J. M. Bunk 1995, *Law, Power, and the Sovereign State,* Penn State Press.

Grinath, A., J.J. Wallis and R.E. Sylla 1997, "Debt, Default and Revenue Structure: the American State Debt Crisis in the Early 1840s", *NBER Working Paper Series* on historical factors in long run growth, No 97, March 1997.

Hatchondo, J. C., L. Martinez and H. Sapriza 2007, "The Economics of Sovereign Defaults", *Economic Quarterly*, Federal Reserve Bank of Richmond, spring issue, pp. 163-187.

International Monetary Fund 2006, Cross-Country Experience with Restructuring of Sovereign Debt and Restoring Debt Sustainability, report prepared by the Policy Development and Review Department, August 2006.

Lindert, P.H. and P. J. Morton 1989, "How Sovereign Debt Has Worked", in *Developing Country Debt and Economic Performance*, Jeffrey D. Sachs, Volume 1: The International Financial System, Vol. 1 (University of Chicago Press), pp. 39-106.

Manasse, P. and N. Roubini 2005, "Rules of Thumb" for Sovereign Debt Crises, *IMF Working Paper* 05/42.

Mitchener, K. and M. Weidenmier 2005, "Empire, Public Goods, and the Roosevelt Corollary", *The Journal of Economic History* 65 (3), pp. 658–92.

Özler, S. 1993, "Have Commercial Banks Ignored History?", *American Economic Review*, 83(3) pp. 608–20.

Reinhart, C.M. and K.S. Rogoff 2009, *This Time is Different: Eight Centuries of Financial Folly*, Princeton University Press.

Reinhart, C.M., K. S. Rogoff and M. A. Savastano 2003, "Debt Intolerance", *Brookings Papers on Economic Activity*, 1 pp. 1-62.

Rieffel, L. 2003, *Restructuring Sovereign Debt: The Case for Ad Hoc Machinery*, Washington, D.C.: Brookings Institution Press.

Stoica, T. and A. Leonte 2011, "Estimating a Fiscal Reaction Function for Greece", 2011 International Conference on Financial Management and Economics.

Sturzenegger, F. and J. Zettelmeyer 2005, "Haircuts: Estimating Investor Losses in Sovereign Debt Restructurings 1998-2005", *IMF Working Paper* No 05/137.

Sy, A. 2004, "Rating the rating agencies: Anticipating currency crises or debt crises?", *Journal of Banking & Finance*, vol. 28(11), pp. 2845-2867.

Tomz, M. and M.L.J. Wright 2008, "Sovereign Theft: Theory and Evidence about Sovereign Default And Expropriation", *CAMA Working Papers* 2008-07, Australian National University, Centre for Applied Macroeconomic Analysis.

Trebesch, C. 2008, "Delays in Sovereign Debt Restructurings: Should we Really Blame the Creditors?", *Working Paper, Free University of Berlin*, March 2008.

Yue, V. 2006, "Sovereign Default and Debt Renegotiation", *Working Paper, New York University.*

11. Default of Systemically Important Financial Intermediaries: Short-Term Stability vs. Incentive Compatibility

Yves Mersch

1. INTRODUCTION

The recent crisis has brought to the forefront not only new themes (e.g., the compensation schemes prevailing in the financial industry or the limits of the originate-and-distribute model of securitisation), but also rekindled old ones. An old theme is the perceived trade-off between policies that prevent that the failure of a systemically important financial institution (SIFI) at a point in time generates financial instability and reduces welfare, and the effects of such policies on economic agents' future behaviour. There are several facets of this perceived trade-off, all of them linked to a fundamental aspect of human action: the role of incentives in the process of learning and its impact on constrained decision-making under uncertainty.

SIFIs are singled out in discussions about systemic risk because, given the magnitude of their interdependence with other financial and non-financial institutions, the fate of the economy tends to be attached to their viability. There are several reasons for this situation currently discussed in an ever-growing literature. First, given SIFIs' direct cross-exposures and the large share of SIFIs in total lending and financing, doubts about their liquidity or solvency can quickly and negatively affect agents' perceptions of the viability of other financial institutions, and ultimately, of the stability of the real economy. Even without taking into account the negative price effects that the failure of a SIFI may cause, the risk of contagion is one main reason advanced to justify special attention to SIFIs and managing efficiently the implications of their eventual failure.

Second, SIFIs are sometimes headquartered in jurisdictions that are small, at least when the jurisdiction's GDP is compared to the assets managed by the

The views presented here are my own and do not necessarily reflect those of the other members of the ECB Governing Council. I would like to thank the staff of the Financial Stability Unit of the Central Bank of Luxembourg, in particular Francisco Nadal De Simone, for their help in producing this chapter.

troubled SIFI, and thus protecting them with domestic public funds may have to be ruled out. Classic examples are UBS in Switzerland or Fortis in Belgium.

Third, and intimately related to the previous point, some SIFIs are global institutions which are active in multiple jurisdictions with disparate legal systems, and subject to different regulators and monetary authorities, and which in case of a liquidity crisis are expected to provide lending-of-last-resort (LLR) services. In addition, they are subject to different sovereign public authorities that are called to rescue them by taxing their own citizens in case they run into solvency problems. This is why addressing the issue of SIFIs has been among the key goals of the G20 objective to design a more resilient global financial regulatory framework via the work of the Financial Stability Board (FSB) and other standard setters (FSB 2010b). In the European Union, in particular, the on-going discussions regarding the design of a bank resolution framework include, quite conspicuously, bail-in, a statutory tool providing the supervisory authorities with the power of writing down or converting into equity subordinated and senior unsecured debt to the extent deemed necessary to absorb losses and ensure a bank's return to solvency. SIFIs are particularly targeted in these discussions which are expected to result in a new framework for banks' resolution to be announced in early June 2012.[1]

Other SIFIs, while not global but domestic, are nevertheless large, complex, and maybe interconnected financial institutions. Similar in nature to global systemic financial institutions, these features of domestic SIFIs also call for cooperation, information exchange and burden sharing across sovereign jurisdictions, and for coordinated measures via colleges of supervisors, cross-border financial stability groups, and (in the European Union) the new bodies in charge of supervision.

Preserving financial stability may require public support policies including emergency liquidity assistance (ELA) and deposit guarantee schemes (DGS). However, those public support policy measures taken at a point in time have an effect on the way rational economic agents make decisions in the future and may induce future risk-taking activities that are in excess of what otherwise would have been taken. Therefore, those actions increase the likelihood of future financial instability and welfare losses. This has long been recognised as *moral hazard*, deeply engrained in the fact that information is asymmetric.

Because asymmetric information is pervasive and learning is costly and takes time, moral hazard can be quite insidious. Therefore, the way in which public support is provided is key for minimising moral hazard. In the case of SIFIs, moral hazard is certainly more likely to be present as economic agents' current decisions depend in part upon future policy actions, and rational agents have reasons to expect that those future policy actions will be determined by the same

---

[1] These issues are not covered in this chapter as the main elements of the framework, especially bail-in, are under discussion at the time of writing.

type of arguments that today justify public support policies of SIFIs. This chapter deals with the question of the design of a policy framework that preserves financial stability over time in the presence of SIFIs, i.e., that minimises the trade-off between financial stability today when consistent discretionary policies are called upon in the presence of SIFIs, and future financial stability given that today optimal agents' decisions depend also on tomorrow's policy measures.

The rest of the chapter is organised as follows. The next section presents an application of the Basel Committee on Banking Supervision criteria for determining systemically important banks to Luxembourg-registered banks. Section 3 discusses moral hazard issues posed by SIFIs and section 4 addresses the aspects of moral hazard covered by the FSB's multipronged framework to deal with it. Section 5 takes up emergency liquidity assistance (ELA), resolution mechanisms and deposit guarantee schemes (DGS) relating them to regulation and supervision, the structure of the interbank market, and banks' incentives. The final section concludes.

2. SYSTEMIC IMPORTANCE OF GLOBAL FINANCIAL INTERMEDIARIES: WHAT DOES IT MEAN AND HOW IS IT REFLECTED IN LUXEMBOURG?

One key outcome of the joint work of the FSB, the International Monetary Fund and the Bank for International Settlements, is the Basel Committee on Banking Supervision (BCBS) methodology for the identification of global systemically important banks (G-SIBs), and the determination of their additional loss absorbency requirement (BCBS 2011). This is justified by the financial and economic costs of public interventions aimed at restoring financial stability, as conspicuously shown by the last crisis, as well as the associated expected increase in moral hazard in a regulatory environment that does not address the cross-border negative externalities generated by those large banks.

While G-SIBs are the focus of the BCBS' proposed regulation, domestic systemically important banks (D-SIBs) may entail the same implications at national level by generating negative externalities and moral hazard as a result of public policies to preserve financial stability. Therefore, in Luxembourg, where almost all banks are affiliates of large and complex financial institutions, many of which are on the list of G-SIBs,[2] it seems pertinent to apply the BCBS methodology in order to identify the D-SIBs registered in the country, at least until on-going work on criteria to identify D-SIBs becomes operational.

The methodology proposed by the BCBS is indicator-based, which is viewed as more robust than model-based ones which are at a very early stage

---

[2] See list of G-SIBs for which the resolution-related requirements will need to be met by end-2012 in Annex to FSB (2011c).

of development. The chosen indicators reflect the different aspects of the negative externalities G-SIBs generate: size, interconnectedness, substitutability,
global activity and complexity. Each category has the same weight and the
indicators within each category also have the same weight (BCBS 2011, p.
5).[3] SIBs are grouped in buckets of systemic importance based on the score
produced; buckets are of equal size in terms of those scores. Banks in different
buckets have different magnitudes of additional loss absorbency requirements
which should be met with Common Equity Tier 1 (Basel III).

Applied to a sample of 76 banks – about 90% of total bank assets – using
prudential and statistical bank level data for September 2011, the BCBS approach determines as D-SIBs five banks amounting to over five times Luxembourg's 2011 GDP.[4] Figure 11.1 shows the score obtained by each individual
bank as well as the cut-off value (red vertical line) and the buckets' thresholds.
Three banks are classified in bucket 1, CACEIS Bank Luxembourg, Société
Générale Bank & Trust and Clearstream Banking S.A., and two in the next
bucket of importance, BIL and Deutsche Bank Luxembourg S.A. (Giordana,
2011).

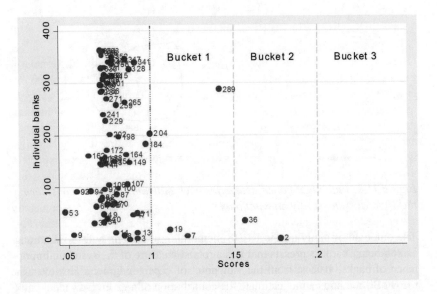

Figure 11.1: Distribution of the banks' scores and their allocation to buckets

---

[3] For the categories of *substitutability* and *complexity*, data constraints allowed only two out of
the three indicators in each of them to be considered. Weights were adjusted accordingly to sum
up to 20% each.
[4] Individual bank's total assets range between 40% to 225% of Luxembourg's 2011 GDP.

An in-depth analysis of individual banks' scores is useful. Note, first, that BIL as part of Dexia group and Clearstream Banking S.A. are the most systemically relevant banks due to their high score in the substitutability category (figure 11.2). Second, complexity is the main driver of the systemic relevance of CA-CEIS bank. Third, size and cross-jurisdictional activity are the main indicators that explain the systemic position of Deutsche Bank. Finally, Luxembourg's banks are quite similar in terms of interconnectedness as the score is close to one for almost all institutions, an important result for financial stability.

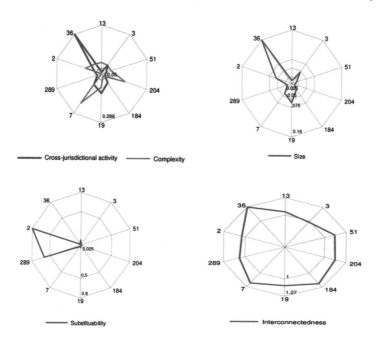

Figure 11.2: Individual banks' scores for each indicator category considering the 30 most systemically relevant banks

The outcome of applying the BCBS methodology to identify D-SIBs among Luxembourg banks suggests that it is a robust measure of the systemic importance of banks, at least from the viewpoint of expert judgment. However, as the BCBS method cannot estimate the contribution of a given individual bank to systemic risk, results from a BCL model-based approach are shown here for the same banks (table 11.1) (Jin and Nadal De Simone forthcoming).[5] As of end-September 2011, according to one possible metric to assess individual

---

[5] The study uses a generalised dynamic factor model applied to a macro-financial database as well as copula analysis to model interdependence among the marginal probabilities of default of 39 Luxembourg banks estimated using Delianedis and Geske (2003) structural credit risk model.

banks' contribution to systemic risk, i.e., the largest probability of at least one other bank becoming distressed if a specific bank became distressed was associated with Bank C becoming distressed. This is a useful indication of the bank's contribution to systemic risk: if Bank C failed, the conditional probability that at least one other bank in the group of five banks became distressed was 87% at end-September 2011.

Table 11.1: PAO at 2011Q3

Bank A	0.76
Bank B	0.76
Bank C	0.87
Bank D	0.80
Bank E	0.75

PAO: conditional probability that at least one other bank becomes distressed given that a specific bank becomes distressed.

Finally, network analysis is a methodology complementary to the BCBS method for the determination of systemic banks which can deepen understanding of the Luxembourg banking sector (Buisson 2012). Given the lack of detailed data regarding bilateral cross-border interbank transactions, this network analysis is conducted at the domestic level including the banks that have reported large exposures in their prudential reporting as of September 2011. The domestic interbank network is composed of 95 nodes (i.e., banks) and 228 arcs (direct links between the banks). The representation of the Luxembourg domestic banking sector as a network shows the importance of some banks due to the size of their balance sheets, the number of links with other banks as well as the volume of their interbank exposures. This is useful to visualise potential contagion channels and systemic risk.

Luxembourg domestic interbank network is characterised by nodes with very heterogeneous degrees of interconnectedness (figure 11.3). The distribution of the links between banks is asymmetric given the existence of a small number of banks highly interconnected, playing the role of "hubs", while most of the other banks are at the periphery, with a low number of connections.

A "core network" showing banks that have at least five links with other domestic banks can be extracted (figure 11.4). Various types of measures can be used to determine the relative importance of a bank within the network and its degree of interconnectedness. Among others, the *degree of centrality* shows how central in a network is a bank according to the number of links it has with other banks; the *closeness of centrality* shows a bank is central if its total distance to the other banks is low; and the *betweenness of centrality* shows a bank is central if it lies on several shortest paths among other pairs of banks in the network. Another indicator is the *prestige* of a bank measured as the number of links directed to the bank. The 25 banks represented on the core network exhibit higher measures of centrality and prestige than the total network.

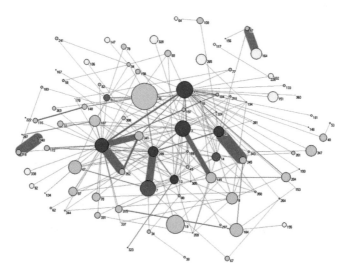

Figure 11.3: Luxembourg domestic interbank network, 30 September 2011

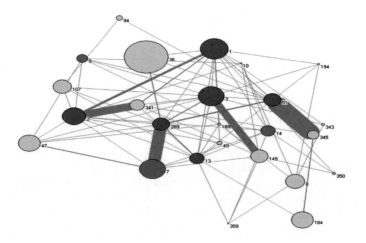

Figure 11.4: Core network

As the analysis suggests, the size of a bank is not sufficient to define its systemic importance: a small bank can play an important role on the interbank market, not only due to its degrees of centrality and prestige, but also due to the volume of its interbank exposures. These methodologies are complementary ways to assess D-SIBs.

3. ASYMMETRIC INFORMATION AND MORAL HAZARD AND RULES VERSUS DISCRETION

The empirical analysis of the previous section illustrates the importance of D-SIBs for the stability of the Luxembourg banking sector. Default of a D-SIB would first entail consequences for other banks given that all Luxembourg banks display a high degree of interconnectedness and second, for the real economy as well, given their relative size. The same can be claimed for other countries within the EU and in the US or Japan. As a result, a framework to minimise the occurrence of liquidity- and solvency-related distress is of paramount importance. This entails a macroprudential set of rules and regulations and a monitoring system that limits systemic risk so as to minimise the costs of financial instability on the economy (ECB 2010) in its three main forms (ECB 2009): (1) as contagion risk,[6] (2) as the risk of macro shocks that cause simultaneous problems to the economy, and (3) the risk of a disorderly unravelling of imbalances that have built up over time. It is clear, however, that despite recent advances in models and policy instruments for dealing with the cross-sectional dimension of systemic risk (e.g., CRD IV) and with the time-dimension of systemic risk (e.g., time-varying Loan-to-Value ratios, and time-varying margins or haircuts), financial distress cannot be avoided altogether (Goodhart and Hofmann 2007; CGFS 2010). From time to time, financial institutions will get distressed, and some SIBs will eventually fail.

Preserving financial stability will require public support policies such as government guarantees, banks' recapitalisation, or other policies to complement more generally-applied measures, such as ELA to deal with a financial institution's liquidity problems, and certain forms of DGS to protect consumers. Those public support policy measures taken at a point in time may have an effect on the way rational economic agents make decisions in the future inducing risk-taking activities in excess of what otherwise would have been taken. In that case, those actions may increase the likelihood of future financial instability and welfare losses. This has long been recognised as *moral hazard* by which it is implied that an agent takes undue risks because part of the ensu-

---

[6] The concept refers to the occurrence of an idiosyncratic shock affecting an important financial institution which in turn gets transmitted through the financial system and ends up affecting the real economy.

ing cost is going to be borne by other agents. This possibility is the result of the fact that information is asymmetric: one party has more information about its actions or intentions than the other, and while the former has incentives to behave *inappropriately* from the perspective of the party with less information, it is costly for the latter to monitor the former's behaviour over time.

Asymmetric information is pervasive and learning is costly and takes time. As a result, moral hazard can be quite insidious. Therefore, how public support is provided is the key for minimising moral hazard. In the case of SIFIs, this problem is certainly more likely to be present given that SIFIs have been publicly identified and economic agents know that they will, if necessary, receive support. Economic agents will internalise these future policy actions in their behaviour and undertake relatively riskier decisions. Yet, not taking the public policy actions needed to safeguard financial stability today would reduce today's welfare. This raises several important questions:

- What are the conditions for moral hazard to be present in the case of SIFIs?
- Is all additional risk undertaken by economic agents excessive?
- What is the nature of the trade-off between financial stability today and financial stability tomorrow?

Moral hazard is pervasive and variants of it are numerous. Yet, the basic characteristics of the phenomenon can be summarised into the conditions present in the famous "principal-agent" problem. A risk-neutral principal's return depends on the *unobservable effort* of a risk-averse agent whose activities are also subject to *unobservable random factors*. If the agent were paid up to the point where the marginal return from effort equalled his marginal disutility of effort, there would not be moral hazard. This is not feasible, however, because the principal cannot observe the agent's effort level. Notice that even if, as an alternative, the agent were paid according to the *observed return* of his actions, the agent would have incentives to supply less effort than optimal because he has more information than the principal about the random effects that affect his activities. Moral hazard would be present even in this case. The typical example is often taken from insurance, but examples abound. If a company insuring against automobile collision risk could monitor the driver and all factors affecting the insured risk, there would not be moral hazard. Similarly, there would not be moral hazard if a bank manager could easily assess the effort and the uncertain payoffs of a trader; or if shareholders were certain that not raising new capital that dilutes their position and strengthens creditors' would trigger bail-in clauses or resolve the institution without taxpayers' money. Therefore, correct pricing excludes moral hazard. To remain within the insurance example, premia charged would reflect all risks that follow the driver's actions and the external factors affecting him. On the other hand, it is also clear that the existence of insurance encourages the insured to take up risks that otherwise would not have been taken; risks that increase welfare. By compensating correctly priced risks, insurance enables higher diversifiable risk-taking activities and increases welfare.

But when the agent's actions are unobservable, correct pricing is not feasible. As a result, the agent can by his actions affect the *size* and/or the *probability* of losses. Insurance in this case subsidises risk taking; there is too much of it. Therefore, normally, insurers charge a premium that includes the potential economic consequences of moral hazard so that the insurance company can remain in business. Given that both parties are aware of this situation, they have incentives to reduce moral hazard ex ante. Those incentives translate into mechanisms that make the insured share part of the losses in case the insured risk materialises. Examples are co-payment in medical insurance, the obligation to have fire extinguishers in case of fire insurance, or conditionality in loans.

How does this analysis apply to public support policies? If public authorities provide regular support to banks in distress, most observers would agree that such policy will create the expectation of such help in the future and induce banks to undertake risks that would not have been taken otherwise. This is especially more likely if the bank is an officially-declared SIFI. It is pertinent to ask how serious this moral hazard is.

Assume that a non-risk based framework to bail out distressed SIFIs is in place. Depositors are fully paid back, and creditors are compensated for their losses. Given that costs of failed, risky investments will be borne by others, there is a clear problem of moral hazard: stakeholders will take up more risk than otherwise because they anticipate that when losses occur, taxpayers will bear the costs.

Given the arguments discussed here, it is useful to ask how large are the losses associated with this case of moral hazard when it is assumed for simplicity that banks only face credit risk, and when they fail, they are compensated with public grants. As resources used could be invested in numerous other activities of similar credit risk, the supply curve can be assumed to be flat. The downward sloping demand curve would reflect the net value of the numerous activities (in descending order of value per unit of resources) that could be undertaken. At equilibrium, where the demand curve intersects the supply curve, resources are used up to the level where activities undertaken are those whose value, net of expected losses, exceeds their resource cost. The distortion introduced by public policies' grants is like the distortion introduced by a subsidy of amount p per unit of invested resources, where (p) is the probability of losses in the event of a bank failure. With this subsidy, resources invested subject to credit risk rise above the optimal level up to the level on the demand curve where the sum of the marginal value of the expected net product from the last unit of resources, *plus the amount of the subsidy*, equals the unit cost of the resources. So the loss from the moral hazard distortion is, for the additional resources that are artificially encouraged to go into risky activities, the excess of the alternative opportunity cost of these resources over the value of what they produce when deployed in activities subject to credit risk. The cost is not the budgetary cost of the implicit subsidy times the unit of resources invested as these represent transfers rather than real resource costs.[7]

Now assume that public policies do not involve grants, but a combination of deposit insurance and loans to banks. Let us consider first *deposit insurance*. If deposit insurance is ex ante and based on an actuarially fair premium, there is no moral hazard problem, even though substantial amounts of compensation may be needed in case of a run on a bank, for example. The fact that an appropriate premium is charged to those that undertake risky activities with those deposits leaves incentives for risking resources to credit risk activities undistorted. If such insurance were not available without government intervention, economic efficiency would be improved by government provision at a fair price as this would enable risk-averse agents to undertake an economically appropriate amount of activities subject to credit risk.

What about the *loans to banks* once their capital is proven to be insufficient to absorb losses? These loans are available because of market distortions that make liquidity and capital scarce when they are most needed, a subject which is not explored here. If the interest rate charged on those loans did not contain a subsidy, then there would be no moral hazard distortion. To the extent that government loans do contain a subsidy element, the cost of moral hazard can be estimated as follows, assuming that their amount equals the full amount necessary to cover losses while leaving banks' capital at the regulatory minimum. Now, the amount of the subsidy is not equal to the probability of losses from credit risk as it was in the previous case of full compensation grants. The subsidy distortion is only equal to that fraction of the initial loan value that is represented by the present value of the interest subsidy. By the same principle as before, the budgetary cost of the interest subsidy (in present value terms) is an overestimate of the economic efficiency loss generated by the moral hazard distortion.

Given the global nature of many SIFIs, it is pertinent to analyse the moral hazard that may result from international financial support as provided, for instance, by the International Monetary Fund (IMF). Detractors of the IMF have argued that its financing activities generate moral hazard. Yet, as shown by Jeanne and Zettelmeyer (2005), as long as the IMF lends at an actuarially fair interest rate and the sovereign debtor maximises the welfare of its taxpayers, i.e., no principal-agent problem is present, changes in policy and work effort, capital flows, or borrowing costs following IMF support are efficient. Under these conditions, IMF lending does not cause moral hazard.

To stress the main points, let us look at two ways in which moral hazard in international lending could be reintroduced. First, if decision-making by policy-

---

[7] Budgetary costs overestimate the distortionary costs of moral hazard.

makers was based on the maximisation of their own utility rather than based on the maximisation of citizens' welfare, this would become nothing more than a variant of the principal-agent problem in disguise. Second, if loans were given at a subsidised rate, moral hazard would appear in the same manner that it occurs when deposit insurance is not risk-based and ex ante. In both cases, there would be "excessive" capital flows, which in the first case would be diverted toward groups favoured by the policy-maker, with the cost being borne by investors, and in the second case, with the cost being borne by IMF's financiers.

As the discussion above suggests, even if there were no publicly designated SIFIs, economic agents would expect that financial stability considerations would lead future public authorities to bail them out. Given the absence of a technology that credibly ties policy-makers' hands over time, the presumption will exist that when the moment comes, policy discretion will be exercised, and the failing SIFI will be bailed out. Future public policy actions vis-à-vis SIFIs will be justified by the same time-consistent, but suboptimal arguments that justify today's public policy actions. As a result of that expectation, agents' decisions today will imply taking a higher level of risk (alternatively, paying a lower price of risk) than otherwise. Policies will be consistent given the prevailing situation, but suboptimal, echoing Kydland and Prescott's conclusion: optimal plans are suboptimal (Kydland and Prescott 1977).[8]

To summarise, dealing effectively with moral hazard requires a framework with mechanisms inducing future policy-makers to take into account the effects of their policies, via expectations, upon current agents' decisions. This needs ex ante, a first line of defence consistent with SIFIs' contribution to systemic risk; mechanisms that improve SIFIs monitoring; that strengthen market infrastructures; and that resolve SIFIs without taxpayers' money. While this is not a foolproof system against moral hazard, it seems a robust framework to minimise the trade-off between short-term financial stability and incentive compatibility.

4. THE FSB MULTIPRONGED FRAMEWORK FOR MINIMISING MORAL HAZARD POSED BY SIFIS

The discussion so far suggests a number of principles that can minimise moral hazard and alleviate the perceived trade-off between short-term and long-term financial stability. Prevention is key, and it includes planning for negative events at the SIFIs level and at the supervisory level; effective supervision with sufficient powers, and capacity of acting fast and coordinating cross-border

---

[8] It is likely that the known bad performance of economic agents in pricing risk over time, as discussed by Borio et al. (2001) for example, recognise prevailing regulatory, supervisory and policy frameworks as an important cause.

transfer of information; credible resolution tools based on ordinary liquidation of distressed institutions, their orderly wind down, or restructuring, in that order; losses borne by shareholders and creditors, and if necessary, by the banking industry, and not by taxpayers; smooth cross-border groups' resolution taking due account of home and host supervisors' divergent incentives; legal certainty about the rights of all involved parties; and preserving the level playing field when public interventions become anyway unavoidable.

Those broad principles (and corollaries of them) have been the subject of numerous discussions both at global and regional fora. Ever since the Pittsburgh Summit in 2009, the FSB has been implementing the G20 recommendations to strengthen financial stability (FSB 2009). Those measures cover a significantly large spectrum including increasing banks' capital quality; reducing financial system procyclicality; eliminating wrong incentives in compensation practices and credit rating agencies' behaviour; improving OTC derivatives markets; strengthening resolution regimes, supervisory colleges and crisis management. This has been a joint work of the FSB with the IMF and other standard setters such as the CPSS (Committee on Payment and Settlement Systems) and IOSCO. In the EU, the European Commission has helped to shape the work of the FSB and the G20, and it is proposing a number of legislative measures to enhance financial stability. Also national authorities have been improving the intensity and effectiveness of SIFIs' supervision and developing frameworks to resolve them. Among those numerous measures and proposals, given this chapter's objective, what follows concentrates in providing a critical assessment of the major steps taken to minimise the moral hazard posed by SIFIs.

At the Seoul Summit in 2010, the G20 Leaders endorsed the FSB (2010a) recommendations for reducing the moral hazard posed by SIFIs. The FSB policy framework has a *four-pronged approach*: (1) increasing the loss-absorption capacity of SIFIs; (2) making SIFIs' resolution a viable option; (3) improving the intensity and effectiveness of SIFIs' supervision; and (4) strengthening financial market infrastructures.

4.1. Increasing the Loss-Absorption Capacity of SIFIs

Following the request from the FSB (FSB 2010a), the BCBS put out a methodology to identify SIFIs and an additional loss absorbency requirement. The criteria to identify SIFIs were discussed and illustrated in section 2. For the determination of the additional loss absorbency requirement, the overriding principle used by the BCBS is that SIFIs should have a higher share of their balance sheets funded by capital and eventually other instruments such as bail-inable debt, that increase their resilience and are commensurate to their importance for the financial system and the risk their failure may pose to the real economy. After an analysis of the pros and cons of bail-inable debt, both at the point of non-viability as well as a going concern, the BCBS concluded that G-SIBs be required to meet their additional loss absorbency requirement with only common equity tier 1. This requirement will be phased-in in parallel with the capital conservation and countercyclical buffers between 1 January 2016 and year end 2018, and will be fully effective on 1 January 2019.

Using the same indicators and bucketing approach used to identify SIFIs (i.e., size, interconnectedness, substitutability, global activity and complexity), and based on policy judgment and different empirical approaches, the BCBS agreed that the magnitude of additional loss absorbency for the highest populated bucket be 2.5% of risk-weighted assets (RWA) at all times, with on top an empty bucket of 3.5% of RWA, and a lowest bucket with a requirement of 1% of RWA. These buckets are on table 12.3 of the BCBS paper (2011), which is reproduced here.

Table 11.2: Bucketing approach

Bucket	Score range*	Minimum additional loss absorbency (common equity as a percentage of risk-weihted assets)
5 (empty)	D –	3.5%
4	C – D	2.5%
3	B – C	2.0%
3	A – B	1.5%
1	Cut-off point – A	1.0%

* Scores equal to one of the boundaries are assigned to the higher bucket.

These are minimum levels and national authorities could, if deemed necessary, impose higher requirements. The assumptions made to determine these percentages are that banks fail when their risk weighted capital ratio falls to 4.5%, the reference non-SIB holds capital of 7%, and the failure of the SIB has an impact on markets that is 3 to 5 times larger than the reference non-SIB. Two approaches were followed to link the regulatory capital ratios and the probability of default of banks: first, the historical distribution of return on RWA and second, Merton credit risk model. Regarding the first approach, the additional loss absorbency ranges from under 2% to just over 2.5%, while in the latter it ranges from 5% to 8%. Thus, it can be argued that, even without questioning the incremental impact of SIBs on markets relative to non-SIBs, minimum additional loss absorbency according to BCBS's table 12.3 is a true minimum.

Regarding the use of Merton credit risk model as an alternative to the historical return on RWA, two points seem worth mentioning. First, the Merton model estimates the probability of default within a year. A more complex model allowing for a time-structure of the probability of default, such as Delianedis and Geske (2003), would suggest a higher loss absorbency capacity. The total probability of default, i.e., the short-term probability plus the forward probability of default conditional on not having defaulted in the short run, is higher than the short-term probability of default. Second, Merton model does not model systemic effects. As indicated in the previous section, the BCBS procedure to determine G-SIBs (and by extension, D-SIBs) cannot measure the contribution of SIBs to systemic risk. The methodology illustrated there to measuring the systemic impact of D-SIBs suggests that the failure of one of the five D-SIBs in Luxembourg can have a large systemic effect. Therefore, these two reasons would argue in favour of a higher loss absorbency requirement to take into account expected impact effects.

As a result of this analysis, policy-makers and supervisors may wish to consider the possibility of phasing-in over time a loss-absorbency capacity larger than the minimum levels suggested by the BCBS. If performed over a moderately long period of time, this will reinforce SIBs value as going concerns and boost financial stability.

4.2. Effective Resolution of SIFIs

Effective resolution of SIFIs implies that unviable SIFIs are allowed to fail. In turn, this requires dealing with the "too-big-to-fail" syndrome. This syndrome is perhaps the most conspicuous source of moral hazard plaguing international financial markets. It is the best example of time-consistent, but suboptimal regulatory and supervisory approaches. Balance sheet growth of some (large) financial intermediaries via capturing returns fully inside the firm while sharing part of the associated risks with society at large is bound to reduce welfare. Financial stability requires that those financial institutions fail when they become insolvent, but most importantly, requires that there are no more too-big-to-fail SIFIs (TBTF-SIFIs). It is not the place to discuss the historical process by which TBTF-SIFIs did come to exist, but it is the place to discuss what is being proposed to deal with the existent SIFIs that could endanger financial stability by a disorderly collapse.

In the EU, since the Ecofin principles in 2007 stating that the objective of crisis management is to preserve financial stability and not to prevent bank failures, the European Commission has issued several regulations covering a significantly wide range of interrelated matters, such as conditions for national guarantees to be in compliance with state aid rules (EC 2008a); conditions for national funds to be able to recapitalise banks (EC 2008b); conditions to clean balance sheets from toxic assets (EC 2009a); a framework for cross-border crisis management in the banking sector (EC 2009b); funds to resolve banks avoiding contagion (EC 2010a); an EU framework for crisis management in the financial sector (EC 2010b). Currently, an Euro area level crisis resolution framework is being discussed, which will possibly include a framework for bail-inable debt and for deposit guarantee schemes.[9] At a global level, the FSB has proposed a series of recommendations to deal with the resolution of SIFIs effectively (FSB 2011a, 2011c). Similar basic principles transpire in all these pieces of legislation, namely, that SIFIs should be allowed to fail without severe disruption to the financial system and the economy and without using taxpayers' money. Given the commonality of principles of those different pieces of legislation and the aim of relating this chapter to SIFIs, the following discusses what the FSB proposes to resolve SIFIs effectively from the viewpoint of reducing moral hazard.

Ex-ante rules are vital to minimise moral hazard when dealing with SIFIs' resolution. Instead, the current situation is largely characterised by ex-post and discretionary national approaches. The most glaring example is the inconsistency between allowing SIFIs registered in a jurisdiction to engage in transactions with worldwide economic and financial implications, and the national and disparate nature of SIFIs' resolution regimes. This suggests that distress planning by SIFIs and public authorities is one vital pillar. *Recovery and resolution plans* (RRP) or "living wills" should be part and parcel of a framework that reduces moral hazard. Those RRPs should be updated regularly so that in the event of a crisis there are detailed and clear contingency plans for the bank to perform its critical functions, preserve asset values, reduce contagion, and if necessary, wind down the bank. RRPs should be approved by home and host supervisors working together given that SIFIs' structures and business models often comprise several legal entities in different jurisdictions and large intra-group exposures (as illustrated in the previous section). RRPs will have a disciplinary role in that firms will need to make sure that the actions they intend to take in case of reasonable doubts about their solvency prospects will ensure that they can be resolved without affecting financial stability and without tapping public resources.

If the SIFI needs to be resolved, it is paramount that the resolution regime is effective. Such effective regime must recognise that SIFIs are different in that their value can change abruptly and their failure may have negative confidence implications well beyond the financial system. That regime should provide a broad set of resolution options to resolve the firm, including via the creation of a "bridge bank" to preserve systemically important operations and buy time, if necessary. Given that confidence is of essence, an administrative resolution authority with a mandate to enhance financial stability is necessary to act expeditiously. This authority should have ample powers within that mandate and be protected against lawsuits when acting in good faith.

---

[9] This will include features already proposed by the EC in its "Proposal for a Directive on Deposit Guarantee Schemes" (EC 2010c).

Like with RRPs, administrative authorities resolving SIFIs will often need to involve several jurisdictions. Effective cross-border resolution will inevitably require legislative changes to allow the resolution authorities of different jurisdictions to cooperate and coordinate their actions while sharing information preventatively and during crises. Cooperation needs to ensure that resolution measures contemplate the property rights of both home- and host-country parties. Regulatory authorities, central banks and ministries of finance in all involved jurisdictions should have the power to share information and transfer assets and liabilities freely duly considering the impact of their joint actions on financial stability at home and abroad. In contrast, currently, most countries have only a few bank-specific regulations; bankruptcy laws often focus on the rights of claimholders; or laws do not allow recapitalisation or make it very expensive. These legal frameworks certainly do not consider the need to preserve financial stability, maintain essential services or protect depositors. Insolvency proceedings are lengthy, and in the case of reorganisation, they require complex negotiations and agreements with creditors, with some potential negative effects for debtors and creditors in the form of delays, costs and outcome. National laws sometimes even discriminate on the basis of the nationality of creditors, or the location of their claims, or on the basis of the jurisdiction where they are payable. In the absence of an agreed international framework for resolving SIFIs, cooperation is of the essence.

A very much discussed issue is the *bail-inable debt*. This is a provision by which a debt instrument can be converted into equity, a creditor-financed recapitalisation. There is an on-going debate on practically all aspects of this approach, including the scope of debt that is to be bail-inable; the role of DGS in the framework; whether firms should hold a minimum of bail-inable debt as a share of RWA; the treatment of derivative contracts; and whether the resolution authority should or not have bail-in powers. These issues are complex, both individually and in terms of the legal and economic interconnections among them as well as regarding the appropriate time for their implementation.

As a matter of good economic principle, a contingent financial "instrument" such as bail-inable debt should be allowed to be traded if it were priced by markets freely and it should be regulated to avoid negative financial stability implications. In contrast to trading bail-inable instruments, there are some diverging views with respect to a regulatory-driven introduction of bail-in. This seems to transpire also from a similar discussion by the BCBS on the use of going-concern contingent capital (BCBS 2011, pp.17-20). To illustrate, and based on the theoretical discussion above, principal-agent problems between shareholders and debt holders could be alleviated by the introduction of bail-inable debt. For example, if shareholders authorise investments that result in losses that may trigger a bail-in, they may lose their principal. Thus, bail-inable debt has a disciplining effect; it reduces this source of moral hazard. However, it can also have the opposite effect when the bank approaches the point at which bail-in kicks in by making shareholders engage in reckless investments as they recognise that they will share the losses, but appropriate the gains fully. At the time of writing, it could be argued that the introduction of this type of financial instrument would require further reflection.

4.3. Strengthening Core Financial Market Infrastructures

Contagion arising from interconnectedness as illustrated at the beginning of this chapter can be reduced by increasing transparency about counterparty risk and liquidity risk. Transparency reduces asymmetric information facilitating the pricing of risk. The FSB has highlighted the role of strengthening financial market infrastructures to reduce moral hazard. Also, work by the CPSS and IOSCO to enhance standards for financial market infrastructure is crucial in this respect.

Recently, the CPSS and IOSCO issued a report on principles for financial market infrastructures (FMI). These principles contribute to reducing the moral hazard posed by SIFIs including the requirement of risk-based margins, the measurement and monitoring of credit, operational and liquidity risk as well as via default management rules and disclosure of market data via trade repositories (CPSS 2012). These standards will contribute to boosting the financial system resilience by making central clearing of standardised OTC derivatives mandatory and being applicable to all systemically important payment systems, central securities depositories, securities settlement systems, central counterparties and trade repositories. CPSS and IOSCO members will strive to adopt the new standards by the end of 2012. FMI are expected to observe the standards as soon as possible.

The FSB second report on implementing derivatives market reforms (FSB 2011b) noted advances in several areas bound to reduce moral hazard in derivative markets. This is being sought by substantially increasing the share of standardised contracts so as to increase transparency and mitigate systemic risk using increased central clearing and trading in organised platforms. Recommendations for authorities to work with market participants to increase standardisation include the use of incentives and, where appropriate, regulation. Regarding central clearing the report also addresses mandatory clearing requirements; discusses requisites for robust risk management for non-centrally cleared markets; and supervision, oversight and regulation of central counterparties. Further work will be needed to fully achieve the G-20 commitment that all standardised products be traded on exchanges or electronic trading platforms. Finally, as authorities must have a global view of the OTC derivatives markets through full and timely access to the data needed to carry out their respective mandates, trade repository data must be comprehensive, uniform and reliable, and in a form that facilitates aggregation on a global scale.

4.4. Improving the Intensity and Effectiveness of SIFIs' Supervision

The crisis made it clear that supervision had to be strengthened on several fronts including especially via a multidisciplinary approach that is forward looking and takes into account macroeconomic and financial trends, is able to timely identify the development of vulnerabilities, efficiently deals with the multi-jurisdictional risk of SIFIs and gathers and disseminates information among supervisors and between supervisors and the financial industry. To that effect, the FSB proposed 11 sets of recommendations for SIFIs' effective and sufficiently intense supervision. They contain a wide range of desirable features that, if implemented, will minimise the moral hazard SIFIs pose to the financial industry (FSB 2010b). Recommendations cover supervisors' mandates, their powers, resources and independence, as well as supervisory techniques, both from a national and a cross-border dimension.

It is hard to disagree with the gist of the FSB recommendations. However, it seems opportune to address three principle-related points. They concern the tension between changing the future rules of the game and market interference; the use of several tools to achieve the same objective; and the need to develop the macroprudential facet of supervision.

First, it seems obvious to most observers that there is tension between removing the causes of incentive incompatibility and supervisors' (micro) managing of SIFIs' activities. There are abundant examples of suboptimal banks' behaviour. It suffices here to illustrate the inefficiency implied by certain financial institutions' compensation schemes that concentrated the benefits of successful business strategies in the hands of shareholders and CEOs while distributing the associated risks exclusively among shareholders and, in certain cases, even among taxpayers. These compensation schemes were not only socially suboptimal, but also suboptimal from the viewpoint of the institutions that adhered to them. On-going regulatory changes are intended to eliminate the causes of such incentives' structures so that in the future there is a better alignment of principal and agent incentives. However, on-going regulatory developments seem also to aim at eliminating the consequences of the old structure of incentives. This is the case of some features of the current recommendations for the assessment of SIFIs' boards; for example, supervisors would be in charge of monitoring whether the business lines continue to operate within the parameters of risk appetite set by the board (FSB 2010b, p. 9). This is inefficient, costly, and unduly intrusive. In general, supervisory approaches that mix administrative- and principle-based features have not performed well and tended to move toward a corner solution (Cihak and Tieman 2008).

Moreover, having supervisors attending and observing SIFIs' board meetings may raise concerns of incompatibility between the FSB recommendations for a better supervisory assessment of boards and the (independence-related) FSB recommendation that supervisory agencies should not manage or otherwise run the enterprises they supervise. It is true that in the US, some regulatory agencies have personnel permanently on site. It remains to be proven, however, that this practice has enough advantages in terms of better knowledge of firms' decisions and their motivations so as to offset the disadvantages in terms of preserving supervisors' independent judgment, operational costs, and intrusiveness. It also raises the fundamental question of why rules and regulations, risk-based controls to enforce them, a speedy and impartial judiciary and market discipline are still insufficient to preserve a sound financial sector. The recent crisis does not seem to suggest that this supervisory model protected financial stability more than one that excludes the presence of supervisory personnel permanently on site.

Second, if history is of any use, it may seem that some of the recommendations put forward regarding Business Models and Product Analysis (FSB 2010b, pp. 10-11) are too invasive and represent an overlapping with other tools applied with the same aim. As stated by the FSB (2010b, p. 10), it is hardly debatable that many financial intermediaries "and their supervisors did not fully understand the risks embedded in the products being offered" in the run up to the crisis. This was clearly the case with asset-backed securities, CDOs, and other even more complex derivative instruments. But it is also clear that securitisation was born out of the "originate and distribute" model which allowed banks to save on relatively expensive capital and circumvent capital requirements. Offloading loans to third parties such as Special Purpose Vehicles (SIVs), however, raised moral hazard issues by weakening banks' monitoring incentives as they transferred the loans and the associated credit risk. With loans offloaded from their balance sheets, banks had the possibility of issuing further loans. In addition, SIVs funded the loans they received with short-term debt. This process, while novel in terms of actors and financial instruments, contained the same characteristic features of long-time recorded credit crisis which point to an infatuation with the perception that "this time is different": an inverted credit pyramid, i.e., an exaggerated build-up of credit on the basis of the same available capital. Furthermore, a pernicious link to liquidity risk via the originating banks' extension of liquidity support lines to the SIVs for emergency cases compounded risks and fragility.

The BCBS new liquidity and capital regulations, the leverage ratio, the elimination of the distorted incentives of credit rating agencies via the conflict of interest implied by rating the very same firms that they advise in their issuance activities, as well as a battery of macroprudential tools, such as more prudent compulsory loan-to-value ratios and similar measures, are targeting precisely the causes of widely spread moral hazard. But it seems debatable that regulation should simultaneously remove the causes of moral hazard and target the consequences of moral hazard inherited from history. True, the history of regulation is one of the pendulums moving from one extreme to the other, such as from administrative-driven regulation to regulation via prudential stand-ards, and now, apparently to a mixture of both. While this may be an expected outcome of the worst crisis suffered by the world economy since the Great Depression, it does not preclude that good policy should strike a balance be-tween the benefits of intervention to alleviate the negative systemic aspects of SIFIs' operations and the costs of interference with banks' business lines. The temptation that public authorities know best should be avoided, as the crisis is also a striking reminder of the contrary.

As a corollary of the previous discussion, supervisory powers should be ex-panded along the lines suggested by the FSB as glaring gaps still remain, and are regularly identified in Financial Sector Assessment Programs – IMF driven exercises. However, it would be convenient to make it clear that some supervi-sory powers are best associated with a *going-concern* while others are best as-sociated with a *gone-concern*. Supervisory imposed dividend cuts, for example, have been considered by some commentators as an intrusion in the economic life of financial intermediaries. Nevertheless, cutting dividends may be an ef-fective tool for reinforcing the resilience of a SIFI through an increase in own funds for as long as there are public funds involved. Therefore, for economic ef-ficiency reasons, such a tool would be best reserved for situations when it is rea-sonable to assume that the prospects of the SIFI as a going-concern are bleak.

Third, the FSB suggests that supervisory authorities have a well-developed macroprudential surveillance and multidisciplinary approach with forward-looking characteristics designed to identify trends and developments that might negatively impact the risk profile of banks. Further, it is suggested that supervisors gather data and consult and coordinate with all government stake-holders, the industry and markets in general. A discussion of alternative regula-tory and supervisory regimes clearly is beyond the scope of this chapter. The complexity, variety and inter-linkages among issues is enormous, e.g., which institution(s) should be responsible for macroprudential policy, mechanisms for sharing information, independence and accountability of the institution(s) in charge, and even country-specific historical and regulatory characteristics (Nier et al. 2011). However, the scope of the task described in the FSB recom-mendations blurs any remaining divide between micro and macroprudential supervision. By proposing that microprudential supervisors develop skills, knowledge, data and statistical infrastructure that is already available even in central banks not in charge of microprudential supervision, it seems to push microprudential supervisors to take on also macroprudential responsibilities. This may result, at least in certain jurisdictions, in a duplication of work and a wasteful use of rare and costly human resources.

Yet, the issue of which government entity should be responsible for a for-ward-looking macroprudential policy aimed at preserving financial stability cannot be eluded. As argued by Blanchard et al. (2010), central banks are a natural candidate to become the macroprudential regulator and supervisor. They are ideally positioned to monitor macroeconomic developments, and in several countries they already regulate the banks. The requirement to monitor trends and macrofinancial developments is part of everyday work in central banks. They have already a great deal of expertise concentrated in achieving an as good as possible understanding of the state of the economy; the crucial surveillance of the development of systemic vulnerabilities falls into the central bank's role. In addition, the urgency of data gathering, of sharing information and communication during periods of stress point to the problems involved in coordinating the actions of two separate agencies. This is also a claim for giving central banks a prominent role in macroprudential policy. Finally, the conduct of monetary policy implies taking decisions that have potential implications for leverage and risk taking.

4.5. The BCBS Criteria for Identifying G-SIBs, Systemic Risk and Knightian Uncertainty

This section would not be complete without an excursion, albeit short, into the links between the BCBS criteria for identifying G-SIBs and the chosen working definition of systemic risk. As discussed above, systemic risk implies a diffusion of financial instability to the real economy recognising as causes either a process involving the build-up of vulnerabilities that unravel in a disorderly manner, or an idiosyncratic shock that affects a financial institution and gets transmitted to the rest of the financial system, or a common shock that hits the entire financial system simultaneously. G-SIBs, by their cross-border activities, their size, specificity, complexity and interconnectedness, are undoubtedly more likely transmitters of instability following an idiosyncratic shock affecting them than regular banks. Similarly, following a financial system shock in a jurisdiction with local affiliates of G-SIBs, it seems more likely that the real economy will be relatively more affected than if the same shock affected another financial market without G-SIBs; contagion in a world with *fiat* currency may follow psychology-related, more subtle channels than those that result from accounting-determined inter-bank exposures. Finally, asset price effects, liquidity spirals (Brunnermeier and Pedersen 2009) and financial distress are more likely when G-SIBs are present than otherwise. Similarly, the implications of abrupt and disorderly unwinding of financial imbalances will reverberate, *ceteris paribus*, more when G-SIBs are at stake than otherwise.

Furthering the implementation of the institutional and regulatory changes discussed above, and the ensuing adjustment in market participants' behaviour will be beneficial for financial stability. This can be expected both for the cross-section dimension of risk and the time-series dimension of risk. However, risk is different from uncertainty (Knight 1921, pp. 19-20).[10] Uncertainty is bound to be responsible not only for profits à-la-Knight, but obviously also for losses, i.e., for divergences between expected relative prices and realised relative prices. Similarly, while business cycles' characteristics can and have been categorised in terms of duration, amplitude, accumulation and excess, it is a fact of economic life that cycles' characteristics do change over time and are different across countries over time as well (Harding and Pagan 1998). Uncertainty affecting the constellation of future prices is bound to play an important role in this "regularity". It is likely that in addition to natural shocks, technological change and financial innovation, and changes in preferences are key driving forces behind uncertainty. This state of affairs suggests two important conclusions. First, the macroprudential policy components of the framework to deal with G-SIBs which have been described above, while undoubtedly necessary, will not be able to fully eliminate the sources of financial instability and the trade-off between short-term stability and incentive compatibility. This first conclusion calls for modesty and further analysis and research. Second, the build-up of vulnerabilities that contribute to systemic risk should be monitored in its cross-section dimension and in its time-dimension. Of the three distinct forms that systemic risk may take, the build-up of vulnerabilities that may disorderly unravel takes up on this light a particular importance. The second conclusion is, therefore, a call for strengthening data collection and information provision to better capture risk-build up; to improve data on network connections; and to monitor the vulnerabilities of the economy. It is also a call for more comprehensive and accurate tools and models that improve our understanding of the channels through which the financial sector is interconnected, via which it interacts with the real economy, and in particular, how it interacts with fiscal and monetary policies.

5. ADDITIONAL FEATURES OF THE FRAMEWORK

5.1. Lender of Last Resort and SIFIs

A key reason often advanced for justifying emergency liquidity assistance (ELA) provision is the prevention of systemic risk in the form of contagion.

---

[10] "Uncertainty must be taken in a sense radically distinct from the familiar notion of risk, from which it has never been properly separated.... The essential fact is that 'risk' means in some cases a quantity susceptible of measurement, while at other times it is something distinctly not of this character; and there are far-reaching and crucial differences in the bearings of the phenomena depending on which of the two is really present and operating.... It will appear that a measurable uncertainty, or 'risk' proper, as we shall use the term, is so far different from an immeasurable one that it is not in effect an uncertainty at all. We shall accordingly restrict the term 'uncertainty' to cases of the non-quantitative type. It is this 'true' uncertainty, and not risk, as has been argued, which forms the basis of a valid theory of profit and accounts for the divergence between actual and theoretical competition."

Once again, and as observed during the recent crisis, the negative impact of such actions on banks' future risk-taking behaviour takes the back seat. It is fair to argue that this state of affairs in policymaking is to a certain extent justified given that Bagehot's advice to provide ELA only to solvent banks against good collateral and at a penalty rate has come under attack. In practice, it is rarely possible to perform a clear-cut distinction as to whether solvency or liquidity is the predominant cause of a given bank's distress (Goodhart 1987). In addition, before the crisis, it was often assumed that banks in difficulty could always tap interbank markets, secured or unsecured. Recently, Freixas et al. (2004) stressed the inherently contradictory nature of the suggestion that banks can always tap interbank markets for liquidity when at the same time solvency and liquidity cannot be clearly disentangled in reality. They argue that even when there is no danger of systemic risk posed by contagion from an ailing institution, there is a role for ELA. However, whether ELA will be consistent with an efficient allocation of liquidity will depend on the nature of the incentives – or the type of moral hazard – faced by banks as well as on macroeconomic conditions. ELA should be provided at a penalty rate only when banks face *screening moral hazard* due to less-than-perfect market discipline, i.e., when banks have difficulties in screening the investment projects they finance.[11] In this circumstance, the interbank market should be unsecured and ELA's task would be to limit the occurrence of asset fire sales. In contrast, when banks face *monitoring moral hazard*, i.e., when market discipline is strong, there is no reason to provide ELA and banks can finance themselves in the secured interbank market.

But not only the structure of incentives matters; macroeconomic conditions also play a role. It is to be expected that the screening of projects will be more difficult during the trough of a cycle than during the upswing; it will be also more prevalent when institutions are weak and when financial statements are not transparent; it will be more important if banks are poorly capitalised and their capital level does not take into account the externalities they pose, especially when they are systemically important. Therefore, the quality and quantity of capital, the efficiency of interbank markets and the types of incentives banks face are intimately linked in determining whether ELA provision is efficient or not.

It is not superfluous to stress that one necessary condition for ELA to be efficient is that supervision is not effective in detecting, managing and resolving unviable banks. To the extent that the framework being built to reduce the moral hazard posed by SIFIs has effective supervision as a key pillar, the role of ELA should be diminished. While not discussed here in detail, effective supervision should minimise the build-up of vulnerabilities that may unravel in a disorderly manner, another way in which systemic risk is manifested. In

---

[11] Freixas et al. use the term *screening moral hazard* to refer to some form of adverse selection.

addition, to the extent that the robustness of market infrastructures and the transparency of financial information are also important pillars of the new framework, ELA's role should also be reduced as SIFIs will have better incentives to screen projects. In addition, SIFIs' collateral which is acceptable for ELA should be commensurate with the size of the shocks they face suggesting an important role for collateral policy and risk management, the treatment of which goes beyond the objective of this chapter.

Finally, the lender of last resort (LLR) can lend at a lower rate than the interbank market by using as collateral the assets of the bank in distress and overriding thereby the DGS. As noted by Freixas et al. (2004), this capacity of the LLR to change the priority of the claims on banks' assets argues for a compartmentalised structure for ELA and DGS so that there is no cross-subsidisation. Most fundamentally, this link highlights the importance of developing a consistent framework for the prevention, management and resolution of banks' crises.

5.2. Deposit Guarantee Schemes, SIFIs, and Moral Hazard

Relatively little attention has been paid to whether DGS in different countries affect financial stability and how they interact with prudential supervision. Minimising the moral hazard posed by SIFIs and reducing the probability of future crises require also considering the role of DGS in a cross-country environment. DGS, if not properly designed, while reducing the likelihood of bank runs, or even stopping bank runs and contagion and reducing systemic risk, can themselves fuel bank crises by providing incentives to banks to take unnecessary risks. In contrast to traditional insurance contracts that protect against defined risks such as illness or accident, DGS normally reimburse depositors for losses from bank failures regardless of the reason for the failure. This reduces depositors' incentives to monitor banks and induces banks to take more risks as they anticipate that the risks will be shared, but not the profits. The prevalence of some form of DGS around the world poses the question of the interaction between the moral hazard posed by SIFIs and by DGS, and the question of which principles can be followed to reduce their negative impact on welfare.[12]

Research profiting from two databases on DGS and regulation and supervision around the world, i.e., the World Bank's "Deposit Insurance Around the World Dataset" (Demirgüc-Kunt et al. 2005), and the "Regulation and Supervision of Banks Around the World" database (Barth et al. 2001), points at the necessary interaction between regulation in the cross-border environment where many SIFIs operate and DGS. The first key result from this research is

---

[12] According to the International Association of Deposit Insurers, as of 2011Q1, 111 countries had some form of explicit DGS and another 41 countries were studying or considering the implementation of an explicit DGS.

that worldwide, explicit deposit insurance has been shown to increase the likelihood of crises. However, across several possible institutional environments, it also results from this research that it is possible to make DGS compatible with financial stability. The key ingredients for achieving such an outcome are effective banking regulation and supervision; strict bank resolution regimes; risk-based DGS; market monitoring and discipline; and strong institutions.

Previous sections of this chapter have already addressed the role of effective regulation and supervision as well as strict bank resolution regimes in reducing SIFI-induced moral hazard. The same applies to DGS-induced moral hazard and will not be discussed here any further. However, those preconditions, while necessary to reduce the moral hazard risk posed by DGS, are not sufficient. Research has pointed out the need to apply to DGS some measures that control risk in insurance. The first one is *coverage*. Given the importance of the ratio of deposit insurance to per capita GDP in explaining the frequency of bank crises, credible coverage limits on DGS are important to limit large banks' creditors and convey the signal that their deposits are not totally safe. This will give them incentives to monitor banks (for the same reason, interbank deposits should not be included in DGS). The second measure is *risk-adjusted premia*. While risk-adjusted premia tend to be backward-looking, difficult to price, and subject to political interference, empirical evidence suggests that they perform better than flat-rate premia. Third, *coinsurance*, while not entirely free of difficulties such as the possibility that it increases the likelihood of bank runs by making every deposit partly uninsured and by being regressive, some evidence suggests that DGS with coinsurance are more stable than without coinsurance, ceteris paribus. Finally, it is important that banks not only carry the cost of deposit growth and existing and future participants are treated equally, but that eventually needed pay-outs are also risk-related. For example, if following distress the DGS is activated, it would be desirable from a moral hazard viewpoint, that solid banks bear relatively lower costs by pay-outs being first drawn from the balance account of the defaulting bank; then, from the risk balance; and only at the end, from other banks' individual balances. However, such a mechanism is very difficult to implement in practice and the second best solution with less complexity could be a deposit guarantee scheme based on an equal and ex-ante contribution from all actors.[13]

Market discipline and monitoring by uninsured depositors, by holders of bank subordinated debt and shareholders should also be part of an effective DGS. Evidence suggests that uninsured depositors and holders of subordinated debt demand higher returns on their accounts. While shareholders have been shown to be part of the problem with banks' short-term profitability search in the recent crisis, shareholders also play a disciplining role by their sales of shares and, in certain legal regimes, their liability for part of the depositors'

---

[13] An example could be the July 2010 European Commission's proposal.

losses. Finally, corporate governance rules and regulations such as those that make banks' directors liable for conflicts of interest and other types of misconduct also contribute to reducing moral hazard.

Yet, what was stated above cannot be effective unless rules and regulations are *enforceable*. Clearly, none of the safeguards discussed will matter if they are not systematically implemented and enforced. Good institutional features such as a strong judiciary, lack of protracted judiciary processes that increase uncertainty, and transparency and enforceability of rules and regulations have been shown to reduce moral hazard.

In the case of SIFIs, it is particularly important to take into account that regulators and supervisors across countries may have different preferences in terms of the relative importance they attach to banks' profitability and financial instability; the effects of banking supervision and deposit insurance on crises probabilities due to different institutional frameworks; and the different magnitude of spillovers due to the different size of cross-border activity (Hardy and Nieto 2008). When countries in which SIFIs operate are asymmetric in any of those aspects, then it becomes crucial that premia based on the riskiness of individual banks, for instance, take into account the quality and the effectiveness of supervision and the potential externalities that ensue from the cross-border activity of SIFIs. For example, a country that is strongly affected by the conditions of banks in another country will gain significantly from coordination of supervision and DGS. Also, a country that places a heavy weight on banks' capitalisation will be less sensitive to cooperative actions with other countries since a country that favours financial stability will not benefit much from stronger supervision abroad. On the other hand, if countries differ significantly in terms of concerns about banking sector soundness and financial stability, it may be even virtually impossible to find a cooperative solution with harmonisation.

The literature suggests that the first best approach is simultaneous strengthening of supervision and limiting deposits protection according to the principles discussed, while ensuring an enforcement mechanism such as countries' mutual evaluations or adherence to internationally-agreed standards to avoid "free riding" behaviour. Stronger regulation and supervision to strengthen banks such as via the CRD IV is part of the framework to limit national supervisory discretion. Finally, DGS premia should also take into account the potential negative externalities of supervisory discretion with SIFIs.

6. CONCLUSION

Financial stability is a multifaceted reality; SIFIs are major actors in modern financial markets; moral hazard is ubiquitous. While some SIFIs are global and others are domestic, both are large, complex and may be highly interconnected posing similar risks to financial stability. Preserving financial stability while avoiding that public policy becomes hostage of trade-offs dictated by consistent, but suboptimal policy actions, requires a multipronged strategy and a comprehensive, global framework. Avoiding that the default of SIFIs puts public policy in a situation in which preserving today's financial stability is bought at the expense of making future financial stability less likely requires clear, ex-ante rules of the game to minimise (screening-related and monitoring-related) moral hazard. This framework is composed not only of microprudential, but also of macroprudential tools, and it should be able to offset, ideally completely, economic agents' biased incentives that result from the large size of financial institutions, aggravated by the official and public label of systemic importance attributed to them.

The first leg of such a framework must be preventive. First, it requires SI-FIs that are sufficiently capitalised and liquid not only from a microprudential perspective, but also in tandem with their potential contribution to systemic risk. Second, it needs solid and transparent financial market infrastructures that minimise credit, operational and liquidity risk and as such reduce contagion derived from interconnectedness. Third, it is necessary to have independent and well-funded supervisory authorities with a "through-the-cycle" view which resists leniency and that shares SIFIs' information on a real time basis with peers from other jurisdictions.

The second leg of such a framework must inevitably be curative as despite the existence of preventive, well-thought-out financial market frameworks, it would be ingenuous to believe (and perhaps even inefficient) that SIFIs will never fail. Therefore, the framework must include rules for an efficient management and resolution of SIFIs that do become non-viable. These rules must prevent that a SIFI's default causes systemic damage and that taxpayers' money is lost. ELA, even with efficient supervision, may be also needed when it becomes too costly for banks to screen projects and interbank markets are impaired.

That framework should minimise the chances of materialising states of the world during which short-term stability considerations require policy measures that impair future financial stability. The discussion in this chapter has endeavoured to show that incentive-compatible rules and policies to preserve financial stability *over time* are feasible, and that a significant amount of work is being done at global and regional levels to that end.

BIBLIOGRAPHY

Barth, J. R., G. Caprio, and R. Levine 2001, "The Regulation and Supervision of Banks Around the World: A New Database", *World Bank Policy Research WP* No. 2588.

Basel Committee on Banking Supervision 2011, "Global Systemically Important Banks: Assessment Methodology and the Additional Loss Absorbency Requirement", Rules Text.

Blanchard, O., G. Dell'Ariccia, and P. Mauro 2010, "Rethinking Macroeconomic Policy", *IMF Staff Position Note*, International Monetary Fund.

Borio, C., C. Furfine, and P. Lowe 2001, "Procyclicality of the Financial System and Financial Stability: Issues and Policy Option", *BIS Papers* No. 1, Bank for International Settlements.

Brunnermeier, M. K. and L. H. Pedersen 2009, "Market Liquidity and Funding Liquidity", *The Review of Financial Studies*, 22, pp. 2201-38.

Buisson, B. 2012, *Les Canaux Interbancaires de Contagion au Luxembourg : l'Apport des Analyses de Réseaux*, Banque centrale du Luxembourg, mimeo.

Committee on the Global Financial System 2010, "The Role of Margin Requirements and Haircuts in Procyclicality", BIS Papers No. 36, Bank for International Settlements.

Cihak, M. and A. Tieman 2008, "Quality of Financial Sector Regulation and Supervision Around the World", *IMF Working Paper* WP/08/190, International Monetary Fund.

Committee on Payment and Settlement Systems 2012, *Principles for Financial Market Infrastructures*, April.

Delianedis, G. and R. Geske 2003, "Credit Risk and Risk Neutral Default Probabilities: Information about Rating Migrations and Default", *Working Paper*, University of California at Los Angeles.

Demirgüc-Kunt, A., B. Karakoivili, and L. Laeven 2005, "Deposit Insurance Around the World Dataset", *World Bank Policy Research WP No. 3688.*

European Central Bank 2009, "The Concept of Systemic Risk", *Financial Stability Review*, pp. 134-142, December.

European Central Bank 2010, "Macro-prudential Policy Objectives and Tools", *Financial Stability Review*, pp. 129-37, June.

European Commission 2008a, "Banking Communication", October.

European Commission, 2008b, "Recapitalization Communication", December.

European Commission 2009a, "Impaired Assets Communication", February.

European Commission 2009b, *EU Framework for Cross-border Crisis Management in the Banking Sector*, October.

European Commission 2010a, *Bank Resolution Funds*, May.

European Commission 2010b, *EU Framework for Crisis Management in the Financial Sector*, October.

European Commission 2010c, "Proposal for a Directive on Deposit Guarantee Schemes", http://ec.europa.eu/internal_market/bank/docs/guarantee/20100712_proposal_en.pdf.

Financial Stability Board 2009, "Progress since the Pittsburgh Summit in Implementing the G20 Recommendations for Strengthening Financial Stability", November.

Financial Stability Board 2010a, "Reducing the Moral Hazard Posed by Systemically Important Financial Institutions", October.

Financial Stability Board 2010b, "Intensity and Effectiveness of SIFI Supervision", November.

Financial Stability Board 2011a, "Effective Resolution of Systemically Important Financial Institutions", July.

Financial Stability Board, 2011b, "OTC Derivatives Market Reform", October.

Financial Stability Board, 2011c, "Policy Measures to Address Systemically Important Financial Institutions", Annex, November.

Freixas, X., B. M. Parigi, and J-C. Rochet 2004, "The Lender of Last Resort: A 21st Century Approach", *mimeo*.

Giordana, G. 2011, "Systemically Important Banks in Luxembourg: An Application of the BCBS Proposed Methodology", *mimeo*, Banque centrale du Luxembourg.

Goodhart, C. 1987, "Why Do Banks Need a CB?", *Oxford Economic Papers*, vol. 39, pp. 75-89.

Goodhart, C. and B. Hofmann 2007, *House Prices and the Macroeconomy*, Oxford University Press.

Harding, A. and A.R. Pagan, 1998, "Dissecting the Cycle", *Melbourne Institute Working Paper*, No. 13/99.

Hardy, D. C. and M. J. Nieto, 2008, "Cross-border Coordination of Prudential Supervision and Deposit Guarantees", *IMF Working Papers* WP/08/283.

Jeanne, O. and J. Zettelmeyer 2005, "The Mussa Theorem (and Other Results on IMF-Induced Moral Hazard)", *IMF Staff Papers*, vol. 52, pp. 64-84.

Jin, X. and F. Nadal De Simone 2012, "Indicators of Banking Sector Systemic Vulnerability: a Dynamic Tail-risk CIMDO Approach", *Banque centrale du Luxembourg, Working Paper*, forthcoming.

Knight, F. H. 1921, *Risk, Uncertainty and Profit*, The University Press, Cambridge, Massachusetts.

Kydland, F. E. and E. C. Prescott 1977, "Rules Rather than Discretion: The Inconsistency of Optimal Plans", *Journal of Political Economy*, vol. 85, pp. 473-91.

Nier, E. W., J. Osinski, L. I. Jacome and P. Madrid 2011, "Towards Effective Macroprudential Policy Frameworks: An Assessment of Stylized Institutional Models", *IMF Working Paper* WP/11/250.

Reinhart, C. M. and K. S. Rogoff 2008, "This Time is Different: A Panoramic View of Eight Centuries of Financial Crises", *mimeo*.

12. Systemically Important Banks – Possible Options for Policy Makers

Klaas H.W. Knot and Hanne van Voorden

1. INTRODUCTION

In the past decades, the global banking sector has grown rapidly, outpacing the world economy. At the forefront of this expansion were a small number of financial institutions. In 1990, assets of the top 25 global banks totalled almost USD 7,000 billion, which accounted for about 30% of worldwide GDP. Just before the start of the current financial crisis, their total assets came to almost USD 40,000 billion, 70% of worldwide GDP.

The literature on financial deepening suggests that the growth of the banking sector has contributed to economic prosperity and globalisation (Levine 2005). Also, large financial institutions provide benefits of scale and scope, and facilitate international capital flows (Poelhekke 2011). However, during the current financial crisis that started in 2007, it became clear that the large size of the banking sector had also become a potential source of financial instability. This is confirmed by another strand of literature, which suggests that excessive financial growth can exacerbate the economic cycle and be a source of financial instability (Easterly, Islam and Stiglitz 2000; Rousseau and Wachtel 2001).

The fear that some of the large financial institutions had become too big and too interconnected to fail became reality. Authorities have sought to deal with this in different ways. At one end of the spectrum is the decision not to rescue Lehman Brothers, an institution that was actually too-interconnected-to-fail. Not rescuing Lehman was partly motivated by a long-term consideration of the fear of moral hazard. And at the other end is Ireland, where the government provided guarantees for the entire banking system and capital support to a number of large institutions, which in the short term contributed to stability, but in the longer term contributed to the sovereign debt crisis. In the end, these institutions proved to be *too-big-to-save* (TBTS), in the sense that they cannot be rescued from failure without severe negative consequences for public finances.

Following the large-scale government interventions made in 2008 and 2009, there is broad consensus that the risks associated with systemically important institutions need to be addressed. The international policy agenda has focused on two issues in particular: systemic risk and moral hazard. Systemic risk is the notion that financial problems or a default of a single financial institution may have negative externalities on the broader financial system and/or the real economy. In other words, the social cost of failure exceeds the private cost of failure. Not only does this create risks to financial stability, but it also causes market distortions that are often summarised as moral hazard. The root cause of moral hazard lies in the (implicit) government guarantees given to these systemically important institutions, eroding market discipline and stimulating excessive risk taking. Furthermore, moral hazard and systemic risk can exacerbate each other. For instance, implicit government guarantees, by creating a funding advantage, may stimulate systemically important banks to increase their leverage, which in turn fuels systemic risk. As a result, policies aimed at mitigating the too-big-to-fail (TBTF) issue need to focus both on decreasing systemic importance itself, and on mitigating the moral hazard effects that follow from it.

We will first discuss the concepts of systemic risk and moral hazard, and try to provide some empirical support for the existence of these concepts. Section four will review various policy options and compare their relative merits and shortcomings.

2. THEORETICAL CONCEPTS

2.1. Systemic Risk[1]

Many different definitions exist for systemic risk. Here we will adhere to the definition as recorded in a paper by De Bandt and Hartmann (2000): '*the risk that multiple institutions or markets fail that would otherwise not have failed.*' Systemic risk can be caused by a 'narrow' or a 'broad' event. In this chapter, we will refer to systemic risk in the 'narrow' sense as this is related to the concept of systemic importance. It refers to an event where the release of bad news about a single financial institution, or even its default, leads in a sequential fashion to considerable adverse effects on one or several other financial institutions or markets (contagion). Systemic risk in the broad sense is then defined as a situation where severe and widespread shocks simultaneously affect a large number of institutions or markets. This is often referred to as 'systematic' or 'system-wide' risk. An example of system-wide risk is the bursting of an asset price bubble. De Bandt and Hartmann further define two main propagation channels through which the problems of a single institution can culminate in a systemic crisis: the real (or exposure) channel, and the information channel. The first relates to contagion caused by financial exposure between institu-

---

[1] See also chapter 9 by Jaime Caruana on the identification of systemic risk.

tions, or linkages through interbank markets, payment systems or other financial markets. And the second refers to changes in behaviour based on (often imperfect) information. This channel may materialise in bank runs by consumers or in herding behaviour (e.g., fire sales) by other market participants.

2.1.1. Definition of a systemically important financial institution (SIFI)[2]

Consequently, a systemically important institution is an institution whose failure will have large negative externalities for the broader financial system. In a joint paper the FSB, BIS and IMF (2009) provided guidance for the assessment of the systemic importance of institutions. They argued that the systemic importance of an institution can be assessed by its size, its interconnectedness with other institutions and markets, and its limited substitutability.[3] Size measures the volume of services the institution provides to the financial system and the real economy, and also proves to be a reliable indicator (proxy) of systemic importance. The interconnectedness factor measures to what extent problems at an institution may affect the financial system. This may happen through an institution's direct links with other institutions, through its role in the financial infrastructure or financial markets, or through reputational effects such as herding behaviour. The third factor, limited substitutability, indicates that if crucial functions or services cannot be quickly and easily taken over by another party, the financial system can become seriously disrupted. A final factor that can increase the systemic importance of an institution is the complexity of its organisational structure. Some of today's banking groups have over 1,000 independent legal entities and operate in more than 40 countries. Obviously, it is not easy to wind up such banks or transfer their crucial functions to another party if necessary. In other words, systemically important institutions are often not easily resolvable.

2.1.2. Measuring systemic importance

Although everyone would agree on the high-level definition of systemic importance as outlined above, it is not an easy task to identify systemically important institutions. First of all, limited data is available to measure systemic linkages. The initiative on data gaps by the Financial Stability Board (FSB) will be an important step in the right direction (FSB 2011). Starting in 2013, the largest global banks will be required to report more comprehensively on their activities and exposures. This detailed information will improve the understanding of systemic risk, particularly the network of banks in which risks may spread. This information will, however, only be available to supervisors and central bankers.

---

[2] Throughout this chapter we have used the terms systemically important financial institutions (SIFIs) and systemically important banks (SIBs) interchangeably. The focus of our attention, however, is on banks, and not on non-bank financial institutions or insurance groups.
[3] For a practical example see section 2 of chapter 11 provided by Yves Mersch.

Academic literature is often based on market data. This brings us to a second difficulty in measuring systemic risk. Systemic importance is a dynamic concept that changes over time. Not only does systemic importance change as an institution evolves, but it is also highly dependent on the state of the financial system and the real economy. Hence, systemic risk may be underestimated in times of relatively calm financial markets and overestimated during periods of financial stress. This may be of particular importance when using market data.

A growing body of literature exists on the measurement of systemic risk, using different procedures and variables. One strand of the literature uses high-frequency market data like asset prices or Credit Default Swap (CDS) premiums. Adrian and Brunnermeier (2009) have for example introduced a type of Value-at-Risk model, called CoVaR. CoVaR measures the marginal effect of an institution's tail risk on the tail risk of the system. More recently, Acharya et al. (2010) and Brownlees and Engle (2011) have calculated systemic risk contribution using the concept of Marginal Expected Shortfall (MES). MES lists companies by the expected loss on equity that they would experience in the event of a significant downturn in markets. Ultimately, the Systemic Risk Contribution Index ranks institutions by the percentage of total systemic risk each of them is expected to contribute in a future crisis. This method takes into consideration size, exposure to loss of market capitalisation, and leverage.

Another strand of literature tries to capture contagion effects by constructing a network of the banking system (Allen and Gale 2000; Van Lelyveld and Liedorp 2006; Haldane and May 2011). This method more directly measures systemic risk in the 'narrow' sense, whereas the methods discussed above may also capture system-wide events not related to the systemic importance of individual institutions. Network analysis can be used to measure the system's resilience to contagion and to identify the major triggers and channels of contagion. It can be used for the identification of systemically important institutions: critical players in the web of exposures. Network analysis is often based on accounting data, like balance sheet data or large exposure data.

Policy makers have also developed methods to measure systemic importance, as input for enhanced regulation for these institutions. These methods generally make use of balance sheet data rather than market data and are often more judgemental than the methods used by academic research. Some authorities only look at size as a proxy for systemic importance. Others, like the Basel Committee on Banking Supervision (BCBS) and De Nederlandsche Bank, use multiple indicators for measuring systemic importance and combine market data with balance sheet information. Still, the mathematical background is relatively simple (e.g., equal weighting between indicators). The assumption underlying such methodologies is that the dispersion of shocks experienced by an institution depends on indicators like size and its share in a particular market.

Evidence on the relative systemic importance of the recognised submarkets being absent, such schemes typically assign equal weighting to all indicators.

For the calibration of capital surcharges for global systemically important banks (G-SIBs), the BCBS has introduced the term 'expected impact' to break down the notion of systemic importance. It defines a G-SIB as a bank whose expected impact of default on the financial system and/or real economy is above the acceptable threshold. Expected impact is a function of loss given default (LGD) and probability of default (PD). LGD is measured by the indicator approach described above: higher scores on the BCBS-indicators mean that the impact of an institution's failure, the LGD, is larger. The supervisory response aims at reducing the expected impact of default by in turn reducing the PD. This is accomplished by requiring that these banks hold higher levels of loss absorbing capacity.

2.2. Moral Hazard

As the term suggests, the concept of *too-big-to-fail* leads market participants and consumers to assume that the authorities will not allow such an institution to fail if it runs into trouble. Due to this implicit government guarantee, these banks are perceived to be safer than other banks. The resulting market distortions are often summarised as 'moral hazard'. These distortions can further increase the systemic importance of an institution. Below we will briefly discuss how this affects the management of banks, market participants, and consumers.

Firstly, moral hazard causes market discipline to decline. Market discipline consists of market monitoring and market influence (Bliss and Flannery 2002). Market monitoring refers to the notion that investors are able to detect changes in a bank's risk condition and incorporate them into yield spreads. Market influence refers to investors' ability to change the risk-taking behaviour of banks. The perceived government guarantee for SIFIs dampens both the incentive and the ability of debt holders (both market participants and consumers) to monitor a bank. Incentive is reduced because of the perceived low risk of default. In addition, it may be more difficult to monitor an institution if it has a very complex organisational structure. Reduced market discipline may cause these banks to take additional risks.

Secondly, as a result of reduced market discipline systemically important banks (SIBs) enjoy a relatively low cost of funding. The perceived low probability of default of a SIB implies that investors would be prepared to lend money at a lower cost to SIBs than to non-SIBs. This in turn creates distortion; it induces systemically important banks to increase their leverage (see also Box 12.1), which increases systemic risk. It also induces banks to become systemically important, and it creates a non-level playing field between SIBs and non-SIBs.

Thirdly, apart from the indirect effects brought on by investor behaviour, there is a direct effect of the implicit government guarantees on the incentives to the bank's management. The safety net provided by the government creates unlimited upward potential for the bank's management, but zero downward risk. From a social perspective, this leads to an inappropriate level of risk taking by private shareholders. So, on the one hand SIBs become more vulnerable to tail risks, because of their higher leverage, while on the other they may be prone to taking on even more tail risks, thereby further increasing their systemic importance.

BOX 12.1: Modigliani & Miller and Too-Big-To-Fail

Modigliani & Miller in a nutshell

The Modigliani & Miller theorem (1958) argues that the value of a firm is invariant with respect to its financial structure, such as its degree of leverage. This result is based on several assumptions, including that the value of the assets does not depend on that of the liabilities, and markets are perfect (no taxes, no bankruptcy costs). Although most assumptions do not hold in the real world (and especially not in the banking sector), the M&M framework does provide us with a useful analytical framework for thinking about bank's capital structure and in particular for thinking about certain market distortions related to the concept of *too-big-to-fail* (TBTF).

   One important conclusion of the M&M theorem is that for any institution there should be a link between the cost of debt and the amount of equity. If we consider that additional equity makes the debt safer, then the cost of debt should fall. That is, the apparent higher costs of raising additional equity (i.e. the required return on equity) may be potentially offset by cheaper debt costs leaving the firm's overall weighted average cost of finance roughly unchanged. At the same time, it means that the total cost of capital cannot be lowered by issuing 'cheaper' debt. Although debt may be relatively cheaper than equity, it also increases the riskiness of a company's debt and in turn the cost of equity.

Modigliani & Miller and too-big-to-fail

In real life, several market distortions exist that interfere with the above reasoning and change the private optimum capital structure for banks. The private optimum level of debt is often higher than the social optimum. First, the existence of taxes distorts the picture, because it makes debt extra cheap in comparison to equity. Thus, ceteris paribus, a bank can increase value to its shareholders by increasing its leverage. The higher its leverage, the more a bank will benefit from tax deductibility. Consequently, shareholders will benefit only to some extent from a lower risk profile following an equity issue; the majority of the benefit of lower risk will be a social benefit for taxpayers.

Another assumption that does not hold true in the banking world is that of zero bankruptcy costs. Especially for systemically important institutions, both economic and social costs of bankruptcy can actually be very high. This is the very reason for providing the banking sector with a safety net. Examples of safety nets are deposit insurance schemes or (implicit) government guarantees for systemically important banks. The safety net – as described in section 2.2. – further decreases the cost of debt, especially for TBTF banks. This induces banks to increase their leverage above the socially acceptable level. Lastly, positive outcomes benefit banks, whereas the government absorbs the most negative outcomes. This may lead to excessive risk taking on the asset side of banks' balance sheets.

Implications for policy

One logical implication for policy would be to limit or abolish tax deductibility of debt payments. We will discuss the pros and cons of this policy tool in section 4. In addition, the incentive structure described above provides a clear justification for setting robust capital requirements for systemically important banks. If banks hold more capital, the first loss for shareholders becomes greater before the government steps in. This improves market discipline and reduces incentives for excessive risk taking.

3. EVIDENCE FOR THEORETICAL CONCEPTS

How did systemic risk build up in the years before the crisis and how did it materialise in the financial crisis that started in 2007? Can we find evidence for the theoretical concept of moral hazard, such as the funding subsidy for TBTF banks? In this section we will explore some more examples of moral hazard and systemic risk.

3.1. Examples of Systemic Risk

The most commonly used measure for indicating the systemic importance of financial institutions is simply their size. Both in absolute terms and in relation to the real economy, the size of the largest global banks increased tremendously between 1990 and the start of the current financial crisis (table 12.1). Size in relation to GDP not only is an indication of the too-big-to-fail issue, but also of the TBTS problem (see also figures 12.1 and 12.2). Table 12.2 shows a number of other indicators for measuring systemic importance at the start of the current crisis in 2007. For instance, its number of subsidiaries is an indication of the complexity of an organisation, whereas a relatively large dependency on wholesale funding indicates interconnectedness, which the BCBS also uses as an indicator for the identification of global systemically important banks.

Table 12.1: Size as a proxy for systemic importance

	1990		**2007**	
	Absolute size	**Size / GDP**	**Absolute size**	**Size / GDP**
Minimum	171,239	5%	707,966	9%
Average	272,764	14%	1,642,910	98%
Maximum	428,167	71%	3,807,892	538%

Panel consists of the 25 largest banks worldwide. Absolute size in USD million, GDP refers to GDP of home country.

Source: Bankscope.

Table 12.2: Selected indicators of systemic importance (2007)

	Total loans (USD million)	**No. of recorded subsidiaries**	**Wholesale funding dependency ratio**	**Leverage**
Minimum	489,050	160	34%	15
Average	795,600	3660	60%	33
Maximum	1,661,500	7990	75%	70

Based on a sample of the 25 largest banks worldwide, availability of data varies by indicator. Leverage (inverse of the equity ratio) is calculated as Total assets/Tier 1 capital.

Source: Bankscope.

A clear example of the impact of the TBTF and TBTS problem on the real economy is via its impact on public finances. Worldwide, large-scale interventions by authorities (in the form of direct capital support, guarantees, etc.) were necessary to maintain financial stability in the short term (figure 12.1). A large proportion of these interventions was aimed at preventing the failure of systemically important financial institutions. At the same time, however, this caused public finances to deteriorate, and the interaction between the health of the banking sector and that of government finances has increased significantly, leading to additional risks to financial stability. To assess this effect we developed a co-exceedance indicator. To calculate this indicator we first made a distinction between normal and large shocks in the CDS spread (a shock is considered large if it is beyond the 95th percentile). Next, we measured the percentage of shocks occurring on the same day. If several shocks occur simultaneously this is a strong indication that multiple governments or banks are simultaneously affected by tail events. However, we should note that this indicator does not distinguish between systemic risk in the narrow sense and in the broad sense (system-wide risk). Still, our co-exceedance indicator clearly shows an increase in interconnectedness between governments and banks (figure 12.2). Until mid-2008, the financial crisis was primarily evident in an increasing connection between shocks in banks' CDS premiums. Since the government interventions of 2008, we have also seen this link reflected in the risk premiums paid by governments.

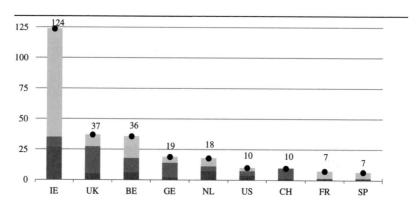

Figure 12.1: Government support during the financial crisis
As % of GDP

Source: CGFS.

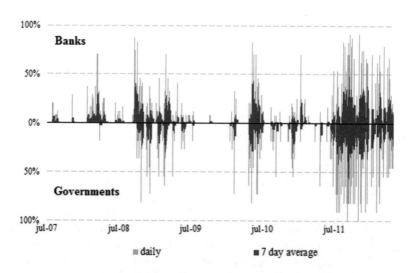

Figure 12.2: Systemic risks of banks and governments – CDS premiums
Co-exceedance of CDS premiums, in percentages

Chart reflects the percentage of banks and governments that simultaneously show an extreme rise in CDS premiums. Governments are EU-12 excluding Luxembourg plus Japan and the US.

Source: Datastream and author's calculations.

3.2. Evidence for Moral Hazard

Moral hazard can present itself as increased risk taking by SIBs (e.g., increased leverage) or decreased market discipline (e.g., lower funding costs for SIBs). In this section we will examine the existence of a funding subsidy for SIBs by looking at three different counterparties: participants in wholesale markets, non-financial institutions and households.

3.2.1. Wholesale markets

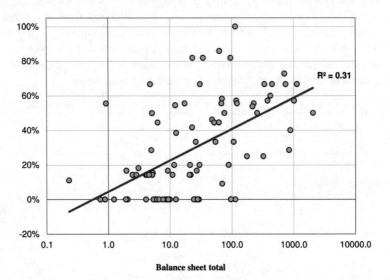

Figure 12.3: Impact of too-big-to-fail perception on credit rating
Rating upgrade in percentages and balance sheet total in EUR billion, 2009 (year-end)

The upgrade is the difference, in number of notches, between the rating including the implicit external support and the bank's financial strength rating divided by the number of notches between Aaa and the bank's financial strength rating.

Source: Moody's and Bankscope.

There is a small but growing body of empirical literature on the measurement of a funding subsidy for SIBs (Morgan and Stiroh 2005; Baker and McArthur 2009; Ueda and Weder Di Mauro 2012). As it is fairly difficult to measure a funding subsidy directly, an often used approach is to derive it from information on ratings and average funding costs per rating category. The reasoning behind this two-step approach is the following. Rating agencies, including Moody's and Standard & Poor's, first assign a rating to a bank based on the intrinsic financial strength of the institution. This rating is then upgraded by one or more notches based on the anticipation of external support. This support may come from a parent company, but in the case of systemically important banks, rating agencies take into account the anticipation of external government support. Non-systemically important banks often do not receive this rating upgrade from expected government support. Then, as a second step, the difference between the intrinsic bank rating and the final bank rating can be used to measure the funding subsidy. A higher rating means lower funding costs.

We have used a similar approach. First, we looked at the correlation between the size of a bank (as a proxy for TBTF status) and the size of the rating upgrade related to the expectation of government support. We then calculated the average funding costs per rating category, using data from unsecured debt issues (variable notes and fixed notes) denominated in euro between 2007 and 2011. We only looked at unsecured funding, as the linkage between the cost for secured funding and the rating of the issuer is less straightforward. Also, government guaranteed notes were deleted from the sample.

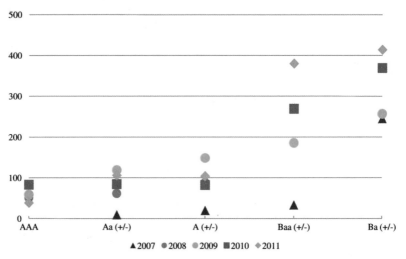

Figure 12.4: Average spreads banks' debt securities

Source: Datastream and author's calculations

The funding subsidy can then be estimated using the approach described above, and we indeed found a clear indication of a funding subsidy for SIBs. First, figure 12.3 shows that the rating upgrade increases with size, and figure 12.4 shows the risk premiums per rating category for each year in the sample. This is calculated based on euro-denominated fixed notes and variable notes issued between 2007 and 2011. Based on a sample of 20 large, systemically important banks we then calculated the average funding subsidy related to the rating upgrade. Over a five-year period, we found an average benefit to these banks of 40 bps, though, for some banks and some years the subsidy was even higher than 100bps. The question remains what this means in terms of funding costs for the average systemically important bank. Using a stylized example of a systemically important bank, we estimated the yearly benefits of the combination of funding subsidies on wholesale and retail funding in Box 12.2.

3.2.2. Households

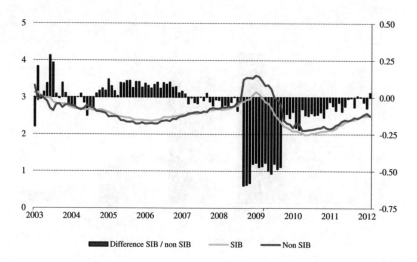

Figure 12.5: Average rates on retail demand deposits
All demand deposits in %

SIBs are the five largest banks in the Netherlands. Non-SIBs are all other banks, including small foreign subsidiaries. AAA banks fully or partly owned by the government have been excluded from the sample.

Source: DNB.

We also assessed whether SIBs enjoy a funding advantage in the retail savings market, as retail funding is an important part of the total funding base. We did this by looking at the difference in savings rates offered by SIBs and non-SIBs on demand deposits. As there is no international data available for individual banks, we have used data for the Dutch market. Figure 12.5 shows the rates offered on consumer demand deposits in the Netherlands from 2003 onwards. Fixed-term deposits show a similar trend. The figure shows that in the years before the crisis there was no TBTF-funding subsidy in the retail savings market. The difference between deposit rates is negligible and is even to the benefit of smaller banks. Since the start of the financial crisis at the end of 2008 this trend has reversed, where rates offered by SIBs have only slightly increased, but those of smaller banks have increased by almost 100bps on average. This resulted in an average funding subsidy of 15bps. Figure 12.6 shows the total funding subsidy in absolute terms, which is estimated by taking the difference in rates found in figure 12.6 and multiplying this by the volume of demand deposits and total deposits (including term deposits), respectively. For the four SIBs that were active in 2008 and 2009, the total funding subsidy amounted to around EUR 750 million on a yearly basis.

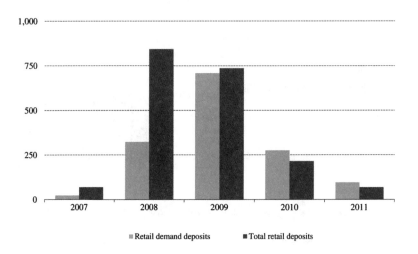

Figure 12.6: Funding subsidy on retail deposits
in EUR mln

Funding subsidy measured by multiplying the difference in rates offered by SIBs and non-SIBs on demand deposits by volume and by total retail deposits.

Source: DNB, author's calculations.

The increase in the difference in deposit rates offered may be explained by the government support given to a number of systemically important banks. These findings should, however, be interpreted with some caution, since other market dynamics distort the picture. First, in the Netherlands there is a deposit guarantee scheme in place that protects a part of consumer deposits from bank failures, independent of a possible TBTF status of the bank. Secondly, banks that received capital support from the government are not allowed to offer competitive rates on retail deposits. Thirdly, the sharp increase in deposit rates offered by small banks during the height of the crisis may be explained by the fact that smaller banks have no or only limited access to the wholesale funding markets.

BOX 12.2: A Stylized Example of a Bank Enjoying a Funding Subsidy

In the sections above, we found a funding subsidy for the main components of the liability mix of banks ranging between 15 and 40 bps. Here, we will estimate how this translates into total funding benefits in absolute terms, using a stylized example of a systemically important bank. The liability mix of our hypothetical bank is based on average data for SIBs as described in section 3.1. The equity ratio and wholesale funding dependency ratio are based on worldwide averages seen in 2007 and are 3% and 60%, respectively (see table 12.2). The mix between consumer and corporate funding is based on averages for Dutch banks (see sections 3.2.2 and 3.2.3), which is 80/20.

Table 12.3: Funding benefits hypothetical SIB

	Total liabilities in EUR billion	*Funding subsidy in bps*	*Funding subsidy in EUR million*
Wholesale funding	582	40	2,328
Retail funding, of which:	388		
Consumer deposits	310	15	466
Corporate deposits	78	29	225
Equity	30		
Total	1000		3,019

Based on this stylized balance sheet and the funding subsidy in bps as derived from our data analysis between 2003 and 2011, the estimated average yearly benefit of reduced funding costs would be around EUR 3 billion for a bank with total liabilities of EUR 1,000 billion. Hence, we may conclude that the funding subsidy is indeed sizeable for systemically important banks. Of course, these estimates need to be interpreted with caution. They are based on a limited data set of 20 systemically important banks for the wholesale funding subsidy, and the Dutch banking sector only for retail and corporate deposits. Furthermore, in our analysis we have not explicitly accounted for possible other factors that may influence funding costs.

Due to the lack of international data for the corporate sector, we have looked at the Dutch savings market to estimate the funding subsidy. Here it is easier to highlight the relationship between TBTF status and funding costs, because there is no distortion from a market-wide deposit guarantee scheme. We have

3.2.3. Non-financial institutions

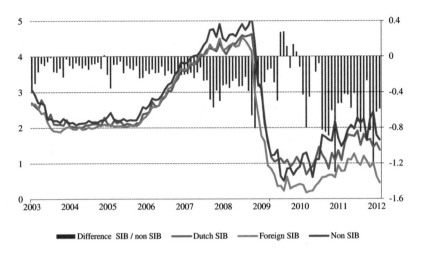

Figure 12.7: Average rates on corporate term deposits
Fixed-term deposits (based on new contracts)

Two AAA banks partly owned by the government have been excluded

Source: DNB.

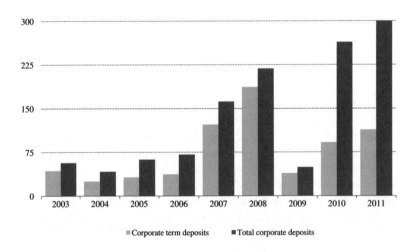

Figure 12.8: Funding subsidy on corporate deposits
in EUR mln

Funding subsidy measured by multiplying the difference in rates offered by SIBs and non-SIBs on term deposits by total term deposits and by total corporate deposits.

Source: DNB, author's calculations.

made a distinction between small banks, Dutch systemically important banks and subsidiaries of foreign systemically important banks. Here we have found an indication of a funding advantage even in the years before the crisis started, as deposit rates offered by SIBs are consistently lower than those offered by non-SIBs. Since the start of the crisis in 2007, the subsidy has increased even further, except for a short period in 2009 when especially deposit rates offered by smaller banks were volatile. On average, the funding subsidy was almost 30bps. In absolute terms, the yearly funding subsidy ranges from EUR 20 to EUR 80 million. Especially in the last two years, when interest rates of non-SIBs were almost twice as high as those offered by SIBs, total funding costs of corporate deposits fell significantly.

4. POLICY OPTIONS

This section lists a number of possible policy solutions and discusses their pros and cons in the context of the two comprehensive policy objectives discussed above: limiting systemic and moral hazard associated with the TBTF problem. Hence, the ultimate policy framework should combine tools aimed at decreasing both PD and LGD, while at the same time aim to address moral hazard. Some policy tools are aimed at directly decreasing the systemic importance, for instance by setting limitations on the organisational structure (UK Vickers recommendations) or restrictions on activities (US Volcker rule). We will not go into these country-specific initiatives.

4.1. Reducing Probability of Default

The rationale behind the capital surcharge for global systemically important banks (see section 2.1.2.) says that SIBs must have a lower probability of default than non-systemically important banks, in order to achieve the same expected impact of default. We will discuss three different policy options that aim to improve the liability side of a bank and hence its capacity to absorb losses.

4.1.1. Capital requirements

An easy way of improving the liability side of a bank is by increasing the required ratio of capital to (risk-weighted) assets. Capital can be used as a buffer to absorb losses and hence to reduce the risk of failure. Systemically important banks would need to hold higher levels of loss absorbing capacity than other banks, because their failure would cause wider effects on the financial system and the economy. A second benefit of setting higher capital requirements is the positive effect that this has on banks' shareholders incentives. Higher capital requirements will transfer more risks to the shareholders. This will limit incentives to take excessive tail-risks by offering products with higher returns, but at the expense of potentially disproportionally high losses. Hence, higher capital buffers will make these banks more stable by increasing their loss absorbing capacity.

What then are the possible drawbacks of setting higher capital requirements? One often heard argument is that setting higher capital requirements may harm the real economy. Banks have argued that the increased cost of funding will result in higher spreads to customers and higher capital requirements would force them to shorten their balance sheets. Together this would lead to more expensive and restricted lending to the real economy. Admati et al. (2011) have shown, based on the Modigliani & Miller propositions as outlined in Box 12.1, that this argument is flawed. They argue that there is no automatic need for balance sheet reduction. The level of equity can be increased as well, through retaining earnings or issuing new equity. The latter does not need to be costly, as banks often argue, because the required return on equity is most likely to decline when leverage decreases and the cost of debt will also fall. This will of course, not happen overnight. This is the very reason for the relatively long transition phases of the new Basel III agreement. In addition, one should note that the relative expensiveness of equity in relation to debt is merely a result of the – socially undesirable – tax benefits for debt. Another possible drawback of setting (very) high capital requirements is that this may induce regulatory arbitrage. One possible consequence is the shifting of activities to non-regulated entities (e.g., shadow banking entities).

4.1.2. Going concern bail-in instruments (CoCos)

As a substitute or complement to increased capital requirements, banks could be required to hold contingent capital instruments (CoCos) to increase their loss absorbing capacity. CoCos are a specific type of bail-in instruments, debt instruments that convert into equity in the event of a predetermined trigger, usually defined in terms of the regulatory capital ratio. With going concern CoCos, a bank's equity is automatically increased in times of distress, but well in advance of an actual default. Gone concern CoCos trigger at a much later stage, for instance when the capital ratio reaches the minimum requirement of 4.5% CET1/RWA. Gone concern bail-in instruments will be discussed in more detail below.

From a theoretical point of view, going concern CoCos have several advantages over regular capital requirements. Indeed, several academic researchers plea in favour of the introduction of contingent capital instruments (e.g., Calomiris and Herring 2011). One advantage is related to funding costs, as debt instruments (including CoCos) are less costly for banks to issue than common equity. This is however partly due to deductibility of debt in many jurisdictions. Essentially, this is more of a private benefit to banks than a social benefit. Another 'real' advantage of CoCos is that it improves market discipline for going concern by improving incentives for management, bond-holders and shareholders. For instance, the risk of conversion of CoCo debt instruments into equity itself may provide incentives for management to either pre-emptively raise equity, to hold higher buffers above the minimum, or to improve the management of tail risks (Calomiris and Herring 2011). The risk of dilution will put shareholders on the alert and increase their interest to monitor the bank. Here the choice of conversion rate is important: the higher the number of new shares created, the higher the dilution. As said, holders of CoCo debt will have an extra incentive to monitor the bank, due to the risk of its conversion into equity.

Going concern CoCos therefore have a number of important theoretical advantages over regular capital requirements, but they remain untested. They may have unknown effects that either increase or decrease the probability of default relative to common equity. One possibility is that the conversion of CoCo instruments is viewed as a warning about the health of the bank, and in itself may exacerbate the problems and create financing problems for the bank in question.

4.1.3. Limit the preferential tax treatment of debt over capital
Another option for increasing the capital ratios of banks is to reduce incentives to hold high levels of debt. One reason for the low equity to debt ratios could lie in the preferential tax treatment of debt over equity (see Box 12.1). One could think of a number of different policy tools that aim at reducing or eliminating these incentives.

Full neutrality between the treatment of debt and equity can be achieved by no longer allowing the deduction of interest payments on debt or to extend deductibility to equity returns (De Mooij 2011). The first method is rather theoretical by nature and has several practical obstacles. Currently no real-life example of this policy tool exists. The second method extends the tax deductibility of interest payments to a hypothetical notional return on equity. A number of countries have this tool in place or have used it in the past. A drawback of this option may be the negative impact that it will have on tax revenues, especially in the short run. For both examples, the question remains whether to apply the new tax system only to the banking sector or to the corporate sector as a whole. A third option does not aim at full neutrality, and is often called the 'thin capitalisation rule'. With this rule, tax deductibility of debt interest payments would depend on a company's leverage, i.e. deductibility decreases according to leverage. Various OECD economies use this rule and it has proven to be effective in reducing leverage, but it also has some drawbacks. The rule complicates the overall tax system, because of the introduction of company-specific tax rules, and it may have adverse consequences on the investment level.

Another possible incentive-based solution to limit leverage is not to change the existing corporate tax scheme, but instead to levy additional taxes on liabilities, which aims to offset gains from the interest deductibility. In theory, full neutrality could be achieved if the level of tax levied is sufficiently high. Following the large-scale government interventions during the financial crisis, the IMF in 2010 proposed a '*financial stability contribution*'. Since then, several countries, including the Netherlands, have indeed introduced a bank tax. Most of these bank taxes have been introduced with the primary goal of recovering the cost to taxpayers of the current crisis or to create an insurance fund to prevent taxpayers from having to foot the bill again in a future crisis. Nevertheless, they can still be effective in taking away incentives for high leverage. In a few years, empirical studies will need to show the effectiveness and potential adverse effects of imposing a bank tax.

So although the partial or full elimination of the preferential treatment of debt over equity has important theoretical benefits, the practical implementation of tools to achieve this is a complicated issue. For all these tools, international implementation would be preferred. Especially in the case of internationally active banks, unilateral introduction of such tools may not be effective and may distort the international level playing field.

4.2. Reducing Loss Given Default

Notwithstanding the importance of decreasing the probability of default (PD), a bank's PD can never be brought down to zero. This would actually not be desirable in a market-based financial system, where in principle institutions should be allowed to fail. This also improves market discipline. This is why various policy measures are currently being implemented with the specific aim of reducing loss given default or, in other words, improving the resolvability of SIBs. Several authorities have improved their bank resolution regimes, and SIBs need to prepare recovery and resolution plans. We will not discuss these agreed policy measures. One necessary precondition for limiting capital support from the government in a resolution is to make debt holders also bear their part of losses. From a theoretical point of view, bail-in instruments may be the necessary component of a resolution toolkit.

4.2.1. Gone concern bail-in instruments
Low-trigger bail-in instruments are resolution tools, as the trigger is set off when a bank reaches a capital ratio that is below or at the minimum requirement, often called the 'point-of-non-viability'. Bail-in provides the authorities with the power of writing down or converting into equity subordinated and senior (unsecured) debt. Bail-in debt has two important functions that are relevant for solving the TBTF issue.

The main benefit of gone concern bail-in is to allow for recapitalisation in resolution, to ensure the continuity of a bank's critical economic functions, without using taxpayers' money. However, there are some practical issues that need to be considered, such as the exact definition of the 'point-of-non-viability', the scope of application (all unsecured debt instruments, or only specific instruments), or the conversion rate. In the proposals made by the European Commission, consumer deposits and short-term debt are excluded from bail-in. This limits the risk of bank runs when a bank comes into financial problems. This may however also have undesirable effects, e.g., inducing banks to issue more short-term debt. One solution would be to require a minimal level of bail-in debt as a percentage of (risk-weighted) assets. The European Commission has indicated that a minimum level of 10% may be appropriate.

The second benefit of a bail-in tool is that it reduces moral hazard by allocating losses to debt holders in case of failure of a bank. In this sense, a bail-in tool may have benefits already in going concern like the benefits of early trigger CoCos. Indeed, rating agencies have indicated that the introduction of a bail-in tool would be effective in limiting the funding subsidy of systemically important banks. A recent paper by Standard & Poor's (2012) states that downgrades may be possible due to reduced likelihood of government support that they currently factor into the ratings on systemically important banks. This may be a clear benefit in the longer term, although it also implies that the timing of the introduction of bail-in instruments needs to be carefully considered, especially in light of the current European debt crisis.

5. CONCLUDING REMARKS

The importance of finding a solution to the *too-big-to-fail* issue has become clear once again. The failure of a systemically important bank has large, unacceptable externalities to the financial sector, the real economy and to government finances. These externalities are related to the mere size of these institutions, their interconnectedness, substitutability and complexity. On top of that, when the financial crisis started in mid-2007, a large number of banks did not have sufficiently robust capital buffers to withstand the huge losses experienced during the crisis. This led to large-scale government interventions, which confirmed the notion of *too-big-to-fail*.

While the problem at hand is complex, the solution needs to combine several policy measures. The ultimate goal of these measures should be to restore market discipline and reduce systemic risk to the financial system. For this, both the probability of default and loss given default needs to be reduced. Starting with the latter, we wonder whether the negative externalities of a bankruptcy of large, international banks can truly be reduced to an acceptable level. Also in the future, policy makers will therefore still need to try and avoid disorderly bankruptcies of systemically important banks. This would imply that the trade-off for the authorities between short-term considerations (i.e. rescuing a bank to guarantee financial stability) and long-term considerations (i.e. allowing a bank to fail) will most likely still exist in the future.

In our view, this has two main implications for policy. First, it increases the need for high levels of loss absorbing capacity to reduce the probability of default. The most effective way is to simply raise common equity requirements. Second, it means that market discipline can only be restored by making market participants bear losses before a bank goes bankrupt. This would call for the introduction of either going-concern CoCos or point-of-non-viability bail-in instruments. If designed adequately these instruments may be an important ingredient for providing the solution to the too-big-to-fail issue.

BIBLIOGRAPHY

Acharya, V., L. Pedersen, T. Philippon, and M. Richardson 2010, "Measuring Systemic Risk", *Federal Reserve Bank of Cleveland, Working Paper* 10-02.
Admati, A., P. di Marzo, M. Hellwig and R. Pfleiderer 2011, "Fallacies, Irrelevant Facts, and Myths in Capital Regulation: Why Bank Equity *is Not* Expensive", *Stanford University Working Paper* No. 86.
Adrian, T. and M. Brunnermeier 2009, "CoVaR", *Princeton University Working Paper*.
Allen, F. and D. Gale 2000, "Bubbles and crises", *The Economic Journal* 110, pp. 236–256.
Baker, D. and T. McArthur 2009, The Value of the 'Too Big to Fail' Big Bank Subsidy, cepr Issue Brief, September.
Basel Committee on Banking Supervision (BCBS) 2011, *Global systemically important banks: assessment methodology and the additional loss absorbency requirement Rules text*, November 2011.
Bliss, R. and M. Flannery 2002, "Market Discipline in the Governance of US Bank Holding Companies: Monitoring versus Influence", *European Finance Review*, 6, pp. 419–437.
Brownlees, C. and R. Engle 2011, "Volatility, Correlation and Tails for Systemic Risk Measurement", *Working Paper*, New York University.
Calomiris, C. and R. Herring 2011, "Why and How to Design a Contingent Convertible Debt Requirement", *Working Paper, Wharton Financial Institutions Center*.
De Bandt, O. and P. Hartmann 2000, "Systemic risk: A survey", *ECB Working Paper* no. 35, Frankfurt.
De Mooij, R. 2011, "Tax Biases to Debt Finance: Assessing the Problem, Finding Solutions", *IMF Staff Discussion Note*, SDN/11/11.
Easterly, W., I. Islam, and J. Stiglitz 2000, "Shaken and Stirred, Explaining Growth Volatility", *Annual Bank Conference on Development Economics*, The World Bank, April.
Financial Stability Board (FSB) 2011, *Understanding Financial Linkages: A Common Data Template for Global Systemically Important Banks,* Consultation paper.
Haldane, A. and R. May 2011, "Systemic Risk in banking ecosystems", *Nature*, 469, pp. 351-355.

IMF 2010, *A fair and substantial contribution by the financial sector, Final report to the G20*, June 2010.

IMF, BIS and FSB 2009, *Guidance to Assess the Systemic Importance of Financial Institutions, Markets, and Instruments: Initial Consideration*.

Levine, R. 2005, "Finance and Growth: Theory and Evidence", in *Handbook of Economic Growth* edited by Philippe Aghion and Steven Durlauf. The Netherlands: Elsevier Science, pp. 865-934.

Modigliani, F. and M. Miller 1958, "The Cost of Capital, Corporation Finance and the Theory of Investment", *American Economic Review*, 48(3), pp. 261–297.

Morgan, D. and K. Stiroh 2005, "Too Big to Fail after All These Years", *FRB NY Staff Report* 220.

Poelhekke, S. 2011, "Home Bank Intermediation of Foreign Direct Investment", *DNB Working Papers* 299.

Rousseau, P. and P. Wachtel 2001, "Inflation, financial development and growth", in *Economic Theory, Dynamics and Markets: Essays in Honor of Ryuzo Sato*, edited by T. Negishi, R. Ramachandran and K. Mino. Boston: Kluwer.

Standard & Poor's 2012, "How A Bail-In Tool Could Affect Our Ratings On EU Banks", *Global Credit Portal, Ratings Direct*.

Ueda, K. and B. Weder Di Mauro 2012, "Quantifying Structural Subsidy Values for Systemically Important Financial Institutions", *IMF Working Papers*, 12,128.

Van Lelyveld, I. and F. Liedorp 2006, "Interbank contagion in the Dutch banking sector: a sensitivity analysis", *International Journal of Central Banking*, 2, pp. 99-134.

13. A Paradigm Shift: Resolution of Banks

Jean-Pierre Landau

1. INTRODUCTION

When deciding on financial regulation, policy-makers often face difficult tradeoffs between efficiency, fairness and potential instability.

Such tradeoffs are apparent when dealing with large and systemic institutions, usually considered as "too-big-to-fail". On the one hand, large and internationally active banks cannot be allowed to go bankrupt (as the experience with Lehman has unfortunately illustrated). On the other hand, the anticipation of public bail-out creates an enormous moral hazard problem and raises significant tensions with national budgets and public opinions.

Governments and regulatory authorities are very anxious not to get caught again in the policy dilemmas they faced over the last years. Since the beginning of the crisis, taxpayers in almost all developed economies have been called to support ailing financial institutions and baling them "*out*" of their troubles. Those rescue packages have met with increasing political resistance from elected Parliaments and public opinions. In addition, public finances in most advanced economies have significantly deteriorated and national budgets may not be able in the future to sustain further efforts to cover losses and recapitalise banks. Indeed, in some countries, Sovereigns would face serious prospects of downgrading and rising borrowing costs if they were seen as rescuing their domestic financial sectors. All in all, there is a strong feeling that, in the future, money for recapitalisation of distressed banks will have to come from other sources than national budgets.

Resolution, possibly with bail-in of existing debts, offers a way out of this policy dilemma. Several major policy initiatives have been developed over the last two years. All major jurisdictions have now adopted broad ranging resolution frameworks.

In the US, the Dodd Frank Act has significantly expanded the scope of resolution to include bank holding companies, non-bank financial institutions supervised by the Federal Reserve as well as any other company that is primarily engaged in activities that are financial in nature, and pose a significant risk to financial stability of the United States.

In 2011, the Financial Stability Board (FSB) has issued its Key Attributes of Effective Resolution Regimes that include the bail-in of subordinated and unsecured senior creditors in failing financial entities.

In spring 2012, the European Commission has published a draft Directive on bank recovery and resolution that also contains bail-in powers to be implemented in 2018.

Resolution has been practised for many years, notably in the US, for regional and local banks. It remains to be tested for large and internationally active complex organisations. *Bail-in* is a new concept, still very much today the product of academic and legal research and has never been implemented in the real world. Both have the potential to significantly transform the banking and financial landscape with consequences that are hard to predict. Accordingly, this chapter strikes a cautious note, as consequences of resolution and bail-in on financial stability, funding and credit distribution may be currently underestimated. Rather than describe in detail (existing or proposed) regulatory arrangements, the discussion concentrates on the main questions and challenges from a conceptual and implementation perspective.

2. RESOLUTION

Resolution involves two different steps. First the authority (which may be the supervisor or another – specifically created – entity) takes control of the management of the bank. And, second, it uses its legal (special) powers to restructure the balance sheet by, inter alia, imposing losses on shareholders and creditors. In addition, there may be elements of public support, either through public recapitalisation or liquidity provision by the Central Bank. The goal is to ensure that a distressed financial institution may continue to operate, with none of the trauma and disruptions associated with a legal bankruptcy process. Ultimately, an orderly resolution process will minimise overall losses to creditors and the economy.

Resolution rests on the assumption that, if remedial measures are taken, the institution can survive as an "ongoing" concern, i.e. remains intrinsically viable. If that assumption is verified, then resolving a bank offers many benefits, as compared to pure liquidation. If no legal insolvency occurs, balance sheet can be restructured discretionary and speedily by the resolution authority, thus avoiding the stress and systemic consequences of disorderly liquidation. Specifically:

- Most existing debt can be honoured, reducing the risk of direct and indirect contagion to other institutions, something very valuable when the bank is entangled in a complex network of derivatives contracts;

- depositors, including non-insured, will be protected, ensuring stability of the bank's funding and lowering the probability of a run;
- disposition of assets, if necessary, can be managed to avoid fire sales, contagion on other institutions and acute stress on market liquidity . This is especially important if the resolved institution is large, systemic, and its operations have significant impact on markets' equilibrium.

Obviously, for those benefits to materialise, something more has to happen. Capital must be rebuilt and part of the existing debt must be restructured or forgiven. This is where bail-in can prove to be useful.

3. BAIL-IN

Bail-in has only recently emerged as a major item in the international regulatory agenda. The term refers to a forced conversion of senior debt into equity. The authorities trigger that conversion as part of the resolution process. The basic idea seems straightforward: if banks are constrained to issue debt discretionary convertible into equity, the resolution authority can kill two birds with one stone, both reducing debt and increasing capital through a single decision.

4. RESOLUTION AND BAIL-IN: MAIN ISSUES

4.1. Treatment of Debt

When a bank is subject to resolution, shareholders can generally expect to be wiped out and junior debt would take a significant haircut. Questions arise for senior debt.

One possibility would be to force haircuts as well. There are good arguments for requiring senior creditors to take a loss whenever a bank faces difficulties:

- It reduces moral hazard and will be conducive to market discipline;
- it establishes burden sharing between private and public sectors' contributions, protects taxpayers' money and minimises the costs to public finances.

At the same time, whenever policy-makers have been confronted with the issue, they have chosen, implicitly or explicitly, not to impose losses on senior debt holders. It is striking that none of the numerous bank rescue operations in the US in 2008-2009 has involved any senior debt taking losses. In Europe, Governments have struggled with the treatment of bank debt when designing and implementing EU-IMF programmes.

The issue first came out for Irish banks. When the Irish programme was launched in late 2010, the Irish Government came strongly in favour of imposing burden sharing on senior debt. Other authorities, including the ECB, resisted this, however, on the grounds that it would create uncertainty on existing debt and threaten financial stability. At the time of this writing, the issue seems to be revisited in the light of Spanish banks' rescue. According to press reports, the ECB seems now to favour requesting even senior debtors to accept burden sharing. If confirmed, that policy stance would mean that the *balance of arguments has shifted in favour of protecting public finances and restoring market discipline.*

This ongoing debate illustrates the fundamental complexity of the issue.

Current contracts do not legally provide for bailing-in or forcing haircuts on senior creditors. Imposing it ex post would therefore be equivalent to a compulsory debt relief and unilateral default on senior debt. While this could be contemplated – and indeed unavoidably – for bankrupt institutions, it hardly seems appropriate for viable banks, where resolution aims at re-establishing confidence and normal funding conditions.

Bail-in is precisely attractive because it avoids reneging on existing debt by providing ex ante for the possibility of conversion into equity. Compared to pure haircuts, bail-in also offers one major benefit: by converting debt into equity, it automatically provides for additional capital, always necessary when a bank is resolved. Bail-in offers an attractive alternative to public recapitalisation. It can be done without issuing new shares to the public, something very difficult to achieve in a distressed, even if ongoing, situation.

However, providing legally for such a conversion changes the nature of the debt. The prospect of being called to participate to a bank rescue may deter prospective lenders or, at the very least, change their behaviour when tensions start to appear in the financial system. In times of stress, this may result in increased instability and in normal times it can make bank funding more difficult. The behaviour of creditors will depend both on intricate legal aspects and unforeseeable dynamics, which arise in times of stress. Overall, the consequences on credit availability and financial instability are highly uncertain.

One question relates to the demand for – and pricing of – bail-inable debt. No one can be sure that those new debt instruments will prove attractive to investors. The uncertainty attached to the possibility of conversion may carry a high, and variable, risk premium. One cannot exclude that bail-inable debt ultimately comes out *more expensive* than pure equity. True, equity is fully wiped out in case of bankruptcy (or even resolution) while debt stands to be partially recovered. Contrary to equity, however, debt does not benefit from upside risks. The ultimate pricing will depend on the perceived risk profile of the bank, something obviously difficult to predict ex ante and subject to huge potential volatility. Regulators seem acutely aware that issuance of bail-inable debt may prove very costly and that banks will have no incentive to do so. The current EU draft Directive therefore incorporates a mandatory minimum of 10% of total debt to be issued in bail-inable form.

4.2. Discretion and Financial Stability

Preparatory work conducted in the FSB and the IMF has clearly outlined some main technical and legal features of an efficient resolution and bail-in framework. Two points stand out, in particular:

- Hierarchy between creditors should be honoured, which means bail-in can only be considered and implemented after subordinated creditors have taken haircuts at least equivalent to market prices.
- Resolution (and bail-in) should be triggered by a decision of the resolution authority, i.e. there is an unavoidable discretionary element. This makes bail-in different from contractual "contingent capital" where an external private entity would commit to bring additional capital if and when some market indices (or balance sheet ratios) break predetermined thresholds.

That *discretionary component* puts a heavy burden on the judgment of the resolution authority. Should it wait for the institution to be obviously insolvent or should the trigger occur at an earlier stage when rescue might prove less costly? Should it refer to objective or quantitative criteria or base its decision on a combination of quantitative and qualitative assessments? There are no available theoretical answers to those questions; nor is there any previous experience. Depending on how those issues will be solved, the financial dynamics and ultimate impact of bail-in may be very different.

By nature, resolution introduces a discontinuity, together with threshold effects, which may not prove conducive to financial stability. As soon as any doubts will appear on the solvency of a given institution, markets will try and anticipate the triggering point. This, in turn, might generate additional volatility in the relative and absolute pricing of equity and debt. Self-fulfilling spirals may easily develop where doubt and uncertainty could generate both a fall in equity prices and a sudden stop in debt funding. Alternatively, the authorities could give up their discretionary power and rely on pure quantified indicators to trigger the bail-in. It is not clear that the outcome would be better if resolution can be predicted with certainty, as volatility will likely manifest itself in the vicinity of the trigger point.

4.3. International Coordination

This very crucial issue remains unsolved to date, although significant progress has been made in the FSB.

Most, if not all, systematically important financial institutions are internationally active and/or have significant cross border activities. Some form of international regime has to be developed for those institutions to be effectively resolved. It is generally assumed that harmonisation of bankruptcy legal frameworks is a prerequisite. That needs not be the case. Since such harmonisation would take years, or even decades, to achieve, it is worth exploring viable alternatives.

What is essential is to reach an international understanding on common principles for the treatment of different categories of debt. It may not be easy. Host and home countries usually have different interests and divergent views on how to resolve a foreign subsidiary. Depending on who the creditors are, national authorities may be more or less enthusiastic to bail them in. Finally, intra group lending raises interesting questions: should debt incurred between different entities, based on different jurisdictions, be bailed-in or should it be protected?

Once sufficient intellectual and political convergence has been achieved, agreement can take many possible legal forms. One especially attractive possibility would consist in an *"OECD type" framework agreement on guiding principles* for liquidation and resolution of banks. Contrary to full-fledged harmonisation, it would not require that national bankruptcy regimes are identical or similar. Rather, it would ensure that they are mutually compatible by making sure that each of them respects a set of agreed principles. Such a framework agreement could also allow for verification procedures and dispute settlement. Compared to the present situation, this may seem a very ambitious goal. It is difficult to see, however, how resolution of internationally active banks could proceed if such a framework for cooperation between national authorities could not be established.

4.4. Banks' Capital Structure

Resolution forces regulators to confront in great detail the question of banks' capital structure. Resolution mechanisms are meant to be *predictable*. Each and every category of debt holders should know in advance how they would be treated in case resolution occurs. This is a condition for efficient working of capital markets and adequate pricing of different instruments.

In turn, predictability requires that regulators define ex ante the hierarchy, hence the characteristics and specificities of all sources of financing and funding (and, maybe, their relative proportions). Making those choices and drawing the lines will prove extremely difficult. Consider, for instance, the following dilemma on the definition of bail-inable debt. Economic neutrality would demand that all debt (including short term and repos) be subject to bail-in. That, however, would significantly increase the cost of lending between banks and impair the liquidity of the interbank market. So, most likely, short term secured and unsecured debt will be excluded. In turn, this would create for banks an additional incentive to do maturity transformation, hardly a positive evolution for the robustness and stability of the financial system.

Overall, resolution frameworks may accentuate an already visible trend towards more segmentation in banks' liabilities. To secure stable and cheap funding in a difficult environment, banks already resort to a variety of techniques, including debt with redemption options or covered bonds (where some assets are in effect earmarked to serve as debt collateral). Resolution and bail-in are likely to add new categories of debt instruments, with pre-specified attributions and hierarchy. It may be that increased diversification of funding sources will provide banks with more flexibility and ultimately will prove helpful to financial intermediation. Complexity in capital structure can also contribute to creating uncertainty, higher risk premia and raising the cost of bank credit.

4.5. The Future of Bail-In

Ultimately, the benefits and cost of bail-in have to be compared to other potential alternatives. Regulators may want to keep their hands free and manage resolution on a pure discretionary basis. In some cases, imposing haircuts and/ or bail-in may be optimal. In others, protection of existing creditors may prove necessary. It is noteworthy that never in the recent past have banks' senior creditors been asked to take losses. In the US, in particular, there was no bail-in at any stage of senior debt, which was fully honoured, even when major investment banks were granted significant amounts of public support.

While bail-in does contribute to protect taxpayers in times of stress and crisis, there are other ways to achieve the same goal. Regulators may require higher capital buffers from systemically important financial institutions (SI-FIs), and indeed are currently doing so according to the international agreement on SIFIs. Other possibilities include the establishment of *resolution funds*, which would help and recapitalise distressed institutions and could be funded themselves by a tax on the financial sector. It is likely that such a fund will be considered in the framework of the Euro Banking Union.

5. CONCLUSION

Resolution and bail-in are only two of the many regulatory changes that will affect the environment of banking for the next decade. They are emblematic, however, of the difficulties and dilemmas confronting regulators and governments.

On the one hand, there is an urgent need to act. The crisis has created enormous economic and social harm. Public opinion wants to be assured that all necessary measures have been taken to avoid the recurrence of such trauma. One legacy of the crisis has been the jump in public deficits and debts, which makes it impossible, in the future, to grant public support to ailing financial institutions. Both for political and budget motives, the financial sector must be protected from its own excesses and be able to sustain itself in case of trouble.

Not surprisingly, the crisis has been followed by an exceptionally intense effort in reforming financial regulations. Decisions have been extraordinarily fast. It had taken more than six years to agree on Basel II. By contrast, Basel III, much more elaborated and complex, has been achieved in less than two years.

Rapidity has a cost, however. In many cases, new regulation has been adopted on the basis of informed intuition rather than deep analysis. Only now do regulators start to consider the "unintended consequences" of some of their recent decisions. As regards resolution and bail-in, there are clearly many issues that would need to be clarified before finalising and implementing the new frameworks.

As previous developments have shown, there is great uncertainty on the impact on funding costs, the distribution of credit and, ultimately, the whole economy. As regards resolution of banks, regulators assume that an orderly process will enhance the perception of solvency; and they further assume that, with increased confidence in the solvency of resolved banks, the risk of runs and liquidity crisis will be significantly reduced. These are not unreasonable assumptions. They have been proved right in numerous cases of isolated resolution for small banks. They remain to be tested, however, in a more troubled environment for large, diversified and internationally active financial institutions.

At this stage of the reform process, it may be best to recognise what is known and what is not known about the financial system. It is no exaggeration to say that policy-makers lack a comprehensive and internationally consistent representation of how a bank works. There is no accepted theoretical reference on the optimal structure of its capital and liabilities. The benchmark Modigliani Miller model asserts that the value of a firm is independent of its capital structure. There is considerable debate as to whether this result holds true for banks, due to tax distortions between debt and equity, implicit guarantees given by governments, and possible myopia by equity investors. In parallel to building a robust and commonly agreed legal framework for resolving systemic banks, there is a considerable and urgent agenda for research on those basic issues in order to best inform future regulatory decisions.

14. Consequences of Financial Shocks for the Real Economy

Hiroshi Nakaso

1. INTRODUCTION

Japan's banking crisis in the 1990s[1] was perhaps the initial salvo in the recent series of financial crises that clearly demonstrated how financial shocks can exert negative consequences on the real economy over a protracted period of time. For some time, Japan's ordeal was considered to be idiosyncratic. However, today, behaviour of Japanese banks and policy makers then does not seem so unique. Indeed, we often hear today the term "Japanisation" to indicate the lasting severity inflicted on the economy when the soundness of its financial system is heavily impaired. In this chapter, after an overview on what happened to Japan's economy during the financial crisis, some policy implications are drawn that might be applicable to the global financial and economic challenges facing us today.

2. JAPAN'S FINANCIAL CRISIS IN THE 1990S

This section first provides an overview of what happened to Japan's financial system in the 1990s and then points out possible reasons why it took so long to overcome the financial crisis and bring the economy back on track towards a sustained growth path.

2.1. Chronology

In a little more than a decade after the asset bubble burst in Japan, as many as 181 deposit-taking institutions failed. Among them were several internation-

The author is Assistant Governor of the Bank of Japan. The views expressed in this chapter are based on his personal experience of dealing with the crises and do not necessarily represent the official views of the Bank of Japan.

[1] For more details about Japan's financial crisis in the 1990s, see BIS Paper No 6 (2001).

ally active banks. This was a financial crisis of an unprecedented scale for Japan. Most of the failed institutions, if not all, went under, because of the funding difficulties that eventually developed into solvency problems. Therefore, too rigid a differentiation of the solvency problem from a liquidity standpoint does not make much sense in a real crisis. In the early stages of the crisis, the Japanese authorities were often criticised as doing "too little, too late" or "muddling through" in implementing the crisis management measures. The authorities had been aware of the need to resort to the use of public money at an earlier stage, when the crisis could have been more manageable. But, the stigma on the part of the authorities that the use of taxpayers' money could only exacerbate, rather than calm, the crisis and the fear that this could invoke public resentment prevented them from taking any decisive measures. This has resulted in what may be called a "forbearance policy".

In November 1997, which is today remembered as the Dark Month or Dark November, as many as four financial institutions failed in succession, almost on a weekly basis. They included Hokkaido Takushoku Bank, which was then one of the internationally active banks, and Yamaichi Securities, which used to be one of the "big four" Japanese security houses with a global presence. Only once the crisis became visible to anyone's eyes did the discussion for capital injection using public money became realistic in the Diet and, more broadly, in the general public.

A series of capital injections to the banking sector was conducted using public money. The first capital injection took place in March 1998, four months after Dark November, when the necessary legislation was completed. However, the size of JPY 1.8 trillion (USD 23 billion) proved far too small to convince the market. A year after, in March 1999, another round of capital injection – this time JPY 7.5 trillion (USD 94 billion) – was conducted, a scale large enough to impress the market. This temporarily restored market stability, but the effect was not long-lasting, as banks saw continuous build-up of non-performing loans against the background of the sliding economy and the resultant increases in loan-losses that eroded their capital positions. Among banks, the painful exercise of cleaning up the balance sheets dragged on. It was not until early 2003, a full five and a half years after Dark November, that, most experts agreed, the financial crisis was finally left behind.

During the years of crisis management, the central bank's Lender of Last Resort (LLR) function was used extensively, along with the government's recapitalisation of banks using public money. The LLR function of the central bank was guided by a set of principles.[2] It included various forms. The LLR

---

[2] The Bank of Japan adopted the following four principles to be met in the actual provision of LLR assistance. They are: i) There must be strong likelihood that systemic risk will materialise, ii) There must be no alternative to the provision of central bank funds, iii) All parties involved are required to take clear responsibilities to avoid moral hazard, and iv) The financial soundness of the Bank of Japan should not be impaired.

at the time comprised emergency liquidity assistance to deposit taking institutions and to non-bank financial institutions that were judged as systemically important,[3] as well as provision of risk capital to financial institutions. At its peak in late 1997, the outstanding of the LLR loans reached JPY 3.8 trillion (USD 48 billion). A total of JPY 207.5 billion (USD 2.6 billion) of the Bank of Japan's LLR loans became unrecoverable (losses incurred by the Bank of Japan).[4] The painful experiences of the crisis management during the 1990s were crystallised into a piece of legislation that shapes the current financial safetynet in Japan. The key features of the safetynet include the retention of access to public money in case of a systemic crisis, but under a more stringent procedure. Under the current framework, a committee called the Conference for Financial Crisis is expected to play a key role. The Conference is chaired by the Prime Minister and relevant ministers and key financial officials including Finance Minister, Minister for Financial Stability, Commissioner of the Financial Services Agency and Governor of the Bank of Japan. If the Conference judges a case to be systemic, the central bank's LLR loans can be extended and the public funds can be mobilised for the purpose of capital injection to banks and/or protecting creditors to maintain financial stability. The current safetynet is a product of the decade long cumulative experiences of dealing with the financial crisis.

2.2. Why has it Taken so Long?

One aspect of Japan's financial crisis during the 1990s is the length of time that was required to bring the problem under control. The reasons behind it taking all those years are perhaps also the underlying elements of "Japanisation" or the so-called "lost decades", terms so frequently used to describe Japan's economic and financial ordeal after the bubble burst. A combination of reasons may be attributable. Some are uniquely Japanese, but others are more universal.

2.2.1. A paradigm shift

During the 1980s, financial deregulation progressed but the concept of the "convoy system" remained almost intact. Under the convoy system it was assumed all banks, including the weakest ones, will always be taken care of and thus every depositor at any bank is protected. This, together with the fact that there were no major bank failures in the postwar period, created a strong belief –

---

[3] In November 1997, the Bank of Japan decided to extend emergency liquidity support to Yamaichi Securities, a non-bank firm which had banking subsidiaries in the UK and several other jurisdictions, thus judged to be highly systemic, in order to promote an orderly winding down of the firm.
[4] The losses were recorded in the early phase of the crisis when the nation's safety net arrangement was still in a primitive form. The Bank of Japan had to mobilise its functions for the purpose of maintaining financial stability, which was a part of its policy mandate along with keeping price stability.

even what may be called a myth – that big banks would never fail. The conviction was tenacious. It survived the waves of financial deregulation in the first half of the 1990s, when the vulnerabilities of the financial system had become already apparent. As the series of large bank failures unfolded in the latter half of the 1990s, the myth began to crumble. Bank managers were forced to recognise that they could no longer expect unconditional rescue and protection by authorities when banks faced serious problems. People realised they must choose safe and sound banks to place their deposits. The authorities recognised that the option of failure would generally be preferable to a bailout unless there was a clear economic rationale for the latter. This was a full reversal of fundamental concepts that underlay the previous banking regime under the convoy system. The fact that the convoy system had worked so well – it had served the purpose of successfully channelling household savings into the industrial sector, thus supporting the nation's sustained economic growth – made a rapid shift to the new deregulated system difficult. In other words, the myth that big banks would never fail was a die-hard perception so deeply embedded in the economy and society that it took a long time to demolish it.

2.2.2. The central bank's dilemma

Evidence suggests that the Bank of Japan had detected by early 1993 that the risks building up in the financial system could be far larger than widely believed. As mentioned above, however, comprehensive measures – including capital injections using public money – were only taken after Dark November in 1997. An argument may well be made today that the Bank of Japan should have warned about the risk and called for an urgent improvement of the safety net. While acknowledging the truth in such an argument, it was difficult in practice to take decisive actions at that time, because the central bank faced a dilemma.

To embark on a comprehensive reinforcement of the safety net, including mobilisation of taxpayers' money, the Bank had to first convince the general public that the risks building up in the financial system were larger than widely believed and could endanger financial stability. But this ran the further risk of unduly frightening the market participants and retail depositors, thus triggering the very crisis it intended to contain. Moreover, the Bank of Japan was not absolutely sure that the information that they had obtained had clearly indicated an imminent financial crisis. This dilemma of the central bank must have been more or less shared by other government agencies. In the end, the authorities chose to avoid the possibility of triggering a crisis and continued with what may be called a piecemeal approach, at least until they encountered a full-blown crisis in 1997. The resultant cost of addressing the crisis would naturally have been smaller had the authorities taken decisive measures at an earlier stage.

2.2.3. Recognition lag of non-performing loans

During the financial crisis in Japan, there used to be a time-lag between the generation of non-performing loans (NPLs) among banks and the recognition of credit costs. This means the recognition of credit losses by banks tended to lag behind the actual point in time when the loans became non-performing. This may be explained by several factors. Until the mid-1990s, banks were required to meet strict criteria in setting aside provisions against loans. This was due to the fact some of the provisions were granted tax-deductibility. To set aside provisions against certain loans, banks had to report to the regulator and convince them that those loans had a relatively high probability of default. This might have resulted in banks being behind the curve in their provisioning policies and thus the recognition of credit losses. It is therefore conceivable that the banks' financial statements did not adequately capture the *true* status of their asset quality. In 1997, the provisioning policy was replaced by a new one that was based on banks' self-assessment of the loan portfolio. This approach allowed for more flexible provisioning, reflecting the actual quality of the borrowers as well as past default experience.

This was a significant step forward, but still not enough to close the time lag. This was presumably because of the fact that, as mentioned above, the provisioning policy of banks was based on the historical default rates observed in the past. In calibrating expected losses, the default rates were assumed to remain more or less constant. But in an economy that was continuing to deteriorate, like Japan's was after the asset bubble burst, what were judged to be performing loans at a certain point in time subsequently turned sour. The credit costs should have been assessed in a more forward-looking manner, taking into account the outlook for macroeconomic developments. Lack of market price or fair-value for loans, unlike the instruments in capital markets, may have also made it more difficult to capture the credit costs.

2.2.4. Adverse feedback loop between the financial sector and the real economy

Another element that was grossly overlooked or underestimated was the negative feedback loop between the financial sector and the real economy. The mechanism had much to do with the recognition lag of NPLs. When banks recognised they needed more charge-offs and provisions than they had expected, their capital positions were inevitably damaged to some corresponding extent. This resulted in stricter lending criteria among banks and thus tighter credit. Furthermore, to preserve risk-weighted assets, there was a general tendency for banks to prefer investing in risk-free assets, typically government securities, rather than lending to corporate borrowers. Tighter credit conditions exerted downward pressure on the real economy, which in turn generated more NPLs. And so the vicious cycle went on: banks' asset quality deteriorated while the economy continued to slide.

After all, it must have been this adverse feedback effect that dragged Japan's economy into a protracted period of economic sluggishness. For an economy like Japan's, which was heavily dependent on the credit intermediary function of banks, this mechanism had been fatally underestimated at that time.

3. WHAT JAPAN'S PROBLEM OF YESTERDAY TELLS US ABOUT THE PROBLEMS OF TODAY

Japan's experience indicates that the main channel through which the shocks of financial disruption were transmitted to negatively affect the real economy was the dysfunctional banking sector. Japan's banking sector had been heavily impaired by the bursting of the asset bubble. This was exacerbated by such other factors as the die-hard belief in the "invincible Japanese banks" and the central bank's dilemma described earlier. The length of time it required for banks to restore their credit intermediary function to support the economic recovery is a painful reminder of the fact, that once entrapped in an adverse feedback loop between the financial system and the real economy, it is very difficult to get out of it, particularly for a bank-centric economy like Japan's.

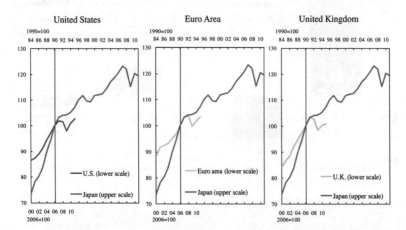

Figure 14.1: Real GDP after the collapse of the bubble economy: comparison with Japan's experience

Sources: ONS; Eurostat; BEA; Cabinet Office.

When we look at the current global financial crisis, we see *striking similarities* with what happened in Japan in the 1990s, notwithstanding the different backgrounds and circumstances. The nature of Japan's financial crisis and the authorities' responses to it has been considered to be uniquely Japanese. But the sequence of events that took place after the summer of 2007 in the US and Europe suggest there are in fact a number of common elements. For example, one might point out the reluctance and agony on the part of authorities and governments preceding the eventual decisions to resort to public funds.

Japan's crisis was brought about by its broken banking system. The US subprime loans problem was a consequence of over-stretched borrowing by the household sector. The crisis in Europe is an outcome of deteriorated fiscal positions and banking systems in some peripheral countries. The common factor is the impaired balance sheets of economic agents and the negative effects inflicted on the economy during the adjustment process. As a matter of fact, the economic performances after the financial crises appear strikingly similar. Figure 14.1 compares the paths of real GDP in the US, Euro area, and the UK with that of Japan after the bursting of the bubbles. For the benchmark years, 1990 is chosen for Japan and 2006 for the US, Euro area, and the UK. The paths seem to look very much alike, at least thus far. This might raise the question: *Is the developed world following Japan's long and winding road?*[5]

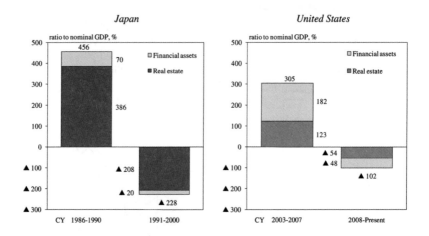

Figure 14.2: Scale of asset price bubbles

Note: Ratios are derived from the cumulative sum of capital gains and losses from each year.
Sources: Cabinet Office; FRB; BEA.

Of course, a simple comparison is misleading, given the differences in nature of each of the crises. For example, one can argue that the sheer scale of the asset price bubble was far bigger in Japan than those elsewhere. Figure 14.2 illustrates this point. The cumulative capital gains during the bubble years in

---

[5] See speech delivered by Masaaki Shirakawa, Governor of the Bank of Japan, at the London School of Economics and Political Science in January 2012.

Japan amounted to more than 450% of nominal GDP. The bursting of the bubble resulted in a large swing in the number in the subsequent years with the cumulative capital losses equivalent to almost -230% of the nominal GDP. Japan's sharp swing contrasts with that of the US, where the corresponding numbers were +300% and -100% respectively. They are large enough, but the magnitude of the problem seems to have been significantly more serious in Japan in the 1990s than the US in the current context.

4. POLICY IMPLICATIONS

Notwithstanding the differences, the basic mechanisms and channels through which financial crisis manifested itself and inflicted Japan's real economy are perhaps still relevant to the current problems we face and therefore offer a lot of insights into contemplation of policy responses. Whatever lessons may be drawn from *Japan's experience of the past*, they are presumably *more relevant to the Euro area today*. This is because of the fact that the Euro area economy is as bank-centric as the Japanese economy is. This is illustrated in figure 14.3, which shows the dependence of non-financial firms on bank loans exceeding 80% in these economies, which contrasts with a corresponding figure of 30% among US non-financial firms. The following section outlines policy implications that can be drawn from the past experiences of Japan.

4.1. Disconnecting the Adverse Feedback Loop

As mentioned earlier, it was the adverse feedback loop between the financial system and the real economy that brought Japan's economy into a protracted period of economic sluggishness. Clearly, the banking crisis initiated the vicious cycle. Japanese banks had already been overloaded with NPLs generated by the bursting of the asset bubble. On top of that they had to face NPLs newly created in the adverse feedback loop. It is true that the magnitude of the problem in the banking sector as of today in the Euro area may be smaller than that of Japan in the 1990s, since the problem is confined to some banking sectors in the peripheral countries. However, it has a potential risk to develop further in the feedback loop, which, in the case of Euro area, is more complex. It is a vicious cycle involving the financial system, the real economy, and sovereign debt. The last element was missing in Japan's crisis.

In the *Euro area*, the potential risk is a further deterioration in fiscal positions across a wider group of countries. This would imply lower market values for sovereign debt. This could undermine the balance sheet of banks that are large holders of sovereign debt. Impaired balance sheets would induce more cautious lending attitudes. Tighter credit conditions could exert negative impacts on the real economy. The slower growth could result in lower tax revenue, which could worsen the fiscal position. And so the cycle could go on.

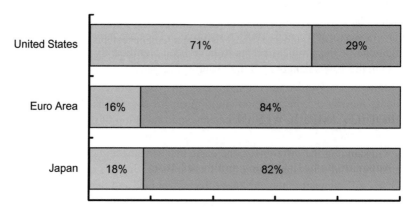

Figure 14.3: Ratio Between Bonds/CP and Loans Concerning Liabilities of Non-financial Corporations

Note 1: All the figures are based on the flow of funds.

Note 2: The current figure for Euro area is at the end of 2011/4Q, while the other figures are at the end of 2012/1Q. Trade receivables are excluded for Japan and the US.

Sources: FRB, ECB, BOJ.

It is, therefore, of *paramount importance* to disconnect the loop at an earlier stage, before it gets out of control. The deeper the vicious cycle proceeds, the more difficult it becomes to escape the loop. Admitting one could be wise only after the event, we see that one of Japan's mistakes was the underestimation of the magnitude with which the feedback negatively affected the real economy. Comprehensive measures involving bank recapitalisation, fiscal consolidation, and growth strategies must be implemented promptly and simultaneously to avoid the unbearably high price and misery that can last unendurably long. In this regard, the Euro area Summit Statement, issued on 29 June 2012, which affirms the imperative need to break the vicious cycle between banks and sovereigns, and sets forth key measures, including recapitalisation of banks, is definitely a step in the right direction.

4.2. Bank Reforms and Consolidation

The banking sector has to proceed with structural reforms to remove the unwanted legacies of the past that led to the financial crisis. For a banking sector with overstretched balance sheet, systematic disposal of NPLs and deleveraging may be of foremost importance. This will contribute to improved cash flow and thus to restoring banks' credit intermediary function, which is a prerequisite to economic recovery. Individual banks must identify the areas of relative advantage and re-establish business models to build stronger basis for profitability over the medium term. Improved profitability would contribute to increased resilience to overcome future difficulties. In the meantime, banks must also establish sound and robust risk management systems underpinned by good corporate governance. Finally, where overcapacity persists in the banking sector, consolidation must proceed.[6] These measures, however, usually take a long time to prove effective, often preceded by pains. For example, reshaping business models or consolidation could mean for some banks organisational restructuring, sometimes with redundancy and relocation of management and staff members.

4.3. Adequate Bank Regulation and Supervision

Requiring banks to hold higher capital buffers is undoubtedly the right approach, because, at the end of the day, it is the capital buffer for an individual bank that absorbs losses and thus withstands a systemic shock. The new capital standard under Basel III will soon start to be implemented. It is important that the implementation process of the new capital rule remains on track to restore the resilience of the global financial system. *Equally important as the capital standard is the regulation on liquidity.* Liquidity regulation is an important pillar under the Basel III. Although some revisions may be made before the introduction, it would be important to ensure the effectiveness of the liquidity regulation. As Japan's experience of the 1990s shows, most bank failures, if not all, started with funding pressures and the liquidity crunch developed into a solvency crisis that eventually killed off the bank. The liquidity regulation is intended to prevent such a process from being initiated by requiring banks to hold enough liquidity buffer that can be drawn down in times of stress.

There is an argument that implementing the capital and liquidity rules under the current turbulent financial environment would exacerbate the turmoil by placing tougher constraints on banks that could discourage them from lending. It is, therefore, argued that this could negatively affect the growth trajectory. This may be a fair point when observing what happened in Japan after the crisis. In their capital restoration process, Japanese banks competed fiercely to reach the newly needed higher capital ratio ahead of others, because they thought this could earn them a better reputation and thus a higher rating. This "race to the top" strategy was completely rational from an individual bank's point of view, but the collective behaviour of Japanese banks exacerbated the credit crunch and the resultant negative effects dragged Japan's economy into a recession.

---

[6] In Japan, there were more than 20 internationally active banks before the financial crisis in the 1990s. These banks were consolidated into basically three mega-banks during the post crisis years.

However, for the very reason of avoiding these kinds of unintended consequences, the *phase-in period* was put in place. For example, in the case of the new capital rule under the Basel III, the minimum Common Equity Tier 1 and Tier 1 requirements will be phased in between January 2013 and January 2015. Bank supervision is expected to play an instrumental role in discouraging banks from being engaged in the "race to the top". The core part of the liquidity regulation[7] is scheduled to be introduced in January 2015 after any revisions are made. In the meantime, national supervisors should pay due attention to the possibility that ring-fencing of liquidity in each jurisdiction under the crisis situation, even if warranted from a national perspective, could jeopardise the smooth cross-border flow of funds and worsen liquidity conditions. The long-term objectives of the capital and liquidity regulation should not be compromised to satisfy the short-term needs to adapt to the crisis situation.

4.4. Timely Recognition of Credit Losses

It is of paramount importance for banks to recognise the losses on their balance sheets in a timely manner. As the Japanese experience shows, there is an inherent mechanism that delays banks' recognition of bad loans. General reluctance on the part of banks to charge off or set aside provisions on a large scale may be understandable, since it could damage their capital positions and/or reputation. Lack of market value or fair value for loans could also make timely recognition of NPLs more difficult than the capital market instruments. Their market prices enable a timely assessment of valuation gains and losses. More importantly, lack of means to capture the negative feedback loop to be adequately reflected in banks provisioning policies could result in underestimating the credit losses at an earlier stage of a crisis. Historical events show that potential NPLs snowball in the feedback process and eventually require huge write offs from banks, often in a merciless manner. This could undermine the credit intermediary function of banks and thus exert negative impacts on the real economy.

To restrain such negative effects on the real economy, it would be essential to install a mechanism, with which the potential credit losses of banks are captured in a timely manner. Several measures are conceivable. First, a means that enables banks to write off or set aside provisions in a forward-looking manner, taking into consideration the economic and inflation outlook. Second, creating a vehicle that purchases loans, including NPLs from banks could promote recognition of losses, because the transaction price with the vehicle may be regarded as fair value. The difference between the face and fair value may be used as a

---

[7] The liquidity regulation under Basel III comprises Liquidity Coverage Ratio (LCR) and Net Stable Funding Ratio (NSFR). LCR and NSFR will be subject to an observation period beginning in 2011. At the latest, any revisions would be made to the LCR by mid-2013 and to the NSFR by mid-2016. The LCR, including any revisions, will be introduced on 1 January 2015. The NSFR, including any revisions, will move to a minimum standard by 1 January 2018.

basis for provisioning. The transfer of bad assets at fair value would almost inevitably accompany losses that result in further impairment of the seller bank's capital position. Therefore, some mechanism must be introduced in tandem to facilitate restoration of the seller bank's capital position, if needed. Third, enhancing public disclosure on banks' credit portfolio would impose more discipline on banks in terms of provisioning policy. Banks may endeavour to avoid delay in loss recognition because not doing so would be ill-perceived by the market and impair reputation. Finally, bank supervision and examination may also play an instrumental role in ensuring timely recognition of credit losses.

4.5. Resilient and Operational Safety Net

Given the important role that the banking sector plays in supporting the economy, it is necessary to establish a resilient safety net ensuring financial system stability and uninterrupted credit intermediary function even if a shock occurs at a corner of the financial system. Installing such a safety net would be a prerequisite to minimising the negative consequences of a financial shock on the real economy. In designing a safety net, several factors seem essential in view of the experiences of the recent past.

First, a deposit insurance system is required that guarantees a certain portion of the deposit base of a failed bank. The coverage of deposit protection must be carefully designed so as to strike a good balance between restraining moral hazard and minimising financial shock. The financial resources of the deposit insurance system should be sufficiently large to gain the confidence of depositors. In principle, it should be based on the premia collected from the beneficiary banks. A temporary borrowing arrangement from the government may be necessary in case the deposit insurance becomes underfunded.

Second, it would be necessary to establish a bank resolution scheme in which a failed bank may be resolved in a timely and smooth manner. The scheme should desirably be endowed with the flexibility to choose from various policy options, ranging from liquidation to transfer of business of the failed bank to a solvent bank. Depending on the degree of a financial turmoil, an option to inject capital into a problem bank should not be ruled out. After all, it would be the borrower firms and households that would benefit most from retaining the franchise value of the lender bank by injecting capital to it. If this option is chosen, the actual injection should happen as quickly as possible to boost confidence, by proving that the safety net is indeed operational.[8]

---

[8] In the Japanese financial crisis, there were two major cases of capital injection to the banking sector using public money. The first case was in March 1998, when capital of JPY 1.8 trillion was injected to 21 banks one month after the necessary legislation. The second injection took place in March 1999, which was five months after the legislation. During the interval period, assessment was made as into how much was needed to recapitalise individual banks. A total of JPY 7.5 trillion of capital was injected into 15 banks.

In an environment where the negative feedback loop is at work, the longer the interval, the larger the credit losses, and thus the larger the necessary size of capital injection would become. The policy to promote timely capital injection would be consistent with the policy objective of minimising the negative consequences of a financial shock on the real economy.

Third, principles to restrain moral hazard must be articulated. In a bank failure, in principle, existing shareholders must be wiped out, and the management must assume responsibility for the mismanagement. General creditors, too, will get a haircut, depending on the remaining net value of the failed bank. However, under an exceptional case, depositors and general creditors outside the deposit insurance system may have to be protected for the sake of financial stability and thus minimising the negative consequences on the economy. In such a case, access to public money should be granted, if the private financial resources fall short of what may be required to address the systemic nature of a financial crisis. An ex-post arrangement should be in place to repay to the government the amount of public money needed to deal with the crisis. *The cost may most likely be borne by the entire banking sector, since it is the collective beneficiary of surviving the systemic crisis.*

Such an exceptional treatment should be processed according to predetermined criteria under stringent procedure. In Japan, what may be called a "systemic risk exception" is installed into the safety net. As noted earlier, if a case is judged to be systemic by the Conference for Financial Crisis, the LLR function by the central bank may be extended and government resources be made available to protect all depositors and creditors. This scheme was developed in an evolutionary manner in the actual dealing with the financial crisis, and finally crystallised in 2000 in Article 102 of the Deposit Insurance Act, generally known as the "*systemic risk exception clause*". It has been activated in the past and has proven operational.[9]

4.6. Right Set of Policies

The global financial crisis that started in the summer of 2007 prompted central banks to take accommodative monetary policies. When the policy rates in the major economies reached the effective nominal lower bound, the central banks embarked on so-called *unconventional monetary policies*. Whatever they may be called – Quantitative Easing, LTROs, or the Asset Purchase Programme

---

[9] This comprehensive safety net was not introduced overnight and without sacrifices. There used to be anger and resentment to the banking sector for the use of taxpayers' money. Policy makers were heavily criticised for failing to bring the crisis under control. Bank CEOs resigned, giving up retirement allowances, not to mention bonuses. Some of them were arrested, brought to court and indicted. Under pressure, about half a dozen senior bankers committed suicide. The Bank of Japan's two Executive Directors were among them. Only then did the public pressure subside, paving the way to the creation of a comprehensive safety net.

– the common feature of these unconventional monetary policies is the *substantial expansion of the central banks' balance sheets*. The balance sheet size relative to nominal GDPs has reached 20-30% in these economies. As a result, market interest rates remain very compressed. There is no doubt that these policies were effective in underpinning the economy and maintaining financial system stability. But if these exceptional policies are to remain in place for an extended period of time, central banks may have to pay due attention to *possible side effects* that could partially offset the positive effects obtained from the unconventional policies. In view of the experiences in the recent past, several such side effects are conceivable.

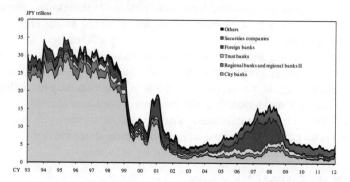

Figure 14.4: Amounts Outstanding in the Uncollateralised Call Market by Borrower

Note: Monthly data. The latest data are as of February 2012.

Source: Bank of Japan.

An example is the possibility of *money market contraction*. The money market may become increasingly dysfunctional as more transactions are replaced by the central banks' operations. Market participants simply borrow from the central bank and place the money with the central bank. Japan's precedence is illustrated in figure 14.4. During the period of March 2001 to March 2006, when the Bank of Japan implemented the so-called "Quantitative Easing Policy", the uncollateralised call market, the benchmark money market, shrank. As a result, the market became a place like the Sea of Tranquility on the moon's surface, with no signs of life. This also implied that the core of the transmission mechanism for monetary policy was undermined. The contraction resumed in 2008, as the Bank of Japan started to expand its balance sheet by pumping massive liquidity into the banking sector to address the global financial crisis.

   Another possible side effect is the possibility that *unconventional policy deprives banks of lending incentives*. Many forms of unconventional policies resulted in compressing the yield curve towards the longer end. This could squeeze banks' profit opportunities as they typically make profits by taking advantage of the slope in yield curve. Thus, banks may be discouraged from extending loans. This could be counterproductive when the very intention of the aggressive monetary easing was to encourage banks' lending and stimulate the economy.

Moreover, the very benign financial environment created by the accommodative policies could delay rather than promote much-needed structural reforms such as the balance sheet repairs of economic agents. This could mean that inefficiencies are to be embedded in the economy. The ultra easy monetary condition could also undermine banks' credit intermediary capacity, because banks may focus more on building up a portfolio of risk-free assets and become less interested in extending loans that involve credit risks insufficiently rewarded with very narrow margins. These factors could ultimately lead toward lower growth potential.

It would, therefore, be essential to minimise the side effects that may arise from policy responses to the current financial crisis by implementing complementary and counterbalancing policies. This would pave the way to a balanced and sustained economic growth in the long run. In order to identify the right set of policies, more empirical studies are needed to have clearer views on possible long-term effects of the crisis management policies on the real economy.

5. CLOSING REMARKS

Financial shocks spill over to affect the economy in various channels. There is the trade channel through which the economies dependent on exports to the crisis-struck countries are affected. There is the foreign exchange channel, where the real economy is affected by changes in foreign exchange rates. Finally, there is the financial channel, in which banks' impaired credit intermediary function affects the real economy. This chapter focused on the financial channel, as lessons learned from Japan's financial crisis in the 1990s have probably more relevance to the Euro area crisis today, given the bank-centric nature that the two economies share in common.

For policy implications based on Japan's experience, the chapter cited the significance of disconnecting the adverse feedback loop, bank reforms, bank regulation/supervision, timely recognition of credit losses, resilient safety net, and identification of right set of policies. The search for a right set of policies is a reminder that the policy responses themselves, in addition to the financial shocks, have consequences for the real economy. Given the complex policy repercussions through various channels, it may not be possible to fully assess the extent to which the crisis management policies were successful until the policy cycle is completed.

The economic distress that the world faces today is not only the result of a larger-than-otherwise swing in the business cycle, but also the outcomes of various structural problems. These include deficiencies in the banking sector and the sovereign debt problems. For some countries, the root cause is labour market inflexibility and the resultant losses in industrial competitiveness. For another country, more imminent is the demographic issue. To the extent that the structural elements are involved, placing the global economy back on track toward sustained economic recovery under price stability is a policy agenda that can only be achieved by the joint efforts of governments, central banks, and the private sector. It must be guided with clear growth strategies and implemented through a combination of enlightened policies.

BIBLIOGRAPHY

Bank for International Settlements 2001, *"The financial crisis in Japan during the 1990s: how the Bank of Japan responded and the lessons learnt"*, *BIS Paper* No 6, October 2001.

Hannoun, H. 2012, *"Monetary policy in the crisis: testing the limits of monetary policy"*, speech given at the 47th SEACEN Governors' Conference.

Shirakawa, M. 2012, *"Deleveraging and Growth: Is the Developed World Following Japan's Long and Winding Road?"*, lecture given at the London School of Economics and Political Science (Co-hosted by the Asia Research Centre and STCERD, LSE).

PART III:

Prevention of Financial Instability

15. The Economics of Financial Regulation

Ewald Nowotny

1. INTRODUCTION

Discussing the economics of financial regulation is quite a daunting task, as it encompasses a broad body of literature building on different conceptual frameworks. I will therefore present a selective overview of the respective approaches and results. Historically, they developed in parallel and with the growing specialisation in academic economics the different perspectives on financial regulation advanced increasingly in isolation and sometimes even yield conflicting results. To underpin sound policy making, I advocate a comprehensive view, which I will develop in this chapter highlighting the relative strengths and weaknesses of each of the frameworks.

Given the degree of uncertainty resulting from the economic and financial crisis, I am convinced that financial regulation has to be firmly rooted in rigorous theoretical and sound empirical foundations. Particularly at the current juncture: the great financial crisis not yet over, but the (re-)regulation of the financial system internationally already under way. Financial regulation itself is under fire in some quarters ("regulatory failure"). I will therefore critically evaluate the methods and results from the point of view of a practitioner in the field.

I will open with the standard rationale for financial regulation based in welfare economics (section 2) and its critique, because this conceptual framework serves as benchmark model for policy discourse. I highlight the limits of partial equilibrium analysis and the neglect of politico-economic considerations. Based thereon, I will structure the remainder of the chapter along the identified blind-spots of the welfare theoretic approach. Without insinuating that the respective conceptual frameworks were developed in reaction to these gaps, I review the theoretical fields that I read as essential complements to the welfare theoretic approach, starting with the Public Choice approach to the behaviour of regulators and supervisors (section 3). Going forward I will discuss some recent innovations that try to broaden the horizon of traditional models with regard to systemic risk and the "*too-big-to-fail*" problem in the banking sector

I want to thank Stefan W. Schmitz and Claus Puhr for their collaboration in writing this chapter.

(section 4). Finally, in section 5 I will show that the economics of financial regulation need to pay more attention to politico-economic considerations to gain relevance in both process and substance of financial regulation (see Kopp et al. 2010; Elsinger and Summer 2010).

2. WELFARE ECONOMICS AND MARKET FAILURE

The first fundamental theorem of welfare economics states that any Walrasian general equilibrium is Pareto optimal, i.e. it is impossible to increase the utility of at least one individual in the economy without decreasing that of another. The second fundamental theorem of welfare economics asserts that any Pareto efficient allocation can be achieved by pure market exchange by redistributing the initial endowments of all individuals. Under the conditions of general equilibrium economics, any intervention in the market, e.g., through regulation, distorts equilibrium allocations and reduces welfare. These are very strong results. However, they only apply if a unique and stable equilibrium exists.[1] It took half a century until John K. Arrow published the standard proofs of the existence, uniqueness, and stability of a general equilibrium with Gerard Debreu and Leon Hurwicz, respectively (Arrow and Debreu 1954; Arrow and Hurwicz 1958).

However, these seminal achievements came at a high price: the conditions for the existence, uniqueness, and stability of the general equilibrium were very restrictive. Hence, in the end there is no rationale for banking in the model. In order to analyse the implications of bank regulation, some form of friction has to be introduced.[2] Most models relax the condition of complete information. For the institutional and contractual arrangements that constitute financial intermediation and banking in these models it is crucial which interaction is subject to information asymmetries: bankers (owner-managers) versus depositors, shareholders versus bank managers, owner-managers versus new outside shareholders. The vast theoretical literatures about deposit insurance and solvency can serve as illustrative examples.

2.1. Deposit Insurance – Regulation versus Market Solution

Diamond and Dybvig (1983), for example, model banking as contractual arrangement between the bank and depositors that seek liquidity insurance.

---

[1] Walras and Pareto assumed that any system in N linear equations and N variables would have a solution. This is not necessarily true; but if it were, it would not address uniqueness and stability. Abraham Wald (1935, 1936a, 1936b), a participant of the Vienna Mathematical Colloquium of Hans Hahn and Karl Menger, tackled these issues in 1935/6. Also John von Neumann (1937), another participant of the Colloquium, studied the problem by applying a generalisation of Brouwer's fixed point theorem.

[2] For an overview of the various approaches to the theory of financial intermediation see Freixas and Rochet (2008); Goodhart (1989); Greenbaum and Thakor (1995).

The bank cannot observe depositors' liquidity shocks. As a consequence, the model establishes an incentive problem that can lead to a bank run. Regulatory intervention (tax financed deposit insurance) removes these incentives. The equilibrium is stable and the distortionary tax never has to be imposed. Deposit insurance improves efficiency in the Diamond-Dybvig model and it is costless. This is a strong and intuitively plausible result, but it does not imply that public intervention is a necessary and unique solution to the problem (Green and Lin 2000). In the past bank-runs were often addressed by imposing bank holidays; once depositors calmed again, banks re-opened. Under the restrictive assumptions of the model, this institutional arrangement yields identical results as deposit insurance. Charles Jacklin (1987) proposes yet another solution: unlike the Diamond-Dybvig model, his model allows for bank shareholders. He shows that based on an ex-ante dividend, the market price of ex-dividend shares will establish the same efficient allocation of consumption over individuals and time as the deposit banking solution under some specifications of individuals' utility.[3] Finally, Freixas and Rochet (2008) argue that the Diamond-Dybvig model could also be adapted by removing the restriction on the tradability of deposit contracts after the realisation of individual liquidity shocks. The resulting deposit market-price would then ensure that the sequential service constraint would not be binding anymore and the efficient allocation would also be stable.

While the models differ with respect to the necessity of regulatory intervention, they all agree that full insurance is efficient. Diamond and Dybvig, as well as Jacklin assume that individuals are uninformed about banks' asset quality. A large body of theoretical literature emerged that assumed the opposite: depositors can be informed about bank asset quality. Short-term liabilities – and the fragility of banks – are a disciplining device to limit banks' risk taking (e.g., Calomiris and Kahn 1991). Full insurance, then, leads to moral hazard of depositors (e.g., Freixas and Rochet 2008). The proponents of the moral hazard effect of deposit insurance propose co-insurance arrangements, i.e. deposit insurance that does not provide full coverage.[4] Experience during the financial crisis casts some doubt on the time-consistency of these results, because political pressure to shield depositors from losses might be very high. Thus, the results of the models in this framework need to be complemented by models

---

[3] Diamond (1984) and a substantial body of literature building thereon aim at responding to this challenge.

[4] The empirical evidence on the impact of deposit insurance on bank risk-taking is inconclusive (see inter alia Demirgüc-Kunt and Detriagache 2002, versus Gropp and Vesalla 2001). Some authors model the information available to depositors. While the latter cannot monitor the banks' portfolios directly, they can observe macro-economic variables (e.g., Gorton and Winton 2002). In these set-ups bank runs are not just an inefficient coordination failure, but a rationale response to worsening expectations of deteriorating bank portfolio quality. That would imply that banks experience large deposit outflows during recessions, but the opposite is usually the case (Gratev and Strahan 2003).

that take into account the political economy of bank regulation. Another strand of the literature focuses on the impact of full coverage and reduced market discipline on moral hazard by banks. Deposit insurance premia should thus be risk-sensitive which might not be always feasible (Chan,et al. 1992).

2.2. Solvency Regulation – Realigning Incentives versus Unintended Consequences

Turning to the extensive literature on solvency regulation within this framework yields a similar picture of contradicting results sensitive to model assumptions and structures:

In many models on solvency regulation bank owners/managers are assumed to have more information about the underlying assets than depositors (see inter alia Diamond 1984; Winton 1995). First, they argue in favour of risk-weighted minimum capital requirements. Otherwise, the portfolio manager had incentives to increase the risk of the risky part of the portfolio to increase the expected return per unit of deposits (Koehn and Santomero 1980). Second, even under risk-weight capital ratios, portfolio managers' incentives are distorted by limited liability. This could be addressed by an absolute minimum value of bank capital independent of size (Rochet 1992). Third, some of the models are very critical of minimum capital requirements; if banks are risk-averse, the failure probability might even increase after minimum capital requirements are imposed, if the risk weights are not always in line with market estimates.[5] Since the latter condition cannot be fulfilled, I conclude that the results of this strand of literature are very sensitive with respect to the model set-up and yield conflicting results.

Another approach highlights the principal-agent problem between banks (bank owners) and the public safety net. Banks' limited liability implies that depositors and other unsecured debtors are exposed to substantial uncertainty regarding the underlying real value of their nominally fixed claims. Often these costs are shifted to the general public; either ex-ante by imposing a public safety net (i.e. deposit insurance, lender of last resort) or ex-post (e.g., EU bank rescue packages; Posch et al. 2009). Consequently, the public is exposed to substantial costs of bank failures. The main results of this strand of research link the costs of public funds to the risk structure of the banking system. If public funds are extremely costly, narrow banking (banks under the public

---

[5] See Kim and Santomero (1988). In their model, Hellman et al. 2000 provide a formalisation of the argument: minimum capital requirements can have the unintended negative consequence of reducing the banks' charter value, if the costs of capital are very high. That in turn can lead to disincentives to invest in the safe project. In order to compensate for this effect, the authors argue that deposit rates should be capped to increase the banks' charter values again. However, Greenbaum and Thakor (1995) blame non-price competition in the face of price controls for the misallocation of resources (i.e. oversupply of branches).

safety net are only allowed to invest in "safe" assets) is optimal. Otherwise, optimal capital regulation allows for some risk transformation; i.e. the optimum probability of bank failure remains positive. The level of the optimal minimum capital ratio depends on the negative externality generated by the individual bank in terms of expected losses to the public safety net. Minimum capital ratios are then calibrated in a way that the additional marginal costs for banks equal a Pigovian tax that internalises the externality. In addition, the minimum capital ratio should not only be risk-weighted. In a mature banking system strong credit growth is likely to be accompanied by decreasing credit quality. The marginal minimum capital ratio should therefore be higher than the average ratio.

A further approach studies a combination of different principal-agent problems. First, large banks are owned by many dispersed shareholders rather than the banks' managers (market failure: asymmetric information between bank owners and managers). Second, the bank's debtors are usually small and uninformed depositors (market failure: coordination failure of small depositors and asymmetric information with respect to managers' efforts). Dewatripont and Tirole (1994) argue that shareholders have an incentive to gamble for resurrection, while debtors would like to close the bank early enough to ensure that capital does not turn negative. The role of minimum capital requirements is then to provide the supervisor with the legal power to seize control of the bank and the continuation decision, before the expected liquidation value of the distressed bank turns negative. This also addresses the second kind of market failure; the public good characteristic of monitoring the bank and enforcing bank insolvency. Shareholders can avert the shift in control by voluntary recapitalisation of the bank. In both cases solvency regulation promotes the interests of the depositors. However, given that the regulator cannot observe managerial effort either, the solution is only a second best solution: the shareholders now face the risk that the bank will be closed, despite a potential non-negative liquidation value after the second period. The decision of the supervisor can have strong distributive implications for shareholders and/or debtors (see Mayes 2004). Furthermore, the decision is taken under a great deal of uncertainty. From a supervisory perspective models of solvency regulation would gain, if more attention would be paid to modelling the decision problem of the supervisor and the political-economic consequences of their decision.

2.3. Expanding the Welfare Economic Framework

To sum up, the welfare-economic framework has generated a very large body of literature on banking regulation. However, I suggest that its applicability to banking policy could be enhanced taking into consideration the following observations:

First, once the necessary conditions for the uniqueness, existence, and stability of a general equilibrium are no longer fulfilled, the models are restricted to partial equilibrium analysis. This has three unpleasant effects: *(i)* Small changes in the model assumptions have strong implications for the normative results, which gives rise to a very large literature with often conflicting – and misleading – results. In some cases even the very same model has more than one optimal solution including one interventionist and another purely market driven. *(ii)* The institutional solutions to the imperfections do not evolve endogenously and do not constitute global optima. As such the models are mostly confined to providing an economic rationale for historic policy innovations (e.g., deposit insurance). *(iii)* The partial analytic solutions often have unintended consequences (e.g., impact of deposit insurance on bank risk taking incentives). The examples concerning deposit insurance and solvency regulation demonstrate that even the most fundamental results generated by the literature within this framework are very sensitive to specific assumptions and to the exogenously imposed institutional framework (also Wallace, 1988). For policy makers this limits the information content and applicability of research within this tradition. In this respect, recent contributions to integrate financial intermediation and regulation in general equilibrium models are to be welcomed (Goodhart 2003; Goodhart et al. 2011).

Second, while some key conditions of general equilibrium are relaxed, the conceptual framework itself is not questioned: *(i)* The public is assumed to trust the institutional arrangement (be that the market solution or public intervention); such trust hinges on transparency, legality, legitimacy, accountability – traditionally issues of politics and political economy (see section 5). These pre-conditions for the suggested solutions are not discussed under the welfare theoretic framework. The state is introduced as omniscient dictator whose omniscience is known and trusted. *(ii)* The state mechanically acts in the interest of depositors and the general public, although she has no incentives to. She is not accountable to the public. While all agents in the model are purely self-interested, the state is purely altruistic. Public Choice theory contributes to our understanding of banking regulation. It complements the welfare theoretic approach, as it explicitly investigates the motives, constraints, and behaviour of regulators and supervisors (see section 3).

Third, policy makers have to develop regulation under substantial uncertainty about the correct model of the economy, the significance of market failure, the future development of banking, and the impact of regulation on bank behaviour and the economy. But the models discussed so far do not encompass uncertainty, endogenous innovation, feedback-effects and complexity. Their approach to banking regulation as optimisation problem might therefore be misleading, in principle. Once we look at banking as dynamic industry that reacts to regulatory intervention, our approach to regulation should become more dynamic and adaptive. In this respect, research on banking regulation could learn from other fields like political economics, in which "*really responsive regulation*" was developed to address challenges posed by rapid innovation and complexity (Baldwin and Black 2007). Another line of research with regard to complexity tries to integrate dynamic interdependence within the welfare economic approach – such as feedback-effects and network complexity – under the heading of systemic risk. Mostly partial equilibrium models and therefore closer in spirit to the conventional approach to regulation, it nevertheless took the financial crisis to haul "*macro-prudential*" regulation onto the policy makers' agenda (see section 4).

Fourth, in the models regulators and supervisors are not subject to political deliberations, democratic decision making, or the rule of law. It is assumed that there is no political sphere; interaction between individuals remains confined to the price system. Hence the models abstract from conflicts of interest and distributional effects of banking regulation as well as the distribution of political power. The recent crisis demonstrated that political pressure strongly impacts the distribution of costs of banking crisis, the shape of deposit insurance, and that some ex-ante optimal regulatory arrangements prove time-inconsistent. Hence, the results of the models in the welfare-economic framework need to be complemented by models of the political-economic environment (see section 5).

3. PUBLIC CHOICE THEORY OF FINANCIAL REGULATION

In response to the focus on the benefits for financial regulation, a literature evolved that highlighted the potential costs of regulation. It looked at the administrative costs of regulation ("red tape"), such as reporting requirements, the operating costs of the supervisory institution(s), and compliance costs. Under oligopolistic competition bank managers and bank shareholders earn rents. Incumbent banks have an incentive to deter market entry. Rent seeking behaviour leads to efficiency losses over and above the efficiency losses associated with entry restrictions themselves (Krueger 1974).

This literature also deviated from the assumption that regulators and supervisors act as altruistic, omniscient dictator. On the one hand, bureaucracies might be biased towards excessive intervention: given that public officials have limited tenure, the distribution of costs and benefits over time matter for them. If the societal costs of excessive regulatory intervention materialise only in the long-term, but the stability gains materialise immediately, myopic regulators might be biased towards excessive intervention. Similar conclusions are reached, when regulators and supervisors derive utility from high reputation due to banking stability. That would lead them to over-weight the benefits of stability. At the same time the costs of excessive regulation are spread across society. This might entice reputation-focused regulators to attempt to reduce failure probabilities too much. On the other hand, myopia and high reputation sensitivity might have the contrary effect and lead to regulatory forbearance. In this setting, closing a bank is interpreted as revealing past mistakes by the regulator (Boot and Thakor 1993). If the bank is allowed to continue as going concern, the regulator still has the chance that the bank recovers and his/her reputation remains unscathed or that the bank fails after he/she has retired – and his/her successors would be blamed.

Naturally, bank regulators and supervisors frequently interact with bank managers and bank shareholders, quite often individuals change sides (*"revolving doors"*). But even before regulators or supervisors change side, the prospect of job opportunities in the future can compromise his/her integrity (Kane 2012). This might lead to regulatory capture, the promotion of the interest of the industry rather than the public interest (Admati and Hellwig 2011; Boyer and Ponce forthcoming).

What are the implications of this strand of literature for regulatory and supervisory policy? I strongly believe that *(i)* administrative costs ("red tape") must be watched very closely; e.g., the benefits of existing and new reporting standards must be weighed carefully against these costs. *(ii)* Banking markets should remain contestable: licensing requirements and procedures need to be transparent, unambiguous, and no ex-ante quantitative limits should provide incentives for rent seeking behaviour. The EU takes decisive action in this field; the Capital Requirements Directive (CRD) and the EU passport as well as the on-going initiatives by the EU Commission removing barriers to competition in retail banking (EU Commission 2007) have contributed to the integration of the banking market.[6] *(iii)* We need to address regulatory capture in a comprehensive manner. The Eurosystem has in place strict cooling-off rules for management and senior staff. Regulatory capture can be reduced by high levels of transparency of the policy process. Public consultations and hearings are now common tools at the international, EU, and national levels. However, the delineation between legitimate lobbying and illegitimate capture can be challenging. Members of the European Parliament have drawn public attention to excessive lobbying pressure (Die Welt, June 22, 2010). The foundation of the not-for-profit organisation Finance Watch aims at "... *strengthen[ing] the voice of society in the reform of financial regulation by conducting advocacy and presenting public interest arguments to lawmakers and the public as a counterweight to the private interest lobbying of the financial industry.*"[7] *(iv)* The critique of the Public Choice approach must be taken seriously by regulators

---

[6] But admittedly the current crisis is a temporary backlash with some previously integrated areas like money markets showing signs of segmentation again.

[7] See the organisation's mission statement at www.finance-watch.org/mission.

and supervisors. Regulatory initiatives need to carefully demonstrate that the expected benefits of regulation outweigh its potential costs. The welfare theoretic framework constitutes an important benchmark model for this purpose; it provides a common language for regulatory impact assessments and shifts the burden of proof to regulators. Impact assessments, therefore, need to be based on sound theoretical and empirical research. However, regulatory development is path-dependent and can aim at gradual improvements of a given regulatory framework (Streeck 2004). Any regulatory impact assessment therefore needs to take into account the legal, economic, and political environment. Both, a theoretical, welfare theoretic justification alone or a critique focusing only on potential costs of regulation cannot do justice to the objectives of rigorous and policy relevant analysis. Many aspects of the current regulatory reform underwent those rigorous impact assessments, both, at the international, at the EU, and at the national level (see Macroeconomic Impact Assessment Group 2011; EU Commission 2011; Kopp et al. 2010).

4. MORE RECENT DEVELOPMENTS: SYSTEMIC RISK AND TOO-BIG-TO-FAIL

The financial crisis has accelerated fascinating dynamics in research on the economics of banking regulation that had already started in the late 20th century, both, with respect to the number of papers and with respect to the conceptual frameworks employed. I will firstly touch upon the research under the heading of systemic risk and move in the latter parts of this section to large and complex institutions that are often deemed too-big-to-fail. Regarding the former, the precise meaning of systemic risk itself is ambiguous, i.e., it carries different meanings to different authors. But considering the discourse amongst policy makers and the recently growing body of literature reveals frequently three common narratives (not all of which are highlighted by each author): *(i)* correlated exposures and common shocks, *(ii)* the collective behaviour in an interconnected network, which is often discussed as "*contagion*", and *(iii)* the economic interactions between financial markets and the macro economy.

Of these three narratives, correlated exposures and common shocks is the most straightforward: banks hold correlated exposures and, if severe enough, an adverse economic shock may directly result in simultaneous, multiple bank defaults. Moreover, the origins of the initial shock might stem anywhere from cyclical credit risk, to concentrated large exposures, to unforeseeable market price shocks originating well beyond the immediate financial system. Of all the aspects of systemic risk, I am of the opinion this is the best covered by supervisors. After all, stress tests expose banks to common shocks and assess the risk bearing capacity of individual institutions against their capital and in comparison to their peers.

4.1. Spiralling out of Control: Contagion in the Financial System

However, more subtle transmission mechanisms of systemic risk exist and the available literature on collective behaviour in an interconnected network takes three different approaches: examining direct linkages *(a)* via prices and *(b)* interbank exposures and finally indirect, *(c)* informational linkages.

The first, contagion via prices, is obviously related to the correlated exposure category above. Either in a bank-run type scenario or a more general panic – i.e. whenever there is demand for liquidity – a funding constrained bank might be forced to raise money quickly enough and hence has to sell assets at distressed prices. These distress prices reduce asset values at other banks and cause (fair value) losses (Cifuentes et al. 2005). Moreover, funding and market illiquidity can reinforce each other, leading to vicious liquidity spirals multi-plying the initial shocks (Brunnermeier and Pedersen 2009). Contrary to common exposure, I have the feeling that – although intuitively obvious – these "*fire sale*" type scenarios are not well covered by regulators and/or supervisors as of yet. This is obviously related to the difficulties of modelling banks' and other financial market participants' behaviour under stress, a necessary precondition to quantify worst case outcomes.

Second, a more immediate contagion channel propagates losses in case of the default of one bank via direct exposures to the stricken bank's creditors, potentially leading to default cascades in the system. Early research by Rochet and Tirole (1996) focused on central bank policy options in a model of interbank lending. Allen and Gale (2000) studied how the banking system responds to contagion when banks are connected under different network structures. And Eisenberg and Noe (2001) formalised a hypothetical clearing of the interbank market.[8] The latter, in particular, have been influential amongst regulators and supervisors and I am happy to say that our own research department has led the way in not only promoting but putting to use their seminal work amongst policy makers.[9]

Beyond fire sales and interbank linkages, a third kind of transmission mechanism is more subtle but nonetheless material. It relates to spillovers from an initial exogenous shock, but depends on weaker and more indirect connections. A bank becomes exposed if it shows certain similarities, shared traits with a stricken bank (Kaufman and Scott 2003). Under uncertainty with regard to the actual exposure of the bank in question, this leads investors to reassess their exposure and limit potential losses by withdrawing funding. Just recently formalised models are usually enhancements of fire sale type scenarios (amongst others Caballero and Simsek 2009). The mentioned authors in particular show,

---

[8] For an overview of more recent attempts at modelling direct contagion see Allen and Babus (2009); and ECB (2010).
[9] See Elsinger et al. (2006) for the theoretical foundations and Boss et al. (2006) for the operationalisation at Oesterreichische Nationalbank.

that complexity and thereby uncertainty about future pay-outs increases the likelihood and severity of fire sales even when markets are deep and the initial shock is small in comparison to the capital endowment in the model system.

It is important to note that all of these dynamics might be at play independently or, with all likelihood in a severe financial crisis, reinforce each other. The most important take-away from the recent surge of financial network literature – addressing direct as well as indirect contagion channels – is therefore the system's "robust-yet-fragile"-property. As Andrew Haldane (2009) observed,

"the intuition behind this result is beguilingly simple, but its implications profound. In a nutshell, interconnected networks exhibit a knife-edge, or tipping point, property. Within a certain range, connections serve as a shock-absorber. (...) Connectivity engenders robustness. Risk-sharing – diversification – prevails. But beyond a certain range, the system can flip the wrong side of the knife-edge. Interconnections serve as shock-amplifiers, not dampeners, as losses cascade. (...) Risk-spreading – fragility – prevails. The extent of the systemic dislocation is often disproportionate to the size of the initial shock. Even a modest piece of news might be sufficient to take the system beyond its tipping point."

Historically, financial regulation was confined to micro-prudential regulation: systemic stability is simply seen as the consequence of micro-prudential stability. The authors of the Geneva Report on *"The Fundamental Principles of Financial Regulation"* have labelled this a fallacy of composition (Brunnermeier et al. 2009) and by discussing the insights of research above, I believe I have strongly made the case of why regulation has to move beyond its prevalent micro-prudential stance. But with regard to systemic risk, contagion is not the end-it-all of issues.

The ECB has been instrumental in promoting the idea of a slow build-up and quick unravelling of imbalances, within the financial system and beyond, in coining its definition of systemic risk (de Bandt and Hartmann 2000; Trichet 2009). Discussing the intricate interlinkages and feedback effects between the financial system and the banking system goes well beyond the scope of my contribution. But let me emphasise that no individual bank has an incentive and/or the ability to contain the inherent pro-cyclicality of boom-and-bust cycles in the economy. I would refer the readers to my colleague Andreas Ittners' contribution (chapter 7 this volume) for a plethora of arguments why intervention is necessary, the issues it needs to be aware of, and in fact what regulatory initiatives are currently under way in Europe.

4.2. Too-Big-To-Fail: Moral Hazard in the Financial System

Closely related to systemic risk and with great significance for any discussion of the economics of bank regulation are so called *"too-big-to-fail"* banks. Historically, large insolvent banks were more likely to be bailed-out by governments than smaller insolvent banks.[10] This has a number of negative consequences: first, large banks receive an implicit subsidy, which provides them with an unfair competitive advantage versus smaller rivals (Kopp et al. 2010; and Ueda and Weder di Mauro 2012); second, the expectations of a bail-out lead to excessive risk-taking (moral hazard), and a lack of market discipline; third, the implicit subsidy leads to a risk and wealth transfer from the public to bank shareholders and managers; fourth, bank managers and shareholders have an incentive to become too-big-to-fail.[11] A large literature addressing these issues has put forth various proposals: *(i)* a Pigovian tax that increases with the size of the institution and feeds into systemic risks funds that are empowered to intervene early (Doluca et al. 2010; Freixas and Rochet 2010); *(ii)* an additional capital levy similar to the operation of margin accounts calibrated so that the bank's CDS spread remain below a certain maximum (Hart and Zingales 2010); *(iii)* an additional capital levy based on the interconnectedness of the bank (Chan-Lau 2010); *(iv)* ring-fencing the systematically important part of the institution (Vickers Report 2011); *(v)* banks that are too-big-to-fail are too big and should be broken up.[12]

Much of the literature on the too-big-to-fail problem is firmly rooted in the traditional welfare theoretic framework of the economics of banking regulation: e.g., an omnipotent, omniscient regulator determines the optimal Pigovian tax and implements a credible bank resolution regime. However, one important contribution to the literature takes a wider perspective and addresses the roots of the problem beyond banking regulation. Admati et al. (2009, 2010, 2012) deviate substantially from the welfare theoretic framework in which the existence of banks is inherently incompatible with the Modigliani-Miller theorem. As root-causes of the too-big-to-fail problem, they identify the high leverage of the banking system. This in turn is a consequence of the tax wedge between equity and debt and the implicit and explicit (deposit insurance) government guarantees on debt. Consequently, the problem should not be tackled by banking regulation alone, but also by abolishing that tax subsidy. After it is removed, bank minimum capital requirements should be drastically raised to, say, 25 per cent of total assets (rather than risk-weighted assets). Instead of providing a partial equilibrium model to calibrate the exact level, they discuss the pros and cons of alternative approaches. Their main argument is that the fo-

---

[10] During the Savings and Loans Crisis a "too-big-to-fail" doctrine was introduced in the US in 1984. Although the Federal Deposit Insurance Corporation Improvement Act (FDICIA) of 1991 aimed at removing it, large banks continued being perceived as too-big-to-fail. The Dodd-Frank Act (2010) constitutes another attempt to address the problem. During the financial crisis following the collapse of Lehman Brothers the EU explicitly pledged to "support relevant institutions" (EU Summit October 12, 2008). The term too-big-to-fail is often used synonymously with too-interconnected-to-fail.

[11] Brewer and Jagtiani (2011) find a substantial premium banks are willing to pay in mergers to become too-big-to-fail.

[12] See Willem Buiter on his FT Maverecon Blog, 24 June 2009.

cus on minimising bank capital requirements to lower the costs of intermediation is flawed in the first place. Once the frictions (tax wedge and government
guarantees) are removed, the average costs of funding should be (almost) neutral with respect to capital structure (Modigliani and Miller 1958). Comparing
ex-ante self-insurance (low leverage) with ex-post bank resolution the authors
highlight that the latter might overburden supervisors and politicians alike, so
that it is unlikely to be credible. They also refute the claim that higher capital
requirements would lead to a lending contraction or to a migration of business
to shadow banking. In an accompanying paper Admati and Hellwig (2011)
explicitly tackle politico-economic considerations.

In sum, the recent literature on the economics of regulation has substantially advanced the field from a practitioner's point of view. The breadth of the
discussion of policy alternatives is a distinct advantage. However, I think any
approach that remains embedded in the welfare theoretic framework is incomplete from a practitioner's point of view. Chancellor Merkel put it bluntly: *"No
bank must grow to a size that puts it in a position in which it can blackmail
governments."* (Bloomberg, September 1, 2010). The size of the very large
banks and unpredictable impacts of their failure constitute a shift in power
from policy makers, regulators and supervisors to the managers, shareholders,
and debtors of these banks. Taking this power constellation seriously, I regard
the time-inconsistency problem of large bank resolution as most challenging. I
am convinced that any analysis of the too-big-to-fail problem and any solution
would have to rigorously account for this challenge; hence, it would have to
place politico-economic considerations centre stage.

5. THE POLITICAL ECONOMY OF FINANCIAL REGULATION

The Public Choice approach to banking regulation questioned the assumption
that regulators and supervisors would inherently act in the public interest. The
political-economy literature focuses explicitly on the redistributive effects of
banking regulation within and beyond the banking sector. It highlights potential conflicts of interest and discusses requirements of reform processes with
respect to their legitimacy, transparency, accountability and participation.

The economic rationale for deposit insurance as efficiency enhancing and
Pareto improving institutional arrangement for a system of fractional reserve
banking system was discussed in section 1. However, the private-interest view
(Stigler 1971; Peltzman 1976) of banking regulation looks at the adoption of
deposit insurance from a different perspective. First, the analysis is embedded
in the specific political, economic, and societal environment in which the decision is taken. Second, the redistributive effects of the introduction of deposit

insurance are investigated. Third, the motives and behaviour of political actors are studied empirically. The conclusions differ from those of the welfare theoretical models. In the US, the introduction of federal branching restrictions in 1927 and federal deposit insurance in 1933, both, were instituted for political and not for efficiency or stability reasons (Economides et al. 1996). They benefited small US banks at the expense of geographically well diversified large banks. Deposit insurance reduced market discipline that would have forced smaller banks to hold more capital; branching restrictions reduced the contestability of local markets.[13] Studies looking at the international evidence also conclude that the private-interest theory is not rejected by the data (Laeven 2004; Demirgüc-Kunt et al. 2008).

The private-interest view of banking regulation still *(i)* operates on the basis of a market (coordination of private interest via market prices) versus state (coordination of public interest via political institutions) dichotomy and *(ii)* restricts the distributive impact to first-round effects within the financial system.

The simple market versus state dichotomy is a convenient conceptualisation in the area of banking regulation. However, the banking sector is not composed of atomistic price-takers. The dominant firms are power structures with strict hierarchies. Some of them are very large and their viability becomes akin to a public good (see too-big-to-fail, section 4.). Banks operate in a number of input and output markets which are shaped or even require political intervention (regulation) to function (e.g., labour markets) (North 1990). Similarly, states are not monolithic decision makers with coherent values and interests. They consist of constitutional institutions in which conflicts of interests and coordination take place. However, beyond these strict boundaries of the state, a "*market place*" of competing ideas, political parties, and NGOs ("*civil society*") operates and complements the constitutional fora of deliberation and action.

An alternative view conceptualises the state and the market as state-market condominium (Underhill 2006): the political and the economic spheres are intertwined in a simultaneous process of interdependent change. Market players take political processes into account in their strategies (e.g., concentration of banking activities in financial centres) which often include a political agenda as well (e.g., privatisation and financialisation of retirement pensions). In some cases, their objectives are coherent and lead to temporary alliances among market participants, in others they are antagonistic and are accompanied by competitive business and political strategies. The boundaries of the state change in reaction to the internationalisation of banking markets. Banking regulation is shifted to the international level (e.g., Basel Committee on Banking Supervision). The representatives of public institutions have more than one objective (e.g., global public good of financial stability, promotion/protection of local banking structures). Consequently, sub-groups of representatives of public in-

---

[13] From 1925 to 1930 the market share of branching banks increased from 35 to 46 per cent.

stitutions and industry can form (temporary and issue-specific) coalitions to promote common policy objectives within the deliberations at the international level.

Regulatory reform of the banking sector can have an impact on the distribution of income and wealth beyond the immediate impact on *"winners"* and *"losers"* in the banking sector. They can initiate a transformation of the banking sector that shifts its governance structure, its balance-sheet structure, and its fragility in the face of shocks. For example, a shift from a bank-based financial system towards a market-based financial system can lead to a more active market for corporate control. On the one hand, this could lead to increased efficiency through takeovers of inefficiently managed companies (Ruback and Jensen 1983); on the other, it can lead to a redistribution of income to shareholders from other stakeholders (Shleifer and Summers 1988; Deakin and Singh 2008). The shift from bank-based to market-based system is accompanied by a shift of the asset structure of households. In the financial system banks holding loans as assets are substituted by other intermediaries (pension funds, investment funds) holding tradable debt and equity. The weight of volatile assets in households' financial wealth increases at the expense of nominally fixed bank deposits exposing households to higher asset price risk (Allen and Gale 2004).

Closely related to the redistributive impact of banking regulation are studies that focus on the effects of imbalances of structural power on shaping banking regulation.[14] The financial industry is well organised and resourceful relative to the general public (Olson 1982). The interpretation of banking regulation as an efficiency-enhancing, purely technical subject (see section 2) further enhanced the structural power of the industry in the policy process (after all, bankers are supposed to know more about the complex technical details of financial products and markets). Lobbying of the financial services industry has reached dimensions that started to annoy policy makers (*Die Welt*, June 22, 2010). The institutional structure of the European system of financial supervisors aims at rectifying the structural imbalances of power – each of the European Supervisory Authorities has a stakeholder group. They are composed of representatives of consumers, users of financial services, EU financial market participants, employees in the financial sector, academics and small and medium-sized enterprises.

What are the conclusions I would draw from this brief overview of research on the political economy of financial regulation? Banking regulation is not just about the elimination of technical inefficiencies, but can have strong repercussions on the distribution of income and wealth in society. Thus, it is important to find a balance between, on the one hand, expert-led technical implementation and supervision of regulation and, on the other hand, democratic legiti-

---

[14] See the papers published in Mooslechner et al. (2006).

macy. Since banking regulation has redistributive effects beyond the banking sector, it has to be legitimated by elected representatives. A concrete example concerns the policy process that shapes the future banking regulation in the EU.[15] The political preferences among member states are hard to reconcile. In order to shorten the political deliberations, a number of controversial issues are referred to by the European Banking Authority (EBA) as "*technical standards*". While some of these are clearly technical and warrant such a procedure,[16] others constitute decisive decisions regarding the impact of new regulation.[17] The latter decisions fundamentally affect the expected benefits and the potential costs of regulation; as such they should be democratically legitimated.

The Lisbon treaty has increased the role of the European Parliament in the policy process. I believe that the process of increasing input legitimacy in the area of banking regulation should be continued and strengthened at all levels of financial system governance. Moreover, regular consultations by the EU Commission, the European Supervisory Authorities and the Eurosystem, and the frequent public hearings of the Committees of the European Parliament have substantially increased the transparency of the policy process. Nevertheless, more needs to be done. While the involvement of a complex web of institutions in banking regulation can increase transparency and participation, it is not directly conducive to the accountability of the responsible actors. Especially, the various lobbying and expert groups, as well as academics are not accountable to the general public.

Finally, interpreting the process of international banking regulation in the sense of a state-market condominium opens the door for new strategies for regulators. I suggest to seek temporary and issue related "*coalitions of the willing*" to promote the global public good of financial stability. Such a coalition could comprise states with a low risk tolerance regarding banking crisis, well-capitalised and well-funded banks, and relevant non-governmental organisations that seek to reduce the future societal costs of banking crisis.

6. CONCLUSION

The economics of banking regulation needs to broaden its theoretical and empirical foundations to increase its relevance for policy makers. In parallel, policy makers are called to increase resources for sound policy development processes that evaluate and translate the – often contradictory – results of re-

---

[15] I refer in my example to the Capital Requirement Directive (CRD) IV and the Capital Requirement Regulation (CRR).
[16] E.g., IT formats of reporting requirements Art. 403 (3) CRR.
[17] E.g., the definition of certain aspects of capital instruments regarding eligibility as core capital Art. 26 (3) CRR or the definition of liquid assets in the Liquidity Coverage Ratio (LCR) Art. 481 (2) CRR.

search into implementable policy options. These have to take into account uncertainty, path-dependency, and the governance of the political system.

I have shown that the traditional welfare-economic framework has generated an important basis for the assessment of banking regulation. However, these models are restricted to partial equilibrium analysis and, hence, their approach to banking regulation might not always suffice in terms of covering endogenous innovation, feedback-effects and externalities. Problems my peers and I have to tackle going forward. Fortunately, the financial crisis has initiated noteworthy dynamics in research, both, with respect to the number of papers and the conceptual frameworks employed. These should provide us novel foundations on which to base regulation and supervision that address the dynamics and complexities of the financial system, and its interaction with the broader economy better than ever.

But as I have argued above, no matter how fanciful those new theories or complex those new models, regulatory development is path-dependent and has repercussions on society at large, i.e. it is established at a particular point in time under particular circumstances and has significant redistributive effects beyond the banking sector. Therefore banking regulation is not just about the elimination of technical inefficiencies so that the expected regulatory benefits outweigh potential costs, but it is also about legitimacy, transparency and accountability. I firmly believe that in our current drive to improve on the regulation in place, we better heed these insights to seize the historic opportunity afforded to us.

BIBLIOGRAPHY

Admati, A. R., P. M. DeMarzo, M. F. Hellwig and P. Pfleiderer 2009, "Fallacies, Irrelevant Facts, and Myths in the Discussion of Capital Regulation: Why Bank Equity is Not Expensive", mimeo.

Admati, A. R., P. M. DeMarzo, M. F. Hellwig and P. Pfleiderer 2010, "Improving Capital Regulation for Large Financial Institutions", paper presented at the Joint Research Workshop of the OeNB and the Max Planck Institute for Research on Collective Goods on The Economics of Bank Insolvency, Restructuring and Recapitalisation, Vienna, September 16-17.

Admati, A. R., P. M. DeMarzo, M. F. Hellwig and P. Pfleiderer 2012, "Debt Overhang and Capital Regulation", *mimeo*.

Admati, A. and M. F. Hellwig 2011, "Good Banking Regulation Needs Clear Focus, Sensible Tools, and Political Will", *mimeo*.

Allen, F. and A. Babus 2009, "Networks in Finance", in *Network-based Strategies and Competencies*, P. Kleindorfer and J. Wind (ed.), pp. 367-382.

Allen, F., A. Babus and E. Carletti 2010, "Financial Connections and Systemic Risk", *NBER Working Paper* 16177.

Allen, F. and D. Gale 2000, "Financial Contagion", *Journal of Political Economy* 108, pp. 1-33.

Allen, F. and D. Gale 2004, "Comparative Financial Systems: A Discussion", in *Credit Intermediation and the Macroeconomy: Models and Perspectives*, S. Bhattacharya, A. Boot, A. Thakor (eds), pp. 701-70.

Arrow, J. K. and G. Debreu 1954, "Existence of an Equilibrium for a Competitive Economy", *Econometrica* 22, pp. 265-90.

Arrow, J. K. and L. Hurwicz 1958, "On the Stability of a Competitive Equilibrium", *Econometrica* 26, pp. 522-52.

Baldwin, R. and J. Black 2007, "Really responsive regulation", *LSE Law, Society and Economy Working Paper* 15/2007.

Bhattacharya, S., A. W. A. Boot and A. V. Thakor 1998, "The Economics of Bank Regulation", *Journal of Money, Credit, and Banking* 30(4), pp. 745–70.

Boot, A. W. and A. V. Thakor 1993, "Self-interested bank regulation", *American Economic Review*, 83(2), pp. 206–12.

Boss, M., G. Krenn, C. Puhr and M. Summer 2006, "Systemic Risk Monitor: A Model for Systemic Risk Analysis and Stress Testing of Banking Systems", *OeNB Financial Stability Report* 11, pp. 83-95.

Boyer, P. and J. Ponce, forthcoming, "Regulatory capture and banking supervision reform", *Journal of Financial Stability*.

Brewer, E. and J. Jagtiani 2011, "How much did banks pay to become too-big-to-fail and to become systemically important?", *Research Department Working Paper*, Federal Reserve Bank of Philadelphia, pp. 11-37.

Brunnermeier, M. K. and L. H. Pedersen 2009, "Market Liquidity and Funding Liquidity", *Review of Financial Studies* 22(6), pp. 2201-38.

Brunnermeier, M., A. Crocket, C. A. E. Goodhart, A. D. Persaud and H. Shin 2009, "The Fundamental Principles of Financial Regulation", *Geneva Reports on the World Economy* 11.

Caballero, R. J. and A. Simsek 2009, "Fire Sales in a Model of Complexity", *NBER Working Paper* 15479.

Calomiris, C. and R. Kahn 1991, "The Role of Demandable Debt in Structuring Optimal Banking Arrangements", *American Economic Review* 81, pp. 497-513.

Chan, Y. S., S. I. Greenbaum and A. V. Thakor 1992, "Is fairly priced deposit insurance feasible?", *Journal of Finance* 47, pp. 227-45.

Chan-Lau, J. A. 2010, "Regulatory Capital Charges for Too-Connected-to-Fail Institutions: A Practical Proposal", *IMF Working Paper* 10/98.

Cifuentes, R., G. Ferrucci and H. S. Shin 2005, "Liquidity Risk and Contagion", *Journal of the European Economic Association* 3, pp. 556-66.

de Bandt, O. and P. Hartmann 2000, "Systemic risk: A survey", *ECB Working Paper* 14.

Deakin, S. and A. Singh 2008, "The stock market, the market for corporate control and the theory of the firm: legal and economic perspectives and implications for public policy", Centre for Business Research, *University of Cambridge Working Paper* No. 365.

Demirgüç-Kunt, A. and E. Detragiache 2002, "Does deposit insurance increase banking system stability – an empirical investigation", *Journal of Monetary Economics* 49, pp. 1373-406.

Demirgüç-Kunt, A., E. J. Kane and L. Laeven 2008, "Determinants of deposit-insurance adoption and design", *Journal of Financial Intermediation* 17(3), pp. 407-38.

Dewatripont, M. and J. Tirole 1994, *The Prudential Regulation of Banks*, MIT Press.

Diamond, D. W. 1984, "Financial Intermediation and Delegated Monitoring", *Review of Economic Studies* 51(3), pp. 393-414.

Diamond, D. W. and P. H. Dybvig 1983, "Bank Runs, Deposit Insurance, and Liquidity", *Journal of Political Economy* 91(3), pp. 401-19.

Doluca, H., U. Klüh, M. Wagner and B. Weder Di Mauro 2010, "Reducing Systemic Relevance: A Proposal", paper presented at the Joint Research Workshop of the OeNB and the Max Planck Institute for Research on Collective Goods on The Economics of Bank Insolvency, Restructuring and Recapitalisation, Vienna, September 16-17.

ECB 2010, "Recent advances in modelling systemic risk using network analysis", Financial Stability Report June 2010, pp. 155-60.

Economides, N., R. G. Hubbard and D. Palia 1996, "The Political Economy of Branching Restrictions: A Model of Monopolistic Competition among Small and Large Banks", *Journal of Law and Economics* 39, pp. 667-704.

Eisenberg, L. and T. H. Noe 2001, "Systemic Risk in Financial Systems", *Management Science* 47(2), pp. 236-49.

Elsinger, H., A. Lehar and M. Summer 2006, "Risk Assessment for Banking Systems", Management Science 52(9), pp. 1301-14.

Elsinger, H. and M. Summer 2010, "The Economics of Bank Insolvency, Restructuring and Recapitalization", Joint Research Workshop of the OeNB and the Max Planck Institute for Research on Collective Goods on The Economics of Bank Insolvency, Restructuring and Recapitalisation, OeNB Financial Stability Report 20, 115-20.

EU Commission 2007, Sector Inquiry under Article 17 of Regulation (EC) No 1/2003 on retail banking (Final Report), *COM 33 final*.

EU Commission 2011, Impact Assessment – Accompanying the document Regulation of the European Parliament and the Council on prudential requirements for the credit institutions and investment firms, Commmission Staff Working Paper SEC 949.

Freixas, X. and J.-C. Rochet 2008, *Microeconomics of Banking*, MIT Press.

Freixas, X. and J.-C. Rochet 2010, "Taming SIFIs", paper presented at the Joint Research Workshop of the OeNB and the Max Planck Institute for Research on Collective Goods on The Economics of Bank Insolvency, Restructuring and Recapitalisation, Vienna, September 16-17.

Goodhart, C. A. E. 1989, *Money, Information, and Uncertainty*, MacMillan.

Goodhart, C. A. E. 2003, "What Can Academics Contribute to the Study of Financial Stability?", *The Economic and Social Review* 36(3), pp. 189-203.

Goodhart, C. A. E., A. K. Kashyap, D. P. Tsomocos and A. P. Vardoulakis 2011, "Financial Regulation in General Equilibrium", *mimeo*.

Gorton, G. and A. Winton 2002, "Financial Intermediation", *NBER Working Paper* 8928.

Gratev, E. and P. E. Strahan 2003, "Banks' Advantage in Hedging Liquidity Risk: Evidence form the Commercial Paper Market", *Wharton Financial Institutions Centre Working Paper* 03-01.

Green, E. and P. Lin 2000, "Diamond and Dybvig's Classic Theory of Financial Intermediation: What's Missing?", *Federal Reserve Bank of Minneapolis Quarterly Review* 24, 3-13.

Greenbaum, S. I. and A. V. Thakor 1995, *Contemporary Financial Intermediation*, Dryden Press.

Gropp, R. and J. Vesala 2001, "Deposit Insurance and Moral Hazard: Does the Counterfactual Matter?", *mimeo*.

Haldane, A. G. 2009, "Rethinking the financial network", speech delivered at the Financial Student Association, Amsterdam.

Hart, O. and L. Zingales 2010, "A New Capital Regulation For Large Financial Institutions", paper presented at the Joint Research Workshop of the OeNB and the Max Planck Institute for Research on Collective Goods on The Economics of Bank Insolvency, Restructuring and Recapitalisation, Vienna, September 16-17.

Hellmann, T. F., K. C. Murdock and J. E. Stiglitz 2000, "Liberalization, Moral Hazard in Banking, and Prudential Regulation: Are Capital Requirements Enough?", *American Economic Review*, American 90(1), pp. 147-65.

Jacklin, C. J. 1987, "Demand Deposits, Trading Restrictions, and Risk Sharing", in *Contractual Arrangements for Intertemporal Trade*, E. C. Prescott and N. Wallace (eds.), Minnesota Studies in Macroeconomics.

Kane, E. J. 2012, "Missing Elements in US Financial Reform: a Kubler-Ross Interpretation of the Inadequacy of the Dodd-Frank Act", *Journal of Banking and Finance*, Vol. 36(3), 654-61.

Kaufman, G. G. and K. E. Scott 2003, "What Is Systemic Risk, and do Bank Regulators Retard or Contribute to It?", *The Independent Review* VII 3, pp. 371– 91.

Kim, D. and A. M. Santomero 1988, "Risk in banking and capital regulation", *Journal of Finance* 43, pp. 1219-33.

Koehn, M. and A. M. Santomero 1980, "Regulation of bank capital and portfolio risk", *Journal of Finance* 35, pp. 1235-44.

Kopp, E., C. Ragacs and S. W. Schmitz 2010, "The Economic Impact of Measures Aimed at Strengthening Bank Resilience – Estimates for Austria", *OeNB Financial Stability Report* 20, pp. 86-114.

Krueger, A. O. 1974, "The Political Economy of the Rent-Seeking Society", *American Economic Review* 64(3), pp. 291-303.

Laeven, L. 2004, "The Political Economy of Deposit Insurance", *Journal of Financial Services Research* 26(3), pp. 201-24.

Macroeconomic Impact Assessment Group 2011, *Assessment of the macroeconomic impact of higher loss absorbency for globally systemically important banks*, BIS, Basel.

Mayes, D. G. 2004, "Who pays for bank insolvency?", *Journal of International Money and Finance* 23 pp. 515–51.

Modigliani, F. and M. H. Miller 1958, "The Cost of Capital, Corporation Finance and the Theory of Investment", *American Economic Review*. 48, pp. 261–97.

Mooslechner, P., H. Schuberth and B. Weber (ed.) 2006, *The Political Economy of Financial Market Regulation – The Dynamics of Inclusion and Exclusion*, Edward Elgar, Cheltenham.

North, D. C. 1990, *Institutions, Institutional Change, and Economic Performance*, Cambrige University Press, Cambridge.

Olson, M. 1982, *The Rise and Decline of Nations: Economic Growth, Stagflation, and Social Rigidities*, Yale University Press.

Pareto, V. 1906, *Manual of Political Economy*.

Peltzman, S. 1976, "Towards a more general theory of regulation", *Journal of Law and Economics* 19, pp. 109-48.

Posch, M., S. W. Schmitz and B. Weber 2009, "EU Bank Packages: Objectives and Potential Conflicts of Objectives", *Financial Stability Report* 17, pp. 63-84.

Rochet, J. C. 1992, "Capital requirements and the behaviour of commercial banks", *European Economic Review*, 36(5), pp. 1137-70.

Rochet, J. C. and J. Tirole 1996, "Interbank Lending and Systemic Risk", *Journal of Money, Credit, and Banking*, 28, pp. 733-62.

Ruback, R. S. and M. C. Jensen 1983, "The Market for Corporate Control: The Scientific Evidence", *Journal of Financial Economics* 11, pp- 5-50.

Shleifer, A. and L. Summers 1988, "Breach the trust in hostile takeovers", in *Corporate Take-overs: Causes and Consequences*, A. J. Auerbach (ed.), University of Chicago Press, pp. 33-68.

Stigler, G. J. 1971, "The Theory of Economic Regulation", *Bell Journal of Economics and Management Science* 2, pp. 3-21.

Streeck, W. 2004, "Taking Uncertainty Seriously: Complementarity as a Moving Target", *OeNB Workshops*, 101-15.

Trichet, J. C. 2009, "Systemic Risk", Clare Distinguished Lecture in Economics and Public Policy, Cambridge, 10 December.

Ueda, K. and B. Weder di Mauro 2012, "Quantifying Structural Subsidy Values for Systemically Important Financial Institutions", *IMF Working Paper* 12/128.

Underhill, G. R. D. 2006, "Theorizing Governance in a Global Financial System", in *The Political Economy of Financial Market Regulation – The Dynamics of Inclusion and Exclusion*, Mooslechner, P., H. Schuberth, B. Weber (eds.), Edward Elgar, Cheltenham, pp. 3-33.

Vickers Report 2011, Independent Commission on Banking, UK.

Von Neumann, J. 1937, "Über ein ökonomisches Gleichungssystem und eine Verallgemeinerung des Brouwerschen Fixpunktsatzes", *Ergebnisse eines mathematischen Colloquiums* 8, pp. 73-83.

Wald, A. 1935, "Über die eindeutige positive Lösbarkeit der neuen Produktionsgleichungen", *Ergebnisse eines mathematischen Colloquiums* 6, pp. 12-20.

Wald, A. 1936a, "Über einige Gleichungssysteme der mathematischen Ökonomie", *Zeitschrift für Nationalökonomie* 7, pp- 637-70.

Wald, A. 1936b, "Über Produktionsgleichungen der ökonomischen Wertlehre", *Ergebnisse eines mathematischen Colloquiums* 7, pp. 1-6.

Wallace, N. 1988, "Another Attempt to Model an Illiquid Banking System: The Diamond-Dybvig Model with Sequential Service Taken Seriously", *Federal Reserve Bank of Minneapolis Quarterly Review*, pp. 3-15.

Walras, L. 1874, *Elements of Pure Economics*.

Winton, A. 1995, "Delegated Monitoring and Bank Structure in an Infinite Economy", *Journal of Financial Intermediation* 4/2, pp. 158-87.

16. A Strategic Approach to Post Crisis Regulation – The Need for Pillar 4

David T. Llewellyn

1. KEY ISSUES AND PERSPECTIVES

1.1. Introduction

Banking crises inevitably bring forth more and different regulation of banks, and the recent global crisis is no exception. There are many reasons why a comprehensive review of regulatory, supervisory, and intervention arrangements are being made in the wake of one of the most serious banking crises ever. Firstly, given the enormity of the crisis, there were evident fault lines in regulatory and supervisory arrangements: the rules enshrined in thousands of pages behind the Basel Capital Accords did not prevent the crisis. Secondly, the crisis imposed substantial costs and risks on tax-payers in several countries which implies a perverse scenario of privatising bank profits while socialising bank risks. In effect, the tax-payer became an insurer-of-last-resort but on the basis of a very inefficient insurance contract. The EU Commission indicates that between October 2008 and October 2011, the Commission approved EUR 4.5 trillion (equivalent to 37 percent of EU GDP) of state aid to financial institutions. Thirdly, regulatory arbitrage always finds routes round particular regulations which leaves open the question whether detailed and prescriptive rules are necessarily the right approach. Fourthly, it has become evident that reform strategy needs to be framed in terms of a risk matrix which considers measures both to lower the probability of bank failures and the cost of those failures that do occur. Fifthly, there is the important issue about whether the focus should be on individual banks or the system in aggregate because, *pace* the *fallacy of composition*, it does not follow that regulating individual nodes in a network is necessarily the optimal approach to ensuring the stability of the network as a whole. Because of increased connectedness (between banks and between banks and markets) network externalities increased steadily in the decade before the onset of the crisis which increases the probability of bank failures and their costs. Finally, the need to address the Too-Big-To-Fail problem became increasingly evident.

It is also evident that, prior to the onset of the crisis, many countries did not have clearly-defined resolution arrangements in place which created uncertainty about how governments would respond to serious bank distress. A series of *ad hoc* responses were made which were generally handled well. A central issue, however, is the moral hazard created by the massive interventions made by governments and central banks. The UK authorities reacted quickly to establish the Special Resolution Regime which, *inter alia*, gives the authorities power to activate resolution before a bank becomes technically insolvent. In June, 2012, the EU Commission also agreed to an EU-wide resolution Regime.

As a result, there is likely to evolve one of the biggest-ever reforms in the regulatory regime and, most especially with respect to the EU, also in the basic regulatory architecture. Regulation is at a turning point as the trend towards deregulation and "light-touch" supervision has given way to more intensive and extensive regulation and supervision. *In effect, faith in markets has given way to faith in regulation.*

The focus of this chapter is on this post-crisis regulatory regime and regulatory strategy. As a structure of complex and extensive regulation did not prevent the recent crisis, a key issue is whether the failure was due to fault-lines in the regulatory regime or whether the underlying methodology of regulation has been inappropriate. The chapter discusses the "endogeneity problem" whereby, through financial innovation and the incentive structures created, problems such as excessive risk-taking by banks may be partly endogenous to the regulatory regime itself (Llewellyn 2011).

The structure of the chapter is as follows. This section offers an opening perspective by outlining some general principles to guide the regulatory reform process, and makes a distinction between *incremental* and *strategic* approaches to reform. A Regulation Matrix is outlined based on the two central objectives of any regulatory regime: lowering the probability of bank failures (Objective 1), and minimising the costs of those failures that do occur (Objective 2). The nature of a possible trade-off between the two objectives is reviewed. Section 2 discusses the *endogeneity problem* and its implications for regulatory strategy. Section 3 considers the various instruments in a regulatory regime. Section 4 reviews the alternative approaches to reducing the probability of bank failures, and section 5 considers the various options to minimise the costs of bank failures. Section 6 brings together the main themes by outlining a regulatory reform strategy.

The objectives of the chapter are to consider structural fault-lines in the pre-crisis scenario and to establish a general paradigm for regulatory reform. The main themes are summarised at the outset:

- In terms of systemic stability, the two objectives of the reform agenda are: (1) to lower the probability of bank failures (Objective 1), and (2) to reduce the costs of those failures that do occur (Objective 2).
- To some extent there is a trade-off between the two in that the more the costs of failure can be reduced, the less intensive regulation to lower the probability of failure needs to be.
- What will be defined as the *endogeneity problem* suggests that crises associated with bank failure are partly endogenous to the regulatory regime for Objective 1.
- The optimal intensity of regulation for Objective 1 is indeterminate until the arrangements for Objective 2 (resolution structures, etc.) are known.
- The danger is that the two are addressed separately with a resultant potential for over-regulation for Objective 1.
- Because of this, regulatory reform needs to be strategic (addressing both objectives simultaneously) rather than incremental (refining the existing regulatory regime).
- Within this strategic approach, more emphasis than in the past needs to be given to minimising the social costs of bank failures. Emphasis needs to be given to the resolution of failing (failed) banks.
- Because of the endogeneity problem, Basel N (the perfect model) will never be achieved and attempts to achieve it would create avoidable regulatory costs.
- In the context of cross-border banks, and the increased connectedness of banks, resolution arrangements of each country have an international dimension and need to be incorporated in a Pillar 4 of the Basel Accord.

1.2. Some General Principles

Several structural features of the pre-crisis environment have proved to be unsustainable and themselves contributory causes of the crisis. A basic perversity in the regime is that bank profits were privatised while risks were socialised with the tax-payer effectively acting as an "insurer-of-last-resort" on the basis of an inefficient contract as no *ex ante* premia were extracted. Overall, as there was a reluctance to require creditors to absorb a proportionate share of the costs of bank distress and failures, burden-sharing was disproportionate with an excessive share borne by tax-payers. In the absence of pre-determined resolution arrangements, the perception of banks being Too-Big-To-Fail (TBTF) weakened the incentives for private monitoring of banks.

In the absence of credible and predictable resolution arrangements for failing banks, in many cases there was little choice about whether bail-outs and official support operations for TBTF banks should be undertaken. Given the potential costs of bank failures (largely due to the absence of credible resolution arrangements), rescue operations or bail-outs may be the least-cost option in the short run. However, given the time-consistency issue, such bail-outs create serious moral hazard for the future. A distinction is therefore made between short-run and long-run optimality with respect to rescue operations. Only if the costs of bank failures can be minimised will a no-bail-out policy be credible or even desirable. It is argued that this is a major unsustainable feature that needs to be corrected. In effect, arrangements need to be in place that allow banks to fail without imposing substantial systemic and social costs and tax-payer liability. Given the increased cross-border interconnectedness that developed over the decade or so before the onset of the crisis, the absence of agreed cross-border resolution arrangements surfaced as a particular issue that needs to be addressed most especially within the EU.

Before considering regulatory reform in more detail, the context is set by outlining some *guiding principles*:

- The regulatory regime has two key objectives: to lower the probability of bank failures (Objective 1), and to lower the social cost of those failures that do occur (Objective 2). Both dimensions need to be considered in regulatory strategy.
- A holistic approach to Objectives 1 and 2 needs to be adopted on the basis that the optimal regulation for Objective 1 is indeterminate in the absence of known arrangements for Objective 2.
- As much focus is needed on Objective 2 as on Objective 1 and it is in this sense that a *strategic* rather than *incremental* approach to regulatory reform is required.
- A central requirement of any regulatory reform strategy must be to limit claims on tax-payers, and to prevent risks being shifted to them.
- As part of this, credible, predictable, and timely resolution arrangements for failing institutions are needed to enable banks to fail without causing disruption to customer services, or imposing costs on tax-payers.
- Because of the moral hazard it creates towards excessive risk taking and potential tax-payer liability, the TBTF issue needs to be addressed. The moral hazard of bail-outs is to be avoided and arrangements are needed to confer credibility on a "no-bail-out policy" which addresses the time-consistency problem.
- The perversity of the privatisation of bank profits and the socialisation of bank risk (without *ex ante* insurance being paid) needs to be reversed.
- Burden-sharing between the various stakeholders in the event of bank failure needs to be explicit, fair and coherent. The costs of any bank failure are to be borne by private stakeholders (mainly bank shareholders and unsecured creditors) rather than tax-payers.
- Regulatory strategy needs to be based on the principle of competitive neutrality: all institutions (and not exclusively banks) that can potentially create

systemic stability problems need to be included within the orbit of regulation: the "boundary" issue.

- The loss-absorbing powers of (at least) systemically important institutions (SIFIs) need to be increased.
- Clearly-defined crisis management strategies are needed with an added dimension when cross-border institutions are involved.
- The role for market discipline within the overall regulatory regime needs to be enhanced. In principle, enhancing resolution arrangements (allowing banks to be closed with creditor losses) should enhance the role of market discipline.

1.3. Objectives of Regulation: A Risk Matrix Trade-Off

A central theme is that regulatory reform needs to be *strategic* rather than *incremental* implying that regulatory reform goes back to basics including considering both what the ultimate objectives of regulation are, and also what role is appropriate for banks to play in the economy. This requires a different paradigm than with *incremental* reform which restricts itself to refining existing regulatory requirements (capital ratios, etc.). Abstracting from issues of consumer protection, the two broad objectives of any regulatory regime are:

(1) to reduce the *probability* of bank failures (Objective 1), and

(2) to lower the *social cost* of those failures that do occur (Objective 2).

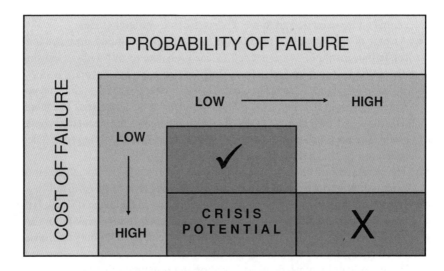

Figure 16.1: Regulation Matrix: Probability v. Cost Trade-Off

In a *regulation matrix* (figure 16.1), the probability of a bank failing is measured on the horizontal axis, and the costs of failure are identified on the vertical axis. The social costs of bank failures arise through externalities and relate to those incurred directly or indirectly by *inter alia* the system as a whole (the systemic stability dimension), tax-payers who might be called upon to finance rescue operations, depositors, deposit protection funds, and customers in general if banking services are disrupted and uncertainty is created.

The matrix illustrates the possibility of a trade-off between the two: if the social *costs* of failure can be lowered, there need be less concern about the *probability* of failures. In the extreme (totally unrealistic) case, if the social costs of bank failures could be reduced to zero, the probability of failures would be of no concern, there would be no potential tax-payer liability, no need for bail-outs, and no moral hazard attached to bail-outs. Furthermore, there would be no need for regulation to reduce the probability of bank failures. Of course, such a utopia is just that! Nevertheless, it serves to illustrate the nature of the trade-off implicit in the *regulation matrix*.

There may, therefore, be less need for measures to lower the cost of failures if their probability were to be reduced to a low level. Conversely, if this were to be either impossible (or achievable only with draconian and high-cost regulation), the greater will be the need to have in place measures to minimise the social costs of those bank failures that do occur. The central strategic issue in any comprehensive regulatory and institutional reform programme is the positioning to be made on the regulation matrix.

Given that all regulatory measures to reduce the probability of bank failures have costs, and the costs that would arise in seeking to reduce the probability of failure to zero (supposing it were possible even with the most draconian regulation) would be substantial, the trade-off between the two dimensions is central to decisions about the optimal intensity of regulation. Greater emphasis needs to be given to Objective 2 in two circumstances: (1) the more intensive that regulation needs to be in order to achieve the aim of lowering the probability of bank failures, and (2) the greater are the costs of such regulation. The central strategic issue in any holistic regulatory reform is the positioning to be made on the *regulation matrix*. The less confidence there is that the probability of bank failures can be reduced, the greater the need for institutional arrangements designed to reduce the costs of failures. In practice, a combined strategy is likely to be optimal.

Historically, the focus of the regulatory regime has been on reducing the probability of failures rather than minimising their costs. Indeed, in many countries the second issue has only been addressed in a serious way since the current crisis. For instance, the UK adopted a Special Resolution Regime in 2009 in the context of the absence of any special insolvency arrangements for banks, and weak and ill-defined institutional arrangements for dealing with failing institutions.

2. REGULATORY STRATEGY: THE *ENDOGENEITY PARADIGM*

Regulatory strategy conventionally assumes that problems to be addressed (e.g., excessive risk-taking by banks) are *exogenous* to the regulatory process. In which case a problem is observed and a regulatory response is made to deal with it: i.e. to reduce the probability of it happening. This is a bold assumption because problems may be at least partly endogenous to regulation, i.e. caused by the very regulation designed to reduce the probability of them emerging. This arises as banks seek to circumvent regulation through financial innovation and by changing the way that business is conducted. This in turn calls forth more regulation: Kane's Regulatory Dialectic (Kane 1987).

As regulation responds to the endogeneity problem by successive adjustments, the cost of regulation rises. As the costs of regulation designed to lower the probability of bank failure rise, the trade-off between the two objectives in the risk matrix changes in favour of minimising the cost of bank failures rather than their probability. The endogeneity problem is likely to raise the cost of effective regulation because it engenders a rules-escalation strategy. By raising regulatory costs, this becomes part of the trade-off between the two core objectives. Overall, optimality shifts towards Objective 2 the more costly effective regulation to lower the probability of bank failures becomes, and the more that the costs of bank failures can be reduced. However, in a complex cost-benefit analysis, the costs of measures for Objective 2 also need to be considered.

The process of regulatory arbitrage diverts the nature of the problem. Because of this, regulation is often shooting at a moving target, and the target moves partly because of regulation itself. For instance, the Basel 2 capital regime (hailed at the time as a decisive breakthrough in the regulation of banks) created incentives for banks to remove assets from banks' balance sheets, for securitisation, the creation of Structured Investment Vehicles and other off-balance sheet vehicles, excess gearing, and the use of credit risk-shifting derivatives. All of these featured as central aspects of the banking crisis (Llewellyn 2010). It is evidently the case that detailed regulation at the time did not prevent the crisis and, to some extent, contributed to it, although a more serious failing was in supervision rather than regulation.

In addition to regulatory arbitrage, under some circumstances, capital requirements may induce banks into more risky business. Blundell-Wignall et al. (2008) show a positive correlation between losses and banks' Tier 1 risk-weighted capital ratio, although a negative correlation between losses and the leverage ratio. A similar conclusion is found in a recent Centre for European Policy Studies report (Ayadi et al. 2011). This suggests that the risk-weight approach to capital adequacy may induce banks to incur more risk through increased leverage. Regulatory arbitrage will always be a major feature of bank business models. As noted in Haldane et al. (2010), "risks migrate to where regulation is weakest, so there are natural limits to what regulatory strategies can reasonably achieve."

The *endogeneity problem* can be considered in the context of the history of the Basel Capital Accord. The original Basel regime established in 1988 was revised in Basel II and again in 2010 in Basel III. One interpretation is that subsequent adjustments imply moving towards the perfect model (Basel N) by correcting for past errors. An alternative interpretation is that there are fault-lines in the regulatory process itself and that the methodology is flawed because banks will always engage in regulatory arbitrage. In this sense, the view that "regulators are always behind the curve" is not a critique of regulators but is endemic within the regulatory process. Successive adjustments over time have not solved the problem of periodic crises.

Unless regulation is to become grossly repressive, regulatory arbitrage will always be a major feature of bank business models. Given the weaknesses and limitations of regulation, whilst rules designed to lower the probability of bank failures are a necessary part of an overall regulatory regime, they are not sufficient. An alternative approach is to lower the cost of bank failures by keeping risks private rather than, as has massively been the case in the recent crisis, socialised by shifting risks to tax-payers.

In practice, both approaches are needed: lowering the probability of bank failure, and limiting the social costs of failures. The debate about the role of regulation and supervision for financial stability should be about the appropriate weight to be given to the two dimensions. Whilst both approaches are needed, more emphasis than in the past needs to be given to Objective 2 given that, however carefully constructed, regulation will never remove the possibility of banks failing and neither should it attempt to do so.

In principle, and returning to the trade-off in the *risk matrix*, if the costs of bank failures can be reduced there can be greater tolerance of the probability of bank failures, and a lesser need for intensive and extensive regulation for Objective 1.

3. INSTRUMENTS IN A REGULATORY REGIME

With respect to the two core objectives of the regulatory regime, eight broad strategic options are summarised in table 16.1:

(1) *Structural* regulation (such as Glass-Steagall-type measures and Narrow Banks) is designed to limit the size and/or allowable business of those banks that are deemed to be TBTF.

(2) *Behavioural* regulation (such as capital and liquidity requirements) designed to lower the probability of failure.

(3) *Supervision* by official agencies.

(4) *Intervention* measures (such as Structured Early Intervention and Resolution (SEIR) regimes) designed to maintain a deteriorating bank as a going concern.

(5) *Tax and Insurance* whereby banks pay *ex post* to recoup the costs of past bail-outs (tax), and/or *ex ante* to cover the costs of possible future interventions (insurance), and to offset the implicit subsidy received by TBTF institutions.

(6) *Resolution* arrangements for closing banks and their subsequent resolution (bank bankruptcy laws, etc.), and how, in the event of a failure, the process is managed in order to minimise costs.

(7) *Living Wills* (or Recovery and Resolution Plans) designed to make explicit how banks will respond to problems that threaten solvency (recovery), and how, in the event that a bank fails, different parts of the business are to be separately identified so that some can be rescued while others are not (resolution).

(8) *Market Discipline* which relates not only to transparency and disclosure (Pillar 3) but also to the use of market data in the supervisory process conducted by official agencies.

We refer to this eight-fold paradigm, and the instruments within it, as the *regulatory regime*. A wider definition (including the role of corporate governance) is given in Llewellyn (2001).

Table 16.1: Regulatory Regime Instruments

	OBJECTIVE 1 Lower Probability of Failure	OBJECTIVE 2 Reduce Costs of Failure
Structural Measures	* Glass-Steagall * Narrow Banks * Equity Banks * Derivatives trading	* Limits on size * SIFIs * Glass-Steagall * Narrow Bank * Ring Fencing
Behavioural Measures	* Capital	* Capital

	* Liquidity	* Connectedness
	* Remuneration	
	* Connectedness	
	* Funding rules	
	* Macro-prudential focus	
Supervision	* Interventionist	
Intervention Measures	* PCA /SEIR	
Taxation and Insurance		* Taxation of banks
		* Ex ante insurance
Resolution Measures		* Bank insolvency laws
		* Ring Fencing
		* Pillar 4
		* Private purchase of banks
		* Bridge Bank
		* Bad bank
		* Nationalisation
		* Business transfers
Living Wills	* Recovery measures	* Resolution measures
		* Wind-up plans
Market Discipline	* Disclosure	
	* Use of market metrics	

The following sections discuss some of these in the context of the distinction between objective 1 and objective 2.

4. OBJECTIVE 1: LOWERING THE PROBABILITY OF BANK FAILURES

Measures to reduce the probability of bank failure can be categorised as *structural, behavioural,* or *intervention* (table 16.1). There is a long history of structural regulation in many countries and many of the arguments considered after the recent crisis are not new. However, in practice many of the proposed structural measures are either impractical or largely irrelevant.

4.1. Structural Regulation

Structural measures relate to regulation that prescribes the nature, structure and allowable business of banks and other financial firms, rather than the way business is conducted. Only a brief overview of structural measures (such as Glass-Steagall and Narrow Banks) is outlined here: a more detailed review is given elsewhere (Llewellyn 2011).

Our theme is that in practice most of the proposed structural measures are either impractical or largely irrelevant, at least as far as Objective 1 is concerned. Evidence from the crisis indicates that a wide range of different types of banks failed: large, small, highly diversified, focused, commercial banks and investment banks. Thus, in the UK, the most spectacular bank failure was that of Northern Rock which was quintessentially a retail commercial bank even though it adopted a different model of banking with heavy use of securitisation and wholesale funding (Llewellyn 2008). Equally, not all universal banks which combined the full range of activities encountered serious problems in the crisis.

This raises three general questions about structural measures: whether, in practice, a clear distinction can be made between different types of institution and business; whether it is possible to define institutions that are systemically important, and whether issues of size and business lines are the key issues. Prohibiting commercial banks from conducting some forms of speculative activity would not reduce it in total but shift that activity elsewhere in the system and there can be little confidence that the institutions conducting this business would not be systemically significant even though they may not be conducting core commercial banking business. For instance, Lehman Brothers was not a commercial bank conducting core banking business, and yet its failure clearly did impose substantial systemic costs.

Several problems are associated with structural measures: it is not always clear what an optimal structure is (e.g., the allowable business mix of banks), and arbitrage will often be able to circumvent them (e.g., the various ways around the Glass-Steagall Act). The practical difficulties of making a formal distinction between different types of business are formidable and the distinction between different types of business is fuzzy at the margins. In fluid markets, and with constant financial re-engineering, it is difficult in practice to separate different types of risks. In particular, a Glass-Steagall-type approach is based on a faulty diagnosis of the causes of the crisis. A further consideration is that systemic problems arise largely through cross-sector contagion and the connectedness of banks, and it is not clear that a formal separation of different types of banking activity would address this central issue.

Some of the proposed structural measures – such as Narrow Banks (Kay 2009), Equity Banks (Kotlikoff 2010; Kotlikoff and Leamer 2009) and measures to drastically reduce maturity transformation by banks – amount almost to solving the problem of bank failures by abolishing banks. Maturity transformation, for example, is an integral part of the functioning of banks in the financial system. The question arises as to whether it is appropriate for regulatory and structural reform to undermine the basic functionality of banks.

There are often superior behavioural alternatives (e.g., differential capital requirements) to structural measures. Furthermore, reformed resolution and living wills arrangements can be superior ways of addressing the issues that structural measures are designed to deal with. A higher degree of regulatory intensity could be applied to banks which are judged to be systemically significant by, for instance, calibrating regulatory requirements on the basis of institutions' contribution to systemic risk (Acharya and Richardson 2009; Brunnermeier et al. 2009; Bernanke 2009). The Financial Services Board has also proposed a global capital charge on systemically important banks.

4.2. Behavioural Regulation: Bank Capital

Most regulation is behavioural in that it imposes requirements that affect the way business is conducted and is designed to create incentives for prudent behaviour. Because of its central importance, we focus in particular on the role of bank (equity) capital.

A central issue is the extent to which (if at all) imposed capital requirements are a real cost either to banks or society generally. It is frequently claimed (mainly by bankers) that imposing higher capital requirements would lead to a rise in the costs of banking and financial intermediation services, lower bank lending, and lower rates of return on equity and hence returns to shareholders.

We argue the case for a substantial rise in bank (equity) capital as a major contribution to lowering the probability of bank failures. This is based in part on the proposition that many of the concerns about raising equity capital requirements are unfounded when the systemic perspective (rather than the interests of banks themselves) is adopted:

- Various versions of the standard Modigliani-Miller theorem (e.g., Admati et al. 2010) suggest that a rise in equity capital ratios should produce at least some offsetting fall in risk premia (both in equity and debt) as the bank becomes less risky. This in turn lowers the required rate of return on equity to satisfy shareholders. Overall, whilst the impact of higher equity ratios on the overall cost of capital might be modest, the offset is unlikely to be total (Llewellyn 2011).

- Empirical research (conducted, for instance, by the Basel Committee, the Bank of England, Financial Services Authority in the UK, and the National Institute of Economic and Social Research) supports such an intermediate position. Most empirical studies suggest that the macro-economic costs of higher equity ratios are modest most especially when viewed in the context of the trade-off with enhanced systemic stability. However, a distinction is made between the stock-adjustment effect (moving from low to high equity capital) and the new steady-state outcome: the costs of moving from one capital regime to another are likely to be greater than the new steady-state outcome. For this reason, a phase-in period is optimal as proposed in the Basel 3 arrangements.
- Even if there were to be net costs arising from higher imposed equity capital ratios, the benefits of a potentially more stable banking system need to be considered as part of the equation of balancing costs and benefits. Such benefits include avoidance of the output costs of bank crises, greater confidence in the banking system which should also contribute to lowering the cost of capital, and lower costs to tax-payers associated with bank failures. This would amount to the consumer paying the higher costs of bank intermediation as the price of a more stable system.
- There is a systemic benefit in lowering the cost of bank failures given the higher equity cushion: a higher proportion of losses are met by equity shareholders.
- Higher equity ratios are likely to create more powerful incentives for private monitoring as equity holders have more to lose which compensates the cost of monitoring. Moral hazard in terms of risk-taking should also be moderated to the extent that shareholders have more to lose with high equity capital ratios. Low capital ratios can be an incentive for shareholders to take (or tolerate) high risk strategies.
- Banks could benefit by lowering the monitoring costs of their bank counterparties to the extent that they also have higher equity cushions.
- There is currently a bias in favour of debt financing of banks because of the different tax treatment of debt and equity. A rise in required equity capital ratios can be viewed as a contribution to minimising this perverse bias. Again, while this will be a cost to banks (and hence one reason why they prefer high gearing) it is not a social cost to the extent that it corrects for market distortions.

Admati et al. (2010) argue that higher capital requirements are likely to produce more stable returns to bank shareholders, albeit lower in buoyant times, but higher in distressed times because of a lower appetite for risk.

Bankers have argued that the proposed rise in equity requirements under Basel 3 is disproportionate and excessive (as they are based on low-probability risks) and will result in a disproportionate decline in lending and a higher cost of credit. The argument here is that the costs are exaggerated. It can also be argued that banks were extending too much credit in the years prior to the crisis because risks were being under-estimated and under-priced. In any case, the costs associated with Low-Probability-High-Impact (LPHI) risks can be very substantial when they do occur even though they may not happen very frequently. The benefits of avoiding these occasional costs may be greater than the higher costs in normal times created by the requirement to hold more equity.

The key point is that a distinction is made between *private* and *social costs* when adjusting regulatory capital requirements. The cost of capital is likely to rise if the perception is that risks are shifted from tax-payers to shareholders. However, social costs are not increased if banks are required to pay for the subsidies and implicit guarantees they receive. Our overall assessment is that higher (perhaps substantially higher) capital requirements are likely to imply little social cost but significant systemic benefits.

The overall conclusion is that the costs of higher equity capital requirements is probably exaggerated by bankers; there is a crucial distinction between private and social costs; the benefits of more stability are an important offset; it is appropriate that consumers pay for the benefits of lower costs associated with instability; and the costs of LPHI risks can be very high.

One of the central features of the recent crisis was the high degree of connectedness between banks with the corollary that it is difficult to measure risk exposures of individual banks, and that shocks in one part of the system can magnify and have a substantial systemic impact (Haldane 2009b). This increased interconnectedness of risks (and the resultant network externalities) applies both as between banks and also between banks and various financial markets. Such network externalities also mean that, in practice, the number of banks that are potentially systemically significant has risen over time.

One possibility to address this key issue is greater transparency of connectedness so that banks, other market transactors, and supervisory agencies are able to make more informed judgments both about the risks attached to individual institutions, but also system risks. On the strength of more accurate and extensive data, higher regulatory capital and liquidity requirements could be imposed on banks which are deemed to be highly connected with others. This in turn might create incentives for banks to manage their connectedness, and hence vulnerability to shocks emanating from other banks, more effectively.

4.3. Intervention

A key component of any strategy to lower the probability of failures is the nature, timing and form of *intervention* in the event of a failing bank. Intervention strategies can be based on Prompt Corrective Action (PCA) programmes (i.e. intervention being made early), and Structured Early Intervention and Resolution (SEIR) regimes as in the US. These are similar to the recovery and resolution arrangements within living wills discussed in section 5.6. below.

Intervention arrangements have incentive and moral hazard effects which potentially influence future behaviour of banks and their customers. These arrangements may also have significant implications for the total cost of intervention (e.g., initial forbearance often has the effect of raising the eventual cost of subsequent intervention), and the distribution of those costs between tax-payers and other agents. A central issue focuses on when intervention is to be made. The experience of banking crises in both developed and developing countries indicates that well-defined strategies for responding to the deteriorating position of banks are needed.

A key issue relates to rules *versus* discretion in the event of bank distress: the extent to which intervention should be circumscribed by clearly-defined rules (so that intervention agencies have no discretion about whether, how and when to act), or whether there should always be discretion simply because relevant circumstances cannot be set out in advance. The obvious *prima facie* advantage for allowing discretion is that it is impossible to foresee all future circumstances and conditions for when a bank might become distressed and close to insolvency.

However, there are strong arguments against allowing discretion and in favour of a rules approach to intervention. Firstly, a rules approach enhances the credibility of the intervention agency in that market participants have a high degree of certainty that action will be taken. Secondly, allowing discretion is likely to increase the probability of forbearance which usually leads to higher costs when intervention is finally made. It guards against hazards associated with risk-averse regulators who themselves might be disinclined to take action for fear that it will be interpreted as a regulatory failure, and the temptation to allow a firm to trade-out of its difficulty: a policy that amounts to the regulator "gambling for resurrection". Kane (2000), for instance, argues that officials may forbear because they face different incentives from those of the market: their own welfare, the interests of the agency they represent, political interests, reputation, future employment prospects, etc. Thirdly, a rules-based approach removes the danger of undue political interference in the disciplining of banks. Fourthly, a rules approach guards against supervisors focusing on the short-term costs of intervention compared with the longer-term costs of delaying intervention. Fifthly, it guards against a "collective euphoria" syndrome whereby all agents (including supervisors) are swept along by a common euphoria (Llewellyn 2010). Finally, and related to the first, a rules approach to intervention is likely to have a beneficial impact on *ex ante* behaviour of financial firms, and create incentives for management to manage banks prudently so as to reduce the probability of insolvency. Above all, a rules approach is designed to address the time-consistency problem and add credibility to a no-bail-out strategy and thereby create appropriate incentives within banks. SEIR strategies can, therefore, act as a powerful incentive for prudent behaviour.

Put another way, time-inconsistency and credibility problems can be addressed through pre-commitments and graduated responses with the possibility of over-rides. This could be achieved via various forms of pre-determined intervention through a general policy of SEIR.

An example of the rules based approach is the Prompt Corrective Action (PCA) rules in the US specifying graduated intervention by the regulators with pre-determined responses triggered by, *inter alia*, capital thresholds. Several other countries have such rules of intervention.

4.4. Market Discipline

The role of market discipline needs to be enhanced not only via the elements already within Pillar 3 of the Basel Accord, but also by the use of market metrics and the use of market signals in triggering discretionary supervisory intervention. Market approaches have the advantage of being simple metrics, being transparent, model-free, timely and observable in real time, and create incentives for monitoring and shareholder activism. In contrast, the quest for enhanced risk-sensitivity of capital requirements has created complexity, opacity and has to some extent impaired the incentives for market discipline.

There is evidence that market-based capital ratios and measures of Tobin Q yield useful information to supervisors which can be utilised in the supervisory process, and that market-based measures of capital have greater predictive value than do book-based measures. Haldane (2011) observes that market-based metrics perform well in distinguishing between good and more vulnerable in that they give advance warning of distress.

5. OBJECTIVE 2: MINIMISING THE COSTS OF BANK FAILURES

5.1. Lowering the Costs of Bank Failures

Our central theme is that regulatory reform needs to focus not only on measures to reduce the probability of bank failures (Objective 1), but also on measures to reduce the cost of those failures that inevitably will occur under any regulatory regime (Objective 2). This section reviews measures designed to lower the cost of bank failures borne by tax-payers, the system, depositors or deposit protection funds, and bank customers.

The *main elements* (in table 16.1) are: (1) structural measures; (2) ring-fencing within conglomerate banks; (3) taxation; (4) explicit and predictable resolution arrangements; and (5) living wills. Without credible and predictable arrangements for the allocation of losses, resolution will always be delayed.

A central issue in regulatory reform centres on the TBTF syndrome. Furthermore, banks might also be too big to rescue because of the size of the potential tax-payer liability. Several problems emerge when a financial system is populated with banks that are deemed to be too-big-to-fail:

- the system may be exposed to more risk,
- a moral hazard is created if banks or depositors know that a rescue will be mounted in the event of a potential insolvency which may both induce such banks to take excessive risks and weaken the incentive for market monitoring of the risk-taking of banks,
- incentives may be created for banks to become big in order to secure TBTF rents, especially because empirical evidence indicates that there is a "TBTF ratings premium",
- competitive neutrality between banks of different size is compromised,
- tax-payers are potentially exposed to a large liability in the event of a failure of a TBTF bank: the tax-payer may be called upon to be an insurer-of-last-resort,
- the possibility arises (as in Iceland) that banks might also become "too big to rescue" because of the burden placed on the tax base.

A key issue is how to break out of a potential vicious circle: expectations of some banks being TBTF create a moral hazard and excess risk-taking which may lead to failures and the rescue of those banks. The resurrected banks are then free to repeat the process. In this vicious circle, the apparent solution to one problem sows the seeds of the next (Haldane 2009a). The central objective is to lower the systemic costs of failure.

5.2. Structural Measures

Five broad alternative strategies to limit the TBTF problem can be identified. Firstly, although in practice unrealistic, a limit might be placed on the size of banks. Secondly, large banks could be broken up. A third option, and more realistic than limiting size, is to impose capital charges based on the size of banks and their systemic significance. In practice to date there has been something of a negative correlation between bank size and capital ratios which, to some extent, has been perversely encouraged by the Basel Capital Accord and especially Basel II. A fourth alternative is to impose a tax on size. Finally, as part of resolution arrangements, "wind-up" plans and/or living wills could be imposed on large institutions designed to ring-fence some bank activities so that parts can fail without bringing down the whole bank. Overall, large or systemically important banks could be subject to a higher degree of regulatory intensity.

One option to deal with banks regarded as potentially systemically important is to impose higher capital charges on such institutions as advocated, for instance, by Acharya and Richardson (2009), Brunnermeier et al. (2009) and Bernanke (2009). The Financial Services Board has also proposed a global capital charge on SIBs. Chan-Lau (2010) suggests a practical methodology for levying capital charges based on degrees of interconnectedness. These would be based on a bank's incremental contribution to systemic risk and its contribution to increased risk of other institutions. The approach is designed as a way of internalising negative externalities associated with too-connected-to-fail institutions. The BIS has argued that the rationale of a systemic capital charge would be to create a distribution of capital that reflects the systemic risk posed by individual firms (BIS 2010).

There are, however, several problems with such structural measures. Firstly, it is difficult in practice to define the size of a bank which triggers the TBTF problem. For instance, in the UK while Northern Rock was not a large bank (it had assets of around £100 billion), the government judged that, faced with a run on the bank in August 2007, it needed to intervene with a rescue operation. Secondly, in a world of network externalities and high connectedness, even the failure of relatively small banks has the potential to create systemic problems: Lehman Brothers was not a particularly big bank. It cannot be claimed that only large banks pose systemic vulnerabilities, and in a crisis a wide range of banks can become systemically significant. Thirdly, to the extent that there are economies of scale in banking (though the empirical evidence is at best ambiguous), there could be costs associated with any structural regulation that sought to limit size. Furthermore, if regulatory arbitrage and competitive neutrality problems are to be avoided, any such measures would need to be internationally coordinated and this is unlikely in practice. Such measures could also impose a "tax" on efficiency in that large banks may have got to their size because of their superior efficiency and performance.

5.3. Ring-Fencing

The Glass-Steagall model requires a total separation between commercial and investment banking business. An alternative approach – outlined, for instance, in the report of the UK's Independent Commission on Banking (ICB 2011) and in the Liikanen Report (2012) – is to allow the two activities to be conducted within the same bank but to have an internal separation between the two. This would imply, for instance, having dedicated capital assigned to the two parts of the business. Under the ICB approach, any excess capital within either business can be transferred to the other business providing the required minima are kept in each. The principle is that, in the event of distress, the investment banking part of the business would not be rescued though the core commercial banking arm (however that is defined) could be rescued if necessary. The central idea is two-fold: commercial banking operations should not be contaminated by the risks in investment banking, and the ring-fenced commercial banking operation would be rescued in the event of distress.

As in the original Litan model of the Narrow Bank (Litan 1987), banks would not be able to use protected or insured deposits for speculative and casino-like activities. Some Narrow Banking proposals argue that banks should not hold any risky assets and that, while banks should be free to originate loans, these should then be securitised. The business of a Narrow Bank would be restricted to accepting deposits and supplying basic banking services (such as payments facilities) and holding low-risk and highly liquid assets. The key property of the model is that retail deposits (and the assets backing them) would be segregated from any other business that the institution incorporating a Narrow Bank might conduct, and that the allowable business of a Narrow Bank would be severely restricted. Furthermore, if they are incorporated within the same organisation (such as a bank holding company) the structure of the bank should allow for the "utility" part of the bank to be easily separated from the "casino" part in the event of a failure of the bank.

The central advantage to ring-fencing is that commercial banking operations of a financial conglomerate would be rescued if necessary whilst the investment bank would not be, but while maintaining any economies of scale and scope advantages that might exist within a financial conglomerate. Specifically, resolution would be made easier because of a simplified business structure, and there would be no implicit subsidy to investment banking activity by virtue of a bank being judged to be TBTF. In principle, the overall cost of a bank failure is reduced as one part of the bank can be allowed to fail without undermining core commercial banking activity.

While such models might appear attractive in terms of shielding depositors from excessive risk taking in the investment part of the business, and possibly allowing the latter to fail without a bail-out, there are limitations:

- How are crucial ring-fenced services to be defined in practice?
- All types of institutions can have powerful and destabilising systemic implications which means that, in practice, there is no clear-cut division between ring-fenced parts of banks that will be supported and the other parts which will be allowed to fail.
- The key systemic issues arise through connectedness and it is difficult to imagine that in practice the ring-fenced part of a bank would be entirely immune from the failure of a "casino" operation. All banks become vulnerable in a crisis.
- To some extent, the same objectives could be achieved through a combination of higher capital requirements on the investment business of a universal bank, more intensive regulation and supervision generally, and living wills.

Furthermore, many of the banks that failed in the recent crisis (e.g., in Ireland, Spain, and elsewhere) were the result of bad property lending undertaken within what would become the "ring-fenced" part of a bank. This indicates that the ring-fencing strategy is largely irrelevant for Objective 1, but may nevertheless be relevant for Objective 2 to the extent that problems arise outside of the ring-fenced part of the bank and that this part will not be a claim on tax-payer support.

5.4. Taxation

The wide range of intervention measures applied by governments and central banks in the wake of the crisis involved a substantial tax-payer commitment. Tax-payers became what amounted to an "insurer-of-last-resort" but with an inefficient insurance contract in that no *ex ante* premiums were paid by the insured entities. The contract was implicit. In effect, tax-payers became exposed to bank credit risks that they themselves had no part in creating and for which no *ex ante* premiums were received. In order to minimise the cost to tax-payers, banks could be required to pay *ex ante* premiums and/or *ex post* for the costs of rescue operations. Each bank's liability to pay could in principle be related to a measure of its systemic significance. In other words, whether banks should be required to pay for the costs of the crisis and the benefits received through public intervention.

The rationale for imposing special taxation on banks is three-fold: (1) to recoup the costs of past bail-outs and intervention, (2) to compensate for the effective subsidy received by banks by virtue of possible future bail-outs and being TBTF, and, (3) creating incentives to alter funding structures and perhaps against becoming "too big". The incentive structure with regard to funding is seen in the UK case where a new tax relates to each bank's balance sheet size minus the sum of core capital, insured (retail) deposits, and cash raised against holdings of government bonds: this is, in effect, a tax on wholesale market borrowing. It amounts to a systemic risk levy whereby the tax internalises to banks the social (systemic) costs they potentially create.

The IMF has made two proposals: a *Financial Stability Contribution* and a *Financial Activity Tax*. In the former case, banks would be required to make payments *ex ante* through a levy on their balance sheets. This would imply payments to cover Intervention and Resolution costs.

An alternative approach is to charge banks *ex ante* insurance premiums to cover the possibility of tax-payer liabilities emerging through future rescue operations. Such *insurance premiums* would be based on assessments of banks' potential contribution to systemic risk.

A key issue arises as to whether such premiums would be allocated to a dedicated "rescue fund" (and invested in appropriate assets such as government debt), or whether such payments would be regarded as contributions to general government revenues and used to reduce budget deficits and/or finance higher government expenditure or lower taxation. There are problems with both. A possible drawback of creating a "rescue fund" would be the moral hazard associated with all forms of insurance: if funds are known to be available for rescue operations, insured banks might be induced to take excessive risk. A second problem is that it might be viewed as undermining a government's commitment not to bail out failing banks. Thirdly, the logic of creating alternatives to bail-outs (such as living wills and SEIR regimes) would be undermined as the creation of a fund would appear to be an admission that the planned alternative strategy might not work. This would amount to a public policy that says that mechanisms have been introduced to avoid the need for any future bail-outs, and yet a fund has been created in case a bail out is needed. This could undermine credibility, and create uncertainty about what government policy is.

On the other hand, if any premiums were to go to governments' general accounts, the credibility of the scheme could be undermined in that there might be doubt about whether, notwithstanding that premiums have been paid, the government would have the resources to rescue a large failing bank. This could also raise the potential hazard of weakening pressure on governments to pursue responsible fiscal policies. Furthermore, in the event that the proceeds of the premium payments were taken into the government's general accounts, the tax-payer would receive the benefits of higher public spending and/or lower taxation as the compensation for possibly having to use public resources for future bank bail-outs. But this might be resisted at the time.

5.5. Resolution Arrangements

Whatever regulatory regime exists to reduce the probability of bank failures, it can never reduce the probability to zero, and neither should it attempt to do so as this would imply gross over-regulation which would undermine the effectiveness and efficiency of the banking sector. As there always will be bank failures, it is prudent to have explicit resolution regimes so as to reduce the costs of those failures that do occur.

Prior to the onset of the recent crisis, few countries had clearly-defined resolution arrangements in place, or a legal structure giving powers of intervention before insolvency is reached. This meant that uncertainty was created about how governments would respond to serious bank distress. Exceptions were the US, Canada, Italy and Norway with the last-mentioned having put in place special resolution arrangements following the banking crisis in the 1990s. To avoid this uncertainty, the regulatory regime needs to encompass credible, predictable, and timely resolution arrangements for failed institutions which limit the potential liability imposed on tax-payers, maintains systemic stability, and protects depositors. The ultimate objective is for resolution arrangements to be in place to deal with distressed banks with the minimum of costs and disruption. This implies allowing banks to fail without disturbing customer business or compromising systemic stability, and to ensure that the costs of default fall on equity, bond holders and other non-insured creditors. In effect, the "socialisation" of the costs of failure is to be avoided. Bail-outs are to be avoided as they impose costs on tax-payers, create serious moral hazard, may support inefficient banks, and weaken market discipline. Banks need to be put into a resolution procedure if they are unable to survive without public support, and cannot re-finance maturing debt. A key objective is to minimise the moral hazard created by bank rescues.

Problems emerge when resolution arrangements are not clear. Firstly, uncertainty and unpredictability is created for all stakeholders including depositors and other banks in the system. Secondly, it creates time-consistency problems (and hence credibility issues) as governments may be induced to behave differently over time. Thirdly, stakeholders are inclined to bargain for economic rents often (if not usually) at the expense of the tax-payer. Fourthly, as argued above, it can lead to political pressures for forbearance and the moral hazard attached to it, and can lead to costly and unnecessary delays in resolution. Fifthly, uncertainty is created with respect to rights and obligations in the event of bank failures and the absence of predictable rules on burden allocation creates delay in resolution. Two further considerations in the case of cross border banks is the extent to which countries have different resolution regimes, and how burden sharing is to be distributed.

To address this, we argue for the addition of a fourth Pillar to the Basel Capital Accord: whilst Pillars 1-3 focus predominantly on reducing the probability of bank failures, Pillar 4 would focus on resolution arrangements designed to lower the cost of those banks that do fail. Competitive distortions between different nationalities of banks can arise just as much through different approaches to resolution as with different rules and procedures within Pillars 1 to 3 (see section 5.7. below).

Given the strong presumption in favour of clearly-defined, explicit and predictable resolution procedures to be in place, a set of key criteria are outlined for constructing such a regime:

- Failed banks to exit in an orderly way and without disrupting customers' business.
- Minimal, or zero, loss or risk to tax-payers.
- Banks that cannot survive without public support to be placed in the resolution procedure.
- Resolution to be activated before a bank becomes technically insolvent: this should have the beneficial effect of enhancing market discipline.
- Resolution procedures to be activated very quickly so as not to jeopardise customers' banking arrangements: there should be no disruption to the business of the bank for its customers.

- Any pay-outs to insured depositors to be made with minimal delay.
- Shareholders never to be protected.
- Non-insured creditors to share in any costs of insolvency.
- Resolution arrangements not to create moral hazard for the future.
- Minimal distortion to competitive neutrality between banks: for EU countries this also implies adherence to EU competition requirements.
- Large, and systemically significant, banks to be required to construct their own resolution plans (living wills as discussed below).
- The avoidance of any potential for stakeholders (most especially banks) to bargain for economic rents.

Several elements can be included in resolution arrangements some of which are included in the UK's Special Resolution Regime: the facility for private sector purchases of failed banks, transfer of engagements to a bridge bank, partial transfer of assets and liabilities to other institutions, temporary public ownership, the ability to re-structure claims of an institution (e.g., debt-equity conversions, and the writing down of unsecured creditors' claims), forced merger/acquisitions without shareholder consent, the creation of bad banks, the suspension or termination of powers, and forced private sector hair-cuts.

5.6. Living Wills

Prior to the crisis, most countries did not have in place the necessary tools to wind-down their domestic financial conglomerates. Huertas (2010) argues that living wills can in theory create a financial system that is "resilient to shocks and one that assures that banks are not 'too big' or 'too interconnected' to fail." Living wills can be a superior and more realistic alternative to structural measures to address the TBTF issue. Living wills seek to prevent the failure of one bank having broad systemic consequences leading to the failure of other innocent banks. As put by Huertas (2010): "Living wills offer the prospect that society can create a lower impact/lower cost solution to the problem posed by large, systemically important banks."

The two key components of living wills are *recovery* and *resolution* arrangements with the resolution component kicking in when the recovery component has failed. In principle, clearly-defined and credible recovery plans should lower the probability that resolution will be needed because such plans outline how a bank is to respond to distress situations. They are designed to maintain banks as going-concerns. Living wills dictate that a bank has in place a clear recovery plan by requiring it to outline in advance what is to be done in the event that it falls into extreme stress. As put by Huertas (2010): "the bank is forced to think through in advance what it would do if the bank were to fall under extreme stress." In particular, banks are required to have plans in place to ensure that, in such circumstances, they can maintain adequate capital and liquidity. The requirement to have convertible bonds as part of a bank's capital base could be part of living will arrangements with the circumstances under which the conversion takes place being specified in advance. Other possible routes to recovery include selling parts of the business, exiting from some business lines, running down the scale of the bank, selling the entire business, etc.

The essence of living wills is that there are clearly-defined and credible recovery plans established in advance, resolution arrangements are made explicit, and arrangements are in place to enable a bank to be broken up when in distress so as to protect core depositors' business. They amount to a form of SEIR. There are further advantages to living wills in the case of complex and potentially systemically important institutions. Firstly, to the extent that they induce simplified structures in complex banks, interconnectedness might be lowered. Secondly, they are designed to lower the probability of failure through the recovery component. Thirdly, systemic costs of any failures that occur should be lowered because clear and credible resolution plans are put in place in advance. Fourthly, the resolution process should be made easier and less complex. Fifthly, they would give more information to supervisors in the process of resolution operations. Finally, there could be general advantages through reducing the need for rescues or bail-outs because credible and explicit alternative resolution mechanisms would be in place. This should enhance the credibility of a no-bail-out policy. The ultimate rationale is that the "recovery" component should lower the probability that a bank would require intervention by the regulatory authorities, and the resolution part should lower the costs to society of a bank failure.

Above all, living wills would mitigate moral hazard to the extent that they make it clear to creditors that resolution can take place without a bail-out and, as a result, market discipline should be enhanced. The rationale of living wills is that the "recovery" component should lower the probability that a bank would require intervention by the regulatory authorities, and the "resolution" part should lower the social costs of a bank failure.

Living wills make recovery and resolution plans more explicit. Banks are particularly complex organisations and generally have more subsidiaries than most other types of company. Banks can be horrendously complex with subsidiaries, SIVs, SPVs, and with complex relationships between different parts of the business. HSBC, for instance, has in excess of two thousand entities although in many cases they are separately capitalised. The structural complexity of large, conglomerate banks creates particular problems for the resolution regime most especially when the objective is to separate the essential parts of a bank (which are to be sustained) from its other activities. Living wills need to be designed to give information about how any wind-down would be executed in practice. They are also designed to include mechanisms to separate the components of a financial firm that are critical as opposed to those that are not

(Hupkes 2009): in particular, deposits, some lending business, and payments services are to be ring-fenced in the event of a resolution. This suggests having simple structures so that parts of the bank can easily be sold (Tucker 2010). The main purpose is to lower the cost, and speed up the process, of resolution by making it easier to sell different parts of the bank, and to protect the tax-payer by giving an alternative to bail-outs. It needs to be clear which parts of a bank's business are to be supported and kept solvent. A key feature is that core business should be effectively ring-fenced in the event of bank distress.

The British government has imposed a requirement on large banks to cre-ate recovery and resolution plans (living wills) which explain how a bank is to be broken up in the event of resolution. The Group of Thirty has made a similar proposal in order to "develop internationally consistent firm-specific resolution plans" (Group of Thirty 2009). The UK Financial Services Author-ity requires that such plans should: be capable of execution within a fairly short period and with a high degree of certainty; be of a size that would have a substantial impact and be capable of turning round a distressed institution, and contain a wide range of alternative options to bolster capital and liquidity when necessary.

The central rationale of explicit ex ante resolution arrangements is to allow banks to fail whilst minimising social costs. A "no bail-out" policy will only be credible in the market if it is clear that bank failures will not incur substantial social costs.

5.7. Where is Pillar 4?

Many of these issues are particularly relevant in the case of the EU. What might be termed an *incompatible trinity* has three elements: (1) integrated cross-bor-der banking markets with strong externalities, (2) global financial stability, and (3) autonomous national regulation and supervision. The incompatibility arises as any two can be chosen but not all three. As argued in Masciandaro et al. (2011): "a fragmented supervisory structure is increasingly inadequate to fully internalise the negative externalities stemming from cross-border banking".

A central problem in many cases is that banks are cross-border in terms of business operations while resolution arrangements tend to remain national. In this sense the regulatory regime has not kept pace with business structures.

The Basel Capital Accord has three pillars: in essence, regulation, supervi-sion, and market discipline. A crucial element in any regulatory regime (the resolution arrangements) is *not explicitly covered* and yet this is an area which needs as much international coordination as do the three existing pillars. Dif-ferent national resolution arrangements have as much potential to create com-petitive distortions between different nationalities of banks as would different capital adequacy rules within Pillar 1. A Pillar 4 in the Basel Accord would contribute to making the overall regulatory regime more competitively neutral as between countries.

There are several problems with not having an internationally agreed Pillar 4 within the Basel Capital Accord:

- There is potential for non-competitive neutrality as between countries in resolution arrangements which could, under some circumstances, lead to regulatory arbitrage.
- There remains a temptation to adopt bail-out strategies which create moral hazard.
- Banks are global in nature and hence a degree of coordination and compatibility in resolution arrangements is desirable because of the negative externalities associated with interconnectedness.
- The international dimension raises difficult issues of burden-sharing if in practice there are bail-outs.
- Resolution requires quick and predictable action which is likely to be difficult in the case of global banks. Resolution can be particularly time-consuming when negotiations are needed about procedures between different countries (this was demonstrated in the case of Fortis bank).
- Information sharing is essential and yet this is not always practised.
- Uncertainty is created regarding how different countries will react to banks in distress.
- Different countries have differing legal powers with respect, for instance, to bankruptcy laws.
- Countries are tempted to adopt national interests.

Clearly, difficult political and logistical issues are involved with a coordinated approach. Nevertheless, the advantages of more predictability and compatibility in resolution arrangements are clear.

There are currently formidable problems with respect to coordinated resolution arrangements with regard to cross-border banks: some supervisory agencies are constrained in their ability to share information with agencies in other jurisdictions, there are major differences between countries with respect to resolution powers and procedures, legal structures (including with regard to bankruptcy procedures) vary considerably, and coordination can be time-consuming. Furthermore, primacy is often given to national interests. All of these, together with a requirement for there to be a degree of convergence in resolution regimes, need to be addressed if an effective and efficient cross-border resolution and burden-sharing regime is to be established.

A basic set of requirements (most especially within the EU) needs to be agreed and enforced with regard to key elements: each country should have effective resolution powers and instruments; a degree of harmonisation of bankruptcy laws; an agreed framework for coordination in the case of cross-border banks; a reasonable degree of convergence in resolution arrangements between countries; living wills to simplify the resolution procedure; the free exchange of information between national supervisory agencies with the removal of some current legal impediments; a consistent approach to SEIR, and an agreed model to determine burden sharing.

The EU Commission in June, 2012 issued a long-awaited draft Directive on bank resolution in the EU area which includes proposals for living wills, funding arrangements for the resolution of cross-border banks, and proposals for a bail-in regime. The proposed tools for resolution are divided into three categories: prevention, early intervention, and resolution. Under the draft Directive, banks will be responsible for creating recovery plans, and supervisory authorities will be required to produce resolution plans. The plan is that there will be harmonised resolution tools and powers. Overall, the objective is to create a Union-wide framework to manage banks in distress and to move towards a greater integration and coherence in the resolution requirements applicable to cross-border banks.

6. SUMMARY OF THE ARGUMENT: A REGULATORY STRATEGY

The over-arching conclusion is that regulatory reform needs to be *strategic* rather than *incremental*. By strategic is meant that the regulatory reform process needs go back to basics including considering what the ultimate objectives of the regulatory regime are, and what functions are required to be performed by banks in the economy. This requires a different paradigm. "Incremental" reform, on the other hand, is simply refining existing regulatory requirements (capital ratios, etc.). Two broad objectives of any regulatory regime need to be considered: (1) to reduce the probability of bank failures, and (2) to lower the cost of those failures that do occur. In a regulatory matrix the possibility of a trade-off between the two is outlined.

A particular argument is that structural regulation for Objective 1 is largely irrelevant because it was not structural issues that were the root cause of the banking crisis: in this sense, it is the wrong solution to a wrong definition of the problem.

The implication is that, because of the "endogeneity problem", more weight needs to be given to arrangements to lower the cost of bank failures and, therefore, intervention and resolution with the latter including the ability to "close" a bank (but without disturbing customer business) before the bank is technically insolvent. It also includes the creation of living wills. This also leads to a consideration of whether taxation and insurance arrangements related to banks are to be considered. The former suggests that taxation could be used to require banks to recompense (*ex post*) the tax-payer for past "bail-outs", and insurance could be an *ex ante* protection for the tax-payer.

The conclusion regarding regulatory strategy is that most, if not all, of the objectives of the regulatory regime can be achieved without major structural measures or ever-more refinements to the existing regime, but through a combination of:

- A significant rise in equity capital requirements applied to banks. This would relate to a simple gearing ratio rather than further detailed refinements to the Basel risk-weight methodology. Capital regulation should also include explicit "bail-in" requirements, and contingent capital. The case for less complex capital regulation is made in Haldane 2012. Overall, banks need to have greater loss-absorbing power.
- Differential capital requirements applied to banks that are regarded as systemically significant.
- More stringent liquidity requirements on banks related both to asset holding and funding positions.
- More timely and intensive supervision of banks to encompass more focus on business models and strategies, the testing and monitoring of risk analysis and management systems of banks, earlier direct intervention by supervisory agencies, governance arrangements of banks, internal incentive structures, and a particular focus on high-impact institutions.
- Measures to make Pillar 3 of the Basel Accord more effective including a focus on internal incentive structures within banks, and more use to be made of market metrics in supervisory and intervention processes.
- Tax and insurance impositions on banks.
- Ring-fencing within banks with a resultant more simple organisational structure. While stopping short of breaking up banks or applying a rigid Glass-Steagall-type approach, one structural measure to be incorporated in living wills would be "subsidiarisation" whereby banks that are deemed to be potentially systemically significant would have dedicated capital allocated to different areas of the business.
- A commitment to PCA and SEIR strategies implying early and decisive direct intervention by supervisory agencies.
- The requirement for major banks to have living wills incorporating recovery and resolution plans.
- Clearly-defined and credible resolution arrangements. The objective is to allow banks to fail without disturbing business and customer relationships, and to ensure the costs of default fall on equity and bond holders and other non-secured creditors.
- Resolution arrangements at the international level to be covered in a Pillar 4 of the Basel Capital Accord.

This strategy implies greater emphasis and effectiveness of Pillars 2 and 3, and the addition of a Pillar 4. Pillars 1-3 focus predominantly on Objective 1, while the proposed Pillar 4 is relevant for Objective 2.

BIBLIOGRAPHY

Acharya, V. and M. Richardson 2009, "Government Guarantees: Why the genie needs to be put back in the bottle", *The Economists Voice*, November, The Berkeley Electronic Press.

Admati, A., P. DeMarzo, M. Hellwig, and P. Pfleiderer 2010, "Fallacies, Irrelevant Facts and Myths in the Discussion of Capital Regulation: Why Bank Equity Capital is not Expensive", *Stanford University Working Paper* No 86, Graduate School of Business, Stanford University.

Ayadi, R., E. Arbak and W. P. de Groen 2011, *Business Models in European Banking: A pre- and post-crisis screening*, Centre for European Policy Studies (CEPS), Brussels.

Bernanke, B. 2009, "Financial Regulation and Supervision after the Crisis – The Role of the Federal Reserve", speech at the Federal Reserve Bank of Boston 54th Economic Conference, October.

BIS 2010, *Annual Report*, Bank for International Settlement, Basel, June.

Blundell-Wignall, A., P. Atkinson and S.G. Lee 2008, "The Current Financial Crisis: Causes and Policy Issues", *OECD Financial Market Trends*, OECD, Paris.

Brunnermeier, M., A. Crockett, C. Goodhart, A. Persaud and H.-S. Shin 2009, "The Fundamental Principles of Financial Regulation", *Geneva Reports of the World Economy*.

Chan-Lau, J.A. 2010, "Regulatory Capital Charges for Too-Connected-to-Fail Institutions: A Practical Proposal", *IMF Working Paper*, Washington.

Group of Thirty 2009, *Financial Reform: A Framework for Financial Stability*, New York.

Haldane, A. 2009a, "Rethinking the Financial Network", available on Bank of England website.

Haldane, A. 2009b, "Banking on the State", speech to Federal Reserve Bank of Chicago International Banking Conference on "The International Financial Crisis: Have the Rules of Finance Changed?", September. Available at http://www.bankofengland.co.uk/publications/speeches/2009/speech386.pdf.

Haldane, A. 2010, "The $100 billion Question", Comments at the Institute of Regulation and Risk, Hong Kong, March. Available at Bank of England website.

Haldane, A. 2011, "Capital Discipline", paper based on a speech given at the American Economic Association, available on Bank of England website.

Haldane, A. 2012, "The dog and the frisbee", paper presented at the FRB Jackson Hole Conference, August.

Herring, R. 2010, "Bank Wind-down Plans", *EBR Advisory Board Report*, Italian Bankers Association, Rome.

Huertas, T.F. 2010, "Living Wills: How can the Concept be Implemented", speech to Wharton School of Management, 12th February, 2010. Available on FSA website at www.fsa.gov.uk.

Hupkes, E. 2009, "Too Big, Too Interconnected, and too international to resolve? How to deal with Global Financial Institutions in Crisis", *mimeo.*

ICB 2011, "The Independent Commission on Banking: The Vickers Report", Final Report, Recommendations, http://bankingcommission.independent.gov.uk.

International Monetary Fund 2009, *Global Financial Stability Report*, April.

Kane, E. 1987, "Competitive Financial Regulation: an International Perspective", in *Threats to Financial Stability*, eds. Portes, R and Swoboda, A., Cambridge University Press, Cambridge

Kane, E. 2000, "Designing Financial Safety Nets to Fit Country Circumstances", mimeo, Boston College.

Kay, J. 2009, *Narrow Banking: The Reform of Banking Regulation*, Centre for the Study of Financial Innovation, London.

Kotlikoff, L. 2010, *Jimmy Steward is dead: Ending the World's Ongoing Financial Plague with Limited Purpose Banking*, Wiley, London.

Kotlikoff, L. and E. Leamer 2009, "A Banking System We Can Trust", *Forbes*, 23 April.

Liikanen Report, 2012, "High Level Expert Group on reforming the structure of the EU banking sector", Final Report, EU Commission, October.

Litan, E. 1987, *What Should Banks Do?*, Brookings Institution, Washington.

Llewellyn, D.T. 2001, "A Regulatory Regime for Financial Stability", in *Bank Fragility and Regulation: Evidence from Different Countries*, G. Kaufman, ed., JAI, Amsterdam.

Llewellyn, D.T. 2008, "The Failure of Northern Rock: A Crisis Waiting to Happen", *Journal of Financial Regulation and Compliance*, March.

Llewellyn, D.T. 2010, "The Global Banking Crisis and the Post-Crisis Banking and Regulatory Scenario", Topics in Corporate Finance, Amsterdam Centre for Corporate Finance, University of Amsterdam, October.

Llewellyn, D.T. 2011, "A Post-Crisis Regulatory Strategy: The Road to 'Basel N' or 'Pillar 4'?, Austrian National Bank Conference Proceedings, Annual Economics Conference, 2011, Austrian National Bank, Vienna.

Masciandaro, D., M. Nieto and M. Quintyn 2011, "Exploring Governance of the New European Banking Authority: a Case for Harmonisation?", *Journal of Financial Stability*, Vol 7, Number 4, pp 204-214.

Tucker, P. 2010, Remarks to European Commission's Conference on Crisis Management, available on Bank of England website.

17. Regulation of Banks and the "Level Playing Field" – The Case of Shadow Banking

Otto Lucius

1. INTRODUCTION

The financial crisis that evolved out of the subprime mortgage crisis in 2007 and then turned into a banking crisis – or, to be more precise, turned out to be a crisis of the financial system – has revealed fundamental weaknesses of the financial system. These weaknesses could easily turn into disaster triggered by systemic risks. This was one of the reasons why the focus of discussion shifted away from a microprudential supervisory regime to put more emphasis on a macroprudential view of the financial system. The phenomenon of systemically important financial intermediaries, the so-called SIFIs, attracted more and more attention. Martin Blessing in chapter 1 of this volume calls the new focus on systemic risk a 'paradigm shift'. Some of the other contributions in this volume deal with systemic risk per se, especially chapter 9 written by Jaime Caruana, but also Luiz Pereira da Silva et al. in chapter 4 discusses systemic risk. And other authors in this volume touched the problem of SIFIs, or SIBs and G-SIBs, like Yves Mersch (chapter 11) as well as Klaas Knot and Hanne van Vorden in chapter 12.

With the crisis forcing governments to put substantial amounts of money into the rescue of banks the question is legitimate if financial stability can be re-established this way. The answer is twofold. We have seen the actions taken by the US Government to stabilise their financial system. However it is too early to give a positive answer if they had successfully restored financial stability. Financial stability is not only dependent on the regulatory framework, or on the capital requirements imposed on the banks. It is also dependent, as convincingly laid out by Paul Tucker (chapter 8 of this volume), on a "tendency to excessive risks" inherent to the system. This is largely due to agency problems and myopia (see Paul Tucker in this volume, chapter 8, section 2.).

A different but nevertheless very exciting topic is the complexity of the regulatory work designed. It is not without some irony that Andrew Haldane as economist of one of the regulators responsible for designing the Basel framework and his co-author are now calling for less complexity (Haldane and Ma-douros 2012). Their arguments are very convincing. But the fact remains that the Basel III regime is under way, like the Titanic, and that a small sailing boat tied to the Titanic, i.e. some regulators now calling for less complexity, will not be able to change the course of the "Titanic" rapidly. Hopefully the Basel III regime will not end up like the Titanic. And to reduce the complexity of the financial system itself might be an even bigger challenge.

2. REGULATION OF BANKS – A LEVEL PLAYING FIELD?

We have already entered the discussion of banking regulation. Given the huge importance of banks for a country's economy in the case of a bank-based financial system (Diamond 1984) regulation of bank activities is of vital importance. It is common sense that banking activities shall be regulated in order to secure proper functioning of the banking system and as a secondary goal to maintain depositor's confidence in bank stability. We might state that without a safety net banking is unstable. This proposition finds support in economic theory. In their well-known analysis, Diamond and Dybvig (1983) showed that banks without deposit insurance exhibit multiple equilibria – one of which is a bank run. And financial history confirms this hypothesis. Banking panics were common in the US before the enactment of deposit insurance, but nonexistent thereafter. And indeed it is more philosophical to argue that a properly functioning banking system will have the full confidence and trust of depositors and therefore will never experience a bank run. Depositor protection is only needed in case of a malfunction of the banking system. However a lot of legislators explicitly strive for both goals, e.g., the Official Comments on the Austrian Banking Act (Bankwesengesetz – BWG).

Largely due to the efforts of the Basel Committee on Banking Supervision, the BCBS, a huge step towards harmonisation of banking regulation was initiated. The Basel II regime, which has now evolved into the Basel III regime, based the regulation of banks on three pillars: pillar 1 with all the capital requirements, even for reputational risk; then pillar 2 with internal and external risk assessment; and lastly pillar 3 with its disclosure requirements (market discipline). This is not the place to discuss the appropriateness of the EU Commission's decision to extend Basel II requirements to all credit institutions located within the EU. And it is not the place to argue if the US were right in not introducing the Basel II framework for all their banks, as the Basel II framework was from the very beginning designed for large internationally operating banks (and not for small savings banks or credit unions). The case of complexity has already been mentioned above.

There is another issue: the current regulation is largely based on sufficient own capital held by financial institutions. And the crisis has shown that own funds can quickly be consumed thus leaving the bank without any further protection. One of the reactions was to step up capital requirements. This is a right step in the right direction. However it makes a huge difference if we consider an investment bank's own capital or a universal bank's own capital. Needless to mention that any investment bank very easily can raise own capital up to 15 or 20 percent as the balance total is rather small – due to the nature of its business. The case of a commercial bank is totally different. The business case of a commercial bank requires a large (or very large) balance total. Therefore it is much more difficult (and much more costly) to raise the capital ratio up to say 10 or 12 percent. This is another case of an uneven playing field. Instead of focusing on capital ratios it might be more successful to focus on leverage ratios and/or on liquidity ratios. Basel III has already started to evolve in this direction. Other instruments to be discussed could be loan-to-value ratios and debt-to-income limits. There are already experiences available from Hong Kong and South Korea (Hartmann 2011).

Now let us assume that we succeed in designing a perfect banking regulation. Let us assume that we are able to solve one of the rather urgent issues, the TBTF syndrome. This will prove rather difficult, because resolving a bank which is too-big-to-fail without letting the taxpayer pay might rather turn out to be a challenge. Perhaps we might be able to act in a forward looking way. But what to do with all the existing banks already too-big-to-fail? If the unthinkable should happen and one of the truly European banks gets into trouble, then even the envisaged resolution fund will quickly turn out to be ineffective. And politics has let gone the chances to act. Not only in Spain it happened that banks merged in order to become one of those too-big-to-fail institutions that had to be or will have to be rescued. Furthermore the preferred TBTF status with its implicit guarantees provides incentives to reach that status. Brewer and Jagtiani (2011) showed that banks are willing to pay a substantial premium for mergers to become TBTF. Another dimension of the TBTF problem is not the question if a bank is really too-big-to-fail but if the markets believe it would be bailed out in case of a crisis. This in turn has a lot to do with moral hazard.

Regulation is necessary, without doubt. But as David Llewellyn has repeatedly stated, regulation is an endless race between regulators and the regulated industry (Llewellyn 2011; Llewellyn in this volume, chapter 16). Once we impose stricter regulation the industry will immediately start trying to find ways to circumvent regulation. Thus it might not help to step up Basel III towards Basel IV and perhaps V. Even reaching a regime of Basel N will be of little use (Llewellyn 2011). The regulated industry will definitely try to find loopholes. Perhaps legislators should become more familiar with certain patterns of human behaviour. Only if the shareholders of a financial institution have to fear total loss of their investment, and only if there are grave consequences for the management in case of insolvency or resolution, will there be a strong incentive to avoid such a situation. So the real challenge lies in the equilibrium of tackling bank resolution and at the same time maintaining trust and confidence in the banking system.

3. SYSTEMIC RISK

For a long time regulation has focused on microprudential measures, regulating a single financial institution. The macroprudential dimension had been rather neglected. This split seems to be similar to the split economists live with, microeconomics and macroeconomics (Caruana 2010). A lot of definitions of systemic risk are available (ECB 2010; FSB-IMF-BIS 2011). Despite all differences in defining systemic risk there are two commonalities: firstly the disruption of functions in the financial system, as opposed to an individual institution not being able to perform. The relations and interactions between the components of the system are the key factor for stability and/or instability. This is something we should keep in mind when looking at shadow banking activities. The second commonality is the relation between the financial sector and the real sector. Malfunctions of the financial sector might not only lead to losses to portfolios, it might also end up in disruption of vital functions of the financial services industry, like a credit crunch, eventually resulting in missed growth and lower employment rates.

In chapter 9 of this volume Caruana has described, based on Borio (2003) and Caruana (2010), two dimensions of systemic risk, the cross-sectional dimension and the time dimension. According to this chapter the cross-sectional dimension refers to the way risk is distributed in the system at a certain point of time. It is dependent on weaknesses in the organisation of markets and their infrastructure and to the concentration of risks in specific institutions or even segments of the financial sector (e.g., large exposures to similar risks or large bilateral counterparty exposures). Insufficient diversification across institutions may result in bulges of risk in the system and give rise to vulnerabilities. Thus even a slight exogenous shock can spread quickly through a system exhibiting such weaknesses. On the other hand the time dimension refers to the dynamic profile of systemic risk. We may also call it procyclicality in the financial system, a phenomenon that can also be observed when looking at bank regulation. In general an upward trend in the markets leads to exuberance with highly lifted investors' expectations and boosted confidence. Such boom phases lead to risky attitudes and high leverage. Imbalances building up gradually during booms will in most cases be ignored. Therefore any correction leading to a bust is coming abruptly, with potentially disastrous consequences for the financial and real sectors. Caruana rightly points out that systemic risk in the time dimension is best understood as arising largely endogenously: the seeds of crises are sown during the boom.

Now regulators all over the world led by the Financial Stability Board are searching for ways to make the financial system more resilient and to minimise systemic risk. Looking at the cross-sectional dimension of systemic risk as laid out above we might succeed in minimising possible impacts of systemic risk. This holds true only if we look at the financial system, as the financial services industry is already (heavily) regulated. But what if an exogenous shock hits the financial services industry, and this shock is coming from part of the financial sector not being regulated or only poorly regulated? This sector is commonly called the shadow banking sector.

4. SHADOW BANKING

The crisis revealed structural weaknesses in the regulated part of the financial services industry. And soon it became apparent that there is a unregulated part of the financial sector, the so-called "shadow banking sector". It was the G20 that pushed towards regulation and oversight of the shadow banking sector. After the completion of the new capital standards for banks, the Basel III regime, the G20 leaders at their Seoul Summit of November 2010, realised the potential threat that regulatory gaps may emerge in the so-called shadow banking system. They therefore mandated the Financial Stability Board (FSB) to develop recommendations to strengthen the regulation and oversight of the shadow banking system (G20 2010) and the G20 Cannes Summit Action Plan of November 2011 reaffirmed this mandate (G20 2011).

4.1. Defining Shadow Banking

In starting work on its mandate the FSB had to develop working definitions of shadow banking. Following the concept that banks mainly deal with credit intermediation (seen aside from payment system services) it was obvious to base a definition of "shadow banking" on the function of credit intermediation. Thus FSB defined the shadow banking system broadly as "the system of credit intermediation that involves entities and activities outside the regular banking system" (FSB 2011). The ECB closely follows this definition (Bakk-Simon et al. 2012, p. 4). The EU Green Paper Shadow Banking (EC 2012) is based on the FSB definition by describing the possible shadow banking entities and activities on which the Commission will focus its analysis:

Entities:
- Special purpose entities which perform liquidity and/or maturity transformation; for example, securitisation vehicles such as ABCP conduits, special investment vehicles (SIV) and other special purpose vehicles (SPV);

- Money market funds (MMFs) and other types of investment funds or products with deposit-like characteristics, which make them vulnerable to massive redemptions ("runs");
- Investment funds, including exchange traded funds (ETFs), that provide credit or are leveraged;
- Finance companies and securities entities providing credit or credit guarantees, or performing liquidity and/or maturity transformation without being regulated like a bank; and
- Insurance and reinsurance undertakings which issue or guarantee credit products.

Activities:
- Securitisation; and
- Securities lending and repo.

Tucker (2012a) states that the definition of "shadow banking" employed by the FSB and the EU Commission is very close to the definition he used in a speech in 2010 calling for work on shadow banking. The only difference would be that he included "monetary services" in addition to leverage and maturity transformation.

Of course there are lot of other definitions of shadow banking. For those interested Deloitte (2012) provides a good overview of some widely referenced definitions.

The debate taking place internationally tends to see "shadow banking" as one of the triggers for financial instability. Perhaps this impression was due to the fact that at first, in the time span 2007/08, the crisis did not look like a traditional banking crisis, but rather one related to a new phenomenon: shadow banking (Turner 2012). As Pozsar et al. 2012 put it: shadow banks conduct credit, maturity and liquidity transformation similar to traditional banks. But a decisive difference vis-à-vis traditional banks is their lack of access to public sources of liquidity such as the Federal Reserve's discount window, or public sources of insurance such as Federal Deposit Insurance (Pozsar et al. 2012).

As Tucker points out, the problems in the financial sector seemed initially concentrated in the US, with non-bank credit intermediation being most advanced. Many of the events which marked the developing crisis related to non-bank institutions and markets. As one of few Tucker (2012a) has emphasised in a speech at the EC High Level Conference that shadow banking is not the same as the non-bank financial sector. And he also highlighted that non-bank credit intermediation per se is nothing bad. On the contrary, it can help to make financial services more efficient and effective, and it may help making the system more resilient (see also FSB 2012a).

Last but not least it should be mentioned that some authors claim governments act like shadow banks. In a paper from September 2011 Viral Acharya examines the hypothesis that governments often have short-term horizons and are focused excessively on the level of current economic activity. But they ignore whether it will lead to stable long-term growth. By allowing excessive competition, providing downside guarantees and encouraging risky lending for populist schemes, governments can create periods of intense economic activity fuelled by credit booms. This way, governments effectively operate as "shadow banks" in the financial sector. Such government role appears to have been at the centre of recent boom and bust cycles and continues to present a threat to financial stability (Acharya 2011).

Acharya presents as leading examples not only government-sponsored enterprises in the United States, primarily Fannie Mae and Freddie Mac. He also summarises e.g., the Landesbanken in Germany, and the Cajas in Spain, the equivalent of savings and thrift institutions, which are effectively owned by local governments and played a central role in the Spanish housing boom and painful bust, competing aggressively with commercial banks as government-sponsored enterprises. As this is not the place discuss this topic in more depth, interested readers are invited to study Acharya (2011) for more details. Anyway, the intention was to highlight the complexity of the shadow banking issue.

4.2. The Size of Shadow Banking

First let us state the obvious: shadow banking is of different importance in the US than in Europe (Turner 2012). One can only agree with Turner that it is important to bear in mind that much of the financial crisis in Europe did not involve shadow banking activities such as securitised lending, but plain old-fashioned on-balance sheet lending. Unlike in the US, losses on securitised mortgage lending in Europe have been rather small. It is however notable that a bigger hit to European bank balance sheets had been arising from commercial real estate loans – in particular in the UK, Ireland and Spain – primarily lent in the traditional way by traditional banks.

Due to different measuring methodologies different numbers for the size of shadow banking can be found. We prefer to stick to FSB's methodology. FSB (2012d) found that according to its mapping the global shadow banking system, as conservatively proxied by "Other Financial Intermediaries" grew rapidly before the crisis, rising from USD 26 trillion in 2002 to USD 62 trillion in 2007. The size of the total system declined slightly in 2008 but increased subsequently to reach USD 67 trillion in 2011 (equivalent to 111% of the aggregated GDP of all jurisdictions).

The FSB's annual monitoring exercise for 2012 significantly broadened the range of jurisdictions covered to include all 24 FSB member jurisdictions, Chile and the Euro area. This expanded coverage enhanced the comprehensive nature of the monitoring, since participating jurisdictions represented in aggregate 86% of global GDP and 90% of global financial system assets (FSB 2012d). Globally, the shadow banking system, as proxied by other financial institutions (OFIs), represents on average 25% of financial system assets, but nearly 50% of the bank's assets (!) and 111% of the aggregated GDP, for the sample of 20 participating jurisdictions and the Euro area. For more details see the document with accompanying data for the Global Shadow Banking Report (FSB 2012e). However these aggregate numbers mask wide disparities between jurisdictions. The Netherlands (45%) and the US (35%) are the two jurisdictions where non-bank financial institutions (NBFIs) are the largest sector relative to other financial institutions in their systems. The share of NBFIs is also relatively large in Hong Kong (some 35%), the Euro area (30%), Switzerland, the UK, Singapore, and Korea (all around 25%).

As demonstrated inter alia by FSB (2012b; 2012c) and Bakk-Simon et al. (2012) money market funds and repo lending are important constituents of shadow banking. Money market funds (MMFs) flourished in the United States as an alternative to bank deposits, to circumvent regulatory caps on bank interest rates. According to Bakk-Simon et al. (2012) assets under management by MMFs at end of 2008 amounted to EUR 2.4 trillion, EUR 1.6 trillion of which was accounted for by institutional investors and the remainder by retail funds. As MMFs invest in short-term debt, they were an important source of funding for the shadow banking sector through purchases of certificates of deposits and commercial paper and through repo transactions. However we have to be clear that MMFs are a somewhat heterogeneous group in Europe (Bakk-Simon et al. 2012) and do not play as decisive a role as in the US.

The repo market is a key source of financing for the US shadow banking sector. Again according to Bakk-Simon et al. (2012) the data available, collected by the Federal Reserve System for primary dealer banks, reported repo financing for EUR 2.9 trillion in March 2008, but its overall size was estimated to be more than EUR 6.4 trillion.

4.3. Reasons for Regulation of Shadow Banking

It is an illusion to believe that shadow banking can be removed. The "traditional" banking system and the shadow banking system are too much intertwined and dependent on each other. We must accept that shadow banking is not something parallel to and separate from the core banking system, but is deeply interconnected to it.

According to the ECB study by Bakk-Simon et al. (2012) the identified interconnections between shadow banks and the banking system include: (i) originating loans to be packaged into ABS; (ii) providing liquidity facilities to conduits; (iii) providing repo financing; (iv) issuing short-term paper for MMFs; (v) marketing their own MMFs to customers.

As already mentioned shadow banking activities are not per se detrimental. Not many will find such kind words for shadow banks as Jean-Pierre Jouyet, Chairman of AMF, the French Capital Markets Authority:

"As a conclusion, I would like to stress that we need a shadow banking system as much as we need banks. Properly monitored or regulated, a healthy shadow banking system is probably one of the conditions for more growth in Europe tomorrow. And to highlight this role of shadow banking, maybe the entities of the shadow banking system should be rebranded with a more appreciative word, like alternative financing mechanisms, once they are properly regulated." (Jouyet 2012)

However, the shadow banking system can also pose risks to the financial system, be it on its own or through its links with the regular banking system. According to FSB (2012f) these risks can become acute especially when transforming maturity/liquidity and creating leverage like banks.

Risks in the shadow banking system can easily spill over into the regular banking system as banks often comprise part of the shadow banking credit intermediation chain or provide support to non-bank entities. Another aspect not to be neglected is that the shadow banking system can also be used to avoid financial regulation and may lead to a build-up of leverage and risks in the system. For example, securitisation was widely used by banks during the pre-crisis period to take on more risks and facilitate the build-up of leverage in the system, while avoiding the regulatory capital requirements posed by the Basel Accord (FSB 2012f).

We have to recognise that the way in which shadow banking contributed to financial instability just reflects fundamental developments in the financial system which are relevant both to banks and to shadow banks, which remain important today, and which could produce new problems in the future. Banks can also be exposed to the shadow banking system through temporary exposures, through the provision of finance or through contingent credit lines (FSB 2011). There can also be important links on the liabilities side, as banks may be funded by entities like money market funds which form part of the shadow banking system.

In past years the interconnection between regulated and non-bank-regulated segments of the financial sector has increased, likely resulting in a higher risk of contagion across sectors and countries (Bakk-Simon et al. 2012). This interconnection is underestimated by the available data because these are not accurate enough, due to reasons not to be discussed here.

In general shadow banking activities can take a variety of forms. These have evolved in the past in response to changing market and regulatory conditions, and they will continue to evolve (FSB 2012a). According to FSB this insight has consequences for a forward looking approach to regulation.

However there is one development giving every reason for caution: shadow banks in their activities started to behave more and more like banks, as Pozsar

(2008) put it. He demonstrated that SIVs and conduits relied on short-term financing in the asset-backed commercial paper market to invest in long-term assets. Thus they were exposed to the classic maturity mismatch typical of banks. By borrowing short and lending long, conduits and SIVs were involved in the classic bank business of maturity transformation. In this sense, conduits and SIVs were an alternative form of traditional banking! A similar view is presented by the Financial Stability Report in its Progress Report to the G20 when addressing short-term deposit-like funding of non-bank entities (FSB 2012f).

The crucial differences were that shadow banks as "alternative banks" were not funded by depositors, but by investors in the wholesale funding market. Maturity transformation did not occur on bank balance sheets but through capital markets in off-balance-sheet vehicles outside the oversight of regulators (and also investors, as prior to the crisis not too many market participants had heard of SIVs). Last but not least the traditional safety nets for regulated banks (borrowing at the Fed's discount window and FDIC insurance) were unavailable for the shadow banking system of SIVs and conduits, and no alternatives existed (Pozsar 2008; Pozsar et al. 2012). Pozsar (2008) compared shadow banks with traditional banks, in that shadow banking system must have the ability to continuously roll over its asset backed commercial paper (ABCP) debt to perform the same functions. This is very similar to regulated banks that need to be able to continuously roll over their deposits in order to fund their loans and provide liquidity to those who need it. That banks are able to continuously roll over their deposits is grounded in their reputation as prudent risk takers and the quality of the loans they carry on their books. The shadow banking system's ability to roll over ABCP depends on the quality of the structured credit products and warehoused loans it held; any sign of trouble with their assets could trigger ABCP investors, so to say their "depositors", to dump and refuse to roll over their debt, and a run on the shadow banking system would ensue (Pozsar 2008).

But there are not only connections between banks and shadow banks. Insurance companies too might be affected by shadow banking and its regulation. In a speech to the Association of British Insurers Paul Tucker told the audience that (already unpopular) regulations on liquidity swaps, whereby banks pay insurers a fee to switch lower quality assets for high quality ones, did not go far enough. Regulators feared that the current all-consuming focus on banks could result in risk being passed on to insurers, putting them at the epicentre of the next financial crisis. The reason why liquidity swaps are seen as potentially dangerous is because insurers might end up holding risky bank loans.

"The importance of this will be underlined as we move towards a world without a safety net for banks, leaving holders of bank bonds exposed to risk. Insurers are significant investors in bank paper. In the future, whether in the

*UK or elsewhere, you will not be protected by an implicit guarantee from the
state for those investments."* (Tucker 2012b).

5. THE WAY FORWARD IN REGULATION OF SHADOW BANKING

Shadow banking activities can perform a useful role within the financial system, due to one of the following functions (EC 2012): (i) they provide alternatives for investors to bank deposits; (ii) they channel resources towards specific needs more efficiently due to increased specialisation; (iii) they constitute
alternative funding for the real economy, which is particularly useful when
traditional banking or market channels become temporarily impaired; and, (iv)
they constitute a possible source of risk diversification away from the banking
system.

However, as the financial crisis has demonstrated, the shadow banking system may create a number of risks and can also become a source of systemic
risk, both directly and through its interconnectedness with the regular banking
system (FSB 2011; EC 2012). Moreover, risks in the shadow banking system
can easily spill over into the regular banking system as banks are often part of
the shadow banking credit intermediation chain or provide support to shadow
banking entities. These risks may be amplified as the chain becomes longer
(and therefore less transparent).

It should be stressed again that the shadow banking system may be used to
avoid financial regulation and lead to a build-up of leverage and risks in the
system. Thus highest priority should be given to enhancing supervision and
regulation of the shadow banking system in areas where these concerns are
highest (FSB 2011; Smolders 2012).

In general shadow banking creates possibilities for regulatory arbitrage.
Shadow banks being less regulated than banks have a competitive advantage
and operate on an uneven playing field. This makes it possible for the shadow banking system to grow at the expense of the regulated banking system
(Smolders 2012).

Until recently there was implicit easing for shadow banking activities. In
the US (much less in the EU) superior bankruptcy rights as safe harbour provisions were massively expanded in a coordinated legislative push in 2004
(Perotti 2012). This supported an extraordinary expansion of shadow banking
credit and mortgage risk taking. The guaranteed ease of escape fed the final
burst in maturity and liquidity mismatch in the 2004-2007 subprime boom.
This safe harbour regime made it possible for shadow banks upon Lehman's
default to take massive stocks of repo and derivative collateral and to resell
it within hours. This produced a shock wave of fire sales of ABS holdings by

safe harbour lenders. While these lenders broke even, their rapid sales spread losses to all others, forcing public intervention. It became evident that shadow banks need the safe harbour privileges to replicate banking. No financial innovation to secure escape from distress can match the proprietary rights granted by the safe harbour status, which ensure immediate access to sellable assets. Traditional unsecured lenders have taken notice, and now request more collateral, squeezing bank funding capacity and limiting future flexibility (Perotti 2012). This is another aspect to be taken into account when tackling shadow banking regulation, and FSB has already addressed this special problem (FSB 2012a).

The FSB is convinced that the authorities' approach to shadow banking has to be a targeted one. The objective should be to ensure that shadow banking is subject to appropriate oversight and regulation to address bank-like risks to financial stability emerging outside the regular banking system. At the same time it should not prevent sustainable non-bank financing models that do not pose such risks (FSB 2012a).

Given the interconnectedness of markets and the strong adaptive capacity of the shadow banking system, any proposals in this area necessarily have to be comprehensive. A piecemeal or incomplete approach would be quickly arbitraged (FSB 2012a).

So what exactly does FSB propose to strengthen regulation of the shadow banking system? Based on the initial recommendations and work plans set out in its October 2011 Report, the FSB, working with the BCBS and IOSCO, have developed policy recommendations. The detailed design and implementation of these recommendations have been guided by the following five general principles for regulatory measures (FSB 2012a):

(i) Regulatory measures should be carefully designed to target the externalities and risks the shadow banking system creates;

(ii) Regulatory measures should be proportionate to the risks shadow banking poses to the financial system;

(iii) Regulatory measures should be forward-looking and adaptable to emerging risks;

(iv) Regulatory measures should be designed and implemented in an effective manner, balancing the need for international consistency to address common risks and to avoid creating cross-border arbitrage opportunities against the need to take due account of differences between financial structures and systems across jurisdictions; and

(v) Regulators should regularly assess the effectiveness of their regulatory measures after implementation and make adjustments to improve them as necessary in the light of experience.

The recommendations as laid out in the Financial Stability Board's recent document (FSB 2012a) cover the following topics:

Banks' interactions with shadow banking entities

Since the crisis, BCBS members have implemented or are in the process of implementing a number of measures (through Basel II.5 and Basel III) that should strengthen the resilience of the banking sector against some risks posed by shadow banks.

Separately, the BCBS considerations in the following three areas (i) scope of consolidation, (ii) large exposures, and (iii) banks' investment in funds have been presented to FSB in July 2012 and should lead to detailed policy recommendations by mid-2013.

Concerning capital requirements relating to banks' short-term liquidity facilities to shadow banking entities FSB asked the BCBS to ensure that banks' support to money market funds and other sponsored vehicles are adequately captured by its work on the scope of consolidation and/or its treatment of reputational risks and implicit support.

Money market funds

Given the demonstrated potential for a systemic run risk among money market funds (MMFs), the FSB requested IOSCO in October 2011 to develop policy recommendations for MMFs. IOSCO's recommendations (IOSCO 2012a) cover a range of issues associated with MMFs including (i) MMFs should be explicitly defined in collective investment schemes (CIS) regulation as they present several unique features; (ii) MMFs should comply with the general principle of fair value when valuing their assets; (iii) Liquidity management for MMFs; (iv) MMFs offering a stable NAV should be subject to risk-reducing measures and additional safeguards; (v) Use of credit ratings; (vi) Disclosure to investors; (vii) MMFs' practices in relation to repos.

Other shadow banking entities

The presented high-level policy framework consists of the following three elements:

(i) Authorities must identify the sources of shadow banking risks in non-bank financial entities in their jurisdictions by referring to the following five economic functions: 1) management of client cash pools with features that make them susceptible to runs (e.g., credit investment funds with stable NAV features, leveraged credit hedge funds); 2) loan provision that is dependent on short-term funding (e.g., finance companies with short-term funding structure or that take deposits); 3) intermediation of market activities that is dependent on short-term funding or on secured funding of client assets (e.g., securities brokers whose funding is heavily dependent on wholesale funding); 4) facilitation of credit creation (e.g., credit insurers, financial guarantee insurers); and 5) securitisation and funding of financial entities (e.g., securitisation vehicles).

(ii) Authorities should adopt overarching principles and apply policy tools from a policy toolkit for each economic function as they think best fits the non-bank financial entities concerned, the structure of the markets in which they operate, and the degree of risk posed by such entities in their jurisdictions, following certain overarching principles.

(iii) Authorities will share information via FSB, in order to maintain consistency across jurisdictions in applying the policy framework, and also to minimise "gaps" in regulation or new regulatory arbitrage opportunities.

Securitisation

Again IOSCO was approached by FSB to examine further policy areas. IOSCO proposed three possible policy actions to align the incentives associated with securitisation, and to support confidence in sustainable securitisation markets while avoiding impediments to cross-border activity in those markets: (i) enhance monitoring of the implementation of retention requirements and its impact on the market (especially differences across jurisdictions in the approaches taken to adopt retention requirements such as the forms of retention and exemptions); (ii) improve disclosures by issuers for example on stress testing or scenario analysis undertaken on underlying assets; and (iii) encourage standardisation of securitisation products through, e.g., development of standard detailed disclosure templates on the basis of existing initiatives such as those developed by the industry. IOSCO has published its final report with policy recommendations on 16 November 2012. These recommendations cover a roadmap toward convergence and implementation of risk retention requirements, work to build on recent developments in terms of standardised templates for asset level disclosure, and other disclosure-related aspects to assist informed investment decisions, as well as further issues for consideration for the sound regulation of sustainable securitisation markets (IOSCO 2012b).

Securities lending and repos

Securities lending and repo markets are central to financial intermediaries' abilities to make markets, and facilitate the implementation of various investment, risk management, and collateral management strategies. Repo markets are also core funding markets for some financial institutions and instrumental in monetary refinancing operations in many jurisdictions. However, securities lending and repos are also used to conduct "bank-like" activities, such as creating money-like liabilities, carrying out maturity/liquidity transformation, and obtaining leverage. Therefore a separate work stream was set up to assess financial stability risks and develop policy recommendations, where necessary, to strengthen regulation of securities lending and repos. Now 13 policy recommendations have been developed and presented in a separate report (FSB 2012c).The recommendations comprise improvements in regulatory reporting, market transparency, corporate disclosures and reporting by fund managers to end-investors; further the introduction of minimum standards for haircut practices, limitation of risks associated with cash collateral reinvestment, addressing risks associated with re-hypothecation of client assets, strengthening collateral valuation and management practices, evaluating the establishment or wider-use of central clearing where appropriate, and changing bankruptcy law treatment of repo and securities lending transactions.

In advancing these proposals, FSB is aware that shadow banking activities have taken a variety of forms, responding to changing market and regulatory conditions, and they will continue to evolve. Looking ahead, FSB recommends authorities to be mindful that, by strengthening the capital and liquidity requirements applying to banks (an essential pillar of the G20's financial reform programme), the Basel III framework may increase the incentives for some bank-like activities to migrate to the non-bank financial space. Other forms of regulatory reform may have similar effects. The FSB therefore believes that oversight and regulation for shadow banking must incorporate a system of "embedded vigilance" through on-going review and be capable of evolving in response to market changes (FSB 2012a).

6. CONCLUDING REMARKS

In autumn 2013 we will know more details about the planned regulation. However, despite the already very detailed proposals of the FSB there is still no definitive agreement on how to best reach protection against systemic risks and spillovers from the shadow banking system to traditional financial system.

First we have the case that shadow banks are really part of banks: many forms of shadow banking have been or still are sponsored by banks or are operated by them, or both. They are effectively part of their "parent" bank (Tucker 2012a). In the run up to the present crisis, prominent examples were SIVs, ABCP conduits, and MMFs. Many benefitted from financial support from their "parent" during 2007–08. For such situations, Tucker (2012a) draws the conclusion that shadow banking vehicles or funds that are sponsored or operated by banks should be consolidated on to bank balance sheets. Such consolidation might require changes in accounting rules, which itself could take time. These vehicles and funds should nevertheless be treated as consolidated in the application of Basel 3 regulatory capital requirements etc. If necessary, Pillar 2 should be used to achieve that (Tucker 2012a).

Turner (2012) posed the question: Separate or regulate? That is to say, should the regulator just put a cordon sanitaire around traditional banking, or is there a need also to regulate shadow banking itself? Turner seems to tend more to the concept of "cordon sanitaire", following the example of the Volcker Rule in the US and the proposals of the Vickers Commission in the UK. His argument is the "woefully inadequate trading book capital support", now being addressed by Basel 2.5. In addition he would like to see a reduction in vulnerability of bank balance sheets by regulatory separation of investment banking from classic commercial banking activity (Turner 2012).

There are also cases, where a shadow bank is neither legally nor de facto part of a banking group. In many such cases shadow banking entities are fundamentally dependent on banks through committed lines of credit. If liabilities are being called before assets fall due or before they can be sold in an orderly way (maturity mismatch) an institution is exposed to liquidity risk. Of course banks can provide insurance against such liquidity risk because their deposit liabilities are money; they can lend simply by expanding the two sides of their balance sheet simultaneously, creating money. But from a macroprudential perspective, for the system as a whole providing committed lines to shadow banks is riskier than providing such lines to non-bank businesses. Shadow banks are liable to call on their lines just when the banking system is coming under liquidity pressure itself (Tucker 2012a).

It is exactly for those cases that regulation will have to take place. Despite the understandable desire to keep complexity as low as possible regulators will have to find an answer on how to most effectively regulate shadow banks – and at the same time to avoid an uneven playing field vis-à-vis banks. There will be no quick and easy solution, partly due to the lack of available data on shadow banking (FSB 2012a), and partly due to the complexity of the task. Whatever the regulatory answer will be, one thing is for sure: we should beware of additional complexity. Haldane and Madouros (2012) have called for reducing complexity of the financial system and of the regulation itself. We also have to bear in mind that a new mindset in regulation could affect other parts of the financial sector like the insurance industry. In a speech at the Association of British Insurers (ABI) on 13 March 2012 Tucker (2012b) seemed to join the growing number of critics of Solvency II, the new European rules for insurers due to come into effect in 2014. Inter alia he stated: *"We are also concerned that it risks being too complicated. We need to be wary of regulators drowning in masses of data. Unless we are careful, it risks distracting supervisors from the big risks."*

So there is definitely a need to regulate shadow banking in order to minimise systemic risk. But if it holds true that regulation of traditional banking has become far too complex, and if out of that insight regulators avoid complex regulation of shadow banking, then it is only fair to call for a more simple banking regulation.

BIBLIOGRAPHY

Acharya, V. 2011, "Governments as shadow banks: The looming threat to financial stability", paper prepared for the Federal Reserve Board of Governors' conference on "Regulating Systemic Risk" on 15 September, 2011, http://www.federalreserve.gov/events/conferences/2011/rsr/papers/Acharya.pdf, accessed October 2012.

Bakk-Simon, K., S. Borgioli, C. Girón, H. Hempell, A. Maddaloni, F. Recine and S. Rosati 2012, "Shadow Banking in the Euro Area – An Overview", *ECB Occasional Paper Series* No. 133, April.

Borio, C. 2003, "Towards a macroprudential framework for financial supervision and regulation?", *BIS Working Paper*, no. 128, February.

Brewer, E. and J. Jagtiani 2011, "How much did banks pay to become too-big-to-fail and to become systemically important?", *Research Department Working Paper*, Federal Reserve Bank of Philadelphia, pp. 11-37.

Brunnermeier, M. K. 2009, "Financial Crises: Mechanisms, Prevention and Management", in *Macroeconomic Stability and Financial Regulation: Key Issues for the G20*, edited by M. Dewatripont, X. Freixas and R. Portes, CEPR, London, p. 91-103.

Caruana, J. 2010, "Systemic risk: how to deal with it?", speech, BIS publications, http:// www.bis.org/publ/othp08.htm, accessed October 2012.

Deloitte Center for Financial Services 2012, "The Deloitte Shadow Banking Index. Shedding light on banking's shadows", http://www.deloitte.com/assets/Dcom-UnitedStates/Local%20Assets/Documents/CFO_Center_FT/US_FSI_The_Deloitte_Shadow_Banking_052912.pdf, accessed September 2012.

Diamond, D.W. 1984, "Financial Intermediation and Delegated Monitoring", *Review of Economic Studies*, 51(3), pp. 393-414.

Diamond, D. W. and P. H. Dybvig 1983, "Bank Runs, Deposit Insurance, and Liquidity", *Journal of Political Economy* 91, pp. 401–19.

ECB 2010, "Analytical models and tools for the identification and assessment of systemic risks", *Financial Stability Review*, June, pp. 138–46.

European Commission 2012, "Green Paper Shadow Banking", COM(2012) 102 final, Brussels, 19.3.2012.

Financial Stability Board 2011, "Shadow Banking: Strengthening Oversight and Regulation. Recommendations of the Financial Stability Board", 27 October 2011, http://www.financialstabilityboard.org/publications/r_111027a.pdf, accessed August 2012.

Financial Stability Board 2012a, "Strengthening Oversight and Regulation of Shadow Banking. An Integrated Overview of Policy Recommendations", Consultative Document, November, http://www.financialstabilityboard.org/publications/r_121118.pdf, accessed November 2012.

Financial Stability Board 2012b, "Strengthening Oversight and Regulation of Shadow Banking. A Policy Framework for Strengthening Oversight and Regulation of Shadow Banking Entities", Consultative Document, November, http://www.financialstabilityboard.org/publications/r_121118a.pdf, accessed November 2012.

Financial Stability Board 2012c, "Strengthening Oversight and Regulation of Shadow Banking. A Policy Framework for Addressing Shadow Banking Risks in Securities Lending and Repos", Consultative Document, November, http://www.financialstabilityboard.org/publications/r_121118b.pdf, accessed November 2012.

Financial Stability Board 2012d, "Global Shadow Banking Monitoring Report 2012", November, http://www.financialstabilityboard.org/publications/r_121118c.pdf, accessed November 2012.

Financial Stability Board 2012e, "Global Shadow Banking Monitoring Report 2012 Exhibits 2-1, 2-2, and 2-3", November, http://www.financialstabilityboard.org/publications/r_121128.pdf, accessed November 2012.

Financial Stability Board 2012f, "Strengthening the Oversight and Regulation of Shadow Banking. Progress Report to G20 Ministers and Governors", 16 April 2012, http://www.financialstabilityboard.org/publications/r_120420c.pdf, accessed October 2012.

FSB-IMF-BIS 2011, "Macroprudential policy tools and frameworks", Progress Report to G20, October.

Group of 20 2010, "The Seoul Summit Document", 12 November 2010, http://www.g20.utoronto.ca/summits/2010seoul.html, accessed September 2012.

Group of 20 2011, "The Cannes Action Plan for Growth and Jobs", 4 November 2011, http://www.g20.org/documents, accessed September 2012.

Haldane, A. and V. Madouros 2012, "The Dog and the Frisbee", paper presented at the Federal Reserve Bank of Kansas City 36th economic policy symposium, Jackson Hole, August.

Hartmann, P. 2011, "Framework, Data and Models for Macropru: A European Perspective", paper presented at the Office of Financial Research and Financial Stability Oversight Council conference, Washington (DC), December.

International Organization of Securities Commissions 2012a, "Policy Recommendations for Money Market Funds. Final Report", October, http://www.iosco.org/library/pubdocs/pdf/IOSCOPD392.pdf, accessed November 2012.

International Organization of Securities Commissions 2012b, "Global Developments in Securitisation Regulation. Final Report", November, http://www.iosco.org/library/pubdocs/pdf/IOSCOPD394.pdf, accessed November 2012.

Jouyet, J.-P. 2012, speech at the European Commission High Level Conference, Brussels, 27 April 2012, http://www.amf-france.org/documents/general/10376_1.pdf, accessed September 2012.

Llewellyn, D. T. 2011, "A Post-Crisis Regulatory Strategy: The Road to 'Basel N' or 'Pillar 4'?"*Austrian National Bank Conference Proceedings*, Annual Economics Conference, 2011, Austrian National Bank, Vienna.

Perotti, E. 2012, "The roots of shadow banking", Vox EU Column 21 June 2012, http://www.voxeu.org/article/roots-shadow-banking, accessed September 2012.

Pozsar, Z. 2008, *The Rise and Fall of the Shadow Banking System*, Moodys's Economy.com, *Regional Financial Review*, July, http://www.economy.com/sbs, accessed September 2012.

Pozsar, Z. 2011, "Can shadow banking be addressed without the balance sheet of the sovereign?", Vox EU Column 16 November 2011, http://www.voxeu.org/article/shadow-banking-what-do, accessed October 2012.

Pozsar, Z., T. Adrian, A. Ashcraft and H. Boesky 2012, "Shadow Banking", *Federal Reserve Bank of New York Staff Report* No. 458, July 2010, revised version February 2012, http://www.ny.frb.org/research/staff_reports/sr458.pdf, accessed October 2012.

Pozsar, Z. and M. Singh 2011, "The Non-Bank-Bank Nexus and the Shadow Banking System", *IMF Working Paper*, December.

Smolders, N. 2012, "Casting more light on shadow banking", *Rabobank Special Report* 2012/04, April, https://www.rabobank.com/en/research/Economic_Research/index.html?prettyu=economics, accessed August 2012.

Tucker, P. 2010, "Shadow banking, financing markets and financial stability", remarks at a Bernie Gerald Cantor (BGC) Partners Seminar, London, 21 January, BIS Review 6/2010, pp. 1-8.

Tucker, P. 2012a, "Shadow banking – thoughts for a possible policy agenda", speech at the European Commission High Level Conference, Brussels, 27 April 2012, http://

www.bankofengland.co.uk/publications/speeches, accessed October 2012.

Tucker, P. 2012b, Speech to Association of British Insurers (ABI), 13 March 2012, http://
www.telegraph.co.uk/finance/newsbysector/banksandfinance/insurance/9141690/
Insurers-face-curbs-on-shadow-banking-risk.html, accessed September 2012.

Turner, A. 2012, "Shadow Banking and Financial Instability", Cass Lecture 2012,
March, http://www.fsa.gov.uk/static/pubs/speeches/0314-at.pdf, accessed October
2012.

18. Enhancing Financial Stability – A Global Bank's Perspective

Ulrich Körner

The financial crisis has laid bare the risks emerging from adverse economic and regulatory incentives, including the fuelling of a housing bubble by loose monetary policy as well as ineffective controls for the related risks at large and small financial institutions. Sensible re-regulation is thus needed, and the financial industry is committed to play its part in this process.

Ultimately, the authorities and the industry share the same goal: to enhance the stability and resilience of the financial system and its institutions. Only a sound and stable financial system can fulfil the economic functions it is designed for, generate sustained profits for market participants and improve overall social welfare.

This chapter provides a practitioner's perspective on how the global mandate for financial regulatory reform is being put into practice. In doing so, it will focus on *three main theses*:

First, *financial services regulation is increasingly determined by national priorities*. The post-crisis push for a global level playing field is fading.

Secondly, *an increasingly complex and uneven regulatory framework is putting at risk the global cross-border banking model* and the substantial benefits that come with it.

Thirdly, *there are ways to mitigate related risks*, at least in part by means of enhanced cooperation between the private and public sectors as well as by improved coordination within the regulatory community.

Section 1 will give an overview of key elements of the regulatory reform agenda, followed in section 2 by an analysis of the benefits of cross-border banking.

Section 3 deals with the tensions that exist between global rules and national implementation, followed in section 4 by an analysis of the consequences that an unlevel playing field in this area would have for a globally operating bank.

The chapter concludes in section 5 with suggestions on how to address these inherent challenges and to improve financial stability.

1. REGULATORY REFORM FOLLOWING THE FINANCIAL CRISIS

The financial crisis that started in late 2007 – and that in a different form continues today – has exposed the inherent fragility of the financial system as well as the inadequacies of the global regulatory framework then in place. While it is up to banks to do their homework by strengthening their control and risk management frameworks, the reform of the regulatory system is a necessity in order to return to a more stable financial system and, crucially, to rebuild trust in the proper working of the financial system itself. This is a task for both regulators and the financial industry.

Getting the incentives in this new framework right is a complex undertaking and it will take an iterative process in order to eventually reach an acceptable and robust outcome. A compromise has to be found between banks' incentives to take on financial risks – a necessary characteristic of banking activities in the first place – and their ability to do so.

The original starting point for the re-regulation push has been promising, deriving from determined and bold decisions that were made at the G20 level at the height of the financial crisis during 2008 and 2009. The G20 mandate represents the global consensus on the need for regulatory reform (G20 2009a, 2009b). The financial industry supports the G20 process and the commitment to working out a comprehensive, internationally consistent framework defined therein. At the same time, banks are determined to fulfil their commitments towards their clients, shareholders, employees and the communities they are active in.

BOX 18.1 Important international regulatory initiatives

The push to overhaul the regulatory framework for the financial sector has spawned a whole set of initiatives that authorities have launched internationally in order to address perceived weaknesses – and to implement the G20 agenda into national and regional legislation. The following overview provides a brief illustration of the most important initiatives, in order to illustrate the scope of the overall ambition.[1]

Basel 3

The Basel 3 framework forms the centrepiece of the new regulatory framework. Agreed by the Basel Committee on Banking Supervision (BCBS), it

---

[1] This overview is not meant to be complete, but rather aims to illustrate the general thrust of the most important individual initiatives. Many reform projects, often more granular, are not included here, but nevertheless form an important part in the overall regulatory environment (e.g., Volcker rule, regulation of credit rating agencies, regulation of the shadow banking system, etc.).

introduces new – and substantially more onerous – minimum capital and liquidity requirements for all banks (BIS, June 2011). In particular, Basel 3 aims to improve the quality as well as the quantity of capital by requiring banks to hold 7.0% of risk-weighted assets (RWA) in the form of common equity tier 1 (CET1; including a 2.5% capital conservation buffer) and another 3.5% in the form of additional tier 1 or tier 2 capital. On top of this, a counter-cyclical capital buffer can be applied by regulators during periods of excessive credit growth in order to temporarily improve banks' loss-absorbing capacities, adding up to 2.5% of CET1. Next to increasing capital ratio requirements and to restricting the eligibility of capital instruments, a number of changes are also envisaged for the calculation of risk-weighted assets (e.g., changes to credit valuation adjustments, counterparty credit risk using stressed inputs, etc.). In addition to such risk-based requirements, Basel 3 introduces a mandatory leverage ratio of 3%.

In terms of liquidity requirements, the framework introduces two new quantitative measures. The Liquidity Coverage Ratio (LCR) aims to bolster banks' resilience in a crisis situation, mandating them to ensure the availability of sufficient liquid funds such as to survive a 30-day stress period. The Net Stable Funding Ratio (NSFR) aims to structurally reduce the portion of short-term funding in banks' liability structures by requiring a higher proportion of longer-dated liabilities.

Frameworks for G-SIFIs
Basel 3 formulates requirements for all banks subject to the BCBS's remit. In view of large banks' importance for the global financial system, the G20 mandate had explicitly called for global systemically important financial institutions (G-SIFIs) to be subjected to even more onerous requirements given the potentially large impact of a G-SIFI failure on overall financial stability. By means of an indicator-based approach determining relative systemic importance, banks deemed systemically relevant will have to hold additional CET1 of between 1.0% and 2.5% of RWA (BIS November 2011; FSB November 2011).

Cross-border resolution regimes and recovery and resolution planning
The FSB – mandated by the G20 – established further policy measures to deal with the too-big-to-fail issue. Specifically, the FSB published a new international standard in relation to effective national resolution regimes and recovery and resolution planning. The global standard sets out the responsibilities, instruments and powers that national resolution regimes should have to resolve a failing SIFI; it also sets out requirements for resolvability assessments and recovery and resolution planning for global SIFIs (G-SIFIs), as well as for the development of institution-specific cooperation agreements between home and host authorities.

Following on the G20 mandate and the FSB recommendations, all major financial market jurisdictions are currently putting conceptual frameworks for recovery and resolution frameworks into practice. Recovery plans are meant to *ex ante* define a menu of options available for a SIFI to deploy in times of stress, that is, to recover from or avoid liquidity or capital difficulties. Such options could include, for example, asset sales, cutting dividends, etc. Resolution plans, in contrast, are meant to provide the resolution authority with a considerable amount of the necessary information needed to resolve a failing bank in an orderly manner.

Reform of the over-the-counter (OTC) derivatives markets
Another cornerstone of the G20 reform agenda is central clearing and increased transparency of the OTC derivatives market, which had been largely excluded or exempted from regulation prior to the 2008 financial crisis. OTC derivatives, or swaps, had been arranged on a bilateral basis and were not reported to regulators. The size of this unregulated market came to light during the financial crisis and regulators were surprised by the substantial positions in swaps held by AIG, Lehman Brothers, and Bear Stearns, among others. The notional size of this market had been quoted as greater than 600tn USD and regulators credit its lack of regulation and transparency as exacerbating the financial crisis. Primary among the reforms to this market is the mandate that all standard OTC contracts be cleared centrally by central counterparties (CCPs) – and all swaps transactions (whether cleared or uncleared) be recorded in so-called trade repositories. Non-standard derivatives will be subjected to higher margin requirements (see also the case study in section 3).

It is clear from the above that the regulatory environment for banks is undergoing a fundamental overhaul, as new rules are defined in rapid succession and a raft of new regulatory bodies are established. The immediate consequence for the banking industry has been a rash of uncertainty, which, even if it has subsided somewhat by the time of writing, still continues to date. The prospect of an unprecedented administrative and logistical challenge, coupled with an explosion of operational costs, is causing concerns among banks' stakeholders, including shareholders that are implicitly expected to provide large amounts of capital and / or tolerate the dilution of their existing holdings.

At the same time, fundamental changes always hold opportunities as they force us to re-think the way our business is conducted. Remaking a bank's operating model offers the chance to put a potentially more efficient and more resilient one in place, and to ensure that the new setup is geared even more towards putting the essential focus on clients.

2. THE BENEFITS OF CROSS-BORDER BANKING

2.1. Corporate Globalisation defines Corporate Banking

International trade has proven to be one of the fundamental engines of economic growth over the last decades. Cross-border banking chiefly exists to service the international needs of a bank's client franchise – be it corporate, institutional or individual. To that extent, cross-border banking facilitates the international movement of goods, services and capital and helps reducing the risk related to the default of international counterparties. It makes sure that payments are made in the desired currency and helps hedge risks related to changes in commodity prices, interest rates and other variables. Purely domestic institutions will have little insight into mid-sized corporations in other countries, while those with funding in only one currency will be poorly positioned to provide reliable financing to globally active companies.

The story, however, does not end here. Fundamentally, supply chains and individual companies now operate internationally. They need to finance new subsidiaries, provide funds in flexible ways from one operation to another, and pay staff in different places. Retail deposits are domestic, but corporate cash may need to be fungible into different term structures and currencies. Crucially, such financing flows will not always be one-way only. As the last few years have shown, surpluses and deficits of countries, and therefore the companies that operate within them, can reverse. A domestically focused financial sector neither has the capacity nor the capability to provide the necessary flexibility to support internationally operating multinational companies in a dynamic and fast-changing external environment.

2.2. Global Asset Management needs Global Banks

Next to such corporate banking services, cross-border investment banking as well as asset and investment management capabilities primarily serve to match global sources of savings with investment needs and opportunities. Their international dimension directly reflects the desire of investors to diversify risk by country, instrument and currency: institutional money must seek the best balance between risk and return for its providers. A large, sophisticated long-term investor, especially if situated in the countries which are the growth engines of the global economy, cannot be well served by a narrow range of purely domestic investments. Indeed, history has proven that the greatest risk may be in holding only domestic-currency investments.

How should this money be intermediated into suitable investments in non-local assets and currencies? Clearly, the capital markets are important, but depending on securities markets alone introduces expensive constraints. By way of example, consider infrastructure projects in Central and Eastern Europe. These countries have relatively under-developed savings markets, with short-term bank deposits in local currency being the dominant form of savings, along with cash held outside the banking system. With convergence to Western European economies the key policy goal of the authorities in both East and West, it can be argued that it makes no sense to constrain infrastructure finance to what can be financed today by short-term local currency deposits. International capital markets could enhance economic growth by providing access to euro or dollar funding available for greater durations, eliminating dependency on the limited savings pool available from the domestic market. Indeed, the authorities recognised this problem with the creation of the European Bank for Reconstruction and Development (EBRD) almost twenty years ago. The EBRD provides non-local currency financing, equity, long-term bonds and loans and, crucially, co-invests with the private sector in order to make best use of its (constrained) official resources. Global banks partner with official institutions to make change and growth possible.

2.3. A Well-Managed, Interconnected Financial System is a Stabilising Factor

While the recent crisis exposed the interconnected character of global banks' operations, as shocks were rapidly transmitted, the case for an internationally interconnected financial system of global reach is still immensely strong. This point needs to be intensely reinforced as the risks of interconnectedness are often cited to justify measures curtailing the global character of certain business segments and to ring-fence national financial systems. The benefits, however, are rarely mentioned, either because they are taken for granted or because they are not sufficiently transparent.

Empirical evidence shows that cross-border banking is beneficial for the stability of the financial system for a number of reasons:

- It generates diversification benefits and allows for international risk-sharing (Schoenmaker and Wagner 2011).
- Due to their global footprint, international banks – on a group level – have a more diversified risk exposure than purely domestically focused credit institutions. This reduces the likelihood that they will abruptly cut back domestic lending due to deteriorating conditions. As such, assets of cross-border banks are less exposed to country- or region-specific adverse shocks (Allen et al. 2011).
- In turn, local branches of foreign banks, backed by their parent institutions, can substitute for ailing domestic banks in the lending market, thereby helping to smooth economic fluctuations.
- Opening markets up to international competition that were previously highly concentrated or closed to foreign financial institutions helps to bring

about increases in overall efficiency, lower lending rates and an expansion of the product offering.

● Finally, the penetration of hitherto closed markets by cross-border banks carries positive spill over effects in that financial innovation and advanced risk management technologies are introduced to new markets.

Unlike domestic finance, where knowledge of local credit conditions can create opportunities for small and medium-sized banks, cross-border finance is the domain of larger institutions. In some markets, such as foreign exchange or commodities, that is because these markets are deep, liquid and largely homogeneous. Transaction costs are low and accordingly only institutions with sufficiently large economies of scale can operate profitably. In other areas of cross-border finance, such as global equities, credit or government bonds (and their derivatives), high fixed costs in trading, research and, more recently, capital charges, also restrict most activities to large institutions with sufficient operational scale.

In a nutshell, the coincidence of global markets for goods and services based on the provision of cross-border finance and the fact that global finance needs large cross-border banks creates the *necessity for an effective international regulatory framework*. While cross-border banking may carry some risks that need to be managed in an effective way, the benefits of a globally integrated financial system clearly outweigh the related risks (Schoenmaker and Wagner 2011).

Regulation today risks driving in the opposite direction. While recognising that the excesses of the early 2000s drove many poor investment and lending decisions by overleveraged banks across national borders, it is erroneous to conclude that the principle of intermediating savings between countries is flawed. Banks have reduced leverage dramatically since 2007 and the significant reputational damage from losses made in the past is proving a powerful constraint on making similar mistakes again in the future.

3. TENSIONS BETWEEN GLOBAL RULES AND NATIONAL IMPLEMENTATION: AN UNEVEN PLAYING FIELD

3.1. General Remarks

Despite the existence of a common global regulatory reform agenda, substantial differences have emerged in their translation to national rules and legislation. A very important example is the implementation of regulatory requirements specifically for the largest global banks. Despite a supposedly globally agreed set of requirements, *some countries* are *significantly ahead of others* in terms of spelling out the requirements for large banks. In Switzerland, the

"TBTF commission of experts" recommended to concentrate the regulatory response on materially higher capital requirements as well as the implementation of a specific framework for emergency measures to be enacted in case of a crisis and aimed at facilitating an orderly resolution of a large bank[2] (see also the case study in section 3.2. below). In the UK, the Independent Commission on Banking (ICB) proposed a different approach to protect the critical operations, focusing on a strict, organisational "ring-fence" for retail activities as well as differentiated, higher capital requirements for this part of banks' activities to shield critical businesses from the consequences of insolvency (Independent Commission on Banking 2011). In light of the fierce competition among the largest international banks, such different approaches will have consequences on how the portfolio of global activities will be conducted.

But it doesn't only relate to differences in requirements for large banks. The *implementation of Basel 3*, the centrepiece of re-regulation efforts, is *subject to significant differences* in the way it is being transcribed into concrete national legislation. While there are very large gaps in the respective timelines and thus different levels of clarity on the different regimes that banks will eventually have to comply with, some areas of concrete divergence are already emerging, such as those related to the definition of capital under the revised Capital Requirements Directive (CRD 4) in the EU.

An important part of the G20 mandate, which is looked after by the FSB, is thus a *comprehensive international (peer) review process* that, by means of detailed implementation reviews as well as regional and thematic peer reviews, aims to ensure that divergences are being kept to a minimum. As the first reviews have clearly demonstrated, *neither speed nor content of implementation efforts are close to international alignment.*

From the perspective of a global bank it is of the essence that these efforts are successful in establishing a global level playing field. The *risk* is that the international regulatory framework could morph into a *patchwork of national initiatives, rendering global cross-border banking unviable* due to operational constraints *or uneconomical* due to a surge in costs. Demands by regulators to comply with capital and liquidity requirements on a solo basis at the subsidiary level are increasing and are further illustrating this dangerous trend.

The stability of the financial system would be negatively affected as incentives for market participants are skewed towards seeking to exploit regulatory gaps and regulatory arbitrage. This would undermine the ambition of a global level playing field and violate the original mandate set by the G20. Furthermore, it probably does little to prepare us for the next crisis, as there seems to be an emerging consensus also in the regulatory community that the next crisis will most likely not exhibit the same features or be caused by the same factors as the last one (Oliver Wyman 2011).

---

[2] "Too big to fail" commission of experts in Switzerland, "Final Report"; September 2010.

A certain degree of divergence from international compromise provisions has to be acceptable. The characteristics of financial systems and legal frameworks differ by country and their banks have not necessarily been prone to the same weaknesses, justifying differences in emphasis. This means that, in any case, global finance faces a vast net of differing local regulations. What should be prevented in my view is that the fragmentation of the regulatory framework brings about a fragmentation of the global banking model, which could become unviable in the current reform drive.

3.2. Case Studies – International Consensus Framework vs. National Implementation

3.2.1. Recovery and resolution planning

During the financial crisis of 2008 it became clear that banking systems were not equipped to handle the failure of large, systemically important financial institutions. Next to forcing banks to hold more capital to increase their capacity to absorb losses and thereby to reduce the likelihood of a failure in the first place, another key component in developing a credible answer to the too-big-to-fail problem includes bolstering governments' ability to actually allow complex banks to fail. Authorities need to be prepared to intervene and resolve a large, complex bank in a timely and orderly fashion, should initial rescue measures enacted by the firm itself have failed. To that end, policy measures are being established, requiring banks to maintain plans for their own recovery, restructuring and resolution.

Policy-makers and regulators strongly support the concept of recovery and resolution plans, and have been advocating its implementation. The US, the UK and Switzerland, following recommendations set out internationally by the FSB, have been among the first countries to ask systemically important financial institutions to develop recovery and resolution plans, while the EU is also developing its own regime.

However, the effectiveness of such a far-reaching concept beyond the general framework set forth in the regulatory community is broadly untested and heavily dependent on a number of aspects that in themselves are very much problematic, in particular where they relate to cross-border insolvency cases.

Effective resolution of an internationally active, systemically important financial institution needs to be specifically based on a robust coordination mechanism, enabling a rapid and effective resolution process. Work to date by banks on their RRP capabilities has demonstrated that the single most important condition for a SIFI's effective resolution will be that the various national regulators involved in a given situation act collectively in a coordinated and predictable way.

While there is an international consensus that institution-specific agreements among a SIFI's different regulators need to be achieved, there remains a *fun-*

damental open issue: harmonisation of national laws and creation of an agreed toolkit of measures do not fully address the relevant issues at stake in a complex resolution case, which asks for clear, well-established and permanent solutions. Policy responses that envisage radical measures such as limiting size, mandatory breaking up of financial institutions, or national ring-fencing are disproportionate and destroy economic value. Not only do these types of measures give rise to potentially very large unintended consequences, but they would also inevitably curb the freedom of banks to determine their own business model.

It is essential that resolution authorities act to increase the levels of certainty as to the potential outcome of a bank's resolution. Governments and resolution authorities are inherently national and therefore no single resolution authority will have the comprehensive legal authority needed to resolve a financial institution with cross-border activities. In particular, *international standards* should be established *for dealing with critical issues* such as the suspension of cross-default provisions in contracts with group members, including unregulated entities in third-country jurisdictions. In the absence of such a regime and its enforceability in relevant jurisdictions, whole-bank resolutions – or bail-ins that may often be the best vehicles to achieve the overall FSB resolution goals – may not be possible for certain types of systemically important banks.

In our discussions with supervisory authorities in many jurisdictions we feel that while a common understanding and willingness to rely on a globally agreed set of common principles is clearly present, compliance with these and their incorporation in drafting concrete rules and regulations is still a distant goal. By having started to set out their own rules, national authorities risk contributing to a *fragmented regulatory environment*, which would ultimately be detrimental to financial stability and economic growth.

3.2.2. Financial market infrastructure and OTC derivatives regulation
G20 countries agreed in 2009 that all standardised OTC derivatives contracts be traded on exchanges or via electronic trading platforms, where appropriate, and cleared through CCPs by the end of 2012 at the latest. Non-centrally cleared derivatives were to be subjected to higher capital requirements. While implementation is still in a somewhat fluid state, as rule-making efforts are moving ahead only slowly, progress to date on harmonisation between the EU and the US is not encouraging, as regulators on both sides struggle to avoid divergence of requirements despite public commitments to convergence and mutual recognition from policy-makers and regulators (see also Barnier 2011).

Implementation progress

The varying pace of implementation is the first worrying area of divergence. US rules will apply before their European equivalents, giving rise to regulatory arbitrage at least in the short term. In the US, the Dodd-Frank Wall Street

Reform and Consumer Protection Act (DFA), covering the execution, clearing and reporting of derivative contracts, was signed into law in July 2010 and the rule-making phase is now already at an advanced stage. In the EU, the OTC derivatives market regulation is being shaped by European Market Infrastructure Regulation (EMIR), the review of MiFID and CRD 4. It is now clear that EMIR, which mandates the clearing of OTC derivative contracts by CCPs and reporting of all derivative contracts to trade repositories, will not meet the G20 timeline. The earliest clearing mandate is expected to take effect around end-2013 with a likely phase-in by types of counterparties and products. The draft MiFID package, covering inter alia the mandatory trading and clearing of eligible and sufficiently liquid OTC derivatives on venue, is still in the middle of the EU legislative process. The pace of implementation in the US compared to the EU could be reversed in the case of Basel 3 / CRD 4. For example, if the counterparty credit risk provisions of Basel 3 are implemented in their current guise in the EU, US market participants could have a significant cost advantage over EU counterparts as they would not have to hold as much capital to support the clearing business since the US may be delayed with Basel 3 rules.

Treatment of FX instruments

A second area of divergence potentially relates to the treatment of foreign exchange (FX) instruments. While US authorities have exempted FX swaps and forwards from certain clearing and trading requirements and won't require these instruments to be collateralised, EMIR does not contain an explicit exemption of FX products from the clearing mandate yet. This could be a costly difference if realised. More broadly, regulators have been working on a global solution to align the margin requirements for uncleared swaps. In the meantime, US regulators have already displayed a strict stance on this issue with only a narrow range of eligible collateral and quantitative requirements for calculating initial margin. If the European Securities and Markets Authority (ESMA) doesn't follow a similar strict approach, disputes will arise here as well.

To ensure the safety of the clearing house, both DFA and EMIR propose segregation models of customer collateral for cleared trades. The US "Legally Segregated Operationally Commingled" model appears, however, to offer more protection than envisaged under the EMIR "omnibus" solution. Such differences in customer asset protection are likely to push clients to clear eligible OTC derivatives in the US.

Duplication of requirements

There is currently a lack of clarity around the mechanics for ensuring that firms are not subject to conflicting or duplicative regulations. Duplicative clearing requirements will be costly for cross-border business if, for example, the CFTC mandates that the UK branch of a US SIFI clears the trade on a US CCP when it might also be mandated to clear on a UK CCP as the transaction is between two London domiciled counterparties. While EMIR includes provisions to avoid duplicative or conflicting rules as well as recognise third country CCPs and Trade Repositories, they centre on the currently elusive concept of equivalence. How this equivalence concept will be implemented in practice remains very unclear. Global banks are also currently uncertain as to whether the intra-group OTC derivative transactions between their EU and non-EU entities will be exempted from the clearing obligation, which is contingent on the equivalence determination.

The above examples are only few selected pieces from a wider array of worrying inconsistencies arising and areas of uncertainty persisting in the technical implementation of the US and EU rules. They are likely to distort competition as market participants choose counterparties based on regulatory rather than economic factors. More fragmented markets eventually make regulatory oversight more challenging, thereby putting in peril the original G20 objectives to allay systemic risk and boost transparency in OTC derivatives markets.

4. CONSEQUENCES OF THE UNEVEN FRAMEWORK

4.1. General Remarks

The clash between authorities' desire for full control of entities incorporated or resident in their home jurisdiction with globally organised corporate structures that are not necessarily aligned along national borders is prevalent in a number of regulatory areas.

As a consequence, *a more fragmented approach will require banks to adjust their operational model to become more "multi-local" than truly global.* While this would be done under the cover of improving financial stability, as outlined in section 2, it would have direct economic consequences. On a very general level, it is *set to sharply increase inefficiencies*, which in turn are likely to drive up the cost of financial services and could potentially also restrict the availability of credit.

Most global banks are organised in a centralised way in order to exploit economies of scale and scope in steering their global business activities. This is primarily true for internal processes such as treasury / funding or control functions (e.g., risk management), for which it is vital that they can be managed across regions and business divisions from a group perspective.

A fragmented "multi-local" setup entails a significant increase in administrative costs as local subsidiary entities of global groups would have to operate their own, stand-alone funding and / or risk management functions, including the related compliance and validation teams. As a consequence, the cost of doing business in other jurisdictions increases materially. The situation is compounded by the duplication of other regulatory requirements, caused, for example, by conflicting national recovery and resolution planning requirements, ring-fencing provisions, or other far-reaching organisational / structural requirements that have a bearing on the entire organisation.

The main consequence of this approach is a sharp increase in operating costs, which to some degree will have to be passed on to end users in order for banks to remain profitable, making the provision of financial services *across the board* more costly, thereby reducing welfare. But it is not only the immediate financial costs that need to be taken into account here. There are also a number of *macroeconomic or systemic aspects* that have to be included in a cost-benefit analysis and that regulators should consider before moving ahead with current provisions.

First, a greater focus on the regionalisation of rules will ultimately lead to a greater level of domestic market concentration: banks operating on a cross-border basis have a lesser incentive to compete in markets abroad. As a consequence, larger domestic banks would gain, likely at the expense of smaller players and thus counteracting the initial aim of reducing the influence of larger institutions.

Secondly, and related to this point, is the observation that the development of a whole new suite of regulatory rules and procedures increases banks' fixed operating cost base, as control functions have to be built out disproportionately. This raises barriers to entry and inadvertently protects incumbent firms and materially favours large over smaller banks, equally contradicting the stated aim of tackling the too-big-to-fail problem.

Thirdly, such higher cost pressure on the banking system has a direct impact on the incentives to shift certain financial services to the unregulated part of the financial industry. A growing unregulated, non-traditional financial services sector is in itself detrimental to financial stability. While the regulatory community aims to take a deep look at these so-called "shadow banking" institutions, too, it remains somewhat uncertain as to where these efforts eventually will lead.

Moreover, some indications point to a heavy reliance on an "indirect" approach to shadow bank regulation, that is, by means of regulating banks' exposures to shadow entities. Arguably, if not well conceived, these regulatory endeavours might even intensify the incentives for certain activities to migrate to the unregulated sphere. Finally, and from a purely macroeconomic perspective, local savings will have to suffice to a much larger extent for local investment purposes than before, as savings in advanced economies will no longer be available to the same degree to extend credit in emerging markets.

Generally speaking, the desire by national authorities to make locally incorporated entities individually safer might ultimately lead to a less optimal outcome from a systemic, macroprudential perspective.

4.2. Case Study: Extraterritoriality and Third-Country Access – Benefits and Pitfalls of Current Approaches and Potential Alternatives

International financial centres are increasingly being challenged as regulators attempt to extend their reach more and more into other jurisdictions. There are many reasons why legislators would adopt rules with extraterritorial effect:

- The extraterritorial reach of certain rules is an immediate consequence of a seeming determination of regulators and policy-makers to primarily look after their national constituency – and only then consider any potential implications this might have for third-country firms.
- Market access rules for third-country firms are often used to protect domestic businesses – even if this tends to enhance the fragmentation of markets, protectionism, and regulatory arbitrage.
- Finally, there is a lack of confidence by legislators and supervisors in the effectiveness of rules in other jurisdictions. Therefore, in the name of investor protection, legislators set up barriers for market access requiring equivalence of legislation and supervision or adopt rules with extraterritorial effect for the prevention of systemic risks.

In any event, *extraterritoriality and extensive market access rules* for third country firms *are creating more and more unnecessary complexity and barriers for the global financial business*, not only for service providers but also for consumers and investors.

For global financial services providers the extraterritorial application of legal provisions brings a set of complexities and additional costs. Without material coordination between the rules of the different jurisdictions, firms may be confronted with duplicative, inconsistent or even contradicting legal obligations. This means that they need to comply with two or more sets of rules. This increases complexity and costs without any meaningful benefit for the service provider, consumers or investors. In certain cases, it is even impossible to obey all applicable rules due to their incompatibility and due to a lack of international coordination. Finally, a company may end up being prevented from doing business in some jurisdictions. This may result in severe disadvantages also for the domestic industry, investors and consumers as they may be isolated from global capital flows. Furthermore, if foreign companies avoid a jurisdiction, the diversity of the financial service portfolio available will be substantially smaller. This may also result in a substantial bulk risk for domestic investors and financial service providers due to a lack of international diversification.

As the extraterritoriality of legislation depends on the factual ability of the legislature in question to impose its authority, it is usually either the US or the EU legislation that seeks to apply their legislation with extraterritorial effect. The pure scale and factual power of these jurisdictions gives them the possibility to act this way. While some of the US legislation tends to be applicable directly within other jurisdictions (e.g., Dodd Frank and FATCA, which is explicitly designed for financial institutions abroad), EU legislation mainly concentrates on third-country rules for market access (e.g., MiFID II; AIFMD; EMIR).

The EU's approach of handling market access of third-country companies – the so-called *equivalence approach* – was only recently confirmed by the Commission with its proposals for the MiFID review. Furthermore the Commission proposed on that instance that cross-border services needed to be performed through an EU-located branch. Compared to other EU legislation, the scope of the Commission's proposed MiFID II is substantial, covering market infrastructure, operation, governance, and investor protection. This broad scope will make it difficult for third countries to achieve equivalence without a substantial rewrite of domestic law. If the EU would require strict equivalence with the relevant EU legislation (i.e. the third-country legislation would be required to replicate EU legislation word by word) together with the branch requirement, it would basically result in a complete market foreclosure as third countries will hardly be able or even willing to establish such strict equivalence. Furthermore, the EU regulator will not be able to perform the equivalence test within a reasonable timeframe. However, this effect would be less severe if it would be sufficient for the third country to have rules with similar effect compared to the European regulatory framework. However, as part of the rationale behind the proposed rules seems to be protectionism, it is questionable whether a reasonable approach with regard to third country access within the EU may be established.

With regard to the direct extraterritorial effects of some US legislation, it seems that third-country firms simply need to find a way to live with it unless they want to refrain from doing any business with any link to the US whatsoever. It is, however, virtually impossible for a financial institution to avoid any link that would trigger the application of US law. FATCA stands for a piece of legislation with a very intense extraterritorial effect, as it is basically only applicable to financial institutions abroad. With FATCA, US legislators force even pure domestic companies to participate and implement the rules. Otherwise, such companies risk losing access to other participating financial institutions, as different, more burdensome rules would have to be applied vis-à-vis non-participating financial institutions. Consequently, participating institutions will tend to require their business partners to participate as well because it would be too costly for them otherwise.

The challenges for legislators and regulators will increase further and they will be global in nature. Instead of extending the scope of legislation to foreign jurisdictions, *the more efficient approach would be to coordinate and find rules on an international level*. This would ensure that relevant interests of different countries may be taken into account. However, as consensus on an international level seems to be almost impossible to achieve due to lack of confidence in partner states and due to protectionist behaviour, it is safe to say that in the future we will see more unilateral legislation with extraterritorial effect. It will be a huge challenge for global firms to find efficient ways to comply with such legal frameworks. In more and more cases the answer to such legislation will be to give up the affected cross-border business.

5. THE WAY FORWARD – HOW TO ENHANCE FINANCIAL STABILITY?

The case for a re-regulation of the financial sector following on the experiences of the financial crisis of 2008 is strong. But so are the arguments for the maintenance of a global, cross-border banking model. In putting the G20 mandate for financial reform into practice, national authorities will have to find a compromise that takes national specificities and political pressures into account as well as global banks' need for an internationally consistent framework. Three topics in particular might be helpful in shaping the thought process on approaching such compromise.

5.1. Global Rules for Global Finance

The ultimate aim of the push for re-regulation should be to develop "global rules for global finance". Temptations for national solo attempts must be clearly restricted. Current efforts in particular by the FSB to carry out regular peer reviews on the implementation of international rules are therefore welcomed. This process needs to be kept as strict as possible, in order to ensure that it leads to tangible results, for example in the form of rule revisions, should deviations from agreed guidelines be observed.

From a Swiss perspective in particular, these efforts should categorically include an obligation by regulatory authorities of all major financial centres to perform an analysis of "policy spillovers" into other jurisdictions. Third-country issues can unduly cause substantial problems for affected financial institutions, and clear, proportionate equivalence criteria are of utmost importance. The *IMF* is conducting "*spillover analyses*" in order to gauge the transmission channels of financial shocks between different national and regional financial systems. A similar exercise should become a standard part of the regulatory and rule-making processes in order to treat such issues already prior to the actual legislative process.

5.2. Improve Collaboration

A central means to this end has to be a clear reinforcement of the dialogue *within* the regulatory and rule-making community. Developing policy frameworks together in the relevant supranational forums is important; but implementing them in a coordinated fashion is even more important. Clear deference by all relevant authorities to the home regulator would be the best way to ensure consistency in the application of regulatory requirements. At the same time, home authorities need to act responsibly vis-à-vis host authority sensitivities, underlining the need for a robust multilateral dialogue that naturally also involves banking organisations themselves. In light of the paradigmatic change that the financial sector is undergoing, investors and clients are very sensitive to risk factors. This needs to be taken into account in formulating regulatory requirements.

5.3. Balancing Objectives

On a more general note, one should remain conscious of the fact that the regulatory environment in the financial industry is cyclical in nature. Upon each and every financial crisis, the regulatory environment has been tightened in attempts to correct the conditions that had contributed to bringing about the crisis in the first place. While understandable from a political perspective, such an event-driven and essentially backward-looking approach has in the past failed to stem the emergence of new crises. An overly tight regulatory framework has proven conducive to increasing the incentives for regulatory arbitrage.

The case therefore needs to be made for a tempered regulatory response that prevents the policy "pendulum" from swinging too far in the one direction, only to come back and haunt market participants and regulators alike at a later point in time. The case needs to be made for arresting the pendulum at such a level that the amplitude of its swings comes down to something resembling a steady state.

It has to be added here that this would clearly not only cater to the self-interest of the banking industry. The financial sector plays a pivotal role in the economy, supporting growth through the provision of credit and taking on reasonable risks, as well as facilitating the creation and management of wealth. The further it is constrained in its activities, the more likely unintended consequences will become. In view of current trends, certain concessions on behalf of regulators and supervisors will have to be made in order to ensure that "stability" does not become the only policy objective, threatening to suffocate innovation, entrepreneurial spirits, and necessary risk-taking.

The financial industry and regulators should engage in a robust, longer-term dialogue, setting out the conditions that could describe such a balanced scenario. Our times are highly volatile and uncertainty about the future remains exceptionally high, rendering the desire for stability perfectly understandable. But the quest for stability must not become an end in itself that ultimately risks becoming self-defeating.

BIBLIOGRAPHY

Allen, F., T. Beck, E. Carletti, P. R. Lane, D. Schoenmaker and W. Wagner 2011, *Cross-Border Banking in Europe: Implications for Financial Stability and Macroeconomic Policies*, Center for Economic Policy Research, 2011, http://www.cepr.org/pubs/books/cepr/cross-border_banking.pdf.

Bank for International Settlements 2011a, *Basel III: A global regulatory framework for more resilient banks and banking systems – revised version*, June, http://www.bis.org/publ/bcbs189.pdf.

Bank for International Settlements 2011b, *Global systemically important banks: assessment methodology and the additional loss absorbency requirement – final document*, November, http://www.bis.org/publ/bcbs207.htm.

Barnier, M. 2011, speech/11/420, Brookings Institute, Washington, 3 June 2011.

CFTC and SEC 2012, "Joint report on the progress and harmonization of international swap regulation", as required by Section 719(c) of the Dodd-Frank Act, http://www.sec.gov/news/studies/2012/sec-cftc-intlswapreg.pdf.

Financial Stability Board 2011, *Policy Measures to address systemically important financial institutions*, November, http://www.financialstabilityboard.org/publications/r_111104bb.pdf.

G20 2009a, "Declaration on Strengthening the Financial System", statement issued by the G20 leaders in London, 2 April 2009, http://www.g20.utoronto.ca/2009/2009communique0402.pdf.

G20 2009b "Declaration on Strengthening the International Financial Regulatory System", statement issued by the G20 leaders in Pittsburgh, 25 September 2009, http://www.g20.utoronto.ca/2009/2009communique0925.html.

Independent Commission on Banking in the UK 2011, "Final Report", September, http://bankingcommission.independent.gov.uk.

Oliver Wyman 2011, *The Financial Crisis of 2015*, State of the Financial Industries report 2011.

Schoenmaker and Wagner 2011, Cross-Border Banking in Europe and Financial Stability, November 2011, http://ssrn.com/abstract=1790882.

Too big to fail commission of experts in Switzerland 2010, "Final Report", September, http://www.sif.admin.ch/dokumentation/00522/00715/index.html?lang=en.

19. Stable Liquidity and Funding Flows

José Manuel Campa Fernández

When thinking about the issue of global liquidity management within the international monetary and financial systems, I like using the analogy of comparing our economies to plots of land. A plot of land needs the right amount of water to realise its productive potential. Water supply can neither be too scarce nor too abundant. In our economies, if liquidity is scarce, there are negative consequences for output and employment. If there is an abundance of liquidity, inflation distorts the price system, compromising future growth.

A significant amount of pages have been written about the causes of the financial turmoil that we are currently experiencing. It all began with unprecedented distress in money markets in early August 2007, when the Eurosystem reacted by injecting EUR 95 billion into the banking sector in an overnight operation, but, like a virus, it quickly passed on to all funding markets to the point of limiting, to an unsustainable extent, private and public sources of funding for a large part of agents. Financial institutions, and more specifically, although not exclusively, credit entities suffered and continue to suffer from market uncertainty regarding their solvency soundness linked to questions on asset quality and asset valuation. Such doubts have consistently become the cause of liquidity stress as depositors and creditors head for the exit at the same time and, ultimately, solvency difficulties arise. This cycle has taken place in different jurisdictions and with an emphasis on different financial assets or financial institutions but with the same underlying dynamics.

A large number of measures have been needed to address the failures of the system. Central banks have deployed monetary tools which had been the discussion of academic circles and unprecedented in modern history of financial policy. Supervisors and regulators are struggling to develop and implement solutions both to address the current collapse of the system and to avoid future ones. Nevertheless, the dynamics of the markets continue to seem being ahead of public reactions and new leakages keep appearing, while the capacity of the financial system to withstand the precarious conditions of its irrigation system seems exhausting.

In such a context, what are the mechanisms needed to guarantee credit entities liquidity? Will the new Basel III framework procure the adequate amount of water for our banks, as it promises? What other sources of liquidity, other than central banks, should we be thinking about?

This chapter reviews the evolution of liquidity within financial markets, with a strong emphasis on the current difficulties confronted and the challenges to ensure a more robust provision of liquidity in the future. The next section reviews the conditions under which the international monetary and financial system has been operating over the recent past. The following two sections propose two sets of measures. A first set is oriented to repair the functioning of liquidity to what could be considered normal levels, i.e. measures to fix the irrigation system of the global economy in our initial analogy. The third section focuses on a second group of measures oriented to increase the resilience of the system and its actors to withstand future strains. The chapter concludes with some remarks on the evolution of global safety nets for liquidity provision.

1. CREDIT BOOMS, COUNTERPARTY RISK AND ASSET QUALITY CONCERNS

During the last decade, the irrigation system of the global economy has grown in complexity through its four interconnected elements: monetary policies, capital flows, exchange rates, and domestic financial systems. At the same time, there has been a lack of policy coordination at the global level, characterised by a prevalence of un-coordinated policy decisions made at the national level. The experience from the crisis has shown that the international monetary system has, in fact, *three major problems* regarding global liquidity management. *First*, an unbalanced pattern of liquidity creation and distribution that endangers the sustainability of global demand and the incentives for current account adjustment. *Second*, the extremely cyclical behaviour of financing conditions can jeopardise financial and macroeconomic stability in the world economy. *Finally*, the inability of the system to detect and/or address these issues in time to avert a crisis.

Indeed, the beginning of this crisis confirms the "*paradox of financial stability*" (Borio 2009), that is, the financial system looks strongest precisely when it is most vulnerable. When we all believed that financial markets had developed to the point of making the theory of efficient markets a tangible truth; when we struggled to find problems in an environment where credit risks where thought to be under absolute control; and when financial authorities were happy to having found what looked like an adequate regulatory and monetary framework to allow this perfect world to go on, it all unravelled in front of our eyes. To understand this phenomenon, it is worth going through the underlying causes of the credit boom and asset quality deterioration that was experienced prior to the crisis. Credit booms have been a recurrent feature in economic history and they have existed in both developed and under-developed nations. They always tend to occur in a context of low volatility, increasing risk taking and good funding and liquidity conditions. The more profound, complex and inter-connected the financial system is, the more intense the credit cycle can be and its unravelling most disruptive.

The simplest policy implication would be that, in order to ensure financial stability and avoid credit busts, credit booms must be prevented. However, the experience shows that one of the most difficult challenges for policy-makers is to determine the existence of unhealthy credit booms and bubbles during good times and determine the appropriate mechanisms to stop them in due time. In real time, as the boom grows over time there are always good arguments to justify the rationality of the process in place, and the majority of economic agents are favoured by the evolution of events leading them to be reluctant to any changes. Risk tends to be underscored during good times and the assess-ment that excess returns on investment are compensation for risks that have not yet aroused but will materialise is often ignored.

Concerning the link between risk taking and economic performance, the level of risk tolerance depends partly on economic agents' risk aversion and partly on the objective valuation of uncertainty. Assuming that risk aversion does not substantially change over time, most of the fluctuation that underlies a higher risk taking in good times is an undervaluation of risks. This has been accentuated partly by policy and modelling techniques in recent times. Current methods to price risk often entail *pro-cyclical* estimates of probability of de-fault, loss given default, volatility and correlation. Moreover, when examining the viability of a project, users of funds treat the risk as an exogenous variable which depends on the risk of the sector over a period of time, which might not interiorise eventual downturns or shocks. Models to estimate an asset's funda-mentals imply an important dose of subjectivity which is inevitably influenced by the underlying current pulse of markets.

2. MEASURES TOWARDS RESTORING STABLE LIQUIDITY FLOWS

A comprehensive approach to address the stability in financial market liquidity should include: measures that address problems of complexity and uncertainty around financial products, enhancing transparency in financial markets, the role of national central banks, and the evaluation of funding management prac-tices to ensure financial stability.

Liquidity always disappears first in complex customised products. The high level of complexity and opacity of current financial markets can be tackled by a number of policy options both from a preventive and a corrective perspective. From a preventive point of view measures should aim at increasing the level of transparency of financial markets and institutions. In this vein, current proposals to foster financial exchange infrastructures to reduce OTC trading, where appropriate, and increasing transparency requirements for financial agents and financial markets certainly go in the right direction. Enhancing disclosure requirements for institutions, such as banks and their balance sheets, and for some specific instruments, such as structured products, can also reduce uncertainty and limit spillover effects.

On a related matter, an adequate improvement of resolution and supervisory tools, such as those being fostered by the G20 and the FSB (see FSB 2011), to reduce the risks posed by systemically relevant financial institutions and markets should also help stabilise liquidity to the extent that they eliminate the potential system risk from distress arising in individual firms. A better knowledge of the mechanisms that global financial firms have to address financial strains in some parts of their business, as it would be reflected in their recovery and resolution plans currently under discussion for the largest international banks, will certainly prove helpful.

Once initial liquidity concerns arise, there are also measures that policymakers and supervisory authorities can implement to contain contagion. Here a correct assessment of risks and potential losses is essential to deliver proportionate and effective solutions. Bank stress tests have looked in this direction and tougher rules for asset valuation and losses provisions have also helped. If public financial assistance is required (bail-outs, asset purchases, public guarantees, etc.) adequate conditionality tends to help also in reducing uncertainty. Compulsory earning retentions, change of management teams, limits to bonuses and similar measures, allow channelling as many resources as possible to recuperating solvency and liquidity positions and so dispel financial concerns.

Despite all preventive measures, a key player in the solution of a liquidity turmoil must be the national central banks. Liquidity provision has been at the core of the functions of central banks and the current crisis has reaffirmed even further their role in this respect. The unprecedented levels of distress experienced in money markets have made essential that the central bank community provide sufficient liquidity to cover the limitations of other private instruments and markets. Not in vain, central bank balance sheets in major advanced economies have doubled as a percentage of GDP since 2007. Although this role was clearly highlighted at the early stages of the crisis, unconventional measures taken by many central banks have intensified and diversified to address the increasing liquidity strains of money and debt markets.

This ex-post reaction to the crisis is welcome and absolutely necessary. Nevertheless, this extraordinary support introduces a number of *additional vulnerabilities* that need to be addressed. In particular, two risks of a very different nature need to be confronted. In the short term, a "*false comfort*" among deposit institutions with access to central bank facilities can delay the normalisation of money markets. The stigma effect on financial institutions that are persistently relying on liquidity access to their central bank has progressively decreased. It is good that firms are not stigmatised from accessing central bank liquidity in moments of financial stress. Nevertheless it may also create a perception of normality in the function of financial markets when it does not really exist, and it reduces banks' incentives to return to normality and restore interbank operations, helping illiquidity to become a structural problem of the system. This situation is particularly worrying when extraordinary access to liquidity provision to the central banks does not transform into a higher access to financing in the private sector in the form of bank loans or debt securities buying.

A second problem is the potential *moral hazard* arising from the implicit belief by the industry that, in the future, support from central banks is assured in crisis times, especially in case of systemic crises, inducing greater risk-taking. This moral hazard may lead institutions to opt to continue in the future with weak and/or illiquid financial structures. Exactly the same problems arise when alternative measures from the public sector are used to support funding, such as state guarantees to financial debt issuance. While being welcomed and needed as a last resort solution to ensure that institutions which had lost access to distorted funding markets recuperate access to the market, risks of excessive reliance on government guaranteed debt instruments and moral hazard problems threaten public interventions.

Taking these two risks into account, we need to realise that extraordinary non-conventional support measures need to be deployed taking into account a good balance between liquidity support and moral hazard. Such measures should be withdrawn progressively and as soon as possible in order to allow for a quick normalisation of money markets and reduce the moral hazard effect. Otherwise, *prolonged easing responses may generate new financial imbalances*. Once we have avoided the risk of doing too little, too late we should not underestimate that of doing too much, too prolonged. Paradoxically, in this context low inflation and weak (recession-prone) economic conditions can be a hurdle by delaying the need for normalisation of interest rates and other unconventional measures.

Additional measures in this toolbox should aim at promoting changes in liquidity and funding management practices. The industry has responded to the crisis adjusting the funding composition and the way liquidity management is conducted at the group level. Although most banks defended their pre-crisis approach to liquidity management in the initial stages of the crisis, some *new patterns on liquidity management* seem to be emerging (CGFS 2010): i) increased reliance on retail funding as opposed to wholesale funding; ii) increased recourse to capital markets, in volume and frequency, especially for long-term funding; iii) more decentralisation in funding among international banks, increasing local funding; iv) decreased reliance on cross-currency funding in order to avoid cross-currency maturity mismatches; and v) overhaul of internal transfer prices in order to better reflect the cost of liquidity.

Although the global trend in fundraising seems to be heading towards some degree of decentralisation, certain aspects move in the opposite direction. In particular, the industry appears to be responding to the current challenging environment with a higher degree of centralisation in liquidity control (not necessarily fundraising) for the head office to gain more information over existing holdings of liquidity and collateral, as well as to coordinate access to central bank facilities at the group level. Monitoring of liquidity risk and funding conditions is becoming more intense and frequent. Improvements in monitoring have to be one of the most visible outcomes of the crisis also from an industry point of view. Furthermore, some of these policies for centralised liquidity management are encouraged by national supervisors as a form to strengthen the stability of their national financial system. These measures can quickly become beggar-thy-neighbour in their essence and imply and increase fragmentation of global financial markets.

An initial evaluation of these changes in liquidity management leads us to a number of *conclusions*. Increased reliance on retail funding should lead to more competition and, possibly, to an increase in the cost of funding. Increased recourse to the capital markets to the detriment of wholesale funding markets may lead to disintermediation and a slow recovery of interbank markets. Although the latter effect is undesirable, the effect of a certain degree of disintermediation, especially if referred to longer-term capital funding, might be neutral. Some degree of disintermediation in Europe, where recourse to capital markets has a relative lower weight in funding, could even be desirable. The remaining changes (more decentralisation in funding among international banks, decreased reliance on cross-currency funding, overhaul of internal transfer prices, and increased liquidity risk monitoring) are aimed at reducing liquidity risk, and go in the direction marked by the regulatory changes. The final outcome of private and regulatory measures will likely be a *different banking business model*, with a lower position in the risk-return frontier and more resilient banks. In this new environment, access to funding and liquidity could be eased in the medium term.

All these changes are an answer to the increased market pressure on banks, but go in a similar direction to that imposed by regulation. For example, risk management committees have been given higher profiles inside banks and their role has been reinforced by the recommendations of the Financial Stability Board to improve intensity and effectiveness of the supervision of Systemically Important Financial Institutions (SIFIs).

3. MEASURES TO REINFORCE THE SYSTEM IN ORDER TO PREVENT FUTURE CRISES

We have previously discussed the reasons behind the development of credit bubbles and we have also anticipated the difficulties in identifying and preventing them from occurring in the future. Nevertheless, efforts to provide better assessment of future vulnerabilities are an essential part of policy to pursue financial stability. A number of measures have been discussed and are being implemented to improve this area of financial policy in the future. Among others we would highlight supervisory measures to ensure institutions have sufficient buffers and appropriate risk management to weather future turbulence.

3.1. New Capital and Liquidity Buffers

Although the industry has reacted to the crisis environment with its own new patterns for funding and liquidity management, some of the most relevant regulatory initiatives that have been launched in this crisis are those to improve banks' solvency and liquidity. Among these, I would like to highlight the Basel Committee on Banking Supervision (BCBS) proposals to reinforce the Basel Capital Accord (bank solvency requirements) which were backed by the G20 nations in 2010 and is currently in the process of national implementation. This agreement, known as Basel III, enhanced existing solvency provisions by increasing capital requirements and it also introduced new liquidity standards.

Since its inception in 1988, the Basel solvency framework has been based on the establishment of minimum capital requirements for banks to be able to address three types of risk: market risk (potential loss due to adverse market fluctuations), counterparty or credit risk (potential loss due to the borrower's inability to fulfil its commitments), and operational risk (potential loss due to a system or operation failure). Although the capital ratios were not directly designed to contain liquidity risk, the benefits in terms of solvency they produce should have helped to manage liquidity risk in an indirect way.

The Basel III framework aims at improving banks' solvency by three means. Firstly it increases banks' capital quantity and quality by fixing a minimum common equity ratio of at least 4.5% of risk-weighted assets from 2015 onwards, and a minimum Tier 1 capital ratio of at least 6%. Secondly it introduces a countercyclical capital buffer, of an additional 2.5% of capital relative to risk-weighted assets that will be phased-in from 2016 to 2019. And finally it proposes a leverage ratio, currently under Pillar II, to ensure that banks operate with sufficient own funds. All these ratios will allow for an improvement in the soundness of financial institutions. This in turn will make them more robust and credible as counterparties, mitigating their credit risk and thus facilitating their access to interbank liquidity and funding.

But the harshness of the current financial crisis has also evidenced that *liquidity risk* on its own can be a major source of concern for financial institutions and that its mitigation requires specific measures aimed at improving liquidity management and granting that banks dispose of an adequate liquidity cushion. The BCBS liquidity standard for internationally active banks, still in an observation phase, includes two regulatory ratios. A *Liquidity Coverage Ratio* (LCR) that establishes that the ratio of the stock of high-quality liquid assets to cumulative expected net cash outflows over a 30-day stress period must equal or exceed 100%. Under this metric high-quality liquid assets are defined as unencumbered assets, central-bank eligible, that can be converted into cash to meet liquidity needs under stressed market conditions. In practical terms only money, reserves in central banks, public debt and high-quality corporate debt and covered bonds that will be subject to valuation haircuts are expected to be liquid assets.

A second ratio, the *Net Stable Funding Ratio* (NSFR), demands that the available stable funding (capital, long-term liabilities and a share of stable deposits) must equal or exceed the required stable funding in a stress scenario in order to avoid serious aggregate maturity mismatches.

The purpose of both ratios is to ensure that a bank maintains an adequate level of unencumbered, high-quality assets to meet short-term liquidity needs under stress. These ratios also create incentives for banks to fund their activities with more stable sources of funding on an on-going structural basis. Both ratios force banks to maintain a certain amount of liquid assets (liquidity demand), although this does not imply per se that access to liquidity is facilitated. Therefore liquidity supply will also be relevant. Banks' ultimate access to liquid assets will depend on internal (solvency, profits, equity value, etc.) and external factors (funding availability, risk and cost of liquid assets, and market conditions).

Although several countries have already put in place measures to tackle the issue of liquidity regulation, such as the UK or the US, they have proved to be insufficient. The impact of Basel lll requirements to improve banks' solvency and liquidity is still uncertain and it creates mixed feelings among industry participants. There is a widespread acceptance that the increased solvency ratios and the introduction of countercyclical capital buffers will enhance banks' solvency and thus their ability to obtain liquidity and funding in better conditions. However credit risk has reached such high levels nowadays that, in the short term, *markets seem to demand solvency ratios well above those established by Basel III*. As a result, although the Basel III capital requirements were conceived to be phased-in between 2013 and 2019 many banks have reacted to the current environment with an immediate and significant increase in their solvency ratios. This step forward has been underpinned by national regulation and by a controversial coordinated initiative in Europe to increase capital buffers based on mark-to-market of all sovereign bond portfolios.

The potential impact of Basel III *liquidity* requirements is subject to higher uncertainty and complexity. By ensuring higher levels of liquidity buffers, credit risks should diminish. This should not only reduce the likelihood of future liquidity crises but also facilitate funding access for banks. Nevertheless, a number of short-term probable unintended effects of these new requirements should be taken into consideration, in order to calibrate their potential impact:

1. The limited set of liquid assets admitted to fulfil the LCR requirements may produce market segmentation, damaging demand for assets not considered as liquid by these standards and thus distorting their markets. Widespread preference for a relatively reduced universe of assets may have a number of consequences: reduced sources of funding, reduced investment alternatives and more likely herding behaviours due to the fact that all banks will be subject to the same liquidity standards.

2. Although the LCR has been designed to reduce banks' dependency on central bank funding, the reform may produce the opposite effect. Indeed there is a risk of an increase of the retention of certain types of liquid assets in banks' balance sheets and of the discount of other non-accepted liquid assets to obtain liquidity in central bank facilities. This could be particularly the case in the Euro zone due to the fact that the Eurosystem accepts more types of assets as eligible collateral for liquidity provision than the LCR. This effect may be damaging, but it can be solved by increasing the types of liquid assets accepted in the LCR or toughening central banks collateral frameworks. A coherent response by central banks to these regulatory changes and new measures to foster alternative liquidity sources in the supply side of the market for liquidity will also be necessary to avoid the undesired effect of increasing banks' recourse to central bank liquidity.

3. Regarding money markets, Basel III liquidity rules will replace demand in the unsecured segment for an increased demand in the repo segment. As a consequence, liquidity may decrease and price volatility may increase in the unsecured segment. It is easy to underline two disadvantages in the short term: a potential reduction in aggregate market volumes in times of intense liquidity needs (if alternative markets are not expanded accordingly) and distortions in the determination of Libor and Euribor rates.

4. In more general terms, the introduction of minimum liquidity ratios enforces shorter asset maturities for internationally active banks (Basel III rules) and money market funds (SEC rules). To the extent that these financial institutions act as fund-providers, this measure induces a shortening of credit and loan maturities to the real economy and to banks. Thus financial institutions subject to liquidity rules may find problems in managing the traditional maturity transformation activities undertaken by banks (relativly long-term assets financed through shorter-term liabilities). Given that final borrowers will still have long-term funding needs there is a danger that an

alternative shadow banking system is developed in parallel to the regulated banking activities.

5. The impact of liquidity rules on liquidity management for internationally active groups depends crucially on whether quantitative liquidity ratios must be satisfied at the group or bank level. Liquidity self-sufficiency rules for banks at a legal entity basis foster a decentralised liquidity management model, which in principle has proved to be more resilient to crises. A centralised model, however, also has some advantages, so we cannot affirm that a simple liquidity self-sufficiency rule is the solution to the liquidity management challenge. Enforcing decentralisation of important aspects of liquidity management with compulsory rules has the benefit of ensuring a certain degree of diversification and reducing intra-group contagion, although it may also lead to a fragmentation of liquidity holdings, interfering with group business strategies and affecting the supervisory monitoring of the global liquidity situation at the group level.

Despite some of these potentially negative short-term effects, if we take into account a longer-term perspective, the Basel III framework should facilitate banks' access to liquidity and term funding. The initial limits to credit expansion and the disintermediation trend prompted by industry and regulatory measures will be soon offset by the long-term benefits of having sounder financial institutions. What is more, we should not forget that Basel III liquidity ratios are in an observation period, and improvements in their design are still possible. Nevertheless, for such longer-term benefits to be fully achieved, new liquidity rules must be part of a comprehensive framework to improve financial regulation and funding and liquidity management. *In this regard, improved supervisory and resolution frameworks and better market infrastructures may prove to be as relevant as liquidity rules.*

Additionally, despite the potential role of NSFR as an indicator of emerging liquidity concerns of banks, its ability is limited and we should not rule out the need for alternative systemic risk indicators, as proposed, among others, by the IMF. According to the IMF, end-2006 data show that seven of the 13 failed banks in a sample of 60 globally-oriented banks had a NSFR below 100% but overall the banks that failed during the crisis were evenly distributed across the range of NSFR (Vàzquez and Federico 2012).

3.2. Financial Cycles, Liquidity and Monetary Policy

One of the questions that were raised at the early stages of the crisis is to what extent low policy rates during the expansion period preceding the crisis induced greater risk-taking by financial institutions. The influence of interest rates on perceptions of risk and attitudes towards it (what Borio (2009) calls the "risk-taking channel") was widely neglected in the past and is now the subject of numerous studies by academics and central bankers. One way in which central banks' rates influence risk-taking is by signalling low return rates of other financial assets (debt securities). As low return rates are attributed to low-risk assets, financial agents in economies where intervention rates are low have incentives to assign low-risk perceptions and widespread low return rates to financial assets. As a self-reinforcing mechanism asset prices, cash flows and high profits have an indirect effect in the measurement of risk and risk tolerance, and therefore in risk premia. If we assume that low policy rates during the expansion period help inducing greater risk-taking strategies, it is consistent to wonder whether monetary policy should lean against the build-up of these strategies and their associated imbalances even if medium-term inflation is under control. This question has been frequently raised in reference to the control of asset bubbles, one of the main imbalances derived from loose monetary conditions.

Arguably the answer is a qualified yes. To the extent that financial imbalances can be built up in long cycles in a context of monetary policy strictly focused on one or two year inflation prospects, central banks should remain vigilant on these indirect shocks and act in a countercyclical manner to prevent them from developing. Although we are still managing the exit of this crisis, a number of reactions from central bankers look in this direction and, very likely, the debate will intensify once financial markets conditions are restored and monetary policy returns to the conventional interest rate fixing strategy we were used to.

3.3. Liquidity and Deposit Guarantees

Retail deposit guarantee schemes as well as other types of insurance schemes (investment protection, insurance protection) have certainly a role in ensuring financial stability and preventing financial (banking) crises. Their existence (assuming an adequate level of protection and solid functioning mechanism) helps prevent runs on banks by protecting retail depositors and ensuring swift payments. Depositors or other guaranteed agents feel a certain degree of protection when these schemes are in place, something that helps banks to buy time to address liquidity shortages and avoid liquidity shortages giving rise to confidence concerns, or even transforming into solvency problems. It can also help authorities and central banks to prevent or delay public measures of intervention.

The capacity of deposit guarantee schemes to prevent risks of runs is well known and has been widely anchored in the current crisis. European governments, for instance, automatically raised the level of protection of these schemes and some of them even took it to the limit of issuing governmental blanket guarantees to retail deposits. However, these instruments are only one tool within a broad (and increasingly broader) toolbox that regulators need to

use to manage a crisis. While deposit guarantee schemes have been quite successful in preventing depositors' runs in this crisis, they cannot impede either
creditors' runs or wholesale funding markets' distress, which are highly more
damaging than the former. The increasing relevance of non-deposit sources
of funding for financial institutions (interbank markets, money market funds,
institutional funding etc.) makes deposit guarantee schemes a very partial and
insufficient tool to address systemic crises. Additionally, faced with large-
scale crises, deposit guarantee schemes have limited capacity to fulfil their
task of deposit coverage. These schemes are not pre-funded in a large number
of countries. Even in those jurisdictions with ex-ante funding and the highest bank contribution rates their size is very limited compared to the volume of insured deposits. In Europe, for instance, deposit coverage ratio (fund
size/eligible deposit) rarely exceeds 1.5%. One has to realise that, if public
authorities had not rescued a large number of financial institutions, deposit
guarantee schemes would not have been able to cover deposit amounts of the
failing institutions.

As a corollary it can be said that deposit guarantee schemes are important
tools for financial stability which have proved successful in the current crisis
to prevent deposit runs and therefore relieve operational strains for banks (and
central banks). Nevertheless their capacity to handle systemic concerns is limited as these problems normally affect segments of the financial system which
are outside its scope.

4. ADDRESSING LIQUIDITY FROM A GLOBAL PERSPECTIVE: SOME FINAL REMARKS

The increasing global nature of capital flows makes global liquidity a key issue to be considered also in this context. On different international fora, such
as the G20, concern is insistently being expressed about global imbalances,
with some advanced economies and most emerging economies having hoarded
vast amounts of reserves throughout a long period with constant and sizeable
current account surpluses, with the counterpart being large accumulated debts
(and persistent current account deficits) by other countries.

The role of certain currencies as reserve currencies is leading some banks
to establish branches in their territory with the sole purpose of obtaining funding in that given currency and sending it to their headquarters. These flows fell
sharply in 2008, immediately after the crisis, but have since recovered. This
channelling of funds through interoffice accounts has implications in terms of
monetary policy spillovers, since the cash transferred to the headquarters is
then allocated in the recipient country. These dynamics cause the quick transmission of monetary policy decisions by some key central banks into global

monetary impacts. These large flows of international liquidity may lead to quick liquidity squeezes in certain economies or certain areas of the global financial system.

Despite the eminent role that national central banks play in preventing bubbles and vulnerabilities deriving from the risk of a quick deleveraging process after a surge in capital inflows, regulators and supervisors also have a very active role to play. This role is especially important when the majority of these flows are channelled through the banking sector. Banks due to their nature are more exposed to leveraging and deleveraging cycles. In this context, the introduction of macroprudential policies and a thorough analysis of the macro aspects of financial stability are essential. Global liquidity constraints are closely intertwined with shortages of foreign exchange currency funding and currency mismatches on bank balance sheets. These shortages have accentuated during this crisis due to the sudden aversion of US money market funds to invest with European banks. Central banks helped financial institutions to overcome these problems mainly by offering reserves, swap lines or special facilities in foreign currency. As for banks, there are two ways by which they can finance foreign currency assets: either they borrow the currency or they convert liabilities through swaps. Either way, they will try to avoid open positions in the foreign currency by matching the level of their foreign currency investments with on- and off-balance sheet liabilities in the same currency.

We need to build on the strengthened governance framework provided by the G20 to introduce a set of measures aimed at better managing global liquidity, within the broader reform of the International Monetary System.

The on-going work should seek two key objectives. The first objective should aim to achieve stability in credit provision to the economy, resulting in more growth and employment. The second objective should aim to achieve a more symmetrical system, and a conduct of fiscal and monetary policies across the business cycle by originators and recipients of capital flows that gets reflected through current account adjustments taking place by both surplus and deficit countries.

As a first step to reach this target, we could improve global liquidity management by strengthening surveillance of the international monetary system. In order to do so, we need to create a *standard for global liquidity*. This is not a trivial pursuit. The concept of global liquidity is subject to broad conceptual and policy controversy. The transmission channels of liquidity mismatches across jurisdictions and different financial markets are only partially understood. Furthermore, the complementarities among markets and the connexions between liquidity, financial markets, and price dynamics are not easy to disentangle. Nevertheless, we need to make progress in at least defining what should be the object of surveillance in global liquidity. The IMF, together with the necessary guidance of the G20, should also be mandated to conduct a much more systematic and visible surveillance process of the determinants of global liquidity and its transmission mechanisms.

Also, we need to focus on surveillance of spillovers in the international monetary system and the transmission mechanisms from reserve-issuing countries to the rest of the world economy and financial system. Systemic economies need particular attention in this respect. In parallel, we can develop guidelines on the management of capital flows with positive consequences for third parties and global financial stability.

As a second recommendation, we could enhance liquidity provision mechanisms that would result in improved global liquidity. This crisis has forced us to set up stronger and smarter mechanisms of this sort at the multilateral level. The IMF took the lead with the creation of Flexible and Precautionary Credit Lines (FCLs and PCLs), and the EU has followed with the European Financial Stability Fund (EFSF) and now with the European Stability Mechanism (ESM). These developments were reactive to the challenges posed by the financial crisis. In my view, it is essential to develop the multilateral and regional financial assistance mechanisms with a common approach based on 3 principles: 1) financial credibility; 2) appropriate incentives for good policies; and 3) strong emphasis on precautionary access. Let me stress this third point, to make the system more robust it is essential to limit the likelihood that self-fulfilling market dynamics may arise. Precautionary access also helps in applying conditionality in a preventive manner and in good times, when it is less costly for countries to follow appropriate policies. Precautionary tools should be incorporated into the Regional Financial Safety Nets currently under discussion in different parts of the world. Regional action should become more effective and proactive than global coordination for localised problems. It has been quite puzzling in the crisis that the IMF membership has been able to agree faster to preventive safety nets (such as the FCL and PCL) than a more homogeneous and integrated group of countries such as Europe and could also effectively rely on the use of these lines in a preventive manner with very limited conditionality in a more effective manner.

We will only be able to make headway in global liquidity management if we acknowledge, at the political level, the full potential benefits of a cooperative approach. As the correct amount of water is necessary to maximise the productivity of land, so too must we carefully manage the liquidity of our economies, keeping in mind a global perspective.

BIBLIOGRAPHY

Borio, C. 2009, "Ten Propositions about liquidity crises", *BIS working paper*, no. 293, November.

Committee on the Global Financial System (CGFS) 2010, "Funding patterns and liquidity management in internationally active banks", *BIS paper* no. 39, May.

Financial Stability Board 2011, "*Key Attributes of Effective Resolution Regime for Financial Institutions*", October.

Vázquez, F. and P. Federico 2012, "Bank Funding Structures and Risk: Evidence from the Global Financial Crisis", *IMF Working Paper* no. 12/29, January.

20. How to Avoid Contagion and Spillover Effects in the Euro Zone?

Michael C. Burda

1. INTRODUCTION

As a rule, issues of contagion arise more frequently in epidemiology and linguistics than in economics and finance, but this has changed dramatically in recent years. While the inherent instability of the banking sector due to liquidity and maturity mismatch has been well-understood for centuries, we never cease to be blindsided after believing that "this time it really is different" (Reinhart and Rogoff 2011). The globalisation of financial markets has created a new era of frictionless finance – a hyper-lubricated environment for the transmission of all kinds of disturbances, real or imagined, fundamental or self-fulfilling. The dramatic increase in levels of global leveraging and risk-shifting using old-fashioned debt and newfangled financial derivatives is unexplored terrain with unimaginable new risks. Yet the fundamental mechanism of financial contagion is the same that existed in the days of carrier pigeons, couriers on horseback, and the telegraph. The current age of heightened trade, frictionless communication, and increased ease of deal-making and execution makes it all the more imperative to examine critically the phenomenon of contagion in light of the anachronistic structure of European banking, as we move forward into the second decade of the new millennium.

In this chapter I outline the positive and normative aspects of financial spillovers in the European context. I do so from the perspective of a *macroeconomist* – i.e. neither that of a private nor a central banker. For all its romantic attractiveness, national heritages and cultural identities – Europe remains a banking backwater and a bank regulator's nightmare. Its mosaic of national dependencies, rivalries and preferences makes banking the Achilles heel in the economic race with North America and Asia. The regulatory vacuum which accompanied monetary union has rendered Europe even more vulnerable to the vagaries of rumour mills that drive international finance. As the

The author is grateful to Benjamin Friedman and Otto Lucius for comments, and to Christina Resniscek for useful research assistance.

cases of Iceland, Ireland and Spain have made evident, the average financial market in Europe can be swamped by a day's adverse financial trading flow or a moderate counterparty incident.

2. WHAT IS CONTAGION?

In the same way we care when colleagues show up to work with the flu, any bank crisis in a globalised financial system is everyone's business. A crisis in one region or nation of the world can have spillover effects on banks and payment systems in others. The great secular increase in global leverage in traditional banking in the 20th century (Schularick and Taylor 2012) has magnified this characteristic feature of banks as going concerns. Often for reasons which are not immediately evident, a failure of a small financial institution operating on the edge of a great financial network can inflict just as much damage as one at the hub.

Contagion arises among banks because they are interconnected. To a great extent this is inherent to the nature of financial institutions, which originate, hold or are liable for investments by others – either nonfinancial entities, or other banks. Banks thrive on trade – trade in financial claims. They intermediate between savers and lenders, large and small – "selling" (collecting) sight and savings deposits and "buying" loans and securities. Bank intermediation means operating very large balances sheets on thin levels of equity or net worth. Many of their assets are liabilities of other financial institutions. Obviously, the aggregate volume of money and credit which an economy and its banking system collectively choose to create is a function of underlying real activity, but also affects that level of activity. The failure of one financial institution can affect all the creditors of that institution, as well as creditors of such creditors. For this reason, bank regulators actively monitor and verify the capitalisation of financial institutions, even if banks were restricted to investments of the highest quality. *This is why contagion and spillovers, across banks and across national boundaries, is such a central problem facing Europe today.*

Yet by their very nature, financial institutions touch large volumes of money in their day-to-day activities and there is an ever-present temptation to "do something with it" – flowing not only from the greed of imperfectly monitored bankers, but also of shareholders, depositors, bank customers, and even employees. It is inevitable that banks take risks – the asset side of a typical balance sheet contains not only short-term debt of governments and high grade borrowers, but also long-term loans to households, nonfinancial and financial entities, as well as to long-term domestic and foreign governments. It is widely accepted that increasing sophistication in financial management has led both to increased risk-taking and lower capital margins in the competition for investors. More expansive deposit insurance has tempted banks to adopt riskier funding models or rely more heavily on the judgment of third parties such as rating agencies. This is why bank regulators monitor the quality of the balance sheets of banks, since very few individuals – depositors, bank owners, or even the bank managers themselves – are completely informed about the quality of those balance sheets.

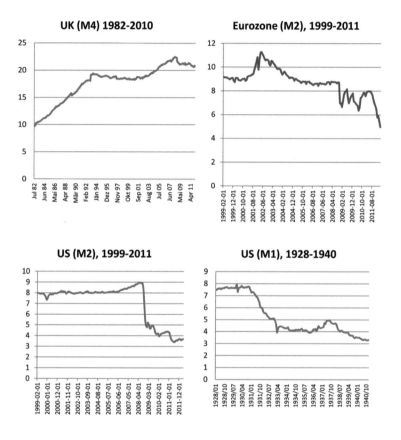

Figure 20.1: Money market multipliers for the UK, Euro zone and US

Money supply (M1, M2 or M4) divided by the monetary base (currency in circulation plus bank vault cash and deposits with the central bank).

Sources: Bank of England, European Central Bank, US Federal Reserve, Friedman and Schwartz (1963).

An efficient secondary or interbank market guides financial resources of the banking system to their most productive uses. The ratio of demand and savings deposits to the volume of central bank reserves plus currency in the hands of the nonfinancial public – the so-called *money market multiplier* – is thus a particularly good indicator of the faith and confidence in the financial system in itself. Contagion strikes at the heart of the fractional reserve banking system and the money and credit creation process. When banks stop lending to each other and suddenly prefer to hold their liquidity with the central bank, the volume of money and credit contracts. Figure 20.1 shows this contraction during the recent financial crisis, but also its resemblance to that of the US financial

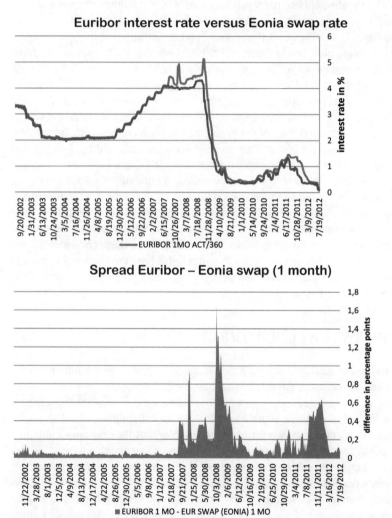

Figure 20.2: Unsecured interbank lending versus swap rates, Euro 1 month, 2002-2012

Source: Bloomberg.

Stability of the Financial System

system at the outset of the Great Depression. It is also striking to see that the latter collapse had already begun in 1930 and not in the years 1932-3, a period of widespread public banking panics.

Contagion works through the erosion of trust. A bank failure in region or country A can affect the system of payments and thus the real or perceived quality of the transactions medium in region or country B, even though the latter may not even be guilty of any particular banking sin. The affected banks may simply have counterparty relationships with each other, or might be suspected of such, or might both have relations with a third, vulnerable financial institution. The collapse of the money market multiplier displayed in figure 20.1 is a rough indicator in the trust that banks place in each other as compared with the central bank. While more money was held in the form of cash (banknotes) and the technology of payments was quite different, the dynamics of bank runs observed today are hardly different from those in the 1930s. The stereotypical lines of private bank customers lined up to withdraw their deposits are only a small part of the problem. The problem lies with the *reserve-holding behaviour of banks*. Then as now, banks simply withhold their funds from interbank markets and deposit them with the central bank in the form of low or no-yield bank reserves. The unwinding of interbank commitments in favour of the central bank deposits is a reflection of shrinking trust. This erosion of trust can be recognised in the behaviour of the spread between interest rates for unsecured interbank lending and the swap rate, which involves no transfer of principal between trading banks. Figure 20.2 plots these two rates for the euro and the spread between them, and highlights how the latter tracks closely periods of bank stress in the past decades, especially the exacerbation of the sovereign debt crisis in 2011.

3. MONEY IS A PUBLIC GOOD

By borrowing and lending, banks collectively – and largely unintentionally – create the means of payment in an economy. For decades now, the money supply in modern economies has not been driven by cash – relevant mostly for those with something to hide – as it is by bank liabilities – bank deposits. Because these liabilities are the essential life-blood of the economy, contagion and spillovers are everyone's problem. Economists say that this form of money possesses characteristics of a *public good*. That a country's money or a particular bank's deposits are sound and widely accepted in payment is its central non-rivalling feature: We – and by "we" I mean private households and firms that comprise the economy – all enjoy the benefit from the fact that deposits at the Deutsche Bank or Commerzbank are recognised by other banks all around the world as a means of payment, even if we as individuals own no deposits with those banks. Nor is this benefit excludable: Deutsche Bank or Commerzbank couldn't prevent me from enjoying those benefits, even if they wanted to. The quality of the transactions medium is intimately related to the financial soundness of the issuing financial institutions, more plainly, the quality of the balance sheet. And this quality depends on all its activities, which are sundry and, while profitable, do not possess the public good aspect of the deposit issuing and payments system function. *Solving the contagion problem means guaranteeing the fundamental quality of deposit-issuing institutions.* This is easier said than done, and will generally require some form of government intervention.

We teach students that banks represent financial conduits between savers – those who forgo consumption – and those who spend beyond their immediate means on the other. Obviously, banks do not restrict their activities to their intermediary and payment functions. Besides essential checking, lending and clearing services, banks provide a spectrum of other services, ranging from cash management, wealth management and family office services. Some engage in significant wholesale refunding activities. Others provide short-term inventory finance and factoring services. Some sell insurance to their retail clients. Many offer trading platforms and brokerage services, while some even engage in aggressive proprietary trading. All these activities contain elements of risk, some greater than others, which can threaten the bank's own equity and solvency in times of financial stress. Management of this risk rises as the capital ratio with which banks work decreases. Competition among banks tends to lower this ratio, because the lower the capital ratio, for a given level of asset quality (performing loans) the higher the rate of return on equity.[1] Only a rigorous and incorruptible level of bank supervision will convince investors to reward those banks with high-quality balance sheets with their money.

Even if banks were forbidden to engage in these other activities, the intermediation function of banks involves maturity transformation – mismatch on the balance sheet, usually borrowing short and lending long. Borrowing short in the form of deposits is even more perilous, as these loans are instantly callable, making them to put options at par value. Risk, liquidity and maturity transformation is usually an invitation for trouble, yet represents the inherent characteristic of modern fractional banking (Diamond and Dybvig 1983). Add to this shadow banks, investment banks and nonbank financial institutions and one has a potentially explosive cocktail for crises. *Spillover effects are no longer bank-to-bank, but also region-to-region, and nation-to-nation.* In past crises in Iceland and Ireland and the current mess in Spain, volatile spillovers immediately involve government finance, with European banks operating in a nationally fragmented banking system. As bizarre and anachronistic as it may seem many Euro zone countries hardly qualify as US states – Finland,

---

[1] The effect of increased bank concentration and decreased competition on risk-taking is theoretically unclear. See Boyd and DiNicoló (2005) and Pedauge (2012) for empirical investigations of the effect of competition on aggregate risk-taking.

Luxemburg, or even Cyprus – and yet have their own central banks. Europe finds itself in the situation of the US states in the 1930s, when a fractionalised Federal Reserve Board exhibited remarkably little national leadership, driven by local interests.

A free-market position on financial market regulation is that banks should do as they please, within the realm of legal activity, and it is up to shareholders and depositors to monitor the riskiness of deposits and investment stakes (Kaufman 1988). Such a libertarian approach ignores the *externality* arising from the public good aspect of money, or assumes that the market will solve the problem. This would require both 1) depositors and investors can readily access information about bank activities and can "vote with their feet" if dissatisfied and 2) that they actually bother to do so, which cannot be taken for granted. When they do not, either due to laziness, turpitude or moral hazard, contagion can easily arise. Free banking regimes, as practiced in 18th century Scotland, 19th century US West or 20th century Hong Kong – presume a high degree of transparency as well as sophistication on the part of the banking public – as well as a commitment by the government not to bail out those who did not exercise due diligence. Yet such commitments are not time-consistent, and governments – especially European ones – inevitably bail out banks. Nor is it time-consistent for "systemically important financial institutions" (SIFIs) to exercise due diligence, if the government will always pick up the bill.

This is why free banking never took off. We face a situation typical of an externality – the lack of due diligence by one party has a negative effect on the viability of the entire financial system.[2] Thus when externalities are involved, there is no excuse for the government to stick its head in the sand; it must actively prevent contagious situations from arising. Every economist must face up to this fact, or face the accusation of being a shill for the financial industry. Naturally, government regulation brings its own difficulties to the table, yet this is no excuse to accept another, more glaring imperfection in the way our economy is managed.

To summarise, some but not all elements of banking involve an externality – the behaviour of each bank affects the integrity of the whole in ways which cannot be mediated by market processes. A certain class of liabilities issued by banks (bank deposits) serves as the means of payment, involving the real economy. In a fractional reserve banking system, the means of payment is backed by the soundness of credit, and in a world in which monetary quantity targets are no longer used by central banks means that the volume of credit is indeterminate and demand-determined. The problem arises when banks, managing such large accumulations of financial resources, conduct activities which are only tangentially related to the means of payment function, and thereby

---

[2] Note that I avoid use of terms "solvency" or "liquidity" as they are notoriously fuzzy, even among the most competent of financial authorities.

threaten its overall stability. In the process, they become "systemically relevant" and are able to take the economy as its hostage. For without a payments system, both real and financial spheres of the economy cannot function.

4. A POSITIVE ANALYSIS: WHO'S TO BLAME FOR THE CURRENT CRISIS?

The pathology of contagion in the European banking and sovereign debt crisis merits particular discussion. The small size of each individual country means that portfolio decisions of large international investors can induce or reinforce a negative assessment by the market, leading to dramatic reassessments of debt quality, higher refinancing rates and, potentially, to self-fulfilling prophecies.[3] Since national banks were less than fully diversified, they are overexposed to national economic problems – which in an age of financial globalisation are increasingly difficult to conceal. The emergence of shadow finance (hedge funds, private equity) has exacerbated idiosyncratic national risk while providing no additional insurance against such risk. Thus a failure of one or more banks in a small country can not only cause a financial crisis, but also a fiscal crisis as governments are forced to move in and save systems of payments and fundamental financial transactions, which are themselves drawn into the maelstrom (Eichengreen 2011). *The dramatic deterioration of the quality of the banking system in a matter of months in Europe is what contagion is all about.* Whether the emperor had no clothes to start with, whether he was in fact clothed in tatters, or whether the garments were torn off in the aftermath of the first global crisis is immaterial.

Who failed? The European financial crisis offers a wonderful exercise in consistent yet circular reasoning, offering every guilty party the obvious way out – by blaming another, equally guilty participant. If we play the *"blame game"* for a moment, we can identify a number of parties, without any particular respect to ordering: 1) the banks themselves, both public and private; 2) bank regulation, regulators and politicians; 3) sovereign borrower governments; 4) the financial rating agencies; 5) academic economists, especially specialists in finance.

---

[3] The example of Greece's interaction with the leading sovereign bond fund manager Pimco – with USD 1.3 trillion in bonds under management – is now legendary. After Greece's public admission in November 2009 that its fiscal deficit had reached 13% – double the original figure – Pimco liquidated its entire Greek sovereign portfolio, coinciding with an almost 100 basis point jump in the yield of the then A-rated 10 year government bond over the month of December. Pimco also dumped its holdings of Portuguese and Spanish sovereign debt, initiating a rapid unravelling of the tight cross-country bond yield structure that had prevailed for more than seven years. For a vivid description of this fateful chain of events, see http://www.thisamericanlife.org/radio-archives/episode/455/continental-breakup?act=3.

4.1. Banks Themselves

European private and public banks have traditionally operated on thinner capitalisation than their US counterparts and have done so for a long time (see, e.g., Bair 2011). Partially this might be due to the fact that, under national regulation with national currency, systemic, macroeconomic risk could always be obviated by an aggressive depreciation of the exchange rate. In the run-up to the 2008 episode, European banks participated enthusiastically in the US financial binge, loading up on highly rated mortgage-backed securities and collateralised debt obligations derived from them. Many of these banks in Germany were *Landesbanken*, publicly backed financial institutions which had come under fire from the European Commission for public guarantees. When these guarantees were removed in 2005, they were expected to earn high rates of returns for their owners (mostly, the German federal states) despite higher cost of funds. For this reason, they were easy prey to aggressive sales pitches of US investment banks for exotic financial products promising high yields and low risk.

4.2. Bank Regulation, Bank Regulators and Politicians

The state has an overriding interest in the stability of the payments system. This is why central banks and bank regulators are almost always associated with national governments. Yet the integrity of the payments system does not merely presume a seamless supply of banknotes to those who want to hold them, or perhaps an acceptably low rate of inflation. As noted above, money in modern economies consists chiefly of negotiable bank liabilities held by nonbanks rather than banknotes (about 80-85% in the Euro zone) which are fungible with cash or central bank deposits at any time. Attenuation of the quality of bank balance sheets has immediate macroeconomic implications. In the US deregulation of the financial sector – starting with the elimination of the Glass-Steagall Act in 1999 and continuing through explicit light touch of derivatives regulation and reduction of margin requirements for broker banks – led to a degradation of the quality of the banking system there, leading to a freeze-up of the interbank market in the aftermath of the Lehman bankruptcy in October 2008.

In Europe, weak or attenuated regulatory authorities have traditionally worked in an already decentralised setting governed primarily by national interests and perspectives. In the past decade, national banking authorities presided over a creeping deterioration of loan portfolios increasingly influenced by inter-European exposure, all against a backdrop of low bank capitalisation. The failure of the Belgian Dexia, with operations in Belgium, France, and the Netherlands, among other places, is a case in point. The failure of this bank was dealt with at a national, rather than international level, an uncoordinated response to an obvious spillover effect. Governments failed to realise that, without clear distinctions between essential and non-essential financial functions, all bank liabilities had become contingent government liabilities, with the relevant contingency becoming increasingly likely.

4.3. Sovereign Borrower Governments

Borrowing by sovereigns in a foreign currency is known as "original sin" (see Eichengreen et al. 2005). Uncontrolled borrowing in the context of a monetary union is a macroeconomic recipe for disaster. This can be seen from many historical episodes involving monetary unions, including the US states in the 1830s and the Argentine provinces in the 1990s. In several ways, the Euro zone situation resembles that of Bretton Woods in the 1960s, with the southern periphery playing the role of the United States and Germany the role of Europe and Japan. In particular, the difference was the lack of an IMF "policeman" which could have intervened at the hint of chronic balance of payments disequilibria (current account deficits not financed by long-term private capital flows). Instead, the Hume mechanism which would otherwise have generated a slowdown in uncompetitive countries was neutralised by passive ECB-refunding of banks in crisis regions (Burda 2012).

4.4. Rating Agencies

The agencies responsible for assessing creditworthiness of borrowers failed massively to anticipate problems arising in the aftermath of the financial crisis in 2008. Banks trusted blindly the quality of government debt and the quality of the rating agencies, so overly optimistic ratings, such as those given to Greek sovereign debt in 2001 or to Irish banks until 2007, led to excessive bank holdings of these securities and rising vulnerability to contagion.[4]

Particularly disturbing was the lack of understanding by rating agencies of macroeconomic implications of monetary union, in particular, on the impact and propagation of fiscal and financial shocks. It is well-known in macroeconomics that fixed exchange rate regimes magnify the short-run effect of real shocks, including unanticipated fiscal austerity programmes. Standard feedback mechanisms which dampen real fluctuations – a change in the exchange rate and domestic interest rate – are ruled out by the fixed parity. A construction boom in a small open economy under flexible exchange rates leads to an exchange rate appreciation and an increase in domestic interest rates, both of

---

[4] Moody's clung to its A rating for Greece government debt until 2010, well after yields had started climbing in December 2009. See "Ratings Firms Misread Signs of Greek Woes", *New York Times* November 29, 2011. Similarly, only after the December 2009 sell-off did Fitch reduce its own rating of Greek sovereign debt from A- to BBB+ and downgrade Greece below investment grade for the first time in a decade.

which would ultimately arrest the boom. When exchange rates are fixed as they are in a monetary union, capital inflows keep interest rates low and the party continues.[5] Furthermore, the effect is symmetric: the negative demand effects of fiscal consolidation are larger for the southern Euro zone; with slower growth and falling tax revenues, it is all the more difficult to meet austerity targets. These basic wisdoms, which have been around for fifty years, were not incorporated in the rating agencies' assessment of sovereign borrowers. For this and a number of other reasons, a critical evaluation of their role in the crisis seems long overdue.

4.5. Academic Economists

To the extent that my profession advised banks, rating agencies and governments – as was the case – it was guilty of either naiveté, hubris, ingenuousness, or some combination thereof. No matter how one cuts it, this is not a great moment for our profession. At the same time, many of our colleagues who did protest were drowned out or driven out of town by the mob with their conviction that "this time was different".

But enough of the blame game: How do we move forward?

5. POLICY OPTIONS: NORMATIVE RECOMMENDATIONS

Economics students are taught that an externality arises whenever some agent fails to bear the social costs of privately chosen actions. Public policy is needed to solve the problem, either because no market exists, or coordination costs are too high to solve the problem in a decentralised way. For the externality to be internalised, the originator of the harm must pay the full social costs of his actions. This principle is enshrined in German environmental law as the *Verursacherprinzip* and justifies the imposition of effluent charges on polluters who dump industrial waste in public waterways. In terms of finance, the poor investment decision of a single bank can pollute the quality of the entire financial system. While obvious to most, few policy-makers in Europe appear ready to take the next logical step: *imposition of a tax on agents responsible for the externality*, which is the degradation of the integrity of the payments system and the overall quality of the banks. Whether this tax is specific (e.g., a progressive tax on the size of a financial institution's balance sheet) or blunt (a stamp or transactions tax) is a matter to be decided in a democratic process. In any case, this discussion must be preceded by a careful analysis of the externality itself.

---

[5] See Mundell (1962), Fleming (1962). For one modern undergraduate exposition of the "Mundell-Fleming model", see Burda and Wyplosz (2009).

Like the blame game, identifying the source of the externality more often than not involves frustrating chains of circular reasoning. First, imperfect supervision of banks with deposit-taking and interbank-systemic functions can lead to (and did lead to) inordinate risk-taking, which in turn threatened the financial systems of not only individual European countries (Ireland, Spain, Germany), but also the trans-European interbank funding market and the international credibility of European financial institutions. Second, imperfect information – fragmented national banking supervision and poorly incentivised rating agencies – distorted investor perceptions of risk, interconnectedness and covariance, thus worsening the original externality. Third, a long-standing moral hazard situation has been fuelled by the nonexistence of cross-border bank and sovereign bankruptcy resolution regimes, making it easier for institutional or individual investors in bank or sovereign liabilities to throw due diligence to the wind, relegating responsibility to rating agencies. Undoubtedly, the favourable risk characteristics attributed to public debt worsened matters.

In its great banking crisis of 1932-3, the United States faced comparable but not entirely identical dilemmas. Bank failures in individual states gave rise to highly uncoordinated, inadequate (and sometimes counterproductive) policy reactions. Only after President Franklin D. Roosevelt applied the tourniquet of a nationwide bank holiday in March 1933 did the bleeding stop. This gave breathing room for banks to be resolved (merged or closed) without being dogged by short-run liquidity problems, justified or unjustified. By closing all banks, the government was able to perform this service without prejudice. Not accidentally, the same shotgun approach was taken by Treasury Secretary Hank Paulson in October 2008, when the US government took a stake in all banks regardless of whether they were affected by the interbank run of the fall associated with the bankruptcy of Lehman Brothers.

Beside the bank holiday and subsequent bank restructuring and resolution, the Roosevelt Administration took comprehensive legislative action in response to the banking crisis. The Banking Act of 1933 (the so-called Glass-Steagall Act) created the Federal Deposit Insurance Corporation, which provides deposit insurance to almost all banks in a manner unprejudiced by state of charter. Banks were also forced more or less to become members of and subject to the rules of the Federal Reserve System. The most well-known and controversial provision of the Glass-Steagall Act of 1933 was the stripping out of risky and highly profitable investment banking from the bland "main-street" provision of commercial and retail banking services, a separation which would last for more than six decades. Moreover, to prevent banks from becoming too-big-to-fail, Glass-Steagall simply prohibited interstate banking! Commercial banks were made too small to matter – some states even prohibited banking across county lines. To solve the problem of adverse selection of credit projects (Stiglitz and Weiss 1981) – "Regulation Q" ceilings were imposed on interest rates payable on bank deposits.

While Glass-Steagall can be likened to cracking a peanut with a sledge hammer, it certainly addressed the externality that investment banking imposed on essential commercial banking functions – in probability, if not with certainty. Its impact was to insulate core social functions of banks in a fractional reserve system from risky proprietary trading, excessive leverage and waves of unbridled malfeasance which have befallen the industry over the past five centuries. If it was impossible for regulators to keep banks away from the candy, Glass-Steagall's approach was simply to take the candy out of the candy store.

For some of my colleagues, the age of Glass-Steagall is seen as a regulatory regime which redirected the best talent to more productive uses and was responsible for the steady growth of the US economy in the second half of the 20th century.[6] While the validity of this claim is difficult to establish, it is equally difficult for economists to justify the present size of the financial sector in some Anglo-Saxon countries on normal welfare measures alone.

With six decades of hindsight and technological progress, more intelligently designed regulatory alternatives should be available to solve the fundamental banking externality described above. Several measures designed to improve financial market stability have been discussed – and after clever lobby work by the financial industry – apparently removed from the table. A "Volker Rule" preventing banks from trading for their own account would attack the problem that obviously plagued US banking in the 1920s and 2000s, but loopholes may doom it to failure before it is even implemented. Higher capital requirements for riskier investments will fail as long as the rating agencies are unable to provide an unbiased and if necessary, contrarian opinion.

Given the experience of the US in the 1930s, a convincing case can be made for *intelligent European-wide financial regulation*. The normative criteria for an international (trans-European) approach – a failure of national governments to achieve the financial stability individually – appear to have been met. Moreover, the positive theory of regulation predicts that the likelihood of trans-European regulation increases with the congruence of interests between the regulated and the regulator (Frieden 2012). In principle, the interests of large banks should guide if not force the hand of European regulation, yet those interests do not appear sufficiently powerful in cross-national banking for that step. Moreover, politically connected local banks (*Sparkassen* in Germany, *cajas* in Spain, *Caisses d'Epargne* in France, for example) are likely to block a truly unified approach to bank regulation. Europe missed a golden opportunity to promote cross-border bank mergers as part of its internal market project starting in 1988. A dozen or so Europe-wide banks emerging from the single market initiative would certainly have lobbied national interests to yield to economic reality, as important US Federal legislation did at the turn of the

---

[6] For a particularly forceful expression of this view see Reich (2012). A similar, but less extreme view can be found in Friedman (2010).

20th century did (Frieden 2012). As it stands, national interests still largely co-incide with nationally based financial structures (and national central banks), so the chances of ceding significant national sovereignty to a European banking union or Europe-wide bank regulator still seems remote.

In the macroeconomic policy sphere, contagion can be contained by preventing systemic *national* risks from arising, which quickly can mutate to banking crises (e.g., Greece). The most direct approach is robust and enforceable fiscal rules – to prevent governmental sub-units (national European governments, localities) from losing control of their fiscal integrity, becoming too-big-to-fail and spilling over to the union as a whole (Beetsma and Uhlig 1999). This was the central objective of the *Stability Pact* in its original and unadulterated form. While it is clear that the Stability Pact was not time-consistent over the business cycle, more work is needed to ensure that countries run surpluses in good times so that deficits are tolerable in bad times, and that they commit to pro-growth policies for the medium run.

Yet the discussion does not stop here. *Contrary to popular opinion, central banking and monetary policy can also contribute towards the containment of contagion.* We now know that the failure of the central credit allocation mechanisms to penalise excessive private sector borrowing is a political problem for which the Euro zone was completely unprepared. The inability of the European Central Bank (ECB) to suppress the political influence of national central banks has become increasingly evident as the crisis progressed. ECB policy is likely to have worsened matters; President Trichet's celebration of rapid interest rate convergence in the early 2000s was not just premature; it was fundamentally misplaced. The regions of Europe need differentiated and responsive structures of interest rates to reflect the different default risks of households, firms and governments, and thus to reward prudent behaviour. Thus, the ECB needs to change the rules of the game and introduce explicit haircuts for the securities it accepts as collateral (Buiter and Sibert 2005). In doing so, it can help prevent *banking* risks from becoming *national and systemic* risks (e.g., Ireland and Spain). If the ECB applied this standard to the credit allocation process in a neutral way, the Target 2 problem (excessive balance of payments imbalances within the Euro zone) would resolve itself through the normal operation of the credit allocation mechanism. This may require more wide-reaching steps, including the abolition of national central banks and the introduction of country-cutting ECB banking districts such as those of the Federal Reserve System.[7]

Finally, robust regulation at the microeconomic level complements macroeconomic measures described above. Bank runs and speculative attacks are fed by a lack of transparency to the average market participant; that is, when a

---

[7] Automatic mechanisms – like the Hume mechanism of the gold standard – could improve credit allocation if scarcity of pledgeable collateral at a bank or in a region leads to higher refinancing rates for that bank or region. For a descriptive discussion of the Hume mechanism in the modern context and how national interests can interfere with it, see Burda (2012).

lack of reliable publicly available information renders liquidation and market exit the most rational response to an increase in market uncertainty. In environments like these, agents naturally suspect that sellers know more than the market, so guaranteeing "skin in the game" for originators of securitised assets is likely to contribute positively to stability. New mechanisms of contagion have arisen in the meantime which truly dwarf anything we could have imagined in the past half-century years. The pervasive use of financial derivatives – current estimates of gross volumes outstanding range anywhere up to USD 700 trillion – (USD 700,000,000,000,000) – a shocking number in a world in which many counterparties are unknown and the counterparty risk is difficult if not impossible to assess (Rajan 2005). In the light of such "weapons of mass destruction", *stopping contagion should receive first priority*. Ultimately, it requires a *realignment of incentives* in the banking business to work towards and not against more stability – trading and risky securities origination versus deposit issuance and payment systems. It may even require taxing those aspects of the former which, in regular intervals, tend to bring hardship on the latter, and lead to additional burdens on the real economy and the taxpayer. One way of dealing with this is the so-called Tobin tax, another might be the institution of a derivative bailout fund or imposition of trading clearinghouse platforms like the Chicago Board of Trade.[8]

6. CONCLUSION

To solve the contagion problem and to deal with the externality, Europe will need to go much farther down the path of financial integration than she has to date. She will need to abandon her traditional national banking identities in favour of a European playing field dominated by cross-border institutions. This will be difficult, as preferences for special arrangements with local and regional lending commitments will always be strong – and to the extent such institutions are exempted, the risk of mischief and contagion will continue to arise. In any case, the nations of Europe will need to surrender most of its sovereignty in the area of bank regulation, deposit insurance, and insolvency rules. Because such a bold step seems unlikely to come from the political realm, it will be necessary for private sector banks themselves to demand it.

In addition to a banking regulatory authority with real teeth, Europe will need an intelligently managed deposit insurance system, which would also contribute to containing contagion. Naturally, such institutions should have been created 10-15 years ago, at the outset of the monetary union experiment, and not in midstream and under duress. As often is the case, a crisis may be

---

[8] EMIR, the new European Market Infrastructure Regulation on trading and clearing of standardised OTC derivatives, is the right step in the right direction.

necessary to fix attention and generate momentum for such deep reforms; at the same time it will be difficult if not impossible to implement them without significant transfers between countries and financial institutions of differing fiscal and financial stress.

The practical implementation of these measures – especially a pan-European banking resolution authority – will be no mean task. It will require delicate respect for the political economy of bank resolution, which requires both democratic legitimacy as well as hard-nosed business decisions on when to rescue or close financial institutions.[9] While this is certainly a task of Herculean dimensions, the alternative – dissolution of the Euro area and the disintegration of European trading relations – is not an option.

My analysis is based on the here and now, and banking will be around for centuries to come – but almost certainly not in the form we observe today. This means that any form of regulation will be outdated in a decade (or even a few years). Glass-Steagall's greatest weakness was its prohibition of cross-state-banking, which threw out the baby (of reasonable geographic asset diversification) with the bathwater (eliminating financial institutions which are too-big-to-fail). While few are calling for a re-institution of Glass-Steagall Act, the railings of Senator Glass and Representative Steagall in the 1930s against unbridled speculation are just as relevant today as they were seven decades ago. The demand for light-touch regulation should not be confused with current realities of no-touch response. We need to think hard about the extent to which banking and finance have become a self-justifying, low-productivity activity except for those individuals at the top who are in charge of the casino and the games that are played there.[10] To the extent that this is true, they will continue to pose a serious risk to financial market stability.

BIBLIOGRAPHY

Bair, S. 2011, "The Eurozone Crisis will not go away until Banks face Reality", *Fortune* November 2, http://finance.fortune.cnn.com/2011/11/02/eurozone-crisis-banks-risk/.

Beetsma, R. and H. Uhlig 1999, "An Analysis of the Stability and Growth Pact", *Economic Journal* 109, pp. 546-571.

Boyd, J. and G. De Nicoló 2005, "The theory of bank risk taking and competition revisited", *Journal of Finance* 60, pp. 1329-1343.

Buiter, W. and A. Sibert 2005, "*How the Eurosystem's Treatment of Collateral in its Open Market Operations Weakens Fiscal Discipline in the Eurozone (and what to do about it)*", mimeo.

Burda, M. 2012, "Hume on Hold?", www.voxeu.org, 17 May.

---

[9] See Rocholl (2012) for a careful analysis of practical problems associated with a European banking union.

[10] For a clear and concise statement of this challenge, see Friedman (2010).

Burda, M. and C. Wyplosz 2009, "*Macroeconomics: A European Text*", Fifth edition, Oxford: Oxford University Press.

Diamond, D. W. and P. H. Dybvig 1983, "Bank Runs, Deposit Insurance and Liquidity", *Journal of Political Economy* 91 (June 1983), pp. 401-419.

Eichengreen, B. 2011, "Fix the Banks, Fix the Currency", *Wall Street Journal* March 8, p.14.

Eichengreen, B., R. Hausmann and U. Panizza 2005, "The Pain of Original Sin", in *Other People's Money*, eds B. Eichengreen and R. Hausmann, Chicago University Press.

Fleming, J. M. 1962, "Domestic financial policies under fixed and floating exchange rates". *IMF Staff Papers* 9, pp. 369–379.

Frieden, J. 2012, "Global Economic Governance after the Crisis", *Perspektiven der Wirtschaftspolitik*, forthcoming.

Friedman, B. 2010, "Is our Financial System Serving us well?" *Daedalus* (Fall 2010), pp. 9-21.

Friedman, M. and A. Schwartz 1963, "*A Monetary History of the United States, 1863-1960*", Princeton, Princeton University Press.

Kaufman, G. 1988, "Bank Runs: Causes, Benefits and Costs", *Cato Journal*, Vol. 7, No. 3 (winter).

Mundell, R. 1962, "Capital mobility and stabilization policy under fixed and flexible exchange rates", *Canadian Journal of Economic and Political Science* 29, pp. 475-485.

Pedauge, L. E. 2012, "Financial Consolidation and Stability: Empirical Evidence Reviewed" University of Granada, mimeo.

Rajan, R. G. 2005, "Has financial development made the world riskier?" *Proceedings*, Federal Reserve Bank of Kansas City, pp. 313–369.

Reich, R. 2012, "How J.P. Morgan Chase has made the case for breaking up the big banks and resurrecting Glass-Steagall", http://robertreich.org/post/22821591303.

Reinhart, C. and K. Rogoff 2009, "*This Time is Different: Eight Centuries of Financial Folly*". Princeton, N.J., Princeton University Press.

Rocholl, J. 2012, "Bankenunion: Ist eine gemeinsame europäische Bankenaufsicht ein neues Instrument der Bankenrettung?", *Ifo Schnelldienst* 14/2012: 65, pp. 15-18.

Schularick, M. and A. M. Taylor 2012, "Credit Booms Gone Bust: Monetary Policy, Leverage Cycles and Financial Crises, 1870–2008", *American Economic Review* 102(2), pp. 1029-1061.

Stiglitz, J. and A. Weiss 1981, "Credit Rationing in Markets with Imperfect Information," *American Economic Review* 71, pp. 393-410.

21. The New European Supervisory System – Harmonisation and Macroprudential Oversight

Sabine Lautenschläger

1. INTRODUCTION

2011 was a turning point for European supervisors. The European System of Financial Supervision (ESFS) entered into force, thus decisively altering the architecture of financial supervision in Europe. At the beginning of 2011, several new authorities started their work: the European Systemic Risk Board (ESRB) and three new European supervisory authorities: the European Banking Authority (EBA), based in London; the European Insurance and Occupational Pensions Authority (EIOPA), based in Frankfurt am Main; and the European Securities and Markets Authority (ESMA), based in Paris.[1] These four new authorities, which have been given extensive powers, and the national supervisory authorities (NSAs) together form the European System of Financial Supervision (ESFS). The establishment of the ESFS is a manifestation of the strong political will to use the experience of the financial market crisis in order to redefine how certain market participants and markets are supervised. The founding fathers of the ESFS had two objectives in mind: first, to link microprudential supervision and macroprudential oversight more closely together; and second, to help strengthen the supervisory "level playing field" in a single market, in which the principle of "same risks – comparable/same rules" applies. They were particularly concerned with harmonising European supervisory rules, going even as far as to create a "single rule book" and to further harmonise supervisory practice.

The measure of the system will lie in its ability to create the basis for a more resilient financial system on the whole. There are two key questions that this raises.

___

This chapter represents the author's personal opinions and does not necessarily correspond with the official position of the Deutsche Bundesbank. It was finalised in June 2012 and reflects the state of discussion at that time.

[1] These three authorities are collectively referred to as European Supervisory Authorities (ESAs).

- First: what is the optimum degree of harmonisation of regulation and supervisory practice in a single market in which financial institutions operate across national borders and in a monetary union?[2]
- Second: how can a new and improved macroprudential oversight contribute to crisis prevention, and how should microprudential supervision and macroprudential oversight be meshed in the future?[3]

2. THE EUROPEAN SYSTEM OF FINANCIAL SUPERVISION (ESFS)

2.1. From the Level 3 Committees to the ESFS

In order to simplify and speed up the complex legislative process in the EU, the "Lamfalussy process" was in place for EU financial market legislation prior to the reform in 2011 of the European supervisory architecture. This four-stage procedure goes back to a "Committee of Wise Men" established in 2000 and chaired by Baron Alexandre Lamfalussy. Introduced in the securities sector in 2001, this process was extended in December 2002 to cover the banking and insurance industries – in effect, the entire EU financial sector. There were four levels: framework principles, implementing measures, comments by the Lamfalussy committees (Level 3 committees[4]) and implementation. The Level 3 committees played a key role here. They developed standards, guidelines and recommendations for the three (nationally) supervised areas, thus fleshing out European legislation. Although the rules they developed were not formally binding, a voluntary commitment by the committee members virtually gave these rules binding effect. They were ultimately the predecessor committees to the current European supervisory institutions.

By the time of the financial crisis, it had become clear that, despite the efforts of the Level 3 committees, there were still deficits in implementing the European rules. At the European level, there was insufficient cooperation, coordination and coherence in the application of Union law.[5] Therefore, in 2009 a further high-level committee, chaired by Jacques de Larosière, proposed enlarging the three committees to form supervisory *authorities* for the banking, securities and insurance sectors.[6] In addition, in the light of the lessons learned

---

[2] See section 3.
[3] See section 4.
[4] These were the Committee of European Banking Supervisors (CEBS), the Committee of European Securities Regulators (CESR) and the Committee of European Insurance and Occupational Pensions Supervisors (CEIOPS). The committees' membership comprised representatives of national supervisory authorities and, in the case of CEBS, also representatives of the national central banks. CESR was established in 2001, CEBS and CEIOPS in 2004.
[5] Regulation (EU) No 1093/2010, recital 1.
[6] See The High-Level Group on Financial Supervision, Report, 25 February 2009. http://ec.europa.eu/internal_market/finances/docs/de_larosiere_report_en.pdf.

from the financial crisis, the de Larosière Commission recommended adding a European macroprudential component to microprudential supervision.

On the basis of the report, in September 2009 the European Commission presented proposals for several regulations[7] which, after passing the Council and Parliament, entered into force on 16 December 2010. The newly created institutions of the European System of Financial Supervision (ESFS) were thus able to take up their work on 1 January 2011. In the following, I will explain the powers of the three new supervisory authorities using the European Banking Authority (EBA) as an example.

2.2. The European Banking Authority (EBA)

The EBA,[8] which is at the focus of this chapter, was given broad powers. Its main tasks are[9]

- to contribute to developing binding supervisory standards by drafting both regulatory technical standards and implementing technical standards which, upon adoption by the European Commission, represent directly applicable Union law;
- to issue guidelines and recommendations;
- to create a common supervisory culture in order to ensure consistent application of supervisory rules;
- to enforce Union legislation, contribute to crisis management and resolve disputes between supervisors in a binding manner, as well as to conduct EU-wide stress tests;
- to cooperate with the other members of the ESFS;
- to analyse developments in the markets and in the area of financial regulation;
- to contribute to the consistent and coherent functioning of supervisory colleges; and
- to inform the public.

In addition, in some areas and under certain circumstances, the EBA, as an *ultima ratio*, has also been given powers to take specific decisions addressed to national supervisory authorities and even individual institutions, for example

---

[7] Proposal for a Regulation of the European Parliament and of the Council on Community macroprudential oversight of the financial system and establishing a European Systemic Risk Board, 23 September 2009, COM(2009)499 final; Proposal for a Regulation of the European Parliament and of the Council establishing a European Banking Authority, 23 September 2009, COM(2009)501 final; Proposal for a Regulation of the European Parliament and of the Council establishing a European Insurance and Occupational Pensions Authority, 23 September 2009, COM(2009)502 final; Proposal for a Regulation of the European Parliament and of the Council establishing a European Securities and Markets Authority, 23 September 2009, COM(2009)503 final. In this chapter, the terms EBA Regulation and ESRB Regulation will be used for short.

[8] A more thorough introduction to the structure and tasks of the EBA may be found in Deutsche Bundesbank, Monthly Report, September 2011, pp 86-91.

[9] See EBA Regulation, Articles 8 and 9.

in the event of breaches of Union law, a crisis situation or when a binding settlement is required.

The central decision-making body is the Board of Supervisors,[10] of which
the heads of the 27 national financial supervisory authorities are voting members. The Board of Supervisors also has non-voting members: the chairperson
of the EBA, a representative of the ECB, a representative of the ESRB and a
representative each from the ESMA and EIOPA. Where the supervisory body
is not a central bank, the respective country's central bank may nominate a
non-voting representative to the Board.

Like the other two supervisory authorities, the EBA has its own legal personality and is designed to have administrative and financial autonomy.[11] It is
accountable to the European Council and the European Parliament.

2.3. The European Systemic Risk Board (ESRB)

The ESRB[12] is a cooperative body without any legal personality or powers of
intervention. According to the EU regulation establishing the ESRB, *"[t]he
ESRB's task should be to monitor and assess systemic risk in normal times for
the purpose of mitigating the exposure of the system to the risk of failure of systemic components and enhancing the financial system's resilience to shocks."*[13]
The ESRB is therefore responsible for macroprudential oversight in Europe.

The ESRB's central decision-making body is the General Board.[14] It unites
the representatives of the national central banks, the ECB, the three new European supervisory authorities and the Commission, and the chairpersons of the
two advisory committees of the ESRB (voting), the EU's Economic and Financial Committee and the national supervisory authorities (non-voting). The
General Board is chaired by the President of the ECB.

If the ESRB identifies risks to financial stability in the European Union, it
can issue public or confidential warnings or recommendations. Addressees may
include the Union as a whole, individual member states, the Commission, or
European and national supervisory authorities. Such recommendations contain a
proposal for remedial action or implementation; the implementation of the proposals is monitored by the ESRB.[15] Addressees must either notify the ESRB of
the measures taken or justify their non-action ("comply or explain" mechanism).

The effectiveness of the ESRB hinges on its ability to enforce the implementation of its proposals for action. Although its recommendations are not

---

[10] See EBA Regulation, Article 43.
[11] See EBA Regulation, Recital 14.
[12] A more thorough introduction to the structure and tasks of the ESRB may be found in Deutsche Bundesbank, Monthly Report, April 2012.
[13] ESRB Regulation, Recital 10.
[14] See ESRB Regulation, Article 6.
[15] See ESRB Regulation, Article 16.

legally binding, public recommendations, in particular, which force the addressee to either "comply or explain", are likely to be of binding effect.

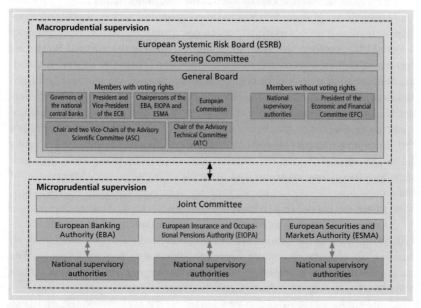

Figure 21.1: The European System of Financial Supervision
Source: Deutsche Bundesbank.

3. HARMONISATION OF SUPERVISORY RULES AND PRACTICES

3.1. Term and Status Quo in Europe

The European Union defines harmonisation as *"bringing national laws into line with one another, very often in order to remove national barriers that obstruct the free movement of workers, goods, services and capital. In other words, harmonisation means making sure that, on any particular issue for which the EU has responsibility, the rules laid down by the different EU countries impose similar obligations on citizens of all those countries and that they impose certain minimum obligations in each country."*[16]

The aim is therefore to harmonise rules and practices in a pre-defined environment, scope or ambit. In a continuous process, albeit at quite uneven speeds

---

[16] http://europa.eu/abc/eurojargon/index_en.htm.

in the various policy areas, Europe's nations have gradually transferred some powers to the Union; in financial market legislation, in particular, a relatively high degree of harmonisation has been achieved, on the whole.

This applies, not least, to banking supervision. In Europe, banking supervision legislation has been gradually harmonised since the 1970s. EU legislators adopted EU directives that need to be implemented at the national level – allowing for certain options and national discretion. Thanks to this progressive, gradual harmonisation and the discretionary scope awarded, national peculiarities or market circumstances, which also reflect a variety of customer preferences, can be maintained while at the same time achieving a convergence of supervisory law in Europe. A milestone in this respect was the introduction of the "European passport" for credit institutions in 1989, which permits banks licensed to operate in one EU member state to open up branches in any other member state. Along with this, the principle of home country supervision of these branches was set, as were supervisory minimum standards – such as uniform minimum capital requirements.

A further institutional milestone was the establishment of the "Level 3 committees", including the Committee of European Banking Supervisors in 2004, which took cooperation among European supervisors to a new level.[17] The most important aim here was to achieve a convergence of supervisory rules and practices by way of voluntary commitments.

Upon implementation of the new Basel capital framework (Basel III) in 2013, the EU will have taken a further step towards even greater harmonisation of banking regulation in Europe, as major sections of the new accord (Pillars I and III) will no longer be implemented at the European level as directives, but as regulations.[18] The EU regulation and the likewise binding prudential supervisory standards co-shaped by the EBA represent directly applicable Union law. Member states therefore no longer have to transpose these European laws into national law and therefore no longer have any discretionary scope for formulating national law.

This further step towards harmonisation, however, should not delude us into believing that the entire legal framework governing credit institutions and their business models will be harmonised any time soon. Even if supervisory legislation is fully harmonised, the complete harmonisation of European banking supervision will remain a gargantuan challenge as, despite the communitisation of many important areas of European law, other equally crucial areas of legislation, such as tax law, company law and administrative law, are still na-

---

[17] See section 2.1.

[18] See the Proposal for a Directive of the European Parliament and of the Council on the access to the activity of credit institutions and the prudential supervision of credit institutions and investment firms (COM(2011)453 final), CRD IV; and the Proposal for a Regulation of the European Parliament and of the Council on prudential requirements for credit institutions and investment firms (COM(2011)452), CRR.

tionally grounded. And it is precisely these areas of law which, alongside banking supervision law, still have a major impact on the activities of banks and supervisors. Attempts to create a uniform supervisory and regulatory structure can therefore lead to conflict with legal regulations from other areas, which still vary quite considerably across Europe. The discussions about provisions in the area of "corporate governance" are a case in point. A strict and uniform orientation to a "one-tier structure", comprising an executive board and a supervisory board, would cause problems in countries whose company law envisages a "two-tier structure", in which the two bodies are separated.

The continued existence of differences in national financial and banking systems, despite all the progress made thus far in integration and harmonisation, poses a further challenge; the effects of an amendment to rules and practices may therefore often vary from one country to the next. In a bank-based system, for instance, the real economy is also indirectly affected more strongly by changes in bank regulation and supervision than in a market-based system. There are, in some cases, significant differences between European financial systems. Whereas, in bank-based Germany, for example, the real economy obtains just over 60% of its financing via banks and just under 40% in the capital market, the ratio in the United Kingdom, for instance, is exactly the opposite.[19]

Further differences also continue to exist in the number of institutions, their size distribution and, concomitantly, the concentration of business and the competitive situation. Here, too, harmonisation rules have varying effects depending on whether a banking industry is dominated by a very few large players or whether market shares are spread across a broader base; large exposure rules or provisions to counteract geographical or product-specific concentration risks will affect a market with a large share of special-purpose or geographically concentrated institutions more strongly than a market with larger, more broadly diversified banks. Higher funding costs will also have a greater impact on a more competitive banking market, in which profit margins are consequently low, than in a banking industry in which competition is less intense.

There are also major differences with regard, for example, to the degree of concentration:[20] whereas in Germany the five largest banks hold a market share of around 33% (measured in terms of total assets), in other large EU member states such as Spain, France, Italy and the UK the figure ranges between 40% and nearly 50%.[21] In some cases, concentration runs as high as over 80% in Finland or even over 90% in Estonia. The provision of banking services to the public likewise varies. Whereas in Germany there is one bank branch for every 2,073 residents, in the UK one branch has to serve 5,107 residents. The number

---

[19] See Allard and Blavy (2011), p 9.
[20] All figures from ECB (2012). The figures refer to the year 2010.
[21] Spain 44.3%; France 47.4%; Italy 39.2%; United Kingdom 42.5%; at the other end of the scale, Finland 83.8%, Estonia 92.3%.

of residents per bank branch in Spain is much smaller, at 1,070.[22] Significant differences also exist regarding the percentage shares of foreign institutions in a given market: foreign institutions hold about 10% of the market share in Germany, France and Spain, but a dominant share of over 90% in countries such as Luxembourg, Slovakia and Estonia.[23]

With regard to key areas of legislation, and especially market structures, Europe still has a long way to go before it achieves harmonisation or convergence. Some current trends in macroprudential instruments could even be interpreted as indicating that differences between the respective national markets are being accorded growing importance and that the aim is to pave the way for a sort of "re-nationalisation" of rules and supervisory practices.

3.2. Opportunities and Risks of Harmonisation in Banking Supervision

The historical – and, by all means, justified – differences in legal systems and market structures in Europe give rise to the question of whether harmonising supervisory rules and practices completely is really the best solution – or whether there is an optimum degree of harmonisation somewhere short of the maximum objective.

The advantages of harmonisation are well-known. Uniform rules create transparency and clarity with regard to their interpretation. Especially for cross-border banks, a single set of rules can reduce the regulatory and reporting burden, and thus the costs of transactions and red tape; by creating a regulatory level playing field, it prevents "regulatory arbitrage". At the same time, it would avoid the importing of risks caused by regulatory and supervisory differences between European countries, which supervisors regard as a desirable aim.

When discussing the advantages of standardised rules and practices, however, it must not be forgotten that harmonisation is not an end in itself. Here, too, we must observe the principle of treating like cases alike and unlike cases differently. Whereas it is desirable to harmonise like with like, unthinking uniformity would be harmful because it would align historically grown market structures and business models and fail to sufficiently address customer preferences. Such harmonisation should only be limited, with a clear idea of the consequences. Otherwise, diversity and competition between different banking services and products across jurisdictions could disappear. Such a development could even run counter to the aim of creating a stable framework for the financial system, as it would fuel trends towards concentration.

---

[22] All figures are from ECB (2012), ECB calculations.
[23] See ECB (2012).

3.3. Variants of Harmonisation and their Consequences

Yet what type of harmonisation is suitable for the European banking industry and for its ability to function in the various national markets? There are many different types of harmonisation and levels of intensity at which supervision can be harmonised in the real world. There are two highly important reference points here: the "framework of rules", which institutions in Europe are required to comply with and which underlie the supervisory approach; and the "competencies of supervisory authorities". In order to give structure to this notion, let us introduce three different options below.

Full harmonisation (*option 1*) is what would result if supervisory rules, their interpretation and their practical application were aligned at the European level, along with powers and opportunities for supervisors to intervene. These uniform supervisory rules and practices would then apply to all institutions in Europe. This would thus create a "single rule book" and uniform practice in the ongoing supervision of all institutions. Supervisory powers would remain with national authorities.

Another possibility would be a "*dual approach*" (*option 2*) with full harmonisation of rules, as described above, for institutions active across Europe (such as the EBA stress test banks), and national rules for nationally operating banks. Even in this dual approach, supervisory powers could remain with national authorities both for banks active across Europe and also for nationally operating banks. The dual approach would involve a departure from a "holistic" approach to supervision and from efforts towards convergence and harmonisation within the European single market. According to the status quo, by contrast, the EU still has a "single rule book", and the differences in systemic relevance and cross-border operations of institutions are taken into account only through additional provisions, such as a capital add-on for systemically important banks. Thus, the single rule book is generally applied at present; in practice, the principle of proportionality guides the intensity and standards of supervision.

In the dual approach with different European and national rulebooks, I believe the attendant disadvantages far outweigh the advantages of the added flexibility to take account of national particularities. First, the mere act of classifying institutions would be anything but trivial. It is difficult to develop meaningful criteria for classifying all institutions active in Europe definitively as either European-regulated or nationally regulated banks. Systemic importance alone is an inadequate criterion for such classification since it does not prevent the feared regulatory arbitrage; for even small and medium-sized institutions can engage in regulatory arbitrage, thus collectively accumulating systemically important risks. This would also nullify the carefully chosen principle of "same business, same risks, same rules". "Same business", such as domestic lending, would be supervised under different rules depending on the type of institution, which would lead to different cost structures and thus have undesirable implications for competition.

Second, nor do I share the view, held by many proponents of the dual approach, that the only way to eliminate the dangers resulting from networking and interdependency in the financial market is through uniform supervision of cross-border institutions. The contagion channels continue to exist. For instance, many institutions – cross-border and regional alike – are interconnected through the interbank market or indirectly by investing in the same or similar asset classes and thus exposed to the threat of contagion. It is precisely in the past few years that we have been forced to realise just how quickly confidence not only in a bank or group of banks, but in the entire financial sector, can vanish. The wish for appropriate harmonisation of supervisory rules and supervisory practice is therefore more than understandable.

A "*double dual approach*" (*option 3*) would constitute a bigger step in the direction of harmonisation in Europe. Institutions active across Europe would be subject to fully harmonised EU regulations and be supervised by a European supervisory authority, while national institutions would be supervised by domestic authorities according to national regulations. This would make the option of a double dual approach a more substantial move and, given that it would involve two supervisory bodies, would probably lead to even greater divergence in the application of supervisory practices. In addition, the separation between financial and functional responsibility would be even more of an issue under this kind of approach, as would the question of whether it is desirable to have a system where one body combats hazards and another entirely different one has to repair the damage if such risks become a reality. A European supervisory authority would be responsible for supervising the category of institutions which holds the greatest potential to cause harm, yet any fiscal burden would still be borne by taxpayers in the individual countries. It is hard to imagine national governments in the EU member states agreeing to shoulder budgetary responsibility for supervision without having the corresponding decision-making rights or powers of intervention. Even a joint deposit guarantee scheme and resolution fund could only be funded by the national taxpayer. A double dual model would therefore necessitate fundamental changes to European primary legislation, involving pan-European burden-sharing which would require the member states to relinquish some of their fiscal sovereignty.

It will become apparent in the coming years which route the EU will choose in its quest for harmonisation. We are currently on course for full harmonisation, despite being a long way from the finishing line. Indeed, supervisors' powers of and options for intervention are precisely the areas that are not yet fully harmonised, and nor are supervisory approaches or, as a result, the methods for applying European law in day-to-day supervisory work. Yet this seems to be the only viable route to creating a true internal market and effectively preventing supervisory arbitrage. EU legislators need to be aware, however, that the differing impact of full harmonisation in the individual countries of Europe must be managed with care and deliberation if it is to be carried out at an appropriate speed and intensity. As outlined above, the structure of banking systems varies across Europe despite the existence of a single market, not least because of differing customer needs. Even so, efforts to harmonise the regulatory framework and supervisory practices must not render national banking sectors incapable of "serving" the real economy by providing it with credit and other financing instruments.

The right balance therefore needs to be struck to enable supervisory legislation and practices to take account of both the specific characteristics of national systems and cross-border integration in the financial markets. The EBA Regulation also contains provisions to this effect: recital 11 requires that the EBA should act "with a view to improving the functioning of the internal market, in particular by ensuring a high, effective and consistent level of regulation and supervision taking account of the varying interests of all Member States and the different nature of financial institutions."

This task will not become any easier for national supervisors in the future. The EBA's specific range of duties will lend an entirely new quality to the harmonisation of regulation and ongoing supervision in Europe. Binding technical standards drawn up by the EBA will have binding legal effect once they have been endorsed by the Commission. To implement the Basel III framework, the EBA will carry out the groundwork for around 80 such standards in the coming three years. The legal provisions devised for this purpose by European legislators would seem to indicate a depth of detail which stands in conflict with principles-based supervision. Yet it is the principles-based approach which provides the leeway needed for a banking system as heterogeneous as Germany's. Both the "single rule book" and the more specific technical standards therefore need to be worded in a way that leaves sufficient scope for differentiation. The principle of proportionality must not be cast aside. It will also be crucial to conduct comprehensive studies of the potential implications of important regulation for the different market structures before it is introduced. We must also ensure that harmonisation does not have the unwanted side-effect of making it harder for the real economy to obtain funding. These impact studies and the subsequent negotiations on the appropriate steps to take towards dovetailing supervision as far as possible are time-consuming but essential to achieving an appropriate and successful harmonisation.

As illustrated above, harmonisation is a process rather than an end in itself. As preferences and market structures are not set in stone and may change, albeit slowly, the appropriate degree of harmonisation is also more of a moving target than a pre-established objective. For this course of action to succeed, it is crucial to have intensive cooperation between the members of the new European supervisory system, the European supervisory authorities, the ESRB and, not least, the national supervisory authorities – not only to identify cross-border risks at a sufficiently early stage and ensure better supervision of institutions that are active across Europe but also to allow any convergence of national supervisory practices at all.

4. MACROPRUDENTIAL OVERSIGHT IN COMPLEMENT WITH MICROPRUDENTIAL SUPERVISION

4.1. Stronger Macroprudential Oversight: A Lesson from the Crisis

The financial crisis has shown just how great the need is for more intense macroprudential analysis and oversight in complement with microprudential financial supervision. Macroprudential oversight can be defined as providing a safeguard for the stability of the entire financial system by monitoring macroeconomic indicators.[24] The G20 leaders are pressing ahead with the expansion of macroprudential oversight at a global level; a number of institutional measures have already been taken, including the strengthening of the Financial Stability Board (FSB) and the IMF.

As outlined above, European macroprudential oversight has found an institutional home in the European Systemic Risk Board (ESRB), which was set up as part of the reform of supervisory structures.[25]

Macroprudential oversight in Germany will be the responsibility of the German Financial Stability Board, which is to be established in accordance with the draft Act to Strengthen German Financial Supervision (*Gesetzentwurf zur Stärkung der deutschen Finanzaufsicht*). This draft act was adopted by the German federal cabinet on 2 May 2012 and is expected to come into effect by the start of 2013.[26] The Federal Ministry of Finance, BaFin and the Bundesbank will each have three voting members on the German Financial Stability Board. The current cabinet draft assigns the Bundesbank an important role on this board, giving it the power of veto. The Bundesbank will also be tasked with using its analyses to identify risks to financial stability and devising proposals for warnings and recommendations to avert such risks, as well as monitoring whether the board's recommendations are being implemented.

4.2. Macroprudential Oversight: What will be Analysed and Why?

Macroprudential oversight is to take more of a "systemic approach" in future. It will identify developments among market participants, products and infra-

---

[24] See Buch (2011), p 4.
[25] See section 2.3.
[26] See Entwurf eines Gesetzes zur Stärkung der deutschen Finanzaufsicht, Bundesrat, Drucksache 249/12 (in German only).

structures which could generate risks to the stability of the financial system. It will also investigate areas of interdependence between participants in the financial sector and between the financial sector and the real economy. It will therefore work in complement with "traditional" financial supervision, which is more focused on individual institutions or market structures.

Macroprudential oversight in Europe is still under negotiation and development; specific macroprudential tools have yet to be created and their interplay with tried and tested microprudential instruments examined. There are already plans to introduce one macroprudential instrument, at least for the banking sector: the countercyclical capital buffer under the Basel III framework. Current discussions on CRD IV – which will transpose Basel III into EU law – are also addressing the possibility of introducing other tools, such as a general systemic risk buffer set by national supervisors. The possibility of lending greater weight to systemic risk, e.g. when setting additional capital requirements for individual institutions, is also being considered. Another option under debate would be to allow member states, subject to the European Commission's endorsement, to impose stricter capital requirements or large exposures regulations and additional disclosure requirements if national financial stability appears to be under threat. By contrast, ideas on the macroprudential instruments needed beyond the sphere of banking regulation, e.g. for the shadow banking sector, are still in their infancy.

To be successful, macroprudential oversight needs a broad focus. It must consider all risks to the financial system, including those created by the real economy itself or the behaviour of other market participants. This is ultimately why, under certain circumstances, it could even go beyond merely analysing the effects of procyclical fiscal policies and also look at the risks induced by incentive structures in the real economy which, for example, stimulate funding via banks or insurance companies. Economic developments among important market participants such as insurance companies are just as important to the stability of the financial system as new trading practices, e.g. high frequency trading, or the security of payments and market infrastructures such as clearing houses or central counterparties. Macroprudential analyses and oversight should also involve intensive scrutiny of the shadow financial sector. Although the body of data in this area is currently rather small, making it difficult to assess risks comprehensively, global initiatives (FSB) to bring this sector into a regulatory framework mean that more possibilities for analysis are likely to arise as it becomes more transparent.

Though somewhat further removed from the financial markets, social security systems (e.g. implicit liabilities created by demographic developments) and, notably, tax systems are nonetheless important to their stability. Tax incentives can, for example, encourage certain forms of investment and be a potential source of asset price inflation (e.g., in housing markets), which could generate bubbles that affect financial stability. Macroprudential analyses also need to examine the effects of monetary policy on the financial systems. An overly expansionary monetary policy can likewise influence financial stability, e.g. when asset price inflation is fuelled by "cheap money".

In all of these areas, macroprudential analysis can deliver important findings which help to improve our understanding of risks to financial stability. However, we must not have unrealistic expectations of macroprudential oversight. Given the deep interlinkages among markets and market participants, risks formed outside of the national or European market can also have a destabilising effect on the European market. A wide range of markets, products, market participants, infrastructures and legislative initiatives would need to be analysed and proposals for action considered in order being able to identify these risks at an early stage and assess their importance to European markets.

Added to the difficulties in identifying such risks would be the no less complex problem of how to use the macroprudential toolkit appropriately. For one thing, this toolkit has yet to be developed and, for another, causal relationships are less clear in macroprudential analysis than in microprudential supervision. When identifying threats to the financial system at a very early stage, it may be difficult to find a sound legal basis for applying measures which could create substantial burdens.

4.3. The Role of Central Banks in Macroprudential Oversight

Based on the cabinet draft, the Bundesbank's role on the planned Financial Stability Board will make it pivotal to macroprudential oversight in Germany. The European central banks have a coordinating function on the ESRB. It makes sense to involve central banks in macroprudential oversight in this way given their in-depth knowledge of and data on the financial market. Further macroprudential analysis would be a logical addition to the economic research and analysis that central banks already carry out today. They also play a key part in payments, a vital component of market infrastructure.

In addition, the tasks that many central banks perform in banking and financial supervision are a good starting point for developing more extensive macroprudential duties. Central banks in 15 (initially 16) EU countries are responsible for banking and financial supervision or – as is the case in Austria and Germany – are substantially involved in banking supervision. These kinds of structures mean that the necessary integration between micro and macroprudential supervision is ensured in-house, at least for part of the financial system. This integration also extends to the European level; all central banks and the national and European authorities working in the area of financial stability are represented on the ESRB, which allows findings to be exchanged between central banks and supervisory authorities and between national and European bodies. This is also illustrated by the exchange of data between the different tiers of supervision; the ESRB provides supervisory authorities with information on relevant risks while also receiving aggregated data from the European supervisory authorities, the European System of Central Banks (ESCB), the European Commission and the national supervisory and statistical authorities. The ESRB can also submit a reasoned request for data from individual institutions in specific cases.[27]

There are therefore a number of good reasons for *giving central banks a macroprudential mandate*. However, the central bank needs to be given the appropriate powers to fulfil this mandate, above all with respect to obtaining the necessary information and data. It is ultimately crucial to ensure that a central bank's macroprudential remit does not encroach upon its monetary policy independence.

4.4. Interplay between Microprudential Supervision and Macroprudential Oversight

To ensure the success of macroprudential oversight at national and European level, it is vital, in particular, that the two "tiers" of supervision – macroprudential oversight and microprudential supervision – are closely intertwined and work in complement with one another. The two tiers must establish an intensive exchange of information on the developments they identify and their assessment of them. Also on the European level, the ESRB and the EBA are required to exchange all important information and inform each other of potential risks. Together, they can issue a confidential recommendation to the Council where they consider that an emergency situation may arise. They cooperate closely on the Union-wide stress tests and join forces to develop criteria for measuring systemic risk.

In this way, macroprudential oversight will benefit, for example, from banking supervisors' insights into systemically important trends and developments. Above all, findings from cross-institutional national and international peer group analyses and other cross-comparisons in modern banking supervision can be key to assessing macroeconomic developments.

For this approach to succeed, there need to be aggregated observations of the banking system and of bank categories that go beyond the microprudential level. At the same time, systemic analyses must include specific criteria for identifying developing risks and possible paths and effects of contagion. The aim is to enable macroprudential findings to be applied in specific prudential strategies and action plans while also ensuring that macroprudential overseers obtain regular feedback from ongoing supervision as "food for thought" to help them identify new sources of risk.

This interplay between macroprudential analysis and microprudential supervision must then be reflected in better regulation and/or supervisory prac-

---

[27] See ESRB Regulation, Article 15 5-7.

tices. Findings on relevant macroeconomic developments will influence the supervisory strategy and planning for individual institutions and categories of institutions. At the same time, however, it is important to maintain a distinction between the two tiers of supervision to ensure that the lines of responsibility are clear and unambiguous.

4.5. Conclusion

It is sensible and advisable to introduce a macroprudential component alongside microprudential supervision. This has been achieved within the ESFS through the creation of the ESRB. The instruments available to the ESRB are not legally binding; they need to be enforced by the EU member states or the national supervisory authorities. However, the "comply or explain" mechanism will probably make them *de facto* binding. The Bundesbank is to make significant contributions to and therefore to play a key part in the German Financial Stability Board. This is the best possible way to address one of the lessons learned from the financial crisis, namely that insufficient account was taken of macroeconomic developments. Expanding the focus of analysis can reduce the number, frequency and severity of crises by broadening the underlying information for recognising threats to stability, even though it is impossible to rule out future crises entirely. Cooperation between all parties involved at national and European level will be an important factor in determining the reform's success.

5. CLOSING REMARKS

This chapter investigates the overarching issue of whether the new European supervisory system has prepared the ground for learning lessons from the financial crisis and contributing to financial stability even in view of the changing structure of the financial industry. We have set out on the right track. To ultimately achieve the set aims and be able to answer the question with a clear affirmative, however, certain important aspects need to be taken into consideration.

We should push ahead with harmonisation in European banking regulation and supervision – with the proviso that sufficient consideration is given to market and customer-driven differences between the national banking markets. Tried and tested structures and products must not be sacrificed at the altar of harmonisation and replaced by a uniform system without due consideration. Diversity can actually help to safeguard stability because one-crop economies are more vulnerable to systemic risk.

Should the European supervisory authorities, specifically the EBA, be given an even more extensive remit or sole responsibility for supervising large complex financial institutions in order to push ahead with harmonisation? Advocates of this approach would be forced to change certain political realities first. The dual supervisory approach would be a departure from the "same rules, same risk" concept. In the absence of a fiscal union, it would also be subject to legal and budgetary limitations and contravene the principle of uniting financial and functional responsibility. The current system is thus a workable political compromise as it strikes the necessary balance between harmonisation and the required flexibility. This is also reflected in the "members-driven approach" chosen by the EBA, which entails a lasting involvement of national supervisory authorities and central banks in supervisory work.

Introducing a macroprudential component will close the gap in the observations of financial systems. The EU has already created an institution tasked with identifying systemic risks in the form of the ESRB. This macroprudential mandate now needs to be fleshed out by developing suitable instruments that have an effective and efficient impact on market participants and the markets themselves. Microprudential and macroprudential supervisory authorities must collaborate closely to ensure that this undertaking is successful.

Safeguarding financial stability in Europe is a complex and difficult task, not least – as the financial crisis has shown – because of the strong impact of developments outside Europe. If the ESFS is structured appropriately, however, it should be possible to provide a firm basis for financial supervision and macroprudential oversight in order to better contribute to maintaining stability.

BIBLIOGRAPHY

Allard, J. and R. Blavy 2011, "Market Phoenixes and Banking Ducks: Are Recoveries Faster in Market-Based Financial Systems?", *IMF Working Paper*, September 2011. WP/11/213.

Buch, C. M. 2011, "Regulierung von Banken und makroökonomische Risiken", speech, Deutsche Bundesbank Stuttgart.

Deutsche Bundesbank 2011, "International cooperation in banking regulation: past and present", *Monthly Report*, September 2011, pp 79-93.

Deutsche Bundesbank 2012, "The European Systemic Risk Board: from institutional foundation to credible macroprudential oversight", *Monthly Report*, April 2012.

ECB 2012, *Structural Indicators for the EU Banking Sector*, http://www.ecb.int/pub/pdf/other/structralindicatorseubankingsector201001en.pdf.

European Commission 2009, "Report by the High-Level Group on Financial Supervision in the EU", Brussels, 25 February 2009.

22. Macroprudential, Microprudential and Monetary Policies: Conflicts, Complementarities and Trade-Offs

Paolo Angelini, Sergio Nicoletti-Altimari and Ignazio Visco

1. INTRODUCTION

Following the outbreak of the financial crisis in the summer of 2007, the reforms of the regulatory framework aimed to address financial instability and introduced macroprudential authorities in many jurisdictions. As these authorities commence operations, the question of how macroprudential policy will interact with monetary, microprudential and fiscal policies has inevitably come to the fore.

A broad consensus has emerged around the idea that macroprudential policy should address systemic risk – externalities which, if unheeded, could jeopardise financial stability. However, this remains a somewhat elusive concept, hard to measure and identify. Furthermore, we still lack a well-defined analytical apparatus and operational definitions of the objectives and instruments of macroprudential policy. Indicators and early warning signals are available, but a coherent framework to interpret them, to assess the need for intervention and to measure the effectiveness of the policies adopted is still lacking. This applies both to the time-series dimension of systemic risk (linked to pro-cyclicality, the accumulation of risk over the business or the financial cycle) and to the cross-sectional dimension (linked to the distribution of risks across intermediaries that may exacerbate vulnerabilities for any given amount of time-varying risk).[1] A related problem is that the set of candidate macroprudential instruments, their effects and interactions – among themselves and with other

All of the authors are with the Bank of Italy. We would like to thank P. Bologna, M. Caccavaio, A. De Vincenzo, F. Panetta, G. Pepe, M. Pietrunti and M. Rocco for their many useful comments and help with the evidence and the arguments. The views expressed by Mr. Visco in this chapter are his own and do not represent those of the Governing Council or of the European Central Bank.

[1] For a discussion of these two aspects, see Borio and Crockett (2000); Borio et al. (2001).

policies – are in need of more in-depth analysis (see, e.g., Bank of England 2009, 2011; Borio 2010).

In the next section we review the recent attempts to analyse macropruden-tial policy and its interaction with other policies, in particular monetary policy. Notwithstanding the advances made, the analytical framework remains far from complete. On the one hand, most of the existing macroeconomic models used to study and simulate macroprudential tools still fail to incorporate op-erational definitions of systemic risk, the very problem which macroprudential policy should address. On the other hand, models that attempt to incorporate systemic externalities are computationally highly intensive and are necessar-ily formulated at a level of abstraction that makes them unsuitable for policy analysis. Moreover, many of the effects associated with asset price misalign-ments and financial crises are highly non-linear. This is at odds with the current generation of macro models, which relies heavily on linearisation techniques. Such non-linearities may be of a kind that are particularly difficult to deal with, i.e. linked to regime shifts and discontinuities in economic relationships. These difficulties represent a challenge for future research.

Several important points emerge from our reading of the literature. First, the most recent theoretical works have identified sources of externalities in the financial sector, often in the form of potentially excessive credit growth. This finding squares well with recent experience and provides a rationale for mac-roprudential policy. Second, the conduct of monetary policy needs to take into account financial stability because the latter is a necessary condition for price stability and because, by doing so, it may improve its performance in terms of output and inflation variability. Third, countercyclical macroprudential instru-ments (time-varying capital requirements or provisioning, loan-to-value ratios, etc.) tend to be effective at moderating economic fluctuations and the financial cycle, although with a number of caveats and uncertainties. Finally, there are complementarities between monetary and macroprudential policies, but also a potential for conflict. This calls for institutional arrangements that favour cooperation and synergies between the two policies.

In sections 3 and 4 we try to relate these key messages to recent events, in particular in the Euro area against the backdrop of the unfolding sovereign debt crisis. We argue that in principle national macroprudential authorities would want to adjust countercyclical instruments to compensate for the highly hetero-geneous real interest rates that have recently materialised in various Euro-area countries. However, at present there is very little room for manoeuvre for such policies: in the run-up to the crisis insufficient capital buffers had been accumu-lated and, also due to market pressures, it is now difficult for macroprudential authorities, especially in the countries with weak sovereign debt conditions, to credibly call for lowering prudential requirements. It follows that there is not, at present, any issue of conflict between macroprudential and monetary policies; by the same token, neither is there any conflict with microprudential policy.

Why was bank capital so low at the start of the financial crisis? Several factors, linked to the regulatory framework and supervisory practices, may have played a role in preventing the build-up of adequate capital buffers. We discuss the role of risk-weighted assets (RWAs); our evidence suggests that the underlying methodologies may have been unable to adequately capture the actual risks borne by banks, confirming that the key features of the microprudential apparatus are crucial for preventing financial instability. Can the banking sector as a whole sustain a significantly higher level of capitalisation, or would the cost be prohibitively high? We review the debate, pointing out that the new regulation already implies an important move in this direction, due to changes in both the numerator (higher quality capital) and denominator (increased risk weights) of the capital ratio. Our conclusions are summarised in the final section.

2. CURRENT MODELLING APPROACHES TO MACRO-PRUDENTIAL POLICY

How should countercyclical macroprudential policy be conducted? To what extent do macroprudential and monetary policies have the capacity to affect the economy independently of each other? May they usefully coexist, or is there a risk of conflict? How should one choose among the multitude of possible macroprudential instruments? Answering these questions requires the development of a theoretical framework in which these policies can be properly modelled, to be used as a guide for empirical investigation. Ideally, this framework should be simple enough to allow a proper understanding of the underlying mechanisms but also realistic enough to offer guidance to policy-makers in this new environment. A very simple framework is unlikely to be adequate. For instance, in a standard AS-AD New Keynesian model, the two policies would be perfectly linearly dependent, as they both end up influencing the only control instrument available to the policy-maker, the interest rate – either via open market operations, or via the macroprudential policy measure.[2] A framework for studying macroprudential policies should have another essential characteristic: it should incorporate the particular distortions that macroprudential policy is supposed to address – the externalities associated with systemic risk.

These features are hard to combine in a single model. To our knowledge, none of the existing analytical frameworks feature a comprehensive modelling of systemic risk. This partly reflects its elusive nature: systemic risk can take different forms with respect to market participants (a bank run or the default of

---

[2] Cecchetti and Kohler (2012) adopt a highly-stylized model to investigate the possibility of using capital requirements to reach traditional monetary policy goals such as inflation and output stability and explore whether coordination is desirable when two separate bodies are in charge of the two goals. The authors find that if a policy-maker is concerned only with price and output stability, the two instruments are perfect substitutes.

an investment firm), markets (stock market crashes or currency crises) and geographical areas (domestic vs. international crises), making it virtually impossible to devise a general modelling approach. Several recent contributions do incorporate systemic externalities, but are too complex and stylized for policy use. By contrast, other model classes lend themselves to policy analysis, but fail to incorporate systemic risk. We review these two strands in the next subsections; we then move to the empirical contributions, and present a summary in subsection 2.4. We should acknowledge at the outset that we confine ourselves to some key strands of the literature on macroprudential policy, without any pretence to completeness.[3]

2.1. Some Models Feature Systemic Risk but are too Abstract for Policy Use ...

Lorenzoni (2008), Bianchi (2010), Bianchi and Mendoza (2010), Mendoza (2010), Jeanne and Korinek (2010) and Korinek (2011) show that when access to credit is subject to an occasionally binding collateral constraint a credit externality arises, driving a wedge between the competitive equilibrium and the planner's allocation. This approach is rooted in the debt deflation theory developed by Fisher (1933), later introduced in formal models by Kiyotaki and Moore (1997) and Shleifer and Vishny (1997). The key driver is that the price of assets is an increasing function of the aggregate level of debt: when a shock hits the economy, investors must reduce their asset positions in order to fulfil their debt obligations. The contemporaneous ("fire") sale of assets brings their price below its fundamental level and this leads to a tightening of credit conditions and exerts a further depressive effect on asset prices, starting a vicious cycle.[4] As agents do not take into account the effects of their aggregate actions on the price of collateral, in such a set-up this externality induces households to over-borrow. One problem is that it is not yet clear how robust this externality is. Depending on certain features and parameterisations, the models can produce over-borrowing as well as under-borrowing (Benigno et al. 2010), and under reasonable assumptions under-borrowing may even predominate (Benigno et al. 2011). Bianchi and Mendoza (2010) also find that over-borrowing arises in the competitive equilibrium for reasonable values of the key parameters, but not for all values.

Brunnermeier and Sannikov (2011) study a continuous-time, global (non-linearised) model in which certain agents ("experts") have superior skills in selecting profitable projects but possess limited net worth. In normal times the

---

[3] See Galati and Moessner (2011) for a recent review of the literature on macroprudential policy, the chapter by Caruana on systemic risk (chapter 9 in this volume) and the papers in BIS (2011) for an overview on systemic risk, financial system procyclicality, early warning indicators, and macroprudential policy implementation.

[4] See Brunnermeier (2009) for the amplification role played by liquidity risk in these circumstances.

economy is in a steady state with low volatility, but it occasionally lapses into a regime with high volatility induced by strong negative feedback from large losses by the "experts". At the heart of the loop lies an externality, in that individually market participants take prices as given but collectively they affect them. Stein (2011) develops a model where the collateral constraint applies directly to financial intermediaries. In his model banks have a strong incentive to issue "too much" collateralised short-term debt because they fail to fully internalise the fact that in a bad state they will need to liquidate assets to repay their debt, thus inducing a fire sales spiral.

Overall, models of this class provide a micro-founded (albeit specific) definition of systemic risk and a rationale for policy intervention, for example regulatory measures to reduce leverage, or an active role for central banks as lenders (or market makers) of last resort. They also provide insights into the undiversifiable nature of systemic risk and may help explain why asset prices tend to become highly correlated in certain conditions, complicating the task of market operators and regulators alike. However, one common problem is that in order to overcome technical and computational complexities they are extremely simplified. Moreover, they often have an insufficient level of detail in the description of the financial sector or in the monetary policy design, or both, and are accordingly unsuitable for policy analysis.

2.2. ... Whereas Others are Suitable for Policy Use but do not Feature Systemic Risk

Several recent papers have examined issues of financial stability in more standard macroeconomic models. While not explicitly considering the financial sector, Cúrdia and Woodford (2010), Woodford (2012), and Gilchrist and Zakrajsek (2012) develop a modelling technique that captures financial risk via proxies of credit risk in the economy (typically, a spread between risky and riskless rates). They show that Taylor-type monetary policy rules that also include indicators of financial distress dominate rules of the standard type. One shortcoming of these models is that they fail to incorporate a meaningful modelling of systemic risk, which makes them unsuitable for welfare analysis.

A step in the right direction is made in the literature that develops and uses models with a simplified financial sector, often using dynamic stochastic general equilibrium (DSGE) models featuring the "financial accelerator" mechanism originally proposed by Bernanke, Gertler and Gilchrist (1999), or building on the alternative approach pioneered by Kiyotaki and Moore (1997). These models share some of the shortcomings of those of the previous strand. On the other hand, they are well-known, relatively easy-to-use workhorses that can be useful for the purposes of a positive analysis. Specifically, they allow us to study countercyclical macroprudential instruments at the centre of the current policy debate – typically time-varying capital requirements or provisioning, loan-to-value ratios, etc. – or the interactions between monetary and macroprudential policies.

Kannan et al. (2009) and Angeloni and Faia (2009) were among the first papers to analyse this interaction, introducing capital ratios as a policy tool into a DSGE model. Kannan et al.'s paper focuses on housing booms; Angeloni and Faia's on banks prone to runs. Their main finding is that countercyclical capital ratios have beneficial real effects. Moreover, the optimal policy mix would involve a reaction of monetary policy to asset prices, or to credit expansion ("leaning against the wind"). Other papers that focus on various macroprudential instruments and reach encouraging conclusions in terms of the effectiveness of monetary and macroprudential policies and their interaction include: N'Dyaie (2009), Covas and Fujita (2009), Roger and Vlček (2011), Angelini et al. (2011b), Lambertini et al. (2011), Beau et al. (2011). Positing that the macroprudential authority can affect mortgage spreads directly, Catte et al. (2010) show that a tighter monetary policy by the Fed between 2002 and 2006 would not have been sufficient to avoid the housing bubble; however, if appropriately combined with macroprudential credit restraints, it could have dampened the housing boom with modest macroeconomic side effects. In many of these papers, however, the extent of the effectiveness of macroprudential instruments depends on various factors, including the way monetary policy is treated. For instance, the benefits of macroprudential policies tend to be smaller if monetary policy rules are optimised to take the effects of the macroprudential instrument into account.

Angelini et al. (2011a), Bean et al. (2010), Beau et al. (2011), Quint and Rabanal (2011), Cecchetti and Kohler (2012) also study the strategic interaction between monetary and macroprudential policy. These papers confirm that macroprudential policy has some potential to stabilise the economy over and above what can be achieved by monetary policy alone, but that this varies depending on the type of shock or set-up considered (model parameterisations, etc.). Furthermore, they point to the risk of conflict between the two policies in the absence of coordination. Ueda and Valencia (2012) claim that when a central bank is in charge of price and financial stability a new time-inconsistency problem may arise. Ex ante, the central bank chooses the socially optimal level of inflation. Ex post, the central bank may choose inflation above the social optimum to reduce the real value of private debt. However, this conclusion is based on the assumption that macroprudential policies cannot be adjusted as frequently as monetary policy.

2.3. Recent Strands of Empirical Literature

The empirical literature bearing on issues related to macroprudential policy is probably too ample to permit an exhaustive review. Accordingly in this section we confine ourselves to recalling two important recent strands. The first concerns the relationship between monetary policy and risk-taking behaviour, and hence financial stability; the second addresses the issue of macroprudential instruments.

There is by now broad consensus around the view that low interest rates tend to encourage excessive risk-taking. This can occur via various channels (see the survey by Panetta et al. 2009). In the presence of an inverse relationship between asset values and interest rates, when rates are low the value of collateral is high, and vice versa. Therefore low rates can drive credit growth above the level compatible with a "normal" value of collateral.[5] Recent evidence confirms this thesis: lower short-term interest rates decrease the probability of default on existing loans but increase it on new loans, so the latter are riskier than average (Jiménez et al. 2008; Ioannidou et al. 2007). Furthermore, periods of low interest rates tend to be accompanied by low volatility and high risk appetite (see, for example, Pericoli and Taboga 2008; Rudebusch et al. 2006; Kim and Wright 2005). Low interest rates may also induce institutional investors to take on excessive risk.[6] Contributions to this strand of literature go under the name of the "risk-taking channel", after Borio and Zhu (2008), who argue that a loose monetary policy may stimulate excessive risk-taking and leverage, or liquidity transformation, thus increasing systemic fragility and ultimately putting price stability at risk. Altunbas et al. (2010) and Maddaloni and Peydró (2012), present empirical evidence in line with this hypothesis.

This literature underlines the need for monetary policy to be aware of these potential channels and to monitor a broad range of indicators, like buoyant credit growth, increasing leverage of financial institutions, and in general leading indicators of financial instability. One key implication is that central banks should not confine their action to intervening after a crash; they should also play an active role in limiting the build-up of systemic risk during the buoyant phases.

Another rapidly developing strand of literature draws lessons from the actual implementation of macroprudential instruments, mostly in developing countries. Lim et al. (2011), using data from a group of 49 countries, find that financial system procyclicality may be dampened by several instruments: caps on the loan-to-value (LTV) ratio, on the debt-to-income ratio (DTI), or on credit, or credit growth, reserve requirements, countercyclical capital require-

---

[5] The financial accelerator may be reinforced by banks' lending policies. Under imperfect information bank managers affected by short-termism have an incentive to adopt an excessively liberal credit policy (Rajan 1994, 2005).

[6] Rajan (2005) describes various possible underlying mechanisms. For instance, insurance companies and pension funds may have a large share of liabilities that are fixed in nominal terms. Therefore, unexpected prolonged periods of exceptionally low rates may put severe strain on their balance sheets and profits and loss accounts, inducing them to seek riskier investments to meet their commitments, since they tend to perceive mainly the upside and to overlook the downside risks.

ments and provisioning. In addition, limits on net open currency positions, and on currency or maturity mismatches may help to reduce common exposures across institutions and markets. Wong et al. (2011) as well as Ahuja and Nabar (2011) present evidence that management of LTV and DTI in Hong Kong and in several other countries proved effective, although the effect on household debt and transaction volumes is more evident, whereas that on real estate prices is less direct, or materialises with a delay.

Overall, the evidence suggests that macroprudential policies may effectively achieve their goals, but several caveats apply. In particular, little is known about the costs of resorting to macroprudential instruments, their calibration, and potential unintended effects. Moreover, several factors that policy-makers may not have taken into account – for example, a rapid reaction by the financial system to the policy move, or gaps in the regulatory framework – can hinder or completely undo the desired effects. For instance, Jimenez et al. (2012) show that dynamic provisioning sustains credit growth in bad times, but does little to stem it in good times, probably due to the fact that firms find substitute credit from less affected banks and/or other financiers. In a similar vein, Aijar et al. (2012) show that UK-owned banks and resident foreign subsidiaries (the regulated sector) reduce lending in response to tighter capital requirements imposed by the national regulator, but that this effect is largely offset by resident foreign branches (unregulated banks), who respond by increasing it.

More generally, in an integrated financial system possible cross-country spillovers need to be taken into account by macroprudential policy-makers, because failure to do so may render policies ineffective. Furthermore, a policy that can be beneficial in one country may have undesired side effects on its neighbours. As argued by Shin (2011), for example, the spectacular rise of gross capital flows through the banking sector in the years preceding the financial crisis provided fertile conditions for excessive credit growth in both Europe and the US. While these issues lie outside the scope of this contribution, in the EU there is an intense debate on the need for cross-border coordination of the actions of national macroprudential authorities.

2.4. Summary

We are still far from a satisfactory state of affairs concerning the theoretical underpinnings of macroprudential policy and its relationship with other policies – in particular monetary policy. The empirical literature is also at a very early stage. The main challenge for the future is to develop models that allow the proper handling of externalities associated with systemic risk, and which are at the same time elaborate enough – especially in terms of financial sector modelling – to permit the analysis of policies to counteract this risk. These models will have to handle the strong non-linearities and complexities associated with financial and asset price imbalances, potentially leading to financial crises.

Notwithstanding these limitations, the literature reviewed above does highlight some important points. First, externalities may induce excessive credit growth followed by sudden busts, providing a rationale for macroprudential policies designed to curb excessive credit volatility. Second, monetary policies that also take into account measures of financial tensions tend to improve upon standard Taylor-type reaction functions in terms of macroeconomic stabilisation. Moreover, there is some theoretical – and empirical – support for the view that a loose monetary policy may lead to excessive risk taking. These conclusions support the view that monetary policy has a role to play in leaning against the development of financial imbalances, and should not just be confined to "cleaning up" after the bursting of financial bubbles. The observation that theoretical developments appear to have followed, rather than anticipated, economic events, does not take away from the fact that these works have contributed to our understanding of the way policies ought to react to unexpected events. This lesson should be heeded as soon as the world economy exits the current crisis. Third, countercyclical macroprudential policies (time-varying management of capital requirements or provisioning, loan-to-value ratios, etc.) can be effective at moderating economic fluctuations and the financial cycle, although with a number of uncertainties (potential unintended effects, offsetting forces which may undo the impact of the policies, etc.). Finally, there are both complementarities and trade-offs between monetary and macroprudential policies, with a potential for conflict; this calls for institutional arrangements that favour cooperation and synergies between the two policies.

3. MACROPRUDENTIAL AND MONETARY POLICIES: LESSONS FROM RECENT EXPERIENCE

The main conclusions emerging from the previous paragraph have a clear bearing on the current situation. There is no doubt that excessive credit growth, causing high levels of leverage in the financial and nonfinancial sectors, and fuelling a real estate boom in several countries, was among the determinants of the current crisis. Moreover, central banks have been very active in contrasting financial distress, as prescribed by several of the models surveyed above. Although rigorous empirical evidence in support of this thesis is still not available, it seems likely that the exceptionally loose monetary policy stance currently prevailing in most advanced economies cannot be fully rationalised in terms of inflation and output dynamics. This is confirmed by a simple Taylor rule that we computed using the expected inflation and output gap: since 2010 the actual short-term rate in the Euro area has been well below the rate suggested by the rule.

Could countercyclical macroprudential policies be adopted to moderate the current negative economic and financial cycle? Is there a material risk of conflict between monetary and macroprudential policies? Restricting the focus to the Euro area at the present juncture, we argue that a selective use of macroprudential instruments at the national level could bring great benefits to the weaker countries, where they are most needed, but that unfortunately there is not much room for manoeuvre for these actions. In this context, monetary policy can cooperate with macroprudential policy, "lending a hand" for financial stability purposes.

Let us have a look on why the selective use of macroprudential instruments at the national level could deliver great benefits at this point in time. In principle monetary policy implements a single short-term, risk-free interest rate in the Euro area, and lets market forces determine the appropriate cost of funds for the various economic actors – firms and households – as a function of several idiosyncratic factors, first and foremost, their creditworthiness. However, this mechanism has been malfunctioning since the onset of the current crisis, as confirmed by several indicators.

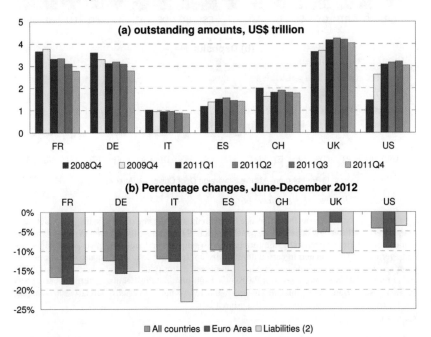

Figure 22.1: Bank foreign claims by nationality of reporting banks (1)

(1) Immediate borrower basis. – (2) Computed as foreign claims by Euro area banks towards the countries in the figure.

Source: BIS.

Figure 22.1 reports the outstanding foreign claims of banks in selected industrialised countries. Panel (a) shows that the four main Euro area economies are
financially very open: at the end of 2008 foreign claims held by their banks
jointly amounted to over USD 9 trillion, a value roughly equal to the sum of
these countries' nominal GDP. The UK banking system displayed a similar
degree of openness, whereas the values for the US were much smaller (about
USD 1.5 trillion, or 10 per cent of GDP).[7] In the last three years banks' foreign
claims have rapidly declined on average in the euro-area countries, whereas
they have grown in the US and UK.

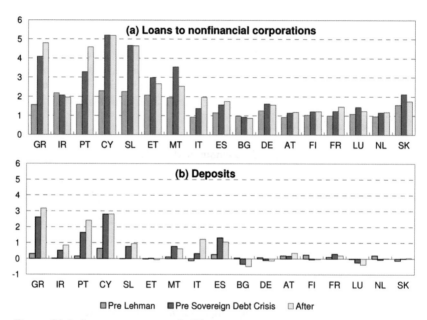

Figure 22.2: Interest rate spreads (1)

(1) Spreads are calculated as the difference between the interest rate on new loans – in panel (a) –
or the interest rate on new deposits – in panel (b) – and the interest rate on the main refinancing operations of the ECB. Specifically, the former interest rates are on loans other than revolving loans
and overdrafts, denominated in euro with maturity up to 1 year, to nonfinancial corporations; the
latter are on deposits denominated in euro with agreed maturity up to 1 year, held by households
and nonfinancial firms. Averages over the relevant sub-period. "Pre-Lehman", "Pre-sovereign crisis" and "Sovereign crisis" indicate, in order, the following sub-periods: January 2007-August
2008, July 2010-June 2011 and July 2011-March 2012.

Source: ECB.

Panel (b) of figure 22.1 focuses on percentage changes in the second half of
2011, which marked the aggravation of the Euro area sovereign crisis. Over

---

[7] The high degree of openness for the EU countries clearly reflects intra-EU interconnections.

this period banks' retrenchment within national borders is somewhat generalised, but it is more intense among the Euro area countries. The panel also reports a measure of foreign liabilities: the sharpest drop is recorded in Italy and
Spain, countries that have been most heavily affected by the crisis. It vividly
illustrates the unwillingness of Euro area banks to lend to each other, which
led to the corresponding dramatic increase in refinancing from the ECB over
the same period.

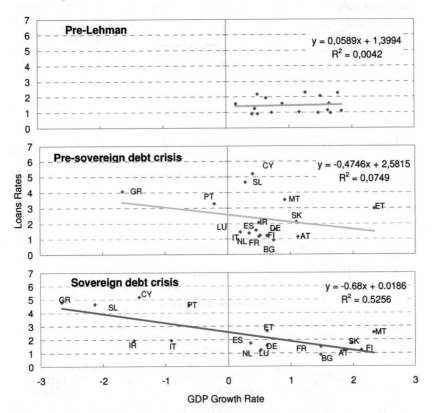

Figure 22.3: Interest rate spreads and GDP growth in the EU
(percentage points)
(1) See the footnote to figure 22.2 for the definition of the loan rates and of the sub-periods.
Source: ECB.

Overall, there is clear evidence of malfunctioning in the interbank market, the
initial stage of the transmission mechanism. Does this have any effect on the
final stage of the mechanism, i.e. on the conditions faced by the nonfinancial
sector in the markets for bank products? Figure 22.2 looks at the behaviour
of interest rates on loans to firms and on households' deposits over three key

sub-periods: the period prior to the Lehman default, in September 2008; the
July 2010-June 2011 period; the period starting in July 2011, characterised by
an escalation of the sovereign crisis in Europe. Both panels display a dramatic
increase in the cross-country dispersion of deposits and lending rates in the
second and third sub-periods. The greatest changes tend to be concentrated in
the programme countries (Greece, Portugal and, to a lesser extent, Ireland),
Cyprus, Malta and Slovenia; relatively strong variations can also be seen for
Spain and Italy.

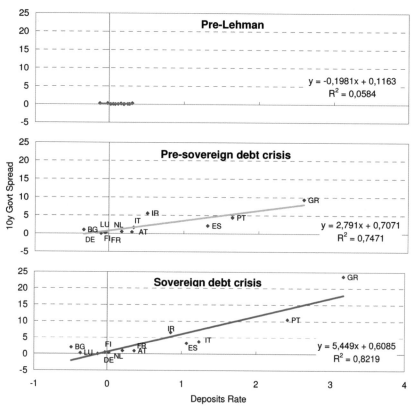

Figure 22.4: Sovereign spreads and deposit rates in the EU
(percentage points)
(1) See the footnote to figure 22.2 for the definition of the loan rates and of the sub-periods.
Source: ECB.

The increased dispersion in lending rates could be due to the fact that firms in
countries that are more exposed to the sovereign crisis have become riskier,
given the poor performance of the respective economies. The evidence in figure 22.3 is consistent with this hypothesis: the relationship between a country's

real GDP growth and average loan prices, apparently non-existent prior to the Lehman default (panel (a)), becomes negative in the July 2010-June 2011 period, and strongly significant afterwards (panel (c)). This seems reasonable, to the extent that nationwide averages can be used to proxy for micro relationships and since low growth is associated with a higher probability of default.

However, strong simultaneity might be at work here: the decline in growth rates may have been to some extent caused by the increase in lending rates, which in turn were triggered by the sovereign crisis. Indeed, there are several direct and indirect channels through which sovereign risk affects the cost and availability of banks' funding (CGFS 2011). Figure 22.4 lends some support to this thesis: it shows that the relationship between sovereign spreads and deposit rates, nil before the Lehman collapse, became increasingly positive and significant in the two sub-periods that followed.

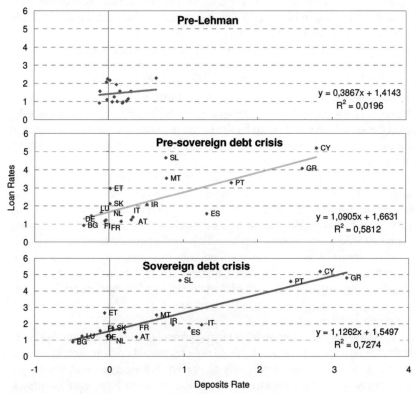

Figure 22.5: Lending rates and deposit rates in the EU
(percentage points)

(1) See the footnote to figure 22.2 for the definition of the loan and deposit rates and of the sub-periods.

Source: ECB.

Figure 22.5, which plots lending vs. deposit rates over the same three sub-periods, further reinforces this point. In principle, deposit rates in EU countries should be close to a risk-free rate: deposit insurance is widespread, and under normal circumstances there is no reason to believe that deposit rates should diverge in an ample and systematic fashion across countries. Since 2010, however, the cross-country dispersion of deposit rates has increased, as shown in figure 22.2, panel (b). Specifically, banks in countries with high sovereign risk have been forced to pay high rates on deposits and new debt issuance. This was a consequence of various mechanisms: competition for stable funds – among banks, but most likely also between banks and the national sovereign – played a role; the increase in perceived sovereign risk also adversely affected the value of the implicit government guarantee on bank deposits. In turn, higher funding rates have fuelled an increase in banks' lending rates. This is shown in figure 22.5: in the pre-Lehman period there is no relationship between the two rates; the relationship becomes positive after the Lehman default and strongly significant since the summer of 2011.[8]

The correlations reviewed above must be approached with caution, since the variables we have been examining are simultaneously determined, and causality links are hard to identify. With this caveat, our evidence suggests that in the countries affected by the crisis the cost of lending borne by firms is not exclusively driven by their fundamentals: it also reflects difficulties faced by local banks, which are affected by the perceived health of their sovereign, and are forced to transfer their higher cost of funds on to borrowers, independently of the latter's creditworthiness.

The medium to long-term consequences of these developments relate to level playing field concerns. The immediate ones are even more worrisome: the economies of the countries with weak sovereign debt conditions and growth problems would require lower real rates, whereas those of the strong countries would in principle require relatively higher real rates; however, the opposite occurs. Among the weaker countries this situation can fuel a vicious circle between economic slowdown, high sovereign debt, and banking system fragility, a distinguishing feature of the latest stage of the current crisis; among the strong countries, it can engender overheating, leading to pressures on both consumer and asset prices.

This situation would be an ideal testing ground for macroprudential policies at the country level. In principle, these policies should act countercyclically in the weak countries, and stand ready to prevent the emergence of asset price imbalances in stronger countries that are experiencing large capital inflows.

---

[8] Indeed, the Eurosystem's Securities Markets Programme, i.e. the direct intervention by the central banks in the sovereign markets most affected by the crisis, has been directed at tackling the malfunctioning in the sovereign bond markets in an attempt to restore the monetary policy transmission mechanism, including the mispricing in the loans market.

Unfortunately, as we argue below, there is at present little room for manoeu-vre for macroprudential countercyclical policies in the countries most affected by the crisis. There is no problem of a potential conflict between monetary and macroprudential policies; rather, the two policies can cooperate, helping to achieve financial stability.

4. MACROPRUDENTIAL AND MICROPRUDENTIAL POLICIES

4.1. Interactions and Potential Conflicts between Micro- and Macroprudential Policies

Why has the scope for countercyclical macroprudential policy been so limited in the follow-up to the crisis? Answering this question leads us to consider the interactions between macro- and microprudential policies.

It has been long recognised that the distinction between micro- and macro-prudential policies is best thought of in terms of the objectives, rather than in terms of the instruments used in the pursuit of those objectives (Crockett 2000). Indeed, much of the discussion following the recent financial crisis has been on how to re-orient typical microprudential tools (such as capital and liquidity requirements, loan-to-value ratios, etc.) to serve the macroprudential goal of limiting systemic risk. If the tools are broadly the same but must serve two purposes and be used by two different authorities, the potential for conflict arises, just as in the case of the interaction between macroprudential and mon-etary policies, reviewed above. It is worth noting that the potential for conflict seems asymmetric: it is likely to materialise mainly (or exclusively) during downturns, when the macroprudential regulator may want to run down equity buffers in order to avoid a credit crunch, whereas the microprudential regula-tor may be reluctant to let that happen owing to the need to preserve the safety and soundness of individual institutions. Is this a cause for concern under the present macroeconomic conditions?

As in the case of the interaction of macroprudential and monetary policy, we believe that the answer is no. In a downturn it may be very difficult for the macroprudential authority to lower the capital requirement, because markets themselves may put pressure on banks to recapitalise (Diamond and Rajan 2009). This problem should be addressed by raising the requirement in normal times by a sufficient amount, so as to make the reduction dictated by coun-tercyclical policies in bad times credible and acceptable to markets. But the current crisis caught banks in most advanced economies off their guard. In practice, it has been impossible for macroprudential authorities to implement countercyclical policies, because good times had not been used to build up

sufficient buffers. In loose terms, we could say that countercyclical macroprudential policies are at their lower bound.[9]

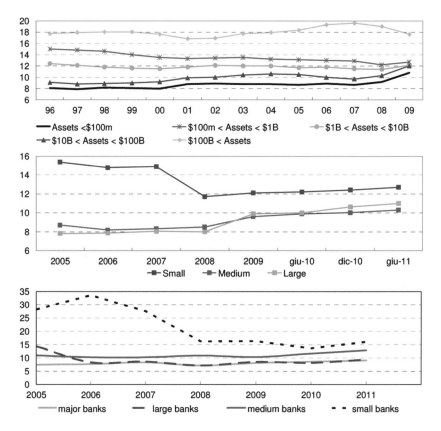

*Figure 22.6: Tier 1 risk-based capital ratios of commercial banks, by bank
size*
(percentage points)

(1) In panel (c) size classes are derived from quartiles of total assets, computed for each year on a
sample of about 100 consolidated bank balance sheets.

Sources: panel (a): Hanson et al. (2011); panel (b): ECB; panel (c): Bank of Italy.

Figure 22.6, extending to Europe the evidence highlighted by Hanson et al.
(2011) for the US, supports this narrative: large banks in the US and in Europe

---

[9] In principle, the macroprudential regulator could force banks to raise new capital (increasing the
numerator of the capital ratio), via retained earnings or by raising equity on the market. In practice,
this is hard to do in a crisis situation, as bank profits tend to be low and shareholders are reluctant
to accept the strong dilution effect that new capital issuance entails in an environment of high risk
aversion and low share prices.

increased their capitalisation levels after the Lehman default. Market pressure was probably an important driver of this effect: at a global level, there was no specific regulatory provision to increase capitalisation levels until the first version of the Basel 3 package appeared in 2010. Another interesting insight we can glean from the figure is that the capital ratio for small banks declined over the same period (2008-2009), effectively playing the countercyclical role that a macroprudential authority would have liked to implement at the aggregate level. This effect was clearly insufficient to offset the opposite trend prevailing among all other size classes, but it suggests that, provided bank capital levels are large enough, capital ratios could be effectively manoeuvred in a countercyclical fashion.[10]

The tier 1 ratios are subject to notable differences in the way they are computed over time and across countries. A degree of caution should therefore be exercised when interpreting and comparing the results presented in figure 22.6. Despite the common international standards set up by the Basel Committee on Banking Supervision, national rules and practices for determining tier 1 ratios still differ substantially across countries. The main differences can be referred to both the numerator of the ratio, tier 1 capital, and the denominator, risk-weighted assets (RWAs). As for the numerator, some jurisdictions allowed a relatively broad definition of tier 1 capital, including instruments that during the crisis showed little loss absorption capacity. These differences are bound to be gradually reduced with the implementation of the new Basel 3 framework, which excludes most of the weaker components of capital and gives a strong preference to equity as the prevailing element of regulatory capital. As for the denominator, concerns have been raised recently about the ability of RWAs to capture risk correctly. We discuss this issue in the next section.

4.2. Risk-Weighted Assets and Leverage

Besides the general disregard of systemic risk, other factors, linked to the regulatory framework and supervisory practices, may have played a role in preventing the build-up of adequate capital buffers in the run-up to the current crisis.

Under the Basel framework the amount of minimum required capital of banks is proportional to the level of risk-weighted assets (RWAs), which aim to measure the actual exposure of individual institutions to risk, or the true amount of risk per euro of exposure. The methodology for computing RWAs has become a cornerstone of supervisory activity since the Basel 1 accord

---

[10] Indeed, the move observed among small banks was arguably spontaneous, suggesting that a macroprudential authority might not even be needed to implement a countercyclical mechanism. The evidence surveyed in Panetta et al. (2009) indicates that the capital buffers that banks hold over and above the regulatory minimum can significantly mitigate the procyclicality induced by capital requirements, but that they are unlikely to fully eliminate it. On this issue see also Repullo and Suarez (2008).

in 1988. It has been refined over time, in particular with the Basel 2 accord (2004). Various factors have contributed to amplify cross-country heterogeneity in RWAs, making comparisons difficult. First of all, not all countries adopted Basel 2 at the same time and to the same extent. In addition, the Basel 2 framework gave banks the option to compute capital requirements based on their own internal models, validated by the supervisor. As a result the computation of RWAs has become increasingly dependent on banks' discretionary choices. Further changes have recently been introduced by Basel 2.5, as it is known, which has radically revised the RWA computation for trading-book items. The phasing-in of Basel 3 will bring about further changes.

It is not surprising, therefore, that RWA measures have recently attracted increasing attention (Bair 2011; Le Lesle and Avramova 2012). One argument is that heterogeneities in the methodologies to compute RWAs may not only hinder comparability across institutions and jurisdictions, but also fail to reflect risk properly (see, among others, Hellwig 2010; Carmassi and Micossi 2012), with potentially negative consequences on the level playing field in financial markets, and most importantly, on financial stability. One main problem is that separating the correct drivers of divergences in banks' RWAs (mainly risk profiles, possibly also differences in business models) from undesired drivers (regulatory arbitrage, differences in supervisory and accounting rules, and supervisory practices) is rather difficult.[11]

Irrespective of the source of the divergences in RWAs, it is interesting to look at the relationship between RWAs across jurisdictions and the actual risk borne by the respective banking sectors, as proxied by public funds used to rescue banks. In panel (a) of figure 22.7 we plot for a sample of European countries and the US the RWA/total asset ratios in 2008 against the maximum amount of government capital injections and asset relief measures in subsequent years. In theory, if RWAs were adequately reflecting the actual risk faced by the different banking sectors we should expect no correlation between the two variables: the materialisation of risk should have been contrasted with adequate

---

[11] As an example of the correct drivers, consider a bank holding only short-term debt securities, and another one holding only a similar nominal value of stocks by the same issuer. Clearly the RWAs of the former will be lower than those of the latter, correctly reflecting each bank's different exposures to risk. As an example of the incorrect drivers, consider the differences in consolidation rules between the US GAAP and the European IAS-IFRS. According to Deutsche Bank (2006), total assets for the group at the end of 2006 were EUR 1.126 trillion based on the former accounting standard, and EUR 1.572 trillion according to the latter. Our point here is not to single out any particular accounting standard for criticism, but to show that different standards may substantially alter the accounting representation of the same balance sheet and make cross-country comparisons very difficult. Cannata et al. (2012) show that a significant portion of divergences in RWAs across a sample of large European financial institutions is explained by the different asset allocations across regulatory portfolios (business models) and the different proportion in which the Internal Ratings-Based and the Standardised approaches (both introduced by Basel 2) are used by banks. Partly due to data limitations, they fail to provide an estimate of the extent to which differences in RWA may reflect undesired drivers.

bank capital. On the contrary, a negative relationship emerges from the figure: in jurisdictions where RWAs were small relative to total assets the need for government interventions has been greater.[12] This evidence suggests that, at least in these cases, RWAs may have been unable to adequately capture risks, due to potential problems in the rules, or in supervisory practices, or in both.

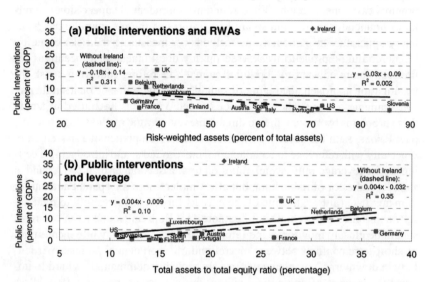

Figure 22.7: Lending rates and deposit rates in the EU
(percentages)

Public interventions include governments' capital injections and asset relief measures, i.e. the amount of assets acquired or guaranteed by the State to improve banks' balance sheets either via a national scheme or via an ad hoc individual rescue operation. The value equals the acquisition value plus the guaranteed value. Risk-weighted assets (RWA) and leverage measures refer to domestic banks.

Sources: Based on ECB, EU Commission and OECD data.

In figure 22.7, panel (b), we replicate the previous exercise by replacing the RWA/total asset ratio with a measure of banks' leverage, given by the ratio of total assets to total equity. The panel provides complementary information with respect to panel (a): while in fact RWAs establish the minimum capital requirements, banks may decide to hold more capital, or may be asked to do so by the supervisors. The figure shows that the higher the leverage ratio the

---

[12] The exercise was replicated using the value of support measures as of end 2011, instead of their maximum value, or using only capital injections (excluding asset relief measures), or constructing these measures as a percentage of banks' total assets instead of GDP. The results are practically unchanged. We also considered the whole banking sector in the computation of RWAs and leverage. In this case as well, the results are not radically different, with the exception of Ireland: its aggregate RWAs over total asset ratio falls (to about 40 per cent), whereas its leverage ratio grows (to about 30 per cent), strengthening the correlations portrayed in figure 22.7.

greater the need for public interventions during a crisis. In particular, leverage ratios higher than 25 are often associated with significant public costs for banking rescue purposes. This suggests that the ceiling value of 33 for the leverage ratio set forth in the Basel 3 package may still be quite high.

Overall, while certainly not conclusive, the evidence presented above prompts two considerations. First, sound microprudential supervision is a pillar of financial stability, and so are key features of the microprudential regulatory apparatus. In particular, the methods for measuring the risks borne by banks tend to be prone to weaknesses, partly due to the strong incentives for financial intermediaries to "optimise capital"; therefore, following a risk diversification approach, the regulator should avoid overreliance on a single risk containment measure. The new Basel 2.5 and 3 accords have tried to tackle these problems by moving in two directions: revising the methodology to compute RWAs, with the objective of ensuring more comprehensive risk capture, especially with reference to complex financial products; and introducing a ceiling on the leverage ratio, which relies on total assets rather than RWAs and is a cruder indicator of risk taking, but also simpler, more transparent and harder to manipulate (although some of the caveats for RWAs also apply to total assets, and hence to leverage; see footnote 11). Both amendments to the rules should be closely monitored and refined over time. *Second*, while there might be short-term conflicts between macro- and microprudential policies, particularly in downturns, complementarities are probably dominant. It is hard to imagine the success of one policy without the success of the other. Regardless of the institutional arrangements, it is therefore crucial to ensure a continuous exchange of information while setting up well-defined mechanisms to resolve possible conflicts between the two functions, should they emerge.

4.3. Are Much Higher Capital Levels Sustainable for the Banking Sector?

Are levels of capitalisation close to 20 per cent, such as those suggested by the evidence in figure 22.6, sensible and feasible? The starting point to address this question is the Modigliani-Miller equivalence result: in the absence of frictions, debt and equity are equivalent sources of funds, as the value of the firm does not depend on the composition of its liabilities. Thus, the debate revolves around the empirical importance of the deviations from the frictionless world hypothesised by the theorem. This debate, dating back at least to Myers and Majluf (1984), has been reopened by the current crisis.

Several commentators, mainly from the side of the banking industry, have argued that forcing banks to abide by higher capital ratios may hamper their ability to finance viable investment projects, with large negative effects on economic growth (see, e.g., IIF 2010). Admati et al. (2010), and Miles et al. (2011) have taken the opposite view, arguing that capital requirements for banks should be raised to values of 20-30 per cent.

While there is broad agreement on the view that the Modigliani-Miller paradigm does not apply to banks, significant uncertainty remains about the practical importance of the various sources of deviations from the paradigm, making it difficult to obtain reliable estimates of the cost of capital for banks. For instance, the debate often overlooks the role of fiscal wedges, which provide strong incentives to use debt to the disadvantage of equity (see IMF 2009). Moreover, higher costs or efficiency losses from regulatory reforms should always be confronted with the social losses deriving from banking crises which, as shown by recent experience, may be very large.

The increase of minimum capital requirements recently adopted by the regulator (Basel 3), relying on original estimates of the economic costs and benefits of the reform (see BCBS 2010; MAG 2010), has taken a pragmatic middle ground between the extreme positions referred to above. The new regulations are designed to increase capital requirements gradually to the new levels in 2019, in order to avoid the procyclical consequences of a rapid drive to these levels when economic conditions are still weak. Overall, it implies significantly higher capitalisation, due to changes in the numerator (higher quality capital) and in the denominator (tighter risk weights) of the capital ratio. Moreover, the recent special provisions regarding global SIFIs move in the direction of further increasing capital requirements over and above the Basel 3 levels (the Swiss regulator has already significantly increased the requirements for its two largest banks, following capital injections by the government into one of the two). Finally, individual countries may also choose to impose higher standards. In the EU, following an ongoing debate, national macroprudential authorities are likely to be granted leeway to impose tougher requirements in their jurisdictions, if properly motivated. In perspective, this may help build precautionary buffers in those countries where they are most needed. It is not surprising that many of the countries advocating for themselves the right to impose higher prudential standards are characterised by financial systems whose total assets are a large multiple of their GDP.

5. CONCLUSIONS

In this chapter we review recent attempts to analyse macroprudential policy and its interaction with other policies, in particular monetary policy. Through the prism of theoretical literature, we then examine the conditions in the Euro area as the sovereign debt crisis evolves. We argue that there is not, at present, any issue of conflict between monetary and macroprudential policies. Because of the sovereign debt crisis, a retrenchment of capital and intermediaries within national borders seems to be taking place, jeopardising the uniform transmission of monetary policy impulses in the area and amplifying the divergences across its economies. The policy action of the ECB, aimed at contrasting these tendencies, has played an important role in preserving financial stability but by its very nature it has limits in tackling cross-country heterogeneities: in theory, the economies of countries with weak sovereign debt conditions and growth problems would require low real rates, whereas those of the strong countries would need higher real rates; however, the opposite occurs. Ideally, in this situation national macroprudential policies would act countercyclically in the countries most affected by the crisis and stand ready to prevent the emergence of asset price imbalances in the economies that are experiencing massive capital inflows. Unfortunately, there is very little room for manoeuvre for countercyclical macroprudential policies, especially in the weaker countries. As a consequence monetary policy is left to shoulder most of the burden (a situation not unique to the Euro area).

Why has the scope for countercyclical macroprudential policy been so limited since the onset of the crisis? Answering this question brings us to that of the interactions between macro- and microprudential policies, and those microprudential tools (capital and liquidity requirements, loan-to-value ratios, etc.) which may be appropriately calibrated to serve macroprudential goals. In the run-up to the crisis insufficient capital buffers had been accumulated, and market pressures prevented macroprudential authorities from credibly pushing for a countercyclical relaxation of capital requirements to avoid a credit crunch.

Banks' behaviour in the US and in Europe during the financial crisis confirms that capital levels were indeed too low to allow for countercyclical policies. We show that in the initial years of the crisis large commercial banks, whose capital was very close to the minimum Basel requirement, increased their capital ratios, mainly because of market pressure. Smaller banks instead reduced their ratios, effectively playing a countercyclical role. They could do this because at the onset of the crisis they had accumulated significantly higher capital buffers.

Several factors, linked to the regulatory framework and supervisory practices, may have played a role in preventing the build-up of adequate buffers. While there is no doubt that the regulation had failed to adequately take systemic risk into account, other pitfalls have also emerged, linked to rules and supervisory practices. A key determinant of banks' capital requirements under the Basel regulatory framework is risk-weighted assets (RWAs), the denominator of the capital ratio, which have recently come under close scrutiny by market analysts, banks and supervisory authorities. We find that RWAs failed to reflect the effective risk borne by the different banking sectors, as proxied by the public funds used to rescue banks in the aftermath of the financial crisis: in jurisdictions where RWAs were small relative to total assets, governments' interventions to shore up national banking systems have been larger. In a similar vein, measures of leverage seem to perform well in predicting the cost of public interventions.

This evidence shows that the key features of the microprudential apparatus are crucial for preventing financial instability. In particular, the methods for measuring the risks borne by banks tend to be prone to weaknesses. The new Basel 3 accord tackles some of these problems by revising the methodology to compute RWAs and introducing a ceiling on the leverage ratio, an indicator that is cruder but also simpler, more transparent, and harder to manipulate. Both amendments to the rules should be closely monitored and refined over time, bearing in mind that financial intermediaries tend to react to the new regulations quickly, reducing their effectiveness.

Can the banking sector as a whole sustain a significantly higher level of capitalisation, or would the cost be prohibitively high? The debate on this issue is still open. Certainly, the recent crisis has been a strong reminder that the social losses associated with financial and banking crises may be very high. As a consequence, the regulatory reform has moved in the direction of imposing significantly higher requirements, in terms of both the levels and quality of capital. The possibility for national macroprudential authorities to impose tougher requirements in their jurisdictions may help build precautionary buffers in those countries where they are most needed.

Overall, we stress complementarities over trade-offs in the interaction of macroprudential policies with other policies. Macroprudential policy should be concerned with the setting of the structural features of the financial system, with a view to limiting risk, reducing procyclicality and increasing resilience by building up adequate buffers in good times for use in bad times. Only if these structural parameters are properly set will there be room left for discretionary and countercyclical macroprudential policy.

BIBLIOGRAPHY

Admati, A.R., P.M. De Marzo, M.F. Hellwig and P. Pfleiderer 2010, "Fallacies, Irrelevant Facts, and Myths in the Discussion of Capital Regulation: Why Bank Equity is Not Expensive", *Stanford GSB Research Paper* No. 2063, and the *Rock Center for Corporate Governance at Stanford University, Working Paper* No. 86.

Ahuja, A. and M. Nabar 2011, "Safeguarding Banks and Containing Property Booms: Cross-Country Evidence on Macroprudential Policies and Lessons from Hong Kong SAR", *IMF Working Paper* No. 284.

Aijar, S., C.W. Calomiris and T. Wieladek 2012, "Does macro-Pru leak? Evidence from a UK Policy Experiment", *NBER Working Paper* No. 17822.

Altunbas, Y., L. Gambacorta and D. Marques-Ibanez 2010, "Does Monetary Policy Affect Bank Risk-Taking?", *BIS Working Paper* No. 298.

Angelini, P., S. Neri and F. Panetta 2011a, "Monetary and Macroprudential Policies", *Banca d'Italia Working Paper* No. 801.

Angelini, P., L. Clerc, V. Cúrdia, L. Gambacorta, A. Gerali, A. Locarno, R. Motto, W. Roeger, S. Van den Heuvel, and J. Vlček, 2011, "BASEL III: Long-term impact on economic performance and fluctuations", *BIS Working Paper* No. 338.

Angeloni, I. and E. Faia 2009, "A Tale of Two Policies: Prudential Regulation and Monetary Policy with Fragile Banks", mimeo.

Bair, S. 2011, "Europe lax on RWA calculations, says Bair", *Risk Magazine*, June 24.

Bank for International Settlements (BIS) 2011, "Macroprudential regulation and policy", proceedings of a joint conference organised by the BIS and the Bank of Korea in Seoul on 17–18 January 2011, *BIS Paper* Nr. 60, December.

Bank of England 2009, "The role of macroprudential policy", *Discussion Paper*, November.

Bank of England 2011, "Instruments of macroprudential policy", *Discussion Paper*, December.

Basel Committee on Banking Supervision (BCBS) 2010 (LEI Report), "An Assessment of the Long-Term Impact of Stronger Capital and Liquidity Requirements", Basel, August.

Bean, C., M. Paustian, A. Penalver and T. Taylor 2010, "Monetary Policy after the Fall", paper presented at the Federal Reserve Bank of Kansas City, Annual Conference, Jackson Hole, Wyoming.

Beau, D., L. Clerc and B. Mojon 2011, "Macro-Prudential Policy and the Conduct of Monetary Policy", mimeo, Banque de France.

Benigno, G., H. Chen, C. Otrok, A. Rebucci and E. R. Young 2010, "Resisting over-borrowing and its policy implications", *CEPR DP* 7872.

Benigno, G., H. Chen, C. Otrok, A. Rebucci and E. R. Young 2011, "Monetary and Macro-Prudential Policies: An Integrated Analysis", mimeo.

Bernanke, B. S., M. Gertler and S. Gilchrist 1999, "The Financial Accelerator in a Quantitative Business Cycle Framework", in *Handbook of macroeconomics*, Volume 1C, ed. John B. Taylor and Michael Woodford, pp. 1341-93, North-Holland.

Bianchi, J. 2010, "Credit Externalities: Macroeconomic Effects and Policy Implications," *American Economic Review*, 100(2), pp. 398-402.

Bianchi, J. and E. G. Mendoza 2010, "Overborrowing, Financial Crises and 'Macroprudential' Taxes", National Bureau of Economic Research, Inc, *NBER Working Paper* No. 16091.

Borio, C. 2010, "Implementing a macroprudential framework: Blending boldness and realism", BIS 22 July.

Borio, C. and A. Crockett 2000, "In search of anchors for financial and monetary stability", *Greek Economic Review*, 20(2), pp. 1-14.

Borio, C., C. Furfine, and P. Lowe, 2001 "Pro-cyclicality of the Financial System and Financial Stability: Issues and Policy Options", *BIS Papers*, No. 1.

Borio, C. and H. Zhu 2008, "Capital regulation, risk-taking and monetary policy: a missing link in the transmission mechanism?", *BIS Working Paper* No. 268.

Brunnermeier, M. K. 2009, "Deciphering the Liquidity and Credit Crunch 2007-2008", *Journal of Economic Perspectives*, 23(1), pp. 77-100.

Brunnermeier, M. K. and Y. Sannikov 2011, "A Macroeconomic Model with a Financial Sector", unpublished manuscript, Princeton University.

Cannata, F., S. Casellina, and G. Guidi 2012, "Inside the labyrinth of RWAs: how not to get lost", *Banca d'Italia Occasional Papers* No. 132.

Carmassi, J. and S. Micossi 2012, "Time to set Banking Regulation Right", *CEPS Paperbacks*, 15 March.

Catte, P., P. Cova, P. Pagano and Visco, I. 2010, "The role of macroeconomic policies in the global crisis", *Journal of Policy Modeling*, 33, pp. 787–803.

Cecchetti, Stephen G. and M. Kohler 2012, "When capital adequacy and interest rate policy are substitutes (and when they are not)", *BIS Working Paper* No. 379.

Committee on the Global Financial System (CGFS) 2011, "The impact of sovereign credit risk on bank funding conditions", report submitted by a Study Group established by the Committee on the Global Financial System, *CGFS papers* No. 43.

Covas, F. and S. Fujita 2009, "Time-varying capital requirements in a general equilibrium model of liquidity dependence", *Federal Reserve Bank of Philadelphia Working Paper* No. 23.

Crockett, A. D. 2000, "Marrying the micro- and macroprudential dimensions of financial stability", remarks before the Eleventh International Conference of Banking Supervisors, Basel, 20-21 September 2000.

Curdia V. and M. Woodford 2010, "The Central-Bank Balance Sheet as an Instrument of Monetary Policy", with Vasco Curdia, paper prepared for the Carnegie-Rochester Conference on Public Policy, "The Future of Central Banking", April 16-17, 2010.

Deutsche Bank 2006, "Transition Report – 2006 IFRS Comparatives". Available at https://www.db.com/medien/en/downloads/Transition_Report_EN_2006_IFRS.pdf

Diamond, D. and G. Rajan 2009, "The Credit Crisis: Conjectures about Causes and Remedies", *NBER Working Paper* No. 14379.

Fisher, I. 1933, "The Debt-Deflation Theory of Great Depressions", *Econometrica*, 1(4), pp. 337-357.

Galati, G. and R. Moessner 2011, "Macroprudential policy – a literature review", *BIS Working Paper* No. 337.

Gilchrist, S. and E. Zakrajsek 2012, "Credit supply shocks and economic activity in a financial accelerator model", mimeo.

Hanson, S. J., A. K. Kashyap and J. K. Stein 2011, "A Macroprudential Approach to Financial Regulation", *Journal of Economic Perspectives*, 25(1), 3-28.

Hellwig, M. 2010, "Capital Regulation after the Crisis: Business as Usual?", *Max Planck Institute for Research on Collective Goods*, 2010/31, Munich, July.

IMF 2009, "Debt Bias and Other Distortions: Crisis-Related Issues in Tax Policy", June 12.

Institute for International Finance (IIF) 2010, "Interim Report on the Cumulative Impact on the Global Economy of Proposed Changes in the Banking Regulatory Framework", June.

Ioannidou, V., S. Ongena and J. Peydró 2007, "Monetary Policy, Risk-Taking and Pricing: Evidence from a Quasi-Natural Experiment", mimeo.

Jeanne, O. and A. Korinek 2010, "Managing Credit Booms and Busts: A Pigouvian Taxation Approach", National Bureau of Economic Research, Inc, *NBER Working Paper* No. 16377.

Jiménez, G., S. Ongena, J. L. Peydró and J. Saurina 2008, "Hazardous Times for Monetary Policy: What do Twenty-three Million Bank Loans say About the Effects of Monetary Policy on Credit Risk-taking?", *Banco de España Documentos de Trabajo* No. 0833.

Jiménez, G., S. Ongena, J. L. Peydró and J. Saurina 2012, "Macroprudential Policy, Countercyclical Bank Capital Buffers and Credit Supply: Evidence from the Spanish Dynamic Provisioning Experiments", mimeo.

Kannan, P., P. Rabanal and A. Scott 2009, "Monetary and Macro-prudential Policy Rules in a Model with House Price Booms", *International Monetary Fund Working Paper* No. 251.

Kim, D. H. and J. Wright 2005, "An Arbitrage-Free Three-Factor Term Structure Model and the Recent Behaviour of Long Term Yields and Distant-Horizon Forward Rates", *Finance and Economics Discussion Series of the Federal Reserve Board*, 33/2005.

Kiyotaki, N. and J. Moore 1997 "Credit Cycles", *Journal of Political Economy*, 105(2), pp. 211-48.

Korinek, A. 2011 "Systemic risk-taking: amplification effects, externalities, and regulatory responses", *European Central Bank, Working Paper Series* No. 1345.

Lambertini, L., C. Mendicino and M. T. Punzi 2011, "Leaning Against Boom-Bust Cycles in Credit and Housing Prices", *Banco de Portugal, Working Paper* No. 8/11.

Le Lesle, V. and S. Avramova 2012, "Revisiting Risk-Weighted Assets", *IMF Working Paper* No. 12/90.

Lim, C., F. Columba, A. Costa, P. Kongsamut, A. Otani, M. Saiyid, T. Wezel and X. Wu 2011, "Macroprudential Policy: What Instruments and How to Use Them? Lessons From Country Experiences", *IMF Working Paper* No. 228.

Lorenzoni, G. 2008, "Inefficient Credit Booms", *Review of Economic Studies*, 75(3), pp. 809-33.

Macroeconomic Assessment Group (MAG) 2010, "Assessing the Macroeconomic Impact of the Transition to Stronger Capital and Liquidity Requirements", group established by Financial Stability Board and the Basel Committee on Banking Supervision, August.

Maddaloni, A. and J.L. Peydró 2012, "Bank Risk Taking, Securitization, Supervision, and Low Interest Rates: Evidence from the Euro Area and US Lending Standards", *Review of Financial Studies*, forthcoming.

Mendoza, E. G. 2010, "Sudden Stops, Financial Crises, and Leverage", *American Economic Review*, 100(5), 1941-66.

Miles, D., J. Yang and G. Marcheggiano 2011, "Optimal Bank Capital", *Bank of England, Discussion Paper* No. 31.

Myers, S.C. and N.S. Majluf 1984, "Corporate financing and investment decisions when firms have information that investors do not have", *Journal of Financial Economics*, 13, 187-221.

N'Dyaie, P. 2009, "Countercyclical macro prudential policies in a supporting role to monetary policy", *IMF Working Paper* No. 257.

Panetta, F., P. Angelini, U. Albertazzi, F. Columba, W. Cornacchia, A. Di Cesare, A. Pilati, C. Salleo and G. Santini 2009, "Financial sector pro-cyclicality – Lessons from the crisis", *Banca d'Italia, Occasional papers*, No. 44.

Pericoli, M. and M. Taboga 2008, "Canonical Term-Structure Models with Observable Factors and the Dynamics of Bond Risk Premia", *Journal of Money Credit and Banking*, 40, 1471-1488.

Quint, D. and P. Rabanal 2011, "Monetary and Macroprudential Policy in an Estimated DSGE Model of the Euro Area", IMF, presentation made at the 12th Jacques Polak Annual Research Conference.

Rajan, R. 1994, "Why Bank Credit Policies Fluctuate: A Theory and Some Evidence", *The Quarterly Journal of Economics*, 109(2), pp. 399–441.

Rajan, R. 2005, "Has Financial Development Made the World Riskier?", *NBER Working Paper* No. 11728.

Repullo, R. and J. Suarez 2008, "The Pro-cyclical Effects of Basel II", *CEMFI Working Paper* No. 0809.

Roger, S. and J. Vlček 2011, "Macroeconomic Costs of Higher Bank Capital and Liquidity Requirements", *IMF Working Paper* No. 103.

Rudebusch, G. D., E. T. Swanson and T. Wu 2006, "The Bond-Yield Conundrum from a Macro-Finance Perspective", *Monetary and Economic Studies of the Institute for Monetary and Economic Studies of the Bank of Japan*, 24, 83-109.

Shin, H. S. 2011, "Global banking glut and loan risk premium", Mundell-Fleming Lecture, presented at the 2011 IMF Annual Research Conference, November.

Shleifer, A. and R. W. Vishny 1997, "The Limits of Arbitrage", *Journal of Finance*, 52(1), pp. 35-55.

Stein, Jeremy C. 2011, "Monetary Policy as Financial-Stability Regulation", National Bureau of Economic Research, Inc, *NBER Working Papers* No. 16883.

Ueda, K. and F. Valencia 2012, "Central Bank Independence and Macro-prudential Regulation", *IMF Working Paper* No. 101.

Wong, E., T. Fong, Ka-fai Li and H. Choi 2011, "Loan-to-value ratio as a macro-prudential tool – Hong Kong's experience and cross-country evidence", *Hong Kong Monetary Authority Working Paper* No. 1.

Woodford, M. 2012, "Inflation Targeting and Financial Stability", National Bureau of Economic Research, Inc, *NBER Working Paper* No. 17967.

23. Why Central Banks need a Macroeconomic Toolkit

Philipp M. Hildebrand

1. FLAWS OF THE FINANCIAL SYSTEM

The ongoing financial crisis has unleashed devastating forces. Persistent financial and economic adversity in much of Europe nearly five years after the onset of the crisis is a stark reminder of how costly the crisis has been.[1] In retrospect, it is obvious that the pre-crisis financial system had a number of built-in flaws. Most importantly, capital and liquidity buffers in the system were far too low, and systemic risks had been grossly underestimated. A far-reaching and global reform effort is now under way to repair these flaws and render the financial system more resilient.

With the benefit of hindsight, central banks have come to recognise that, while monetary policy aimed at ensuring price stability is a key ingredient to ensure long-run macroeconomic stability, price stability provides no guarantee against the build-up of dangerous imbalances in our economies and our banking systems. Indeed, long periods of macroeconomic stability can lead to a state of exuberance in financial markets and, as a consequence, large-scale mispricings of financial risk (Borio 2011). The experience of the crisis shows that systemic risk can be highest precisely at the moment when risk premia are lowest. Or put differently, the procyclical forces in the financial system are much stronger than was previously understood. They exacerbate the dynamics in both directions, in the upswing and in the downturn (Financial Stability Forum 2009).

The conventional wisdom among central bankers before the crisis was that financial imbalances are difficult to identify in a timely manner and that the standard tool of monetary policy, the interest rate, is too blunt an instrument to address a perceived build-up of risks in the financial system. Therefore, all

The author thanks Daniel Heller, Barbara Meller and Alexander Schulz for helpful discussions.

[1] For example, the ILO estimates that nearly 60 million people lost their jobs as a direct result of the crisis. Moreover, debt levels rose dramatically in the aftermath of the crisis (by about 20 percentage points in the Euro area and by about 35 percentage points in the USA).

monetary policy could do was to help "clean up" once the bubble burst.[2] But now that the world has experienced the devastating effects of the financial crisis, a new consensus is emerging: merely focusing on "cleaning up" no longer constitutes a satisfactory policy framework. Systemic imbalances do not emerge without warning. Various credit aggregates, for example, can serve as effective early warning indicators. Because the interest rate tool indeed tends to be a blunt instrument to address financial imbalances, central banks need other instruments – and in many cases more specific formal competences – to mitigate or even prevent the build-up of such imbalances. These instruments, intended to affect the financial system at the macro level, have come to be known as macroprudential instruments.[3]

In many ways, the most interesting country cases with which to examine the state of play with regard to macroprudential instruments are those where central banks ended up playing a crucial role in combating the financial crisis without having any specific and clearly formulated competences in the area of preventive action. Such gaps between actual crisis role and formal preventive competences need to be closed. There is clearly a need to strengthen macroprudential tools that can be deployed to address risks to financial stability – and there is scope to do so.

Since the peak of the crisis, the need for a macroprudential arsenal has become even more compelling. In many countries, interest rates are at a record low level, and are likely to remain there for what could be a long time. Past experience and empirical evidence suggest that long periods of very low interest rates ultimately tend to be associated with excessive credit creation and the build-up of financial imbalances (see, e.g., Altunbaş et al. 2010). An environment of unusually low interest rates thus reinforces the need for macroprudential instruments. Paradoxically, the more resilient a particular country's financial system proves to be during the crisis, the more vulnerable it is to the dynamic of low interest rates leading to excesses in the financial system. Canada, Sweden and Switzerland are noteworthy cases in point. Similarly, in the context of the Euro zone, Germany may become prone to excessive risk-taking in the financial sector if macroprudential policy makers do not take action to counteract regionally inappropriate interest rates.[4]

---

[2] For example, see Greenspan (2002) and Issing (2009). Also, on the policy of "leaning against the wind", Greenspan (2008) wrote: "I know of no instance in which such a policy has been successful. [...] I doubt that it is possible. If it turns out it is feasible, I would become a strong supporter of 'leaning against the wind'".

[3] Clement (2010) traces the term "macroprudential" back to work done at the BIS in the late 1970s. Note that Issing (2011) stresses the need to account for the interaction of monetary policy and asset prices and thus propagates the ECB's two pillar approach. While he reconciles the price stability objective with a financial stability perspective, it seems clear that monetary policy alone cannot and should not be burdened with the objective to counter systemic risk.

[4] In a recent speech in New York, Bundesbank President Weidmann (2012) pointed to the importance of macroprudential instruments in the context of a currency union when countries have different business cycle).

2. THE WAY FORWARD: GENERAL REMARKS

Operationalising and deploying effective macroprudential instruments will not be an easy task. The challenges are formidable. Excesses in our economies, in our banking systems or in financial markets will first have to be not only correctly identified but even forecasted. The identification of systemic risk remains a complex task which is fraught with uncertainty, not least because new types of threats will arise (for an overview of issues see BIS 2011; IMF 2011). Central banks and other institutions have already devoted a great deal of work to this topic and much progress has been made. But still, much remains to be done. Once policy makers have identified potential excesses or imbalances, they will have to decide what instruments might be appropriate to deal with them. Moreover, they will face the difficult task of determining the appropriate timing and the right dosage in the deployment of macroprudential tools.

In the context of the international post-crisis financial stability reform efforts, a range of instruments aimed at mitigating systemic risks are being developed and discussed around the world. In the following, I will identify several potentially useful macroprudential instruments: strengthened and enhanced capital requirements, restrictions on leverage ratios, new liquidity standards, large exposure restrictions, increased transparency and disclosure requirements as well as bail-in instruments.

2.1. Strengthened and Enhanced Capital Requirements

The aim of capital requirements in general is to ensure that risks are adequately backed by capital so that large idiosyncratic or systemic shocks can be absorbed by financial institutions, thus increasing their resilience. The crisis clearly revealed that on the whole, capital levels in the largest global financial institutions were inadequate. *A first order response to the crisis was therefore to increase the quality and quantity of capital* so as to increase the shock absorption capacity of banks. Beyond that, *higher risk weights for specific exposures* are used to address sectoral risks. By increasing risk weights permanently, temporarily, or over the cycle, specific products or activities become subject to higher capital requirement. This will have two salutary effects: first, banks' exposures in products or activities which are considered particularly risky will have to have more capital set against them. Second, since capital is costly, incentives can be expected to work in such a way as to prevent an excessive build-up of risks in these areas in the first place. The current risk-weighted framework does not provide a transparent and common method for calculating risk weights across institutions and geographies. These shortcomings make the risk-based capital framework vulnerable to inconsistencies and, at worst, manipulations. For the risk weights to be truly effective, the Basel Committee and national regulators will need to address this.

A specific form of structural capital buffer is the *surcharge for systemically important financial institutions* (SIFIs). The capital surcharge is expected to enhance the resilience of SIFIs in order to mitigate the systemic impact of their possible failure. Greater resilience by way of greater loss absorbency capacity is an appropriate response to the potentially dramatic systemic impact of their possible failure. In addition, a capital surcharge for SIFIs should force their owners to take greater responsibility for their actions and thus help reduce the misguided incentives to take excessive risks. Since the capital surcharge will be applied in relation to systemic importance, SIFIs will have an incentive to reduce their systemic importance over time. Moreover, the surcharge aims at internalising the negative externalities with regard to lower refinancing costs for SIFIs which enjoy an implicit government guarantee owing to their systemic importance.

The *countercyclical capital buffer* is a temporary and time-varying capital buffer which is intended to, on the one hand, cool off credit-fed booms by increasing the cost of funding for banks and borrowers during economic upswings and, on the other hand, to mitigate credit crunches during recessions, thereby pre-emptively smoothing the supply of bank lending over the cycle.[5] Moreover, setting aside an additional cushion of capital reserves enables banks to absorb greater losses during downturns without constraining the supply of credit.

2.2. Restrictions on Leverage Ratios

A maximum leverage ratio "enhances current risk-weighted capital requirements" (Hildebrand 2008). It addresses inherent and ultimately unavoidable weaknesses related to the risk management of financial institutions: model risk, risk of bypassing risk-sensitive capital requirements and systemic risk when high quality-highly liquid assets become suddenly low quality or illiquid. Since the leverage ratio may provide incentives for banks to take on more risk for a given leverage level, it should only serve as a backstop to a risk-sensitive capital ratio, thereby limiting excessive leverage and reducing procyclicality in the financial system. One great virtue of the leverage ratio is its conceptual simplicity. Ideally, it would be simple to calculate and transparent. Unfortunately, the current definition of the leverage ratio under Basel III is neither simple nor particularly transparent. In fact, it is extremely difficult for market participants to calculate the Basel III leverage ratio themselves.

2.3. The New Liquidity Standards

Next to insolvency, an important aspect of systemic risk is liquidity risk. One of the Basel liquidity ratios is the "*net stable funding ratio*" (NSFR). It is in-

---

[5] Conceptually, the countercyclical buffer is aimed at credit cycles and not business cycles. In practice, the two normally move closely together.

tended to foster a more medium- and long-term refinancing of assets and businesses of banks. The NSFR sets a minimum amount of stable funding, based on the liquidity characteristics of assets and business of a bank over a one-year horizon. This liquidity ratio should ensure, in particular, that long-term assets are backed by stable liabilities. Overreliance on short-term assets should be limited in times of abundant liquidity and a more sound assessment of liquidity risk on all on- and off-balance sheet positions should be encouraged. A greater reliance on stable funding – inter alia in contrast to wholesale financing – should also affect asset markets positively, as occasions of funding stress-induced asset sales should become less frequent.

Besides liquidity risk at the institutional level, we need also to address *systemic aspects of liquidity risk* which arise if multiple financial institutions simultaneously encounter liquidity problems. This could then place severe restrictions on the market liquidity of banks' assets and, at the same time, on liquidity in funding markets, thus endangering the financial system as a whole. A lack of transparency about financial institutions' liquidity situation could in some cases provoke systemic problems or fuel the spread of a crisis.

It is essential to ensure that the incentives and restrictions set out in the liquidity regime do not themselves have any undesired side effects on the financial system, and indirectly on the real economy. Complying with the NSFR at all times – i.e. also under stress – can encourage liquidity hoarding and undermine the pool of liquid assets. Furthermore, the precise criteria for liquid assets influence their own liquidity. These criteria could restrict markets for ineligible assets while conversely expanding markets for eligible assets significantly.

Taking into account system-wide effects in liquidity regulation raises several operational issues. First, the definition of liquid assets is non-trivial. A consistent approach would need to determine the eligibility of assets for the liquidity buffer based on its liquidity characteristics. These would have to be monitored on a regular basis to take changes into account and to modify the buffer accordingly. Secondly, there is a need for safeguards for concentration risk. To avoid concentrating the buffer on a few asset classes, concentration limits may be warranted. Thirdly, it is essential to define what constitutes a systemic liquidity event. Should financial institutions be allowed to run down their buffers, authorities will find it hard to determine an appropriate trigger. While some discretion may be necessary, any judgment call is likely to benefit from the availability of a set of systemic liquidity indicators.

2.4. Increased Transparency and Disclosure Requirements

Increased transparency and disclosure requirements are essential in fostering market discipline. In normal times, increased transparency and disclosure requirements allow investors to exercise their control power and to prevent unhealthy leverage ratios from building up. But high standards of disclosure are also important during busts. If all agents expect that disclosure requirements will not be relaxed to protect single institutions, banks will contain their risk in normal times as they know that their conditions will be revealed and they will be cut off from the interbank market in bad times.

It is often argued that transparency and the disclosure of banks' risk positions may increase the likelihood of a bank's failure especially in times of crisis. However, the insolvency of a single institution that has taken excessive risk might be desirable firstly because it ensures market discipline and secondly because other banks can be identified as sound, thereby ensuring the functioning of the interbank and bank bond market. If there were uncertainty surrounding all banks' risk exposures, not only the affected banks but also healthy banks would find access to liquidity denied. In order for *disclosure requirements* to be an effective tool, they *have to be credible, transparent and of the same high standard throughout time*. It has to be kept in mind that market discipline will only work if, in addition to disclosure requirements, there is a credible threat of resolution of an institution, even a SIFI.

2.5. Bail-In Instruments

The possibility to restructure or resolve any bank, even a SIFI, in an orderly manner, without imposing devastating costs on financial markets and the real economy is essential. In that context, bail-in procedures are particularly promising instruments. Here a distinction must be made between *contractual* and *statutory* bail-in solutions. A contractual solution provides for the creation of a separate category of bail-in-enabled liabilities. This solution avoids some operational and legal problems of the statutory solution. In contrast, the statutory bail-in tool enables the competent authority to enforce the loss of the existing equity rights and then write off a portion of the liabilities and/or convert them into new equity shares. Under this definition, all liabilities are always bailed-in, with very few exceptions, such as collateralised deposits and other secured debts.

By offering a broad basis of the loss-absorbing liabilities, the *statutory bail-in solution* has *significant benefits*. It provides for more recapitalisation, thereby improving the chances of survival of the institution and thus minimising the risk of taxpayer exposure to the risks of the financial sector. Moreover, it prevents regulatory arbitrage by market participants, since the use of debt to bail-in is the rule and the exceptions have to be explicitly defined. Lastly, it gives credit holders an incentive to control managers and equity holders by demanding higher premiums on riskier debt. Admittedly, one important drawback of a statutory bail-in solution is the complexity of its legal implementation, especially in a cross-border context (see Blavatnik School of Government 2012).

The statutory approach provides a unified solution which enhances clarity and transparency. Furthermore, it could be implemented relatively quickly without a transition period. By contrast, a contractual solution requires a transition period, which seems suboptimal from the perspective of financial stability, since continued uncertainty in the market would ensue. Another danger of a contractual solution is that newly issued securities would contain an above-average risk of loss, and their acceptance in the market would suffer as a result.

In the context of resolution regimes and bail-in procedures, *contingent capital instruments* represent another promising avenue. The Swiss authorities, in particular, have made them an integral part of their efforts to tackle the too-big-to-fail (TBTF) problem. Contingent capital instruments aim at avoiding discretionary regulatory interventions by providing a rule-based and automatic strengthening of the capital base of a financial institution in a crisis situation. The incentive effects of these instruments depend on their actual design, especially on their trigger mechanism. As there is still little practical experience with contingent capital instruments, it is too early to tell to what extent these instruments are capable of changing the behaviour of banks ex-ante (i.e. lower moral hazard). Despite a number of successful placements, some commentators continue to doubt whether large volumes of contingent capital instruments can be placed in the market at acceptable prices for issuers. Others argue that simultaneous conversion of contingent capital in several financial institutions could itself be a trigger of extreme market volatility.[6] While these considerations merit attention, it is important to remember that it is above all insufficient levels of capital that has been the root cause of the financial crisis. Few would doubt that common equity is ultimately a better shock absorber than contingent capital. On the other hand, convertible contingent capital instruments are surely preferable to insufficient capital levels. All possibilities to bolster fully loss-absorbing capital need to be explored, including the complementary use where appropriate of convertible contingent capital instruments.

When applying macroprudential instruments, extreme care will need to be exercised to be mindful of the interaction between macroprudential policies with an anti-cyclical character and the transmission channel of traditional monetary policy. This is a crucial point. For instance, it would be completely counterproductive if traditional monetary policy and a particular macroprudential instrument were to cancel each other out. In other words, a lot of conceptual work remains to be done – and done correctly.

3. MACROPRUDENTIAL MANDATES – DEVELOPMENTS IN SWITZERLAND AND GERMANY

In an effort to go beyond discussing macroprudential policy in general terms, Switzerland provides an insightful example. The SNB took aggressive policy

---

[6] The same argument could be made for bail-in solutions.

measures during the crisis to prevent turmoil in its financial system. At the same time, it had very limited formal competences in the area of preventive action. This dichotomy has led to intense discussions amongst the Swiss authorities on the merits of the macroprudential toolkit and, more importantly, how to deploy it in the future.

For background, the new central bank law of 2004 gave the SNB a fairly generic legal mandate to "contribute to financial stability."[7] That is virtually the only passage in the SNB law that can be seen as giving the SNB a preventive action mandate in the area of financial stability apart from its traditional lender of last resort function and its responsibility to oversee systemically important financial market infrastructures. Notably, the SNB has no formal competence in the area of banking supervision. This competence rests squarely with the supervisory and regulatory agency FINMA.

In light of the crisis and in the view of the SNB, this is not a satisfactory situation. Broadly speaking, and based on the experience of the financial crisis, the SNB has called for some time for the SNB's financial stability arsenal to be enhanced in order to augment the resilience of the banking system and moderate its procyclical behaviour. *The SNB's logic is simple and compelling: given its inevitable role as lender of last resort, it is bound to play an active role in combating a financial crisis.* In light of that role and the central bank balance sheet risks associated with it, it is self-evident that the SNB should be able to play a role in reducing the probability of a crisis emerging in the first place. Here, macroprudential supervision has a key role to play.

After careful deliberation, the SNB concluded that the formal legal competences of the SNB in the area of prevention needed to be enhanced carefully (Jordan 2010; Hildebrand 2010). In a joint working group chaired by the Finance Ministry, FINMA and the SNB worked actively towards that objective (Federal Department of Finance 2012). Needless to say, the outstanding analytical work of the BIS in the area of macroprudential policies served as an important reference point in the work of the joint expert group (Caruana 2010).

From the beginning, the SNB argued that its formal competences should be enhanced in two areas. First, it should be in a position to have *independent access to bank data*. The inability to collect and independently assess data from the systemically relevant banks prevented the SNB from assessing the risks related to the rising problems observed in the US subprime market in the run-up to the peak of the financial crisis in 2008 and 2009.

Second, the SNB has long felt that it should have a *more formal role to play in initiating financial stability regulation*. Specifically, the SNB felt it should have a crucial role in the implementation of the countercyclical capital buffer, as set out in Basel III. Any regulation that aims to reduce the procyclicality of the banking sector is bound to have close links to monetary policy. This link

---

[7] See National Bank Act (NBA), which came into force on 1 May 2004.

strengthens the case that the central bank should be in the lead when it comes to proposing or initiating regulation in this area.

Throughout its deliberations on an appropriate macroprudential toolkit, the SNB was always of the firm view that safeguarding price stability must remain the key objective of its legal mandate. The point was simply that if the central bank was going to continue to play a role in crisis prevention, it needed additional macroprudential instruments at its disposal.

In a report published in November 2011, the Ministry of Finance acknowledged that the SNB has a role to play in the future to monitor credit growth and other indicators to determine whether systemic risks are on the rise. The government has now created the legal basis for the SNB to submit a request to the government, upon hearing the view of FINMA, to activate the countercyclical buffer in accordance with Basel III. The final decision to activate the countercyclical buffer therefore rests with the government. In other words, while the SNB was not fully empowered to mandate the countercyclical buffer, the final arrangement does provide a clear division of responsibilities and was publicly welcomed by the SNB (Jordan 2011). The countercyclical buffer has become an available tool in Switzerland. A regulation was accordingly adopted by the government on 1 June and went into effect on 1 July 2012. Indeed, in its most recent semi-annual press conference, the SNB has indirectly signalled its readiness to propose an activation of the buffer to the Government if house prices and mortgage volumes continue to rise.[8] In contrast, nothing has happened yet with regard to the authority of the SNB to collect bank data directly from the systemically relevant banks. FINMA has so far consistently opposed this initiative and deposited a minority view on this point in the final report of the expert commission chaired by the Finance Minster. It remains to be seen to what extent the government will empower the SNB with regard to this point. What the Swiss example shows is that moving from the recognition that macroprudential instruments are needed to creating them is not a straightforward process. The politics are not trivial, especially in times when there is much focus about central banks potentially acquiring too much power in the aftermath of the financial crisis. Even in a case like Switzerland, where the central bank played such a decisive role in combating the crisis by rescuing UBS in a joint operation with the government, there is discernible opposition to ceding full authority over a macroprudential toolkit to the SNB.

Germany is about to set up its new financial stability framework.[9] It has established a Financial Stability Commission which consists of three members each from the Bundesbank, BaFin and the Finance Ministry, as well as a spokesman of the management committee of the Federal Financial Market Sta-

---

[8] SNB press conference on 14 June 2012.
[9] In Germany, a draft law for the strengthening of financial supervision passed the federal cabinet on 2 May 2012.

bilisation Agency[10] as a non-voting member of the commission. The Finance Ministry provides both the chair and vice-chair of the commission.

The *Bundesbank* has been given the *mandate for macroprudential surveillance and analysis*. It is responsible for preparing warnings regarding threats to financial stability and recommendations for averting those threats. Moreover, the Bundesbank prepares the Financial Stability Commission's annual accountability report to the Bundestag (lower house of parliament). The commission can issue warnings regarding threats to financial stability and recommendations for averting those threats. These warnings and recommendations will be prepared by the Bundesbank. The commission will then decide on the possible publication of warnings and recommendations. The main addressees of warnings and recommendations will be the federal government and BaFin.

Addressees are bound to "comply or explain" in response to warnings and recommendations. The federal government and BaFin will report to the commission on the planning and implementation of adopted measures, while the progress and effectiveness of these measures will be assessed by the Bundesbank. BaFin will be responsible for the use of macroprudential instruments, e.g., setting/resetting capital buffers or adjusting risk weights. Decisions are taken by simple majority, but *no major decision can be taken against the will of the Bundesbank*, as it has a special right of veto on warnings, recommendations, and the accountability report.

As these two specific country examples illustrate, the starting point for setting up a macroprudential supervision framework is likely to vary from one country to another depending on that country's history, individual experience of the crisis and legal and operational setups and mandates. So there is unlikely to be one answer that fits all, especially with respect to provisions against the political bias towards inaction. Yet – and here the example of inflation targeting comes to mind – if we look ahead to see which macroprudential policy frameworks have been put in place in 10 years' time, we should not be surprised to see broad international convergence around a small number of core principles.

4. CONCLUSION

It is very important to have a strong and effective regulator focused on microprudential supervision. But that is not enough. Everything we have learned during the financial crisis tells us that someone must keep an eye on and assess the risks at the systemic level. By design, by experience, and by trial and error, central banks are best equipped to do so. However, if central banks are to play that role effectively, they must have both the mandate and the toolbox to carry it out properly. The worst combination would be an implicit – or even an

---

[10] FMSA for short, the agency which controls, inter alia, the stabilisation fund SoFFin.

explicit – expectation that the central bank will fulfil such a role while being deprived of the appropriate mandate and the necessary instruments to do so. That is an outcome central banks all over the world must avoid at all costs. Essentially the whole debate about central banks and macroprudential supervision comes down to a simple choice. One option: central banks can stick to traditional monetary policy. Given what we have learned during the crisis, this is an extremely difficult proposition to uphold. The other option: assign central banks a role in the area of macroprudential supervision. However, in this case it is essential that they have the proper mandate and appropriate instruments.

BIBLIOGRAPHY

Altunbaş, Y., L. Gambacorta and D. Marqués-Ibañez 2010, "Does monetary policy affect risk taking?", *ECB Working Paper Series* 1166.

Bank for International Settlements 2011, *Annual Report*.

Blavatnik School of Government 2012, "Global Banking – The Challenges of Cross-Border Resolution", memos of workshop, Oxford University.

Borio, C. 2011, "Rediscovering the macroeconomic roots of financial stability policy: journey, challenges and a way forward", *BIS Working Paper* No 354.

Caruana, J. 2010, "The challenge of taking macroprudential decisions: who will press which button(s)?", speech in Chicago.

Clement, P. 2010, "The term 'macroprudential': origins and evolution", *BIS Quarterly Report.*

Federal Department of Finance 2012, *Financial Stability Working Group – Final Report.*

Financial Stability Forum 2009, *Report on Addressing Procyclicality in the Financial System.*

Greenspan, A. 2002, "Opening Remarks", in *Rethinking Stabilization Policy*, The Federal Reserve Bank of Kansas City.

Greenspan, A. 2008, "A response to my critics", *FT Economists' Forum.*

Hildebrand, P. M. 2008, "Is Basel II Enough? The Benefits of a Leverage Ratio", Financial Markets Group Lecture, London School of Economics.

Hildebrand, P. M. 2010, "Die geldpolitischen Herausforderungen und der Schweizer Immobilienmarkt", speech in Lugano.

International Monetary Fund 2011, *Macroprudential Policy Tools and Frameworks.*

Issing, O. 2009, "Asset Prices and Monetary Policy", *The Cato Journal.*

Issing, O. 2011, "Lessons for Monetary Policy: What Should the Consensus Be?", *CFS Working Paper* No. 13.

Jordan, T. 2010, "Neue Aufgaben für Zentralbanken?", speech in St. Gallen.

Jordan, T. 2011, "Introductory Remarks", SNB News Conference, December 15th.

Weidmann, J. 2012, "Global Economic Outlook – What Is the Best Policy Mix?", speech in New York.

24. Lender of Last Resort – Which Institution Could Best Fulfil this Function?

Gertrude Tumpel-Gugerell

In the 19th and 20th centuries, financial and monetary crises triggered by bank runs used to be a common phenomenon (Goodhart, 2002). Then, bank runs led to a reduction of central banks' gold reserves, with tightened credit standards exacerbating the situation. Only when central banks responded to such liquidity constraints by stepping up lending was it possible to achieve some stabilisation (Goodhart, 2002). Around that time, the theoretical basis for the lender of last resort (LLR) principle was first established in England by Henry Thornton (1760–1815) and Walter Bagehot (1826–1877). Following the Great Depression, both the theoretical and political debate of the role of LLR had receded into the background as economic and financial crises were few and financial stability was a given. However, since the beginning of the 1970s, when deregulation waves commenced and the global financial system started to become ever more interconnected, the frequency of crises has increased. Naturally, the recent economic, financial and sovereign debt crisis has reinvigorated the debate on the LLR principle. Who should assume this role? To what extent? To the benefit of whom? When? Under which conditions? These are some of the questions that need to be addressed in this context (Kindleberger, 2001).

1. THEORETICAL FOUNDATIONS OF THE NOTION OF A LENDER OF LAST RESORT

History shows that bank runs cause customers to withdraw their deposits and channel them into what they perceive as safe havens, namely cash, gold or foreign currencies (Goodhart and Huang, 1999). In such situations, the LLR is meant to provide liquidity to solvent, yet temporarily illiquid banks ("classical view"), to insolvent banks ("banking view") or to the market ("money view").

The term *lender of last resort* as such was coined by Sir Francis Baring in his work "Observations on the Establishment of the Bank of England" (1797),

---

This chapter was finished in July 2012 and reflects the state of discussion and development at that time.

in which he referred to the Bank of England as *dernier resort*, which should provide all banks with liquidity in times of a crisis (Humphrey, 2010). The theoretical foundations, however, were laid by Henry Thornton (1760–1815) and Walter Bagehot (1826–1877), whose writings must be regarded in their historical context. Both authors set forth principles to be heeded by central banks during a crisis.

The question of whether banknotes should be readily convertible into gold at any given time – which became known as the "Bullionist Controversy" – cropped up in the early 1800s during the Napoleonic Wars. Fear of war among the British population led to a run on banks' gold reserves. As a consequence, the British parliament decided on February 27, 1797, to suspend gold convertibility. This decision was repealed only in 1821 (http://www.mises.de/public_home/article/396/2). The Bullionists, among them Thornton, supported a return to gold convertibility on the argument that otherwise money supply would expand uncontrollably, which would fuel inflation. The Bank of England was at that time a private institution trusted with a monopoly over the issuing of banknotes within a 26-mile radius of London (Bordo, 1990). In his work "An Enquiry Into the Nature and Effects of Paper Credit of Great Britain" (1820), Henry Thornton ascribed to the Bank of England the task of providing the market with liquidity during banking panics. In other words, an LLR has to meet the drastically increased demand for *reserve money* over the short term. Monetary policy, by contrast, must control the monetary aggregate over the medium term (Freixas et al., 1999). Thornton supported *liberal lending* by the Bank of England, provided the collateral was of adequate quality.

Bagehot's works, by contrast, dated from peacetime and a different institutional setting. In 1844, under Prime Minister Sir Robert Peels, a new act was passed which centralised note-issuing powers and restricted the supply of uncovered notes to a set volume. This Bank Charter Act reflected the ideas of the Currency School, which argued that the monetary aggregate should remain relatively stable (Kindleberger, 2001). The Bank of England was restricted to issue no more than GBP 14 million in uncovered notes. No limit was set, however, on the volume of banknotes 100% backed by gold (Eltis, 2001). Within the Bank of England, the Issue Department was separated from the Banking Department (Laidler, 1999). Moreover, the Bank of England had to publish a weekly financial statement covering both departments.

In Bagehot's view, the Bank of England was the sole LLR, given its exclusive note-issuing powers and the fact that it held sufficient reserves to withstand a panic (see Knittel, 2007; Kindleberger, 2001). Yet, loans were to be extended only to illiquid, solvent institutions because support for insolvent banks would entail moral hazard (Thiel, 1995). Such loans were to be granted without any restrictions against adequate collateral, which was assessed at pre-crisis prices, though.

"Theory suggests, and experience proves, that in a panic the holders of the ultimate Bank reserve (whether one bank or many) should lend to all that bring good securities quickly, freely, and readily. By that policy they allay a panic; by every other policy they intensify it." (Bagehot, 1873, p. 173)

This type of lending should, however, come at a penalty rate to ensure that banks do not regularly refinance themselves that way:

"These loans should only be made at a very high rate of interest. This will operate as a heavy fine on unreasonable timidity, and will prevent the greatest number of applications by persons who do not require it. The rate should be raised early in the panic, so that the fine may be paid early; that no one may borrow out of idle precaution without paying well for it; that the Banking reserve may be protected as far as possible." (Bagehot, 1873, p. 197)

Moreover, it must be clear upfront that the Bank of England is ready to act as an LLR:

"The public have a right to know whether the Bank of England, the holders of our ultimate bank reserve, acknowledge this duty, and are ready to perform it."

In Great Britain – unlike in France – it was not clear, in practice, who should assume the role of LLR and when (Kindleberger, 2001, p. 212ff.). In France, the Banque de France, established in 1803, unmistakably took on the role of LLR in the 1830s crisis (Kindleberger, 2001). A former Governor of the Bank of England commented on Bagehot's call for the Bank of England to assume the role of LLR as the most dangerous view in finance and banking ever expressed in Great Britain (Kindleberger, 2001, p. 212).

Lest we forget, the theories advocated by Thornton and Bagehot rested on the assumption of a fixed exchange rate regime (gold standard). Over time, alternative theories came into being, which accounted for the ongoing integration of financial markets.

Some economists of the 20th and 21st centuries (e.g., Goodfriend and King, 1988) embrace the view that the role of central banks during banking crises should be confined to the provision of additional market liquidity e.g., via open market operations ("money view", see Goodhart, 2002). They argue that bailing out individual banks entails negative externalities due to moral hazard (Goodhart, 2002). Furthermore, in light of banks' vested interest in a sound financial system, these economists maintain that a private sector mechanism should be established along the lines of e.g., the private commercial bank clearinghouses in the USA that predated the foundation of the Federal Reserve System (Goodhart, 2002). Individual banks' refinancing through central banks should be avoided at any rate, since the market – in contrast to central banks – disposes of sufficient information about banks' solvency, and illiquid, yet solvent banks may tap into ample liquidity on the interbank market. This theory implies that markets function smoothly and complete information is available. Yet, especially this argument was refuted by the recent financial crisis (http://www.voxeu.org/index.php?q=node/2717). As inadequate transparency and disclosure requirements made the risk profile and creditworthiness of other financial market participants hard to assess, banks ceased to lend each other money and opted for liquidity hoarding at the central bank.

Freixas and Parigi (2008) argue that a private sector mechanism cannot substitute the LLR function because the members of such mechanisms primarily pursue their vested interests and pay less attention to insolvencies and the related contagion effects of banks outside such a mechanism. For them, financial market stability is not a priority. An LLR should, however, carry out such a mandate and be accessible for all banks, not only for those within a particular safety net.

The historical analysis of the LLR concept conducted by Humphrey and Keleher (1984) resulted in the following conclusions:

- *The LLR's emergence depends critically on fractional reserve banking and central bank monopoly over legal tender.*
  According to them, the necessity of an LLR in crisis situations is traceable to two institutional characteristics of the monetary system, namely the fractional reserve banking and the governmental monopoly of legal tender issuance, which, by extension, means that the central bank is the sole guarantor of deposit-to-currency convertibility (Humphrey and Keleher, 1984).
- *The LLR is essentially a monetary rather than a banking or credit function.*
  The ultimate purpose of the LLR is therefore to maintain monetary stability during panics.
- *The LLR function applies to all monetary regimes (...) The LLR function in no way conflicts with the monetary control function of the central bank.*
  The LLR function is applicable to all monetary systems and pursues differing objectives depending on the system.
- *The LLR has a macroeconomic rather than a microeconomic responsibility.*
  The LLR should serve the economy as a whole, and not individual banks. It should provide the market with liquidity during times of panic and thus curb contagion effects. It is necessary to communicate this role to the public upfront. Bailing out banks and publicly absorbing losses should be prevented. Banks must be allowed to go bankrupt.
- *The LLR function can be accomplished either through open market operations or loans made at penalty rate.*

By contrast, proponents of the "banking view" state that liquidity injections might become necessary also for individual banks, given the inherent fragility of the banking system and contagion effects (Goodhart, 2002). Inefficient interbank markets (see below) could result in a situation in which solvent banks can no longer borrow money in the markets (Freixas et al., 1999). What is more, given information asymmetries, it is not possible to draw a line between insolvency and illiquidity. Goodhart (2002, p. 13) argues as follows: "*When-*

ever a commercial bank asks for central bank assistance, there must always be the suspicion of insolvency – otherwise the market would be willing to provide liquidity." It is therefore critical to analyse the costs and benefits of an LLR, the curtailing of contagion effects, adequate crisis management as well as measures in the realm of regulation, supervision, deposit insurance, crisis finance and distribution of losses and not just the fundamental question of whether an LLR should exist in the first place (Goodhart, 2002). With banks relying on a soft landing in a safety net provided by central banks or governments in the worst case, they could be tempted to take on more risk (Goodhart, 2002). For this reason, it is also necessary to devise strategies to contain moral hazard.

In the literature (see Freixas et al. 1999), two reasons are cited for the need of an LLR function, namely

- information asymmetry and
- systemic risks.

Information asymmetries may lead to bank runs and inefficient interbank markets. In the classic model of a bank run (Diamond and Dybvig, 1983), depositors' pessimistic expectations about, for instance, the solvency of a bank give rise to a panic (*self-fulfilling prophecy*), with everyone trying to withdraw their bank deposits as quickly as possible. Bank runs, which could trigger the collapse of the banking system or the expansion of a credit crisis into a monetary crisis, would be averted by an LLR (Deutsche Bank Research, 2008; Humphrey and Keleher, 1984). Other measures to prevent bank runs are (temporarily) suspending payment obligations or setting up a deposit insurance (Gontermann, 2004).

Interbank markets do not always function smoothly and, under certain circumstances, it might happen that solvent banks no longer have access to funding in interbank markets. The recent crisis is a case in point. The literature identifies three sources of interbank market inefficiencies, all of which are due to information asymmetries (Freixas et al. 1999): first, unfavourable rumours about the creditworthiness of a basically solvent bank could have the effect that this bank can no longer refinance itself on the interbank market. The competent supervisory authorities would have to intervene in such a situation as they have more information about the actual performance of the institution than the market. Second, in times of crisis, banks act cautiously and prefer hoarding money over lending to other banks. Third, banks' uncertainty about future refinancing may cause them to build up precautionary reserves, which in turn can cause market failure.

Another compelling argument for an LLR are the significant repercussions one bank's insolvency due to liquidity problems could have on the entire financial system and on financial stability (Freixas et al., 1999). One such insolvency has the potential of clearly impeding the pricing of risks, allocation of resources, smooth functioning of payment systems and lending to households and the real economy. Given banks' interdependencies, domino effects could cause the entire system to falter.

2. THE ECB'S ROLE IN THE CRISIS

According to Article 127 of the Treaty on the Functioning of the European Union (TFEU) and Article 2 of the Statute of the ESCB and the ECB, the primary objective of the European System of Central Banks (ESCB) shall be to maintain price stability. To meet this objective, the ECB and the national central banks may

"*operate in the financial markets by buying and selling outright (spot and forward) or under repurchase agreement and by lending or borrowing claims and marketable instruments, whether in euro or other currencies, as well as precious metals*;

as well as

- *conduct credit operations with credit institutions and other market participants, with lending being based on adequate collateral" (Article 18, Statute of the ESCB and the ECB).*

Moreover, the Governing Council of the ECB may

- "*decide upon the use of such other operational methods of monetary control as it sees fit, respecting Article 2*" (Article 20, Statute of the ESCB and the ECB).

During the financial crisis, the ECB took decisive action to maintain price stability while also preserving its independence. The ECB was the first central bank worldwide to respond resolutely to the financial turbulence, on August 9, 2007, to be precise (http://www.ecb.int/press/key/date/2012/html/sp120516_1. en.html#footnote.1). Against the backdrop of the collapse of Lehman Brothers, the situation on the financial markets worsened over the course of 2008, which sharply affected monetary policy transmission. Market liquidity dried up, to boot. As a consequence, banks' refinancing conditions became much gloomier.

Against this backdrop, and in addition to cutting key interest rates, the ECB extended its set of monetary policy instruments under the above-mentioned legal framework by taking a number of nonstandard monetary policy measures. These measures comprise, above all, refinancing operations with full allotment (against collateral), longer-term refinancing operations as well as the expansion of the list of eligible collateral. Such liquidity provision became necessary because interbank lending had virtually ground to a halt as banks distrusted each other for fear of potential risks in the banking book. Governments' far-reaching bank deposit guarantees and recapitalisations shoring up customers' confidence in the stability of banking systems largely helped ward off a bank run.

In the years that followed, monetary policy-makers again faced major challenges given runaway sovereign debt in some Euro area countries and problems in government bond markets. Some Euro area countries, for instance, faced sharp increases in government bond yields.

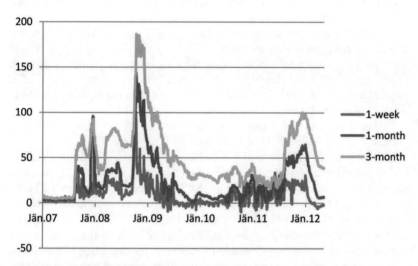

Figure 24.1: Risk Premia in Interbank Market Operations
Source: Thomson Reuters.

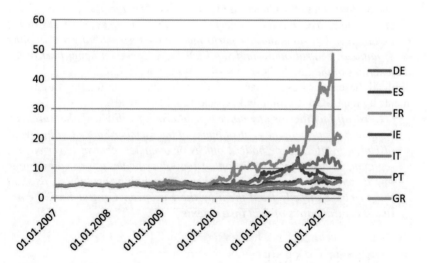

Figure 24.2: Spreads of Selected Government Bonds
Source: Thomson Reuters.

To reduce the tensions, governments decided to set up a European Financial Stability Facility (EFSF), to be complemented by the permanent European Stability Mechanism (ESM) in 2012. In 2013, the ESM is envisaged to fully replace the EFSF. In addition, the Governing Council of the ECB created a Securities Markets Programme, allowing the ECB to intervene on the markets for public and private debt securities should the need arise.

In light of persistent tensions, the ECB, in 2011 and 2012, initiated two refinancing operations with a maturity of three years. Their objective was to guarantee longer-term refinancing of the banking system to support lending to the real economy. Bank demand for these measures was immense. The ECB supplied about EUR 500 billion each; the corresponding net liquidity injection, however, was significantly below that amount (OeNB 2012).

All these nonstandard measures are of a temporary nature, and an exit is possible anytime should risks to price stability be observed.

In principle, the ECB is no LLR in Bagehot's classical definition (i.e. liquidity provision to illiquid, yet solvent banks in crisis situations). This role is assumed by the national central banks (NCBs) under the Emergency Liquidity Assistance (ELA). Under exceptional circumstances, such assistance may be granted by Euro area NCBs to a single, temporarily illiquid bank against good collateral if this bank can no longer refinance itself on the market or via monetary policy operations. Granting ELA is up to the discretion of the NCBs, provided that the Governing Council of the ECB does not object. Any costs and risks must be borne by the respective NCB:

- *"National central banks may perform functions other than those specified in this Statute unless the Governing Council finds, by a majority of two thirds of the votes cast, that these interfere with the objectives and tasks of the ESCB. Such functions shall be performed on the responsibility and liability of national central banks and shall not be regarded as being part of the functions of the ESCB." (Article 14.4, Statute of the ESCB)*

With all these measures one has to bear in mind that direct funding of governments by the ESCB is prohibited. Article 123 TFEU reads,

*"**Overdraft facilities or any other type of credit facility** with the European Central Bank or with the central banks of the Member States (...) in favour of Union institutions or bodies, offices or agencies, central governments, regional, local or other public authorities, other bodies governed by public law, or public undertakings of Member States **shall be prohibited, as shall the purchase directly from them by the European Central Bank or national central banks of debt instruments**."*

3. LESSONS LEARNED

During the crisis, the Eurosystem supplied the market with ample liquidity. These measures were important and effective in guaranteeing the functioning of the interbank market, as monetary policy and financial stability are highly interconnected.

We may draw two lessons for the LLR function from the way the financial, economic and government debt crisis unfolded. An LLR can only function on the basis of

- a stable financial system and
- stability-oriented economic and fiscal policies that are pursued by all Euro area countries.

3.1. Stable Financial System

The crisis has shown that it is necessary to improve the analysis of the inter-linkages between individual risks and systemic risks and their repercussions for the stability of the financial system and for the economy. For this reason, strengthening financial market regulation and supervision both at the national and the international level as well as from the microprudential and macropru-dential perspective was one of the key lessons to be drawn from the financial and economic crisis.

In the international arena, the G-20 responded to the financial crisis by pledging to *"ensure that all financial markets, products and participants are regulated or subject to oversight, as appropriate to their circumstances."*

The LLR function may be fulfilled without any welfare loss only on con-dition that regulatory and supervisory framework conditions rest on a solid foundation. This requires the following reform steps:

- strengthening cross-border and macroprudential supervision,
- improving banks' capital adequacy and liquidity profile both in terms of quality and quantity,
- implementing a comprehensive crisis management framework,
- raising transparency in the financial system, e.g., regarding OTC deriva-tives and shadow banks.

3.1.1. New European supervisory framework

While monetary policy was centralised following the establishment of Eco-nomic and Monetary Union (EMU), financial market supervision still large-ly remained in national hands even though financial market players operate throughout Europe. The supervisory structure lacked a European perspective, i.e. internationally active institutions were supervised primarily at home, and the supervisory role of central banks was reduced considerably in some coun-tries. The combination of microprudential supervision (i.e. of individual banks) and macroprudential supervision (i.e. of the financial system as a whole) was likewise inadequate. For this reason, on January 1, 2011, the *European Sys-tem of Financial Supervision* (ESFS) was put in place. The ESFS consists of the *European Systemic Risk Board* (ESRB) and three *European Supervisory Authorities* (ESAs), namely the European Banking Authority (EBA), the European Securities and Markets Authority (ESMA) and the European Insurance and Occupational Pensions Authority (EIOPA). The ESRB, which is an independent EU body responsible for the macroprudential oversight of the financial system within the European Union, serves as an early warning system for risks to the European financial markets (e.g., to identify asset price bubbles). Its seat is in Frankfurt at the ECB. The three European supervisory authorities EBA, ESMA and EIOPA, the legal successors to the former Level 3 committees CEBS, CESR, CEIOPS, have their own legal personality. The new authorities are meant in particular to foster greater harmonisation and coherent application of Union provisions. To this end, they were entrusted with numerous competences and powers. *Enhancing the macroprudential function of the ESCB strengthens its mandate in the area of financial market stability.* In the same vein, "Europeanising" supervision in a single market for financial services is a natural consequence.

3.1.2. Adequate crisis management mechanisms
Another important lesson from the crisis was to call for improved rules on how to handle and restructure banks in order to prevent them from getting too big or too interconnected to fail, and on how to unwind or reorganise banks at the least possible social cost. Supervisory authorities must be invested with comprehensive intervention powers to initiate the restructuring of banks in a timely manner, and when this is not possible, to unwind banks in an orderly fashion. It is also critical to implement measures governing the distribution of losses in the event of a crisis. Here, setting up *bank resolution funds or harmonised deposit insurance systems* is a welcome solution.

3.1.3. Measures to strengthen banks' resilience
The crisis has exposed some deficiencies in banking regulation, especially as far as banks' capital adequacy and liquidity profiles are concerned. *Basel III* (and the *CRD IV and CRR in the EU*) is set to raise both the quality and quantity of banks' regulatory capital base and improve their capacity to absorb losses. In addition, liquidity regulation should help deal with cases of interbank market turbulence, which had been the reason for the ECB's enormous liquidity support measures. The new provisions are scheduled to make the system much more resilient, in particular with regard to potential interbank market inefficiencies.

3.1.4. Raising transparency: OTC derivatives, shadow banking
Furthermore, it is imperative to raise the transparency in financial markets in order to avoid that banks stop lending to each other on account of mutual distrust. Amid misalignments on OTC derivative markets and given the com-

plex and opaque nature of deals, participants managed to build up excessive risk positions, which went unnoticed by the regulatory authorities and other market participants (Deutsche Bank Research, 2010). *The new obligation to clear OTC derivatives via central counterparties and the extended reporting obligation are vital steps in this context.* Equally important are measures aimed at making currently unregulated shadow banking more transparent.

3.2. Stability-Oriented Economic and Fiscal Policy

Monetary policy can only be effective in sync with national economic and fiscal policies. As has been made evident by the sovereign debt crisis, the rules and procedures currently in place to prevent and resolve such crises are not sufficient. Economic policy flaws must be removed to ensure the stability of EMU also in the future. The institutions responsible for economic and fiscal policymaking as well as the underlying provisions must be strengthened significantly. *In the future, Europe's economic policy must invest in growth and employment and must be based on a fiscal policy that is marked by discipline and social balance.* Such provisions must prevent any individual country's turn toward unsound economic policies.

The reform package adopted by the EU heads of state or government in 2011 – amendments to the Stability and Growth Pact, the introduction of a Macroeconomic Imbalance Procedure ("Euro Plus Pact") and the (earlier) establishment of the European Stability Mechanism (ESM) – must now be implemented or applied resolutely. National balanced budget rules ("debt brakes") are a proactive tool meant to trigger corrective measures in economic policymaking. The evaluation of new sources of income should contribute to a balanced fiscal policy.

4. CONCLUSIONS

Financial crises may impact on monetary policy, financial market stability, payment systems integrity and liquidity management (Padoa-Schioppa, 1999). It is not possible to maintain price stability without financial stability, which is why central banks have a decisive role to play in crisis management to comply with their primary policy objective. In compliance with the applicable legal framework, direct monetary financing of governments by the Eurosystem is strictly out of the question. At the national level, it is possible within the Eurosystem to provide illiquid, yet solvent banks with Emergency Liquidity Assistance (ELA).

During the crisis, insolvent banks received capital injections from the government, ultimately guaranteed by taxpayers. Moral hazard arises when risks are assumed on the assumption that the government will come to the rescue once risks materialise. It is therefore necessary to amend the regulatory framework conditions so that the *financial sector itself*, and not the individual citizen, *bears the cost of crisis management*. The supervisory authorities must be empowered to restructure banks in time and, if all else fails, to unwind them. Such a crisis management framework must incorporate an adequate loss-sharing mechanism (such as a resolution fund). The European Commission has published an *EU framework for bank recovery and resolution* in June and further measures are expected in the course of 2012.

When central banks are to provide the financial system with liquidity in times of stress, they must be thoroughly informed about the system and its participants. Only then can they decide on the scale and type of intervention in an adequate manner (Deutsche Bank Research, 2008). Therefore it would seem only natural for central banks to play an active role in financial market supervision. *The implementation of a banking union is a necessary step*. It follows, in an integrated market, to entrust central European institutions with several functions, such as supervision, crisis management and crisis financing.

It goes without saying that banks must do their homework, too. Otherwise, they may not count on having an LLR on their side during the next crisis. Banks must improve their risk-bearing capacity to become more resilient to shortages of market liquidity.

Also in the 21st century, an LLR is walking a tightrope in balancing out the effects of monetary policy, financial market supervision and financial market regulation. All three of these policy areas must be framed consistently and the role of central banks in these areas (above all regarding financial market supervision and regulation) must be broadly acknowledged. Only then can central banks continue to fulfil the role of lender of last resort in an efficient way.

BIBLIOGRAPHY

Bagehot, W. 1873, *Das Herz der Weltwirtschaft: Die Lombarden Straße*, G.D. Baedecker Verlagsbuchhandlung, Essen 1920.
Bordo, M. D. 1990, "The Lender of Last Resort: Alternative Views and Historical Experiences", *Federal Bank of Richmond Economic Review* 73(3), pp. 257-276.
Deutsche Bank Research 2008, Ziele und Aufgaben der EZB: Preisstabilität vs. Lender of Last Resort; http://www.dbresearch.in/PROD/DBR_INTERNET_EN-PROD/PROD0000000000224194.pdf?jsessionid=DC4E418C5D831420F7D5907EA016C4F6.srv12-dbr-com (accessed June 1, 2012).
Deutsche Bank Research 2010, OTC-Derivate: Grundlagen und aktuelle Entwicklungen; http://www.dbresearch.de/PROD/DBR_INTERNET_DE-PROD/PROD0000000000258017.pdf (accessed June 1, 2012).
Diamond, D. and P. Dybvig 1983, "Bank Runs, Deposit Insurance, and Liquidity", *Journal of Political Economy*, 91, pp. 401-419.

Eltis, W. 2001, "Lord Overstone and the establishment of British nineteenth-century monetary orthodoxy", *Discussion Papers in Economic and Social History* Number 42, University of Oxford, December 2001.

Freixas, X., G. Curzio, G. Hoggarth, and F. Soussa 1999, "Lender of Last Resort: A review of the Literature", *Financial Stability Review*, Bank of England, November.

Freixas, X. and B. M. Parigi 2008, "Lender of Last Resort and Bank Closure Policy", *CESifo Working Paper Series* 2286, CESifo Group Munich.

Gontermann, A. 2004, *Bank-runs und Moral-hazard*, http://epub.uni-regensburg. de/4504/1/Bank-runs_und_Moral-hazard_387.pdf, (accessed June 1, 2012).

Goodfriend, M. and R. King 1988, Financial Deregulation Monetary Policy and Central Banking, in *Restructuring Banking and Financial Services in America*, ed. By W. Haraf and R. M. Kushmeider, AEI Studies, 481, Lanham, Md.: UPA.

Goodhart, C.A.E. 2000, *Which Lender of Last Resort for Europe?*: A Collection of Papers from the Financial Markets Group of the London School of Economics.

Goodhart, C.A.E. 2002, Introduction, in *Financial Crises, Contagion, and the Lender of Last Resort*, ed. by Goodhart, C. and G. Illing, Oxford University Press.

Goodhart, C.A.E. and H. Huang 1999, A Model of the Lender of Last Resort, *IMF Working Paper* 39.

Humphrey, T. M. and R. E. Keleher 1984, "The lender of last resort: a historical perspective", *Cato Journal* 4(1).

Humphrey T. M. 2010, "Lender of Last Resort: What it is, Whence it came, And why the Fed isn't it", *Cato Journal* 30(2) p. 335.

Kindleberger, C. 2001, *Manien, Paniken, Crashs. Die Geschichte der Finanzkrisen dieser Welt.* 3rd edition. Kulmbach Börsenmedien.

Knittel, M. 2007, "Europäischer Lender of Last Resort", in *Hohenheimer Diskussionsbeiträge* Nr. 290/2007. Institut für Volkswirtschaftslehre, Universität Hohenheim.

Laidler, D. 1999, "Highlights of The Bullionist Controversy", http://economics.uwo.ca/ faculty/laidler/workingpapers/highlightsof.pdf, (accessed June 1, 2012).

OeNB 2012, *Annual Report* 2011.

Padoa-Schioppa, T. 1999, "EMU and banking supervision", lecture at the London School of Economics, Financial Markets Group on 24 February 1999; www.ecb.int/ press/key/date/1999/html/sp990224.eu.html.

Thiel, M. 1995, "Die Zentralbank als Lender of Last Resort: theoretische und praktische Grundfragen", *Working Paper* 39, Johann-Wolfgang-Goethe-Universität.

Stability of the Financial System: Illusion or Feasible Concept? An Epilogue

Christine Lagarde

The complexity of the modern global financial system is richly illustrated in the impressive series of chapters presented in this volume. Equally vivid are the challenges facing policy-makers to harness its potential.

It would be difficult, if not impossible, to do justice in just a few pages to the wealth of ideas contained here. By definition, an epilogue is a piece of writing at the end of a work of literature used to "bring closure to the work", and also "provide a brief description of the fates of the characters". While no one can pretend to predict the fates of anything in this global financial drama, this epilogue strives to present a synopsis on the state of play of financial sector reforms, with the humble goal of bringing closure to this volume, though not, of course, to the work herein.

THE QUEST FOR FINANCIAL STABILITY

Like most difficult public policy challenges, the quest for financial sector stability is a delicate balancing act: exploiting the benefits that the financial sector can provide to all citizens by intermediating savings toward productive investment and consumption, while controlling system-wide risks and preventing the build-up of imbalances. The breadth of issues and proposals raised in this book highlight both the considerable ground covered since 2008, but also the unfinished agenda. It recognises that which is not yet known, the financial sector phantoms yet to be created.

Let's save the unknowns for later. As for what we do know, including what still needs to be fixed, policy-makers must keep the reform "pedal to the metal". The global recovery has suffered new setbacks and economic growth has been disappointing. Growth is being held back by fiscal consolidation, private sector deleveraging, policy uncertainty, and weak financial systems. Indeed, despite considerable effort and progress, the financial sector – the source of this crisis – is holding back the recovery in key parts of the global economy.

FINANCIAL SECTOR UTOPIA?

Back in the early days of this crisis, policy-makers set out to build a safer financial system. This better, stronger system would reduce the severity of boom-bust cycles and the burden of distress on taxpayers. It would serve businesses and households better.

More specifically, this new system would provide more transparency and better data so risks could be identified and priced; less leverage to limit contagion risks while reaping the benefits of globalisation; higher and better quality capital with which to absorb losses; more liquidity to manage maturity risks; a better understanding of risks in the nonbank sector; and agreed plans on how to resolve the "too-big-to-fail" problem.

Policy-makers also aimed for an optimal regulatory framework that would ensure that all risks are priced fairly; that would apply prudential standards consistently around the world to stop risks from migrating; and that would discourage institutions from taking advantage of implicit government guarantees.

The outlines of the reform agenda were laid out in more detail in the G-20 Toronto Declaration in 2010. Since then, standard setters, regulators, and supervisors have been working closely with the private sector, the FSB and the IMF toward that goal.

ACCOMPLISHMENTS AND PROGRESS

As noted in the introduction by Mark Carney, there have been some major achievements in regulatory reform and solid progress in other areas. The biggest advance is the new capital and liquidity requirements for banks under Basel III, which has even higher standards for systemically important banks. Recent IMF research shows that higher buffers, like those proposed in Basel III, are also associated with higher rates of growth and lower economic volatility.

Other key accomplishments include progress at the FSB on identifying and supervising SIFIs, and specific features under Basel III on SIFIs aimed at reducing their systemic footprint; a new standard on Resolution Regimes developed by the FSB, as well as notable country specific reforms; commitments to reduce counterparty risks in the derivatives markets; reduction in the reliance on credit ratings and tougher regulation of credit rating agencies; and changes in compensation practices.

In addition, considerable research and cross-country analysis has been undertaken to develop a framework for macroprudential policies and identify the desired institutional structures underlying them. The IMF has taken a central role in developing this work. The Fund has also intensified research and strengthened operational strategies on macrofinancial linkages and their implications for fiscal policy, public debt management and monetary policy. Several essays in this volume touch on these important issues.

Indeed, collaboration between the G-20, the FSB and the IMF has been an integral factor in developing all of these tools. The IMF has been a strong proponent of the reforms and has actively participated in discussions on design, implementation and impact through our participation in the standard setting bodies and the FSB.

All of these new reforms comprise the tools that will help us shape the future financial system. While these new rules and principles are heading in the right direction, the IMF has found that we still have a long way to go before we can see the fruits of this labour.

PROOF WILL BE IN THE PUDDING

While fundamental changes will take time, the basic structures that we found problematic before the crisis are still with us. Systems are still overly complex; banking assets are still highly concentrated with strong domestic bank inter-linkages; some institutions continue to rely excessively on wholesale funding; and many institutions are still too-important-to-fail.

Change is not visible yet because implementation is being delayed in some places, intentionally or unintentionally, and also because some reforms are meeting resistance. First, some financial systems are still under distress and crisis-fighting efforts are inadvertently impeding reforms. In addition, reforms like Basel III have built in generous implementation timetables, rightly to allow the economy to recover.

Second, there are vested interests working against change and pushback in some areas is intensifying. IMF staff recently conducted a study on the costs of regulatory reform and found that the likely long-term increase in borrowing costs would be manageable, at about one quarter of one percentage point in the US, and lower elsewhere. The world is now in the sixth year of crisis, with more than 200 million people out of work. In the US alone, per capita real GDP is estimated to be about 9 percent lower than what it would otherwise have been. Surely the returns from regulatory reforms will be well worth the investment.

RULES GOOD ON PAPER, NEED IMPLEMENTATION

Looking ahead, the next phase involves two important steps: implementation of the new standards on a globally consistent basis, and the development of multilaterally agreed rules or principles in areas where consensus has not yet been reached.

Many countries have committed to adopt the new regulations, and some have moved further ahead with their own national policies. The key word at this stage is implementation: implementation of the new capital and liquidity standards; implementation of derivatives markets reform; implementation of the FSB's principles for compensation; and so on. Importantly, implementation of the Basel Committee's principles for effective banking supervision warrants special mention. Even the best rules are of no value if not implemented and well supervised.

UNFINISHED REFORM AGENDA

With regard to unresolved regulatory issues, the too-important-to-fail conundrum has not yet been satisfactorily addressed. We need a global level discussion of the pros and cons of direct restrictions on business models. For example, the Volcker Rule in the US, the Vickers Commission proposals in the UK, and the Liikanen Report on the EU banking system will have important effects beyond their jurisdictions. Here a global perspective and more coordinated approach are needed.

We also need further progress on recovery and resolution planning for large institutions, especially cross-border resolution. Much work is underway to develop the tools to intervene in distressed institutions, but we need to move to compliance and assessment on an international scale.

Shadow banking remains a concern. The FSB recently released sweeping proposals to strengthen regulation and oversight of the part of this sector with the bank-like attributes of creating credit or engaging in maturity transformation. The IMF looks forward to collaborating closely with our colleagues at the FSB as they take this work forward.

FEAR OF THE UNKNOWN

While these issues are well identified, what about the unknowns? Since the rapid pace of innovation and technological change in global financial markets is not likely to diminish, policy-makers will always be faced with the possibility of "Knightian uncertainty" – those risks that are immeasurable *ex ante*, not possible to calculate. On the face of it, history suggests that we are doomed to follow Minsky's "financial instability hypothesis" that the financial system is inherently prone to inevitable swings between robustness and fragility.

I beg to differ. First, to any policy-maker, this debate is academic. The staggering economic and human costs of this long crisis compel us to no other choice than to do everything we can to avoid future busts.

More importantly, we have one big advantage this time: a more global approach to regulation and supervision, and better international cooperation. If we can strengthen further this global infrastructure of consistent regulation and oversight, and deepen the network of consultation amongst all stakeholders, we should greatly improve the probability of success at avoiding busts and identifying tail risks in time. This is the best way to ensure that we stay ahead of, or at least keep up with, the rapid evolution of financial systems.

ILLUSION OR REALITY?

If we do this well, I maintain that the goal of financial stability is not just an illusion: it is feasible, as long as everyone plays their part. The essays in this volume reflect indeed the breadth of views and the contributions that are needed by all stakeholders to make the approach fully global, and to make the financial system safer. One cannot foretell the fate of the characters or the reforms in this drama, but they are on the right track. The challenge now is to keep up the political momentum and proceed along the reform road all together.

"Perseverance, secret of all triumphs". *Victor Hugo*

Index

Asset backed commercial paper (ABCP)
392, 397, 402
asset price bubbles 9, 105, 324, 522
asset purchase program 149, 330
asymmetric information 259, 266, 275

Bail-in instruments 304–307, 507
bail-inable debt 270, 273–274, 313, 315
bank-based financing 184
bank-based system 184, 463
banking regulation 28, 152, 196, 341–
343, 345, 349–353, 389, 462
Basel Capital Accord 365, 382
Basel II 365, 389, 492
Basel III
    capital conservation buffer 193, 271,
    409
    countercyclical buffer 31, 42, 193,
    229, 271, 431–432, 505, 510
    framework 31, 33, 187, 402, 431, 434,
    467
    liquidity requirements 409, 433
    liquidity rules 433–434
Basel's Committee on the Global Financial System (CGFS) 66, 71
Borio paradox 70

Capital ratio 36, 271, 305, 340–341,
369–370, 374, 390, 431, 445,
490–491, 494–495
Capital Requirement Directive (CRD IV)
32, 152, 469
capital standard 3, 54, 327, 392
capital structure 293, 315–316, 349
capital surcharge 34, 292, 303, 505
Central Counterparties (CCPs) 275, 410,
416–418
collateralised debt obligation (CDO) 12,
18, 277, 448
collective action clauses (CACs) 133,

150, 175, 246
colleges of supervisors 259
consolidation 21, 25, 148, 164, 176, 177,
326, 402
contagion 252–254, 275, 289, 291, 345–
347, 440–455
contingent capital instruments (CoCos)
192, 304–305, 508
core capital ratio 36
cost of funding 292, 304
countercyclical capital buffer 31, 42, 193,
229, 271, 431–432, 505, 510
country risk 8, 173
credit crunch 18
credit default swap (CDS)
    premium 253–254, 291, 296
credit gap 79, 92, 100, 102, 113–115
credit-to-GDP gap 31, 73–78, 229
crisis management framework 192, 524
cross sectional dimension 71, 112, 189,
215–217, 223, 225, 391, 474
cross-border
    banking 411–414, 422
    finance 413
    financial interconnectedness 105
    financial stability groups 259

De Larosière Commission 459
de Larosière Report 30
debt
    category of debt 315–316
    contracts 24, 154, 237, 243
    levels 8–9, 11, 13, 18, 23
    overhang 145–146, 154
    restructuring 150, 175–176, 238, 242–
    247, 254
    treatment of debt 305–306, 312
deposit guarantee schemes (DGS) 282–
284, 300, 435–436
deposit insurance system 329, 454

deregulation 48, 359, 448, 513
disclosure requirements 389, 506–507
Dodd-Frank-Act (DFA) incl. legislation
    53–55, 59, 310, 416–417
domestic systemically important banks
    (D-SIBs) 260–262, 265
    criteria to identify D-SIBs 260–261
domestic systemically important financial
    institutions (D-SIFI) 259
dynamic stochastic general equilibrium
    (DSGE) 102–103, 478–479

Early warning indicators (EWI) 73, 92,
    220–222
Emergency Liquidity Assistance (ELA)
    280–282, 520
Endogeneity 364–365, 384
EU Banking Structures 182–183
European Banking Authority (EBA) 38,
    457, 459–460, 467
European Central Bank (ECB) 163, 170,
    470, 518–520
European Exchange Rate Mechanism
    (ERM) 161
European Financial Stability Facility
    (EFSF) 129, 131, 167, 170–171,
    520
European Financial Stability Framework
    168, 170–171
European Market Infrastructure Regula-
    tion (EMIR) 417
European Monetary Union (EMU) 164,
    167–177, 248–249
European passport 29, 462
European small and medium sized enter-
    prises (SME) 195
European Sovereign Debt Restructuring
    Mechanism (ESDRM) 144–155,
    175–178
European Stability Mechanism (ESM)
    127–133, 520
European Supervisory Authority (ESA)
    38, 522
European supervisory framework 521
European System of Financial Supervi-
    sion (ESFS) 28, 38, 351, 457–461,
    521–522
European Systemic Risk Board (ESRB)
    37–42, 194, 457, 460–461, 470–
    472, 522
Externality 33–34, 238, 261, 284, 289,

    371, 446, 450–452, 475, 477,
    481–482

Federal Deposit Insurance Corporation
    (FDIC) 54, 451
feedback loop 128, 250, 252–253, 322–
    323, 325, 328, 330
financial activity tax 377
financial crisis 49–50, 52
    global financial crisis 1, 64, 249, 323–
    324
    Japan's financial crisis 318–333
financial instability 30–31, 105, 216–
    217, 393, 530
    paradox of financial instability 31,
    69–70
financial markets infrastructure (FMI)
    275, 416
    standards 275
financial repression 20, 51
Financial Services Action Plan 29
financial spillovers 440–441, 444–445
financial stability
    contribution 306, 377
    disruption 117, 120
    indicators of financial stability 109–
    122
    map 109–110
Financial Stability Board (FSB) 189, 290,
    311, 392, 399, 430
Financial Stability Oversight Council
    (FSOC) 53–54
financial system
    bank-based financial system 184, 351
    market-based financial system 184,
    306, 351
Fiscal Compact 130–131, 151
fiscal transfer 143–144, 151–152
flexible credit line (FCL) 171, 438

G20
    recommendations 270
Glass-Steagall Act 451
global systemically important banks
    (G-SIBs) 271, 279, 292
    BCBS methodology for identification
    260
    criteria for identifying G-SIBs 279
global systemically important financial
    institutions (G-SIFI) 409
government debt 10–11, 15–16, 21, 23–

24, 241
government-sponsored enterprises
(GSEs) 49

Harmonisation
advantages 464
optimum degree of harmonization 464
types of harmonization 465
home country control 28
horizontal review 57–58
household debt 9–10, 93
housing boom 10, 394, 479
housing price bubble 9

Implicit subsidy 348, 366, 376
incentive(s) 23, 40, 48, 50, 103, 128–
129, 147, 152–153, 188, 191, 196–
197, 205–207, 211, 243, 249, 258,
266–270, 276–277, 281–282, 292,
303–306, 315, 339, 340–344, 370,
372–374, 377, 385, 390, 401, 414,
419, 432, 435, 469, 494, 504–508
interconnectedness 34, 73, 81–90, 105,
107, 109–110, 262–263, 290, 294,
375, 412
intermediation function 445
internal devaluation 139, 177
international coordination 314–315
international fiscal bailout program 20
International Monetary Fund (IMF) 247,
254, 278, 422, 437–438, 528–529
Intervention 15, 36, 48–49, 64, 295–296,
339, 359, 366–367, 371–373, 377
invisible hand 46, 50, 53

Knightian uncertainty 35, 279–280, 530

Labour productivity 134
Lamfalussy process 458
Landesbanken 448
lender of last resort (LLR) 59, 146, 149–
150, 280–282, 319–320, 513–524
level playing field 388–391, 414, 457, 488
leverage ratio 152, 187, 409, 431, 493–
494, 505
liquidity
global liquidity 104–105, 426, 436–
438
liquidity coverage ratio (LCR) 2, 409,
432–433
management 426, 429–430, 434, 437

provision 428, 438, 518
regulation 327–328, 506, 522
risk 41, 79, 403, 431–432, 505–506
standards 187, 431–434, 505–506
support 146, 151, 522
Lisbon Treaty 129, 352
living will 190, 273, 366, 380–382
loan to deposit ratio (LTD) 79–80
loan loss provision 92
long-run redistributive mechanism 143
long-term refinancing operation (LTRO)
16, 330
loss absorbency requirement 42, 260,
270–272

Macroprudential
analysis 468, 470–471
approach 53, 55, 58, 68, 70
authority 41–42, 479, 489, 491
countercyclical policy 476, 482–483,
489–491, 496–497
instruments 28, 31, 33, 37, 71–72,
464, 469, 474–479, 503–504
mandates 41, 195
oversight 27–31, 37–42, 194, 457–
461, 468–473, 522
regulation 37, 52, 62, 68, 121–122
supervision 53, 55–59, 192–194, 278,
470, 509, 511–512, 521
supervisors 39, 42
tools 33, 36–37, 42, 60–61, 277, 285,
469, 475, 503–504
marginal expected shortfall (MES) 291
market-based finance 48
market-based financial sector 184
market discipline 51, 53, 206, 209, 249,
254, 277, 281, 283, 292, 294, 297,
305–308, 312–313, 340, 348, 350,
362, 366–367, 373, 379, 381–382,
389, 506–507
market equilibrium 312
Markets in Financial Instruments Directive (MiFID) 417, 421
maturity transformation 33, 193, 203–
204, 315, 369, 392–393, 397, 445
microprudential
regulation 28, 52, 67–70, 128
supervision 28, 37–38, 52, 197, 278,
457–459, 470–472, 494, 511, 521
minimum capital requirements 27, 340–
341, 348, 431, 495

monetary financial institutions (MFIs)
    15–16
money market contraction 331
money market funds (MMFs) 41, 393,
    395–396, 400, 433
moral hazard 188, 292, 347–348, 378–383
    minimizing moral hazard 259, 266–
        267, 269–276, 282–284
    moral hazard distortion 267–268

Net stable funding ratio (NFSR) 2, 409,
    432, 505
network analysis 223, 225, 263, 291
no-bail-out clause 129
nominal interest rate convergence 135–
    136
non-performing loan (NPL) 92–94, 109–
    110, 117, 123, 319, 322

Over-the-counter derivatives (OTCD)
    3–4, 55, 410, 416–418, 522–523

Paris Club 244–245
phase-in period 328, 370
point-of-non-viability 306–308
precautionary conditioned credit line
    (PCCL) 132, 171
precautionary credit line (PCL) 154, 171,
    438
present value borrowing constraint
    (PVBC) 241
primary market support facility 132
principal-agent problem 204, 266, 268,
    274, 340
Prompt Corrective Action (PCA) 372–
    373

Quantitative Easing 330–331

Rating agencies 204, 237, 252, 297, 307,
    449–452
real economic convergence 144, 167,
    172, 174
real exchange rate 138–139
real GDP growth rate 74–75, 109, 117
recognition lag 233
recovery and resolution plan (RRP) 190,
    273, 366, 381–382, 385, 409, 415,
    530
redemption fund 146
regulation

behavioural regulation 365, 369
costs of regulation 343, 345, 364
First Banking Directive 28
objectives of regulation 362
Second Banking Directive 29
solvency regulation 340–342
regulatory
    arbitrage 29, 153, 186, 304, 358, 364–
        365, 375, 383, 398, 401, 414, 416,
        420, 423, 464–465, 507
    framework 50, 186–187, 345, 407–
        408, 413–415, 474, 496, 524, 528
    initiatives 408, 431
    instruments 43
    reform 47, 202, 345, 351, 359–363,
        373–374, 384, 402, 407–408, 413,
        495, 497, 528–529
repo 14, 393, 395, 401–402
resolution
    arrangements 359–362, 366, 374,
        378–385
    authority 192, 208, 273–274, 311–
        312, 314, 455
    framework 192, 259, 273, 310, 315,
        434
    plans 273, 366, 380–382, 410, 415
    regime 3, 148, 153–154, 190, 208,
        273, 311, 359, 363, 378–381, 409
    scheme 329
restructuring
    post-default restructuring 242
    pre-emptive restructuring 242–243
ring-fencing 348, 375–377, 416
risk dashboard 35
risk of contagion 29, 128, 258, 396
risk premium 153, 296, 313
risk-weighted assets (RWA) 18, 36, 152,
    303, 322, 409, 431, 491–493

Secondary market support facility 132
Securitisation 11, 50, 202–204, 277, 364,
    393, 401
shadow bank
    shadow banking sector 4, 20–21, 392,
        395
    shadow banking system 4, 36, 392,
        394
Six Pack 130
Social Contract 207–208
social costs 294, 360–365, 450
sovereign debt 130, 135, 172–177, 237–

255, 325
Sovereign Debt Restructuring Mechanism (SDRM) 175, 178, 246
sovereign default
    liquidity problem 241
    sustainability problem 241
    unwillingness to pay 241
sovereign risk 128, 133, 237–255, 487–488
spillover effects 81, 428, 440–455
Stability and Growth Pact 23, 127–130, 151, 163–164, 249, 523
stress test 70, 226–228
structural
    capital buffer 505
    externalities 33
    measures 53, 366, 368–369, 374–375
    reform 51, 53, 128–130, 165, 326,
structured early intervention and resolution (SEIR) 372
supervisory
    colleges 270, 459
    framework 521–522
synthetic indicators of financial stability
    interconnectedness α-index 111
    principal component analysis (PCA) 112
    quantile regression (QR) 117
systemic importance 34, 83, 225–226, 260–262, 289–292, 465
systemic risk
    contribution index 291
    cross-sectional dimension 70, 223–226, 392
    definition of systemic risk 66, 289, 391
    meaning of systemic risk 345
    measuring systemic risk 215–229, 291
    time dimension 69, 217, 391
    transmission mechanism of systemic risk 69, 217, 391
systemic stability 8, 13, 347, 360–363, 378–379
systemically important banks (SIBs) 288–308
systemically important financial institutions (SIFIs)
    criteria to identify SIFIs 270–272
    definition of SIFIs 290
    resolution process 197, 272–275
    supervision 276–279

Target II (im)balances 138
tax
    subsidy 348
    treatment of debt 305, 370
too-big-to-fail (TBTF) 2–3, 190, 272, 289, 292–293, 297, 307, 337, 345, 347–349, 409, 419
too-big-to-save 288
too-interconnected-to-fail 288
trade repositories 3, 275, 410, 417–418
transactions tax 450
Treaty on Stability, Coordination and Governance (TSCG) 130
Treaty on the functioning of the European Union
    no-bail-out clause 129
trilemma 30

Uncollateralised pre-emptive liquidity facilities 171
unfunded public pension liabilities 10
US dollar funding risks 41
US subprime crisis 7

Vienna Initiative 166–167
Volcker rule 55

Welfare economics 337, 338
White Paper 29

Z-score 184